Microsoft® Official Academic Course

Managing and Maintaining Windows 8 Exam 70-688

Richard Watson

WILEY

Credits

VP & PUBLISHER	Don Fowley
EXECUTIVE EDITOR	John Kane
DIRECTOR OF SALES	Mitchell Beaton
EXECUTIVE MARKETING MANAGER	Chris Ruel
MICROSOFT PRODUCT MANAGER	Gene R. Longo of Microsoft Learning
EDITORIAL PROGRAM ASSISTANT	Allison Winkle
TECHNICAL EDITORS	Jeff Parker Guy Thomas
ASSISTANT MARKETING MANAGER	Debbie Martin
SENIOR PRODUCTION & MANUFACTURING MANAGER	Janis Soo
ASSOCIATE PRODUCTION MANAGER	Joel Balbin
PRODUCTION EDITOR	Eugenia Lee
CREATIVE DIRECTOR	Harry Nolan
COVER DESIGNER	Georgina Smith
SENIOR PRODUCT DESIGNER	Thomas Kulesa
CONTENT EDITOR	Wendy Ashenberg

This book was set in Garamond by Aptara, Inc. and printed and bound by Bind-Rite Robbinsville. The covers were printed by Bind-Rite Robbinsville.

ISBN 978-1-118-59193-2

Printed in the United States of America

10 9 8 7 6 5 4 3 2 1

www.wiley.com/college/microsoft *or*
call the MOAC Toll-Free Number: 1+(888) 764-7001 (U.S. & Canada only)

Foreword from the Publisher

Wiley's publishing vision for the Microsoft Official Academic Course series is to provide students and instructors with the skills and knowledge they need to use Microsoft technology effectively in all aspects of their personal and professional lives. Quality instruction is required to help both educators and students get the most from Microsoft's software tools and to become more productive. Thus, our mission is to make our instructional programs trusted educational companions for life.

To accomplish this mission, Wiley and Microsoft have partnered to develop the highest-quality educational programs for information workers, IT professionals, and developers. Materials created by this partnership carry the brand name "Microsoft Official Academic Course," assuring instructors and students alike that the content of these textbooks is fully endorsed by Microsoft, and that they provide the highest-quality information and instruction on Microsoft products. The Microsoft Official Academic Course textbooks are "Official" in still one more way—they are the officially sanctioned courseware for Microsoft IT Academy members.

The Microsoft Official Academic Course series focuses on *workforce development*. These programs are aimed at those students seeking to enter the workforce, change jobs, or embark on new careers as information workers, IT professionals, and developers. Microsoft Official Academic Course programs address their needs by emphasizing authentic workplace scenarios with an abundance of projects, exercises, cases, and assessments.

The Microsoft Official Academic Courses are mapped to Microsoft's extensive research and job-task analysis, the same research and analysis used to create the Microsoft Certified Solutions Associate (MCSA) exam. The textbooks focus on real skills for real jobs. As students work through the projects and exercises in the textbooks and labs, they enhance their level of knowledge and their ability to apply the latest Microsoft technology to everyday tasks. These students also gain resume-building credentials that can assist them in finding a job, keeping their current job, or in furthering their education.

The concept of life-long learning is today an utmost necessity. Job roles, and even whole job categories, are changing so quickly that none of us can stay competitive and productive without continuously updating our skills and capabilities. The Microsoft Official Academic Course offerings, and their focus on Microsoft certification exam preparation, provide a means for people to acquire and effectively update their skills and knowledge. Wiley supports students in this endeavor through the development and distribution of these courses as Microsoft's official academic publisher.

Today educational publishing requires attention to providing quality print and robust electronic content. By integrating Microsoft Official Academic Course products, MOAC Labs Online, and Microsoft certifications, we are better able to deliver efficient learning solutions for students and teachers alike.

Joseph Heider

General Manager and Senior Vice President

Preface

Welcome to the Microsoft Official Academic Course (MOAC) program for becoming a Microsoft Certified Solutions Associate for Windows 8. MOAC represents the collaboration between Microsoft Learning and John Wiley & Sons, Inc. Microsoft and Wiley teamed up to produce a series of textbooks that deliver compelling and innovative teaching solutions to instructors and superior learning experiences for students. Infused and informed by in-depth knowledge from the creators of Windows 8, and crafted by a publisher known worldwide for the pedagogical quality of its products, these textbooks maximize skills transfer in minimum time. Students are challenged to reach their potential by using their new technical skills as highly productive members of the workforce.

Because this knowledgebase comes directly from Microsoft, architect of Windows 8 and creator of the Microsoft Certified Solutions Associate exams, you are sure to receive the topical coverage that is most relevant to students' personal and professional success. Microsoft's direct participation not only assures you that MOAC textbook content is accurate and current; it also means that students will receive the best instruction possible to enable their success on certification exams and in the workplace.

The Microsoft Official Academic Course Program

The Microsoft Official Academic Course series is a complete program for instructors and institutions to prepare and deliver great courses on Microsoft software technologies. With MOAC, we recognize that because of the rapid pace of change in the technology and curriculum developed by Microsoft, there is an ongoing set of needs beyond classroom instruction tools for an instructor to be ready to teach the course. The MOAC program endeavors to provide solutions for all these needs in a systematic manner in order to ensure a successful and rewarding course experience for both instructor and student—including technical and curriculum training for instructor readiness with new software releases; the software itself for student use at home for building hands-on skills, assessment, and validation of skill development; and a great set of tools for delivering instruction in the classroom and lab. All are important to the smooth delivery of an interesting course on Microsoft software, and all are provided with the MOAC program. We think about the model below as a gauge for ensuring that we completely support you in your goal of teaching a great course. As you evaluate your instructional materials options, you may wish to use the model for comparison purposes with available products.

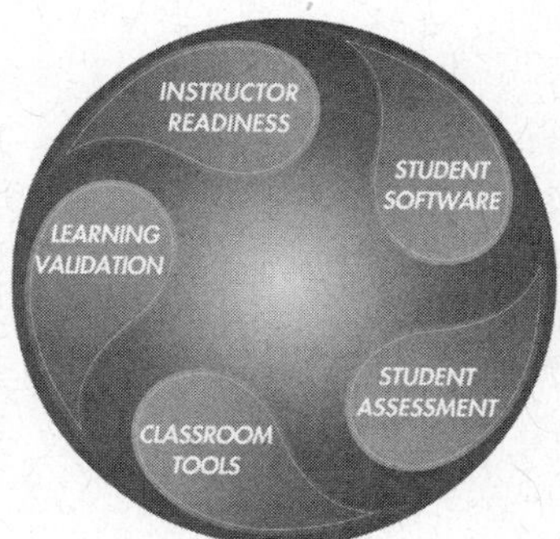

Illustrated Book Tour

■ Textbook Organization

This textbook is organized in sixteen lessons, with each lesson corresponding to a particular exam objective for the 70-688 Managing and Maintaining Windows 8 exam. This MOAC textbook covers all the learning objectives for the 70-688 certification exam, which is the second of two exams needed in order to obtain a Microsoft Certified Solutions Associate (MCSA) certification. The exam objectives are highlighted throughout the textbook.

■ Pedagogical Features

Many pedagogical features have been developed specifically for Microsoft Official Academic Course programs.

Presenting the extensive procedural information and technical concepts woven throughout the textbook raises challenges for the student and instructor alike. The Illustrated Book Tour that follows provides a guide to the rich features contributing to Microsoft Official Academic Course program's pedagogical plan. Following is a list of key features in each lesson designed to prepare students for success on the certification exams and in the workplace:

- Each lesson begins with an overview of the skills covered in the lesson. More than a standard list of learning objectives, the overview correlates skills to the certification exam objective.
- Illustrations: Screen images provide visual feedback as students work through the exercises. The images reinforce key concepts, provide visual clues about the steps, and allow students to check their progress.
- Key Terms: Important technical vocabulary is listed at the beginning of the lesson. When these terms are used later in the lesson, they appear in bold italic type and are defined.
- Engaging point-of-use reader aids, located throughout the lessons, tell students why this topic is relevant (*The Bottom Line*), provide students with helpful hints (*Take Note*), or show cross-references to where content is covered in greater detail (*X Ref*). Reader aids also provide additional relevant or background information that adds value to the lesson.
- Certification Ready features throughout the text signal students where a specific certification objective is covered. They provide students with a chance to check their understanding of that particular exam objective and, if necessary, review the section of the lesson where it is covered.
- Knowledge Assessments provide lesson-ending activities that test students' comprehension and retention of the material taught, presented using some of the question types that they'll see on the certification exam.
- An important supplement to this textbook is the accompanying lab work. Labs are available via a Lab Manual, and also by MOAC Labs Online. MOAC Labs Online provides students with the ability to work on the actual software simply by connecting through their Internet Explorer web browser. Either way, the labs use real-world scenarios to help students learn workplace skills associated with managing and maintaining Windows 8 in an enterprise environment.

Lesson Features

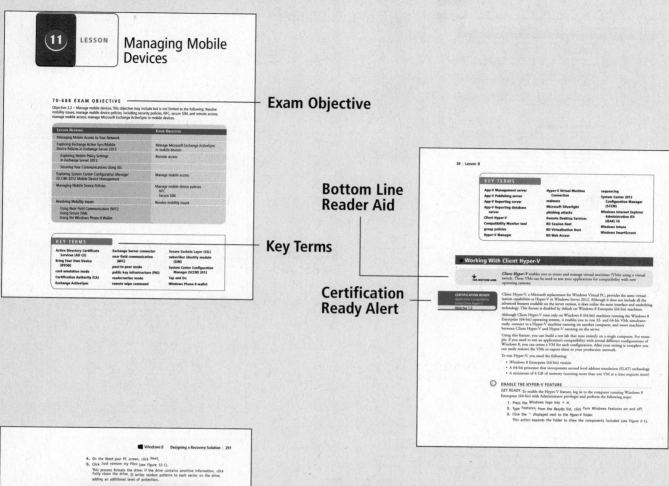

11 LESSON

Managing Mobile Devices

70-688 EXAM OBJECTIVE

Objective 3.2 – Manage mobile devices. This objective may include but is not limited to the following: Resolve mobility issues; manage mobile device policies, including security policies, NFC, secure SIM, and remote access; manage mobile access; manage Microsoft Exchange ActiveSync in mobile devices.

Lesson Heading	Exam Objective
Managing Mobile Access to Your Network	
Exploring Exchange Active Sync/Mobile Device Policies in Exchange Server 2013	Manage Microsoft Exchange ActiveSync in mobile devices
Exploring Mobile Policy Settings in Exchange Server 2013	Remote access
Securing Your Communications Using SSL	
Exploring System Center Configuration Manager (SCCM) 2012 Mobile Device Management	Manage mobile access
Managing Mobile Device Policies	Manage mobile device policies NFC Secure SIM
Resolving Mobility Issues	Resolve mobility issues
Using Near Field Communication (NFC) Using Secure SIMs Using the Windows Phone 8 Wallet	

KEY TERMS

Active Directory Certificate Services (AD CS)
Bring Your Own Device (BYOD)
card emulation mode
Certification Authority (CA)
Exchange ActiveSync
Exchange Server connector
near field communication (NFC)
peer-to-peer mode
public key infrastructure (PKI)
reader/writer mode
remote wipe command
Secure Sockets Layer (SSL)
subscriber identity module (SIM)
System Center Configuration Manager (SCCM) 2012
Tap and Do
Windows Phone 8 wallet

Exam Objective

Key Terms

Bottom Line Reader Aid

Certification Ready Alert

38 | Lesson 2

KEY TERMS

App-V Management server
App-V Publishing server
App-V Reporting server
App-V Reporting database server
Client Hyper-V
Compatibility Monitor tool
group policies
Hyper-V Manager
Hyper-V Virtual Machine Connection
malware
Microsoft Silverlight
phishing attacks
Remote Desktop Services
RD Session Host
RD Virtualization Host
RD Web Access
sequencing
System Center 2012 Configuration Manager (SCCM)
Windows Internet Explorer Administration Kit (IEAK) 10
Windows Intune
Windows SmartScreen

Working With Client Hyper-V

THE BOTTOM LINE

Client Hyper-V enables you to create and manage virtual machines (VMs) using a virtual switch. These VMs can be used to test your applications for compatibility with new operating systems.

CERTIFICATION READY
Application Compatibility Using Client Hyper-V
Objective 1.2

Client Hyper-V, a Microsoft replacement for Windows Virtual PC, provides the same virtualization capabilities as Hyper-V in Windows Server 2012. Although it does not include all the advanced features available on the server version, it does utilize the same interface and underlying technology. This feature is disabled by default on Windows 8 Enterprise (64-bit) machines.

Although Client Hyper-V runs only on Windows 8 (64-bit) machines running the Windows 8 Enterprise (64-bit) operating system, it enables you to run 32- and 64-bit VMs simultaneously, connect to a Hyper-V machine running on another computer, and move machines between Client Hyper-V and Hyper-V running on the server.

Using this feature, you can build a test lab that runs entirely on a single computer. For example, if you need to test an application's compatibility with several different configurations of Windows 8, you can create a VM for each configuration. After your testing is complete you can easily remove the VMs or export them to your production network.

To run Hyper-V, you need the following:

- Windows 8 Enterprise (64-bit) version
- A 64-bit processor that incorporates second level address translation (SLAT) technology
- A minimum of 4 GB of memory (running more than one VM at a time requires more)

ENABLE THE HYPER-V FEATURE

GET READY. To enable the Hyper-V feature, log in to the computer running Windows 8 Enterprise (64-bit) with Administrator privileges and perform the following steps:

1. Press the Windows logo key + w.
2. Type Features; from the *Results* list, click Turn Windows features on and off.
3. Click the + displayed next to the *Hyper-V* folder.

   This action expands the folder to show the components included (see Figure 2-1).

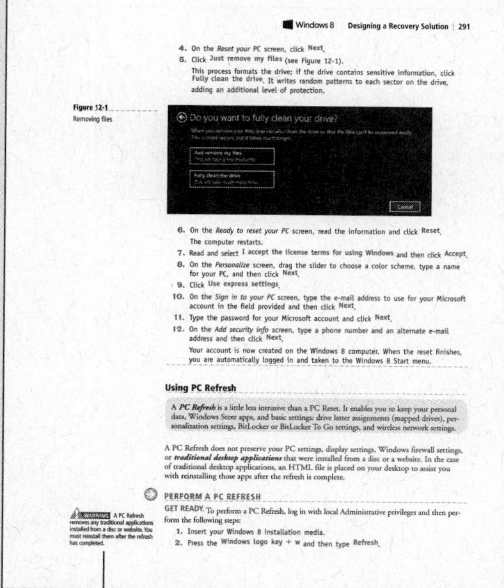

Windows 8 Designing a Recovery Solution | 291

4. On the *Reset your* PC screen, click Next.
5. Click Just remove my files (see Figure 12-1).

   This process formats the drive; if the drive contains sensitive information, click Fully clean the drive. It writes random patterns to each sector on the drive, adding an additional level of protection.

Figure 12-1
Removing files

6. On the *Ready to reset your PC* screen, read the information and click Reset.

   The computer restarts.
7. Read and select I accept the license terms for using Windows and then click Accept.
8. On the *Personalize* screen, drag the slider to choose a color scheme, type a name for your PC, and then click Next.
9. Click Use express settings.
10. On the *Sign in to your PC* screen, type the e-mail address to use for your Microsoft account in the field provided and then click Next.
11. Type the password for your Microsoft account and click Next.
12. On the *Add security info* screen, type a phone number and an alternate e-mail address and then click Next.

    Your account is now created on the Windows 8 computer. When the reset finishes, you are automatically logged in and taken to the Windows 8 Start menu.

Using PC Refresh

A ***PC Refresh*** is a little less intrusive than a PC Reset. It enables you to keep your personal data, Windows Store apps, and basic settings: drive letter assignments (mapped drives), personalization settings, BitLocker or BitLocker To Go settings, and wireless network settings.

A PC Refresh does not preserve your PC settings, display settings, Windows firewall settings, or ***traditional desktop applications*** that were installed from a disc or a website. In the case of traditional desktop applications, an HTML file is placed on your desktop to assist you with reinstalling those apps after the refresh is complete.

PERFORM A PC REFRESH

GET READY. To perform a PC Refresh, log in with local Administrative privileges and then perform the following steps:

1. Insert your Windows 8 installation media.
2. Press the Windows logo key + w and then type Refresh.

WARNING A PC Refresh removes any traditional applications installed from a disc or website. You must reinstall them after the refresh has completed.

Warning Reader Aid

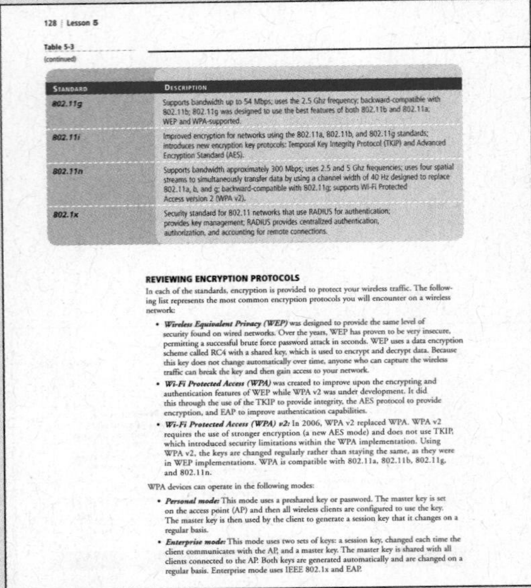

128 | Lesson 5

Table 5-3
(continued)

Standard	Description
802.11g	Supports bandwidth up to 54 Mbps; uses the 2.5 Ghz frequency; backward-compatible with 802.11b; 802.11g was designed to use the best features of both 802.11b and 802.11a; WEP and WPA-supported.
802.11i	Improved encryption for networks using the 802.11a, 802.11b, and 802.11g standards; introduces new encryption key protocols: Temporal Key Integrity Protocol (TKIP) and Advanced Encryption Standard (AES).
802.11n	Supports bandwidth approximately 300 Mbps; uses 2.5 and 5 Ghz frequencies; uses four spatial streams to simultaneously transfer data by using a channel width of 40 Hz designed to replace 802.11a, b, and g; backward-compatible with 802.11g; supports Wi-Fi Protected Access version 2 (WPA v2).
802.1x	Security standard for 802.11 networks that use RADIUS for authentication; provides key management; RADIUS provides centralized authentication, authorization, and accounting for remote connections.

REVIEWING ENCRYPTION PROTOCOLS

In each of the standards, encryption is provided to protect your wireless traffic. The following list represents the most common encryption protocols you will encounter on a wireless network:

- ***Wireless Equivalent Privacy (WEP)*** was designed to provide the same level of security found on wired networks. Over the years, WEP has proven to be very insecure, permitting a successful brute force password attack in seconds. WEP uses a data encryption scheme called RC4 with a shared key, which is used to encrypt and decrypt data. Because this key does not change automatically over time, anyone who can capture the wireless traffic can break the key and then gain access to your network.
- ***Wi-Fi Protected Access (WPA)*** was created to improve upon the encrypting and authentication features of WEP while WPA v2 was under development. It did this through the use of the TKIP to provide integrity, the AES protocol to provide encryption, and EAP to improve authentication capabilities.
- ***Wi-Fi Protected Access (WPA) v2:*** In 2006, WPA v2 replaced WPA. WPA v2 requires the use of stronger encryption (a new AES mode) and does not use TKIP, which introduced security limitations within the WPA implementation. Using WPA v2, the keys are changed regularly rather than staying the same, as they were in WEP implementations. WPA is compatible with 802.11a, 802.11b, 802.11g, and 802.11n.

WPA devices can operate in the following modes:

- ***Personal mode:*** This mode uses a preshared key or password. The master key is set on the access point (AP) and then all wireless clients are configured to use the key. The master key is then used by the client to generate a session key that it changes on a regular basis.
- ***Enterprise mode:*** This mode uses two sets of keys: a session key, changed each time the client communicates with the AP, and a master key. The master key is shared with all clients connected to the AP. Both keys are generated automatically and are changed on a regular basis. Enterprise mode uses IEEE 802.1x and EAP.

Easy-to-Read Tables

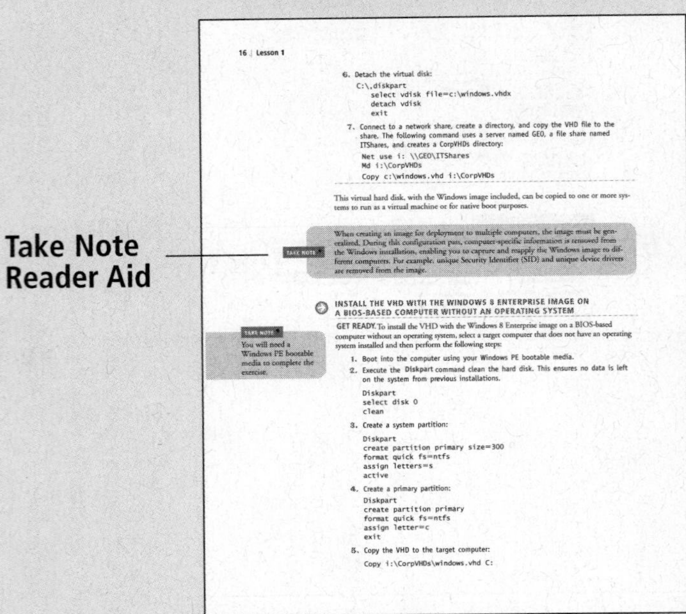

16 | Lesson 1

6. Detach the virtual disk:

```
C:\,diskpart
   select vdisk file=c:\windows.vhdx
   detach vdisk
   exit
```

7. Connect to a network share, create a directory, and copy the VHD file to the share. The following command uses a server named GEO, a file share named ITShares, and creates a CorpVHDs directory:

```
Net use i: \\GEO\ITShares
Md i:\CorpVHDs
Copy c:\windows.vhd i:\CorpVHDs
```

This virtual hard disk, with the Windows image included, can be copied to one or more systems to run as a virtual machine or for native boot purposes.

TAKE NOTE* When creating an image for deployment to multiple computers, the image must be generalized. During this configuration pass, computer-specific information is removed from the Windows installation, enabling you to capture and reapply the Windows image to different computers. For example, unique Security Identifier (SID) and unique device drivers are removed from the image.

INSTALL THE VHD WITH THE WINDOWS 8 ENTERPRISE IMAGE ON A BIOS-BASED COMPUTER WITHOUT AN OPERATING SYSTEM

TAKE NOTE* You will need a Windows PE bootable media to complete the exercise.

GET READY. To install the VHD with the Windows 8 Enterprise image on a BIOS-based computer without an operating system, select a target computer that does not have an operating system installed and then perform the following steps:

1. Boot into the computer using your Windows PE bootable media.
2. Execute the **Diskpart** command clean the hard disk. This ensures no data is left on the system from previous installations.

```
Diskpart
select disk 0
clean
```

3. Create a system partition:

```
Diskpart
create partition primary size=300
format quick fs=ntfs
assign letters=s
active
```

4. Create a primary partition:

```
Diskpart
create partition primary
format quick fs=ntfs
assign letter=c
exit
```

5. Copy the VHD to the target computer:

```
Copy i:\CorpVHDs\windows.vhd C:
```

Take Note Reader Aid

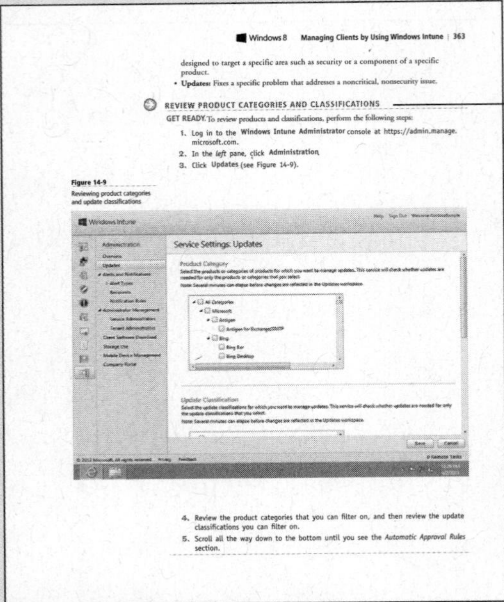

Windows 8 Managing Clients by Using Windows Intune | 363

designed to target a specific area such as security or a component of a specific product.

- **Updates:** Fixes a specific problem that addresses a noncritical, nonsecurity issue.

REVIEW PRODUCT CATEGORIES AND CLASSIFICATIONS

GET READY. To review products and classifications, perform the following steps:

1. Log in to the **Windows Intune Administrator** console at https://admin.manage.microsoft.com.
2. In the *left* pane, click **Administration**.
3. Click **Updates** (see Figure 14-9).

Figure 14-9
Reviewing product categories and update classifications

4. Review the product categories that you can filter on, and then review the update classifications you can filter on.
5. Scroll all the way down to the bottom until you see the *Automatic Approval Rules* section.

Step-by-step Exercises

www.wiley.com/college/microsoft ***or***
call the MOAC Toll-Free Number: 1+(888) 764-7001 (U.S. & Canada only)

Screen Images

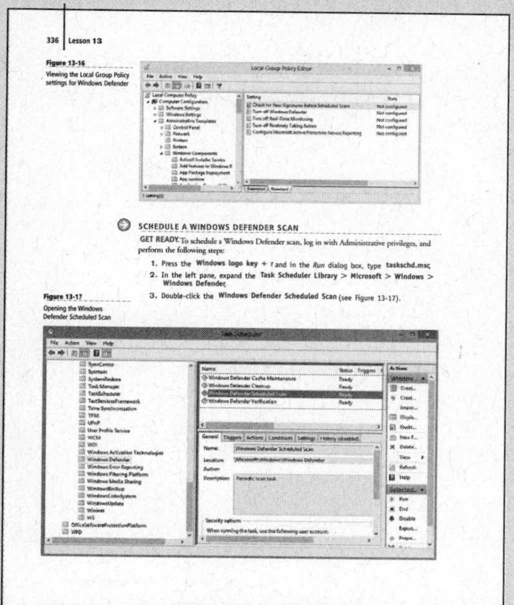

336 | Lesson 13

Figure 13-16
Viewing the Local Group Policy settings for Windows Defender

SCHEDULE A WINDOWS DEFENDER SCAN

GET READY. To schedule a Windows Defender scan, log in with Administrative privileges, and perform the following steps:

1. Press the **Windows logo key + r** and in the *Run* dialog box, type **taskschd.msc**.
2. In the left pane, expand the **Task Scheduler Library > Microsoft > Windows > Windows Defender**.
3. Double-click the **Windows Defender Scheduled Scan** (see Figure 13-17).

Figure 13-17
Opening the Windows Defender Scheduled Scan

Informative Diagrams

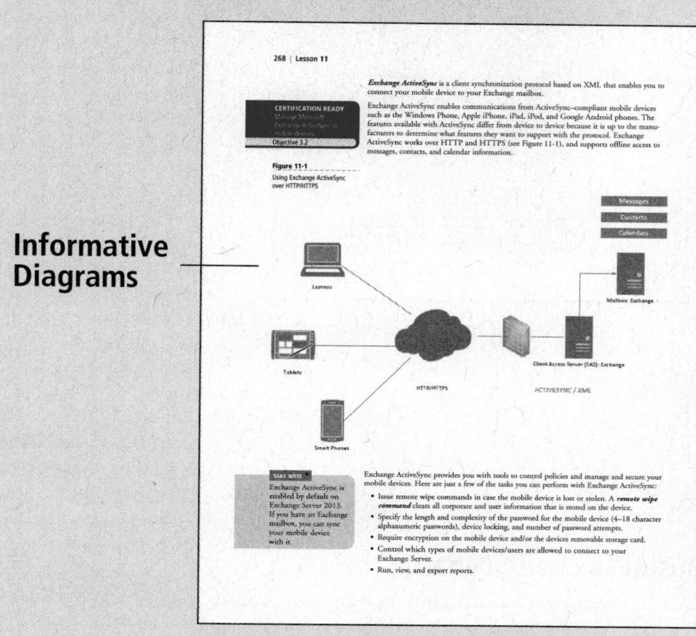

268 | Lesson 11

Exchange ActiveSync is a client synchronization protocol based on XML that enables you to connect your mobile device to your Exchange mailbox.

CERTIFICATION READY
Manage Microsoft Exchange ActiveSync in mobile devices
Objective 3.2

Exchange ActiveSync enables communications from ActiveSync–compliant mobile devices such as the Windows Phone, Apple iPhone, iPad, iPod, and Google Android phones. The features available with ActiveSync differ from device to device because it is up to the manufacturers to determine what features they want to support with the protocol. Exchange ActiveSync works over HTTP and HTTPS (see Figure 11-1), and supports offline access to messages, contacts, and calendar information.

Figure 11-1
Using Exchange ActiveSync over HTTP/HTTPS

TAKE NOTE
Exchange ActiveSync is enabled by default on Exchange Server 2013. If you have an Exchange mailbox, you can sync your mobile device with it.

Exchange ActiveSync provides you with tools to control policies and manage and secure your mobile devices. Here are just a few of the tasks you can perform with Exchange ActiveSync:

- Issue remote wipe commands in case the mobile device is lost or stolen. A ***remote wipe command*** clears all corporate and user information that is stored on the device.
- Specify the length and complexity of the password for the mobile device (4–18 character alphanumeric passwords), device locking, and number of password attempts.
- Require encryption on the mobile device and/or the devices removable storage card.
- Control which types of mobile devices/users are allowed to connect to your Exchange Server.
- Run, view, and export reports.

More Information Reader Aid

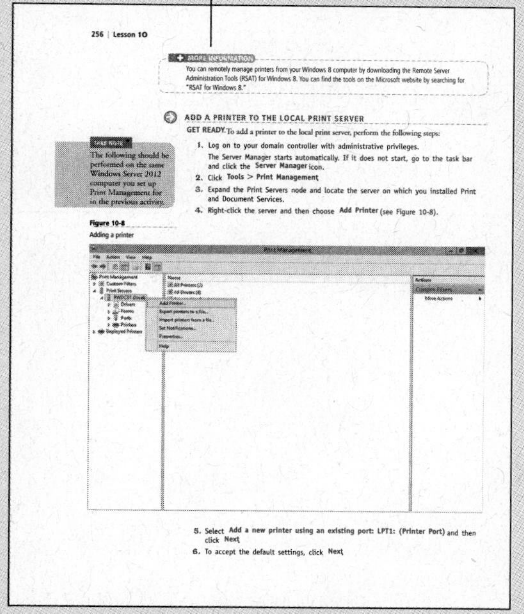

256 | Lesson 10

MORE INFORMATION
You can remotely manage printers from your Windows 8 computer by downloading the Remote Server Administration Tools (RSAT) for Windows 8. You can find the tools on the Microsoft website by searching for "RSAT for Windows 8."

ADD A PRINTER TO THE LOCAL PRINT SERVER

GET READY. To add a printer to the local print server, perform the following steps:

TAKE NOTE
The following should be performed on the same Windows Server 2012 computer you set up Print Management for in the previous activity.

1. Log on to your domain controller with administrative privileges.
   The Server Manager starts automatically. If it does not start, go to the task bar and click the **Server Manager** icon.
2. Click **Tools > Print Management**.
3. Expand the Print Servers node and locate the server on which you installed Print and Document Services.
4. Right-click the server and then choose **Add Printer** (see Figure 10-8).

Figure 10-8
Adding a printer

5. Select **Add a new printer using an existing port: LPT1: (Printer Port)** and then click **Next**.
6. To accept the default settings, click **Next**.

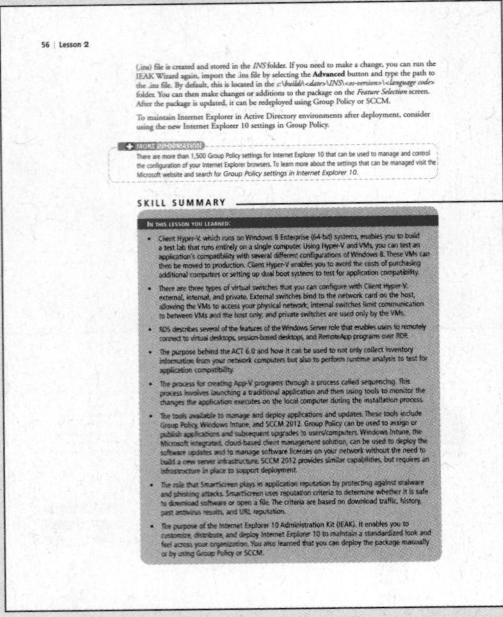

56 | Lesson 2

(.ins) file is created and stored in the *INS* folder. If you need to make a change, you can run the IEAK Wizard again, import the .ins file by selecting the **Advanced** button and type the path to the .ins file. By default, this is located in the *c:\builds\<date>\INS\<os-version>\<language code>* folder. You can then make changes or additions to the package on the *Feature Selection* screen. After the package is updated, it can be redeployed using Group Policy or SCCM.

To maintain Internet Explorer in Active Directory environments after deployment, consider using the new Internet Explorer 10 settings in Group Policy.

MORE INFORMATION

There are more than 1,500 Group Policy settings for Internet Explorer 10 that can be used to manage and control the configuration of your Internet Explorer browsers. To learn more about the settings that can be managed visit the Microsoft website and search for *Group Policy settings in Internet Explorer 10.*

SKILL SUMMARY

IN THIS LESSON YOU LEARNED:

- Client Hyper-V, which runs on Windows 8 Enterprise (64-bit) systems, enables you to build a test lab that runs entirely on a single computer. Using Hyper-V and VMs, you can test an application's compatibility with several different configurations of Windows 8. These VMs can then be moved to production. Client Hyper-V enables you to avoid the costs of purchasing additional computers or setting up dual boot systems to test for application compatibility.
- There are three types of virtual switches that you can configure with Client Hyper-V: external, internal, and private. External switches bind to the network card on the host, allowing the VMs to access your physical network; internal switches limit communication to between VMs and the host only; and private switches are used only by the VMs.
- RDS describes several of the features of the Windows Server role that enables users to remotely connect to virtual desktops, session-based desktops, and RemoteApp programs over RDP.
- The purpose behind the ACT 6.0 and how it can be used to not only collect inventory information from your network computers but also to perform runtime analysis to test for application compatibility.
- The process for creating App-V programs through a process called sequencing. This process involves launching a traditional application and then using tools to monitor the changes the application executes on the local computer during the installation process.
- The tools available to manage and deploy applications and updates. These tools include Group Policy, Windows Intune, and SCCM 2012. Group Policy can be used to assign or publish applications and subsequent upgrades to users/computers. Windows Intune, the Microsoft integrated, cloud-based client management solution, can be used to deploy the software updates and to manage software licenses on your network without the need to build a new server infrastructure. SCCM 2012 provides similar capabilities, but requires an infrastructure in place to support deployment.
- The role that SmartScreen plays in application reputation by protecting against malware and phishing attacks. SmartScreen uses reputation criteria to determine whether it is safe to download software or open a file. The criteria are based on download traffic, history, past antivirus results, and URL reputation.
- The purpose of the Internet Explorer 10 Administration Kit (IEAK). It enables you to customize, distribute, and deploy Internet Explorer 10 to maintain a standardized look and feel across your organization. You also learned that you can deploy the package manually or by using Group Policy or SCCM.

Skill Summary

Knowledge Assessment

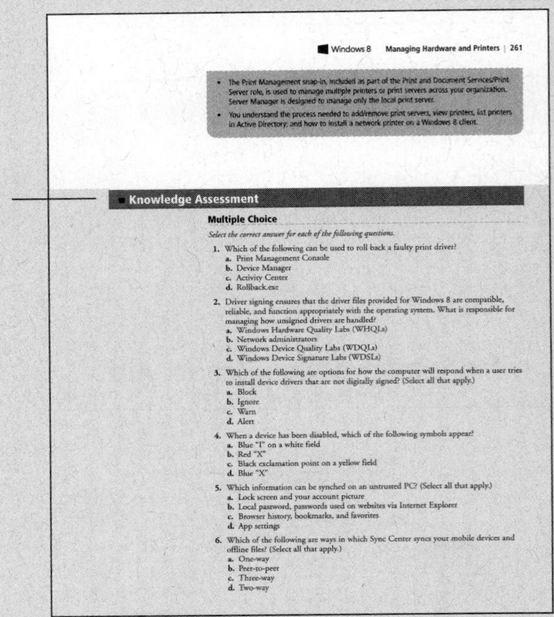

Windows 8 Managing Hardware and Printers | 261

- The Print Management snap-in, included as part of the Print and Document Services/Print Server role, is used to manage multiple printers or print servers across your organization. Server Manager is designed to manage only the local print server.
- You understand the process needed to add/remove print servers, view printers, list printers in Active Directory, and how to install a network printer on a Windows 8 client.

Knowledge Assessment

Multiple Choice

Select the correct answer for each of the following questions.

1. Which of the following can be used to roll back a faulty print driver?
   a. Print Management Console
   b. Device Manager
   c. Activity Center
   d. Rollback.exe
2. Driver signing ensures that the driver files provided for Windows 8 are compatible, reliable, and function appropriately with the operating system. What is responsible for managing how unsigned drivers are handled?
   a. Windows Hardware Quality Labs (WHQLs)
   b. Network administrators
   c. Windows Device Quality Labs (WDQLs)
   d. Windows Device Signature Labs (WDSLs)
3. Which of the following are options for how the computer will respond when a user tries to install device drivers that are not digitally signed? (Select all that apply.)
   a. Block
   b. Ignore
   c. Warn
   d. Alert
4. When a device has been disabled, which of the following symbols appear?
   a. Blue "I" on a white field
   b. Red "X"
   c. Black exclamation point on a yellow field
   d. Blue "X"
5. Which information can be synched on an untrusted PC? (Select all that apply.)
   a. Lock screen and your account picture
   b. Local password, passwords used on websites via Internet Explorer
   c. Browser history, bookmarks, and favorites
   d. App settings
6. Which of the following are ways in which Sync Center syncs your mobile devices and offline files? (Select all that apply.)
   a. One-way
   b. Peer-to-peer
   c. Three-way
   d. Two-way

Business Case Scenarios

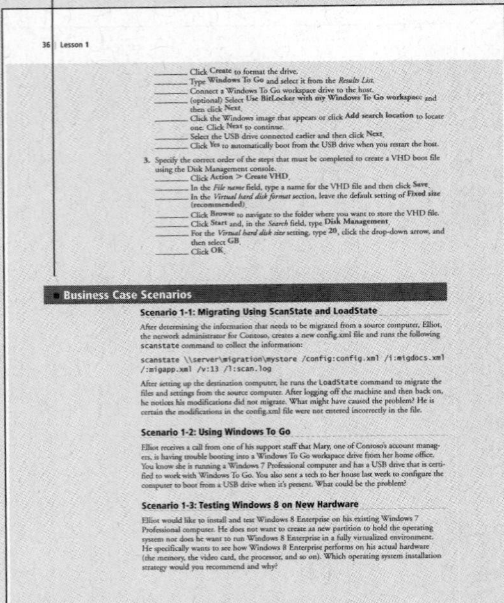

36 | Lesson 1

_______ Click **Create** to format the drive.
_______ Type **Windows To Go** and select it from the *Results List*.
_______ Connect a Windows To Go workspace drive to the host.
_______ (optional) Select **Use BitLocker with my Windows To Go workspace** and then click **Next**.
_______ Click the Windows image that appears or click **Add search location** to locate one. Click **Next** to continue.
_______ Select the USB drive connected earlier and then click **Next**.
_______ Click **Yes** to automatically boot from the USB drive when you restart the host.

3. Specify the correct order of the steps that must be completed to create a VHD boot file using the Disk Management console.

_______ Click **Action > Create VHD**.
_______ In the *File name* field, type a name for the VHD file and then click **Save**.
_______ In the *Virtual hard disk format* section, leave the default setting of **Fixed size (recommended)**.
_______ Click **Browse** to navigate to the folder where you want to store the VHD file.
_______ Click **Start** and, in the *Search* field, type **Disk Management**.
_______ For the *Virtual hard disk size* setting, type **20**, click the drop-down arrow, and then select **GB**.
_______ Click **OK**.

Business Case Scenarios

Scenario 1-1: Migrating Using ScanState and LoadState

After determining the information that needs to be migrated from a source computer, Elliot, the network administrator for Contoso, creates a new config.xml file and runs the following `scanstate` command to collect the information:

```
scanstate \\server\migration\mystore /config:config.xml /i:migdocs.xml
/:migapp.xml /v:13 /l:scan.log
```

After setting up the destination computer, he runs the `LoadState` command to migrate the files and settings from the source computer. After logging off the machine and then back on, he notices his modifications did not migrate. What might have caused the problem? He is certain the modifications in the config.xml file were not entered incorrectly in the file.

Scenario 1-2: Using Windows To Go

Elliot receives a call from one of his support staff that Mary, one of Contoso's account managers, is having trouble booting into a Windows To Go workspace drive from her home office. You know she is running a Windows 7 Professional computer and has a USB drive that is certified to work with Windows To Go. You also sent a tech to her house last week to configure the computer to boot from a USB drive when it's present. What could be the problem?

Scenario 1-3: Testing Windows 8 on New Hardware

Elliot would like to install and test Windows 8 Enterprise on his existing Windows 7 Professional computer. He does not want to create aa new partition to hold the operating system nor does he want to run Windows 8 Enterprise in a fully virtualized environment. He specifically wants to see how Windows 8 Enterprise performs on his actual hardware (the memory, the video card, the processor, and so on). Which operating system installation strategy would you recommend and why?

Conventions and Features Used in This Book

This book uses particular fonts, symbols, and heading conventions to highlight important information or to call your attention to special steps. For more information about the features in each lesson, refer to the Illustrated Book Tour section.

CONVENTION	MEANING
↓ THE BOTTOM LINE	This feature provides a brief summary of the material to be covered in the section that follows.
CERTIFICATION READY	This feature signals the point in the text where a specific certification objective is covered. It provides you with a chance to check your understanding of that particular exam objective and, if necessary, review the section of the lesson where it is covered.
TAKE NOTE* + MORE INFORMATION	Reader aids appear in shaded boxes found in your text. *Take Note and More Information* provide helpful hints related to particular tasks or topics.
! WARNING	*Warning* points out instances when error or misuse could cause damage to the computer or network.
X REF	These *X Ref* notes provide pointers to information discussed elsewhere in the textbook or describe interesting features of Windows 8 that are not directly addressed in the current topic or exercise.
A ***shared printer*** can be used by many individuals on a network.	Key terms appear in bold italic.
`cd\windows\system32\ServerMigrationTools`	Commands that are to be typed are shown in a special font.
Click Install Now.	Any button on the screen you are supposed to click on or select will appear in blue.

Instructor Support Program

The Microsoft Official Academic Course programs are accompanied by a rich array of resources that incorporate the extensive textbook visuals to form a pedagogically cohesive package. These resources provide all the materials instructors need to deploy and deliver their courses. Resource information available at www.wiley.com/college/microsoft includes:

- **DreamSpark Premium** is designed to provide the easiest and most inexpensive developer tools, products, and technologies available to faculty and students in labs, classrooms, and on student PCs. A free three-year membership is available to qualified MOAC adopters.

  Note: Windows 8 can be downloaded from DreamSpark Premium for use in this course.
- **Instructor's Guide.** The Instructor's Guide contains solutions to all the textbook exercises as well as chapter summaries and lecture notes. The Instructor's Guide and Syllabi for various term lengths are available from the Instructor's Book Companion site.
- **Test Bank.** The Test Bank contains hundreds of questions organized by lesson in multiple-choice, best answer, build list, and essay formats and is available to download from the Instructor's Book Companion site. A complete answer key is provided.
- **PowerPoint Presentations.** A complete set of PowerPoint presentations is available on the Instructor's Book Companion site to enhance classroom presentations. Tailored to the text's topical coverage, these presentations are designed to convey key Windows 8 concepts addressed in the text.
- **Available Textbook Figures.** All figures from the text are on the Instructor's Book Companion site. By using these visuals in class discussions, you can help focus students' attention on key elements of Windows 8 and help them understand how to use it effectively in the workplace.
- **MOAC Labs Online.** MOAC Labs Online is a cloud-based environment that enables students to conduct exercises using real Microsoft products. These are not simulations but instead are live virtual machines where faculty and students can perform any activities they would on a local virtual machine. MOAC Labs Online relieves the need for local setup, configuration, and most troubleshooting tasks. This represents an opportunity to lower costs, eliminate the hassle of lab setup, and support and improve student access and portability. Contact your Wiley rep about including MOAC Labs Online with your course offering.
- **Lab Answer Keys.** Answer keys for review questions found in the lab manuals and MOAC Labs Online are available on the Instructor's Book Companion site.
- **Lab Worksheets.** The review questions found in the lab manuals and MOAC Labs Online are gathered in Microsoft Word documents for students to use. These are available on the Instructor's Book Companion site.
- **Sharing with Fellow Faculty Members.** When it comes to improving the classroom experience, there is no better source of ideas and inspiration than your colleagues teaching the same material. The Wiley Faculty Network connects teachers with technology, facilitates the exchange of best practices, and helps to enhance instructional efficiency and effectiveness. Faculty Network activities include technology training and tutorials, virtual seminars, peer-to-peer exchanges of experiences and ideas, personal consulting, and sharing of resources. For details visit www.WhereFacultyConnect.com.

Wiley Faculty Network

DREAMSPARK PREMIUM—FREE 3-YEAR MEMBERSHIP AVAILABLE TO QUALIFIED ADOPTERS!

DreamSpark Premium is designed to provide the easiest and most inexpensive way for schools to make the latest Microsoft developer tools, products, and technologies available in labs, classrooms, and on student PCs. DreamSpark Premium is an annual membership program for departments teaching Science, Technology, Engineering, and Mathematics (STEM) courses. The membership provides a complete solution to keep academic labs, faculty, and students on the leading edge of technology.

Software available through the DreamSpark Premium program is provided at no charge to adopting departments through the Wiley and Microsoft publishing partnership.

Contact your Wiley rep for details.

For more information about the DreamSpark Premium program, go to Microsoft's DreamSpark website.

Note: Windows 8 can be downloaded from DreamSpark Premium for use by students in this course.

■ Important Web Addresses and Phone Numbers

To locate the Wiley Higher Education Rep in your area, go to http://www.wiley.com/college and click on the "*Contact Us*" link at the top of the page, or call the MOAC Toll Free Number: 1 + (888) 764-7001 (U.S. & Canada only).

To learn more about becoming a Microsoft Certified Solutions Associate and exam availability, visit Microsoft's Training & Certification website.

Student Support Program

Book Companion Web Site (www.wiley.com/college/microsoft)

The students' book companion site for the MOAC series includes any resources, exercise files, and web links that will be used in conjunction with this course.

Wiley E-Text: Powered by VitalSource

Wiley E-Texts: Powered by VitalSource, are innovative, electronic versions of printed textbooks. Students can buy Wiley E-Texts for around 50% off the U.S. price of the printed text and get the added value of permanence and portability. Wiley E-Texts provide students with numerous additional benefits that are not available with other e-text solutions.

Wiley E-Texts are NOT subscriptions; students download the Wiley E-Text to their computer desktops. Students own the content they buy to keep for as long as they want. Once a Wiley E-Text is downloaded to the computer desktop, students have instant access to all of the content without being online. Students can also print the sections they prefer to read in hard copy. Students also have access to fully integrated resources within their Wiley E-Text. From highlighting their e-text to taking and sharing notes, students can easily personalize their Wiley E-Text as they are reading or following along in class.

Microsoft Software

Various Microsoft software is available through a DreamSpark student membership. DreamSpark is a Microsoft program that provides students with free access to Microsoft software for learning, teaching, and research purposes. Students can download full versions of Microsoft software at no cost by visiting Microsoft's DreamSpark website.

▪ Microsoft Certification

Microsoft Certification has many benefits and enables you to keep your skills relevant, applicable, and competitive. In addition, Microsoft Certification is an industry standard that is recognized worldwide—which helps open doors to potential job opportunities. After you earn your Microsoft Certification, you have access to a number of benefits, which can be found on the Microsoft Certified Professional member site.

Microsoft Learning has reinvented the Microsoft Certification Program by building cloud-related skills validation into the industry's most recognized certification program. Microsoft Certified Solutions Expert (MCSE) and Microsoft Certified Solutions Developer (MCSD) are Microsoft's flagship certifications for professionals who want to lead their IT organization's journey to the cloud. These certifications recognize IT professionals with broad and deep skill sets across Microsoft solutions. The Microsoft Certified Solutions Associate (MCSA) is the certification for aspiring IT professionals. These new certifications integrate cloud-related and on-premise skills validation in order to support organizations and recognize individuals who have the skills required to be productive using Microsoft technologies.

On-premise or in the cloud, Microsoft training and certification empowers technology professionals to expand their skills and gain knowledge directly from the source. Securing these essential skills will allow you to grow your career and make yourself indispensable as the industry shifts to the cloud. Cloud computing ultimately enables IT to focus on more mission-critical activities, raising the bar of required expertise for IT professionals and developers. These reinvented certifications test on a deeper set of skills that map to real-world business context. Rather than testing only on a feature of a technology, Microsoft Certifications now validate more advanced skills and a deeper understanding of the platform.

Microsoft Certified Solutions Associate (MCSA)

The Microsoft Certified Solutions Associate (MCSA) certification is for students preparing to get their first jobs in Microsoft technology. Whether in the cloud or on-premise, this certification validates the core platform skills needed in an IT environment. Earning an MCSA: Windows 8 certification will qualify you for a position as a computer support specialist.

The MCSA Windows 8 certification shows that you have the primary set of Windows 8 skills that are relevant across multiple solution areas in a business environment. Candidates for the 70-688 exam will show their knowledge in configuring and supporting Windows 8 computers, devices, users, and associated network and security resources. These networks are configured as a domain-based or peer-to-peer environment with access to the Internet and cloud services. This exam will validate the skills necessary to administer Windows 8-based computers and devices as a portion of broader technical responsibilities.

If you are a student new to IT who may not yet be ready for MCSA, the Microsoft Technology Associate (MTA) certification is an optional starting point that may be available through your school.

You can learn more about the MCSA certification at the Microsoft Training & Certification website.

Preparing to Take an Exam

Unless you are a very experienced user, you will need to use test preparation materials to prepare to complete the test correctly and within the time allowed. The Microsoft Official Academic Course series is designed to prepare you with a strong knowledge of all exam topics, and with some additional review and practice on your own, you should feel confident in your ability to pass the appropriate exam.

After you decide which exam to take, review the list of objectives for the exam. You can easily identify tasks that are included in the objective list by locating the exam objective overview at the start of each lesson and the Certification Ready sidebars in the margin of the lessons in this book.

To register for the 70-688 exam, visit Microsoft Training & Certifications Registration webpage for directions on how to register with Prometric, the company that delivers the MCSA exams. Keep in mind these important items about the testing procedure:

- **What to expect.** Microsoft Certification testing labs typically have multiple workstations, which may or may not be occupied by other candidates. Test center administrators strive to provide a quiet and comfortable environment for all test takers.
- **Plan to arrive early.** It is recommended that you arrive at the test center at least 30 minutes before the test is scheduled to begin.
- **Bring your identification.** To take your exam, you must bring the identification (ID) that was specified when you registered for the exam. If you are unclear about which forms of ID are required, contact the exam sponsor identified in your registration information. Although requirements vary, you typically must show two valid forms of ID, one with a photo, both with your signature.
- **Leave personal items at home.** The only item allowed into the testing area is your identification, so leave any backpacks, laptops, briefcases, and other personal items at home. If you have items that cannot be left behind (such as purses), the testing center might have small lockers available for use.
- **Nondisclosure agreement.** At the testing center, Microsoft requires that you accept the terms of a nondisclosure agreement (NDA) and complete a brief demographic survey before taking your certification exam.

About the Author

Richard Watson (MCSE, A+, Network+, iNet+) holds an MBA in Information Technology Management and is the Principal/Owner of Bridgehill Learning Solutions, LLC., which provides content conversion, custom course development, strategic planning, technical writing, and learning management system selection services. Previously, Richard was Manager of Instructional Design for the Audigy Group, whereby he was responsible for the identification, creation/modification, and evaluation of both new and existing learning resources to ensure alignment with companies' business objectives; project management of learning initiatives across multiple departments; working with outside vendors to identify, select, and implement learning programs and systems; and assessing the overall effectiveness of programs through report creation/analysis and surveys/interviews with key stakeholders. Richard has authored several MCSE books covering networking, administration, and security for Windows 2000 and 2003 for Prentice Hall.

Acknowledgements

We thank the MOAC faculty and instructors who have assisted us in building the Microsoft Official Academic Course courseware. These elite educators have acted as our sounding board on key pedagogical and design decisions leading to the development of the MOAC courseware for future Information Technology workers. They have provided invaluable advice in the service of quality instructional materials, and we truly appreciate their dedication to technology education.

Brian Bridson, Baker College of Flint

David Chaulk, Baker College Online

Ron Handlon, Remington College—Tampa Campus

Katherine James, Seneca College of Applied Arts & Technology

Wen Liu, ITT Educational Services

Zeshan Sattar, Pearson in Practice

Jared Spencer, Westwood College Online

David Vallerga, MTI College

Bonny Willy, Ivy Tech State College

We also thank Microsoft Learning's Lutz Ziob, Don Field, Tim Sneath, Moorthy Uppaluri, Keith Loeber, Rob Linsky, Anne Hamilton, Shelby Grieve, Gene Longo, Mike Mulcare, Paul Schmitt, Martin DelRe, Colin Klein, Julia Stasio, and Josh Barnhill for their encouragement and support in making the Microsoft Official Academic Course programs the finest academic materials for mastering the newest Microsoft technologies for both students and instructors.

Brief Contents

Contents

Lesson 4: Designing a Solution for User Settings 88

Lesson 5: Designing for Network Connectivity 113

Lesson 6: Designing for Remote Access 144

Lesson 7: Design for Authentication and Authorization 183

Lesson 8: Managing Data Storage 200

Lesson 9: Managing Data Security 219

Lesson 14: Managing Clients by Using Windows Intune 351

Lesson 15: Managing Public Cloud Services 389

Lesson 16: Managing and Maintaining Clients by Using MDOP 409

Designing an Operating System Installation Strategy

LESSON 1

70-688 EXAM OBJECTIVE

Objective 1.1 – Design an operating system installation strategy. This objective may include but is not limited to the following design considerations: Windows To Go; operating system virtualization; native VHD boot; multi-boot; upgrade vs. migration.

LESSON HEADING	EXAM OBJECTIVE
Creating a Windows To Go Workspace	Windows To Go
Creating and Deploying a Windows To Go Workspace Drive	
Booting into a Windows To Go Workspace	
Virtualizing Operating Systems	Operating system virtualization
Exploring Operating System Virtualization	
Exploring User State Virtualization	
Exploring Application Virtualization (App-V)	
Configuring a Native VHD Boot File	Native VHD boot
Understanding VHD Formats	
Installing Windows 8 on a VHD with an Operating System Present	
Using BCDEdit and BDCBoot	
Configuring a Multi-Boot System	Multi-boot
Setting Up a Multi-Boot System	
Upgrading Versus Migrating to Windows 8	Upgrade vs. migration
Exploring the Application Compatibility Toolkit (ACT)	
Exploring the User State Migration Tool (USMT)	

KEY TERMS

ACT Log Processing Service (LPS)
ACT database
ACT LPS share
Application Compatibility Manager (ACM)
Application Compatibility Toolkit (ACT), 6.0
Application Virtualization (App-V)
Boot Configuration Data (BCD) store
BCDboot (bcdboot.exe)
BCD Editor (bcdedit.exe) or `bcdedit`
BitLocker To Go
Client Hyper-V
Deployment Image Services and Management (DISM)
Disk Management console (diskmgmt.msc)
Diskpart
Dynamically Expanding
Fixed Size
Group Policy Object (GPO)
Group Policy Management console (gpmc.msc)
guest operating system
hardlink folder
Hyper-V
hypervisor (or virtual machine manager)
inventory-collector package
Microsoft Compatibility Exchange
Microsoft Desktop Optimization Pack (MDOP)
Microsoft Enterprise Desktop Virtualization (MED-V)
MED-V workspace
multi-boot (dual boot)
native VHD boot
operating system virtualization
personal virtual desktop
RD Connection Broker servers
RD Gateway servers
RD Licensing servers
RD Session Host servers
RD Web Access servers
RemoteApps
Remote Desktop Protocol (RDP)
Remote Desktop Services (RDS)
runtime-analysis package
session virtualization
thin client
User State Virtualization (USV)
User State Migration Tool (USMT) 5.0
User Experience Virtualization (UE-V)
virtual hard disk (VHD)
virtual machine
virtual machine manager (or hypervisor)
VHD format
VHDX format
Virtual Desktop Infrastructure (VDI)
virtual desktop pool
Windows Easy Transfer
Windows 8 Pre-installation Environment (PE) disk
Windows To Go workspace
Workspace to Go Creator (pwcreator.exe)

■ Creating A Windows To Go Workspace

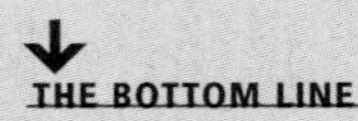

Windows To Go is a feature available with Windows 8 Enterprise clients that allows you to boot a full version of Windows 8 Enterprise from an external USB drive on a host computer.

CERTIFICATION READY
Windows to Go
Objective 1.1

Windows To Go is a feature in Windows 8 Enterprise edition that allows you to create a ***Windows To Go workspace*** on an external USB 3.0 drive. This enables your users to boot a full version of Windows 8 from removable media. The drive uses the same image installed on a corporate desktop and laptop; therefore, you can manage them in the same manner and use the same tools. The drive itself must be connected to a host computer running on a Windows 7 or later certified operating system to function.

Creating and Deploying a Windows To Go Workspace Drive

You can create a Windows to Go workspace drive for employees working from home, contractors on temporary assignment and for employees who travel between sites and need access to corporate resources and applications. This provides them with mobility while also allowing you to manage the devices as part of your corporate policies.

The ***Workspace to Go Creator (pwcreator.exe)*** is used to create Windows To Go workspaces. You can also use a USB duplicator product but that will require you to duplicate the drive before it is booted and initialized.

To create a Windows To Go workspace, you will need:

- A USB drive that supports Windows To Go (32GB or larger).
- A computer running Windows 8 Enterprise edition.
- A Windows 8 Enterprise ISO, Windows 8 Enterprise installation media, or a corporate Windows image (.wim) created from Windows 8 Enterprise media.
- Local administrator access on the computer.

To protect the drive in case it is lost or stolen, you have the option to configure ***BitLocker To Go*** during the setup of the workspace. BitLocker To Go allows you to encrypt a removable drive and restrict access with a password or a smart card.

Once your removable drive is setup, you can deploy the Windows To Go workspace centrally or by allowing individual users to create their own workspaces. Central management and deployment requires System Center Configuration Manager 2012 Service Pack 1.

CREATE A WINDOWS TO GO WORKSPACE

GET READY. To create a Windows to Go workspace, log on as an administrator to a computer running Windows 8 Enterprise edition and then perform the following steps:

1. Connect a Windows To Go USB certified device to the host.
2. Press the **Windows logo key + w.**
3. Type **Windows To Go** and then select it from the *Results* list.
4. Select the USB drive you connected earlier and then click **Next.**
5. Click the Windows image that appears or click **Add search location** to locate one. Click **Next** to continue.
6. Click **Create** to format the drive.
7. (Optional) Select the **Use BitLocker with my Windows To Go workspace** checkbox and then type a password. Click **Next.**

TAKE NOTE*

Enabling BitLocker on the Windows To Go workspace will protect the drive if it is lost or stolen. Using this feature will require you to type a password each time you use the workspace.

8. Click **Create** to setup the Windows To Go workspace.
9. Click Yes to automatically boot from the USB drive when you restart the host or click No if you want to change the PC's firmware settings to use the workspace.

Figure 1-1
Selecting the Windows To Go Startup Option

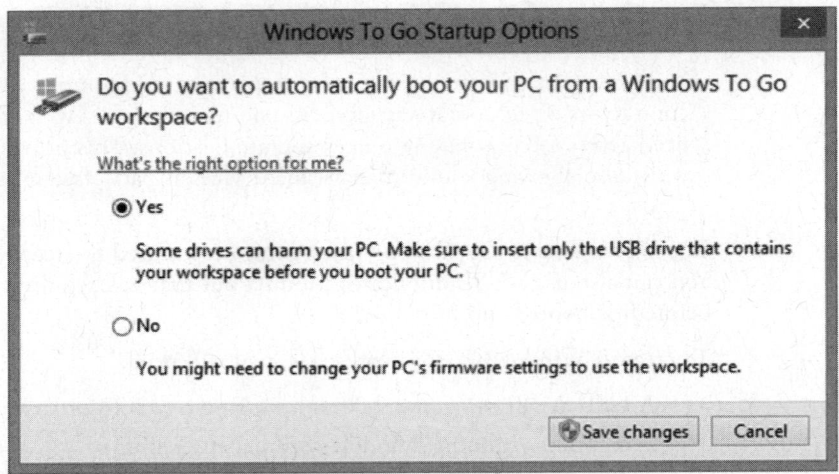

If you click Yes, your computer will automatically boot to the Windows To Go workspace every time a USB drive is detected. If you click No, you will need to change startup options in your computer's firmware. You do this by entering your firmware setup using the appropriate function key for your specific type of BIOS. This is usually the F12 key but you may need to check the manufacturer's website to determine the appropriate key.

If you decide to modify this setting later or want to use the Windows To Go workspace drive on another computer and need to make sure it is configured appropriately, access the Windows To Go control panel using the steps in the following exercise.

CHANGE WINDOWS TO GO STARTUP OPTIONS

GET READY. To change Windows to Go startup options, perform the following steps:

1. Log in to your Windows 8 client device with administrative privileges.
2. Press the **Windows log key + r**.
3. In the *Run* dialog box, type **control panel**.
4. Click the **Hardware and Sound** category.
5. In the *Devices and Printers* category, click **Change Windows To Go startup options**.
6. Click **Yes** to automatically boot from an attached USB drive or click **No** to configure the settings manually.

Booting into a Windows To Go Workspace

To take full advantage of the Windows To Go Workspace, you need to have a good understanding of what the requirements for the host computer are and the resources that can and cannot be accessed on the host.

When deciding on the host to use for a Windows To Go workspace drive, you should make sure it has been certified for use with Windows 7 or Windows 8.

Table 1-1 lists the hardware requirements for Windows To Go workspace hosts.

Table 1-1

Hardware Requirements for Windows To Go Workspace Hosts

Hardware	Requirement
Firmware	Must support booting from USB.
Processor architecture	Must support the image on the Windows To Go drive.
External USB hubs	USB hubs are not supported; you must connect the drive directly to the host computer.
Processor	1 Ghz or faster.
Memory	2 GB or greater.
Graphics	DirectX 9 graphics device with a WDDM 1.2 or greater driver.
USB ports	USB 2.0 or greater. Using a USB 3.0 port will result in increased performance in both drive provisioning and when the drive is used as a workspace.

In addition to the information listed Table 1-1, the Windows To Go image on the USB drive must be compatible with the processor architecture and the firmware on the host PC.

Table 1-2 lists the processor/firmware types and Windows To Go image requirements for Windows To Go workspace hosts.

Table 1-2

Windows To Go compatibility with Host firmware and processor types

Host PC Firmware	Host Processor	Windows To Go Image That Can be Used
32-bit Legacy BIOS 64-bit Legacy BIOS	32-bit 64-bit	32-bit image only
32-bit UEFI BIOS 64-bit UEFI BIOS	32-bit 64-bit	32-bit image only 64-bit image only

Once you have identified a suitable host for your Windows To Go workspace drive, insert the drive and power on the computer. If you configured a BitLocker to Go password, you will need to enter it before you can access the drive. The first time you boot a host from the Windows To Go workspace, it will scan for hardware devices and then install the appropriate drivers. The information it finds is cached; therefore, the next time you boot from the same computer the process will be faster because drivers are loaded automatically. Windows To Go workspace operates just like any other installation of Windows but there are a few differences you will need to be aware of.

Once you log in, you will notice the internal disks on the host system are offline to protect against accidental exposure of data. If you insert the USB drive into a system that is already running, you will also notice that it will not be listed in File Explorer. The Hibernate feature is disabled to prevent data corruption during roaming and the Windows Store is disabled by default. The Windows Store application is disabled because applications licensed through the store are linked to your hardware.

MANAGING WINDOWS TO GO WORKSPACES USING GROUP POLICY

A ***Group Policy Object (GPO)*** that controls the behavior of Windows To Go workspaces can be created and managed at the enterprise level using the ***Group Policy Management console (gpmc.msc)*** and Active Directory. A GPO is a collection of settings that determine how the system for a group of users and/or computers will function. The GPO is then associated with Active Directory containers such as sites, domains, or organizational units.

The settings that are applicable to Windows To Go workspace can be found in the following section of a GPO:

Computer Configuration\Policies\Administrative Templates\Windows Components\Portable Operating System

- *Allow hibernate (S4) when starting from a Windows To Go workspace*: Specifies whether the PC can go into hibernation mode when started from a Windows To Go workspace.
- *Windows To Go Default Startup Options*: This policy controls whether the PC will boot to Windows To Go if a USB device containing a Windows To Go workspace is connected and also controls whether users can make changes to the startup options in the Windows To Go Startup Options Control Panel.
- *Disallow standby sleep states (S1-S3) when starting from a Windows To Go workspace*: Determines if the PC can use standby sleep states (S1-S3) when starting from a Windows To Go workspace. S1 through S4 are sleeping states. When your Windows 8 client computer is in one of these states it is not performing computational tasks and will appear to be off. With each successive sleep state (S1-S4), more of the computer is shut down.

The Windows Store application is disabled by default when booting into a Windows 8 client computer using a Windows To Go workspace. You should enable this policy setting when the workspace will only be used with a single Windows 8 computer.

■ Virtualizing Operating Systems

Developing a strategy to virtualize your desktops, isolate legacy applications and maintain user settings and data will require that you have a good understanding of the tools provided along with their capabilities.

Microsoft solutions in the area of desktop virtualization are designed to allow you to access your applications and Windows environment from anywhere while at the same time, keeping your personal settings when changing to another device. Desktop virtualization focuses on three key deployment models:

- Operating system virtualization (VDI, Client Hyper V, and MED-V)
- Application virtualization (App-V and Remote App)
- User State virtualization (UE-V)

Operating system virtualization is designed to provide your users with the ability to use a single computer to run one or more virtual operating systems. These virtual operating systems can be delivered locally or from a centralized data center. Application virtualization (App-V) provides your users with the ability to run applications side-by-side that would normally cause conflicts or run multiple versions of the same application on the same computer. It also

CERTIFICATION READY
Operating system virtualization
Objective 1.1

provides end users with access to virtually any application anywhere without having to install the application directly on their computers. User State virtualization (UE-V) allows your user's data and personal settings to follow them as they login to Windows 7 and Windows 8 client computers.

Exploring Operating System Virtualization

When determining the appropriate strategy to use for virtualizing your operating systems, you will need to take into consideration hardware, bandwidth, network latency, and costs. You will also need to determine if you want your users to be able to customize their personal desktops and how you will handle application incompatibility issues when moving to Windows 8.

When it comes to operating system virtualization, Microsoft categorizes operating system virtualization according to Virtual Desktop Infrastructure (VDI), Session Virtualization, and Microsoft Enterprise Desktop Virtualization (MED-V).

VIRTUAL DESKTOP INFRASTRUCTURE (VDI)

Virtual Desktop Infrastructure (VDI) is desktop delivery model that allows users to access centrally managed desktops running in a data center.

With VDI, the user has access to a virtualized instance of a client operating system such as Windows 8 that is running on a back-end server instead of on the user's computer. VDI can be deployed by in the form of a ***personal virtual desktop (PVD)*** or a ***virtual desktop pool (VDP)***. In a PVD deployment, each of your users, within Active Directory, will be assigned their own dedicated virtual desktop. The user can customize this desktop and it is for their exclusive use. The means there is a one-to-one relationship between VDI users and PVDs on server running Hyper-V. PVDs can be managed using the same tools used for physical computers and users can have full administrative control over their PVD. In a VDP deployment, users share a pool of virtual desktops that identical in configuration. These are located on servers running Hyper-V in a data center. VDP are dynamically assigned from the pool to users when they log on. Since all of these virtual desktops are the same, the user will see the same desktop regardless of which one they use. When they log off, the virtual desktop is reset to its original state. This represents a many-to-one relationship between VDI users and virtual desktops.

VDI works by virtualizing an entire desktop environment (operating system, user data and applications) on a server that can be accessed by multiple users. VDI then presents the user interface to users' devices by using the ***Remote Desktop Protocol (RDP)***. RDP is a set of rules that specify how the image on the screen of one computer is encoded and sent over a network connection to be displayed on another. The protocol also encrypts data being sent across the connection and increases performance over slow or unreliable connections by only sending data when something on the screen changes.

When combined with App-V and User State Virtualization (USV), users can connect to any available VDI session and access the applications, files, and folders they need while still maintaining their familiar desktop settings.

The typical components of an enterprise VDI include the following:

- A Windows Server running the ***Hyper-V*** role. Hyper-V is a role that provides the tools and services needed to create virtual machines which run multiple operating systems that are isolated from each other on a single physical server.
- A library/repository that contains the virtual machines, the ***virtual hard disks (VHD)***, and the hardware and software profiles. A virtual hard disk is an image format that

allows you to encapsulate the hard disk into an individual file for use by the operating system as a virtual disk.

- A vehicle to deploy applications (App-V) based on user profiles. App-V provides access to applications from any device without the need to install or configure the application on the local device.
- A tool to help manage the VDI, such as ***Microsoft Desktop Optimization Pack (MDOP)***. MDOP is a suite of monitoring, perform emergency recovery, application and desktop virtualization tools.
- The ***Remote Desktop Services (RDS)***. Remote Desktop Services (RDS), formerly known as Terminal Services, allow a Windows 2008/2012 server to host multiple, simultaneous client sessions.

The are several advantages to implementing the VDI model:

- It allows your users to access the virtual desktop environment from several different devices such as a desktop PC, a laptop, or a ***thin client***. A thin client is a computer that relies heavily on another computer to process data, save files and in itself does not perform the tasks normally handled by a computer.
- If the device the user is working on fails, the desktop will continue to run and the user can reconnect from another device providing business continuity.
- The virtual desktops are maintained on a server in the central data center instead of on each of your users' computers providing enhanced security and centralized backup capabilities.

Although there are several advantages to designing and implementing a VDI strategy, you will need to keep in mind the cost of the high-end hardware needed to build the infrastructure, the bandwidth (capacity of connection) available and network latency (time it takes for the packets to traverse WAN links). If you have slow WAN links to branch offices and/or a large number of mobile workers, VDI may not be the solution for your organization. In that case, you might want to consider session virtualization as an alternate strategy.

SESSION VIRTUALIZATION

With ***session virtualization***, your users can access individual applications (RemoteApps) or entire desktops (remote desktops or "sessions"). ***RemoteApps*** are programs that are accessed through Remote Desktop Services (RDS) and appear as if they are running on the client's local computer. RemoteApps removes the need to deliver the entire desktop to the remote system in order to launch an application. Instead, you can launch individual applications from your local computer. Each application will appear in its own window just like a locally running application would. You can also run RemoteApps side by side with local apps; they can be integrated into the Start menu to make it easier for your users to find them. These resources (applications/remote desktops) are running on a server located in a central data center.

The typical components of a session-based deployment include the following:

- ***RD Session Host servers:*** Servers running this role host RemoteApp programs or session-based desktops. Users connect a RD Session Host server to run programs, save their files and use other resources on those servers.
- ***RD Licensing servers:*** Servers running this role manage the licenses required to connect ot the RD Session Host server or a virtual desktop.
- ***RD Connection Broker servers:*** Servers running this role are used to distribute the load across multiple RD Session Host servers and allow users to reconnect to their RemoteApp programs, session-based desktops, and virtual desktops.
- ***RD Gateway servers:*** Servers running this role allow authorized users connecting from the Internet to gain access to their virtual desktops, RemoteApp programs, and session-based desktops located on the internal network.

- ***RD Web Access servers:*** Servers running this role provide the ability for users to access RemoteApp and desktop connection through the Start menu on Windows 7/8 or through a web browser. Both RemoteApp and Desktop Connection provide a custom view of the RemoteApp programs and session-based desktops.

Compared to VDI, session-based virtualization requires fewer resources to implement and is lower in cost to implement. It does not allow users to personalize their environments and in most implementations does not allow users to install their own applications.

MICROSOFT ENTERPRISE DESKTOP VIRTUALIZATION (MED-V)

Microsoft Enterprise Desktop Virtualization (MED-V), another desktop delivery model, is designed to remove barriers from upgrading to a newer version of the Windows operating system due to incompatible or legacy applications. By creating a virtual environment called a MED-V workspace you can run a legacy application that has not been supported or tested on Windows 8. A ***MED-V workspace*** is the desktop environment your user interacts with and consists of both an image and a policy which defines the rules and how the workspace functions. From an administrator perspective, using a MED-V workspace will allow you to move forward with a rollout of Windows 8 instead of getting sidetracked addressing application-compatibility issues.

For example, if you have a user who needs to run an earlier version of an application that is not supported on Windows 8, you can use MED-V to deploy the earlier version as part of a virtual image. The user will then have two copies of the application running simultaneously on her Windows 8 client computer. The current version runs on her host computer and the legacy version runs in the MED-V workspace. To the user, it will appear as if both are running on the local computer. She accesses the legacy application from the desktop of the virtual desktop or by using an application window that is integrated into the local desktop of their host computer.

The typical components of Med-V include:

- MED-V Management Server associates virtual images (located in the Image Repository) with administrator usage policies to Active Directory users and groups. It also stores event information for reporting and monitoring purposes.
- MED-V Management console is used by administrators to control the management server and the image repository.
- MED-V Image Repository stores the virtual images on a standard Internet Information Server (IIS) and handles virtual image version management and requests from authenticated MED-V clients for images.
- MED-V Client allows you to start, stop and lock virtual machines and runs seamlessly on the desktop, making applications appear as if they are running on the local desktop's operating system.

With the MED-V client installed on a desktop computer, the user connects to the MED-V Management Server. The MED-V Management Server queries Active Directory for security settings and access control information. Once approved, the client retrieves the MED-V workspace image from the MED-V Image Repository server.

Administrators use the MED-V Management console to connect to the Management Server where they can update policies; create, manage, and update virtual machines; and provision workspaces to users. The image delivered to the client uses a seamless mode to present the application to the user.

HYPER-V AND CLIENT HYPER-V

The Hyper-V role in Windows Server 2012 provides you with the tools needed to create a virtualized environment. By virtualizing hardware, you can create and manage virtual machines that run an operating system that is isolated from other virtual machines running on the same host computer. The operating system that runs inside the virtual machine is called a ***guest operating system***.

A ***virtual machine*** is a software implementation of a computer that executes programs just like a real physical computer. The software operating inside the virtual operating system is limited to the resources provided by the virtual machine. A component called the ***hypervisor*** or ***virtual machine manager*** is responsible for creating and running the virtual machines.

Hyper-V Server 2012 is an example of a hypervisor. One of the most common uses for it is in VDI environments in which users can access a Windows client operating system running on a server-based virtual machine in the data center. Client Hyper-V, another hypervisor, brings the world of virtualization to a Windows 8 client computers.

Client Hyper-V is available in Windows 8 Professional/Enterprise (64-bit version only) provides the same virtualization capabilities found in Windows Server 2012. Using this feature, you can set up a test environment to troubleshoot your applications, optimize the solution, and once it has been approved for production release, you can then move it to your production environment.

Client Hyper-V allows you to run multiple virtual machines at the same time running both 32-bit and 64-bit operating systems. Although disabled by default, you can access it by searching for Windows Features and enabling the option.

The program comes with a management console and a virtual machine connection component. Using these tools, you can connect to Hyper-V machines on your local computer or on other computers, create a virtual machine, create and manage virtual hard disks, install and run an operating system on a virtual machine, and import/export virtual machines.

INSTALL THE CLIENT HYPER-V FEATURE IN WINDOWS 8

GET READY. To install the Client Hyper-V feature in Windows 8, log on as an administrator to a computer running Windows 8 Professional/Enterprise and then perform the following steps:

1. Press the **Windows logo key + q**.
2. Set the search context to **Settings**, type **Windows Features**, and then click **OK**.
3. Click **Turn Windows features on and off**.
4. Click **Hyper-V** and then click **OK**.
5. Reboot the Windows 8 client computer.

Exploring User State Virtualization (USV)

With the mobility of today's workforce, it is critical that employees can access their files and folders whether they are offline or online and also maintain the look and feel of their desktop across multiple devices. ***User State Virtualization (USV)*** is a collection of technologies that enables data and user settings to follow the user.

Today's users are more mobile and expect to be able to use any device they choose to access their data. Whether it's from a desktop, laptop, or tablet, they want to be able to log on and maintain the same look and feel of their desktops from anywhere anytime. Your information technology staff wants to make sure critical data is backed up and they want to ensure the time to restore users' machines, in a case of loss or damage, is minimal. User State Virtualization can help you to address these challenges by providing the following solutions:

- Folder Redirection: Replicates user data to a centralized folder stored on a server in the data center. This allows users to access their files from any computer they log on from.

- Offline Files: Takes files and folders located on a server and makes them accessible to users. This allows users to continue to work in the event of network outages or while away on travel.
- Roaming User Profiles: Enables users to store their choices in personalization in a centralized folder and then download to another computer when they log on.

User Experience Virtualization (UE-V) provides a similar approach to roaming profiles but maintains the experience across multiple devices (desktop computers, laptops, and VDI sessions) and regardless of the application used. Prior to the release of UE-V, you had to create separate profiles for a user who worked from a physical desktop and then connected over a session-based desktop from home. Using UE-V, for example, you can switch between a laptop running Windows 7 or 8 and a tablet running Windows 8 using the same profile.

You will learn more about how UE-V works in Lesson 4

Exploring Application Virtualization (App-V)

Application Virtualization (App-V) is a set of products that provides virtualization at the application level, which allows you to run applications side by side without conflicts.

App-V provides several benefits to both users and network administrators. By virtualizing an application, you can run applications side-by-side that would normally cause conflicts or run multiple versions of the same application on the same machine.

Application virtualization also provides end users with access to virtually any application anywhere without having to install the application directly on their computers. In fact, virtualized applications will make no changes to the user's computer (registry, files, and application support files), can be isolated from other programs running locally on their machine and allow you to manage and deliver them from a central location. This streamlines the process and time required to update and reconfigure applications across the network. You can also take traditional applications and convert them to a virtualized application through a process called sequencing.

An App-V client, installed on the user's computer, allows the user to interact with the applications after they are published. The publishing process copies the virtual application icons and shortcuts to the computer and allows the users to work with the application. You will learn more about App-V in a later section.

Configuring a Native VHD Boot File

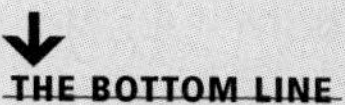

A ***Virtual Hard Disk (VHD)*** is single file on your disk that functions like a separate drive. It can host native file systems (NTFS, FAT, exFAT, and UDFS), function as a boot disk, and support standard disk and file operations. This allows virtual disks to run on a computer that doesn't have a VM or hypervisor and simplifies the image management process.

CERTIFICATION READY
Native VHD boot
Objective 1.1

One benefit provided by VHDs is the ability to run Windows 8 on your computer's real hardware (for example, video, memory, network card, or CPU). This allows you to test its performance and compatibility with your computer system. ***Native VHD boot*** means the computer can mount and boot from the operating system contained within the VHD file. Native VHD boot will also work without an operating system present on the host computer.

TAKE NOTE*

A virtual hard disk in Windows 8 does not require a parent operating system or a virtual machine manager to run. A virtual machine manager (hypervisor) is software that manages and monitors virtual machines.

You can also use VHDs to streamline image management in situations where you support an image library holding multiple formats. Instead of using a different process and toolset to manage and deploy each image format, you can standardize on VHDs and use the same image-management tools to create, deploy, and maintain system images installed on hardware or virtual machines.

Understanding VHD Formats

When setting up a VHD, you have to determine the format and hard disk type. Each is designed to meet a specific goal.

There are two VHD formats to choose from when creating a VHD boot file:

- ***VHD format*** supports virtual disks up to 2TB in size.
- ***VHDX format*** supports virtual disks up to 64TB. VHDX is more resilient to power failure but is only supported on Windows 8 systems.

There are two hard disk types available:

- ***Fixed Size*** is allocated to its maximum size when the VHD is created. It works well with production servers where user data protection and overall performance is critical.
- ***Dynamically Expanding*** will grow to its maximum size as data is written to the virtual hard disk. It should be used in testing and non-production environments. If you are using this disk type, consider storing your critical applications and user data outside the VHD. This reduces the overall file size and makes it easier to recover should the VHD image become corrupted.

To create a VHD file, you can use the ***Disk Management console (diskmgmt.msc)*** and/or the ***Diskpart*** tool. The Disk Management console is used to partition, format, delete, shrink and assign and change drive letters for hard disks (internal/external), optical disk drives, and flash drives. Diskpart is a command-line a tool that enables you to manage objects (disks, partitions, or volumes) by using scripts or direct input at a command prompt.

In the following example, you will create a VHD Boot file on Windows 7 Professional and then install Windows 8 Enterprise to create a dual-boot system to test Windows 8 performance and compatibility with your existing computer's hardware.

CREATE A VHD BOOT FILE USING THE DISK MANAGEMENT CONSOLE

GET READY. To create a VHD boot file using the Disk Management console, log on as an administrator a computer running Windows 7 Professional and then perform the following steps:

1. Clck **Start** and in the *Search* box, type **Disk Management**.
2. Click **Action** > **Create VHD** (see Figure 1-2).

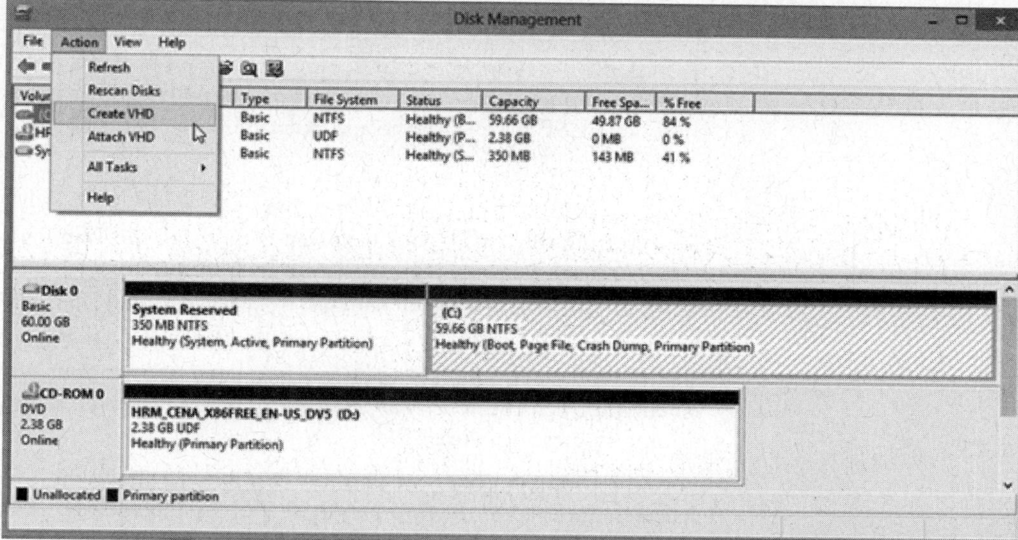

Figure 1-2

Creating a VHD

3. Click **Browse** (see Figure 1-3) to navigate to folder where you want to store the VHD file.

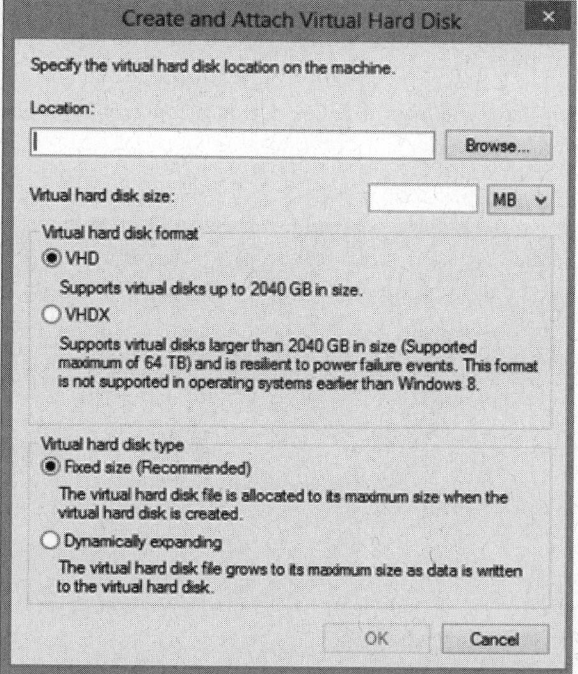

Figure 1-3

Navigating to the folder where you will store the VHD

4. In the *File name* field, type a name for the VHD file and then click **Save**.
5. For the *Virtual hard disk size* setting, type **20**, click the drop-down arrow, and then select **GB**.
6. In the *Virtual hard disk format* section, leave the default setting of **Fixed size (Recommended)**.
7. Click **OK**. The VHD file is created.

Installing Windows 8 on a VHD with an Operating System Present

After creating a VHD, you install an operating system by booting from a DVD or a bootable USB drive with the appropriate image.

After creating the VHD, your next step is to install the Windows 8 operating system on the VHD. You can perform the installation by booting from a DVD or a bootable USB drive that contains the Windows 8 Enterprise image.

Windows 8 setup will take you through the normal setup screens, prompting you for the language to install, time/currency formats, keyboard or input methods, and licensing terms. When you reach the *Where do you want to install Windows?* screen, you can open a command prompt by pressing **Shift+F10**.

From the command line, you can use ***Diskpart*** to attach the VHD. Attaching the VHD ensures it appears on the host as a drive and not a static file. The following example selects and attaches to the virtual hard disk created earlier:

```
X:\Sources>diskpart
select vdisk file="c:\vhdfiles\win8Ent.vhd"
attach vdisk
exit
```

After attaching the VHD, the *Where do you want to install Windows?* screen appears again and you click Refresh. The VHD will display as an option. Click the VHD disk and continue with the normal Windows installation steps.

On reboot, you have the option to select the instance of the operating system you want to run (see Figure 1-4).

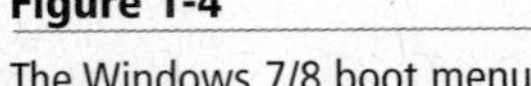

Figure 1-4

The Windows 7/8 boot menu

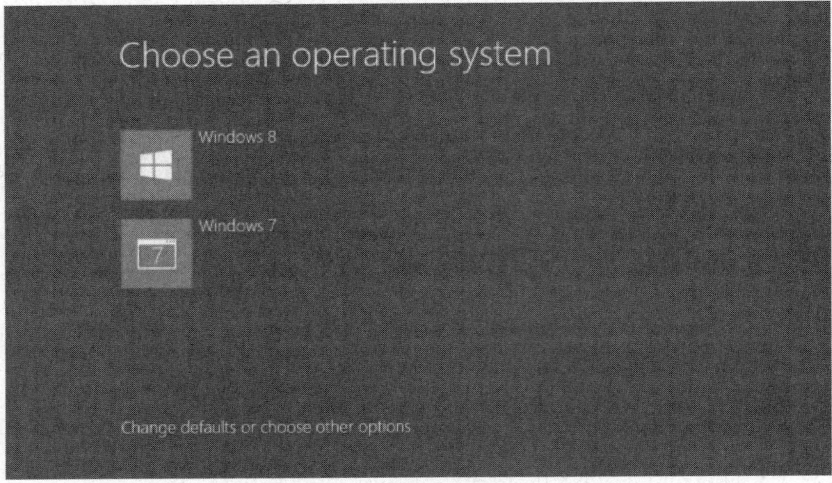

Installing Windows 8 on a VHD Without an Operating System Present

You can apply an existing image to a VHD and use a Windows 8 Pre-Installation Environment (PE) Disk to install the operating system on a computer without a current operating system running.

If you are using the ***Deployment Image Servicing and Management (DISM)*** tool, available on the Windows Assessment and Deployment Kit (Windows ADK), you can apply an existing corporate Windows 8 image (.wim) file to a VHD file. DISM is a command-line tool used to service Windows images offline before they are deployed. It can also be used to install, uninstall, configure, and update Windows packages and drivers. This image can be deployed to computers where an operating system is installed or computers without an operating system present.

To deploy a Windows 8 Enterprise image/VHD Boot file on a computer without an operating system, you need the following:

- A Windows 7/Windows 8 computer running the Windows ADK tools.
- A Windows 8 image (.wim) file.
- A ***Windows 8 Pre-installation Environment (PE) disk***. This disk is used to boot a computer that has no operating system on it. It can be created on removable media such as a CD/DVD, USB flash drive, or a USB hard drive.
- A Windows 7/Windows 8 computer on which to install the VHD; must have a minimum of 30 GB free disk space.

TAKE NOTE *
The Windows ADK can be downloaded at Microsoft's website.

MORE INFORMATION
To learn more about creating a Windows Pre-Installation Environment disk, visit TechNet.

CREATE A VHD BOOT FILE USING DISKPART AND APPLY AN IMAGE USING DISM

GET READY. To create a VHD boot file using DiskPart and apply an image using DISM, log on as an administrator to a computer running Windows 8 Enterprise. You must have the Windows ADK tools installed, a generalized image named install.wim, and a connection to a server providing a network share. Then perform the following steps:

1. Press the **Windows log key** + **r**.
2. In the *Run* dialog box, type **cmd** to open a command console.
3. Start the program by typing **diskpart**.
4. Create a fixed disk, attach to it, create a primary partition, and then perform a quick format:

```
C:\>.diskpart
   create vdisk file=c:\windows.vhd maximum=25600
   type=fixed
   select vdisk file=c:\windows.vhd
   attach vdisk
   create partition primary
   assign letter=v
   format quick label=vhd
   exit
```

5. Use the DISM tool to apply your Windows image file (install.wim) to the primary partition:

```
Dism /apply-image /imagefile: install.wim /index:1
/ApplyDir:V:\
```

6. Detach the virtual disk:

```
C:\,diskpart
    select vdisk file=c:\windows.vhdx
    detach vdisk
    exit
```

7. Connect to a network share, create a directory, and copy the VHD file to the share. The following command uses a server named GEO, a file share named ITShares, and creates a CorpVHDs directory:

```
Net use i: \\GEO\ITShares
Md i:\CorpVHDs
Copy c:\windows.vhd i:\CorpVHDs
```

This virtual hard disk, with the Windows image included, can be copied to one or more systems to run as a virtual machine or for native boot purposes.

TAKE NOTE* When creating an image for deployment to multiple computers, the image must be generalized. During this configuration pass, computer-specific information is removed from the Windows installation, enabling you to capture and reapply the Windows image to different computers. For example, unique Security Identifier (SID) and unique device drivers are removed from the image.

INSTALL THE VHD WITH THE WINDOWS 8 ENTERPRISE IMAGE ON A BIOS-BASED COMPUTER WITHOUT AN OPERATING SYSTEM

TAKE NOTE* You will need a Windows PE bootable media to complete the exercise.

GET READY. To install the VHD with the Windows 8 Enterprise image on a BIOS-based computer without an operating system, select a target computer that does not have an operating system installed and then perform the following steps:

1. Boot into the computer using your Windows PE bootable media.
2. Execute the **Diskpart** command clean the hard disk. This ensures no data is left on the system from previous installations.

```
Diskpart
select disk 0
clean
```

3. Create a system partition:

```
Diskpart
create partition primary size=300
format quick fs=ntfs
assign letters=s
active
```

4. Create a primary partition:

```
Diskpart
create partition primary
format quick fs=ntfs
assign letter=c
exit
```

5. Copy the VHD to the target computer:

```
Copy i:\CorpVHDs\windows.vhd C:
```

6. Attach the VHD file:

```
Diskpart
select vdisk file=c:\windows.vhd
attach vdisk
```

7. Find the letter associated with the VHD, select the volume, and then assign it the drive letter V:

```
List volume
select volume <volume_number_of_attached_VHD>
assign letter=v
exit
```

8. Use **bcdboot** to copy the boot environment files from the \Windows directory (or from the Windows PE media) in the VHD into the system partition. BCDboot creates the BCD configuration to boot from the VHD:

```
cd v:\windows\system32
bcdboot v:\windows
```

9. Detach the disk:

```
Diskpart
select vdisk file=c:\windows.vhd
detach vdisk
exit
```

At this point, you can reboot the computer and the Windows 8 boot manager will load the Windows 8 operating system image contained within the windows.vhd file.

Using BCDEdit and BCDBoot

`bcdedit` and `bcdboot` are command-line utilities used to control the boot process and manage the boot configuration store.

The Windows startup process is controlled by parameters located in the ***Boot Configuration Data (BCD) store***. The BCD store contains information about what boot manager to use and the specific boot application/loaders available.

TAKE NOTE*

The BCD store, which contains the boot configuration parameters and controls how the operating system is started on Windows Vista and later operating systems, replaces the boot.ini text file used in earlier versions of Windows. The location of the store is based on the computer's firmware. On BIOS-based operating systems, you will find it in the \Boot\Bcd directory of the active partition. On Extensible Firmware Interface (EFI)-based systems, it is stored in the EFI system partition.

When you boot your computer, the Windows boot manager displays a menu of boot loader entries. When you select one of the entries, the Windows boot manager loads the system-specific boot loader for that operating system and passes those parameters for that boot entry to the system-specific boot loader.

You will see one instance of boot loader for each installation of Windows Vista or later operating systems present on the computer. If an earlier Windows operating system is installed, an optional legacy boot loader (ntldr/boot.ini) will be present. You might also see an optional boot application present if you are running applications that perform memory diagnostics. You can use the ***BCD Editor (bcdedit.exe)***, a command-line utility, to view and manage the BCD store. For example, you can use it to set a one-time boot sequence for the boot manager to use, create, import, and export the entire store, create, delete, and modify entries in the store, set the default entry the boot manager will use, list entries in the store, and set the timeout value. Figure 1-5 shows the contents of the BCD store when a system is running Windows 8 only. Notice, there is only one boot loader listed.

Figure 1-5

Contents of the BCD store on a system running Windows 8 only

```
C:\>cd \windows\system32

C:\Windows\System32>bcdedit.exe

Windows Boot Manager
--------------------
identifier              {bootmgr}
device                  partition=\Device\HarddiskVolume1
description             Windows Boot Manager
locale                  en-US
inherit                 {globalsettings}
integrityservices       Enable
default                 {current}
resumeobject            {95bc7da5-2d21-11e2-932c-ec4a4369c53a}
displayorder            {current}
toolsdisplayorder       {memdiag}
timeout                 30

Windows Boot Loader
-------------------
identifier              {current}
device                  partition=C:
path                    \Windows\system32\winload.exe
description             Windows 8
locale                  en-US
inherit                 {bootloadersettings}
recoverysequence        {95bc7da7-2d21-11e2-932c-ec4a4369c53a}
integrityservices       Enable
recoveryenabled         Yes
allowedinmemorysettings 0x15000075
osdevice                partition=C:
systemroot              \Windows
resumeobject            {95bc7da5-2d21-11e2-932c-ec4a4369c53a}
nx                      OptIn
bootmenupolicy          Standard

C:\Windows\System32>
```

Figure 1-6 shows the contents of a BCD store on a computer running Windows 7 Professional and Windows 8 Enterprise. Notice the Windows boot manager displays two boot loaders.

Figure 1-6

Contents of the BCD store on a system running Windows 8 and Windows 7

```
Windows Boot Loader
-------------------
identifier              {default}
device                  vhd=[C:]\vhdfiles\win8entvhd11142012.vhd
path                    \Windows\system32\winload.exe
description             Windows 8
locale                  en-US
inherit                 {bootloadersettings}
recoverysequence        {849ab75e-2b7d-11e2-9a4d-10bf4879ebe3}
integrityservices       Enable
recoveryenabled         Yes
custom:17000077         352321653
osdevice                vhd=[C:]\vhdfiles\win8entvhd11142012.vhd
systemroot              \Windows
resumeobject            {849ab75c-2b7d-11e2-9a4d-10bf4879ebe3}
nx                      OptIn
custom:250000c2         1

Windows Boot Loader
-------------------
identifier              {current}
device                  partition=C:
path                    \Windows\system32\winload.exe
description             Windows 7
locale                  en-US
inherit                 {bootloadersettings}
recoverysequence        {849ab75a-2b7d-11e2-9a4d-10bf4879ebe3}
recoveryenabled         Yes
osdevice                partition=C:
systemroot              \Windows
resumeobject            {849ab758-2b7d-11e2-9a4d-10bf4879ebe3}
nx                      OptIn
```

CHANGE THE DEFAULT TIMEOUT VALUE USING BCDEDIT

GET READY. To change the default timeout value using `bcdedit`, log on as an administrator to a Windows 8 Enterprise computer and then perform the following steps:

1. Press the **Windows logo key + r**.
2. In the *Run* dialog box, type **cmd** to open a command console.
3. Type **bcdedit** at the command prompt to view the BCD store. Make a note of the current timeout setting under the Windows boot manager section. It should be set to 30 seconds by default.
3. Type the following at the command prompt. (Entering a timeout value of 0 will boot the default operating system automatically.)

   ```
   C:\Users\Administrator>bcdedit /timeout 10
   ```
4. Type **bcdedit** at the command prompt to confirm the timeout setting has been modified.

Table 1-3 shows the bcdedit commands that can be used on the store.

Table 1-3

BCDedit Commands that Operate on the Store

COMMAND	DESCRIPTION
/createstore	Creates a new empty boot configuration store.
/export	Exports the contents of the system store to a file. This file can be used later to restore the state of the system store.
/import	Restores the state of the system store using a backup file created with the /export command.

Table 1-4 shows the bcdedit commands that can be used to modify entries in the BCD store.

Table 1-4

BCDedit Commands that Operate on Entries in the Store

COMMAND	DESCRIPTION
/copy	Makes copies of the entries of the store.
/create	Creates new entries in the store.
/delete	Deletes entries from the store.
/mirror	Creates mirror of entries in the store.

Table 1-5 shows the bcdedit commands that can be used to control the boot manager.

Table 1-5

BCDedit Commands that Control the Boot Manager

COMMAND	DESCRIPTION
/bootsequence	Sets the one-time boot sequence for the boot manager.
/default	Sets the default entry that the boot manager will use.
/displayorder	Sets the order in which the boot manager displays the multi-boot menu
/timeout	Sets the boot manager timeout value.

BCDboot (bcdboot.exe) is a command-line utility that allows you to set up a system partition when you deploy a new computer, to set up Windows to boot to a virtual hard disk, and to repair the boot environment if your system partition becomes corrupted.

To initialize a system partition, `bcdboot` copies a small set of boot environment files from an installed Windows image. For example, if you want to copy boot environment files from the X:\Windows directory, use the following command:

```
X:\Windows\System32\bcdboot X:\Windows
```

To change the default locale from US English to Japanese, use the following command:

```
X:\Windows\System32\bcdboot /l:ja-jp
```

To copy BCD files from the *C:\Windows* directory to a system partition on another drive to be booted from another computer with the system partition volume letter set to V, use the following command:

```
C:\>bcdboot C:\Windows /s V:
```

Table 1-6 lists some of the common bcdboot command switches.

Table 1-6

Common BCDboot Command Switches

OPTION	DESCRIPTION
`<source>`	Specifies the location of the Windows directory to use as the source for copying boot environment files.
`/l <locale>`	Specifies the optional locale parameter to use. The default is US English (en-us).
`/s <volume letter>`	Specifies the volume letter for the system partition. Use it to specify a system partition when you are configuring a drive that will be booted on another computer (USB flash drive or secondary drive).
`/f <firmware type>`	Specifies the firmware type. Values can include `UEFI`, `BIOS`, and `ALL`.
`/v`	Enables verbose mode.
`/m [{OS Loader GUID}]`	Merges the value from an existing boot entry into a new boot entry.

Configuring a Multi-Boot System

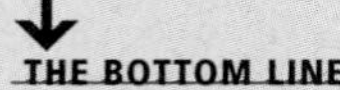

Multi-boot systems provide you with the ability to test a new operating system for hardware and software compatibility prior to deploying it. Each operating system requires its own partition.

A ***multi-boot (or dual boot)*** system is a computer that runs multiple operating systems on the same machine. When you boot the system, a boot menu is presented, allowing you to select the operating system you want to work in.

CERTIFICATION READY
Multi-boot
Objective 1.1

A multi-boot system provides two key benefits:

- It allows you to test a new operating system before fully deploying it to your organization.
- It provides you with the ability to determine how compatible the new operating system will be with your applications and hardware devices.

Setting up a Multi-Boot System

When setting up a dual-boot system, you will need to prepare it for the new operating system.

When you're setting up a multi-boot system, keep the following in mind:

- You should always back up your system before performing a multi-boot setup.
- Each operating system requires its own partition. This differs from the native VHD boot disk previously discussed.
- Programs installed on one operating system are not accessible when booted into the other system; a separate installation is required for each operating system.
- You must reboot the system to switch between operating systems.

You can multi-boot systems running Windows Vista, Windows 7, and Windows 8. In situations where you want to install multiple operating systems, install Windows 8 last. Windows 8 uses a newer boot manager; therefore, installing the older operating last will cause it to be overwritten and disable your ability to boot into Windows 8.

CREATE A WINDOWS 7/WINDOWS 8 ENTERPRISE MULTI-BOOT SYSTEM

GET READY. To create a Windows 7/8 Enterprise multi-boot system, log on as an administrator to a Windows 7 computer and then perform the following steps:

TAKE NOTE*

Before you begin, always back up your files to protect against data loss.

1. Press the **Windows logo key + r**.
2. In the *Run* dialog box, type **diskmgmt.msc** to start the Disk Management console.
3. Make room for your Windows 8 installation by right-clicking the **C:** volume and choosing **Shrink**.

TAKE NOTE*

Shrinking a disk decreases the space used by primary partitions and logical drives by shrinking them into adjacent, contiguous space on the same disk. This is necessary if you need an additional partition but do not have additional disks. Any ordinary files are automatically relocated on the disk to create the new unallocated space.

4. In the *Enter the amount of space to shrink in MB* box, type **20480** (see Figure 1-7) and then click **Shrink**.

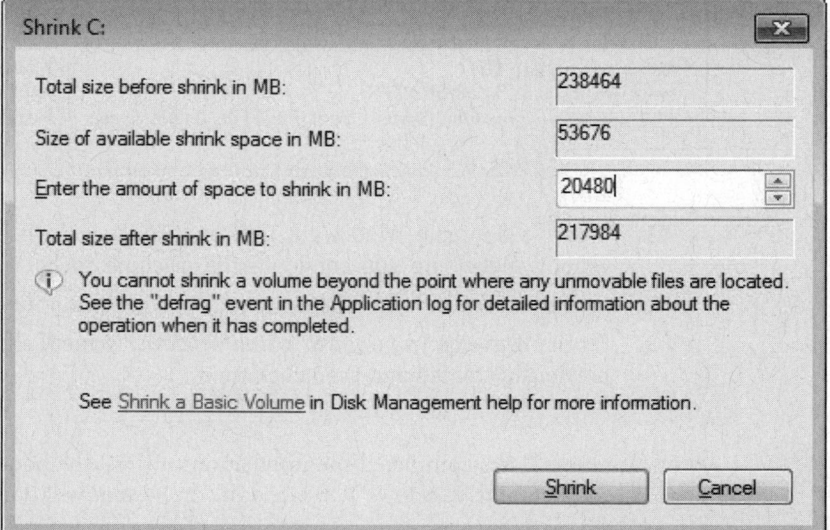

Figure 1-7
Shrinking the basic volume

5. Right-click the unallocated partition and then choose **New Simple Volume**.
6. On the *Welcome to the New Simple Volume Wizard* page, click **Next** to start the New Simple Volume Wizard.
7. On the Specify Volume Size page, click **Next** to accept the default simple volume size.
8. On the Assign Drive Letter or Path page, click **Next** to assign the default drive letter.
9. On the Format Partition page, in the Volume label field, type **Windows 8** and then click **Next** to format the volume with the default settings (see Figure 1-8).

Figure 1-8

Formatting the partition

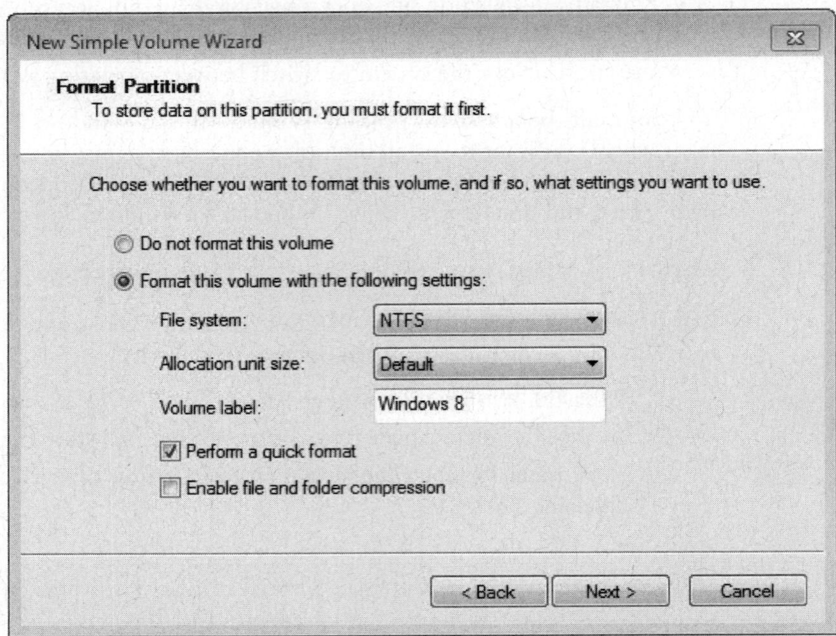

10. On the *Completing the New Simple Volume Wizard* page, click **Finish**. The drive will display as shown in Figure 1-9.

Figure 1-9

Completing the setup of a new simple volume

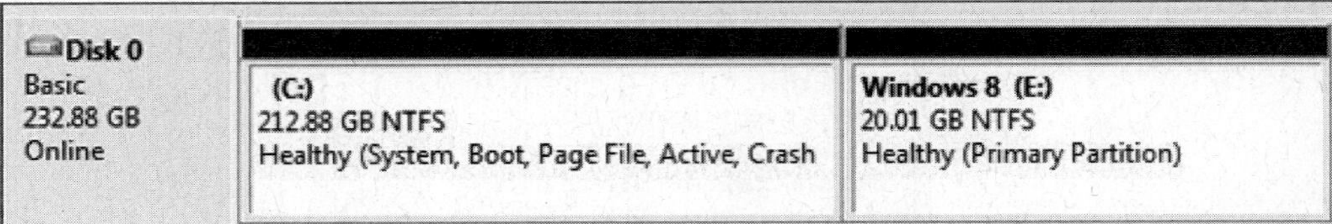

11. Insert a bootable Windows 8 DVD or USB flash drive into your computer and then reboot. Make sure you configure the machine to boot from the device.
12. When prompted, click **Custom: install Windows only (advanced)**.
13. On the *Where do you want to install Windows?* screen, click the new partition you previously created and then click **Next**.

After Windows 8 has completed the installation process, the boot menu will display, showing both Windows 8 and Windows 7. By default, the system will boot into Windows 8 after 30 seconds.

To change the default time and the default operating system to load, click the *Change defaults or choose other options* link. When the options menu appears, you can change the time setting, choose a default operating system to launch when the timer expires, or choose other options to assist in troubleshooting the Windows 8 installation.

Upgrading Versus Migrating To Windows 8

To ensure a successful transition to Windows 8, you need to determine if your current computers' hardware (processor, RAM, disk space, graphics) can support the new operating system, determine if your existing applications are compatible with Windows 8 and understand the tools available to migrate existing user and application settings to the new operating system.

CERTIFICATION READY
Upgrade vs. Migration
Objective 1.1

Prior to beginning your transition to Windows 8, you will need to assess the hardware on your existing computers.

Table 1-7 lists some the minimum hardware requirements for Windows 8.

Table 1-7
Windows 8 System Requirements

HARDWARE	REQUIREMENT
Processor	1 GHz or faster with support for Physical Address Extension (PAE), NX processor bit and Streaming SIMD Extensions 2 (SSE2). PAE allows 32-bit processors to access 4 GB of physical memory. NX helps processor guard against malicious attacks. SSE2 is an instruction set used by third party apps and drivers.
Memory	1 GB (32-bit systems), 2 GB (64-bit systems)
Disk space	16 GB (32-bit systems), 20 GB (64-bit systems)
Graphics	Microsoft DirectX 9 graphics device with WDDM driver

After confirming your computers can support Windows 8 from a hardware perspective, the next step is to determine if you want to upgrade or perform a custom installation of the operating system.

- Custom installations delete the previous installation along with user and application settings. You will perform a clean installation when you can't upgrade from a previous version of Windows, when you want to set up a multi-boot system, or in situations when you need to create a standard configuration that will be used across your organization.
- Upgrade installation results in the new operating system being installed over the older one. This keeps your data intact but depending upon which operating system you upgrade from, some settings (for example, application settings and basic configurations) might not be migrated to the new version. In general, if your existing computer systems support Windows 8, an upgrade makes the most sense because it minimizes the overall disruption to the organization.

Microsoft provides the following tools to streamline your move to Windows 8:

- Application Compatibility Toolkit (ACT)
- User State Migration Tool (USMT) 5.0
- Windows Easy Transfer

Exploring the Application Compatibility Toolkit (ACT)

The ACT Application Compatibility Toolkit (ACT) kit is used to determine whether or not applications, devices, and computers will work with a new operating system. Use it to gather inventory and assess your current environment in preparation for upgrades and migrations.

The ***Application Compatibility Toolkit (ACT) 6.0,*** included with the Windows ADK, can be used to determine if applications, devices, and computers on your company network are compatible with the new Windows operating system.

The following components are included with the tool kit:

- ***Application Compatibility Manager (ACM):*** This is used to create your data-collection package and analyze the collected inventory and compatibility data.
- ***Inventory-collector package:*** This package is deployed to computers in a test environment to gather inventory data to upload to the ACT database.
- ***Runtime-analysis package:*** This is a data-collection package that can be deployed to computers in a test environment to test compatibility with the new operating system.
- ***ACT Log Processing Service (LPS):*** This is a service used to process the ACT log files uploaded from computers where your data-collection packages have been installed. It adds information to the ACT database.
- ***ACT LPS share:*** This is a file share accessed by the ACT LPS to store the log files. The log files will be processed and added to the ACT database.
- ***ACT database:*** A This is a Microsoft SQL Server database used to store the collected inventory and compatibility data.
- ***Microsoft Compatibility Exchange:*** This is a web service that broadcasts application-compatibility issues.

ACT can be installed on Window XP (SP3), Windows Vista (SP2), Windows 7, Windows 8, Windows Server 2008 R2/SP2, as well as Windows Server 2012.

You can deploy inventory-collector packages on the same systems. ACT requires a database component and the .NET Framework 4. The database component can be (Microsoft SQL 2005/2008, Microsoft SQL 2005/2008 Express, Microsoft SQL 2008 R2, Microsoft SQL 2012).

ACT installations can be deployed in the configurations shown in Figure 1-10.

INVENTORYING YOUR COMPUTERS

To determine if your systems are compatible with the Windows 8 operating system, you first need to determine which computers you want to collect information from. If you have a large number of computers on your network and do not have enough resources to manage the information, consider collecting information from a representative subset. For example, if you have a standard build configuration for all laptops on your network and you control the installation of applications, you can inventory a subset of them to get the information you need to determine overall compatibility.

Other factors to consider in your strategy might include role-based applications, the geographic distribution of systems in your organization, and the use of mobile systems.

Figure 1-10

Deployment Options for ACT Installations

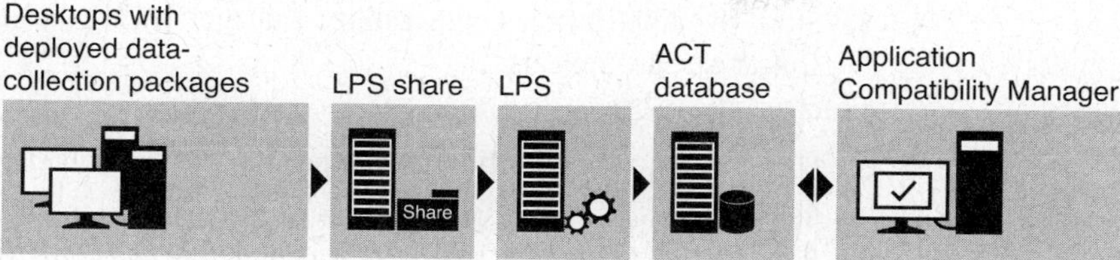

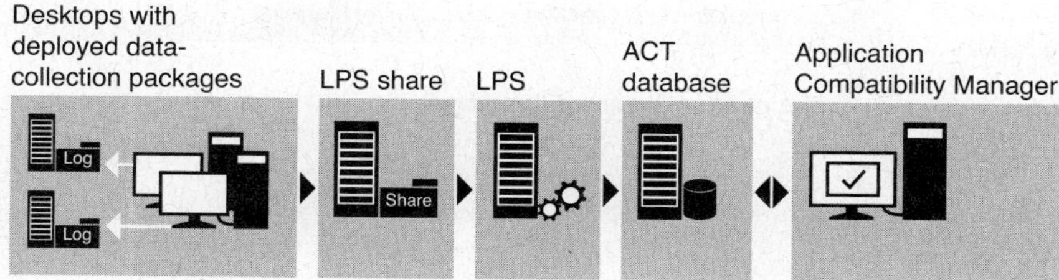

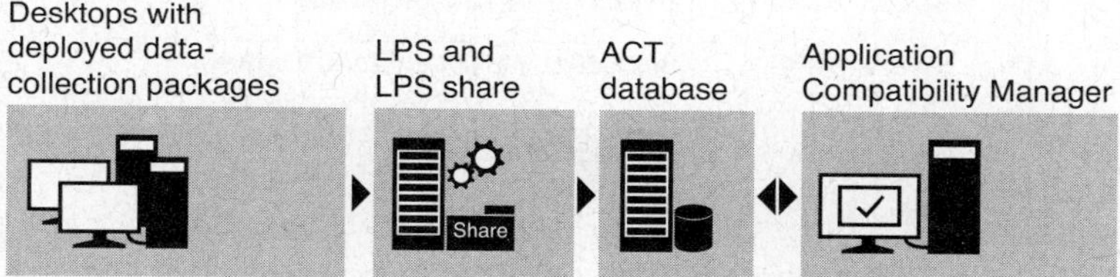

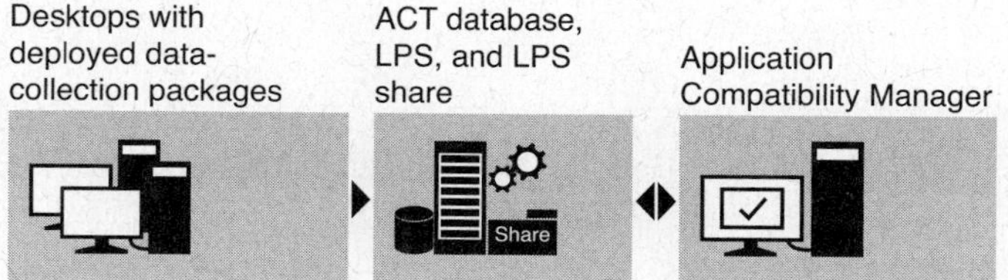

To collect information on your computers, you need to create an inventory-collector package. These packages collect system information (memory capacity, processor speed, and processor architecture), device information (model and, manufacturer), and software information (applications and system technologies).

To create an inventory collector package, you will need to visit Microsoft's website and search for Application Compatibility Toolkit for Windows 8. Download and install the toolkit on your Windows 8 client computer. You will also need to setup a database on your Windows 8 client device.

CREATE AN INVENTORY COLLECTOR PACKAGE

GET READY. To create an inventory collector package, log on as an administrator to a computer running Windows 7 Professional and then perform the following steps:

1. Start the Application Compatibility Manager (ACM) and then click **Collect**. The *Collect* screen appears.
2. Click **File** > **New**.
3. Click **Inventory collection package**. The *Set up your inventory package* page appears.
4. Provide the *Name*, *Output Location*, and the *Label* for the inventory package (see Figure 1-11).

Figure 1-11

Creating an Inventory Package for Sales Desktops

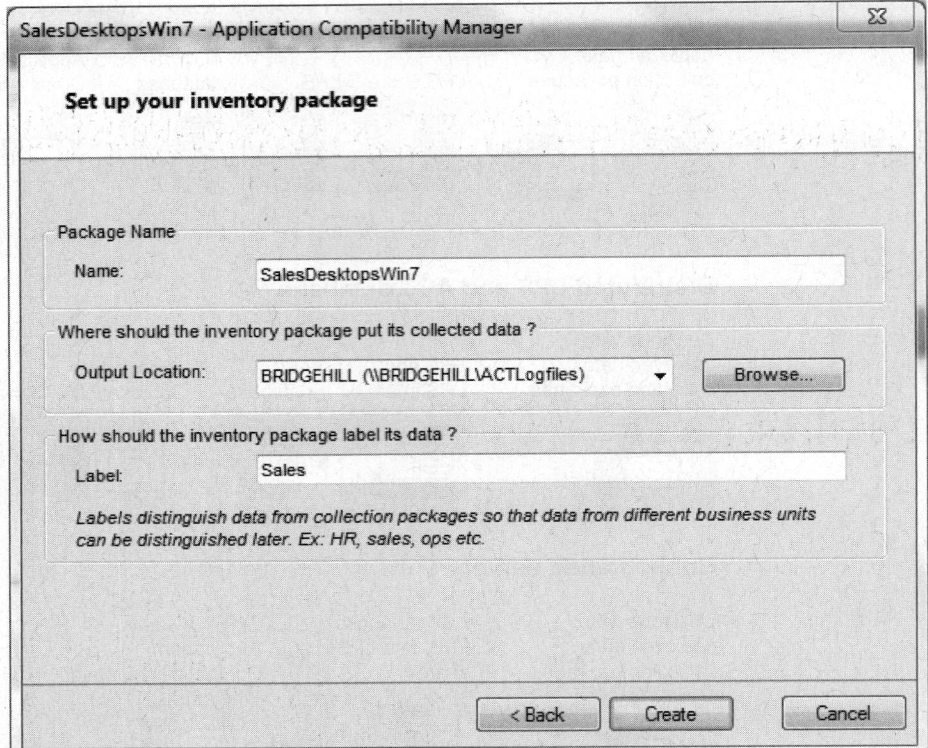

5. Click **Create**.
6. Browse to the location where you want to save the Windows Installer (.msi) file for the package, type a name for the .msi file and then click **Save**.
7. Click **Finish**.

Once your inventory-package has been created, you can choose the following deployment options:

- *Manual distribution:* Stores the package in a shared location on the network; users will need local administrative privileges to install. To deploy, you will need to send an e-mail with a link to the shared folder.
- *Logon script:* Uses the Windows Script Host to create a logon script. Users will need local administrative privileges to install the script

- *Group Policy Software Installation:* All computers targeted for deployment via Group Policy will need to be part of an Active Directory forest.
- *Microsoft System Center 2012 Configuration Manager:* To deploy the package, you will need to target the package to the appropriate users/devices called a collection. You will also have the option to display the application in the Software Center and allow the user to install or hide the application from the Software center and install it whether or not the user is logged on.

TAKE NOTE* To deploy the package to off-line computers, burn it to removable media or send it to the user via e-mail. Users can run the package and then return the log file via e-mail or by later connecting to the network and uploading the log file to a shared folder you create.

Exploring the User State Migration Tool (USMT) 5.0

One of the most time consuming tasks you will perform as an administrator is moving user files and settings between computers and operating systems. The User State Migration Tool (USMT) 5.0 eases this burden.

The ***User State Migration Tool (USMT) 5.0*** is a command-line tool that migrates user data from a previous installation of Windows to a new installation of Windows. It provides you with the ability to customize the user-profile migration experience. This means you can copy the user data that you select and exclude any data that you do not want to migrate. USMT captures user accounts, user files, operating system settings, and application settings to migrate to your new Windows installation.

USMT 5.0 allows you to streamline user state migration for larger deployments and provides a safe and cost-effective way to deploy Windows in your organization. It is not the tool of choice when end-user interaction is required during the installation, when you need to customize individual systems, or when you decide to migrate a small number of systems. In these situations, consider using the Windows Easy Transfer tool.

WORKING WITH USMT 5.0 TOOLS

- The USMT 5.0 includes three command-line tools:ScanState.exe scans the source computer, collects the files and settings and creates a store that contains the user's files and settings.
- LoadState.exe restores the files and settings on the destination computer.
- UsmtUtils.exe deletes hardlink folders in use by applications no longer removable through normal measures; checks the store file's consistency; and restores selected files. A ***hardlink folder*** provides a way for the New Technology File System (NTFS) to point to the same file from multiple locations on the same volume. The store file contains the user state migration data. UsmtUtils can be used to check for corrupted files or a corrupted catalog in the store file.

USMT also includes the following modifiable .xml files. These files can be used with `ScanState` and `LoadState` to perform a targeted migration:

- MigApp.xml includes rules to migrate application settings.
- MigDocs.xml includes rules to migrate user documents from the source computer.
- MigUser.xml includes rules to migrate user profiles and user data.

PLANNING, PROTECTING, AND PREPARING COMPUTERS FOR MIGRATION

Figure 1-12 shows the three-step process you should use when working with USMT 5.0.

Figure 1-12

The three-step process for working with USMT 5.0

Source PC

Destination PC

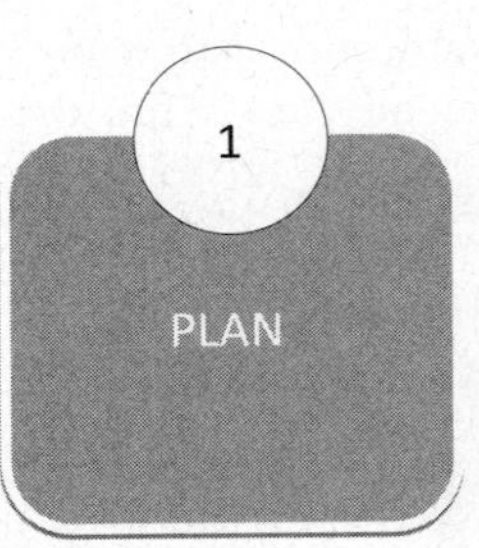
1
PLAN
Plan the migration
• Replace/Refresh
• Determine what to migrate
• Modify/Create the xml file

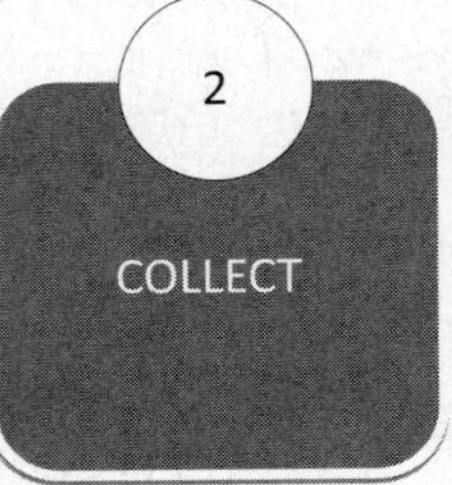
2
COLLECT
Collect files/settings from the source computer
• Back up system
• Run ScanState
• Run UsmtUtils/verify

3
PREPARE & RESTORE
Prepare and restore the files and settings on the destination computer
• Install the OS
• Run LoadState

Step 1: Plan the migration

- Determine whether to refresh or replace your system; identify what you want to migrate (application settings, operating system settings, files, and/or folders), determine where to store it (remotely, locally in a hard link migration store, or directly on the destination computer), and which files will be included in the migration.
- If necessary, modify the MigApp.xml and MigDocs.xml or create and modify a config.xml file. In general, it's best to leave the original .xml files in place and create and modify a config.xml file to keep your changes separate from the default .xml files.

Step 2: Collect the files and settings from the source computer

- Back up the source computer and close all applications before running `ScanState`; otherwise, USMT might not be able to migrate all the data.
- Run `ScanState` to collect the files and settings using an account with administrative privileges. Specify all .xml files you want the command to use:

```
scanstate \\server\migration\mystore /config:config.xml
/ i:migdocs.xml /:migapp.xml /v:13 /l:scan.log
```

- After the store is completed, run `UsmtUtils` with the `/verify` switch to ensure that the store you created was not corrupted. Replace `X` with the store location and `mystore` with the actual name of the store:

```
UsmtUtils /verify x:\mystore\store.img
```

Step 3: Prepare the destination computer and restore the files and settings

- Install the operating system on the destination computer; install any applications that were on the source computer; and then close any open applications.
- Run the `LoadState` command on the destination computer to migrate the files and settings. Make sure you specify the same .xml files you used when you ran `ScanState` during the collection process in Step 2:

```
LoadState \\server\migration\mystore /config:config.xml
/ i:migdocs.xml /i:migapp.xml /v:13 /l:load.log
```

- After completing the LoadState process, you must log off and then log back on the machine to see if some of the settings changed (for example, the screen saver, the fonts, the wallpaper, and so on).

CREATE A CUSTOM CONFIG.XML FILE AND EXCLUDE CONTENT FROM THE MY PICTURES FOLDER

TAKE NOTE*

To complete this exercise, you must have USMT 5.0 installed on your computer.

GET READY. To create a custom config.xml file and exclude content from the My Pictures folder, log on as an administrator to a computer running Windows 8 Enterprise and then perform the following steps:

1. Press the **Windows logo key + q** and in the *Run* box, type **cmd** and click **OK**.
2. From the search results list, right-click **Command Prompt** and then click **Run as administrator**.
3. Change to the directory that contains the USMT tools. In a default installation, this would be found by using the **cd** command as shown:

   ```
   cd "c:\Program Files (x86)\Windows Kits\8.0\Assessment and
   Deployment Kit\User State Migration Tool\x86"
   ```
4. To create a config.xml file, type the following command:

   ```
   scanstate /i:migapp.xml /i:miguser.xml /genconfig:config.xml
   /v:13
   ```

   Log messages regarding the creation of the file will be sent to the scanstate.log file. Both the log file and the config.xml file will be created in the directory from where you run the `scanstate` command.
5. To exclude the My Pictures folder from the migration, change `migrate="yes"` to `migrate="no"`. (The following code is an excerpt from the config.xml file created in Step 2.)

   ```
   <?xml version="1.0" encoding="UTF-8"?>
   <Configuration>
   <Documents>
   <component displayname="My Pictures" migrate="yes" ID="
    http://www.microsoft.com/migration/1.0/migxmlext/miguser/
    my pictures/data"/>
   </Documents>
   ```
6. Save the file.

This file can now be used with `ScanState` to collect information from the source computer and with `LoadState` to prepare the destination computers.

USING WINDOWS EASY TRANSFER

When are migrating information from only a few computers, use ***Windows Easy Transfer***, a utility that lets you migrate files and settings from a Windows 7 computer to a Windows 8 computer. Using this utility, you can transfer user accounts, documents, music, pictures, e-mail, Internet favorites, and videos.

To transfer information to a new computer, you will need one the following:

- A Windows Easy Transfer cable
- A network connection
- An external hard disk or USB flash drive

MIGRATE USING WINDOWS EASY TRANSFER

GET READY. To migrate using Windows Easy Transfer, log on as an administrator to a Windows 7 computer. (This computer will be considered the "old computer" during this exercise.) Perform the following steps:

1. Click **Start** and in the *Search* box, type **Windows Easy Transfer** and click **OK.**
2. On the *Welcome* screen, click **Next.** The Windows Easy Transfer page appears (see Figure 1-13).

Figure 1-13

Choosing a location for storing the files and settings that will be transferred to the new computer

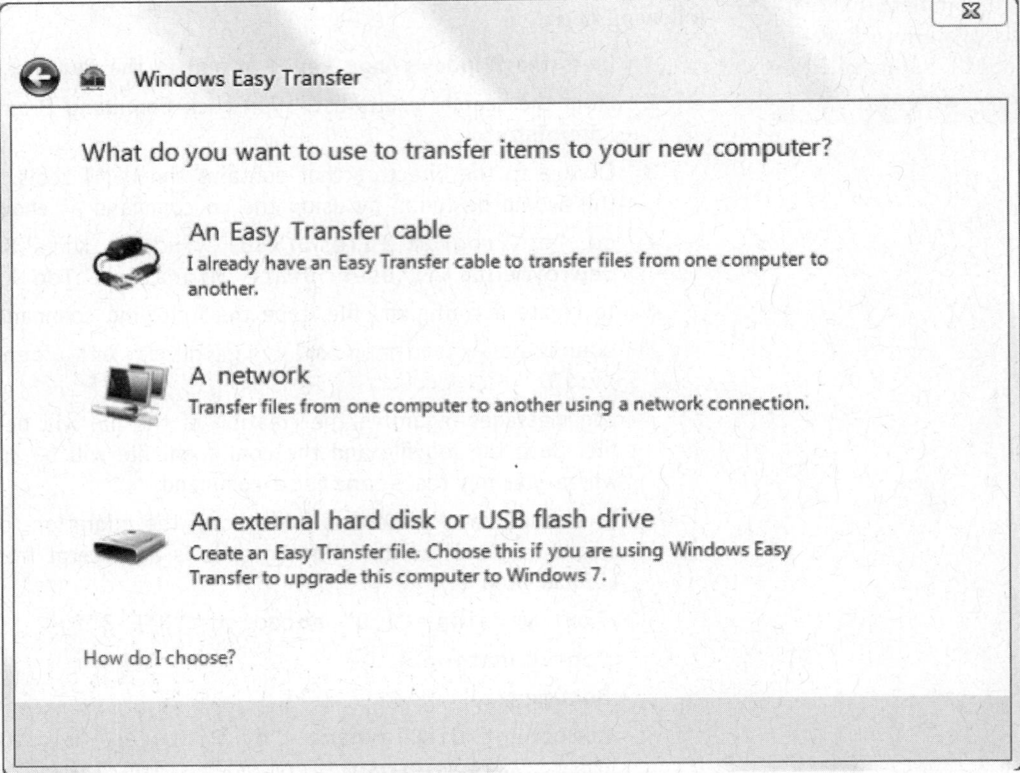

3. Click **An external disk or USB flash drive** as the location for storing the files and settings that will be transferred to the new computer. (The first two options require you to connect to the new computer.)
4. Click **This is my old computer. I want to transfer files and settings from this computer.**
5. To see what will be included in the transfer, click **Customize** (see Figure 1-14). (Clicking **Advanced** opens a file browser to allow you to manually pick additional user profiles and fine-tune the items selected for transfer.)

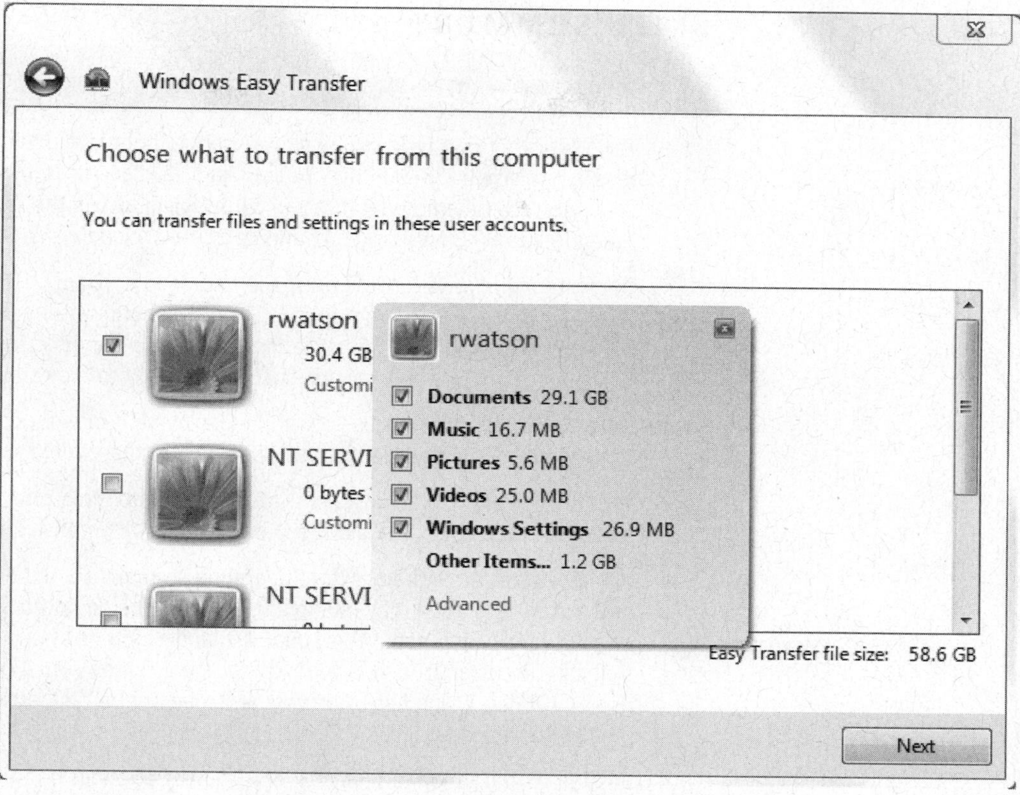

Figure 1-14

Reviewing items that will be included in the transfer

6. Click **Next** to continue.
7. Type a password to secure the transfer process and then click **Save.**
8. Select a location to save the Easy Transfer file to and then click **Save.**
9. Eject the disk and then move it to the New Windows 8 computer after the file transfer has completed.

Complete the following tasks on the new PC running Windows 8:

10. Log on to the new computer running Windows 8 and then start the Windows Easy Transfer program. Click **Next.**
11. On the *What do you want to use to transfer items to your PC?* page, click **An external hard disk or USB flash drive.**
12. When prompted for the PC you are using now, click **This is my new PC.**
13. Connect your USB drive and then select **Yes** to specify the location of your Windows Easy Transfer file.
14. Browse to and then select the file. Click **Open.**
15. Type the password you used to protect the transfer file.
16. Choose what to transfer from the old PC and then click **Transfer.**

After completing the transfer process, you will be presented with a dialog box that shows what was transferred to the new PC as well as a list of programs you might want to install on the new computer. The Windows Easy Transfer Report engine will maintain a log of the data and settings of previously transferred files. It can be accessed by pressing Windows logo key + Q and typing Windows Easy Transfer Reports.

SKILL SUMMARY

IN THIS LESSON YOU LEARNED:

- The Windows To Go workspace allows users to boot into a full version of Windows 8 from an external USB 3.0 drive. You will not have access to the internal disk on the host computer; the hibernate feature will be disabled, as will the Windows Store application. Hiberate and Windows Store settings can be managed via Group Policy.
- To create a Windows To Go workspace, you need a 32 GB USB drive that supports Windows To Go, a computer running Windows 8 Enterprise edition, a Windows 8 Enterprise ISO, Windows 8 installation media, or a Windows image created from Windows 8 Enterprise media and local administrative access to the computer.
- Desktop virtualization focuses on three deployment models: operating system virtualization, application virtualization, and user state virtualization.
- Microsoft breaks operating system virtualization into three components: Virtual Desktop Infrastructure, Session Virtualization, and Microsoft Enterprise Desktop Virtualization (MED-V).
- VDI virtualizes an entire desktop (operating system, user data and applications) on a server that can be accessed by multiple users. It can be deployed as a personal virtual desktop or a virtual desktop pool. A personal virtual desktop gives each user with a virtual desktop that can be customized. A virtual desktop pool shares virtual desktops among multiple users. VDI has a high hardware cost and may not be the best choice if you have lots of mobile users and slow WAN links.
- Session Virtualization requires fewer resources but does not allow users to personalize their environment or install their own installations. Users access their individual applications (RemoteApps) or entire desktops (remote desktops/session).
- MED-V is designed to remove barriers to migrating to a new operating system when you have legacy applications. MED-V runs them in a virtual environment called a MED-V workspace.
- Hyper-V and Client Hyper-V are hypervisors or virtual machine managers that allow you to create and run virtual machines on a single server/computer. Client Hyper-V is available on Windows 8 and is very similar to Hyper-V that runs on Windows Server 2012.
- User Experience Virtualization allows users to maintain the same experience as they move between devices (desktops, laptops, VDI sessions). This means they will see their same desktop and have access to their files and folders when folder redirection, offline files, and roaming user profiles are implemented.
- App-V provides you with the ability to virtualize applications. These applications can then be run side-by-side without causing conflicts, are isolated from other programs running locally and allow administrators to update and reconfigure them across the enterprise network.
- A Virtual hard disk (VHDs) is a file that functions much like a separate hard disk. The computer can mount the file and boot from the operating system that it contains. You can also use VHDs to standardize and streamline your image management process.
- There are two VHD formats: VHD (supports up to 2TB) and VHDX (supports up to 64TB). Hard disk types supported include Fixed Size (allocated to its maximum size when created) and Dynamically expanding disk type that will grow as data is written to it.
- The Windows startup process is controlled by parameters in the boot configuration data store. The BCD Editor can be used to modify and configure settings in the BCD store. BCDboot is a command line utility that allows you to setup a system partition when you deploy new computers.

- A multi-boot system (dual-boot) is a computer that runs multiple operating systems. Multibooting allows you to test a new operating system before fully deploying it and helps you determine if there are any hardware and application compatibility issues. Each operating system requires its own partition, which makes it different from a VHD boot disk. Programs installed on one operating system will not be accessible from the other system.
- The Application Compatibility Toolkit (ACT), User State Migration Tool (USMT) 5.0 and Windows Easy Transfer are all tools you can use to streamline the upgrade and migration to Windows 8. ACT is used to determine if applications, devices and computers will work with Windows 8. The User State Migration Tool (USMT) is a command-line tool that can help you migrate user data to Windows 8 when you have a larger number of systems to transition from. It allows you to copy the user data that you select and exclude any data that you do not want to migrate. Windows Easy Transfer provides a solution for migrating files and settings from Windows 7 to Windows 8 when you are working with only a small number of computers.

Knowledge Assessment

Multiple Choice

1. Which of the following tools should be used to migrate your user settings from a Windows 7 PC to a single Windows 8 PC?
   a. USMT
   b. DiskPart
   c. BCDedit
   d. Windows Easy Transfer
2. You have just set up a system running Windows 7 Professional and Windows 8 Enterprise to test compatibility with your existing hardware. After the installation, the system automatically boots into Windows 8. Which tool and switch should be used to change it so that your computer boots into Windows 7 by default every time?
   a. `BCDEdit /default`
   b. `BCDEdit /displayorder`
   c. `BCDEdit /bootsequence`
   d. `BCDEdit /timeout`
3. Which of the following commands exports the contents of the system store to a file so that you can use it later to restore the state of the system store?
   a. `bcdedit /createstore`
   b. `bcdboot /export`
   c. `BCDEdit /createstore`
   d. `BCDEdit /export`
4. Which of the following are requirements of Windows To Go Workspace?
   a. A USB drive that supports Windows To Go Workspace (32GB or larger).
   b. A computer running Windows 8 Professional edition.
   c. A Windows 8 Enterprise image.
   d. A Windows 7- or 8-certified computer.
5. Which of the following statements is correct? (Select all that apply.)
   a. Client Hyper-V is available on Windows 8 Professional/Enterprise (32-bit) systems.
   b. Client Hyper-V allows you to connect to Hyper-V VMs running on other computers.
   c. Client Hyper-V allows you to create and run virtual machines simultaneously.
   d. Client Hyper-V consists of a Management console and a Virtual Machine Connection component.

6. User State Virtualization includes which of the following technologies? (Select all that apply.)
   a. Folder Redirection
   b. Encrypting File System (EFS)
   c. Roaming User Profiles
   d. Offline files

7. You want to create a new VHD to use on a production server. The VHD file needs to be at least 3040 GB. Which of the following VHD formats and disk types should be used?
   a. VHD, Fixed Size
   b. VHDX, Fixed Size
   c. VHD, Dynamically Expanding
   d. VHDX, Dynamically Expanding

8. Which of the following solutions can be used to deploy an inventory-collector package? (Select all that apply.)
   a. Group Policy
   b. Logon Script
   c. Manual distribution
   d. USMT

9. You have used the `scanstate` command to collect user files and settings. Which of the following tools can be used to verify that your store is not corrupted?
   a. `bcdboot`
   b. `LoadState`
   c. `UsmtUtils`
   d. `bcdedit`

10. When transferring items to your new PC using Windows Easy Transfer, which of the following items can be used to perform the transfer? (Select all that apply.)
   a. A Windows Easy Transfer cable
   b. A network
   c. An external hard disk or USB flash drive
   d. A serial RS232 cable

Best Answer

Choose the letter that corresponds to the best answer. More than one answer choice may achieve the goal. Select the BEST answer.

1. You are implementing VDI and want to provide each user with a virtual desktop that can be customized by the user. Which VDI deployment best fits this requirement?
   a. Virtual Desktop Pool (VDP)
   b. Personal Virtual Desktop (PVD)
   c. Client-Hyper-V PVD
   d. Client Hyper-V VDP

2. You are setting up a virtual hard disk on your Windows 8 client computer. The virtual hard disk will be 3 TB in size and may be used on a production server in the near future. Which of the following combinations provide the best solution?
   a. Use the VHD format/Fixed Size hard disk type
   b. Use the VHDX format/Fixed Size hard disk type
   c. Use the VHD format/Dynamically Expanding hard disk type
   d. Use the VHDX format/Dynamically Expanding hard disk type

3. You have been asked to upgrade a Windows 7 64-bit client computer to Windows 8. Which of the following configurations would ensure a successful upgrade based on its hardware configuration?
   a. 1 Ghz CPU, 1GB of memory, 16GB of disk space.
   b. 1 Ghz CPU, 2GB of memory, 20GB of disk space

c. 1 Ghz CPU, 1GB of memory, 200GB of disk space
d. 1 Ghz CPU, 2GB of memory, 500GB of disk space

4. You would like to reduce the amount of time you system waits to load the default operating system. It currently is set to 30 seconds but you would like to change it to 10 seconds. Which of the following commands accomplishes this task?
   a. bcdedit /default /timeout 10
   b. bcdedit /timeout 10
   c. bcdedit /timeout 10 /default
   d. bcdedit /timeout 10 /set

5. You would like to try out Windows 8 on your current computer running Windows 7. You want to simulate as close as possible the impact the new operating system will have on your existing hardware. You do not want to create a new partition for Windows 8. Which option provides the best solution to meet your needs?
   a. Setting up a multi-boot system.
   b. Creating a Windows 7 image, formatting the drive, and installing Windows 8. After testing, restore the Windows 7 image.
   c. Using a Windows To Go workspace disk.
   d. Configuring a VHD on your Windows 7 computer.

Matching and Identification

1. Match the tool with the tasks it can perform:
   _______ a) `bcdedit.exe`
   _______ b) `pwcreator.exe`
   _______ c) `diskpart.exe`
   _______ d) `gpmc.msc`
   _______ e) `scanstate`
   1. Attach a VHD so that it appears on the host as a drive and not a static file.
   2. Create a new Windows To Go workspace drive.
   3. Create a Group Policy object to apply to all computers in a domain.
   4. Examine a source computer, collect files and settings and create a store to contain a user's files and settings.
   5. Set the order in which the boot manager displays the multi-boot menu.

2. Write the `bcdedit` command for the specified function or scenario:
   _______ Create a copy of the entire BCD store.
   _______ Change the order in which the boot manager displays the multi-boot menu.
   _______ Set the boot sequence (one time only) for the boot manager.
   _______ Change the default entry you want boot manager to use.
   _______ Remove an entry from the BCD store.

Build a List

1. In order of first to last, specify the steps used to install the Client Hyper-V feature in Windows 8.
   _______ Click **Turn Windows features on and off**.
   _______ Click **Hyper-V** and then click **OK**.
   _______ Set the search context to **Settings** and then type **Windows Features**.
   _______ Reboot the Windows 8 computer.
   _______ Press the **Windows logo key + q**.

2. You want to create a Windows To Go workspace on a Windows 8 Enterprise client computer. Specify the correct order of the steps required to create the Workspace.
   _______ Press the **Windows logo key + w**.
   _______ Click **Create** to set up the Windows To Go workspace.

_______ Click **Create** to format the drive.
_______ Type **Windows To Go** and select it from the *Results List.*
_______ Connect a Windows To Go workspace drive to the host.
_______ (optional) Select **Use BitLocker with my Windows To Go workspace** and then click **Next**.
_______ Click the Windows image that appears or click **Add search location** to locate one. Click **Next** to continue.
_______ Select the USB drive connected earlier and then click **Next**.
_______ Click **Yes** to automatically boot from the USB drive when you restart the host.

3. Specify the correct order of the steps that must be completed to create a VHD boot file using the Disk Management console.
_______ Click **Action > Create VHD**.
_______ In the *File name* field, type a name for the VHD file and then click **Save**.
_______ In the *Virtual hard disk format* section, leave the default setting of **Fixed size (recommended)**.
_______ Click **Browse** to navigate to the folder where you want to store the VHD file.
_______ Click **Start** and, in the *Search* field, type **Disk Management**.
_______ For the *Virtual hard disk size* setting, type **20**, click the drop-down arrow, and then select **GB**.
_______ Click **OK**.

■ Business Case Scenarios

Scenario 1-1: Migrating Using ScanState and LoadState

After determining the information that needs to be migrated from a source computer, Elliot, the network administrator for Contoso, creates a new config.xml file and runs the following `scanstate` command to collect the information:

```
scanstate \\server\migration\mystore /config:config.xml /i:migdocs.xml
/:migapp.xml /v:13 /l:scan.log
```

After setting up the destination computer, he runs the `LoadState` command to migrate the files and settings from the source computer. After logging off the machine and then back on, he notices his modifications did not migrate. What might have caused the problem? He is certain the modifications in the config.xml file were not entered incorrectly in the file.

Scenario 1-2: Using Windows To Go

Elliot receives a call from one of his support staff that Mary, one of Contoso's account managers, is having trouble booting into a Windows To Go workspace drive from her home office. You know she is running a Windows 7 Professional computer and has a USB drive that is certified to work with Windows To Go. You also sent a tech to her house last week to configure the computer to boot from a USB drive when it's present. What could be the problem?

Scenario 1-3: Testing Windows 8 on New Hardware

Elliot would like to install and test Windows 8 Enterprise on his existing Windows 7 Professional computer. He does not want to create a new partition to hold the operating system nor does he want to run Windows 8 Enterprise in a fully virtualized environment. He specifically wants to see how Windows 8 Enterprise performs on his actual hardware (the memory, the video card, the processor, and so on). Which operating system installation strategy would you recommend and why?

Designing an Application Strategy for Desktop Applications

LESSON 2

70-688 EXAM OBJECTIVE

Objective 1.2 – Design an application strategy for desktop applications. This objective may include but is not limited to the following design considerations: Application compatibility using Client Hyper-V; Remote Desktop Protocol (RDP); Application Compatibility Toolkit (ACT); App-V; application updates; application coexistence; application reputation; Internet Explorer 10 management.

LESSON HEADING	EXAM OBJECTIVE
Working with Client Hyper-V	Application compatibility using Client Hyper-V
Exploring Remote Desktop Services	Remote Desktop Protocol (RDP)
Working with the Application Compatibility Tool Kit	Application Compatibility Toolkit (ACT)
Using Runtime Analysis Packages and Testing Application Compatibility	
Virtualizing Applications using App-V	App-V
Creating App-V Programs	Application coexistence
Managing Application Updates	Application updates
Managing Apps with Group Policy	
Using Windows Intune	
Using System Center 2012 Configuration Manager	
Protecting Your System with SmartScreen	Application reputation
Using SmartScreen to Implement Application Reputation	
Customizing Internet Explorer 10 using IEAK 10	Internet Explorer 10 management
Maintaining IEAK Packages	

KEY TERMS

- App-V Management server
- App-V Publishing server
- App-V Reporting server
- App-V Reporting database server
- Client Hyper-V
- Compatibility Monitor tool
- group policies
- Hyper-V Manager
- Hyper-V Virtual Machine Connection
- malware
- Microsoft Silverlight
- phishing attacks
- Remote Desktop Services
- RD Session Host
- RD Virtualization Host
- RD Web Access
- sequencing
- System Center 2012 Configuration Manager (SCCM)
- Windows Internet Explorer Administration Kit (IEAK) 10
- Windows Intune
- Windows SmartScreen

Working With Client Hyper-V

Client Hyper-V enables you to create and manage virtual machines (VMs) using a virtual switch. These VMs can be used to test your applications for compatibility with new operating systems.

CERTIFICATION READY
Application compatibility using Client Hyper-V
Objective 1.2

Client Hyper-V, a Microsoft replacement for Windows Virtual PC, provides the same virtualization capabilities as Hyper-V in Windows Server 2012. Although it does not include all the advanced features available on the server version, it does utilize the same interface and underlying technology. This feature is disabled by default on Windows 8 Enterprise (64-bit) machines.

Although Client Hyper-V runs only on Windows 8 (64-bit) machines running the Windows 8 Enterprise (64-bit) operating system, it enables you to run 32- and 64-bit VMs simultaneously, connect to a Hyper-V machine running on another computer, and move machines between Client Hyper-V and Hyper-V running on the server.

Using this feature, you can build a test lab that runs entirely on a single computer. For example, if you need to test an application's compatibility with several different configurations of Windows 8, you can create a VM for each configuration. After your testing is complete you can easily remove the VMs or export them to your production network.

To run Hyper-V, you need the following:

- Windows 8 Enterprise (64-bit) version
- A 64-bit processor that incorporates second level address translation (SLAT) technology
- A minimum of 4 GB of memory (running more than one VM at a time requires more)

ENABLE THE HYPER-V FEATURE

GET READY. To enable the Hyper-V feature, log in to the computer running Windows 8 Enterprise (64-bit) with Administrator privileges and perform the following steps:

1. Press the **Windows logo key + w**.
2. Type **Features**; from the *Results* list, click **Turn Windows features on and off**.
3. Click the + displayed next to the *Hyper-V* folder.

   This action expands the folder to show the components included (see Figure 2-1).

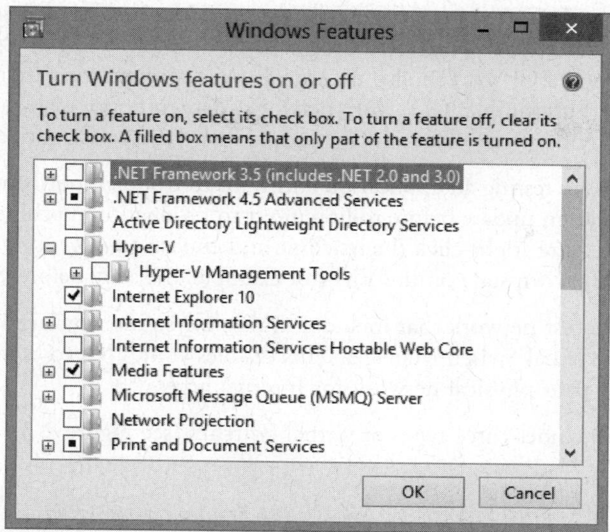

Figure 2-1

Enabling the Hyper-V feature on Windows 8 Enterprise

4. Select the check box next to Hyper-V and then click **OK**.

   Windows searches for the required files and then applies the changes to the computer.

5. Click **Close**.

6. Restart your computer to complete the installation.

   A restart starts the Windows hypervisor and the Virtual Machine Management service.

After installing Client Hyper-V, you see two new tiles after logging in with the administrative account:

- ***Hyper-V Manager*** (see Figure 2-2): This is the management console for creating and managing your VMs and setting up your test network.
- ***Hyper-V Virtual Machine Connection:*** This is used when working with a single VM that you have already created. It is very similar to the Remote Desktop Connection utility.

Figure 2-2

Reviewing the Hyper-V Manager console

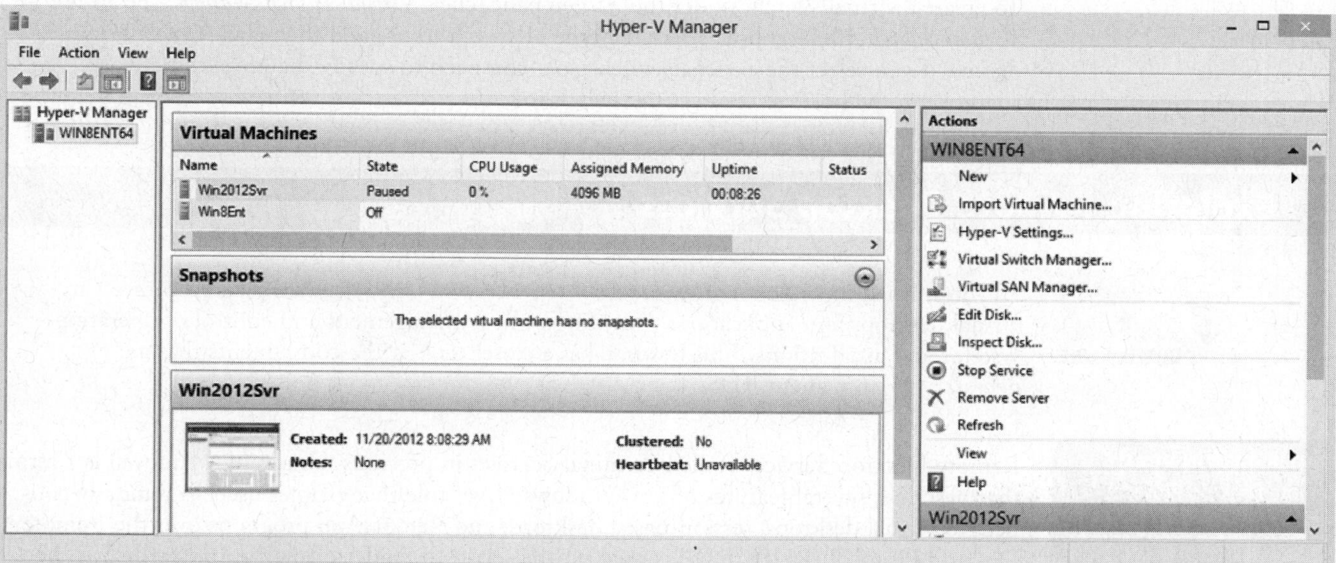

Within the Hyper-V Manager console, you can import VMs (*Action > Import Virtual Machine*) and create virtual hard disks (*Action > New > Virtual Machine*) to be used by VMs or by the host PC. You can also manage a VM's configuration by modifying the startup order of devices (for example, CD, IDE, network adapter, floppy), allocate memory, determine the number of virtual processors to use, and add hard drives/CD drives to an IDE/SCSI controller.

When you are testing an application and want to troubleshoot compatibility issues or test a new application update before rolling it out to production machines, you can use the Hyper-V snapshot feature (right-click the machine and choose *Snapshot*). By taking a snapshot, you can return to a known state on the VM (for example, the state before you installed the application).

To set up a test network that includes multiple systems, you need to configure a virtual switch using the Virtual Switch Manager. This enables your VMs to communicate with each other and access your physical network for Internet access.

Hyper-V includes three types of virtual switches (see Figure 2-3):

Figure 2-3

Reviewing the three types of Hyper-V switches

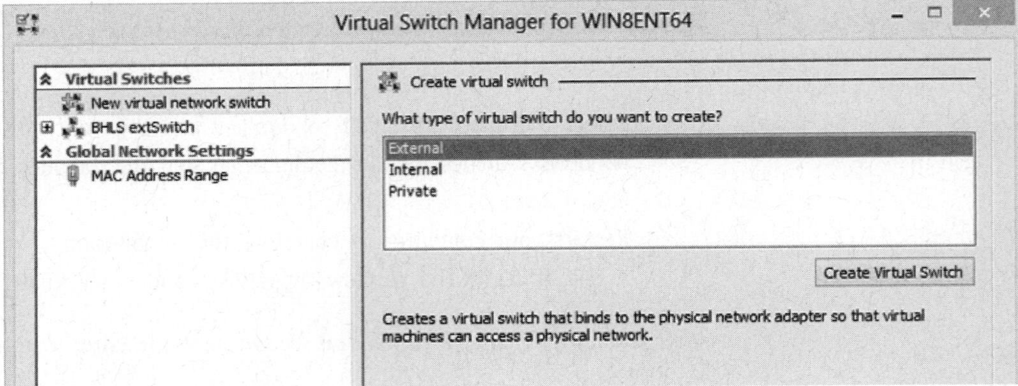

- **External:** Creates a virtual switch that binds to the physical network adapter. This enables your VMs to access your physical network.
- **Internal:** Creates a virtual switch that is used only by the VMs that run on the physical computer and between the VMs and the physical computer.
- **Private:** Creates a VM that can only be used by the VMs running on the computer.

To create a virtual switch, under the *Actions* pane, click *Virtual Switch Manager*. From the *Virtual Switch Manager* box, select the type of switch to use and then click *Create Virtual Switch*. If you select the external switch type, you need to specify the physical network adapter (on the host) to connect the switch to.

Exploring Remote Desktop Services

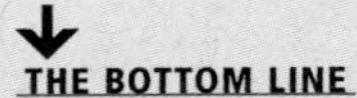

THE BOTTOM LINE

As you learned in Lesson 1, ***Remote Desktop Services (RDS)*** enable users to connect to virtual desktops and applications providing central management and control of operating systems and applications. This lesson takes a closer look at the components that are necessary to implement RDS.

CERTIFICATION READY
Remote Desktop Protocol (RDP)
Objective 1.2

Remote Desktop Services (called Terminal Services in previous releases of Windows) is a term that describes several features of the Windows server role that enables users to remotely connect to virtual desktops, session-based desktops, and RemoteApp programs over the Remote Desktop Protocol (RDP). RDP is used on the server to render display output, which is then sent in the form of packets to the RDP client. On the client, RDP is used to send mouse and keyboard inputs to the server.

The Windows server running the RDS role includes the following services:

- ***RD Virtualization Host:*** Integrates with Hyper-V to enable users to connect to a VM on a server hosting Hyper-V.
- ***RD Session Host:*** Enables a server to host RemoteApp programs or session-based desktops.
- ***RD Connection Broker:*** Used for session load balancing; enables users to reconnect to a virtual desktop and RemoteApp programs, and provides access to virtual desktops in a virtual desktop collection.
- ***RD Web Access:*** Enables users to access RemoteApps and desktop connection via the *Start* menu or through a web browser.
- **RD Licensing***:* Manages licenses needed to connect to the RD Session Host.
- **RD Gateway***:* Enables users to connect to virtual desktops, RemoteApp programs, and session-based desktops from any device connected to the Internet.

An RDS-based Virtual Desktop Infrastructure (VDI) enables you to store, maintain, secure, and manage Windows desktops. When it is configured in combination with Hyper-V, you can assign a unique VM to each user or dynamically assign a machine from a pool of available VMs.

RemoteApp programs stored on a RD Session Host server and virtual desktops hosted on an RD Virtualization Host can be remotely accessed from a client desktop. RemoteApp programs, which look and feel like local applications even though they are accessed remotely, can be accessed via a web console, or can be launched from the users' Start menu or when they open a file associated with the application.

Working with the Application Compatibility Toolkit (ACT)

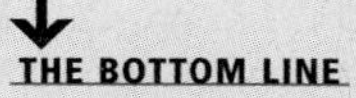

Testing an application's compatibility before installing it onto a new operating system is critical. The Application Compatibility Toolkit (ACT) enables you to collect the information you need to determine where to focus your attention.

CERTIFICATION READY
Application Compatibility Toolkit (ACT)
Objective 1.2

For many reasons, applications become incompatible when they migrate to a current operating system. It can be as simple as the application being designed to check for a certain version on startup or a feature that is no longer present in the latest release. When these applications are critical to your business, it is important to identify them early in the process. The Application Compatibility Toolkit (ACT) 6.0, included with the Windows Assessment and Development Kit (ADK), includes a set of tools, packages, and services that you can use. ACT can help you diagnose and fix problems associated with those incompatibilities.

Using Runtime-Analysis Packages and Testing Application Compatibility

A runtime analysis package can be used to evaluate whether your existing applications are compatible with a new operating system that you are considering deploying to your organization. This package enables you to identify and address any problems prior to deploying the new operating system to your production environment.

In Lesson 1, you learned about the components included in ACT 6.0 and the process to create an inventory-collector package that collects system information and identifies the applications installed on each computer. In this section, you learn a little more about the steps needed to test the applications you find using a runtime analysis package.

A runtime analysis package includes tools you need to monitor applications for compatibility issues and submit compatibility feedback. Before creating this package, you need to decide which applications to test for compatibility issues, make sure you are working with the latest compatibility information from the Microsoft website, and then organize your applications. After these steps are completed, you can then deploy your runtime-analysis packages to your test environment.

CREATE A RUNTIME-ANALYSIS PACKAGE

GET READY. To create a runtime analysis package, log in to the computer running Windows 8 Enterprise (64-bit) with Administrator privileges and perform the following steps:

1. Press the **Windows logo key + q.**
2. From the *Results* list, type **acm** and then select **Application Compatibility Manager**.
3. In the left pane of the *Application Compatibility Manager* window, click **Collect.**
4. From the menu at the top, click **File > New.**
5. In the *Choose the type of package to create* screen, click **Runtime analysis package.**
6. Provide the information requested for the package (see Figure 2-4) and then click **Create.**

Figure 2-4

Providing runtime analysis package information

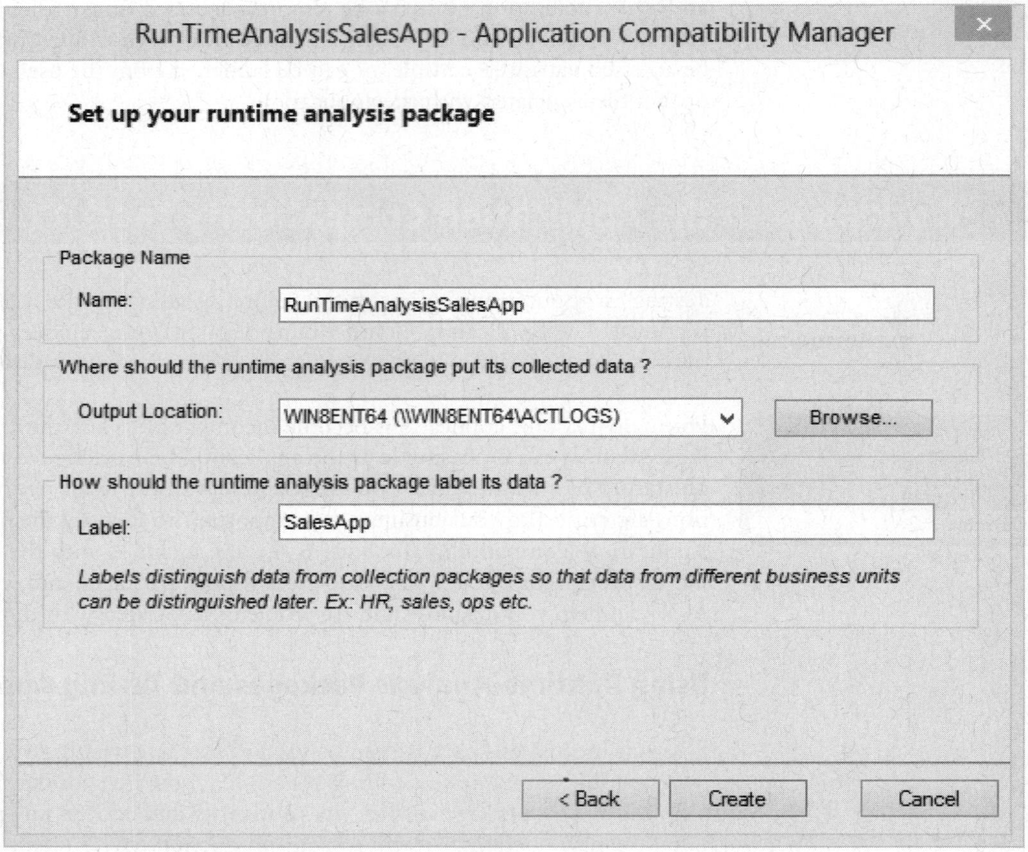

7. Navigate to a folder on your computer where you want to store the Windows installer (.msi) file for the package.

   The .msi file is used to install the runtime analysis package in your test environment.

8. In the *File name* field, type **RunTimeAnalysisSalesApps** and then click **Save**.
9. In the *Next steps for your runtime analysis collection package* screen, review the next steps and then click **Finish**.

You can now deploy the package by using Group Policy, using System Center Configuration Manager (SCCM), via a logon script, storing the file on a network share, or using removable media to distribute it to your Windows 8 test systems.

After it is installed, you can test for application compatibility by using the ***Compatibility Monitor tool***, which is installed as part of the runtime analysis package. The Compatibility Monitor tool is used to submit compatibility information to the ACT database.

To use it on a Windows 8 target computer, type **monitor** from the Windows 8 *Start* menu. From the list of *Results*, select **Microsoft Compatibility Monitor**. The *Compatibility Monitor* tool appears (see Figure 2-5).

Figure 2-5

Using the Compatibility Monitor tool

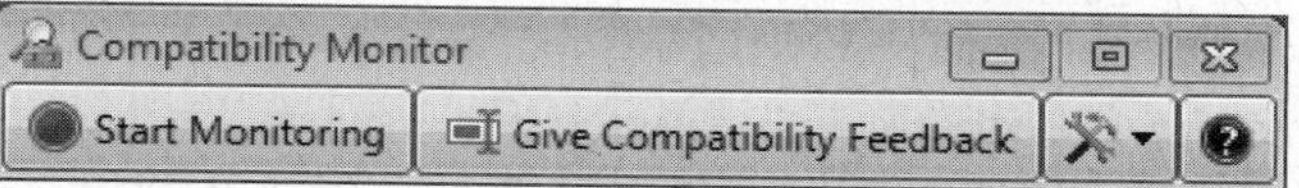

To test for compatibility, click **Start Monitoring** and leave it running while you use the applications to test for compatibility with the new operating system. As compatibility information is detected, the information is sent at regular intervals to the ACT database. When you are done, just click **Stop Monitoring** to complete the data collection.

You can also use the Compatibility Monitor to submit your compatibility rating for the application(s) you are testing. When submitting feedback, you can type a title for the compatibility issue, include a description of the compatibility issue, and then attach a screenshot or a step-by-step recording of the actual issue. After you click **Submit**, the information is sent to the ACT database.

VIEWING YOUR REPORTS

You can view your compatibility report (see Figure 2-6) from within the *Application Compatibility Manager* (ACM).

Figure 2-6

Viewing a sample Windows 8 application report

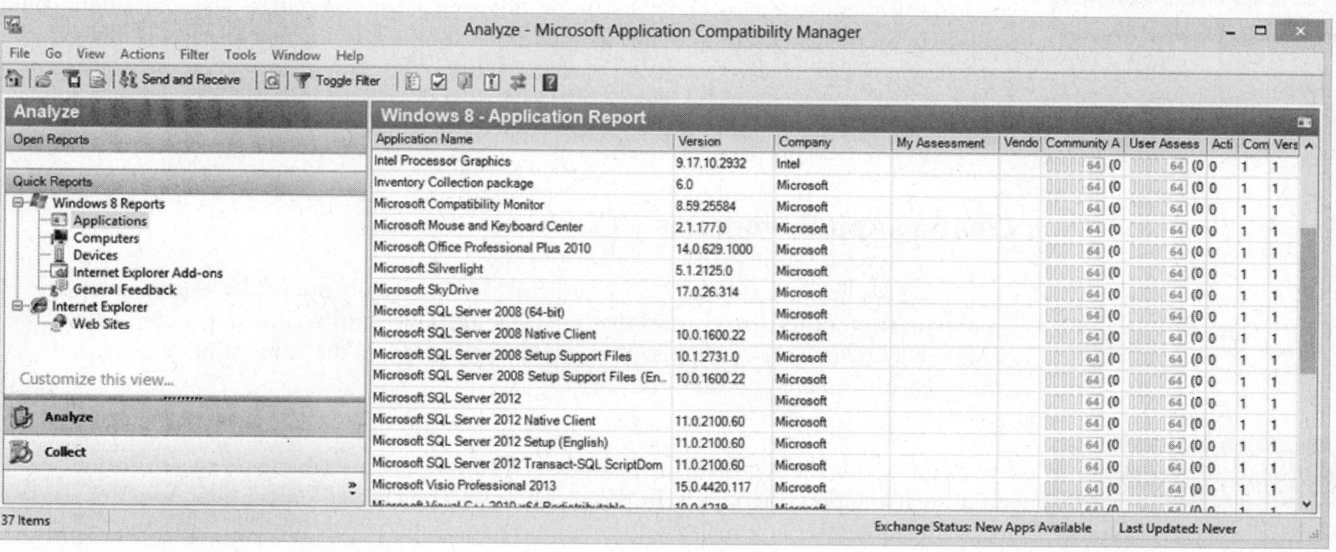

The following reports are available within the ACM:

- **Applications:** This report shows information from the applications from which you have collected information (application name, vendor, version, your organization's compatibility rating, compatibility information from the vendor, the number of computers with the application installed, and so on).
- **Computers:** This report provides information collected from your computers (computer name, domain, operating system, number of applications installed on the computer, and any applications or devices that have issues).
- **Devices:** This report provides information on the model and manufacturer of the device, the number of computers that have the device installed, and whether it works on 32- or 64-bit operating systems.
- **Internet Explorer Add-ons:** This report shows the add-ons that are currently installed for the Internet Explorer browser.
- **Internet Explorer\Websites:** This report provides information on the website URL, your organization's compatibility rating for the internet or internal website, and the number of issues/resolved issues for the website.
- **General Feedback:** This report provides general feedback comments submitted by the Compatibility Monitor. These can include step-by-step recordings with attached screenshots and comments regarding a specific application that was tested.

In addition to these reports, you can also create custom views of each report to filter views. Although these reports are stored in the (.adq) form and can be viewed in ACM, you can also export them to an Excel spreadsheet for further analysis.

■ Virtualizing Applications Using App-V

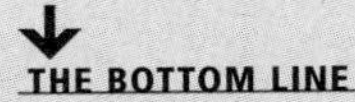

Virtualizing applications enables you to test applications side-by-side, avoid purchasing costly hardware; and, when implementing using Application Virtualization (App-V), centrally manage, maintain, and update your applications.

CERTIFICATION READY
App-V
Objective 1.2

In Lesson 1, you learned that App-V enables you to perform virtualization at the application level. Prior to App-V, if you wanted to test an older version of an application against a newer release, you had to either create a dual boot system or use two separate computers. The applications could not coexist on the same computer due to application conflicts. In the first scenario (a dual boot system), you would have to spend a lot of time restarting the computer to access each version. In the second scenario, it would take time to have your IT staff set up a second system, not to mention the additional cost of the hardware. App-V can address both of these situations.

Creating App-V Programs

Creating applications that can run in a virtualized environment enables you to isolate the program from other applications that might be running on the same target computer. This enables you to avoid application conflicts and reduces the amount of time needed for predeployment application testing.

CERTIFICATION READY
Application coexistence
Objective 1.2

In Lesson 1, you learned that App-V is a set of products that enables you to perform virtualization at an application level. In this section, we take a closer look at how App-V is used to create and deliver a virtualized application to an App-V client through a process called

sequencing. During the sequencing process, the App-V sequencer program monitors the installation and setup process for the application and then records the information necessary to run it in a virtual environment.

App-V is included with the download of the Microsoft Desktop Optimization Pack (MDOP). To use application virtualization in your organization, you need the following App-V components:

- ***App-V Management server:*** Provides the overall management functions for the App-V infrastructure.
- ***App-V Publishing server:*** Provides the functionality needed to host and stream the virtual applications.
- ***App-V Reporting server:*** Enables authorized users to run and view App-V reports and ad-hoc reports to aid in managing the App-V infrastructure.
- ***App-V Reporting database server:*** Facilitates database predeployments for App-V 5.0 reporting.

You can deploy App-V in a standalone configuration in which all the server components are installed on a single computer. This works well when you are testing App-V or in smaller organizations. You can also deploy App-V in a distributed environment in which the components are spread across multiple servers to support future scalability. Electronic software distribution solutions are an option as well.

App-V servers deliver virtual applications either by streaming them to App-V clients or by locally caching them. The applications are stored on the App-V server. When a computer with the App-V client installed requests an application from the server, users are presented with a list of the apps they are allowed to use. Policies controlled by the administrator determine who can and cannot use the virtual applications.

The following represent a few characteristics of running virtualized applications:

- No install or configurations requirements on the client machine.
- No changes to the user's computer after opening and closing the application (registry, files, application support files, and so on).
- The applications are isolated from other virtual and local programs running on the computer. This enables the user to run two versions of the same application simultaneously side-by-side if needed.
- The virtual applications are being managed and delivered from a central location, so updating and reconfiguring applications saves time and resources.

To sequence an application, you need the MDOP from Microsoft, which is available for MSDN and TechNet subscribers. After you have MDOP, you must install the App-V 5.0 sequencer on the Windows 8 computer that will be used to create the sequenced applications.

INSTALL THE APP-V 5.0 SEQUENCER

GET READY. To install the App-V 5.0 sequencer, log in to the computer running Windows 8 Enterprise (64-bit) with Administrator privileges and perform the following steps:

1. Insert the Microsoft Desktop Optimization Pack (MDOP) disc into your computer.
2. When the *MDOP* menu appears, click **Application Virtualization for Desktops**.
3. Under the *App-V 5.0* category, click **App-V 5.0 Sequencer**.
4. Click **Install**.
5. Review the *Software Licenses Terms* screen, select **I accept the license terms**, and then click **Next**.
6. On the *Customer Experience Improvement Program* screen, click **Install** to accept the default.

7. When the message *Setup completed successfully* appears, click **Close**.
8. Close the *MDOP* menu.

The App-V 5.0 sequencer program is ready for use. After you have installed the program, you are ready to sequence an application. Before starting the sequencing process, you need to obtain the application's installer file from the product's website. When creating sequenced packages, you should also set up a single VM that is used only for this purpose.

SEQUENCE AN APPLICATION

GET READY. To sequence an application, log in to the computer running Windows 8 Enterprise (64-bit) with Administrator privileges and perform the following steps:

1. From the Windows 8 *Start* menu, type **sequencer**. From the *Results* list, select **Microsoft Application Virtualization Sequencer**.
2. Click **Create a New Virtual Application Package**.
3. To accept the default setting *Create Package (default)*, click **Next**.
4. On *Prepare the computer for creating a virtual package*, make sure there are no issues listed that need to be resolved and then click **Next**.
   Double-click any issues that appear to read how to resolve them and then click **Refresh** after completing the tasks.
5. To accept the default setting, *Standard Application (default)*, click **Next**.
6. On the *Select Installer* screen, click **Browse** to navigate to the folder in which the application to be sequenced is stored. Select the application and then click **Open**.
7. Click **Next** to continue.
8. On the *Package Name* screen, in the *Virtual Application Package Name* field, type the name for the application (for example, **MySequencedApp**).
9. For the *Primary Virtual Application Directory (required)* field, type **c:\program files\<appname>**
   This is the location where the application would be installed by default. You would need to replace *<appname>* with the actual name of the application you are sequencing and then click **Next**.
10. Install the application to sequence.
    The sequencer program monitors the installation. After your application has completed installing, continue to the next step.
11. On the *You must complete the application installations before you can continue* screen, select **I am finished installing** and then click **Next**.
12. On the *Run each program to manage first use tasks* screen, click **Next**.
13. Review the installation report and then click **Next**.
14. On the *Create a basic package or customize further* screen, select **Customize**.
15. On the *Run each program briefly to optimize the package over slow or unreliable networks* screen, click **Next**.
16. On the *Restrict operating systems for this package* screen, select **Allow this package to run only on the following operating systems**. Select the **Windows 8 32-bit** and **Windows 8 64-bit** options. Click **Next** to continue.
17. Click **Create** to accept the default storage location for the virtualized application.
18. Click **Create**.
    The package is created and placed into a folder with the name you used in Step 8.
19. When the *Package completed* message appears, click **Close**.
20. Close the *Microsoft Application Virtualization Sequencer* window. You have completed the process for virtualizing an application.

You can use the Microsoft installer file you created (*MySequencedApp.msi*) to install the virtual application on a standalone computer, deploy it using Group Policy, or use it with SCCM 2012 to deploy the application to your end users. After the application has been virtualized, you can import it into the Application Management server and manage it via the Application Virtualization Management console. To manage the package, consider using groups to organize the virtual applications (Office Apps, Accounting Apps, and so on.). You can then import the virtual application into the group. After it is in place, you need to determine which group of users will be able to use the application and then assign them to the package.

■ Managing Application Updates

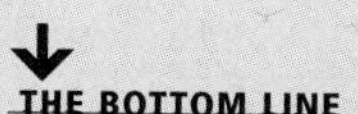

THE BOTTOM LINE

Keeping your applications updated is critical when it comes to maintaining user productivity and keeping your network secure from vulnerabilities. Some of the options require building an infrastructure; others enable you to use the Microsoft cloud. Understanding the options enables you to strategize how to manage your application updates.

CERTIFICATION READY
Application updates
Objective 1.2

Microsoft provides several tools and programs to help keep your applications current and secure. They include Group Policy, Windows Intune, and SCCM.

Managing Apps with Group Policy

Group policies are rules that help you manage users and computers on an Active Directory network or on a local computer running Windows 2000 or later operating systems. Active Directory is a distributed database that stores and manages information about network resources as well as application-specific data.

Group policies comprise rules that help you manage users and computers. To understand Group Policy, you need to first understand the basic hierarchical structure of Active Directory. Active Directory is partitioned into the following:

- Site: Group of TCP/IP subnets.
- Forest: Acts as a security boundary and defines the security scope of authority for administrators. A forest can contain one or more domains. The first domain setup is called the forest root domain.
- Domain: Enables you to partition Active Directory and control where data is replicated to.
- Organizational units (OUs): Designed to enable you to delegate authority to distribute management of resources to a number of people who are trusted to perform them.

Group Policy for your entire enterprise can be managed using the Group Policy Management Console (GPMC), as shown in Figure 2-7. The GPMC provides access to the Group Policy Management Editor, which is used to create and manage policy settings. Policy settings are stored in Group Policy Objects (GPOs) that are assigned at different levels of the Active Directory hierarchical structure based on which computers and users you want them to apply to.

Using Group Policy, you can deploy applications on a per-computer or per-user basis. You make applications available to users or computers by assigning or publishing them.

Figure 2-7

Exploring the Group Policy Management Console

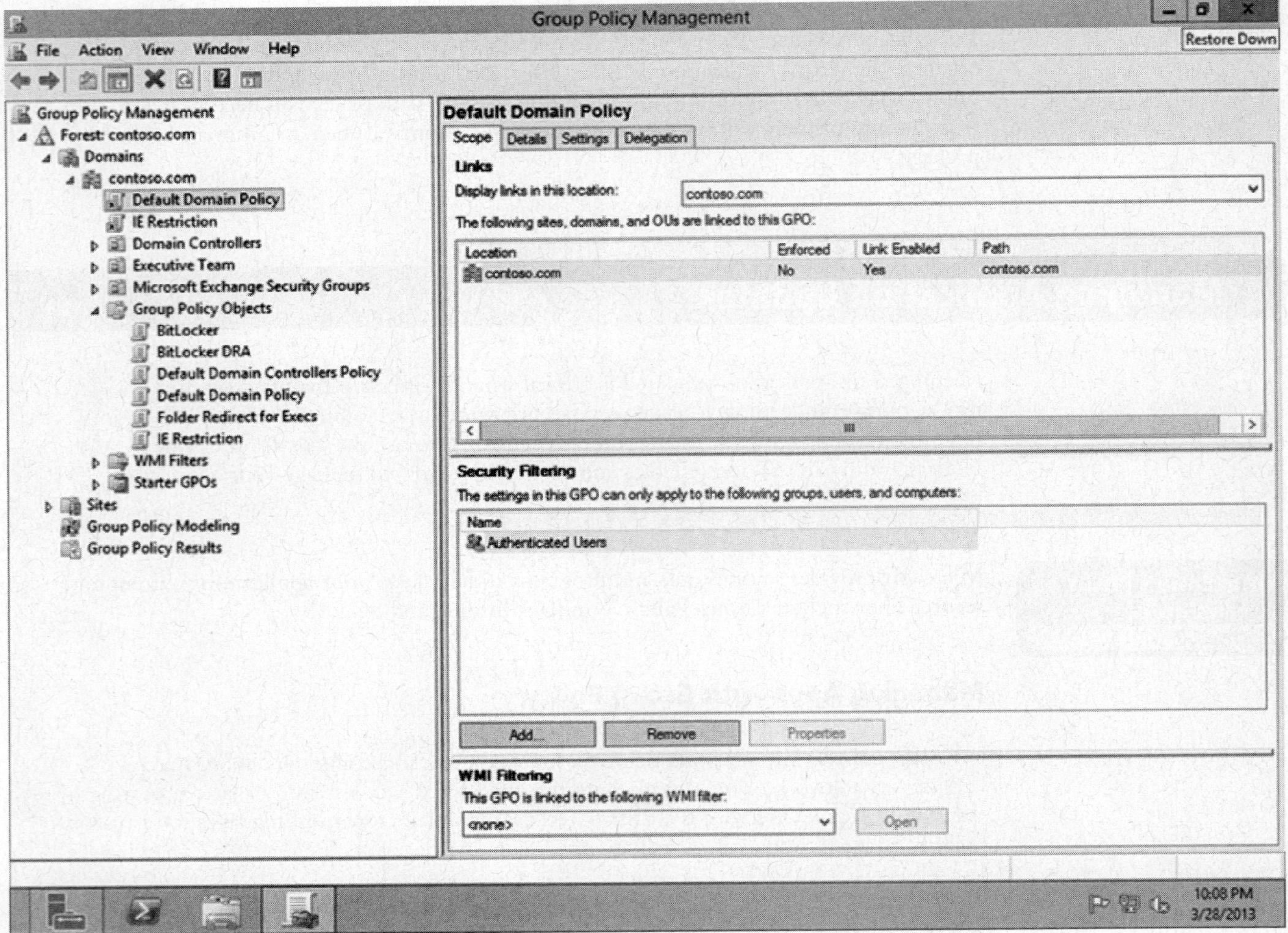

When an application is assigned to a user, the application is advertised to the user at the next login. The application follows the users regardless of which computer they log in from. Depending on how you configure the application, it is either installed when users select it from the *Start* menu or when they open a file that is associated with the application. If you assign the application to a computer, it is typically installed when the computer boots.

If you publish an application to users, the application does not add shortcuts on the user's desktop or in the *Start* menu. Instead, the application can be installed via the Add/Remove programs in Control Panel or when users click a file associated with the application. In other words, it is up to the users when they want to install the program. You cannot publish an application to a computer.

Using Windows Intune

Windows Intune is Microsoft's integrated, cloud-based client management solution for managing computers, tablets, and phones.

Because Windows Intune is a cloud service, you do not have to set up and maintain a server infrastructure to use it. All you need is a Windows Intune subscription.

Windows Intune is composed of two components:

- Web-based administrative console.
- Windows Intune client software: This is downloaded from the Windows Intune account administration website using the Windows Live ID and password associated with your Windows Intune account.

You can deploy the client software manually and have the target computer navigate to the shared folder and launch the installation, or deploy it using software programs such as Group Policy or SCCM.

After the software is installed on the client, it reports its status to the cloud service from anywhere there is an Internet connection. You can then manage the Intune clients using the web-based administrative console (see Figure 2-8) accessed via a browser that supports ***Microsoft Silverlight***. Microsoft Silverlight is a free web-browser plug-in that is designed to provide rich Internet applications and media experiences on the Web.

Figure 2-8

Accessing the Windows Intune administrator dashboard

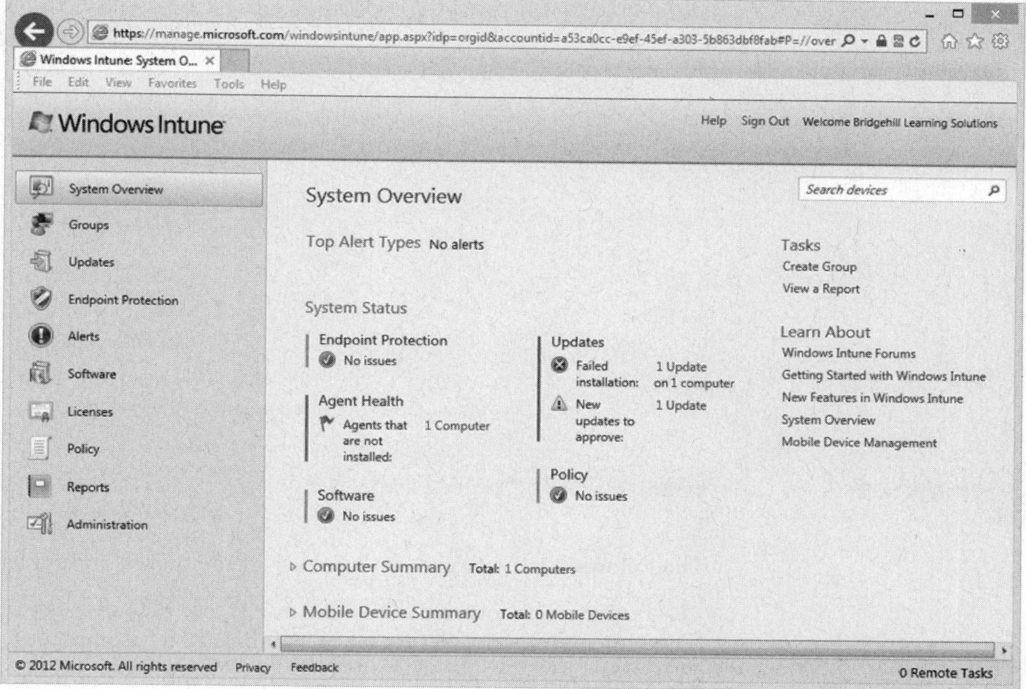

From the console, you can perform the following security and management tasks:

- Protect your computers from malware
- Deploy licensed software (Microsoft Office, third-party applications) to PCs
- Manage the deployment of software updates to Microsoft and most third-party software publishers from a central location
- Receive updates/alerts from the PCs on your network
- Provide remote assistance and perform remote tasks
- Track hardware and software inventory
- Manage software licenses
- Run software update reports, detected software reports, computer inventory reports, and license purchase and installation reports

TAKE NOTE*

Windows Intune can deploy only Windows installer (.msi) or executable (.exe) files that support silent installation.

When deploying software using Windows Intune, you have two installation types:

- A required install automatically installs or pushes the software to the managed computer and requires no user interaction.
- An available install publishes the software to the Windows company portal or on the mobile company portal so your users can choose whether they want to install the software.

The software you upload is stored in the Windows Intune cloud storage that your organization purchased. To deploy software, access the Software workspace (see Figure 2-9).

Figure 2-9

Reviewing the Windows Intune Software workspace

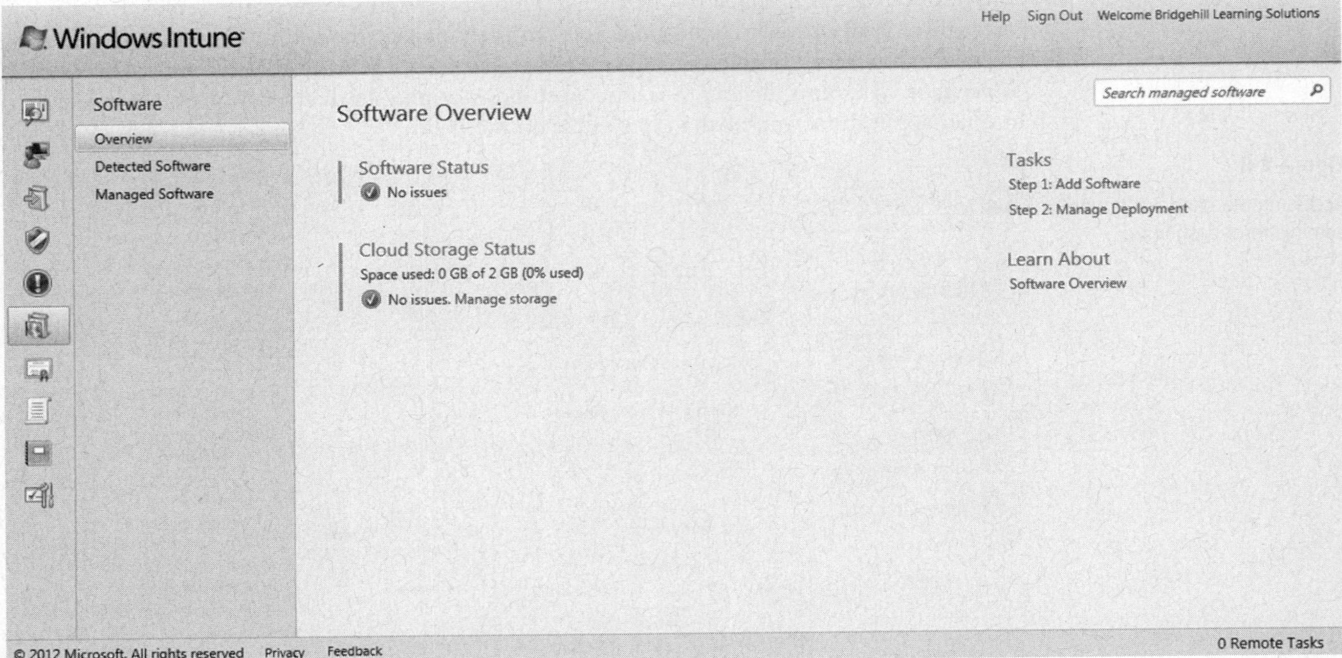

The following steps provide an overview of the process for publishing and updating software:

1. Prepare your software files. The .msi or .exe file must be placed in a single folder along with any supporting files on the administrator's computer.
2. Configure and upload the package. This requires you to type the path to the setup files, the name of the software publisher, the name of the software being deployed, a description, the required architecture (32- or 64-bit), and which operating systems the package will be installed on.

   You also set the detection rule (for example, look for a specific file, registry entry, or MSI product code) to see if the software is already installed when deploying an updated package. After configuration is completed, the file is compressed, encrypted, and uploaded to the Windows Azure storage platform. After it is uploaded, you see the application in the Managed Software workspace.
3. Deploy the package. Within the Managed Software workspace, click the package to deploy and select the group to deploy the software package to. The package is now ready for your users.
4. Client download/installations. If the client meets all the configuration requirements you set in Step 2, it downloads the package to a temporary folder and begin the

silent installation. (The client is configured via a policy to check for new downloads every 8 hours.)

5. Monitor the deployment status. To view the progress of installations across your managed computers, you can use the administrative console.

For many applications, the manufacturer includes options to automatically check for updates directly from the client computer. If you want Windows Intune to manage this process, you have to disable the manufacturer's feature on each of the managed computers.

Using System Center 2012 Configuration Manager

System Center 2012 Configuration Manager (SCCM) provides tools to deploy and manage your applications by setting up a server infrastructure within your network.

SCCM offers another option to deploy and manage your applications. Using the tools provided, you can create, manage, deploy, and monitor applications across your organization. In addition to managing applications, you can also use it to perform the following tasks:

- Assess and track whether the correct operating systems and applications are installed.
- Manage antimalware policies and Windows firewall security.
- Collect and provide inventory reports on hardware, software, and licenses used on your network.
- Create operating system images and deploy them to both computers managed by the SCCM, and to unmanaged computers using PXE boot or other bootable media such as a DVD or USB drive.
- Run queries. For example, you can determine the amount of hard disk space available on all or just a subset of your computers.
- Remotely administer client from the Configuration Manager console.
- Collect software information usage.
- Manage, deploy, and monitor software updates for Microsoft products, third-party applications, custom in-house applications, and hardware drivers.

SCCM takes a very user-centric approach to deploying applications to users based on how they connect to the network. For example, if they connect from a laptop while in the office, they would receive the application via a Microsoft Installer (.msi) package. If they connect from their home computer, SCCM delivers the package through App-V to ensure the data is not stored on the local machine.

Unlike Windows Intune, SCCM requires that you build an infrastructure to support it. This hierarchy of systems for large enterprises can be quite complex involving the use of a centralized administrative site (CAS) along with primary and secondary sites. The CAS is used with large deployments and is used for all administration and reporting for the hierarchy, but it has no clients or client data assigned to it. A primary site, typically deployed in the same location as the CAS, is deployed to manage systems and users. In smaller deployments, you start with the primary site, but you cannot grow the hierarchy later (for example, if a CAS site is not in place, you cannot install additional primary sites). Secondary sites are used to manage a small subset of clients across lower-bandwidth connections.

The sites provide the foundation upon which you manage the users and devices within your network. To support the management of operations at each site, you need to install multiple server roles to include the following:

- Site server: Performs the core functionality of the site.
- Site database server: Holds the SQL Server database.

- Component server: Runs the Configuration Manager service.
- Management point: Provides policy and service location to clients and receives configuration updates from them.
- Distribution point: Contains the source files for clients to download (applications, software packages and updates, operating system images, boot images).
- Reporting service point: Integrates with SQL Server to create and manage reports.

In most situations, multiple roles are run on the same server at each site, but dedicated servers are used to deploy distribution points to distribute the workload. As the company grows, the other roles are distributed across multiple servers. These servers need to have 64-bit operating systems running Windows Server 2008 SP2 (Standard, Enterprise, or Datacenter) or Windows Server 2012 (Standard or Datacenter).

SCCM clients can include workstations, laptops, servers, and mobile devices. The client can be running Windows XP SP3, Windows Vista, Windows 7/8, and Windows Server 2003 and later. SCCM also supports Mac clients running 64-bit OS X (10.6), Snow Leopard, and OS X 10.7 (Lion); and some Linux and UNIX clients (AIX, Red Hat, Solaris, and SUSE).

■ Protecting Your System With Smartscreen

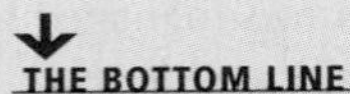

Malware and phishing attacks are common in today's interconnected world. Using SmartScreen filtering, you can protect your end users from downloading malicious files and exposing confidential information on websites masquerading as trustworthy entities.

CERTIFICATION READY
Application reputation
Objective 1.2

In Windows 8, application reputation is designed to provide protection from downloading malware and phishing attacks. ***Malware*** is software designed to either damage your computer or disrupt the use of the system. ***Phishing attacks*** are designed to gain confidential information by masquerading as trusted entities.

With new malware and phishing attacks appearing on a daily basis, there is always a gap between their release and the point at which they can be detected and blocked by anti-virus programs. Application reputation is the early warning system that alerts you before you run unrecognized applications or download files from the Internet during this in-between period.

Using SmartScreen to Implement Application Reputation

Windows 8 can implement application reputation using the Windows SmartScreen feature. SmartScreen is designed to protect users from downloading malicious files or opening malicious websites.

Windows SmartScreen was a feature introduced in Internet Explorer 8 to help detect phishing sites. The primary goals behind the design of SmartScreen were to develop a reliable reputation system that users could trust, and reduce the number of generic warnings seen when visiting websites and downloading files. In Windows 8, SmartScreen protection has been integrated with both Internet Explorer 10 and File Explorer.

When a user visits a website to download a program in Internet Explorer (see Figure 2-10), a file identifier along with the publisher information is sent to a reputation service located in the cloud. The reputation service uses a set of criteria to determine whether the program has an established reputation and whether it is a malicious or phishing site.

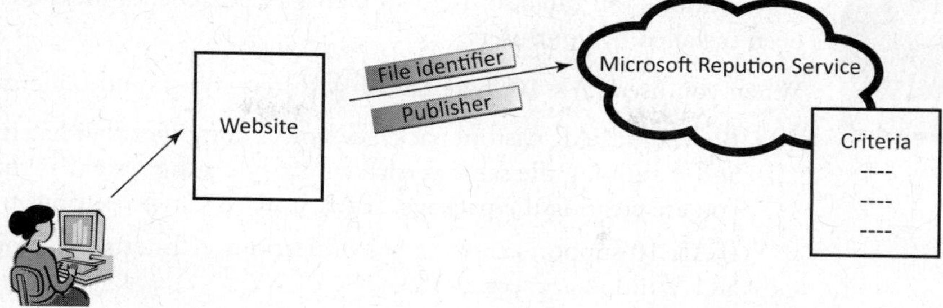

Figure 2-10
Understanding the SmartScreen process

Reputation ratings are based on the following criteria:

- Download traffic
- Download history
- Past antivirus results
- URL reputation

If the program is deemed safe, no warning is issued. If the program is considered malicious, it is blocked. The other option occurs when the reputation service cannot make the determination. In those cases, the program warns you (see Figure 2-11) and lets you decide how to proceed as shown 2. Clicking the *More info* link provides you with the publisher name and the option to run it anyway.

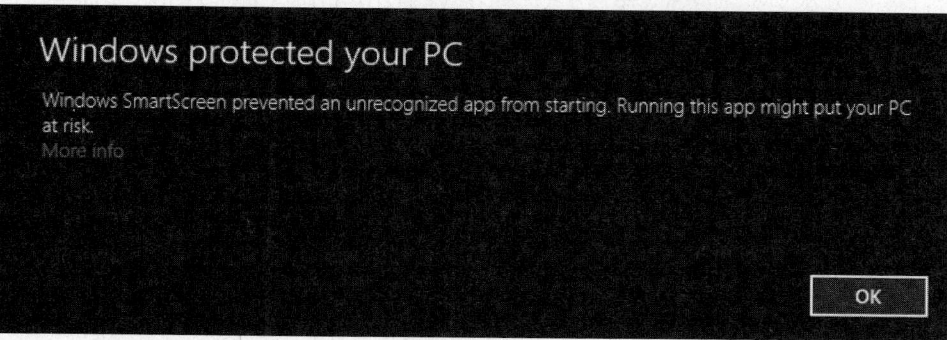

Figure 2-11
A SmartScreen alert

You can disable and enable SmartScreen by pressing *Alt* + *x*, clicking *Safety* > *Turn on SmartScreen Filter*, and then clicking *OK*.

■ Customizing Internet Explorer 10 Using IEAK 10

THE BOTTOM LINE

The Windows Internet Explorer Administration Kit (IEAK) 10 enables you to customize, distribute, and deploy Internet Explorer 10. By using IEAK, you can standardize your browser across all users and control home page settings, add favorites, and set up special links to company help pages.

The ***Windows Internet Explorer Administration Kit (IEAK) 10*** is a tool that enables you to customize, distribute, and manage the Internet Explorer 10 browser to users and computers across your organization. By using IEAK, you can centrally and dynamically control your users' installation of Internet Explorer to ensure that a standard configuration is used across your

CERTIFICATION READY
Internet Explorer 10 management
Objective 1.2

organization. You can also use it to manage updates/modifications to the browser after it has been installed by your users.

When you use IEAK 10, here are a few things you should understand:

- Build the IEAK custom packages from a computer that has Internet Explorer 10 installed and is running the same version of the operating system as the target computers for which you are creating the package. IEAK imports certain settings from the installed browser.
- IEAK 10 supports creating customizations of Internet Explorer 10 only on Windows 8 and Windows Server 2012.
- When building packages, you have two options:
  - Full installation package: This option includes the full installation of Internet Explorer and a Microsoft installer file (msi). These files are named IE10-Setup-Full.exe and IE10-Setup-Full.msi.
  - Configuration-only package: This option includes custom configurations for systems already running Windows 8. The files created using this option are IE10-Setup-Branding.exe and IE10-Setup-Branding.msi.

By using the IEAK Wizard, you can customize the title bar, add additional search providers, specify the home page that opens when Internet Explorer starts, assign accelerators that enhance a user's ability to work with text selected on web pages (map addresses, translate words), and add items under Favorites (company website, help desk links, feeds).

CREATE A CUSTOM INTERNET EXPLORER PACKAGE USING IEAK 10

GET READY. To set up a package that changes the default home page for Internet Explorer 10, log in with Administrator privileges to a computer running Windows 8 Enterprise (64-bit). This computer must have IEAK installed. Then perform the following steps:

1. From the Windows 8 *Start* menu, type **IEAK**. From the list of *Results*, click **Internet Explorer Customization Wizard 10**.
2. When the *Welcome to the IEAK* message appears, click **Next**.
3. For the *Destination* folder, click **Next** to accept the default folder (for example, *c:\builds\<currentdate>*).
4. For the *Target Platform,* select **Windows 8 Systems (x64-Based)** and then click **Next**.
5. For the *Target language,* click **Next** to accept *English (United States)*.
6. On the *Package Type Selection* screen, deselect **Full Installation Package**, select **Configuration-only package**, and then click **Next**.
7. On the *Feature Selection* screen, click **Clear All** (see Figure 2-12) and then select **Important URLs – Home Page and Support**. Click **Next** to continue.
8. When presented with the *Do you want to run this software?* message, click **Run**.
9. Click **Synchronize** to download the latest version of the setup files.

   If the security warning box appears, click **Run** to complete the synchronization. Click **Next** to continue.
10. Under *Add a homepage*, type **http://windows.microsoft.com/en-US/windows-8/meet** for your default home page and then click **Add**. Click any other links that are present and then click **Remove**. Click **Next** to continue.
11. On the *First Run Wizard and Welcome Page Options* screen, click **Next** to use the Internet Explorer 10 *Welcome* page.
12. On the *Wizard Complete* screen, click **Next** to create the custom package.
13. When the message *Your package is now complete and can be found in this folder* appears, click **Finish**.

    Make a note of where the files are stored.

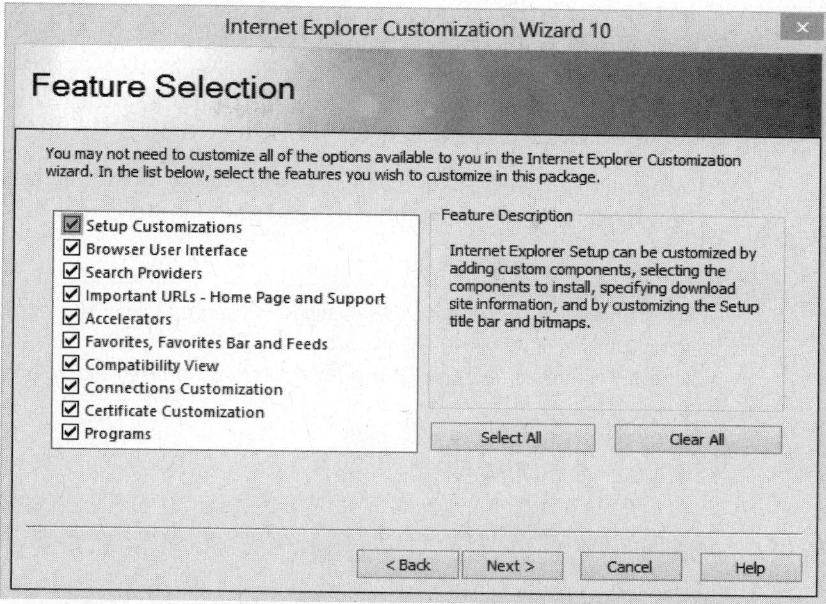

Figure 2-12

Clearing features using the IEAK Wizard

14. Before applying the package on your computer, open the Internet Explorer browser on the computer and notice the URL it defaults to when you open the browser. This URL will change after the package is installed.
15. From your computer, connect to the folder where you stored the package. Right-click **IE10-Setup-Branding.msi**, and select **Install** from the menu that appears.
16. When the *Install Internet Explorer 10* message appears, click **Install**.
17. When the installation is completed, click **OK** and then log off and back on for the changes to take effect.
18. Press the **Windows logo key** to toggle to your desktop. Click the **Internet Explorer** icon on the task bar and confirm that the browser opens to the new home page you configured.

After creating your package, you can easily copy the files to a shared location on the network. From there, you can access the files from your test systems and install the package. You should also test for compatibility with your line of business applications and navigate to critical websites used by the organization to see how the new browser performs.

After the build passes your testing process, you can deploy it to the rest of the organization using Group Policy or SCCM.

Maintaining IEAK Packages

After deploying the Internet Explorer package, you may decide to make changes to include a new home page, add additional favorites to the browser, or make other updates to the program. The IEAK Wizard, which was used to create the original package, can also be used to make these changes.

After deploying your Internet Explorer package, you may need to make changes. In previous versions of IEAK, a tool called Profile Manager was used to create an Internet settings (.ins) file that could then be imported into a new custom package. With the release of IEAK 10, the tool is no longer used. Instead, when you create an Internet Explorer package, an Internet settings

(.ins) file is created and stored in the *INS* folder. If you need to make a change, you can run the IEAK Wizard again, import the .ins file by selecting the **Advanced** button and type the path to the .ins file. By default, this is located in the *c:\builds\<date>\INS\<os-version>\<language code>* folder. You can then make changes or additions to the package on the *Feature Selection* screen. After the package is updated, it can be redeployed using Group Policy or SCCM.

To maintain Internet Explorer in Active Directory environments after deployment, consider using the new Internet Explorer 10 settings in Group Policy.

MORE INFORMATION

There are more than 1,500 Group Policy settings for Internet Explorer 10 that can be used to manage and control the configuration of your Internet Explorer browsers. To learn more about the settings that can be managed visit the Microsoft website and search for *Group Policy settings in Internet Explorer 10*.

SKILL SUMMARY

IN THIS LESSON YOU LEARNED:

- Client Hyper-V, which runs on Windows 8 Enterprise (64-bit) systems, enables you to build a test lab that runs entirely on a single computer. Using Hyper-V and VMs, you can test an application's compatibility with several different configurations of Windows 8. These VMs can then be moved to production. Client Hyper-V enables you to avoid the costs of purchasing additional computers or setting up dual boot systems to test for application compatibility.
- There are three types of virtual switches that you can configure with Client Hyper-V: external, internal, and private. External switches bind to the network card on the host, allowing the VMs to access your physical network; internal switches limit communication to between VMs and the host only; and private switches are used only by the VMs.
- RDS describes several of the features of the Windows Server role that enables users to remotely connect to virtual desktops, session-based desktops, and RemoteApp programs over RDP.
- The purpose behind the ACT 6.0 and how it can be used to not only collect inventory information from your network computers but also to perform runtime analysis to test for application compatibility.
- The process for creating App-V programs through a process called sequencing. This process involves launching a traditional application and then using tools to monitor the changes the application executes on the local computer during the installation process.
- The tools available to manage and deploy applications and updates. These tools include Group Policy, Windows Intune, and SCCM 2012. Group Policy can be used to assign or publish applications and subsequent upgrades to users/computers. Windows Intune, the Microsoft integrated, cloud-based client management solution, can be used to deploy the software updates and to manage software licenses on your network without the need to build a new server infrastructure. SCCM 2012 provides similar capabilities, but requires an infrastructure in place to support deployment.
- The role that SmartScreen plays in application reputation by protecting against malware and phishing attacks. SmartScreen uses reputation criteria to determine whether it is safe to download software or open a file. The criteria are based on download traffic, history, past antivirus results, and URL reputation.
- The purpose of the Internet Explorer 10 Administration Kit (IEAK). It enables you to customize, distribute, and deploy Internet Explorer 10 to maintain a standardized look and feel across your organization. You also learned that you can deploy the package manually or by using Group Policy or SCCM.

Knowledge Assessment

Multiple Choice

Select the correct answer for each of the following questions.

1. When using Client Hyper-V to set up a test lab, which of the following types of virtual switches would you set up to allow your VMs to access the network through the network adapter on the host machine?
   a. Layer 2 switch
   b. External
   c. Internal
   d. Private

2. After creating a runtime analysis package, which of the following tools can you use to deploy the package on your network? (Select all that apply.)
   a. Group Policy
   b. System Center Configuration Manager
   c. Store the file on a network share
   d. Use removable media to distribute it to your systems

3. Which of the following is not a benefit of running virtual applications?
   a. No install or configuration is needed on the client computer.
   b. No changes to the user's computer are made after opening/closing the application.
   c. Two versions of the application cannot be run on the same computer.
   d. Virtual applications can be managed from a central location.

4. Which of the following is an incorrect statement about Group Policy?
   a. Group policies can be managed using the Group Policy Management Console.
   b. The Local Group Policy editor is used to manage policies on a local computer.
   c. Using Group Policy, you can deploy applications to users only.
   d. Using Group Policy, you can deploy applications to users and computers.

5. Which of the following represent security and management tasks that can be handled with Windows Intune? (Select all that apply.)
   a. Track hardware and software inventory.
   b. Provide remote assistance.
   c. Protect computers from malware.
   d. Manage the deployment of software updates.

6. Which of the following is the early warning system in Windows 8 that alerts you before you run unrecognized applications or download files from the Internet?
   a. Windows Defender
   b. Windows Firewall
   c. SmartScreen
   d. ACT

7. IEAK 10 creates custom packages in which directory by default?
   a. c:\windows
   b. c:\IEAK\builds
   c. c:\IEAK\builds\<date>
   d. c:\builds\<currentdate>

8. On which of the following computers can you create an IEAK custom package for a computer running Windows 8 Enterprise 64-bit edition and Internet Explorer 10?
   a. Windows 7 Enterprise 32-bit
   b. Windows 8 Enterprise 64-bit
   c. Windows 7 Professional 64-bit
   d. Windows Server 2012 64-bit

9. Which of the following reports in the ACM provides you with information on whether your application works on a 32- or 64-bit operating system?
   a. Internet Explorer web site report
   b. Device report
   c. Computer report
   d. Application report
10. Which level of the Active Directory hierarchy enables you to delegate authority to distribute management of resources to a number of people who are trusted to perform them?
   a. Site
   b. Forest
   c. Domain
   d. OU

Best Answer

Choose the letter that corresponds to the best answer. More than one answer choice may achieve the goal. Select the BEST answer.

1. Which of the following is necessary to setting up a small lab to test applications on Windows 8 using Client Hyper-V?
   a. Windows 8 Enterprise (32-bit) with Hyper-V enabled
   b. Windows 8 Professional (64-bit) with Hyper-V enabled
   c. Windows 8 Enterprise (64-bit) with Hyper-V enabled
   d. Windows 8 Professional (32-bit) with Hyper-V enabled
2. Which of the following types of packages can be created to monitor applications for compatibility prior to migrating to Windows 8?
   a. inventory-collector package
   b. runtime analysis package
   c. migration package
   d. monitor-analysis package
3. Which of the following tools are needed to sequence an existing application and then deploy it to Windows 8 computers?
   a. Application Compatibility Toolkit (ACT)
   b. Microsoft Desktop Optimization Package (MDOP)
   c. System Center 2012 Configuration Manager (SCCM)
   d. Internet Explorer Administration Kit (IEAK) 10
4. Which of the following tools are used to update a package that brands your installation of Internet Explorer 10?
   a. Profile Manager
   b. IEAK Wizard
   c. Group Policy
   d. System Center 2012 Configuration Manager
5. Which of the following Windows 8 features are used to implement application reputation to provide protection from downloading malware and phishing attacks?
   a. App-V
   b. Group Policy
   c. Client Hyper-V
   d. SmartScreen

Matching and Identification

1. Match the following terms with the related description or usage.
   _______ a) SmartScreen
   _______ b) Windows Intune

_______ **c)** sequencing
_______ **d)** malware
_______ **e)** Client Hyper-V
_______ **f)** Compatibility Monitor
_______ **g)** runtime analysis package
_______ **h)** virtual switch
_______ **i)** RD Session Host
_______ **j)** Application Compatibility Manager

1. A tool installed as part of the runtime analysis package.
2. Used to view general feedback comments submitted by the Compatibility Monitor.
3. A protection feature integrated with both Internet Explorer 10 and File Explorer.
4. Describes the process used to create an application that can run in a virtualized environment.
5. Enables your VMs to access your physical network.
6. A cloud-based management solution for managing your computers, tablets, and phones.
7. Enables a server to host RemoteApp programs or session-based desktops.
8. An .msi package used to monitor applications for compatibility issues and submit compatibility feedback.
9. A Microsoft replacement for Windows Virtual PC.
10. Software designed to either damage your computer or disrupt the use of the system.

Build a List

1. Specify the correct order of the steps that must be completed to enable Hyper-V on a Windows 8 Enterprise computer.
   _______ Press the **Windows logo key + w**.
   _______ Click **Close**.
   _______ Select the *Hyper-V* check box and then click **OK**.
   _______ Restart your computer.
   _______ Type **Features**. From the *Results* list, select **Turn Windows features on and off**.

2. Specify the correct order of the steps that must be completed to create a runtime analysis package.
   _______ Press the **Windows logo key + q**.
   _______ Navigate to the folder where you want to store the Windows installer (.msi).
   _______ Click **Finish**.
   _______ From the menu at the top, click **File > New**.
   _______ On the *Choose the type of package to create* screen, click **Runtime analysis package**.
   _______ In the left pane of the *Application Compatibility Manager* window, click **Collect**.
   _______ Type **acm**. From the *Results* list, click **Application Compatibility Manager**.
   _______ Provide the information requested for the package and then click **Create**.
   _______ In the *File name* field, type a name for the package and then click **Save**.

3. Specify the correct order of the steps that must be completed to install the App-V 5.0 sequencer.
   _______ Click **Install**.
   _______ Insert the Microsoft Desktop Optimization Pack (MDOP) disc into your computer.
   _______ When the *MDOP* menu appears, click **Application Virtualization for Desktops**.

_________ When the message *Setup completed successfully appears*, click **Close**.
_________ Review the *Software Licenses Terms* screen, select **I accept the license terms**, and then click **Next**.
_________ Under the *App-V 5.0* category, click **App-V 5.0 Sequencer**.
_________ On the *Customer Experience Improvement Program* screen, click **Install** to accept the default.
_________ Close the *MDOP* menu. The App-V 5.0 sequencer program is now ready for use.

Choose an Option

1. Which Windows feature turns your Windows 8 Enterprise computer into a host for VMs?

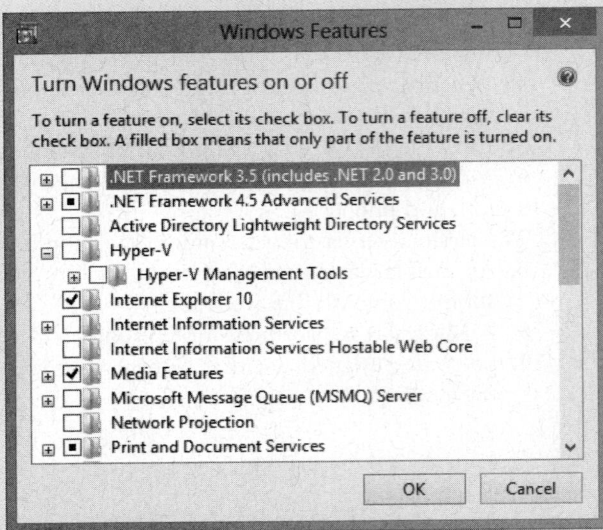

■ Business Case Scenarios

Scenario 2-1: Testing Line of Business Applications

The Director of IT was reviewing her budget and noticed that three application developers requested additional computers. The developers are currently running Windows 7 computers, but she has already determined they will support Windows 8 Enterprise 64-bit. After talking to one of them, she learned they were requesting additional computers to help test their old line of business application on a 32-bit and a 64-bit Windows 8 operating system computer. What other options would help her reduce costs while providing her application developers with the resources they need?

Scenario 2-2: Testing Compatibility

The Director of IT has contacted you to consult with her on the best way to test the compatibility of applications on computers across her network in preparation for an upgrade to Windows 8. She has approximately 200 systems, all located in the same physical location. Explain how you would advise her to approach the testing.

Scenario 2-3: Managing Applications Updates

Over the last few years, Contoso administrators have been managing application updates manually. As they continue to evaluate Windows 8 and as the company continues to grow, they want to find a better solution. The Director of IT asked you to find something that enables administrators to manage the updates from anywhere they have Internet access. She also wants the solution to provide protection against malware, manage deployment of software, provide remote assistance, track applications licenses, perform an inventory of computers, and not require her IT team to have to build an entirely new infrastructure to support it. What should you advise her to consider?

Designing an Application Strategy for Cloud Applications

70-412 EXAM OBJECTIVE

Objective 1.3 – Design an application strategy for cloud applications. This objective may include but is not limited to the following design considerations: Microsoft Office 365; Windows Store applications; restricting Windows Store content; AppLocker; internal content.

LESSON HEADING	EXAM OBJECTIVE
Working with Windows Store Applications	Windows Store applications
Sideloading Windows Apps	
Restricting Access to the Windows Store Using Group Policy	Restricting Windows Store content
Restricting Access Using Group Policy	
Using AppLocker to Manage Applications	AppLocker
Using AppLocker	
Using Microsoft Office 365	Microsoft Office 365
Understanding Microsoft Office 365 Features	
Using SkyDrive to Manage Files/Folders	Internal content
Accessing SkyDrive from a Browser	
Creating a File Within SkyDrive	
Uploading Files to SkyDrive	
Sharing a Document in SkyDrive	
Accessing SkyDrive from the SkyDrive desktop app for Windows	

KEY TERMS

AppLocker
Bring Your Own Device (BYOD)
Certificate Authority (CA)
Deployment Imaging Servicing and Management (DISM)
fetching
file hash
Line of Business (LOB) apps
Microsoft Office 365
path
provisioned apps
publisher
rule collections
sideloading
SkyDrive
SkyDrive desktop app for Windows
Windows Apps
Windows Store

■ Working with Windows Store Applications

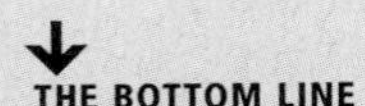

THE BOTTOM LINE Windows Apps are available from the Windows Store. These apps display across multiple devices and are designed to run in a single, full window display.

CERTIFICATION READY
Windows Store applications
Objective 1.3

Windows Apps, also called packaged apps, are available from the Windows Store. These applications differ from traditional applications in that they are designed to run in a single, full window display across multiple form factor devices (desktops, laptops, tablets). These devices can be touch-based or use a standard mouse and keyboard. The ***Windows Store*** (see Figure 3-1) provides a central location for you to purchase and download Windows apps that run on Windows 8 and later operating systems. The applications made available through the store must be certified for compatibility and content by Microsoft. When the user installs a Windows App, it shows up as a tile on the Windows 8 start page that can be clicked or touched to start the program.

Figure 3-1
Accessing the Windows Store

The Windows Store app comes preinstalled on Windows 8 devices. That makes it very easy for your users to connect and access the apps in the Store. When strategizing about how to manage Windows Apps in your organization, you need to consider whether you want to restrict users' access to the Store as a whole or allow access but control which apps the users are allowed to download and install.

Many organizations have policies in place that are designed to standardize the apps being used on company-supplied computers and do not want their users installing any applications they find, even if they are certified to work with Windows 8. ***Bring Your Own Device (BYOD) policies*** may also be in place that require you to control access to the Store. A BYOD policy defines the standards, restrictions and procedures for end users who have authorized access to company data from their personal device (tablet, laptop, smartphone). The policy also includes hardware and related software not approved, owned, or supplied by the company. In either case, as the administrator you will need to make sure your strategy for accessing the Windows Store aligns with your company's policies.

In addition to determining your strategy for controlling access to Windows Apps and the Windows Store, you will also need to consider the deployment of ***Line of Business (LOB) apps***. LOB apps include apps that are critical to running the business of the company as well as apps that are unique to the main business of the company. If you want to use the new Windows Apps format for your LOB apps, you can deploy them via the Windows Store or by a process called sideloading. If you choose to deploy your LOB apps via the Windows Store, they must go through a certification process with Microsoft to ensure they are compatible with Windows 8 and meet criteria for apps being deployed from the Store. The apps will also be available to the public, which may not be what you want. To bypass the Store requirements and make the apps available to your internal users only, consider sideloading them as part of your overall design strategy.

Sideloading Windows Apps

Sideloading Windows Apps provides you with a way to enjoy the look/feel of Windows Apps without having to make them available using the Windows Store.

If you have a Windows App that was created in-house and needs to be leveraged across your organization, you have two options:

- You can make it available from the Windows Store, which means the App has to adhere to certification policies and the processes used by all Apps in the Store. This is designed to ensure the App is compatible and meets the criteria of Apps that are allowed to be deployed via the Windows Store.
- If you choose not to take that approach because you don't want the App available to the public but still want to take advantage of the portability and design of Windows Apps, you can use a process called sideloading. ***Sideloading*** is installing a Windows App without going through the Store by using a tool such as DISM, Windows PowerShell, System Center Configuration Manager (SCCM), or Windows Intune.

To use sideloading, you need to make sure the following are in place with your computers:

- A Windows 8 Enterprise/Professional computer joined to an Active Directory domain.
- Group Policy must be set to *Allow all trusted apps to install.*
- The App must be signed by a ***Certificate Authority (CA)*** that is trusted by the targeted PCs on the network. A CA issues digital certificates that certify a person, organization, server or computer is who it claims to be.
- A sideloading product activation key if the Windows 8 Enterprise/Windows 8 Professional computer is not joined to a domain.

TAKE NOTE*

You can sideload Windows Apps only on Windows Server 2012, Windows 8 Enterprise, and Windows 8 Professional devices that are joined to a domain.

The process for sideloading a Windows App is as follows:

1. Create a Windows Store app using Microsoft Visual Studio Express 2012 for Windows 8 or another similar tool. In order to do this, you will need to have a developer's license.
2. Sign the app with a certificate that is chained to a trusted root certificate.
3. Confirm the computers that will be Sideloaded are running Windows 8 Enterprise, they are joined to the domain and the *Allow all trusted apps to install* Group Policy setting is enabled. If you need to sideload apps on Windows 8 Enterprise/Professional that are not joined to a domain, you will need to install a sideloading product activation key. The key can be obtained from Microsoft's Volume Licensing Service Center (VLSC).
4. Sideload the app using the `add-appxpackage "name of app"` command if you want to make it available for the current user or use the ***Deployment Imaging Servicing and Management (DISM)*** tool if you want to make it available for multiple users. DISM is a command-line tool used to service an online or offline Windows image. When Windows Apps are installed via a Windows image, they are called ***provisioned apps***.

You can set Group Policy for a single Windows 8 computer by opening the Local Group Policy Editor and enabling the *Allow all trusted apps to install* setting, which is located in the following location:

Computer Configuration\Administrative Templates\Windows Components\App Package Deployment

If you want to apply the policy to multiple computers, use the Group Policy Management console (GPMC). The *Allow all trusted apps to install* group policy setting is located in the following location:

Computer Configuration\Policies\Administrative Templates\Windows Components\App Package Deployment

It should be noted that the policy created using the Group Policy Management console can also be applied to a single computer. Local Group Policy is most commonly used in workgroup settings.

If you receive an activation key from the VLSC, you can add it by using the following commands, from a command prompt window (cmd), while logged on as a local administrator. You will need to run this command from an elevated command prompt.

To add the key:

```
Slmgr /ipk <sideloading product key>
```

To activate the key:

```
Slmgr /ato ec67814b-30e6-4a50-bf7b-d55daf729d1e
```

After the computer is prepared, you can install the package on a per-user basis with the following Windows PowerShell command:

```
Add-appxpackage -Path c:\<directory>\<Winappv1.appx>
```

To update the package at a later date, you can manually update the Windows App with the following command:

```
Add-appxpackage -Path

\\<servername>\<share>\<winappv2.appx>
```

MORE INFORMATION

For more information on how to deploy images with Windows Apps, visit TechNet.

Restricting Access to the Windows Store Using Group Policy

THE BOTTOM LINE

Providing users with access to the Windows Store can create problems when you try to standardize applications across your organization. Group Policy can be used to restrict access and maintain your internal policies regarding application usage.

CERTIFICATION READY
Restricting Windows Store content
Objective 1.3

The Windows Store application comes preinstalled on Windows 8 devices. That makes it very easy for a user to connect, download and install Windows Apps. Although the Windows Store can provide a wide variety of Apps and tools to enhance Windows 8, you might decide to restrict access to it for your users. This restriction might be necessary if you want to make sure your users are working only with authorized applications within your organization. There are two ways to prevent users from installing and using Apps from the Windows Store:

- Use Group Policies
- Configure AppLocker

In this section, we'll take a look at Group Policy.

Restricting Access Using Group Policy

To deny access, you can use the Local Group Policy Editor or the Group Policy Management Console to create a policy that restricts access to the Windows Store for users and computers on your network.

TAKE NOTE*

If you create the policy using the Local Group Policy Editor, you can export and import it into a GPO at the domain level. It does not have to be re-created.

To deny access, you need to set up a policy for a single computer/user or for multiple computers and users. The tool you used depends upon where you want to use the policy. For example, if you want to configure the policy and test it, you can use the Local Group Policy Editor on a Windows 8 client machine (see Figure 3-2). If you want to deploy the policy settings across your domain, you need to use the Group Policy Management Console. In either case, the settings are located under the Administrative Templates\Windows Components\Store under the Computer Configuration and User Configuration nodes.

When configuring the policy using the Local Group Policy Editor for a user (User Configuration\Administrative Templates\Windows Components\Store), you have one option to set within the policy:

- Turn off the Store application:
  - o **Not Configured (default):** If you select this option, access to the Store is allowed.
  - o **Enabled:** If you select this option, access to the Store is denied.
  - o **Disabled:** If you select this option, access to the Store application is allowed.

If you set the policy for a computer (Computer Configuration\Administrative Templates\Windows Component\Store) you have the following options available:

- Turn off Automatic Download of updates:
  - o **Not Configured (default):** Download of updates is allowed.
  - o **Enabled:** Automatic downloads are turned off.
  - o **Disabled:** Automatic downloads of updates are allowed.

Figure 3-2

Settings available via the Local Group Policy Editor for users

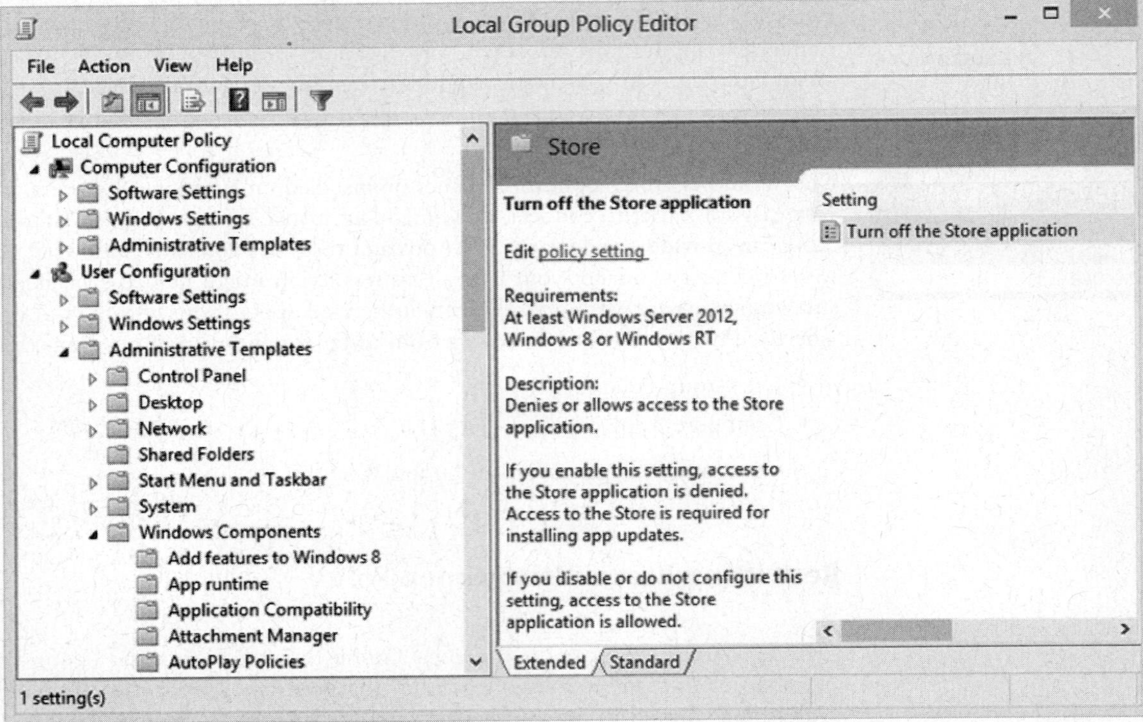

- Allow Store to install apps on Windows To Go workspaces:
  - o **Not Configured (default):** Access to the Store is not allowed.
  - o **Enabled:** Access to the Store is allowed on the Windows To Go Workspace. Use this option only when the device is used with a single PC.
  - o **Disabled:** Access to the Store is denied.
- Turn off the Store application:
  a. **Not Configured (default):** If you select this option, access to the Store is allowed.
  b. **Enabled:** If you select this option, access to the Store is denied.
  c. **Disabled:** If you select this option, access to the Store application is allowed.

RESTRICT ACCESS TO THE WINDOWS STORE USING A LOCAL GROUP POLICY

GET READY. Log on to a Windows 8 computer with administrative credentials. In this activity, you review the policy settings that control the Windows Store access for both computers and users by performing the following steps:

1. Press the **Windows logo key** + **r**.
2. In the *Run* box, type **gpedit.msc**. The *Local Group Policy Editor* appears.
3. Expand **Computer Configuration** > **Administrative Templates** > **Windows Components** and click the **Store** (see Figure 3-3).
4. Double-click the **Turn off the Store application** setting; the *Turn off the Store application* dialog appears. Click **Enabled** (see Figure 3-3).

Figure 3-3

Restricting access to the Windows Store

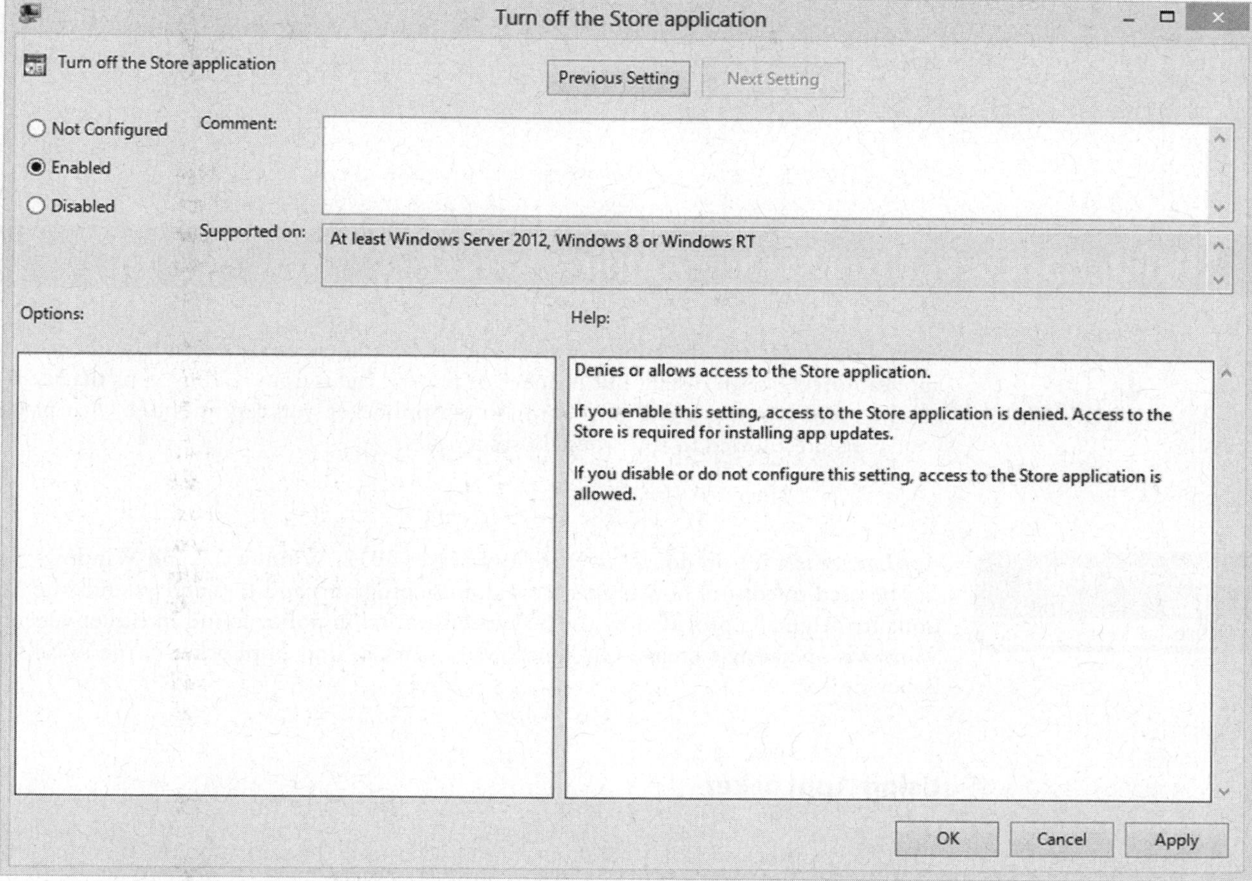

5. Attempt to access the Windows Store by clicking on the Store tile located on the Windows 8 startup screen. The message *Windows Store isn't available on this PC* appears.
6. Return to the group policy setting you enabled in Step 4 and click **Not Configured** to regain access to the Windows Store.

When working with Group Policy settings, you should be aware of the order in which they are applied to your Windows 8 client devices. Having a good understanding of this order will ensure you design them in a way that works for your specific environment. They are processed in the following order:

1. Local Group Policy object.
2. Group Policies linked to the Site container.
3. Group Policies linked to the Domain container.
4. Group Policies linked to the Organizational Unit that is highest in the OU hierarchy are processed first, followed by GPOs linked to the child OU, and so on. If there are multiple GPOs linked to the same OU, they will be processed in the order specified by the administrator.

A shortcut to help you remember the order of precedence is LSDO. This stands for **L**ocal, **S**ite, **D**omain, and **O**rganizational Unit.

In the previous example, you can see that local Group Policy settings are processed first. Group Policy settings linked to the OU that contains the user/computer is processed last, which overwrites the earlier GPOs. In situations where you create a GPO and set it to Enforced (No Override) with respect to the site, domain or OU, its setting will not be overwritten by any GPOs that follow it in the order of precedence. If you have two GPOs that are both set to Enforced (No Override), the one that is highest in the Active Directory hierarchy takes precedence.

Using AppLocker to Manage Applications

Removing users from the administrative role on computers can reduce the number of applications they can install, but it does not prevent them from loading apps that do not require administrative privilege to run. Using AppLocker, you can fine-tune what programs your users are allowed to run by establishing rules.

CERTIFICATION READY
AppLocker
Objective 1.3

AppLocker is a feature found in Windows Server 2012, Windows 7, and Windows 8 that can be used to control how users access and use programs and files and extends the functionality originally provided by the Software Restriction policy found in earlier versions of Windows operating systems. On Windows 8, you can find AppLocker in the Local Group Policy Editor.

Using AppLocker

AppLocker uses rules and file properties to determine the programs and files that are allowed to run on the computer.

You can access AppLocker using the Local Group Policy editor (gpedit.msc) by performing the steps in the following exercise.

ACCESS APPLOCKER

GET READY. To access AppLocker using the Local Group Policy editor (gpedit.msc), perform the following steps:

1. Press the **Windows logo key + r**.
2. In the *Run* box, type **gpedit.msc** and then click **OK**. The *Local Group Policy Editor* appears.
3. Click **Computer Configuration > Windows Settings > Security Settings > Application Control Policies > AppLocker**.

As shown in Figure 3-4, AppLocker includes four ***rule collections:***

- **Executable Rules**
- **Windows Installer Rules**
- **Script Rules**
- **Packaged app Rules**

Figure 3-4

The AppLocker Rule Collections

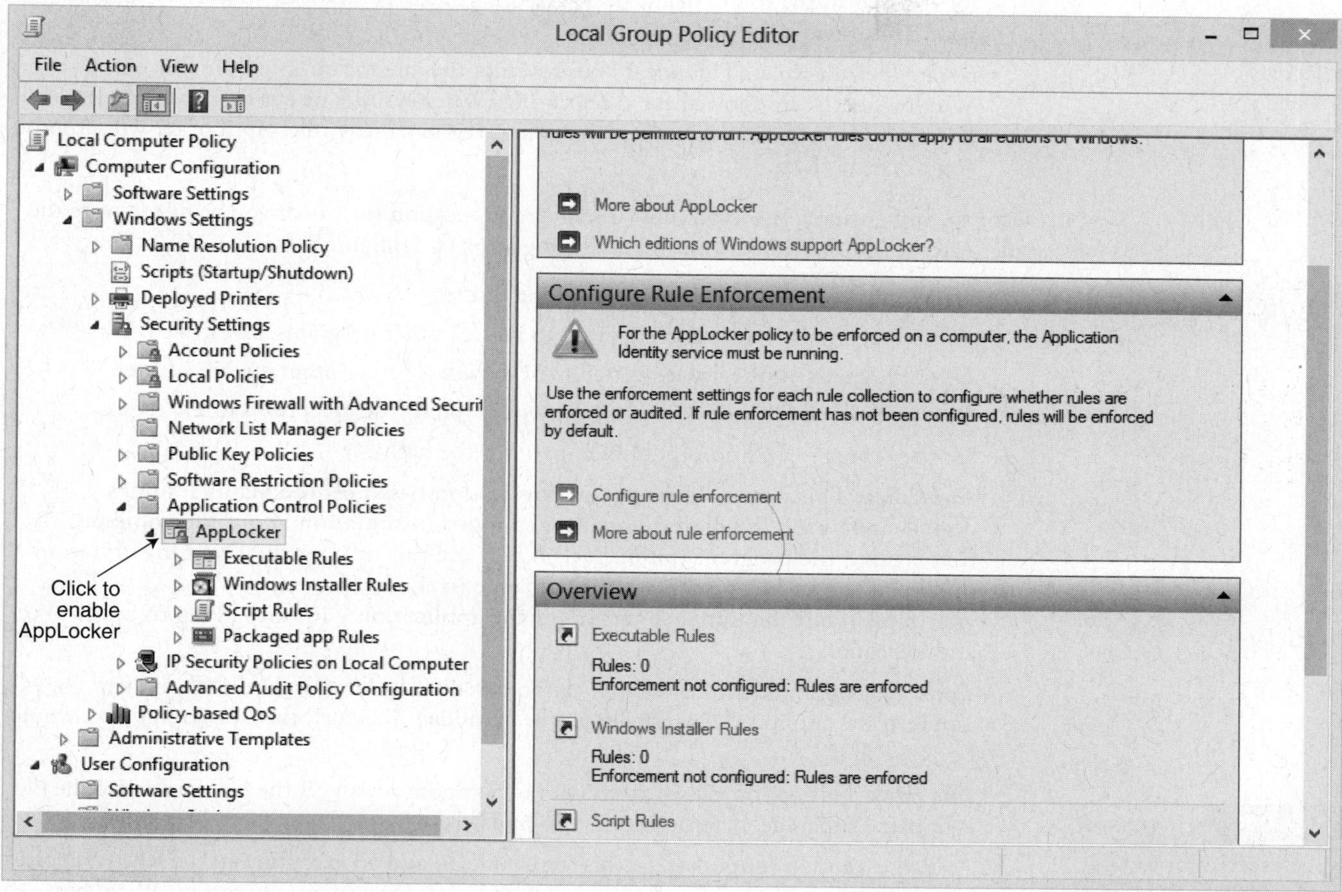

These rule collections allow you to differentiate the rules for different types of applications. AppLocker uses rules and a file's properties to determine whether applications are allowed to run.

A traditional app consists of several components (exe, scripts, and so on). These components may not share the same publisher, product, or product version attribute. In order to manage the traditional app, AppLocker needs to control them using different rule collections. On the other hand, a Windows app (packaged app) shares the same attributes; therefore, you can create a single rule to control the entire application.

Rule collections include:

- Executable files (.exe, .com)
- Scripts (.ps2, .bat, .js, .cmd, vbs)
- Windows Installer files (.msi, .mst, .msp)
- Appx (Packaged apps and Packaged app installers) (.appx) – This includes Windows Apps and side-loaded LOB apps.

By default, there are no rules in any of the rule collections; therefore, AppLocker will allow every file covered in each collection to run.

When creating rules with AppLocker, you have the following options:

- Create New Rule: This wizard walks you through the process of creating one AppLocker rule at a time—setting permissions, publishers, exceptions, and providing a name for the rule.

- Automatically Generate Rules: This wizard creates rules for multiple packaged apps in a single step. You can select a folder and let the Wizard create the applicable rules for the files in the folder or for packaged apps create rules for all Windows apps on your computer.
- Create Default Rules: This wizard creates rules that are meant to ensure that some key Windows paths are allowed for execution (c:\Windows files or c:\Program files). If you do not have the default rules in place, when creating a new rule, AppLocker will prompt you to create them.

Prior to configuring a rule, you must install the application for which you want to create the rule. After it is installed, perform the following steps to configure the rule:

1. Set permissions. AppLocker uses three rule types:

   Allow: Programs on the list are allowed to run; all other programs are blocked.

   Deny: Programs on the list are not allowed to run; all other programs are allowed.

   Exceptions: Used for both allow and deny rules to provide exceptions to the rule.
2. Set the primary condition (publisher, path, or file hash):

   Publisher: This option identifies an application based off the manufacturer's digital signature. The digital signature contains information about the company that created the program (publisher). If you use this option, the rule can survive an update of the application as well as a change in the location of its files. This allows you to push out the updated version of the application without having to build another rule.

   Path: This option identifies an application based off its location in the file system. For example, if the application is installed in the Windows directory, the AppLocker path would be %WINDIR%.

   File hash: This option causes the system to compute a hash on the file. Each time the file is updated (upgrade, patch), you have to update the hash.
3. Add an exception (optional). In this step, you can add an exception to the rule (if applicable). For example, you might have enabled access for a suite (Microsoft Office) but you do not want selected users to be able to use Microsoft Access because you have a limited number of licenses.
4. Type a name for the rule. In this step, you give the rule a name and add an optional description.

TAKE NOTE*

Rules created for a packaged app can use only the Publisher condition. Windows does not support unsigned packaged apps or installers.

CREATE AND TEST AN APPLOCKER RULE

GET READY. To create and test an AppLocker rule that blocks the use of the Remote Desktop Connection client (mstsc.exe), log on to a Windows 8 computer as an administrator and then perform the following steps:

1. Press the **Windows logo key + r** and in the *Run* box, type **services.msc** and then click **OK**. The *Services console* appears.
2. Right-click the **Application Identity** service and then choose **Start**. Close the *Services console* after confirming the service is running.
3. Press the **Windows logo key + r** and in the *Run* box, type **gpedit.msc** and then click **OK**. The *Local Group Policy Editor* appears.
4. Click the **Windows Settings > Security Settings > Application Control Policies > AppLocker**.
5. Right-click **Executable Rules** and choose **Create New Rule** (see Figure 3-5).

Figure 3-5

Creating a new Executable rule for AppLocker

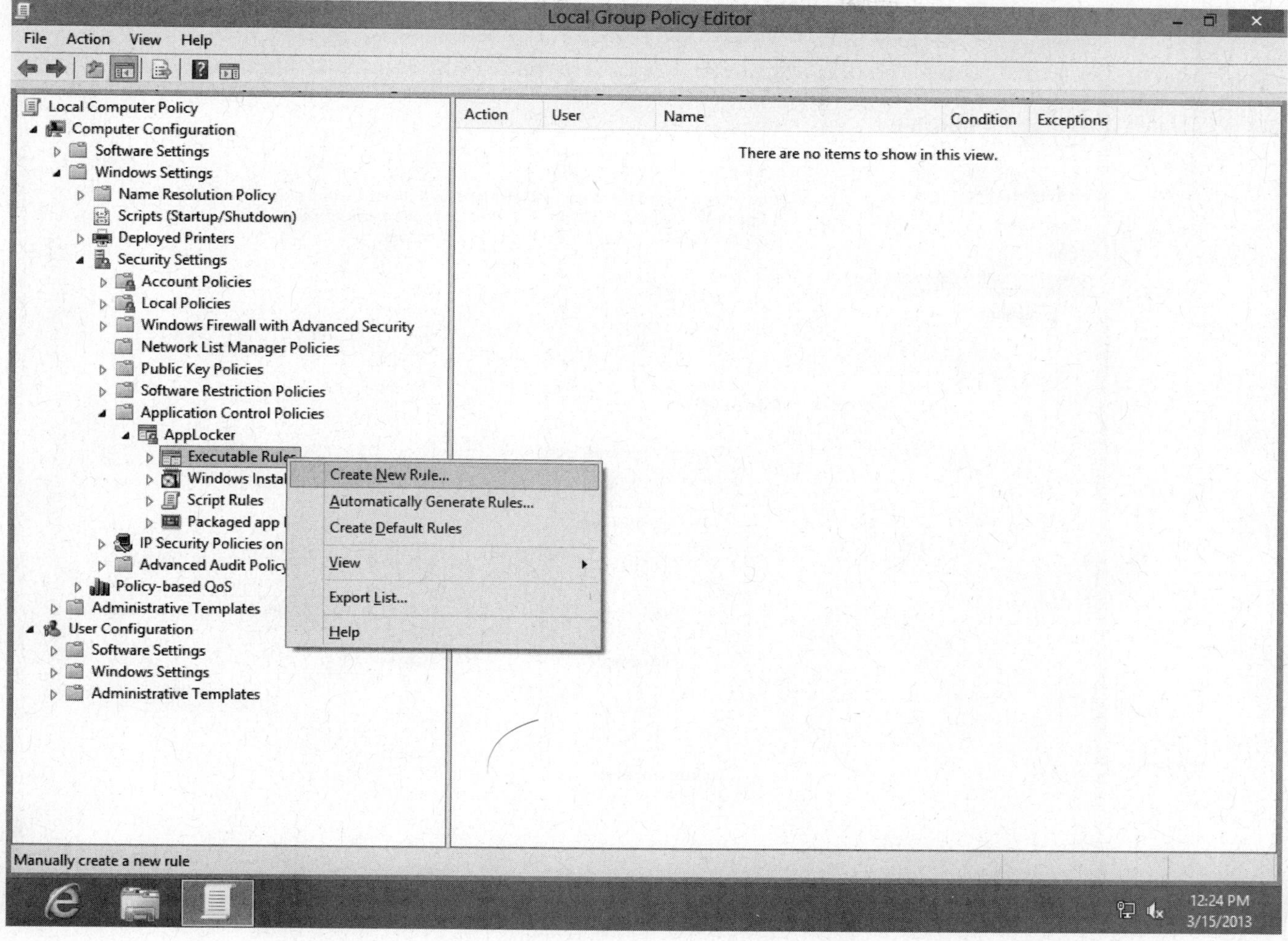

6. Read the *Before you Begin* screen and then click **Next**.
7. Select **Deny** and then click **Next**.
8. Click **Select** and in the *Enter the object name to select* box, type **Users** and then click **OK**.
9. Click **Next** to continue.
10. Select **Publisher** and then click **Next**.
11. Click **Browse** and then navigate to the *C:\Windows\System32directory*. Click the **mstsc.exe** file and then click **Open**.
12. Drag the slider to **File name** (see Figure 3-6) and then click **Next**. This setting ensures the rule will block all instances of the Remote Desktop Connection client (mstsc.exe) regardless of the version.

Figure 3-6

Viewing the Executable Rules/ Publisher Information for the AppLocker rule

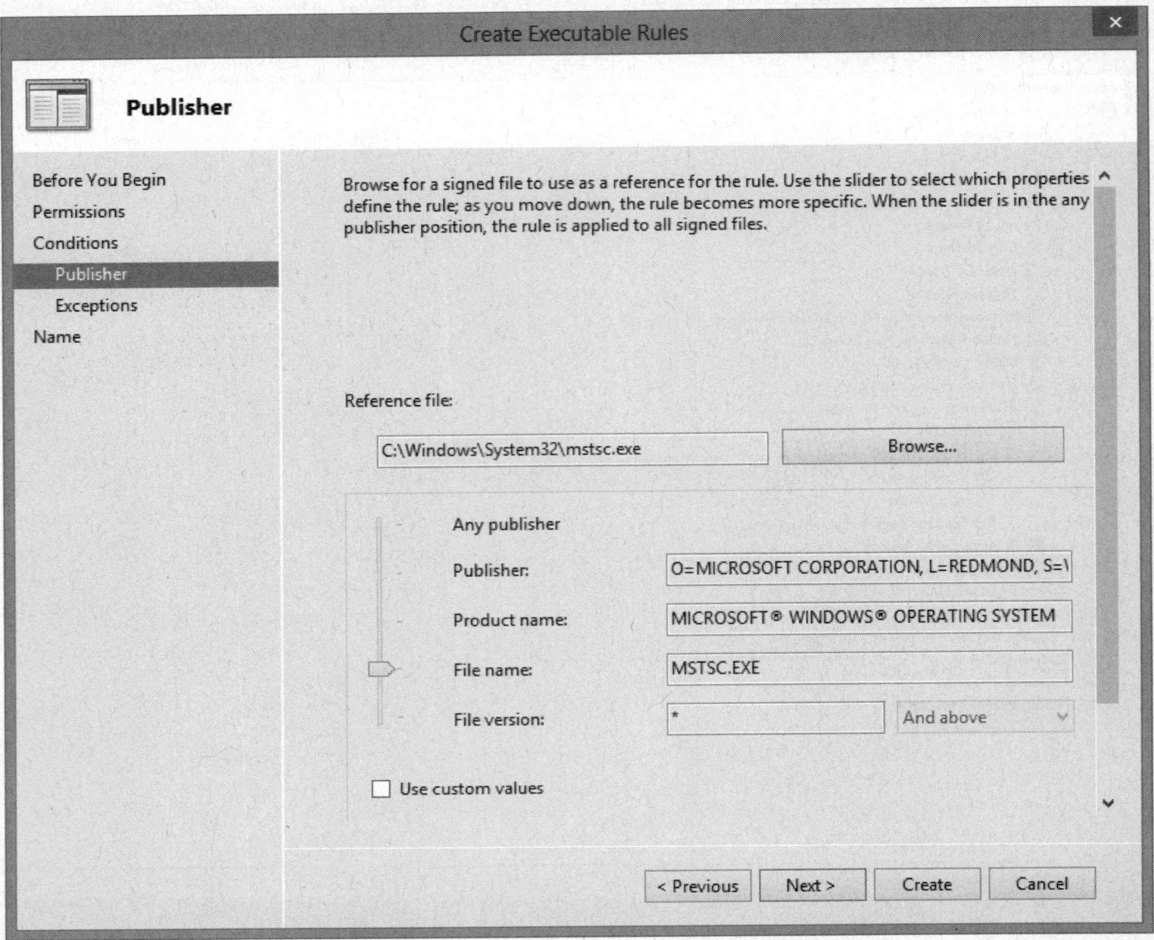

13. Click **Next**. You do not set an exception to this rule.
14. Type a name for the rule and a description (optional). For example, you might type *Disallow Remote Desktop Connection client on Company Systems*.
15. Click **Create**.
16. When prompted to create the default rules, click **Yes**. This ensures important rules are allowed to run as shown in Figure 3-7.
17. Close the *Local Group Policy Editor*.
18. To force Group Policy to update, press the **Windows logo key + r** and in the *Run* box, type **Gpupdate/force** and then click **OK**.
19. Log on with any nonadministrative account and test the policy.
20. Press the **Windows logo key + r** and in the *Run* box, type **mstsc.exe** and then click **OK**.

    The user will see the message shown in Figure 3-8.

Figure 3-7

Reviewing the new AppLocker rules

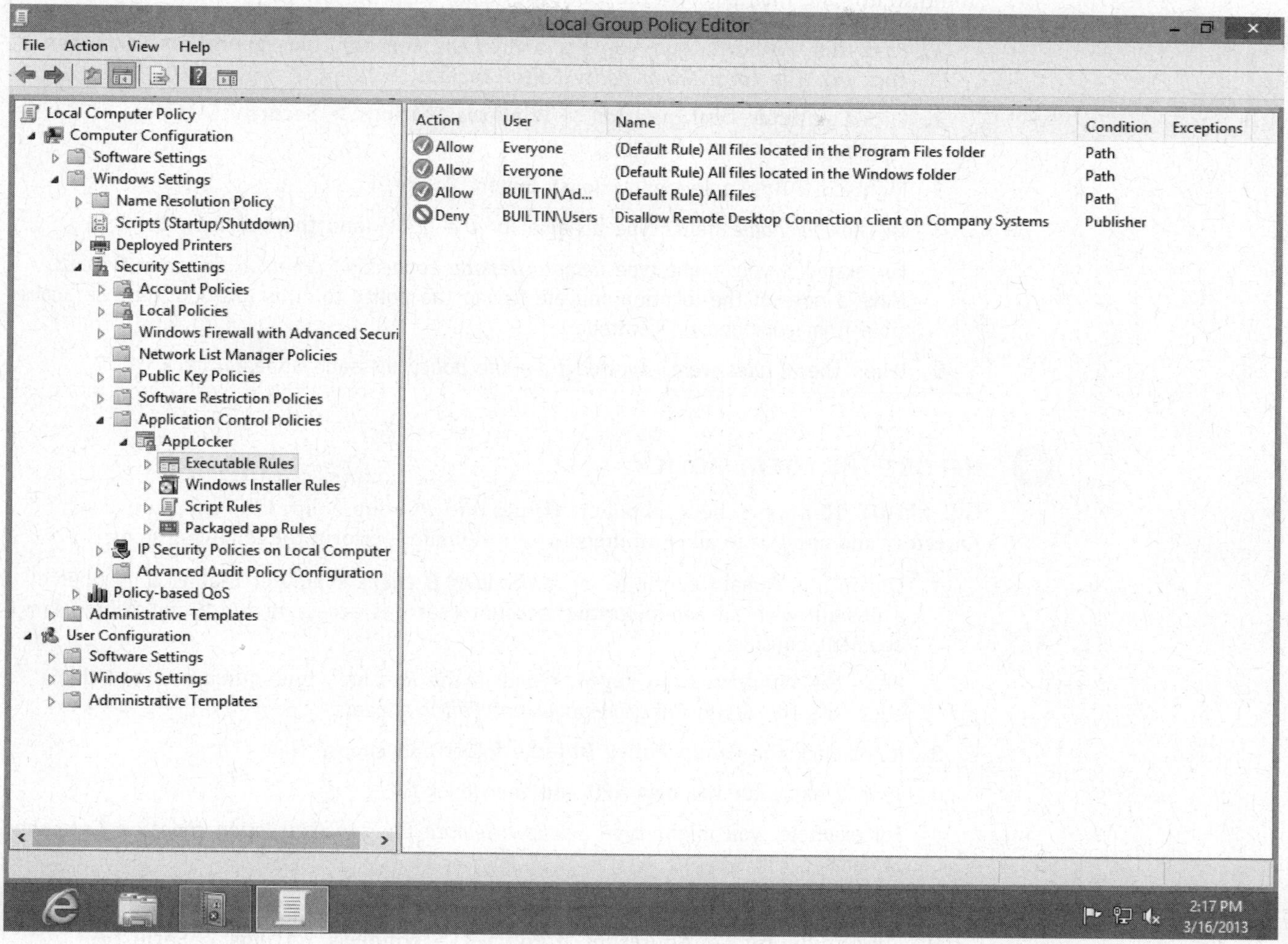

Figure 3-8

An AppLocker warning message

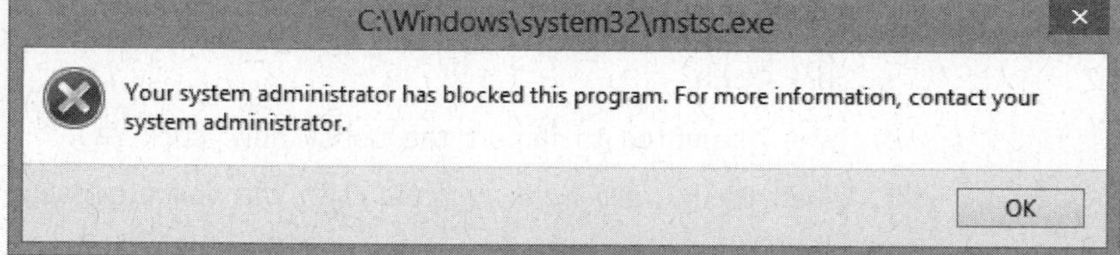

When you create a policy using the Local Group policy editor, you are applying the policy to the local computer and the users who log on to it. If you decide later that you want to use the same policy but apply it to multiple computers across your Active Directory domain, you can simply export the policy and then import it into a Group Policy Object linked to a container in the Active Directory hierarchy (site, domain, or organizational unit). This eliminates the need to recreate the policy settings.

EXPORT THE LOCAL POLICY

GET READY. To export the local policy, log on to the Windows 8 client computer as an administrator and then perform the following steps:

1. Press the **Windows logo key + r** and in the *Run* box, type **gpedit.msc** and then click **OK**. The *Local Group Policy Editor* appears.
2. Click **Computer Configuration > Windows Settings > Security Settings > Application Control Policies.**
3. Right-click **AppLocker** and choose **Export Policy.**
4. In the *File name* field, type a name for the policy and then click **Save.**

   For example, you might type *Remote Desktop Connection client on Company Systems.* Make a note of the location you are saving the policy to. This location must be accessible from your domain controller.
5. When the *4 rules were exported from the policy* message appears, click **OK.**

IMPORT THE LOCAL POLICY

GET READY. To import the local policy settings into a Group Policy Object in Active Directory and apply it to all computers in your domain, perform the following steps:

1. Log into a domain controller or a Windows 8 client computer that is a member of a domain with an administrative account that has access to the Group Policy Management console.
2. Press the **Windows logo key + r** and in the *Run* box, type **gpmc.msc** and then click **OK.** The *Group Policy Management Editor* appears.
3. Right-click the **Group Policy Objects** folder and choose **New.**
4. Type a name for the new GPO and then click **OK.**

   For example, you might type *Disallow Remote Desktop Connection client on Company Systems.*
5. Right-click the GPO and choose **Edit.**
6. Click **Computer Configuration > Policies > Windows Settings > Security Settings > Application Control Policies.**
7. Right-click **AppLocker** and choose **Import Policy.**
8. Browse to the local policy file you exported earlier, select the policy file, and then click **Open.**
9. When prompted to import the policy now, click **Yes.**
10. When the *4 rules were imported from the policy* message appears, click **OK.**
11. Close the *Group Policy Management Editor.*
12. In the *Group Policy Management* console, right-click the domain name (**contoso**) and choose **Link an Existing GPO.**
13. In the *Group Policy objects* section, click **Disallow Remote Desktop Connection client on Company Systems** and then click **OK.**

    Now, no computer in your domain will be allowed to use the Remote Desktop Connection program.

Using Microsoft Office 365

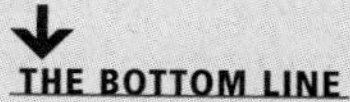

Taking advantage of cloud computing services such as Microsoft Office 365 can reduce the workload on your IT staff. It can also improve the collaboration between your team members.

CERTIFICATION READY
Microsoft Office 365
Objective 1.3

Microsoft Office 365 is a Microsoft subscription–based software service that enables users to access their documents and collaborate with others from anywhere using their computer, the Web, or a smart device. Microsoft Office takes the traditional Office suite and moves it to the cloud. The service includes Office, Exchange, SharePoint, Lync, and Office Web Apps. By using Office 365, you can offload many of the administrative tasks normally handled by your IT department. These tasks include managing software updates, patches, and service packs; and purchasing additional server hardware to support company growth.

Administration is handled through a Web portal/dashboard in which you can create/manage user accounts and oversee the health of all services. Microsoft also provides tools to migrate from your existing on-premise Exchange Server to Office 365.

The service can be used in combination with the desktop version of Microsoft Office and also works if you don't have Office installed on your computers.

Office 365 is available in a number of different plans designed to meet different segments of the market. Each plan uses a per-user/month charge and provides access to either the entire service or subsets of Office 365.

MORE INFORMATION
To compare plans, go to Microsoft's website and perform a search on the phrase "Office 365 Plans."

Understanding Microsoft Office 365 Features

Office 365 provides the software and tools you need to manage a fully collaborated workforce while providing a centralized Web portal to oversee and manage the services.

The following are features available with Microsoft Office 365:

- Access e-mail, calendars, and contacts using the Microsoft Exchange service. They can be delivered to Outlook or Outlook Web Access.
- Create, edit, and store documents you create with the Office Web Apps (browser-based versions of the standard Office suite (Word, PowerPoint, Excel). These documents are fully compatible with the desktop version of the programs created in Office.
- Set up and maintain a company website.
- Connect immediately with co-workers via instance messaging using Microsoft Lync.
- Set up and conduct online meetings (audio, video, and web conferencing) with the ability to share desktops, files, and presentations online.
- Share documents inside and outside of your organization and collaborate with your colleagues using Microsoft SharePoint.

From an administrative perspective, Office 365 offers several benefits:

- Maintenance: Microsoft performs the administrative tasks, so you do not have to worry about backups, patches, and software updates.
- Software upgrades: Office 365 includes them with the subscription price.

- Hardware: Because Office 365 runs in the cloud, you don't have to purchase and maintain expensive server hardware. You can migrate Exchange Server over to Office 365 while at the same time increasing the mailbox storage for users.
- Collaboration on projects: Using SharePoint as a document repository and collaboration workspace, you can connect and work with a geographically dispersed workforce. By using team sites, you can share a portfolio of company projects, enable employees to access project information, share documents, and collaborate on project documents.

Before users can access the services of Office 365, you need to set up user accounts for them by clicking the *Add users* link on the Admin Overview page (see Figure 3-9). Creating new users adds them to your company's subscription. You can also manage domain settings and e-mail address settings from this page.

Figure 3-9

The Office 365 Admin Overview page

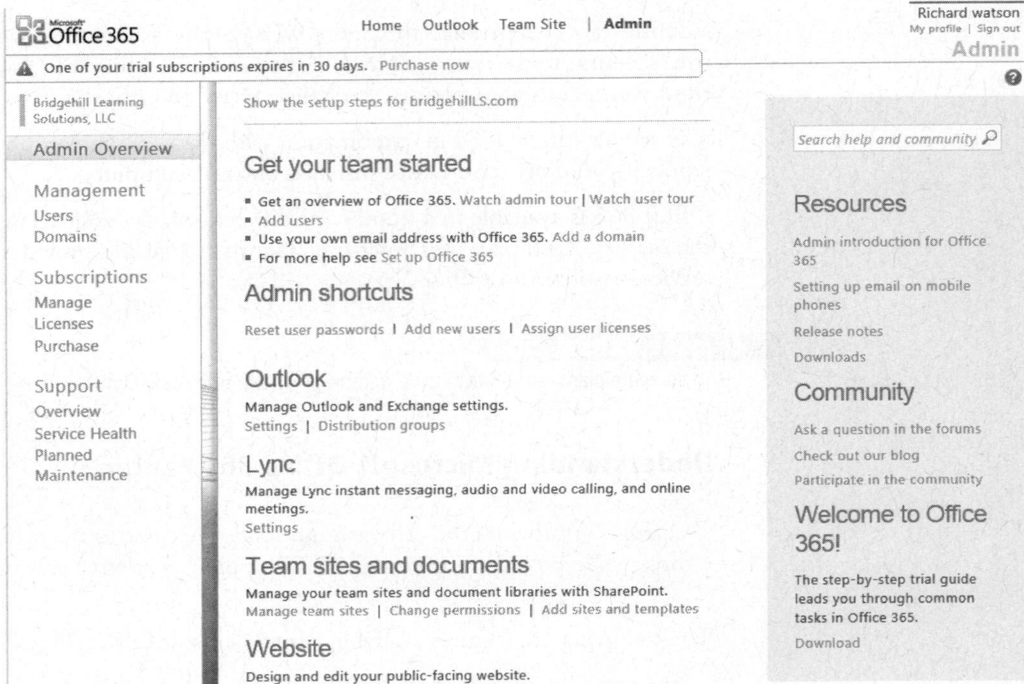

The *Subscriptions* section contains links that enable you to manage/review existing license information, manage license expiration dates, and purchase new subscription plans.

The *Support* link provides you with a connection to Microsoft help services, enabling you to assess the current health of your services (Exchange Online, Identity Service, Lync Online, Office 365 Portal, and SharePoint Online). It also provides you with information regarding planned maintenance.

■ Using Skydrive to Manage Files/Folders

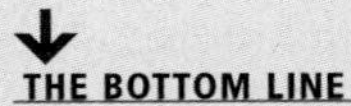

SkyDrive is a file hosting service that allows you to store and create files and folders and share them with other users and groups.

CERTIFICATION READY
Internal content
Objective 1.3

SkyDrive is a free, secure file-hosting service that enables your users to store, synch, and share files across devices using the cloud. It integrates with your Microsoft User Account, offering 7 GB of free space. You can purchase additional storage space as you need it. Using SkyDrive, you can create folders, create or upload files, and share your documents with others. You can also use it to synchronize files and folders that you select across multiple devices. If you forget to include a file within your synch folder, you can use SkyDrive to connect to your remote computer, locate the file, and then upload it to your SkyDrive space. This process is called ***fetching***.

Accessing SkyDrive from a Browser

You can access SkyDrive from a browser using your Microsoft User Account from anywhere you have an Internet connection.

You access SkyDrive from a browser at the SkyDrive website. After reaching the site, you are prompted to log on using your Microsoft User Account. After you are logged in, you see your SkyDrive Dashboard (see Figure 3-10), in which you can upload, download, create, and share folders and files. If your computer is configured to support fetching, you can also connect to it remotely from the SkyDrive Dashboard.

Figure 3-10
The SkyDrive Dashboard

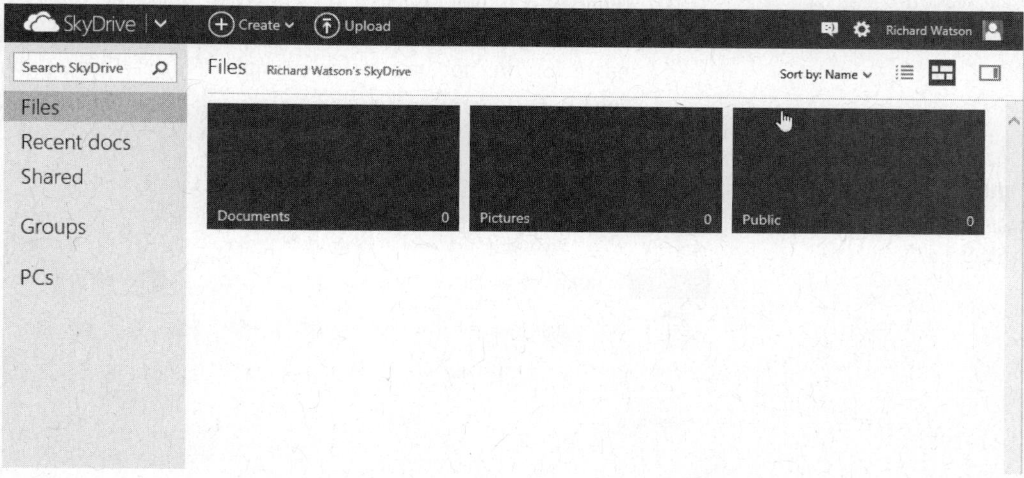

The following provides an overview of each of the options available with the SkyDrive Dashboard:

- **Files:** Includes folders created on the SkyDrive account. You can also see the number of files each folder contains by looking at the number located in the lower-right corner of each folder. Selecting any of these folders opens and displays its content.
- **Recent docs:** Includes a list of documents that have been recently created on the SkyDrive account.
- **Shared:** Provides a list of documents or folders that have been shared with you.
- **Groups:** Displays a list of groups that includes users with whom you frequently communicate and share documents. When you create a group, users receive an e-mail asking them to join. After clicking the link, they are taken to the Groups page, in which they can communicate with other members via e-mail and also view any files that have been shared to the group.

- **PCs:** Provides access through a process called fetching. Use this option if you forget to place a file on your SkyDrive folder, but still need to gain access to it on your PC back in the office. This process requires the SkyDrive for Windows app be installed on the target computer.

Creating a File Within SkyDrive

SkyDrive allows you to collaborate with others on documents provided they have Microsoft accounts.

SkyDrive includes a light version of Microsoft Office apps (Word, Excel, PowerPoint, OneNote). This allows you to create and edit documents directly from your browser.

CREATE A WORD DOCUMENT WITHIN SKYDRIVE USING A WEB BROWSER

GET READY. To create a Word document within SkyDrive using a web browser, log on to a Windows 8 computer with access to the Internet and then perform the following steps:

> **TAKE NOTE***
> To access SkyDrive and complete these steps, you need a Microsoft User Account.

1. Open **Internet Explorer** and go to **http://skydrive.live.com.**
2. Type your **Microsoft User Account** and **Password.**
3. Click the **Documents** folder.
4. From the menu at the top of the page, click **Create** > **Folder.**
5. Name the folder *Project Files* and then click the folder to open it.
6. From the menu at the top of the page, click **Create** > **Word document**, type a name for the document (for example, *Project Scope.docx*), and then click **Create.**
7. Type a few words in the document and then click **Save** (see Figure 3-11).

Figure 3-11

Saving a Word Web document in SkyDrive

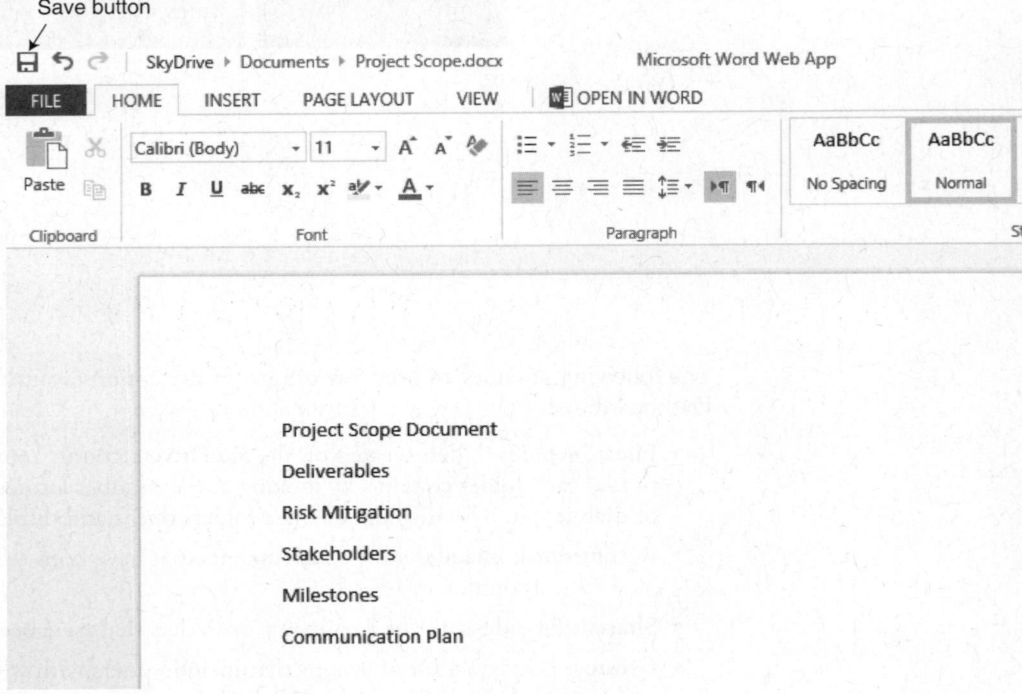

8. Click the SkyDrive link (located at the upper-left corner) to return to the main screen.

Uploading Files to SkyDrive

In the previous activity, you learned how to create a file directly on SkyDrive using the Word Web App. You can also upload files directly to SkyDrive.

If you have existing files on your computer that you want to upload to SkyDrive, you can use either of the following two options:

- From the SkyDrive Dashboard, navigate to the folder in which you want to store the file. On the menu, click Upload, browse to the file you want from your computer, and then click Open.
- From the SkyDrive app installed on your local computer, you can drag and drop the files you want to upload into the SkyDrive folder. This automatically syncs with SkyDrive. You can also configure SkyDrive for the desktop to allow you to fetch files on your PC from other devices.

Sharing a Document in SkyDrive

You can also share a document with others by sending it via e-mail, posting it, or sending others a link to it.

When sharing documents, you have the following options:

- **Send e-mail:** This option should be used if you want to give individual users or groups permission to a file or folder. You can then remove permissions for a specific group or individual if necessary. When users receive the link via e-mail and visit SkyDrive, the file or folder will appear in their list of shared files. You do not have to know their Microsoft user account address. If they do not have one, they can create one for free after clicking on the link.
- **Post to:** This option allows you to share the link on Facebook, LinkedIn, or Twitter. Anyone who views the post on your network can forward the link. If you selected the option to allow recipients to edit the document, anyone the link is forwarded to can view and edit the file or folder.
- **Get a link:** This option should be used if you want to share the file with a larger number of recipients. For example, you could post the link on your blog or your website. You can also include this link in an e-mail or via an instant message. When using this option, you can choose from the following types of links:
  - *View only:* Anyone who receives this link can see the files you share.
  - *View and edit:* Anyone with this link can see and edit the files you share.
  - *Public:* Anyone can search for and view your public files, even if you don't share a link if you decide to make it public.

SHARE A DOCUMENT VIA E-MAIL

GET READY. To share the Word document you created in the previous exercise with others via e-mail, perform the following steps:

1. From the main screen of SkyDrive click **Files** > **Documents** > **Project Files**.
2. Right-click the Word document you saved in the previous exercise (**Project Scope.docx**) and choose **Sharing**.

3. Type the e-mail address of the person you want to share it with and, if necessary, type a message.
4. Click **Share** to send the e-mail message.
5. If you do not want the recipient to be able to edit the document, uncheck the **Can edit** option then click **Done**.

Accessing SkyDrive from the SkyDrive desktop app for Windows

With the ***SkyDrive desktop app for Windows*** installed on your local computer, you can automatically sync files and folders with the SkyDrive cloud. You can then access your resources across multiple devices such as computer web browsers and smartphones.

The SkyDrive desktop app for Windows can be downloaded directly from your SkyDrive account. When you install the app, a folder will be created on your desktop automatically. Anything that you place into this folder is synched with SkyDrive.com as well as with your other computers. You can access the folder from within File Explorer, drag new files into the folder, and choose the folders you want to sync on your computer.

INSTALL THE SKYDRIVE DESKTOP APP FOR WINDOWS

GET READY. To install the SkyDrive desk top app for Windows, log on to a Windows 8 computer with administrative credentials and access SkyDrive.

1. Open **Internet Explorer** and go to **http://skydrive.live.com**.
2. Type your **Microsoft User Account** and **Password**.
3. In the left pane, click and drag the scroll bar to the bottom until you see the *Get SkyDrive apps* link.
4. Click the **Get SkyDrive apps** link.
5. Click the **Windows desktop**.
6. Click the **Download now** link.
7. When prompted with the *Do you want to run or save SkyDriveSetup.exe?* message, click **Run**.
8. After the SkyDrive installation is completed and the *Introducing your SkyDrive folder* dialog box appears, click **Next**.

   By default, the SkyDrive folder will be stored in the *c:\users\%username%\SkyDrive* folder.
9. Leave the default setting *All files and folders on my SkyDrive* and then click **Next**.

   This setting will download everything but the files that are shared with you from your SkyDrive.
10. Click **Done**.

    Do not deselect the Let me use SkyDrive to fetch any of my files on this PC (as shown in Figure 3-12). This is used in the next exercise.

Figure 3-12
Confirming the fetch setting is enabled on this PC

As part of the setup of SkyDrive, you left the option *Let me use SkyDrive to fetch any of my files on this PC* enabled. This setting allows you to use SkyDrive to fetch files from this PC. This process works well when you have a file that is in a folder outside of the SkyDrive folder on your PC or it is a file that you did not configure to synch with SkyDrive when you initially set it up. When a PC has been configured to allow fetching, you see it in your SkyDrive Dashboard, under PCs, when you log on to the SkyDrive website.

FETCH A FILE USING SKYDRIVE

GET READY. To fetch a file using SkyDrive, log on to a Windows 8 computer with access to the Internet and then perform the following steps:

1. Open **Internet Explorer** and go to **http://skydrive.live.com**.
2. Type your **Microsoft User Account** and **Password**.
3. In the left pane, click the remote PC from which want to fetch files. Remote PCs will appear under the PCs section of the left pane.
4. If this is the first time you have attempted to connect to the PC, you will be presented with a security page when you first attempt to connect to it. When the page appears, click **Sign in with a security code**.

   This option automatically sends a seven-digit code to the device you configured when setting up your Microsoft account. This could be your cell phone number or an email address you provided.

5. After you receive the code, type it into the field provided. The folders on your remote PC will appear in SkyDrive (see Figure 3-13).

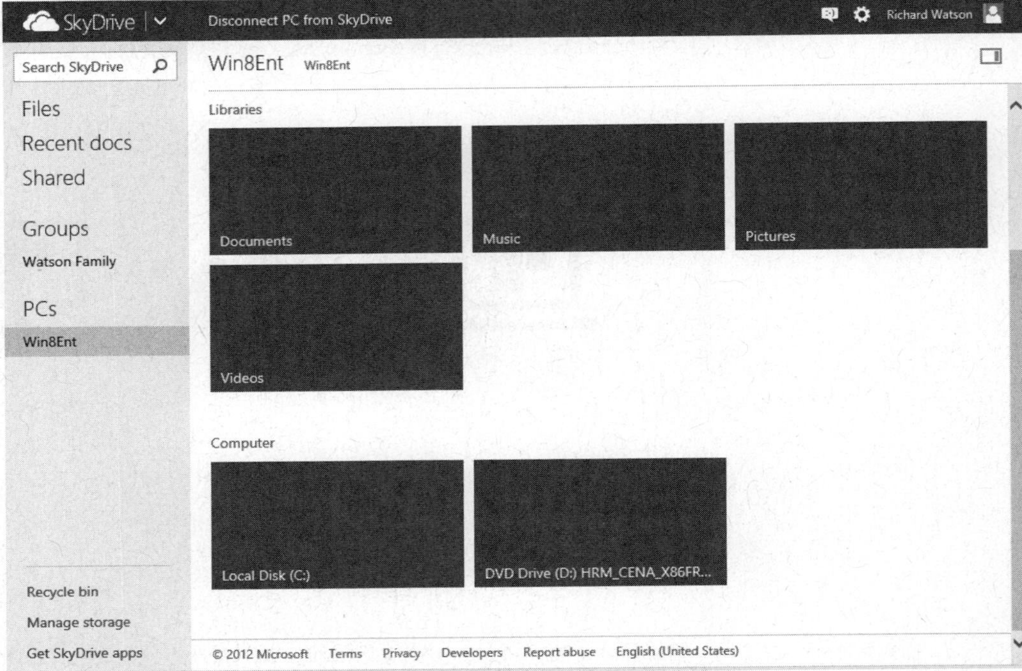

Figure 3-13
Viewing the remote PC's folders and drives

6. Navigate to any folder and select a file that you want to upload. Notice that you have access to your entire PC. This includes all partitions as well as the DVD drive and any externally attached drives on the computer.
7. Right-click the file and choose **Upload to SkyDrive** (see Figure 3-14).

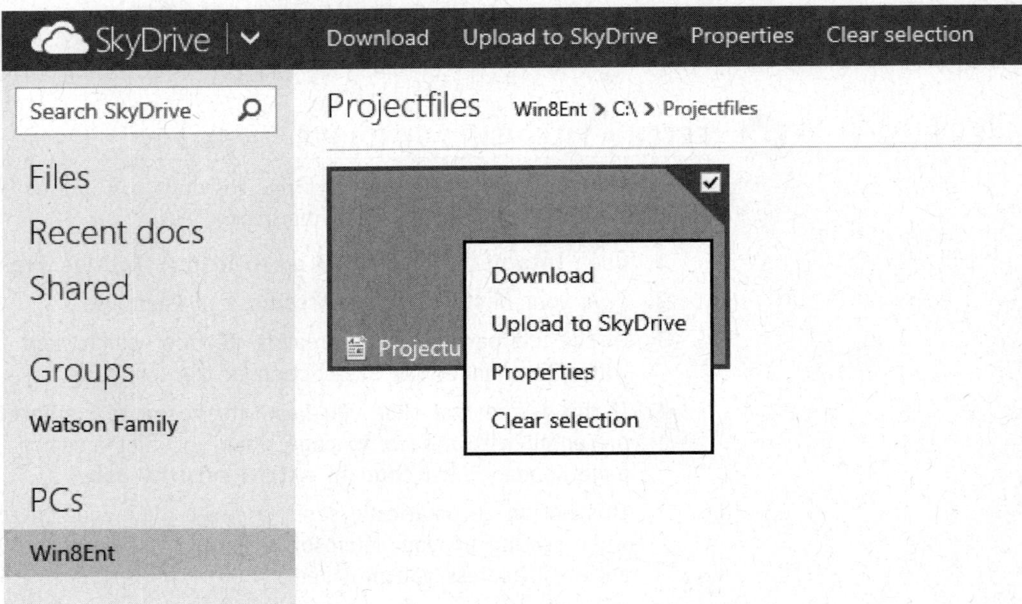

Figure 3-14
Uploading a file from a remote PC to SkyDrive

8. When *The selected item will be uploaded to:* dialog box appears, double-click **Documents**, choose **ProjectFiles**, and then click **Upload**.
9. From the main screen of SkyDrive, click **Files** > **Documents** > **Project Files** and then confirm the file you uploaded appears in the folder.

SKILL SUMMARY

IN THIS LESSON YOU LEARNED:

- When you sideload an app, the PC must be joined to the domain, Group Policy must be set to allow all trusted apps to install, the Windows App must be signed by a CA that the targeted PC trusts, and you must activate a product key to prepare a system for sideloading.
- In situations where you need to restrict access to the Windows Store, you can use Group Policy. To configure the policy on a local machine, you would use the Local Group Policy Editor and for the multiple computers across the enterprise, you would use the Group Policy Management console. Each policy can be set to Not Configured, Enabled, or Disabled. These policies can be found in the Computer or User Configuration\Administrative Templates\Windows Components\Store.
- AppLock can be used to control the way users access and program files. AppLock can be used to configure rules for executables, Windows installers, scripts, and packaged apps (Windows Apps). There are four steps to setting up a rule: set permissions, set the primary condition, add an exception (optional), and enter a name for the rule.
- Microsoft Office 365 is a subscription-based software service that can be used to access documents and collaborate with others from anywhere.
- SkyDrive is a free secure file hosting service that enables your users to store, synch, and share files across devices using the cloud. You also learned the steps involved in accessing SkyDrive from a browser and by using the SkyDrive desktop app for Windows installed on a local computer.

Knowledge Assessment

Multiple Choice

1. Which of the following tools can be used to add and activate the sideloading production activation key received from Microsoft's Volume Licensing Service Center?
   a. GPO
   b. Group Policy Editor
   c. Windows PowerShell
   d. cmd
2. What is the name of the policy setting used to control access to the Windows Store available with the Local Group Policy Editor?
   a. Shut off the Windows Store
   b. Turn off the Store application
   c. Turn off automatic downloads
   d. Shut off automatic downloads

3. Which of the following are requirements of preparing a computer to be sideloaded? (Select all that apply.)
   a. Windows 8/Windows Professional computers must be joined to an Active Directory domain.
   b. Group Policy must be set to *Allow all trusted computers to install.*
   c. A sideloading product key must be activated if the computer is running Windows 7.
   d. The App must be signed by a CA that is trusted by the targeted PCs on the network.

4. When preparing a computer to use a sideloaded app, which of the following commands activates a key?
   a. `Slmgr /ipk <sideloading product key>`
   b. `Slmgr /ato ec67814b-30e6-4a50-bf7b-d55daf729d1e /activate`
   c. `Slmgr /ipk <sideloading product key>`
   d. `Slmgr /ato ec67814b-30e6-4a50-bf7b-d55daf729d1e`

5. Which of the following is a subscription-based software service that enables users to use Office Apps via the Web?
   a. Microsoft Office 365
   b. Skynet
   c. AppLock
   d. GPOs

6. When setting up a rule using AppLock, which of the following primary conditions should be set if you want to use the same rule again after the manufacture updates the application?
   a. Path
   b. Publisher
   c. File Hash
   d. Execute

7. Which of the following options causes the system to compute a hash on the file when using AppLock—and each time the app is updated or patched, you will have to update the hash again?
   a. EFS
   b. Path hash
   c. Folder hash
   d. File Hash

8. Which of the following statements is true about creating a local policy on your computer using the Local Policy Group Editor and wanting to later use it in your domain-based environment? (Select all that apply.)
   a. You cannot use the local policy; you must create a new one for the domain.
   b. You can export it and import it using the Group Policy Management console.
   c. You can export it using the Local Group Policy Editor.
   d. You can import it using the Group Policy Management console and apply it to the domain.

9. Which of the following Group Policy settings can be configured for a computer to control how it interacts with the Windows Store? (Select all that apply.)
   a. Turn off Automatic Download of updates.
   b. Allow Store to install apps on Windows To Go Workspaces.
   c. Turn off the Store application.
   d. Turn on Automatic Download of updates.

10. Which of the following rule collections are used in AppLocker? (Select all that apply.)
    a. Executable files
    b. Scripts
    c. Windows Image files
    d. Appx

Best Answer

Choose the letter that corresponds to the best answer. More than one answer choice may achieve the goal. Select the BEST answer.

1. You have installed an application on your Windows 8 client computer and want to set up an AppLocker rule that denies use of the application. Which of the following primary conditions ensures the rule is still valid even if the maker of the app releases a new version?
   a. Publisher
   b. Path
   c. File Hash
   d. Hash
2. Using the Local Group Policy editor, you disable the *Turn off the Store application* setting. There is also a policy at the domain level that has the same policy setting configured as Enabled. Which of the following statements best describes the result?
   a. You would be able to access the Windows Store.
   b. You will not be able to access the Windows Store.
   c. This policy is not available on Windows 8.
   d. You would be able to access the store but not install Windows apps.
3. Which of the following best represents the order of precedence when processing Group Policy settings in a domain-based environment?
   a. Local, Site, Domain, Organizational Unit
   b. Site, Domain, Organizational Unit, Local
   c. Domain, Organizational Unit, Local, Site
   d. Site, Organizational Unit, Local, Domain
4. Which of the following tools creates a Group Policy object that can be applied to your entire Active Directory domain?
   a. gpedit.msc
   b. gpmc.msc
   c. compmgmt.msc
   d. Active Directory Users and Computers
5. Which of the following rules collections blocks a user from running a specific Windows App in AppLocker?
   a. Executable files
   b. Windows Installer files
   c. Scripts
   d. Appx

Matching and Identification

1. Match the tool to the correct task:
   _______ **a)** `gpedit.msc`
   _______ **b)** `slmgr`
   _______ **c)** `add-appxpackage`
   _______ **d)** `gpupdate /force`
   _______ **e)** Windows logo key + r
   1. Used to install a sideloaded package.
   2. Opens the Local Group Policy Editor.
   3. Adds and activates the sideloading product key.
   4. Refreshes local and Active Directory-based Group Policy settings.
   5. Accesses the Run box.

2. Write the command for the specified function or scenario:
   ________ Add a sideloading product key.
   ________ Install a sideloaded package.
   ________ Update a sideloaded package.
   ________ Activate a sideloading product key.

Build a List

1. Specify the correct order of the steps required to export a local policy on a Windows 8 client computer:
   ________ Click **Computer Configuration > Windows Settings > Security Settings > Application Control Policies**.
   ________ Right-click **AppLocker** and choose **Export Policy**.
   ________ Press the **Windows logo key + r** and type **gpedit.msc** in the *Run* box.
   ________ In the *File name* field, type a name for the policy and then click **Save**.
   ________ Log on to the Windows 8 client computer with administrative credentials.
   ________ When the message *4 rules were exported from the policy* appears, click **OK**.

2. Specify the correct order of the steps required to share a document using SkyDrive:
   ________ Click **Done**.
   ________ Click **Share** to send the e-mail message.
   ________ Type the e-mail address.
   ________ Right-click the document and choose **Sharing**.
   ________ Click **Files > Documents > Project Files**.
   ________ Type your **Microsoft User account** and **Password**.
   ________ Log on to a Windows 8 client computer and open your browser to **http://skydrive.live.com**.

3. Specify the correct order of the steps required to install the SkyDrive App on your desktop computer:
   ________ Click the **Download now** link.
   ________ Click **Next** to keep the default setting *All files and folders on my SkyDrive.*
   ________ When the *Introducing your SkyDrive folder* dialog box appears, click **Next**.
   ________ Log on to a Windows 8 client computer and open your browser to **http://skydrive.live.com**.
   ________ Click the **Get SkyDrive apps** link.
   ________ When prompted with *Do you want to run or save SkyDriveSetup.exe?* click **Run**.
   ________ Click the **Windows Desktop**.
   ________ Type your **Microsoft User Account** and **Password**.
   ________ Click **Done**.

Business Case Scenarios

Scenario 3-1: Troubleshooting Sideloaded Apps

Developers at your company created a Windows App that needs to be sideloaded on a Windows 8 client computer that is part of your Active Directory domain. They ask you to prepare a computer so the sideloaded app can be installed and tested. After setting up the computer, you attempt to sideload the app but cannot complete the process. After reviewing your notes, you are not sure if you have addressed all of the pre-requisites for sideloading the app. What could you have missed?

Scenario 3-2: Multicasting Images

The director of IT noticed that many of the users on the company domain have been installing and playing with apps from the Windows Store. She asks you to figure out a way to restrict access. What is the best approach to solving this problem?

Scenario 3-3: Configuring Cloud Apps and Collaboration

The Executive team has been looking at budgets lately and realizes there is a need to upgrade the company's Exchange and SharePoint Servers. After review, they discover the cost is much larger than expected. Hardware, along with adding another IT staff member to help manage the servers, is considered too costly. They ask you to develop solutions for 250 users or fewer. The Executive team wants e-mail, web conferencing, the ability to share and collaborate between users, and instant messaging capabilities. What solutions might you recommend?

Designing a Solution for User Settings

70-412 EXAM OBJECTIVE

Objective 1.4 – Design a solution for user settings. This objective may include but is not limited to the following design considerations: User profiles; USMT 5.0/WET; Windows Live integration; Folder Redirection; User Experience Virtualization (UE-V)

X REF

The objective item "USMT 5.0/WET" is covered in Lesson 1, in the sections "Exploring the User State Migration Tool (USMT) 5.0" and "Using Windows Easy Transfer."

LESSON HEADING	EXAM OBJECTIVE
Managing User Accounts	
Workgroups and Domains	
User Accounts	Windows Live Integration
Domain-Based Accounts	
Groups	
Deploying User Profiles	User profiles
Folder Redirection and Offline Files/Folders	Folder Redirection
User Profiles (Local/Roaming)	
Virtualizing the User Experience	User Experience Virtualization (UE-V)
Understanding UE-V Templates	

KEY TERMS

Active Directory accounts
Always Offline mode
client-side caching
distribution groups
domain-based accounts
domains
Folder Redirection
group
local user accounts
Microsoft user accounts
Offline Files/Folders
organizational unit (OU)
primary computers
Roaming User Profiles
security groups
Security Identifier (SID)
UE-V Agent
UE-V Generator
user account
User Account Control (UAC)
User Experience Virtualization (UE-V)
User Principle Name (UPN)
user profiles
workgroups

Managing User Accounts

User accounts provide the gateway into your network and its resources. As an administrator, you must be able to identify the type of account to create and configure it appropriately to protect not only your computers and servers but the resources they provide.

A ***user account*** is used by Windows to determine what changes you can make on the computer, which files and folders you can have access to, and is used to track personal preferences such as your choice of desktop wallpaper, color schemes, drive mappings, and/or screen savers. There are standard accounts used to perform daily tasks on the computer which are limited in what they can do as well as administrative accounts which provide full control over the computer.

Before users can access a network and its available resources, they must be authenticated. This involves entering a user name and password that was configured by the network's administrator as part of the initial setup of their user account. Once entered, the computer verifies the credentials against its database and determines whether or not to provide the user with access to its resources. These resources can be located on the local computer, distributed across the network, and/or be located somewhere out on the Internet.

When planning your user account management, one strategy you need to consider a new account type in Windows 8 called the Microsoft user account. This account differs from previous account structures that included local user accounts and domain-based accounts. Before looking at the account types in Windows 8, let's review the concept of workgroups and domains, which play a critical role in determining your user account strategy and how authentication is handled across your organization.

Workgroups and Domains

Workgroups and domains are both networking environments but the way in which user accounts, authentication and security are handled is very different. As an administrator, you must understand the differences between the two to effectively create and manage users in your network.

Workgroups are a collection of computers that interact with each other but have no centralized authority. Each computer in the workgroup manages its own database of user accounts. These accounts are used to authenticate access to resources on that specific computer.

Domains are based on the Active Directory directory service. In a domain, the user accounts are stored as objects in Active Directory, which is maintained on a domain controller. When users log on to a computer in the domain, their user names and passwords are passed to the domain controller for authentication. After they are authenticated, users can gain access to any resources for which they have been given permission on computers across the entire domain.

User Accounts

Each type of user account provides a different level of control over the computers in your network. Matching the right type of account to each user will ensure you provide sufficient privileges to your users without giving them access to areas or resources that might compromise your network's security.

Microsoft user accounts enable you to synchronize your desktop across multiple Windows 8 devices.

Local user accounts are created on individual computers that are members of a workgroup to provide access to resources on that computer.

CERTIFICATION READY
Windows Live Integration
Objective 1.4

MICROSOFT USER ACCOUNTS

When you set up a Windows 8 PC for the first time, you have the option of creating a Microsoft user account using an e-mail address that you provide. The e-mail address you use can come from any provider. After the account is set up, Microsoft will use it along with your password to help manage your settings across all your Windows 8 PCs. After organizing your system the way you want it (desktop background, user tiles, favorite websites in your browser, explorer settings), the information will be associated with your Microsoft user account and will be stored in the cloud. Every time you log in to a Windows 8 device using the account, your settings are synched from the cloud, and any changes you make are updated and available to you on the next device.

Using a Microsoft user account provides a consistent experience when working with the Windows Store apps. Purchased apps will be available from each device, feeds you add will be synched across all devices, and state information will be maintained, so you can start a game or read a book and pick it up later on another device.

Windows Live integration is built around the idea of using a single Microsoft user account (formerly called Windows Live ID) to synchronize multiple Windows 8 devices and provide access to Windows Live services and software products from Microsoft. A primary feature of Windows Live Integration is the Windows Live ID Microsoft user account. Microsoft uses this account as the authentication mechanism for hundreds of web services, Microsoft websites, SkyDrive, Outlook.com, Windows Phone, Xbox Live, and many other services.

Microsoft user accounts can be synched with a domain account, but the capability to do so depends upon Group Policy settings. Using Group Policy, you can determine whether you want to allow the synching of the two accounts and what information can be synched.

You create a Microsoft user account during the initial installation of the operating system or after the system is running. The following steps outline the process you can use to create the account after Windows 8 is installed using the ***Charms bar***. The Charms bar allows you to search, share files and information, gain access to the Windows 8 start menu, access devices connected to your computer, and change settings for both your apps and your PC.

CREATE A MICROSOFT USER ACCOUNT USING THE CHARMS BAR

GET READY. To create the account after Windows 8 is installed using the Charms bar, perform the following steps:

1. Log in to the Windows 8 client computer.
2. Point your cursor to the top- or bottom-right corner of the screen to make the Charms bar appear.
3. Click **Settings** (the gear icon).
4. Click **Change PC Settings**.
5. Click **Users**.
6. Click **Add a user** (see Figure 4-1).

Figure 4-1

Adding a user

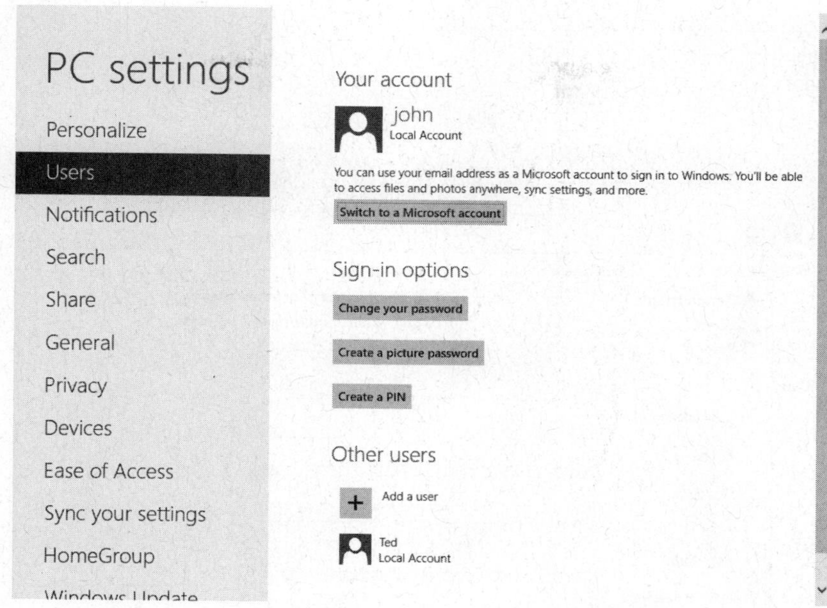

7. Type the email address you want to use and then click **Next.**
8. Click **Finish.**

LOCAL USER ACCOUNTS

To create a local user account, you must be a member of the local administrators group.

In Windows 8, you cannot synchronize your settings with other Windows 8 computers or download applications from the Windows Store. If you use local accounts, you need to create a user account on each Windows 8 computer on which you want to access resources. You can create a local user account during the Windows 8 setup or after the installation is complete.

The following accounts are installed by default on Windows 8:

- Administrator: The administrator account provides complete access to the system. This account is hidden and disabled by default. When you first install Windows 8 you are prompted to create a new user account, which becomes a member of the built-in Administrators group.
- Guest: The guest account, disabled by default, allows for temporary access to the computer.

To create a new local user account using the Computer Management console, right-click Users and choose New User. The New User dialog box appears (see Figure 4-2).

TAKE NOTE*

Although this new account has administrative privileges to the computer, it will still see the ***User Account Control (UAC)*** confirmation box when any administrative tasks are performed. The hidden administrator account will not receive the UAC. The UAC is a feature designed to inform you when you are about to perform an administrative level task. If you click Yes when prompted, you are given the rights temporarily to perform the task and then your permissions are returned to that of a standard user. This ensures changes cannot be made to your computer without you knowing it and also helps protect against malware and spyware. You can enable the hidden Administrator account but it is not recommended in production environments.

Figure 4-2

Creating a local user using the Computer Management console

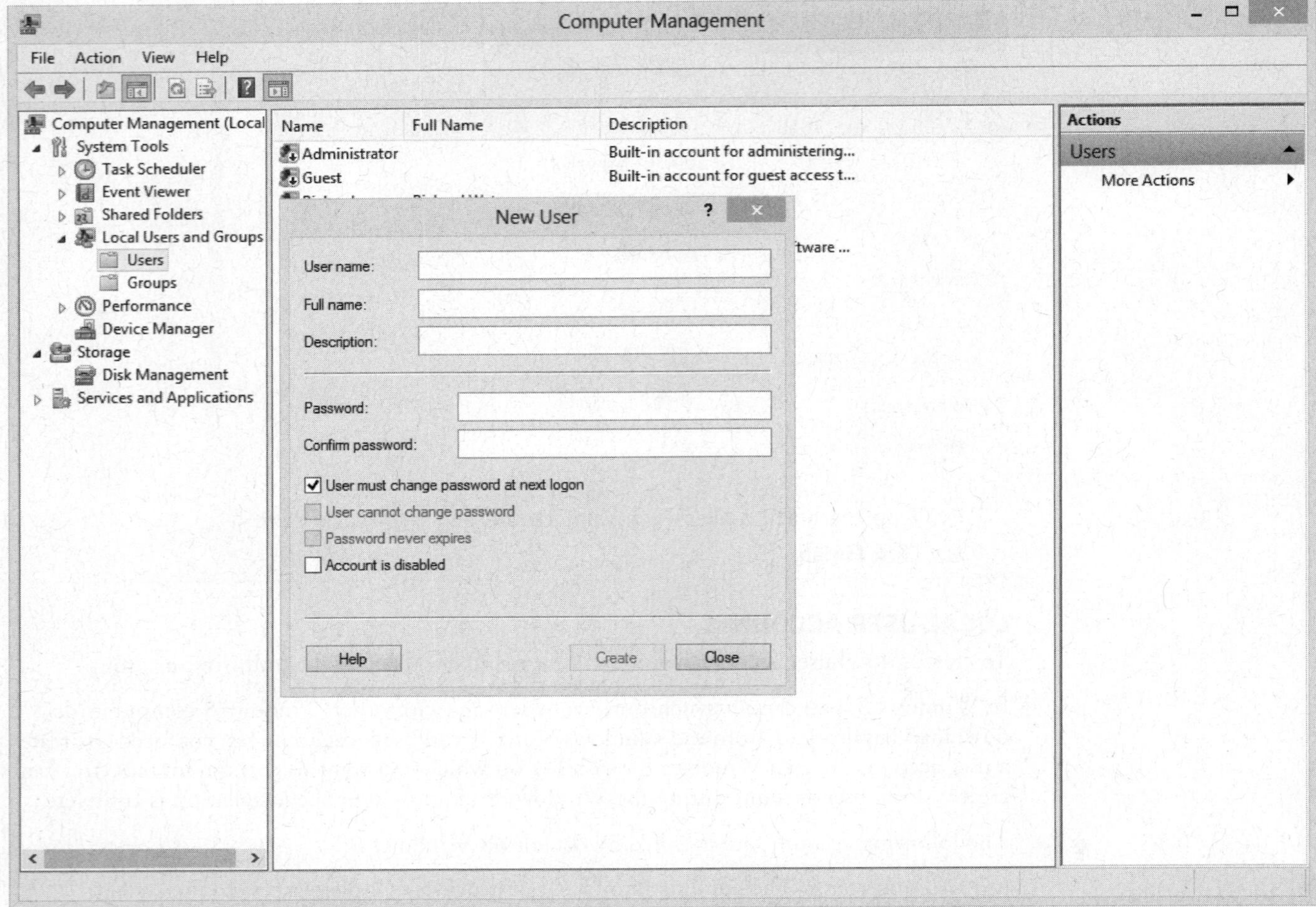

Here are a few things to keep in mind when creating a user account using the Local Users and Groups tool.

- The *User name* cannot be the same as another user or group on the computer. It can contain up to 20 uppercase characters or lowercase characters.
- The *Password* can contain up to 127 characters.
- Enabling *User must change password at next logon* enables users to create their own password when they first log on.

In environments in which you have a small number of computers, using local accounts is manageable, but when your network grows, it can become a problem. Without a centralized computer (a domain controller) managing the accounts, every time you a new user comes onboard, you have to create an account on each computer. As you can see, the administrative workload to manage these accounts can quickly become an issue because the local account is only valid on the local computer. A better solution would be to store the users' credentials in a centralized database. This allows the users to login with a domain-based account from any computer in the domain

Domain-Based Accounts

Domain-based accounts, also called ***Active Directory accounts***, are stored as objects on a domain controller and provide access to resources on multiple systems.

When users log on with a domain account, they are authenticated by a domain controller, not by the local computer they are working on. You create domain-based accounts on a domain controller using the Active Directory Users and Computers console, the Active Directory Administrative Center, Windows PowerShell, or the `dsadd` command.

The following accounts are installed by default on a domain controller:

- Administrator: The domain administrator account provides full control of the domain. It is the first account set up when you create a domain.
- Guest: The guest account, disabled by default, allows for temporary access to the domain. This account does not require a password but should always be left disabled in domain environments.

To set up a domain user account, you must be a member of the Account Operators group, the Domain Admins group, or the Enterprise Admins group (or be delegated the authority by an Enterprise Admin).

The following information is required:

- **First name, Initials, Last name, Full name.**
- **User logon name.** This is the account name the user will log on with and is a mandatory field to complete when setting up the account. This includes the logon name (***User Principle Name*** prefix) and a ***User Principle Name (UPN)*** suffix (@domainname) appended to end of the name. The two combine to create the UPN. The UPN suffix defaults to the domain you are in when creating the account (for example @contoso.com). The UPN must be unique within the Active Directory forest. If multiple accounts have the same UPN configured, users will not be able to log on and be authenticated against the domain controller.
- **User logon name (pre-Windows 2000).** For backward compatibility, each domain has a pre-Windows 2000 name in the form of **domainname\username**. Users who work on pre-Windows 2000 operating systems would use this login name to access their domain. The wizard will automatically enter the first 20 characters from the user logon name you entered but you can change the pre-Windows 2000 login name if you choose. It must be unique within the domain; otherwise, users will not be able to log on and be authenticated against the domain controller.
- **Password.** You can use a password up to 127 characters. The length and complexity are controlled by a password policy set for the domain.

When setting up additional domain user accounts, you can use the Copy feature. The copy feature is very useful when you have several users who work in the same department or have the same permissions and group memberships. Instead of creating an individual account for each one and then assigning them to groups, you simply create a single account and use it as a template to create the others. Copying an existing account does not retain all the information from the original account, but it does retain basic information:

- Address information
- Department and company information
- Group account memberships

If you delete a domain user account and then re-create another account using the same name, you cannot retain the original permissions and access to the same resources because each user account has its own unique ***Security Identifier (SID).*** An SID is a unique alphanumeric character string that is used to identify each user in the network. It is better to disable accounts if you think the employees will return after an absence from the company. When they return, you can easily enable them, providing them with access to all of their original resources.

After creating your user accounts, you may want to make changes that affect all the accounts. You can do this by holding the Ctrl key down and clicking each user and then clicking Action > Properties. For example, if your company moves to a new address, or if you have a group of users that is reporting to a new manager, you can use this approach to streamline management of the accounts.

Groups

When providing users access to resources on the network, you can either assign them permissions to the folders and files separately or assign them to groups, which, in turn, are assigned permissions to the resources.

A ***group*** is a collection of users, computers, contacts, and other group objects within the Active Directory forest.

If you have more than a few users, the administrative process of providing access to shares on an individual user basis will become laborious. A better approach is to create a group, make selected user accounts members of the group, and then assign permissions to a resource to the group. There are two types of groups in Active Directory–based networks:

- ***Security groups*** are used to assign permissions to resources.
- ***Distribution groups*** are used for sending information (such as e-mail messages) to a select group of users in Active Directory.

You will work with security groups primarily to provide access to resources. You will also use them when working with Group Policies.

When working with Active Directory, you will most likely structure your organization and departments around the ***organizational unit (OU)*** container. The OU is a general-purpose container used to group other Active Directory objects together for administrative purposes. An organizational unit in Active Directory is similar to the concept of a directory in a file system; it is designed to hold other objects. For example, the sales, marketing, operations, finance, information technology, and human resources department will each have their own OU. Within the OU would be their associated user accounts, groups, and computer accounts. In the exercise that follows, you will create an OU to store user accounts and a group.

CREATE AN ORGANIZATIONAL UNIT (OU), A DOMAIN GROUP, AND DOMAIN USER ACCOUNTS

GET READY. In this exercise, you will create an organizational unit (OU) for the executive team and then create a domain group and domain user accounts using the Active Directory User and Computer console. Perform the following steps:

1. Log in to a Windows Server 2012 computer that is performing the role of domain controller with administrative credentials.

   The Server Manager console will open automatically. If not, click the Server Manager icon on the task bar
2. Click **Tools > Active Directory Users and Computers.**
3. Right click the domain (see Figure 4-3) and choose **New > Organizational Unit.** This container will be used to store and manage the user accounts.

Figure 4-3

Creating a new OU

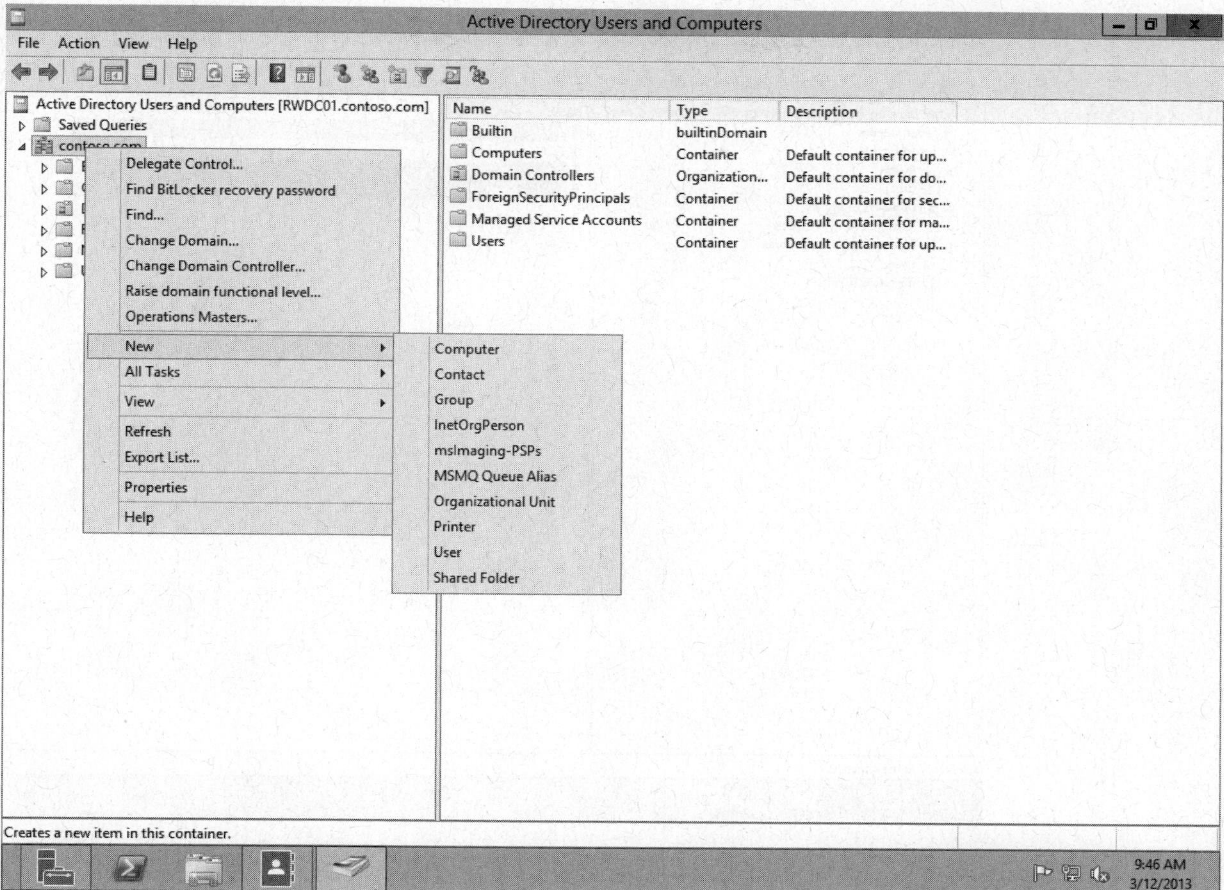

4. Type a name for the OU (for example, *Executive Team*) and then click **OK**.
5. Right-click the **Executive Team** organizational unit and choose **New User**. Create an account using the following properties:

   First name: **Beverly**

   Last name: **Kasik**

   Full name: **Beverly Kasik**

   User logon name: **bkasik**
6. Click **Next**.
7. Type a password, confirm the password for the user, and then click **Next**.
8. Click **Finish**.
9. Right-click the account you created for Beverly Kasik and choose **Copy**.
10. Create an account for **James Elliot** and **Morgan Edwards** using the same steps you used to create Beverly Kasik's account.
11. Right-click the **Executive Team** organizational unit and choose **New Group**. Name it **Execs**.

    This will group all the executive accounts into a single group to streamline the management of their accounts.
12. Click **OK**.

13. Press and hold the **Ctrl** key, select the three accounts you created earlier, and then right-click and choose **Add to a group** (see Figure 4-4).

Figure 4-4

Adding users to the Exec Group

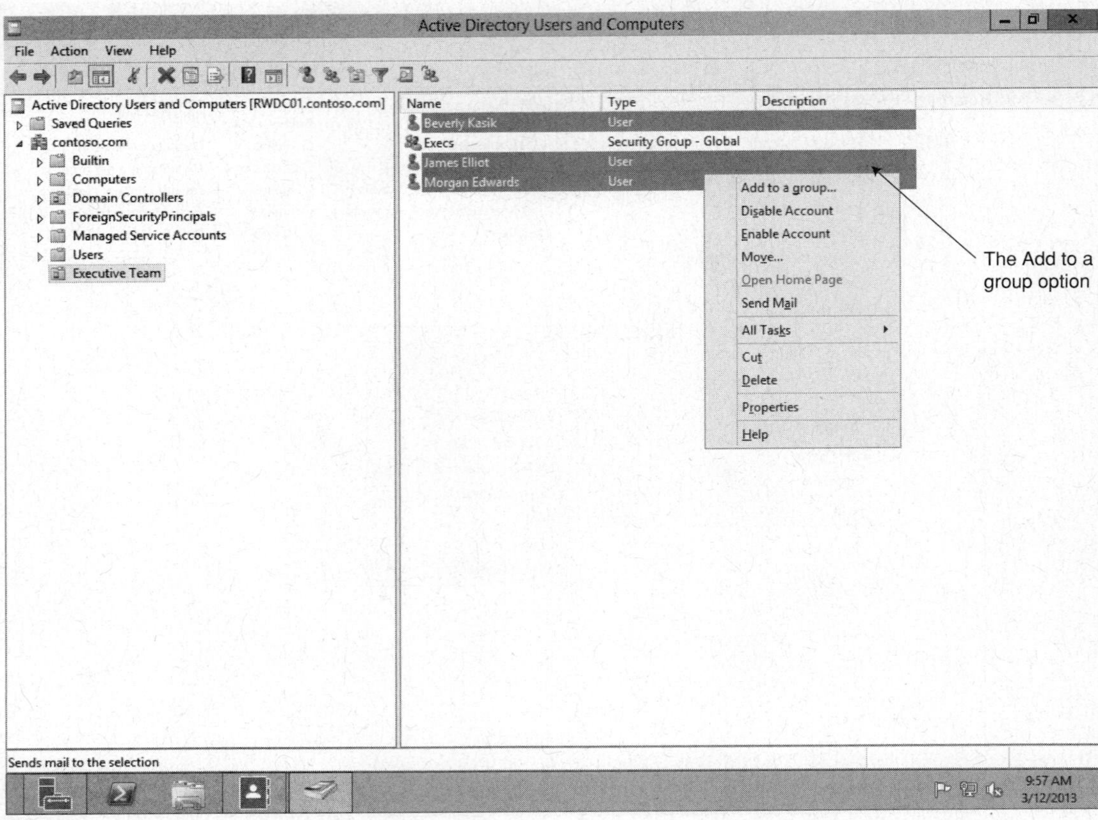

14. In the *Enter the object names to select* box, type **Execs** for the object name and then click **OK**.
15. When the *The Add to Group operation was successfully completed* message appears, click **OK**.

■ Deploying User Profiles

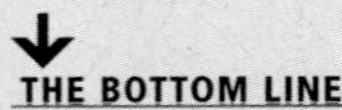

THE BOTTOM LINE

User profiles contain network environment settings as well as desktop configurations. Centralizing these settings along with their data enables your users to access their resources regardless of where they log on.

Offline Files/Folders, Folder Redirection, and Roaming User Profiles are features in Windows 8 that enable you to centrally store user data and settings. This enables users to access resources while working offline or over slow network connections. Because the data is stored centrally, you can back up and maintain your critical information.

CERTIFICATION READY
User profiles
Objective 1.4

We briefly discussed these features in our discussion of User State Virtualization in Lesson 1. In this section, we'll take a closer look. Here is a quick overview:

- ***Folder Redirection:*** Replicates user data to a centralized folder stored on a server in the data center. This enables users to access their files from any computer.
- ***Offline Files/Folders:*** Takes files and folders located on a server and makes them accessible to users. This enables users to continue to work in case of network outages or while away on travel.

- ***Roaming User Profiles:*** Enables users to store their choices in personalization in a centralized folder and then download to another computer when they log on.

Folder Redirection and Offline Files/Folders

Folder Redirection and Offline Files/Folders (also called ***client-side caching***) are designed to complement each other.

By using these Folder Redirection and Offline Files/Folders, you can redirect the path of one or more local folders to a shared folder on the network and then cache the files/folders on the local machine. This makes the resources available to the user from any computer on the network.

CERTIFICATION READY
Folder Redirection
Objective 1.4

Folder Redirection is usually managed by Group Policy in Active Directory–based networks and involves the following steps:

1. Create a security group to contain users whose files you want to redirect.
2. Create and share a folder to hold the redirected files.
3. Create a Group Policy Object (GPO) and configure it to apply Folder Redirection.
4. Enable the GPO.
5. Sign in from a computer in which the policy has been applied to test it.

On Windows Server 2012, a shared folder and its files are configured to be available for offline use. When users connect, they can determine whether they want to make the resource available offline (see Figure 4-5). Using this approach enables users to take advantage of the Always Offline mode feature available in Windows 8. ***Always Offline mode*** provides clients faster access to their files by always working offline, even when they are connected through a high-speed connection. In addition to the default option, you can configure the following offline settings which are available by right-clicking the shared folder, clicking the Sharing tab, choosing Advanced Sharing, and then click Caching.

- **No files or programs from the shared folder are available offline.** This option should be used when you need to protect sensitive files from being cached offsite. It blocks Offline Files on client computers from making copies of the files and programs on the shared folder.
- **All files and programs that users open from the shared folder are automatically available offline.** This option makes the file or program in the folder automatically available to the user offline whenever they access and open it from the shared folder.

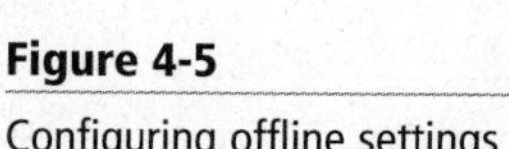

Figure 4-5
Configuring offline settings

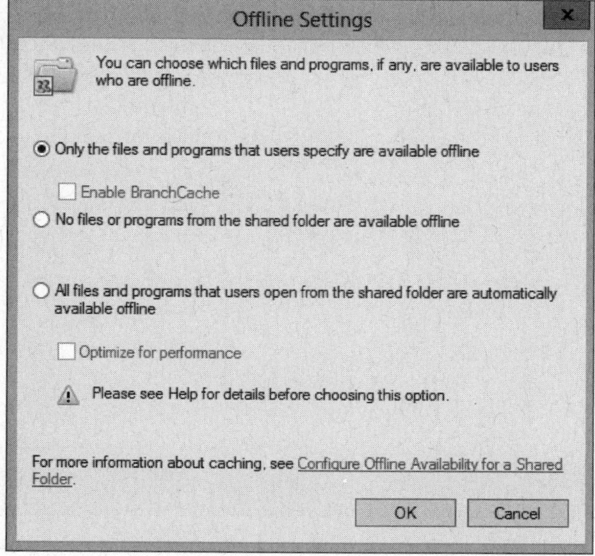

The files and programs remain in the Offline Files cache and are synchronized with the version on the server until the cache is full or the user deletes the files. Files and programs that are not opened are not available offline.

- **Optimize for performance.** This options means that executable files downloaded from the server will be cached and run directly from the client the next time they are accessed.

In the following exercise, you will create a Folder Redirection policy for members of your Executive team.

CREATE A FOLDER REDIRECTION POLICY

GET READY. To create a Folder Redirection policy, log on to the computer running Windows Server 2012 and Active Directory with domain administrative credentials and then perform the following steps:

First, you must create and share a folder for Folder Redirection and configure the appropriate permissions on the folder.

1. Log in to a Windows Server 2012 computer that is performing the role of domain controller with administrative credentials. The Server Manager console opens automatically. If not, click the Server Manager icon on the task bar.
2. Click **File and Storage Services**.
3. Click **Shares**.
4. Click **Tasks** > **New Share** (see Figure 4-6).

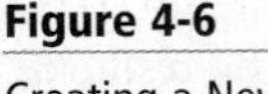

Figure 4-6

Creating a New Share

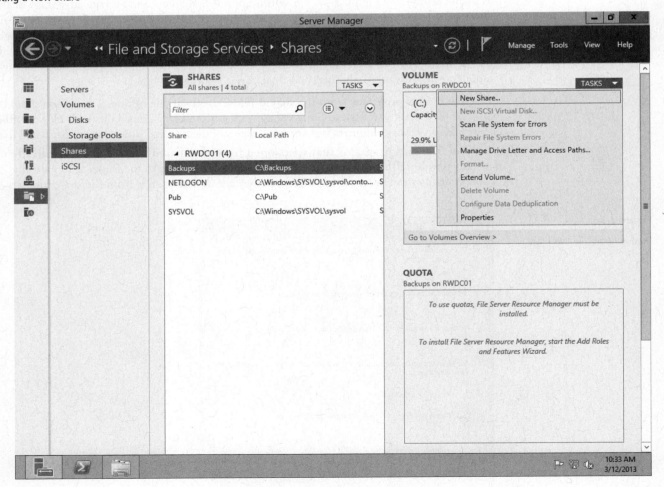

5. Click **SMB Share-Quick** and then click **Next.**
6. Click **Next** to accept the default settings.
7. Type a name for the share (for example, *Execs Folder Redirection*) and then click **Next.**
8. Click **Next** to accept the default *Allow caching of share.*
9. Click **Customize permissions > Disable Inheritance.**
10. Click **Remove all inherited permissions from this object.**
11. Click **Add** and then click **Select a principal.**
12. In the *Enter the object name to select* box, type **Execs** and then click **OK.**
13. Click the drop down arrow next to *Applies to* and choose **This folder only.**
14. Click **Show advanced permissions** and confirm the following advanced permissions are selected:

    Traverse folder/execute file

    List folder/read data

    Read attributes

    Read extended attributes

    Create files/write data

    Create folders/append data

    Read permissions
15. Click **OK.**
16. Click **Add**, and then click **Select a principal.**
17. In the *Enter the object name to select* box, type **SYSTEM** and then click **OK.**
18. Click **Full Control** and then click **OK.**
19. Click **Add** and then click **Select a principal.**
20. In the *Enter the object name to select* box, type **Administrators** and then click **OK.**
21. Click **Full Control** and then click **OK.**
22. Click **Add** and then click **Select a principal.**
23. In the *Enter the object name to select* box, type **CREATOR OWNER** and then click **OK.**
24. Click **Full Control** and then click **OK.**
25. Confirm your permission settings are similar to those shown in Figure 4-7.

Figure 4-7

Setting permissions for Folder Redirection

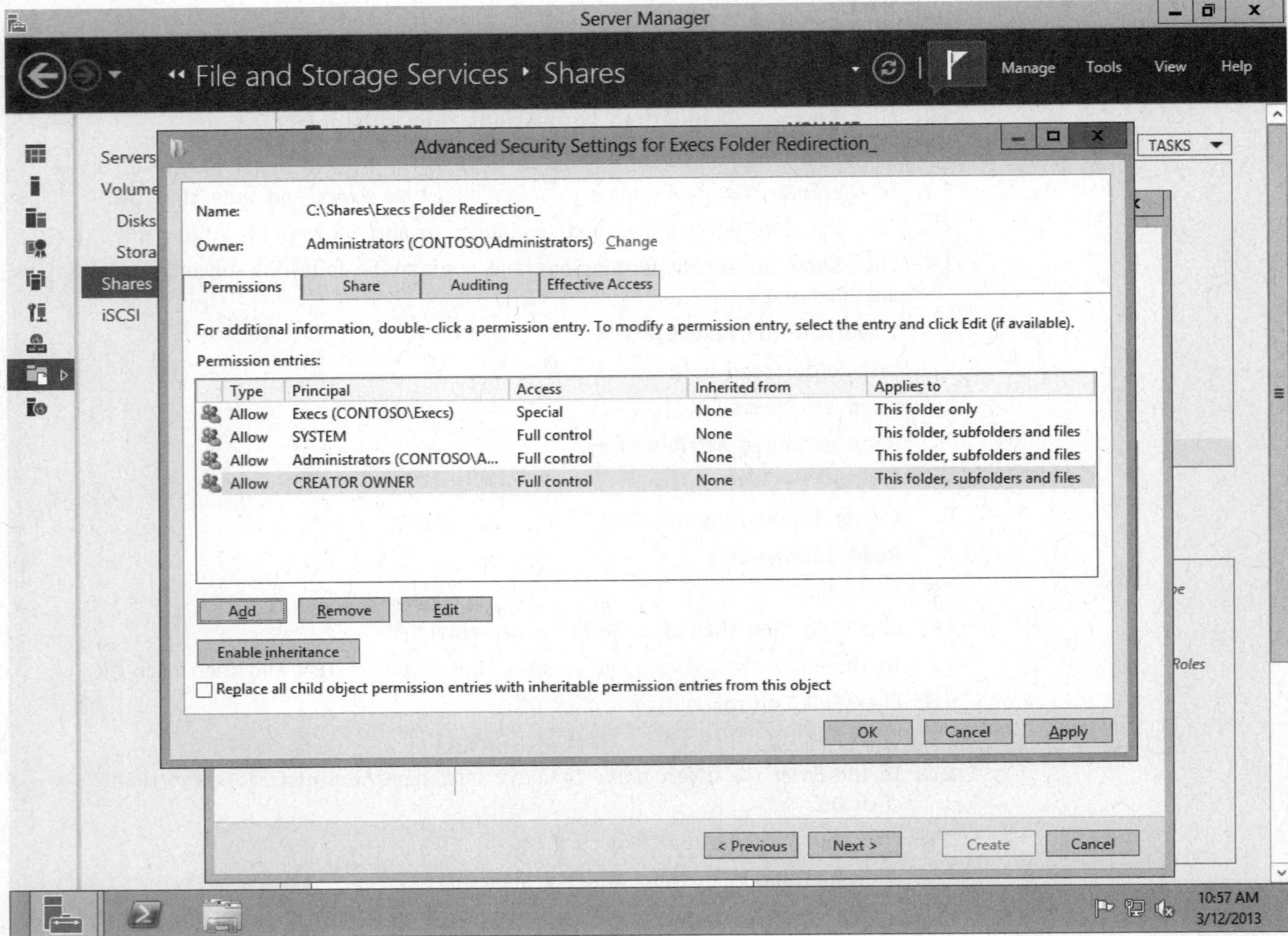

26. Click **OK** to confirm your settings and close the Advanced Security Settings for *Execs Folder Redirection* dialog box.
27. Click **Next**, confirm your settings, and then click **Create**.
28. When the share has completed, click **Close**.

Now you will create a GPO and link it to the Executive Team organizational unit to enable Folder Redirection:

1. Open Server Manager and click **Tools > Group Policy Management**.
2. Right-click the **Executive Team** organizational unit you created earlier and choose **Create a GPO in this domain, and Link it here.**
3. Type a name for the GPO (for example, **Folder Redirect for Execs**) and then click **OK**.
4. Right-click the GPO and click **Link Enabled**.

   As shown in Figure 4-8, the check indicates it is currently enabled and any settings you make will apply immediately to your users.

   Since you want to configure the policy settings first, click **OK** when the message *Do you want to change the Linked Enabled setting for this GPO Link(s)?* appears.

Figure 4-8

Disabling the Link Enabled setting prior to configuring the GPO

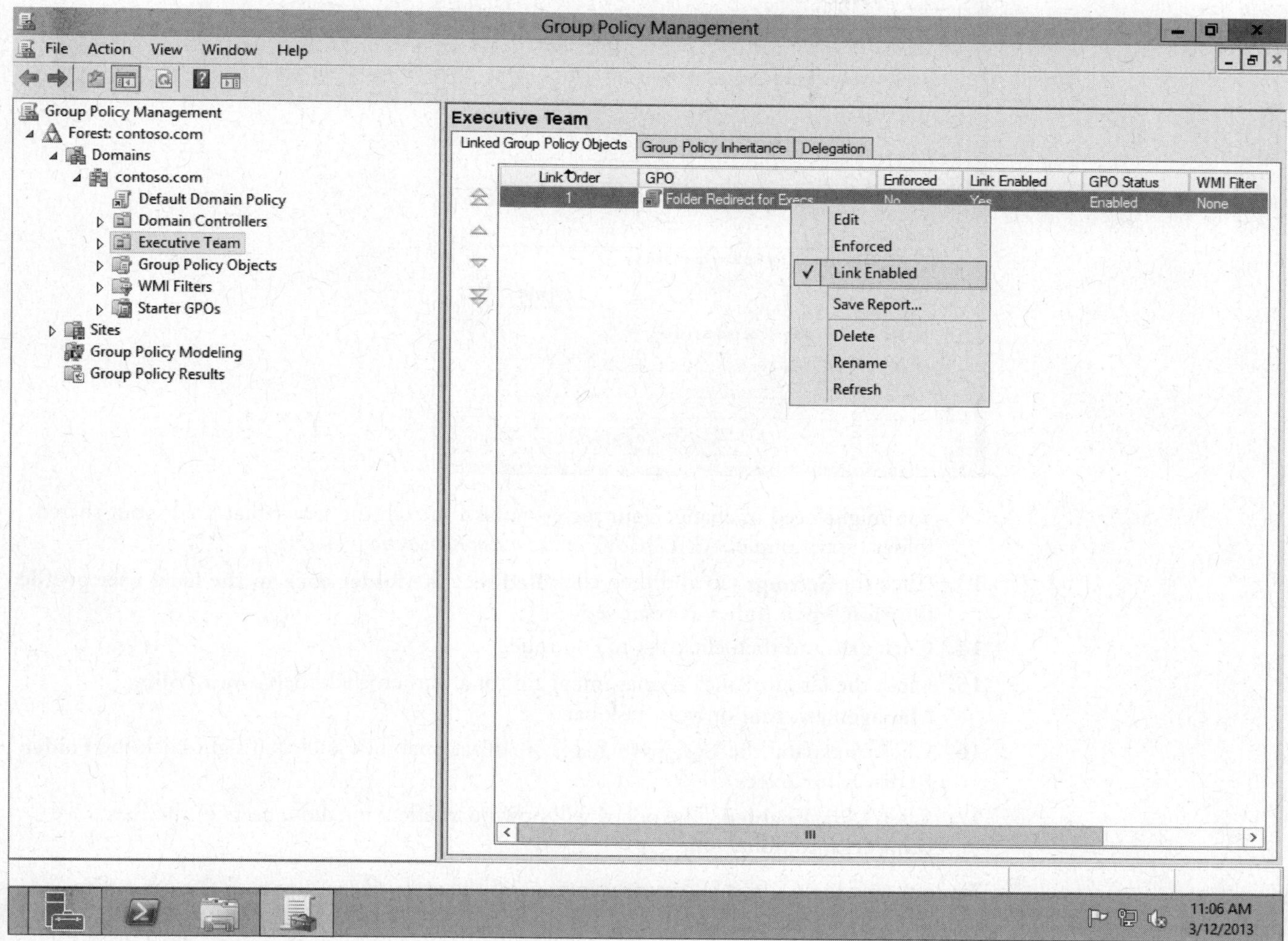

5. Expand the **Executive Team** organizational unit and click the **Folder Redirect for Execs** GPO.
6. Click the **Scope** tab and look in the *Security Filtering* pane. Click the **Authenticated Users** group and select **Remove**.
7. When the *Do you want to remove this delegation privilege?* prompt appears, click **OK** and then click **Add**.
8. In the *Enter the object name to select* box, type **Execs**.

   Execs should be the only group displayed in the *Security Filtering* section.
9. Right-click the GPO and choose **Edit**. Click **User Configuration > Policies Windows Settings > Folder Redirection**
10. Click **Folder Redirection**.
11. Locate the *Documents* folder in the right pane, right-click it, and then choose **Properties**.
12. In the *Setting* box, click the down arrow and choose **Basic - Redirect everyone's folder to the same location** and then set the *Root Path* setting to the shared folder location as shown in Figure 4-9.

Figure 4-9

Setting up folder redirect properties

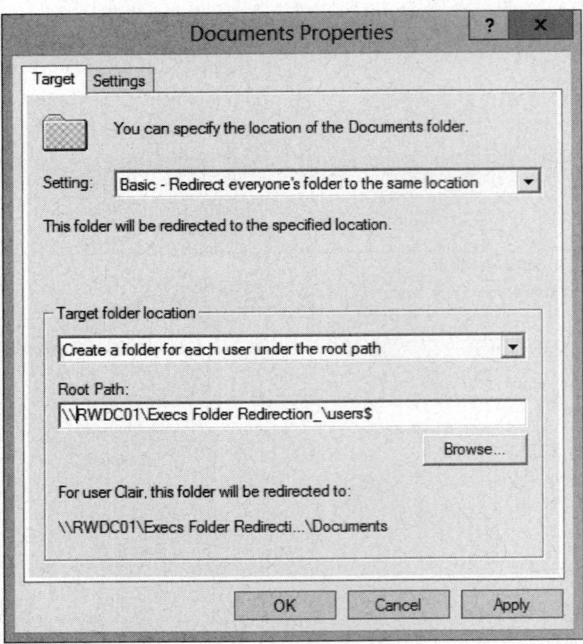

You might need to change your server name to match the server that holds your shared folder (for example, *\\RWDC01\Execs Folder Redirection_\users$*).

13. Click the **Settings** tab and then click **Redirect the folder back to the local user profile location when policy is removed.**
14. Click **OK** and then click **Yes** to continue.
15. Close the Group Policy Management Editor and then click the **Group Policy Management tool** on your task bar.
16. Click to expand the **Executive Team** organizational unit and then right-click the **Folder Redirect for Execs** GPO.
17. Click **Link Enabled**. The policy will now be in effect for those users in the Executive team organizational unit.

You can now log on from a system using one of the executive accounts to test the policy.

User Profiles (Local/Roaming)

Every user has a profile that controls the types of programs available to them as well as how the desktop looks. These profiles can be local or roaming. Roaming profiles can be automatically backed up, allowing users to log into multiple computers and still maintain the same look and feel on each computer. Local profiles allow much faster log-in times because the data is stored locally but a user's settings will not follow them around.

When users move between computers, a separate profile is created on each one. These local profiles, which contain network printer connections; mapped drives; items stored on the desktop (shortcuts); and their screen color, fonts, and wallpaper are specific to the computer where they were created. Every user that logs on to a computer creates a local user profile on the machine.

Roaming User Profiles, which support users who need to work on multiple computers, are local profiles that are stored on a shared network folder. When users log on to a computer with a roaming profile enabled, a copy of their profile is downloaded from the network and is merged with the local profile. When the users log off, their changes are updated both on the local copy and at the profile stored in the network folder. This ensures they get the same look/feel and resources regardless of the computer from which they log in.

Windows 8 introduces a new feature that controls on which computers the user can use roaming profiles and Offline Files/Folders. These assigned systems are called ***primary computers***. By using primary computers, you can protect against exposing sensitive data on a system. For example, you may not want a manager to log on to an employee's computer or on to a computer located in a general conference room. In either case, residual data can be left behind. If a user assigned to use primary computers logs on to only a computer that is not in the group, they will use a local profile instead.

You manage roaming profiles by using Group Policy in Active Directory-based networks and performing the following steps:

CREATE A ROAMING PROFILE

GET READY. Log on to the computer running Windows Server 2012 and Active Directory with domain administrative credentials, and then perform the following steps to create a roaming profile.

First, you must create a roaming user profiles security group. This will contain all users/computers that you want to apply a roaming user profile policy setting to.

1. Log in to a Windows Server 2012 computer that is performing the role of domain controller with administrative credentials. The Server Manager console opens automatically. If not, click the **Server Manager** icon on the task bar.
2. Click **Tools > Active Directory Users and Computers.**
3. Right-click the **Executive Team** organizational unit and choose **New > Group.**
4. Type the name for the security group (for example, **Roaming User Profiles**). In the *Group* scope, make sure **Security** is selected for the *Group type* and **Global** is selected for the *Group scope*.
5. Click **OK.**
6. Right-click **Beverly Kasik** and click **Add to a group.**
7. In the *Enter the object names to select* box, type **Roaming User Profiles** and then click **OK.**
8. After the *The Add to Group operating was successfully completed* message appears, click **OK.**
9. Close the *Active Directory Users and Computers* console.

Next, you must create a folder for the roaming profiles and share it.

1. From within the Server Manager, click **File and Storage Services** and then click **Shares.** If Server Manager is not open, click the Server Manager icon on the task bar.
2. Click **Tasks > New Share.**
3. On the *Select the profile for this share* page, click **SMB Share-Quick** and then click **Next.**
4. On the *Select the server and path for this share page*, click the server and the volume on which you want to create the share and click **Next.**
5. On the *Specify share name page*, in the *Share name* field, type a name for the share (for example, **RoamingUserProfiles$**) and then click **Next.** (Adding **$** after the share name hides it from users who might be browsing the network.)
6. On the *Configure share settings*, click **Next** to accept the defaults.
7. On the *Permissions* page, click **Customize permissions.** The *Advanced Security Settings* dialog box appears.
8. Click **Disable inheritance** and then click **Convert inherited permission into explicit permission on this object.**

9. Set the permissions as follows (see Figure 4-10) and remove any groups that are not listed below:

Figure 4-10

Setting permissions for roaming user profiles

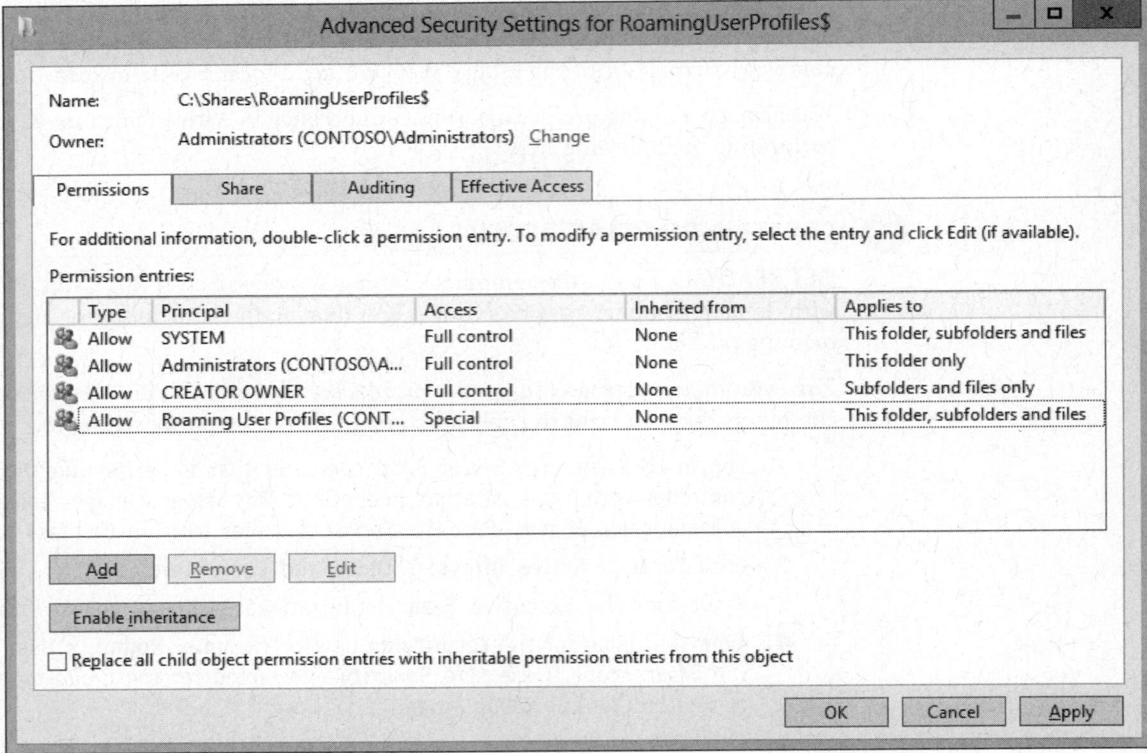

Principal: **SYSTEM**. *Type*: **Allow**. *Access*: **Full control**. *Applies to*: **This folder, subfolders and files.**

Principal: **Administrators**. *Type*: **Allow**. *Access*: **Full control**. *Applies to*: **This folder only**.

Principal: **CREATOR OWNER**. *Type*: **Allow**. *Access*: **Full control**. *Applies to*: **Subfolders and files only**.

Principal: **Roaming User Profiles**: *Type*: **Allow**. *Access*: **Special**. *Applies to*: **This folder, subfolders and files. Special permissions: List folder/read data, create folders/append data**. (To access special permissions, click the **Show advanced permissions** link.)

10. Click **OK** and then click **Next** to continue.
11. After reviewing the *Confirm selections* page, click **Create** and then click **Close**.

Next, create a Group Policy Object (GPO) to configure the Roaming User Profiles settings on your user accounts.

1. From within the Server Manager, click **Tools > Group Policy Management**.
2. Right-click the **Executive Team** organizational unit and then click **Create a GPO in this domain, and Link it here.**
3. In the *New GPO* dialog box, type a name for the GPO (for example, **Roaming User Profile Settings**) and then click **OK**.
4. Right-click the GPO and choose **Link Enabled**.

   This ensures the policy settings do not go into effect until you have finished making the necessary configurations.
5. Click the **Roaming User Profile Settings** GPO and then click the **Scope** tab.

6. In the *Security Filtering* section, click **Authenticated users** and then click **Remove**.
7. When the *Do you want to remove this delegation privilege?* prompt appears, click **OK**.
8. Click **Add** and in the *Enter the object name to select* dialog box, type **Roaming User Profiles**.
9. Click **OK**.
10. Minimize the Group Policy Management console.

Next, set up the path to the roaming profiles folder for your users:

1. From within the Server Manager, click **Tools > Active Directory Users and Computers** and then navigate to the **Executive Team** organizational unit.
2. Select the user(s) for which you want to assign a roaming user profile, right-click, and then choose **Properties** (see Figure 4-11).

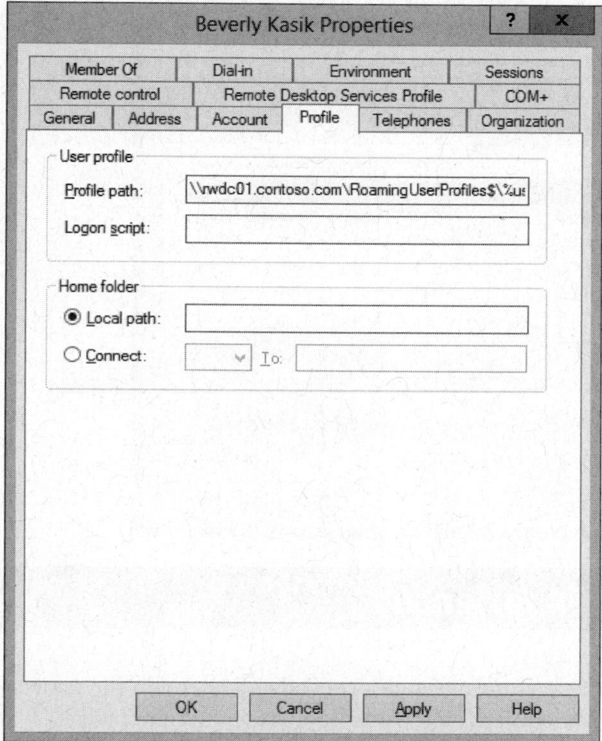

Figure 4-11
Setting the Profile path for a user

In this case, you will assign a roaming user profile only to Beverly Kasik.

3. Click the **Profile** tab. In the *Profile path* field, type the path to the file share where you want to store the user's roaming profile, followed by **%username%**. (This text is replaced automatically with the user's name the first time the user signs in.) For example: **\\rwdc01.contoso.com\RoamingUserProfiles$\%username%**.
4. Click **OK** and then **Close** the Active Directory Users and Computers console.

Next, you need to enable the roaming user profile GPO.

1. Click the **Group Policy Management** icon on your task bar. (It should be minimized. If it's not minimized on your task bar, press the **Windows logo key + r** and then type **gpmc.msc**.)
2. Navigate to the **Executive Team** organizational unit.
3. Right-click the **Roaming User Profile Settings** GPO and choose **Link Enabled**. The GPO is applied.

You can test the remaining profile by having the user (Beverly Kasik) log into a Windows 8 client computer on the domain and then perform the following steps:

1. Press the **Windows logo key + r** and type **control panel**.
2. Click **System and Security**.
3. Click **System**.
4. Click **Advanced System Settings** (you must type administrative credentials to access it).
5. In the **User Profiles** section, click **Settings**.

If you completed the exercise successfully, the account for bkasik will be listed as a roaming profile (see Figure 4-12).

Figure 4-12
Confirming the user account is roaming

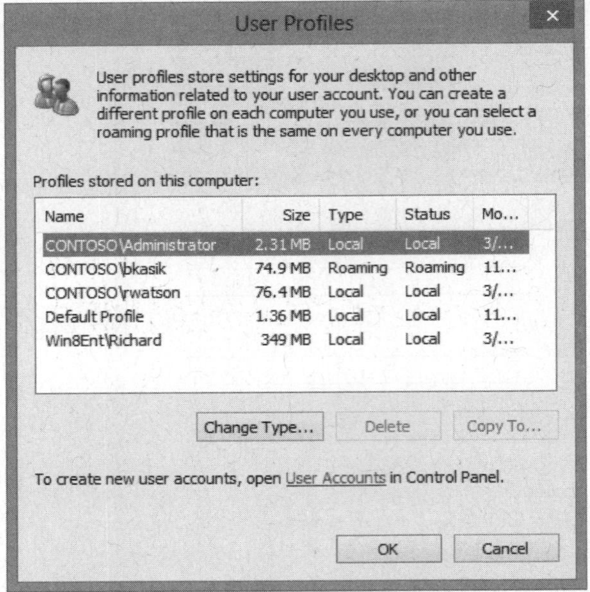

■ Virtualizing the User Experience

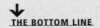

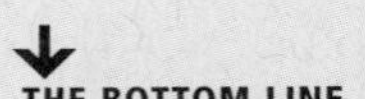
THE BOTTOM LINE

The ability to roam between devices and still maintain the same user experience is important to today's users who work from laptops, desktops, and tablets.

Roaming user profiles, redirecting folders, and accessing offline folder/files are features that enable you to access your resources while maintaining a consistent look and feel when moving between computers.

CERTIFICATION READY
User Experience Virtualization (UE-V)
Objective 1.4

Microsoft's ***User Experience Virtualization (UE-V)*** provides a similar approach across multiple devices (desktop computers, laptops, and Virtual Desktop Infrastructure [VDI] sessions). With UE-V, a user can make changes to his personal settings (operating system or applications) and then log in to a Windows 7 or Windows 8 computer without having to reconfigure them each time. It does this by roaming the operating system settings.

Although the *V* infers virtualization, UE-V does not virtualize system and application settings, but instead monitors those changes using XML templates and then saves them to a file.

TAKE NOTE*
UE-V is part of the Microsoft Desktop Optimization Pack (MDOP) 2012.

Prior to the release of UE-V, you had to create a separate profile for your physical desktop at work and another if you used a session-based desktop to connect when you were away from the office. Using UE-V, you can roam between both while still keeping your application/system settings. For example, using UE-V, you can switch between a laptop running Windows 7/8 and a tablet running Windows 8.

UE-V works on Windows 7, Windows 8 clients and servers, and Remote Desktop Services with App-V.

Understanding UE-V Templates

UE-V templates enable you to control what is stored in your datacenter and differs from a roaming profile that uploads and downloads all the user's desktop/application setting information each time.

UE-V includes the following application settings templates, which are monitored by the UE-V agent (installed on each computer). They are applied when you start the computer and are saved when you exit:

- Microsoft Office 2010 applications
- Internet Explorer 8, 9, and 10
- Windows accessories (Notepad, Calculator)

UE-V Windows settings templates (monitored by the UE-V agent) are applied when you log on, when you unlock the computer, and when you connect remotely to the computer using Remote Desktop Protocol (RDP):

- Desktop background.
- Ease of use (accessibility and input settings, magnifier, narrator, and the on-screen keyboard).
- Desktop settings.

The UE-V components include the following:

- ***UE-V Agent:*** Watches the applications and operating system processes identified within the templates while you are connected. When you close the application or the operating system is shut down/locked, the information regarding the changes is saved to the settings storage location.
- Settings storage location: A network share folder or the home directory in Active Directory.
- Settings location template: XML files that define what the UE-V Agent captures from and applies to your computers.
- Settings package: This is where the application and operating system settings are stored. It is a collection of the information included in the templates.
- ***UE-V Generator:*** A tool used to create your own custom templates. It works by monitoring what the application reads and writes to the registry and what it does with supporting files. After this information is captured, you can use it to create a custom template and deploy it to your computers.

SKILL SUMMARY

IN THIS LESSON YOU LEARNED:

- Windows 8 computers allow you to configure several different account types. They include the Microsoft user account, which enables you to move between multiple Windows 8 devices while maintaining the existing look/feel of your desktop; the local user account that provides access to resources on the local machine only, and the domain-based account that required Active Directory. Domain-based accounts provide a central domain controller to manage authentication across the entire domain.

- Workgroups are a collection of computers that have no central authority and that in domains, user accounts are stored in Active Directory as objects. The user accounts, authentication and security are handled very differently between the two.
- Use profiles contain network environment settings along with desktop configurations. These profiles can either be stored locally or on a central server. The latter are called roaming profiles. Roaming profiles can be backed up and allow users to login to any computer in the domain and be authenticated.
- Offline Files/Folders, Folder Redirection and Roaming User Profiles are all features in Windows 8 that enable you to centrally store user data and settings. Offline Files/Folders take files and folders and make them available when you are not connected to the network. Folder Redirection replicates user data to a centralized folder so you can access your files/folders from any computer. Roaming User Profiles enables you to store your choices in personalization in a centralized folder and then download them to another computer when you log on.
- User Experience Virtualization (UE-V) allows a user to make changes to his personal settings (operating system/application settings) and log in to a Windows 7/8 device without having to reconfigure them. This provides a similar approach to roaming profiles across multiple devices (desktop computers, laptops, and VDI sessions). Although the *V* infers virtualization, UE-V does not virtualize system and application settings, but instead monitors changes using XML template files when they are saved to a file in a network share folder called the *settings storage location.*

■ Knowledge Assessment

Multiple Choice

1. Which of the following accounts can be created and used with Windows 8? (Select all that apply.)
   a. Domain-based user accounts
   b. Local user accounts
   c. Network accounts
   d. Microsoft user accounts
2. Which of the following features can be used to create and manage user accounts in a domain? (Select all that apply.)
   a. useracct.msc
   b. dnsadd
   c. Active Directory Administrative Center
   d. useradd.exe
3. Which type of group is used to assign permissions to resources?
   a. Local user group
   b. Security group
   c. Distribution group
   d. Permissions group
4. Which of the following features provides users with a consistent desktop experience across multiple devices (desktops, laptops, VDI)?
   a. Active Directory Virtualization
   b. App-V

c. User Experience Virtualization (UE-V)
d. Roaming User Profiles

5. Which of the following steps are included in the creation of a Folder Redirection policy? (Select all that apply.)
   a. Create a security group
   b. Create a shared folder
   c. Create and configure a GPO
   d. Enable a GPO

6. Which of the following features is not a component of UE-V?
   a. UE-V Agent
   b. Settings package
   c. UE-V Generator
   d. GPEditor

7. A GPO for Folder Redirection can be applied at which of the following levels of the Active Directory hierarchy?
   a. Domain
   b. Organizational unit
   c. User
   d. Computer

8. Which of the following tools is used to create a Group Policy?
   a. Group Policy Management
   b. Active Directory Users and Computers
   c. gpadd.exe
   d. Group Policy Configuration and Management console

9. Which of the following features enables users to store their choices in desktop personalization in a central folder and then download to another computer when they log on?
   a. Roaming files
   b. Offline Files
   c. Folder Redirection
   d. Microsoft Account Management

10. Which of the following accounts are created by default on a Windows 8 Enterprise system? (Select all that apply.)
    a. Guest
    b. Windows Guest
    c. Administrator
    d. Admin

Best Answer

Choose the letter that corresponds to the best answer. More than one answer choice may achieve the goal. Select the BEST answer.

1. Which of the following caching settings enables users to cache programs and run them directly from the client?
   a. All files and programs that users open from the shared folder are available offline.
   b. All files and programs that users open from the shared folder are available offline/Optimize for performance.
   c. No files or programs from this shared folder are available offline/Optimize for performance.
   d. Optimize for performance.

2. You want access to your files from any computer in the domain even when not connected to the domain. You also want to personalize your desktop settings and be able to maintain them when you log on to other computer in the domain. Which of the following features best help you achieve your goals?
   a. `Folder Redirection`
   b. `Folder Redirection and Offline Files/Folders`
   c. `Roaming User Profiles and Folder Redirection.`
   d. `Folder Redirection, Offline Files/Folders and Roaming User Profiles`

3. You are configuring folder redirection for a user on your network. Which of the following root path settings ensures the folder is redirected correctly?
   a. `\\rwdc01\roamingfoldershare\users`
   b. `c:\rwdc01\roamingfoldershare\users$`
   c. `\\rwdc01\roamingfoldershare\$users`
   d. `\\rwdc01\roamingfoldershare\users$`

4. Which of the following names best represents a UPN name for the domain contoso.com?
   a. `user@contoso.com`
   b. `user/contoso.com`
   c. `contoso/user`
   d. `contoso.com/user`

5. You would like to set up an account on your Windows 8 laptop computer that will allow you to synchronize your personal settings and Windows apps across three other Windows 8 devices. Which of the following accounts would you create?
   a. `Active Directory domain account with roaming profiles in place`
   b. `Local user account`
   c. `Microsoft User account`
   d. `Administrator account`

Matching and Identification

1. Match the term to the task or scenario it is associated with:
   _______ a) `Local account`
   _______ b) `Domain account`
   _______ c) `Roaming profile`
   _______ d) `User Account Control (UAC)`
   _______ e) Organizational unit (OU)
   1. Create this when you want users to be able to store their personalization choices in a centralized folder.
   2. This is a general-purpose container in Active Directory.
   3. These are used in workgroups and must be created on each computer in order to gain access to the resources it contains.
   4. This is a feature designed to warn you when you are about to perform an administrative-level task.
   5. This can be used to log on to multiple computers in the domain using the same user name and password.

2. Write the term that is associated with the task or scenario:
   _______ A group of computers that interacts with each other but has no centralized authority.
   _______ Allows you to synchronize your personal settings across multiple Windows 8 devices.
   _______ If enabled, it bypasses the User Account Control (UAC) warnings.

_________ This is unique to each user account and is the reason you cannot delete the account and recreate it under the same name and still preserve permissions associated with the original account.
_________ A group type used in Active Directory to assign permissions to resources.

Build a List

1. Specify the correct order of the steps that must be completed to create a Microsoft User account after Windows 8 has been installed.
   _________ Click **Settings** (the gear icon).
   _________ Click **Change PC Settings**.
   _________ Point your cursor to the top- or bottom-right corner of the screen to make the Charms bar appear.
   _________ Log in to the Windows 8 client computer.
   _________ Click **Add a user**.
   _________ Click **Finish**.
   _________ Type the e-mail address you want to use and then click **Next**.
   _________ Click **Users**.
2. Specify the correct order of the steps that must be completed when managing Folder Redirection with Group Policy in Active Directory.
   _________ Create a security group that contains the user whose files you want to redirect.
   _________ Enable the GPO.
   _________ Create and share a folder to hold the redirected files.
   _________ Create a GPO and then configure it to apply Folder Redirection.
   _________ Sign in from a computer in which the policy has been applied to test it.
3. Specify the correct order of the steps that must be completed to create a new Group in Active Directory within an organizational unit.
   _________ Click **Tools > Active Directory Users and Computers**.
   _________ Type the name for the group and then click **OK**.
   _________ In the *Virtual hard disk format* section, leave the default setting of **Fixed size (recommended)**.
   _________ Right-click the organizational unit in which you want to create the group account and then choose **New > Group**.
   _________ Log in to a Windows Server 2012 computer that is performing the role of domain controller and then open the Server Manager.
   _________ Right-click a user and choose **Add to a group**. In the *Enter the object names to select* box, type the name of the group and then click **OK**.

Business Case Scenarios

Scenario 4-1: Troubleshooting Folder Redirection

You have set up an OU and added four accounts to it. You want to configure Folder Redirection to allow these four users' Documents folder to be stored on a central server. After configuring the GPO, you disable the Link Enabled setting and then configure it. After making sure you have all the right settings for both the policy and the shared folder permissions, you visit a client computer and log on as one of the users. After checking, you notice the folder redirect did not work. What could have happened?

Scenario 4-2: Managing User Accounts

You created a user account in Active Directory for an employee in HR and added them to a group called HRDocMgrs. A few weeks later, you hear the employee has taken leave and will return in a month. You decide to delete the account and set it up when she returns to maintain security on your network. After a month passes, the user returns, and you are asked to set up her account.

You create the same user name she used last time and send her an e-mail, letting her know that she can log on the network. A few minutes later, you hear back from the user, who states that she can log on but cannot access any of the documents in the HRDocMgrs folder. What could have happened?

Scenario 4-3: Configuring Offline Files/Folders

You have been asked to configure Offline Files/Folders for a directory on your server called Docs. Within the Docs folder is a subfolder called BluePrints that you are told not to make available for caching.

After sharing the Docs folder, the Windows 2012 server uses its default settings to enabled Offline Files/Folders caching. When you connect to the BluePrints folder from a computer on the network, you notice that you can select whether or not to cache files from the folder. What happened?

Designing for Network Connectivity

LESSON 5

70-688 EXAM OBJECTIVE

Objective 2.1 – Design for network connectivity. This objective may include but is not limited to the following design considerations: IPv4 and IPv6; name resolution; wireless; network security; network settings.

LESSON HEADING	EXAM OBJECTIVE
Designing for Network Connectivity	
Exploring the IPv4 and IPv6 Protocols	IPv4 and IPv6
Understanding Name Resolution	Name resolution
Exploring Network Settings	Network settings
Working with Wireless Networks	Wireless
Implementing Network Security for Windows 8	Network security

KEY TERMS

802.11a
802.11b
802.11g
802.11i
802.11n
802.1x
ad-hoc
ANDing
connection security rules
DNS Security Extensions (DNSSEC)
Domain Name System (DNS)
domain profile
Dynamic Host Configuration Protocol (DHCP)
enterprise mode
Extensible Authentication Protocol (EAP)
host ID
host-based firewall
inbound rules
infrastructure mode
Internet Protocol (IP)
key signing key (KSK)
lease period
Link-Local Multicast Name Resolution (LLMNR)
name resolution
name server
network ID
network perimeter firewalls
outbound rules
personal mode
private profile
public profile
Remote Authentication Dial-In User Service (RADIUS) server
resolver
router
Service Set Identifier (SSID)
stateful address configuration
stateless address configuration
subnetting
Transmission Protocol/Internet Protocol (TCP/IP)
Wi-Fi Protected Access (WPA)
Wi-Fi Protected Access (WPA) v2
Windows Firewall with Advanced Security (WFAS)
Windows Internet Name Services (WINS)
Wireless Equivalent Privacy (WEP)

■ Designing For Network Connectivity

THE BOTTOM LINE

Designing network connectivity in today's networks requires you to make decisions about using IPv4/IPv6, designing a name resolution strategy, and understanding how to configure your wired and wireless network for security.

When accessing computers on a network, you typically communicate by using their host names. If you are accessing a website, you enter a friendly name such as www.microsoft.com. Every device that connects to your network or the Internet must have an Internet Protocol (IP) address. You also need a way to associate these names to their assigned IP address. This process is called ***name resolution***.

Internet Protocol (IP) is the key protocol in the TCP/IP suite. It is responsible for adding addressing information to the packets for the sender and the receiver, as well as adding data to help route and deliver the packet. Windows 8 uses TCP/IP as its default networking protocol.

Transmission Protocol/Internet Protocol (TCP/IP) is a set of protocols that allows computers to exchange data within a network and between networks. These protocols (or rules) manage the content, format, timing, sequencing, and error control of the messages that are exchanged between the devices. Every device that communicates over TCP/IP must have a unique IP address. Windows 8 uses a dual-layer architecture that enables it to implement both IPv4 and IPv6 address schemes. Both share the common TCP transport layer protocol.

Before configuring TCP/IP on your network, take time to plan the implementation. For example, how big do you expect your network to be? How will your network be designed from a physical and logical standpoint?

Exploring the IPv4 and IPv6 Protocols

Microsoft, along with other industry leaders, is working hard to make IPv6 the next standard for IP addressing. In the meantime, you have a mixture of IPv4 and IPv6 devices on your network, so you need to understand how these devices are configured and how they interact with each other.

CERTIFICATION READY
IPv4 and IPv6
Objective 2.1

During the 1960s, several universities and research centers needed a network to share information. To address this need, a U.S. government agency called the Advanced Research Projects Agency (ARPA) developed the ARPANET, which initially used the Network Control Protocol (NCP) to handle file transfers, remote login, and e-mail needs. NCP, the predecessor to TCP/IP, was first used in 1972. By 1973, the protocol no longer met the needs of its users, and research was done to find a better solution. TCP/IPv4 was introduced and standardized in 1981 and is still in use today. Microsoft and other industry leaders have been working for years to roll out a newer version: IPv6.

TAKE NOTE*

IPv6 is not backward-compatible with IPv4. An IPv6-only device cannot talk to an IPv4 device. Your current transition strategy should be to use both in the short term.

The goal of IPv6 is to address the exhaustion of the IPv4 address space, which supports about 4 billion addresses. At the time IPv4 was created, no one considered that anything other than computers would be connected. As more computers, smartphones, tablets, and home appliances are being attached to the Internet, the IP4 address space is quickly being exhausted.

Over the years, engineers have found ways to reduce the number of addresses needed through a process called network address translation (NAT). Instead of assigning an IPv4 public address to every device on your network, you can purchase a single IPv4 address and allow all devices behind your router to share the same address. Still, as each year passes and the number of devices connected to the Internet continue to grow exponentially, IPv6 will eventually take over as the main addressing scheme. In the meantime, let's take a closer look at each of the protocols.

UNDERSTANDING IPV4

An IPv4 address is a 32-bit-long number assigned to a host on the network. These addresses are broken into four different sections called octets, which are 8 bits long. For example, the number 192.160.10.2 in binary is 11000000.10100000.00001010.00000010 (see Figure 5-1).

Figure 5-1

Converting binary to decimal

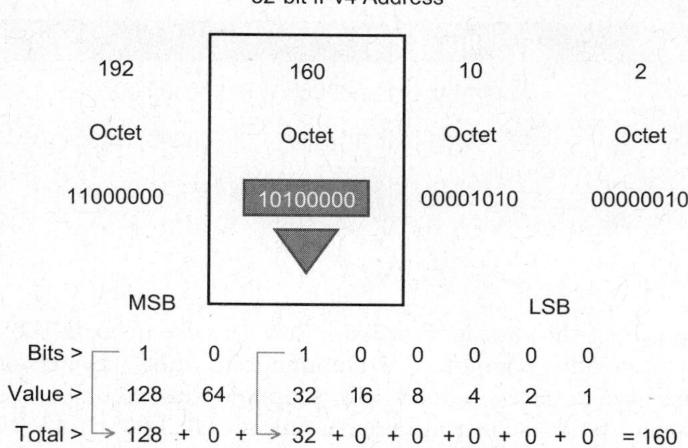

A portion of the 32 bits is associated with the network on which the computer is physically located. This portion of bits is called the ***network ID***. The remaining bits, allocated to the host, are called the ***host ID***. All computers on the same local network share the same network ID, but each has its own unique host ID.

A subnet mask, also 32 bits long, is used to determine which of the 32 bits represent the network ID and which represent the host ID (see Table 5-1). The class of IP address you are using determines the default subnet mask. IPv4 addresses are divided into classes based on the number in the first octet of the IP address. These classes were originally designed to support different organizational sizes. However, classful IP addressing is very wasteful and has mostly been discarded.

There are five classes of IP addresses (see Table 5-1).

Table 5-1

TCP/IP v4 Address Classes

Class	Range	Network ID (Octet)	Host ID (Octet)	Number of Networks	Number of Hosts
A	1–127*	First octet	Second, third, and fourth octet	126	16,777,214
B	128–191	First and second octets	Third and fourth octet	16,384	65,534
C	192–223	First, second, and third octets	Fourth octet	2,097,152	254
D	224–239	N/A	N/A	N/A	N/A
E	240–254	N/A	N/A	N/A	N/A

(*), 0, 127, and 255 are reserved and cannot be used for a specific host. An IP address with all 0s in the host ID describes the network, whereas 127 in the first octet is reserved for loopback testing and handling traffic to the local host. An IP address using 255s in the host ID is a broadcast transmitting to all interfaces on the specified network.

Table 5-2 shows the default subnet masks for each class along with its binary and decimal values.

Table 5-2

Default Subnet Masks for IPv4 Address Classes

Class	Binary	Decimal
A	11111111.00000000.00000000.00000000	255.0.0.0
B	11111111.11111111.00000000.00000000	255.255.0.0
C	11111111.11111111.11111111.00000000	255.255.255.0

If a host is on the same local network (has the same network ID), it can issue broadcast packets to locate other computers. To communicate with computers on a separate network, the packets have to traverse a router. To determine when a computer is on another network, your computer uses the subnet mask and a process called logical ***ANDing***.

Because ANDing is performed using binary, you have to convert the IP address and the subnet mask to binary form. After you complete the conversions, you match up binary 1s (between the IP address and the subnet mask). If there is a 1 in the binary address of the IP and a 1 in the binary address of the subnet mask, set the binary number in the ANDing row to binary 1 (see Figure 5-2). After you complete the process, add up the values, as demonstrated in Figure 5-1. When you are using it for a default subnet mask, it really isn't necessary; but when your network is subnetted, the network ID is a little harder to decipher.

Figure 5-2

Using ANDing to determine network location

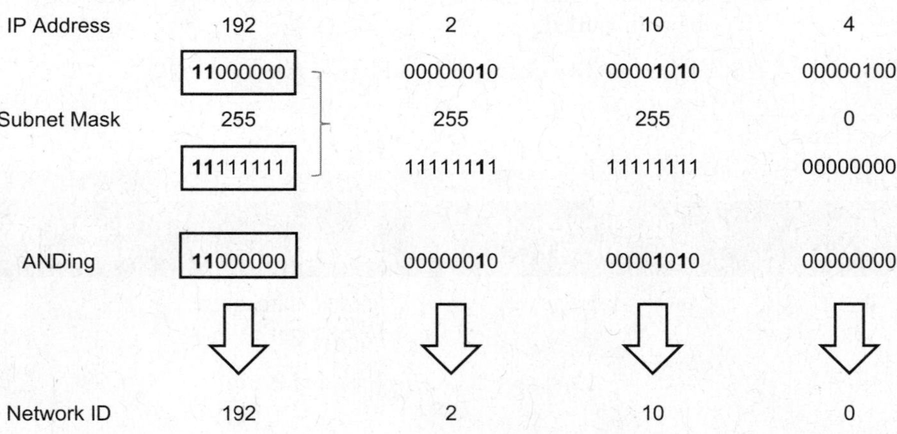

If the computer is determined to be on another network after the ANDing process is completed, the packet is sent to the default gateway configured on the computer (for example, the router's IP address). The router then uses information in its routing tables to locate and transfer your packet to the destination computer.

Subnetting is the process used to break a larger network into smaller segments. For example, a Class B IP address has more than 65,000 host addresses for a single logical segment. Adding that many computers to a single network isn't feasible. If you break the larger network into smaller segments (for example, 254 subnetworks), each can host up to 254 hosts. You accomplish subnetting by stealing bits from the host portion of an address to create a new subnet section.

UNDERSTANDING IPV6

The main advantage that IPv6 has over IPv4 is a much larger address space. An IPv6 address is a 128-bit-long number assigned to a host on the network. These addresses are broken into eight different blocks or groups. Each block is 16 bits long and is represented in hexadecimal, separated by a colon:

- Fe80:0:ac4a:aa04:e713A:0:0:CE2B

A standard IPv6 unicast address uses the first 64 bits to represent the network ID and the remaining bits to represent the host's network interface. The host network interface is generated from the interface's Media Access Control (MAC) address. The MAC address is assigned by the manufacturer of the network interface card and is burned into the hardware.

If a block is set to 0 and is followed by another block set to 0, it can be written as ::. Using this notation, the preceding address would be written as Fe80:0:ac4a:aa04:e713A::CE2B.

TAKE NOTE* When a network card is configured In Windows 8, it automatically has both an IPv4 and IPv6 address by default. This is called a dual stack.

The transition from IPv4 to IPv6 is expected to take several more years. In the meantime, expect to see a mix of IPv4, IPv4/IPv6 (dual stack), and IPv6-only networks.

USE CMD AND WINDOWS POWERSHELL TO VIEW IP ADDRESS INFORMATION

GET READY. To use cmd and Windows PowerShell to view your IP address configuration, perform the following steps:

1. Press the **Windows logo key + r**.
2. Type **cmd** and then press **Enter**.
3. Type **ipconfig** and then press **Enter**.
4. Review your settings. You should see both an IPv4 and IPv6 address.
5. Type **exit** and then press **Enter** to close the cmd shell.
6. Press the **Windows logo key + r**.
7. Type **PowerShell**.
8. Type **Resolve-DNSName** *<website address>* (for example, **Resolve-DNSName** www.cnn.com) and then press **Enter**.
9. Review the address records returned.

   Does the site support IPv6?
10. Type **Resolve-DNSName** www.comcast.net and then press **Enter**.
11. Review the address records returned (see Figure 5-3).

    Does the site support IPv6?

Figure 5-3

Analyzing IPv6 records retrieved using resolve-DNSName

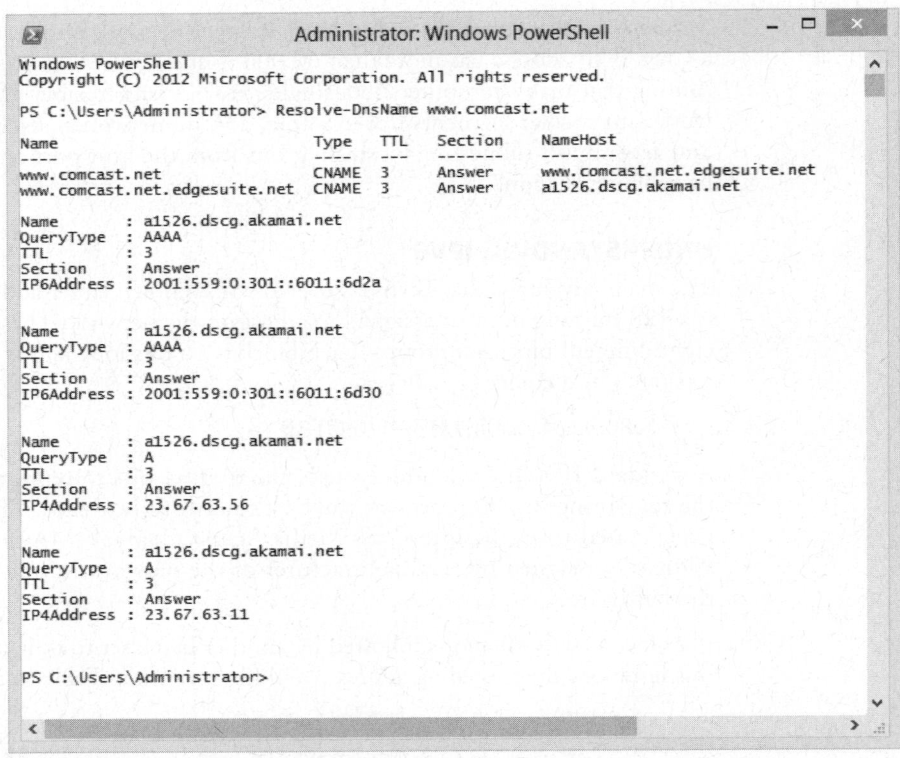

Administrator: Windows PowerShell
Windows PowerShell
Copyright (C) 2012 Microsoft Corporation. All rights reserved.
PS C:\Users\Administrator> Resolve-DnsName www.comcast.net
Name Type TTL Section NameHost
www.comcast.net CNAME 3 Answer www.comcast.net.edgesuite.net
www.comcast.net.edgesuite.net CNAME 3 Answer a1526.dscg.akamai.net
Name : a1526.dscg.akamai.net
QueryType : AAAA
TTL : 3
Section : Answer
IP6Address : 2001:559:0:301::6011:6d2a
Name : a1526.dscg.akamai.net
QueryType : AAAA
TTL : 3
Section : Answer
IP6Address : 2001:559:0:301::6011:6d30
Name : a1526.dscg.akamai.net
QueryType : A
TTL : 3
Section : Answer
IP4Address : 23.67.63.56
Name : a1526.dscg.akamai.net
QueryType : A
TTL : 3
Section : Answer
IP4Address : 23.67.63.11
PS C:\Users\Administrator>

Understanding Name Resolution

Name resolution is the process of converting friendly names to IP addresses. Windows 8 uses DNS, WINS, and LLMNR.

CERTIFICATION READY
Name resolution
Objective 2.1

Name resolution is the process of associating host names to IP addresses. The Windows operating system supports three name resolution systems:

- Domain Name System (DNS)
- Windows Internet Name Service (WINS)
- Link Local Multicast Name Resolution (LLMNR)

EXPLORING THE DOMAIN NAME SYSTEM (DNS)

Domain Name System (DNS) servers are used to associate a computer name such as web1.eastcoast.contoso.com to an IP address. It works over TCP/IP and can be integrated with other services such as WINS, DHCP, and Active Directory. To understand DNS, you first need to review its hierarchical structure. This arrangement, which is called the DNS namespace, is shown in Figure 5-4.

The root domain is managed by the Internet Corporation for Assigned Names and Numbers (ICANN) under the authority of the U.S. Department of Commerce. It is essential for the function of the Internet; without the root domain, services that depend upon DNS (e-mail, browsing the Internet, and so on) would not function. Although the root domain is represented by a single period, it is supported by several hundred root servers spread across the world (to see where they are located, visit the Root Server website). The root servers have a file (zone file) that lists the names and IP addresses of the authoritative DNS servers for all top-level domains.

Figure 5-4

Exploring the DNS namespace

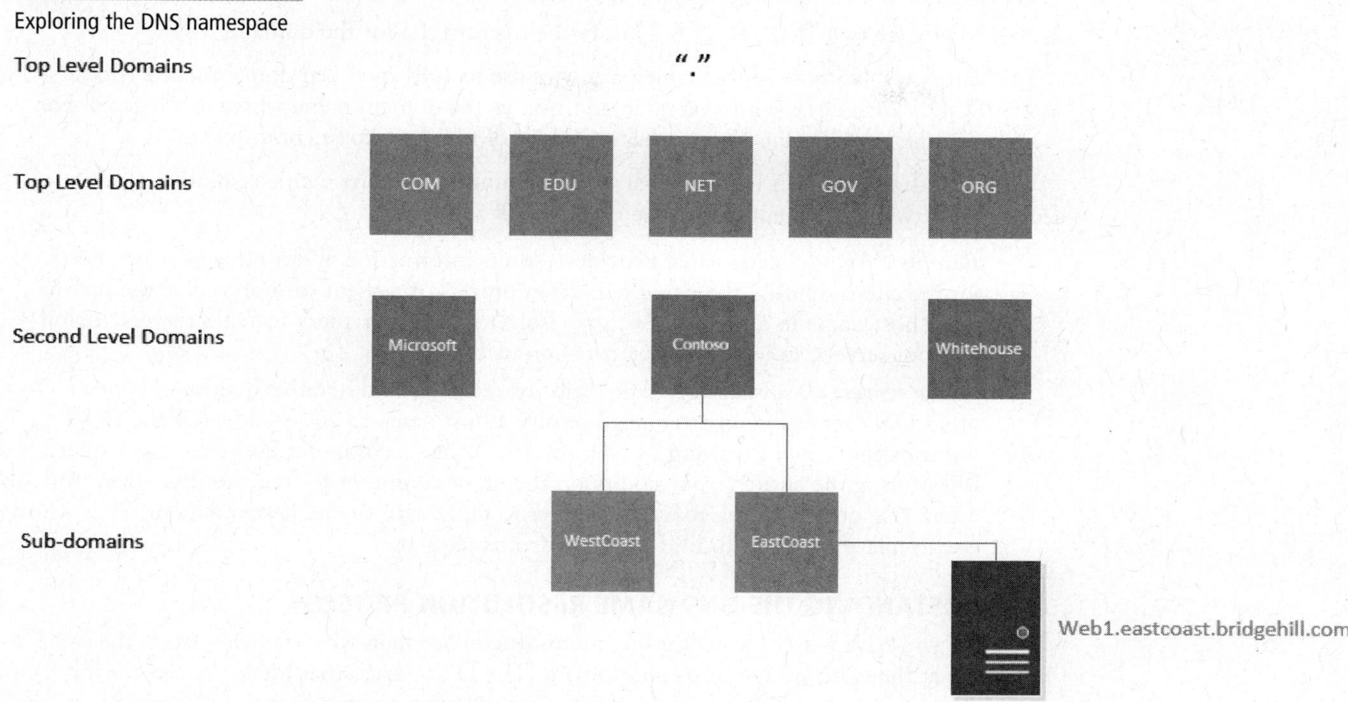

Top-level domains define the organization type or geographic location. For example, .com is for commercial organizations, .gov is for government agencies, .org is for nonprofits, and so on.

Second-level domains, also called parent domains, can be divided into subdomains (child domains). When registering a second level domain for an organization, it is common to register multiple second-level domains (microsoft.com, microsoft.org, microsoft.net) to ensure that users can reach them regardless of whether they type .com, .net, or .org at the end of the address.

Active Directory domains utilize DNS when implementing their hierarchy and naming structure. When you install the first domain controller on a network, you are asked to install DNS automatically. When fully integrated with DNS, all domain controllers can access the data, replicate changes throughout the domain, and register clients into their zone. A zone is a scope of names that are served by a specific DNS name server. The part of the namespace that a zone is responsible for is known as the zone of authority. A zone must contain at least one domain, called the root domain of that zone. All the information about each zone is stored in a file called the zone database file. Inside the zone database file are the resource records that DNS uses to resolve host names to IP addresses.

The DNS server that creates and modifies a locally stored zone file is called the primary name server. A secondary name server is often used and holds a copy of the zone file that it gets from the primary name server. Updates to the primary name server are automatically replicated to the secondary name server. This process, called a zone transfer, provides redundancy for name resolution if one of the servers fails.

Here are a few of the record types you will find in a zone database file:

- Start of Authority (SOA) records are the first records added to a zone. They define parameters for the zone and include the name of the primary name server.
- Name Server (NS) records list any additional name servers for the zone.
- Address (host name) (A) records associate a host name to an IP4 address.
- Address (host name) (AAAA) records associate a host name to its IPv6 address.

- Pointer (PTR) records associate an IP address to a host name.
- Mail Exchange (MX) records identify the mail host(s) for the domain.

To identify a DNS host in the namespace, you use its fully qualified domain name (FQDN). The FQDN includes the host name in addition to the domain name where it is located. For example, the server in the diagram has a FQDN of web1.eastcoast.contoso.com.

Understanding the DNS hierarchy can help you understand how name resolution works. DNS uses two components to resolve names to IP addresses:

- ***Resolver:*** An application that provides address information about other network hosts for the client. During the name resolution process, if a client cannot resolve the destination's host name to an IP address, the resolver will send a query to DNS servers, including root servers, to look up the records on its behalf.
- ***Name server:*** This is a server that performs recursive and iterative queries to contact other DNS servers in an attempt to resolve a host name to an IP address if the DNS server cannot resolve it using its own records. When a computer uses a recursive query, it is putting the entire responsibility on the other computer to find the IP address. An interactive query is a call to a name server to reply with the requested data or tell it who else to talk to in order to find an answer to its request.

UNDERSTANDING THE DNS NAME RESOLUTION PROCESS

Let's say you have a user located in the microsoft.com domain who wants to access the web1 resource at the eastcoast.contoso.com domain. The DNS server that holds the records for web1 (authoritative server) is located in the eastcoast.contoso.com domain. The process works as shown in Figure 5-5.

Figure 5-5

Tracing DNS name resolution

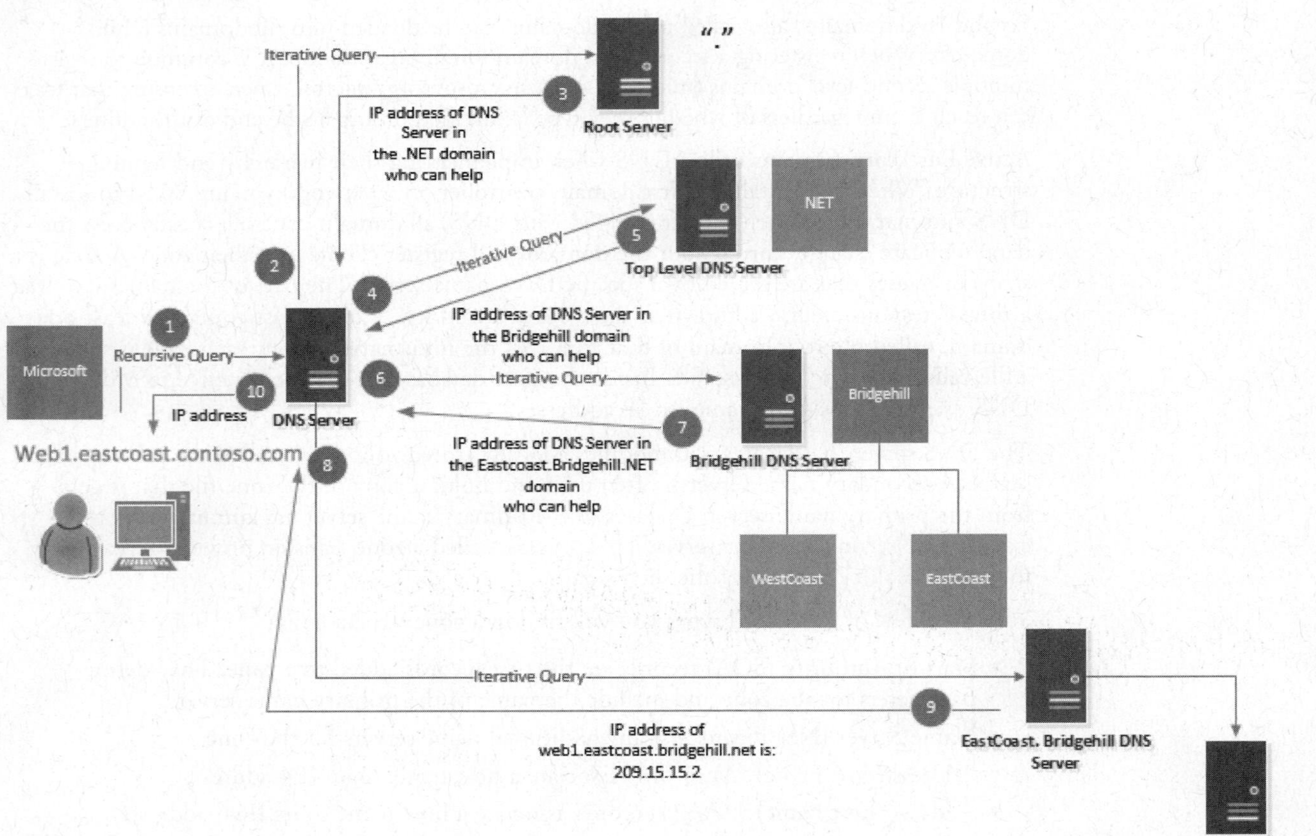

1. The resolver running on the client would send a recursive query to a DNS server located in its local domain, asking it to resolve web1.eastcoast.contoso.com to an IP address. Because this is a recursive query, the client is putting the entire responsibility for finding the answer on its local DNS server.
2. The user's local DNS server would first check its local cache to see whether it has a record on file for web1.eastcoast.contoso.com. Assuming that there was no information available, the DNS server would send an iterative query to a root server.
3. The root server would respond with the IP address of a DNS server located in the top-level domain for .NET.
4. The user's local DNS server would then send an iterative query to the DNS server located in the .NET domain, asking for the IP address to web1.eastcoast.contoso.com.
5. The .NET name server would reply with the IP address of a DNS server located in the contoso domain.
6. The user's local DNS server would then send an iterative query to the DNS server located in the contoso domain.
7. The DNS server located in the contoso domain would then respond with a DNS server located in the eastcoast.contoso domain.
8. The user's local DNS server would send another query to the DNS server located in the eastcoast.contoso.com domain.
9. The DNS server in the eastcoast.contoso.com domain would respond with the IP address for web1.eastcoast.contoso.com.
10. The local DNS server would return the IP address to the client.

The name server's host-to-IP address mappings are collected during the process of receiving and responding to recursive and iterative queries. The name servers use this stored information to resolve host names quickly. This method of storing information is called caching. The information is stored in the cache for a certain amount of time determined by the Time to Live (TTL) setting set by the Administrator on the DNS server located at eastcoast.contoso.com who owns the record. In addition to the local name server storing the information, the client resolver also stores information about recently resolved host names for a time specified by the TTL value.

Now that you have a better idea of how name resolution works, how can you be assured that the name server responding to the request is not a rogue server trying to redirect you to a malicious host or website? That's where DNS Security Extensions comes in.

USING DNS SECURITY EXTENSIONS (DNSSEC) FOR DNS ZONE FILES

In its original configuration, DNS was not designed with security in mind. When a local resolver received a response to its request for a host IP address, it accepted the first response it received. This response could be from a valid server or it could be from a rogue server attempting to redirect it to another host.

DNS Security Extensions (DNSSEC) was implemented to provide a way to confirm that the server sending the response is who it claims to be.

DNSSEC uses public key cryptography to digitally sign a zone that in turn signs all the records in the zone. It adds four new DNS resource records: resource record signature (RRSIG), DNS public key (DNSKey), delegation signer (DS), and next secure (NSEC). These records are called resource record signature (RRSIG) records. The public key is stored inside the DNSKey resource records. The resolver uses the public key to validate the signatures and thus authenticate them.

To sign a DNS zone, right-click the zone and then choose *DNSSEC > Sign the Zone*. As part of the signing process, you choose a key master, which is the DNS server that generates and manages the keys for the DNSSEC-protected zone. Any DNS server that hosts a primary copy of the zone can be the key master. You will also need to configure a ***key signing key (KSK)***. The KSK is an authentication key that corresponds to the private key used to sign one or more other signing keys. In most cases, the private key that corresponds to a KSK signs other keys used for signing the zone.

In Windows 8 and Windows Server 2012, when the DNS client receives a response to a DNS query, it checks to see whether the response has been validated by a DNS server. When issuing queries, the DNS client relies on its local DNS server to confirm that the validation is successful. In both cases, the DNS client only checks for validation; it does not perform the validation itself.

USING WINDOWS INTERNET NAME SERVICE

Windows Internet Name Services (WINS) is another name resolution service that you find on some networks to help pre–Windows 2000 computers to resolve a computer name to an IP address. These older systems use NetBIOS over TCP/IP, which requires either a static LMHOSTS file (located on each computer) or a WINS server to resolve the names. Without a WINS server, these systems rely on broadcast messages to communicate. This introduces extra traffic on the network and also prevents the computers from accessing systems on other subnets. Since the release of Windows 2000, DNS has been the primary mechanism for name resolution.

TAKE NOTE*

LLMNR can be used to resolve both IPv4 and IPv6 addresses.

USING LINK LOCAL MULTICAST NAME RESOLUTION (LLMNR)

Link Local Multicast Name Resolution (LLMNR), enabled on Windows 7 and later operating systems, is a fallback name resolution technique when DNS or WINS is not available. LLMNR works only on the local subnet, so it does not resolve names for systems that are located on another network. LLMNR can be used on a small home network or an ad-hoc network, or in situations in which the DNS server your client is configured to use is not available.

An LLMNR client tries to reach its primary and secondary DNS servers and fails over to LLMNR only if it cannot locate them. It then uses a multicast message for the name it is trying to resolve. Each computer on the local subnet that supports LLMNR checks its own host name. If it matches, it sends a unicast message along with its IP address to the computer. If it does not match, the packet is discarded.

Exploring Network Settings

Network settings can be configured either manually or automatically using DHCP. Using manual settings can introduce configuration issues that can affect communications. Using a centralized approach to IP address management requires you to have a solid understanding of DHCP.

CERTIFICATION READY
Network settings
Objective 2.1

Configuring TCP/IP on a Windows 8 computer can be done manually or automatically. Setting up TCP/IP manually involves configuring it to use a static IP address. This involves entering an IP address, a subnet mask, and (if you need to access computers outside of the local network segment), a default gateway address. In order to resolve friendly names to IP addresses, you also need to configure at least one IP address for a DNS on your network.

CREATE A STATIC IP ADDRESS

GET READY. To create a static IP address, perform the following steps:

1. Press the **Windows logo key + r**.
2. Type **cmd** and then press **Enter**.

TAKE NOTE*

This IP address must be one that is configured for use on the same network segment as your computer.

3. Type **ping** *<ip address>*, where the *<ip address>* is the one you want to manually configure for your computer. If the request times out, the IP address isn't active on the network.

   Write down this IP address.
4. Type **exit** and then press **Enter** to close the cmd shell.
5. Press the **Windows logo key + i** and then click **Control Panel.**
6. Under *Network and Internet*, click **View network status and tasks.**
7. Click **Change adapter settings.**
8. Right-click your network adapter and then select **Properties.**
9. Click **Internet Protocol Version 4 (TCP/IPv4)** and then click **Properties.**

   Write down your current settings. You will reenter this information after completing the exercise.
10. Select **Use the following IP address** and then type the IP address, subnet mask, and default gateway you want to use.
11. Select **Use the following DNS server addresses** and then type an IP address for a preferred DNS server and an alternate DNS server (see Figure 5-6).

Figure 5-6

Entering a static IP address

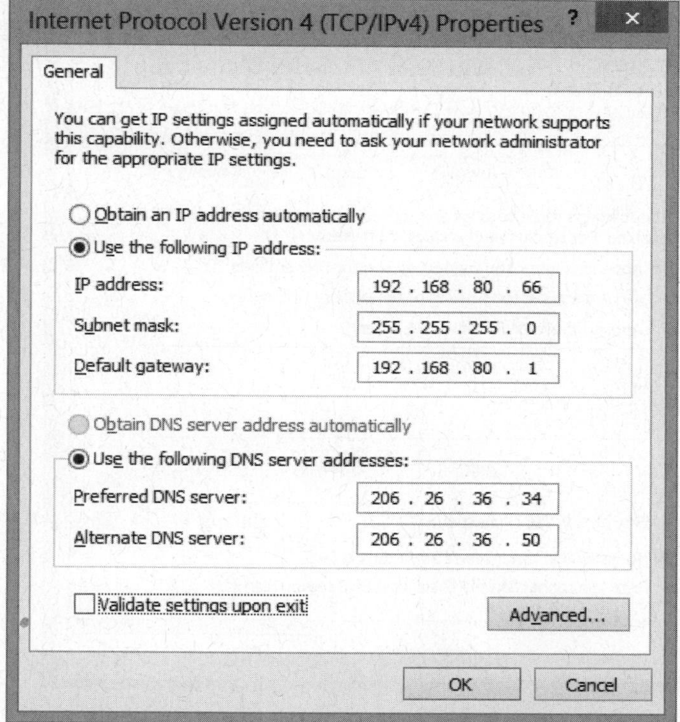

12. Click **OK** to accept your settings and to close the *Internet Protocol Version 4 (TCP/IPv4) Properties* dialog box.
13. Click **Close** to close the *Ethernet Properties* dialog box.

    Do *not* close the *Network Connections* dialog box.
14. Press the **Windows logo key + r** and then type **cmd** to open a cmd shell.
15. Type **ipconfig/all** and then press **Enter** to confirm that your settings have been changed.

16. Type **exit** and then press **Enter** to close the cmd shell.
17. Return to the *Network Connections* dialog box.
18. Right-click your network adapter and choose **Properties**.
19. Click **Internet Protocol Version 4 (TCP/IPv4)** and then click **Properties**.
20. Reenter the settings that were in place in Step 9 to return your system to its original configuration.

If you selected the *Validate settings upon exit* option, Windows 8 performs a network diagnostics test to check your settings for any problems and offers to help to fix them. If you clicked the **Advanced** button, you could make additional configurations to your TCP/IP configuration. For example, in Windows 8, you can configure multiple gateways. When you do this, a metric is used to determine which gateway to use. Multiple gateways are used to provide fault tolerance so if one router goes down, the computer defaults to the other gateway.

You can configure additional DNS settings in the *Advanced TCP/IP Settings* dialog box (see Figure 5-7).

Figure 5-7

Reviewing advanced TCP/IP setting options

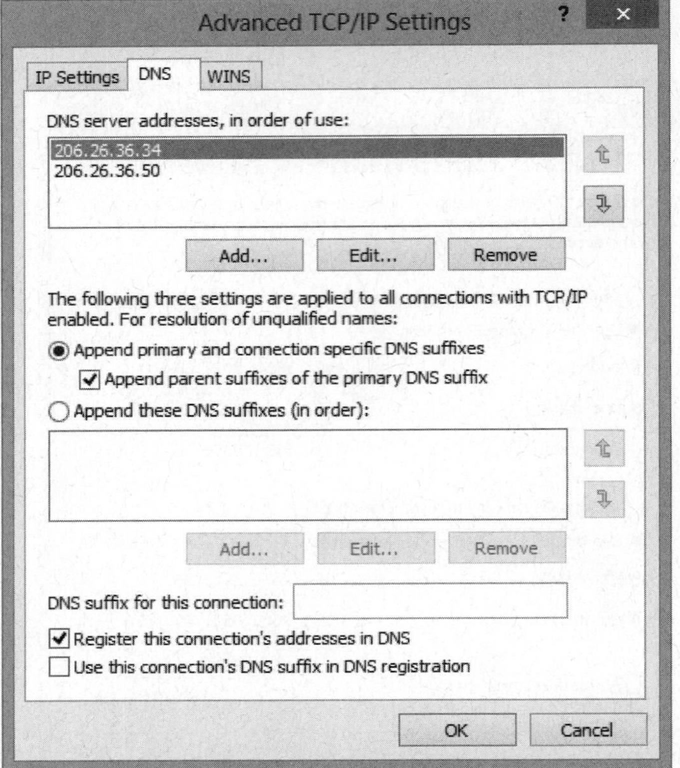

- **DNS server addresses, in order of use:** You can specify multiple DNS servers to use for name resolution. The order listed determines the sequence in which your client will attempt to resolve host names. If the first server does not respond to a name resolution request, the client will contact the next one in the list.
- **Append primary and connection specific DNS suffixes:** This is selected by default. If you attempt to access a computer named FileServer1, and the parent name is contoso.com, the name will resolve to FileServer1.contoso.com. If the FQDN does not exist in the domain, the query will fail. The parent name used (contoso.com) is configured on the *System Properties/Computer Name* tab.

- **Append parent suffixes of the primary DNS suffix:** This is selected by default. It works as follows: If the computer FS2 is in the eastcoast.contoso.com domain, DNS attempts to resolve the name to FS2.eastcoast.contoso.com. If this doesn't work, it tries FS2.contoso.com.
- **Append these DNS suffixes (in order):** Use this option when you want to specify DNS suffixes to use other than resolving names through your parent domain.
- **DNS suffix for this connection**: This setting overrides DNS names that are already configured for this connection. This is typically configured through the *System Properties/Computer Name* tab by clicking the **More** button.
- **Register this connection's addresses in DNS**: This option, selected by default, will automatically enter the FQDN in DNS records.
- **Use this connection's DNS suffix in DNS registration**: If this option is selected, all IP addresses for this connection will be registered in DNS at the parent domain.

UNDERSTANDING AUTOMATIC IP ADDRESS ASSIGNMENT

When you assign static IP addresses (IPv4 or IPv6) to your clients, you run the risk of duplicating IP addresses on your network or misconfiguring the settings, which can result in communication problems. A better approach is to dynamically assign your TCP/IP configurations from a central pool of IP addresses. This is done by using the ***Dynamic Host Configuration Protocol (DHCP)*** server. The DHCP server can also be configured to provide the default gateway, primary, and secondary DNS information; WINS server; and DNS domain name.

Figure 5-8 shows how DHCP communications work.

Figure 5-8

Understanding DHCP communications

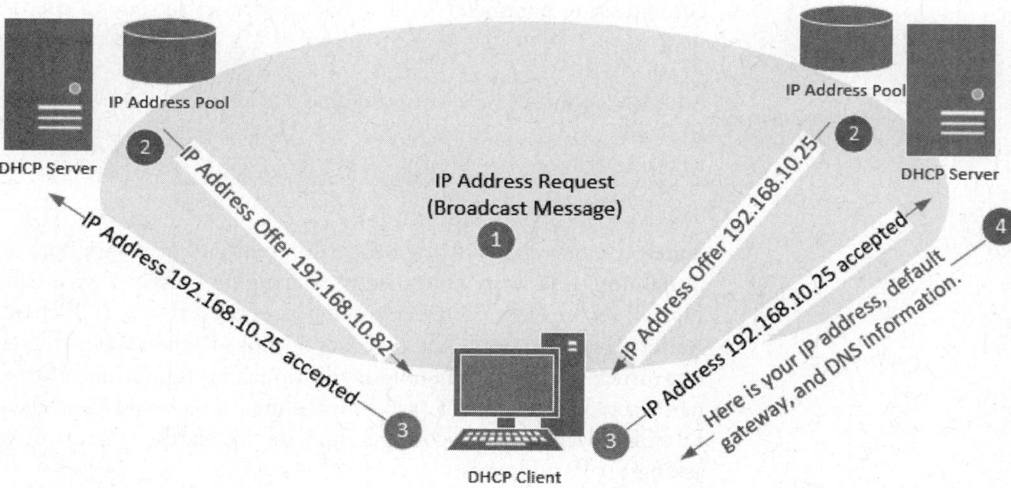

Here is a high-level overview of what happens with DHCP-enabled clients:

1. The DHCP-enabled client starts and broadcasts a request for an IP address over the network.
2. Any DHCP servers that receive the request review their pool of IP addresses (DHCP scope) and select one to offer to the client.
3. The client reviews the offers and broadcasts a message to the servers, letting them know which IP address it has accepted.
4. All DHCP servers see the message. Those whose offers are not accepted place the IP address back into their pool for a future client request. The server the client accepted

acknowledges and provides additional information to complete the client configuration (default gateway, DNS information, and so on).

After a client receives an IP address and additional configuration information, it has it for a specific period of time called the ***lease period***. When the lease is 50 percent expired, the client will try to renew it with the DHCP server. If the client cannot renew the lease, it will try again before the lease expires. At this point, if it cannot renew the lease, it will try to contact an alternate DHCP server. If all attempts fail, and the client cannot obtain a new IP address, it will autoconfigure with a Microsoft class B subnet (169.254.0.0/255.255.0.0).

TAKE NOTE*

You can use DHCP to assign IPv6 addresses through either DHCPv6 stateful mode or stateless mode. If DHCPv6 is used, you need to make sure your routers are configured to support it.

Before it chooses an IP address in this network, the client will check to make sure no other client is using the address it wants to assign. After it has an address assigned, it will attempt to make contact with a DHCP server every 5 minutes. Once found, it will be reconfigured to use an address assigned from the DHCP pool.

USING STATEFUL DHCP AND STATELESS DHCP

There are two ways to configure DHCP when using it for IPv6 implementations: ***stateless address configuration*** and ***stateful address configuration***.

If you are using DHCP to assign IPv6 addresses to stateful mode clients, they work similarly to the IPv4 when obtaining their IP addresses. When a client is configured to use DHCP in stateful mode, it will first use a link local address (IPv6). After it is autoconfigured with the link local address, it will seek out a DHCP server on the network by broadcasting a message every 5 minutes. When the client finally reaches a DHCP server, it will configure itself with the assigned IP parameters.

DHCP servers running in stateful mode will centrally manage the IPv6 addresses and configuration parameters and provide addresses to stateful clients.

TAKE NOTE*

Link local addresses are equivalent to Automatic Private IP Addressing (APIPA) IPv4 addresses using the 169.254.0.0/255.255.0.0 prefix. These address always begin with FE80::/64.

Stateless mode clients work a little differently; they assign both a link local address and additional non–link local addresses by exchanging messages with neighboring routers. When a DHCP server is set up to serve stateless clients, the DHCP clients will autoconfigure using router advertisements. These clients do not use the DHCP server to obtain an IP address, but instead use it to only obtain additional configuration information such as DNS recursive name servers and a DNS search list (domains to be searched during name resolution). If a DHCP server has been configured to service stateless clients, it will not respond to clients asking for IP addresses.

IMPLEMENTING FAULT TOLERANCE AND USING DHCP RELAY AGENTS

Most networks implement at least two DHCP servers to provide fault tolerance by sharing a pool of IP addresses. To avoid duplicating IP addresses, the IP address pools on each DHCP are configured to not overlap.

Because clients send their DHCP requests via broadcast messages that do not cross routers, you must also have a way to allow DHCP-enabled clients to reach a DHCP server located on another subnet. This can be done by using ***DHCP relay agents***, which convert a client's broadcasts into a unicast message that can then be forwarded directly to a DHCP server running on another subnet (see Figure 5-9).

Figure 5-9

Converting broadcasts into unicast messages using a DHCP relay agent

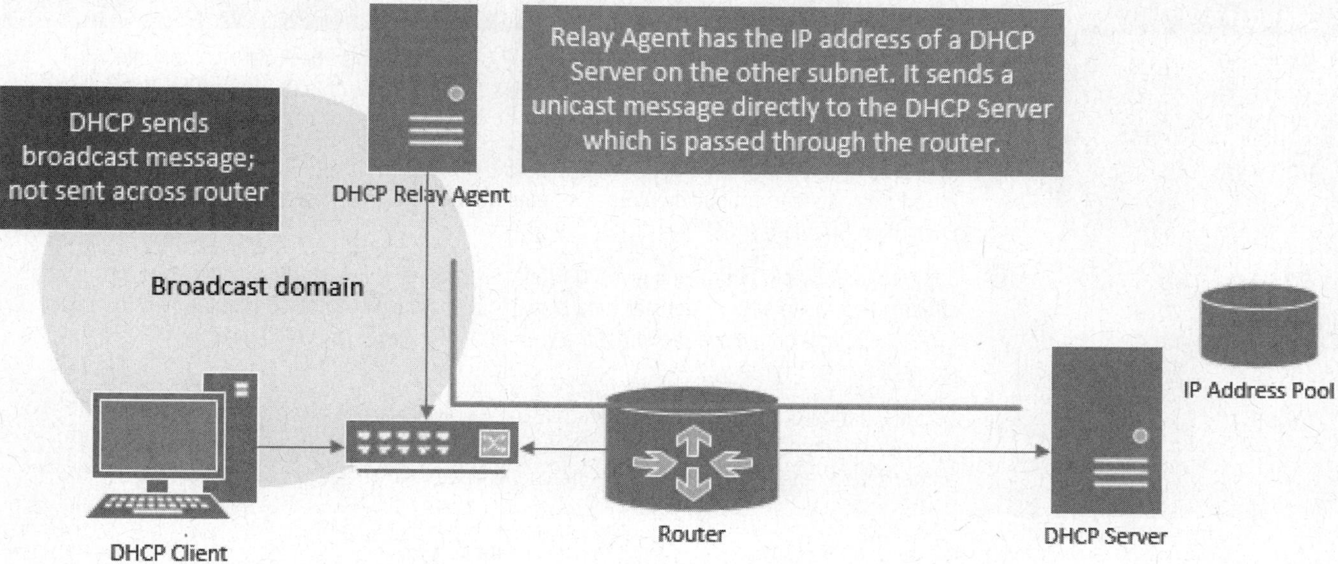

CERTIFICATION READY
Wireless
Objective 2.1

Working with Wireless Networks

Introducing wireless networks and devices into your network involves having a strategy for addressing compatibility issues, addressing encryption capabilities for protecting data, and determining when to use ad-hoc versus infrastructure modes.

When designing your wireless network strategy, you must consider compatibility issues between devices, wireless standards, and security.

EXPLORING COMPATIBILITY ISSUES WITH WI-FI DEVICES

When purchasing wireless network equipment, you need to be aware of issues regarding compatibility between devices. You will face an array of different types of wireless equipment, each built against one or more of the Wi-Fi technology standards. Table 5-3 provides a summary for each standard you may encounter, along with a description of each.

Table 5-3

Wi-Fi Technology Standards

STANDARD	DESCRIPTION
802.11b	Supports bandwidth up to 11 Mbps; uses the 2.5 Ghz frequency; susceptible to interference with cordless phones, microwaves operating in same frequency; WEP- and WPA-supported.
802.11a	Supports bandwidth up to 54 Mbps; uses the 5 Ghz frequency; less interference with common household devices; higher frequency means shorter range compared with 802.11b and also less apt to penetrate walls; incompatible with 802.11b because they use different frequencies; WEP and WPA-supported

(continued)

Table 5-3
(continued)

STANDARD	DESCRIPTION
802.11g	Supports bandwidth up to 54 Mbps; uses the 2.5 Ghz frequency; backward-compatible with 802.11b; 802.11g was designed to use the best features of both 802.11b and 802.11a; WEP and WPA-supported.
802.11i	Improved encryption for networks using the 802.11a, 802.11b, and 802.11g standards; introduces new encryption key protocols: Temporal Key Integrity Protocol (TKIP) and Advanced Encryption Standard (AES).
802.11n	Supports bandwidth approximately 300 Mbps; uses 2.5 and 5 Ghz frequencies; uses four spatial streams to simultaneously transfer data by using a channel width of 40 Hz designed to replace 802.11a, b, and g; backward-compatible with 802.11g; supports Wi-Fi Protected Access version 2 (WPA v2).
802.1x	Security standard for 802.11 networks that use RADIUS for authentication; provides key management; RADIUS provides centralized authentication, authorization, and accounting for remote connections.

REVIEWING ENCRYPTION PROTOCOLS

In each of the standards, encryption is provided to protect your wireless traffic. The following list represents the most common encryption protocols you will encounter on a wireless network:

- ***Wireless Equivalent Privacy (WEP)*** was designed to provide the same level of security found on wired networks. Over the years, WEP has proven to be very insecure, permitting a successful brute force password attack in seconds. WEP uses a data encryption scheme called RC4 with a shared key, which is used to encrypt and decrypt data. Because this key does not change automatically over time, anyone who can capture the wireless traffic can break the key and then gain access to your network.
- ***Wi-Fi Protected Access (WPA)*** was created to improve upon the encrypting and authentication features of WEP while WPA v2 was under development. It did this through the use of the TKIP to provide integrity, the AES protocol to provide encryption, and EAP to improve authentication capabilities.
- ***Wi-Fi Protected Access (WPA) v2:*** In 2006, WPA v2 replaced WPA. WPA v2 requires the use of stronger encryption (a new AES mode) and does not use TKIP, which introduced security limitations within the WPA implementation. Using WPA v2, the keys are changed regularly rather than staying the same, as they were in WEP implementations. WPA is compatible with 802.11a, 802.11b, 802.11g, and 802.11n.

WPA devices can operate in the following modes:

- ***Personal mode:*** This mode uses a preshared key or password. The master key is set on the access point (AP) and then all wireless clients are configured to use the key. The master key is then used by the client to generate a session key that it changes on a regular basis.
- ***Enterprise mode:*** This mode uses two sets of keys: a session key, changed each time the client communicates with the AP, and a master key. The master key is shared with all clients connected to the AP. Both keys are generated automatically and are changed on a regular basis. Enterprise mode uses IEEE 802.1x and EAP.

TAKE NOTE*

The ***Extensible Authentication Protocol (EAP)*** is used in wireless networks to expand the number of authentication methods available. It supports one-time passwords, certificates, smart cards, and public key encryption. When users connect to an AP using EAP, their authentication request is forwarded to a ***Remote Authentication Dial-In User Service (RADIUS) server***. When the RADIUS server receives the request from the AP, it searches its database for the name listed and the password. If the information is correct, the appropriate parameters (IP address, route information, protocol to use) are returned to the AP.

CONNECTING WIRELESS DEVICES

Wireless devices can be connected in two ways (see Figure 5-10):

Figure 5-10

Connecting wireless devices in an ad-hoc network and in infrastructure mode

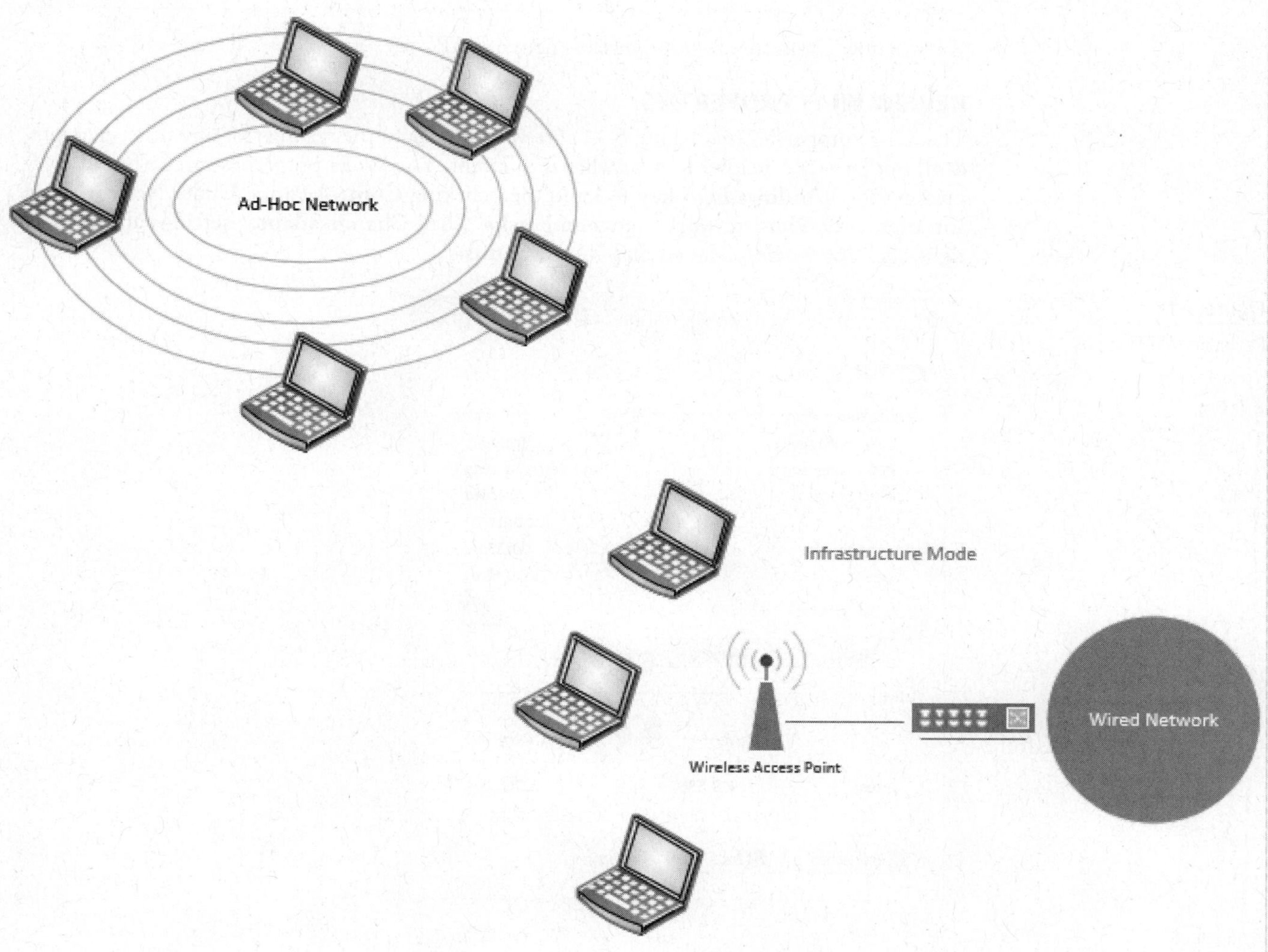

- ***Ad-hoc:*** Wireless clients connect to each other without the use of a wireless AP.
- ***Infrastructure mode:*** Wireless clients connect to a wireless AP. The AP does not have to be connected to a wired network.

After determining how you want to structure your wireless network, you need to configure your Windows 8 systems to connect to the wireless network.

With Windows 8, if you are within the broadcast range of a wireless AP, you do not have to preconfigure the wireless connection; just connect and let Windows determine the appropriate encryption settings.

The available wireless APs are presented, and you can determine which one to connect to. After selecting the AP, you need to enter a key to complete the connection.

CONNECT TO A WIRELESS AP (PRECONFIGURED)

GET READY. To connect to an existing wireless AP, perform the following steps:

1. From the Windows 8 start screen, press the **Windows logo key + i** and then click **Internet access.**
2. Choose the wireless network you want to connect to and then click **Connect.**
3. In the *Enter the network security key* field, type your wireless access key and then click **Next.**
4. Click **Yes, turn on sharing and connect to devices (for home or work networks).**

You are now connected to your wireless network AP.

REVIEW WI-FI PROPERTIES

The Wi-Fi properties (see Figure 5-11) are very similar to the settings for any other network card, but let's take a closer look at what is different. The Wi-Fi properties can be found by pressing the **Windows logo key + i** and then clicking **Control Panel**. Under **Network and Internet**, click **View network status and tasks**. Click **Change adapter settings** and then right-click the wireless adapter and choose **Status**.

Figure 5-11

Reviewing Wi-Fi status

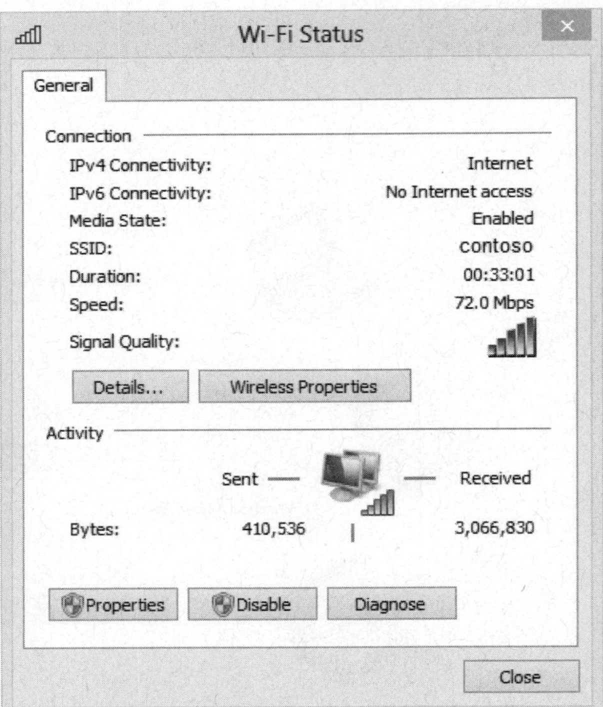

Figure 5-11 shows that additional information is provided for a Wi-Fi connection, including the following:

- **SSID:** This is the name of the wireless local area network. All wireless clients must use the same ***Service Set Identifier (SSID)*** to communicate.

- **Signal Quality:** This is the current signal strength between the wireless client and the wireless AP. More bars mean a stronger signal.
- **Details:** Provides network connection details (address, DHCP-enabled, IPv4/IPv6 configuration information).
- **Wireless Properties:** Provides you with the name of the wireless local area network (SSID), network type (ad-hoc vs. AP), and options for connecting to the wireless local area network (WLAN).
- The **Security** tab provides information regarding the security type used (WPA v2-personal, WPA-enterprise); the encryption type (TKIP, AES); and the network security key, if used.
- **Properties:** Provides access to the connection properties, which are the same types of properties from the earlier discussion on configuring IP manually on a network adapter.
- **Disable:** Disables the wireless adapter and disconnects you from the network.
- **Diagnose:** Launches the Windows diagnostics process that identifies and attempts to correct any problems with connectivity.

If you need to manually connect to a wireless AP, enter information such as the network name, security type, encryption type, and security key. Figure 5-12 provides an example of the settings necessary to make a manual connection.

Figure 5-12

Understanding the wireless AP manual connection requirements

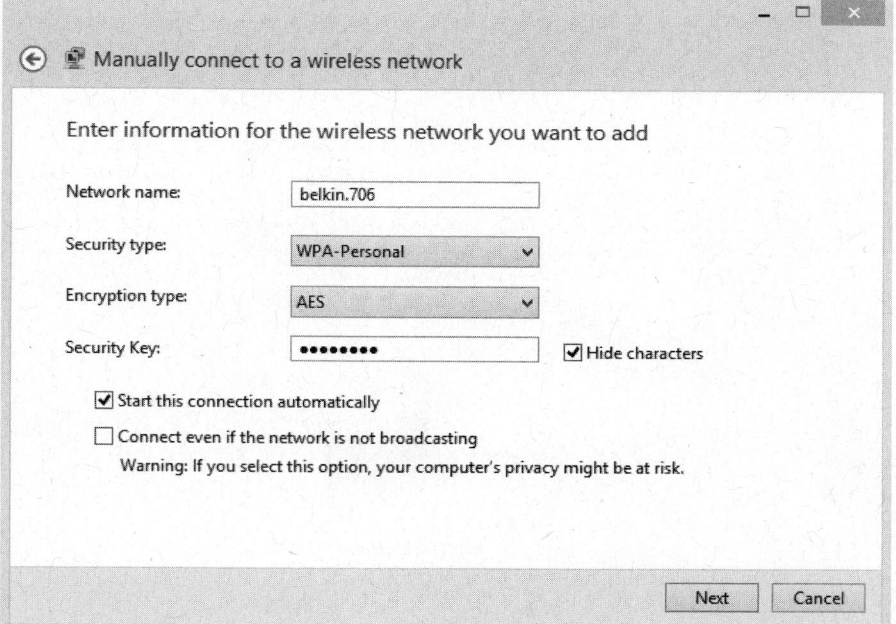

Implementing Network Security for Windows 8

Designing a strategy for protecting your network involves implementing multiple levels of defense. Although most companies have a firewall to protect their perimeter, they don't normally do a good job of protecting the individual hosts behind the firewall.

CERTIFICATION READY
Network security
Objective 2.1

After you determine your IP addressing schemes and how you want to configure your network from a logical/physical layout, it's time to determine how to secure it. This starts with looking at your network perimeter(s), which are the locations in your network in which your trusted network connects to another probably untrusted network. These gateways between networks enable you to implement security, control the types of traffic allowed to enter and exit your network, and reduce your overall network traffic. The most obvious perimeter is where your company's network connects to the Internet, but other perimeters may exist.

It's common for administrators to build network subnets to isolate and control traffic within their own private network so they can restrict traffic to a certain subnet and improve overall performance. It can also help isolate certain areas of the network that contain sensitive information. For example, you might create a subnet that contains just the finance department's systems due to the confidential nature of the information they work with.

The device used to segment a network is a ***router***. Although routers can provide basic traffic management (inbound/outbound), their primary role is to forward traffic between networks. Companies that are serious about their network security will add a commercial-level firewall at the perimeter that leads to the Internet. In most cases, that should be sufficient enough to protect your network, but what happens if something is compromised on that firewall or if misconfiguration allows it to be bypassed? What if mobile users connect behind the firewall and attempt to gain access to a server or computer they are not authorized to use? This is where a host-based firewall can help.

COMPARING NETWORK PERIMETER FIREWALLS TO HOST-BASED FIREWALLS

There are two basic types of firewalls (see Figure 5-13):

Figure 5-13

Reviewing a network firewall and host-based firewall deployment

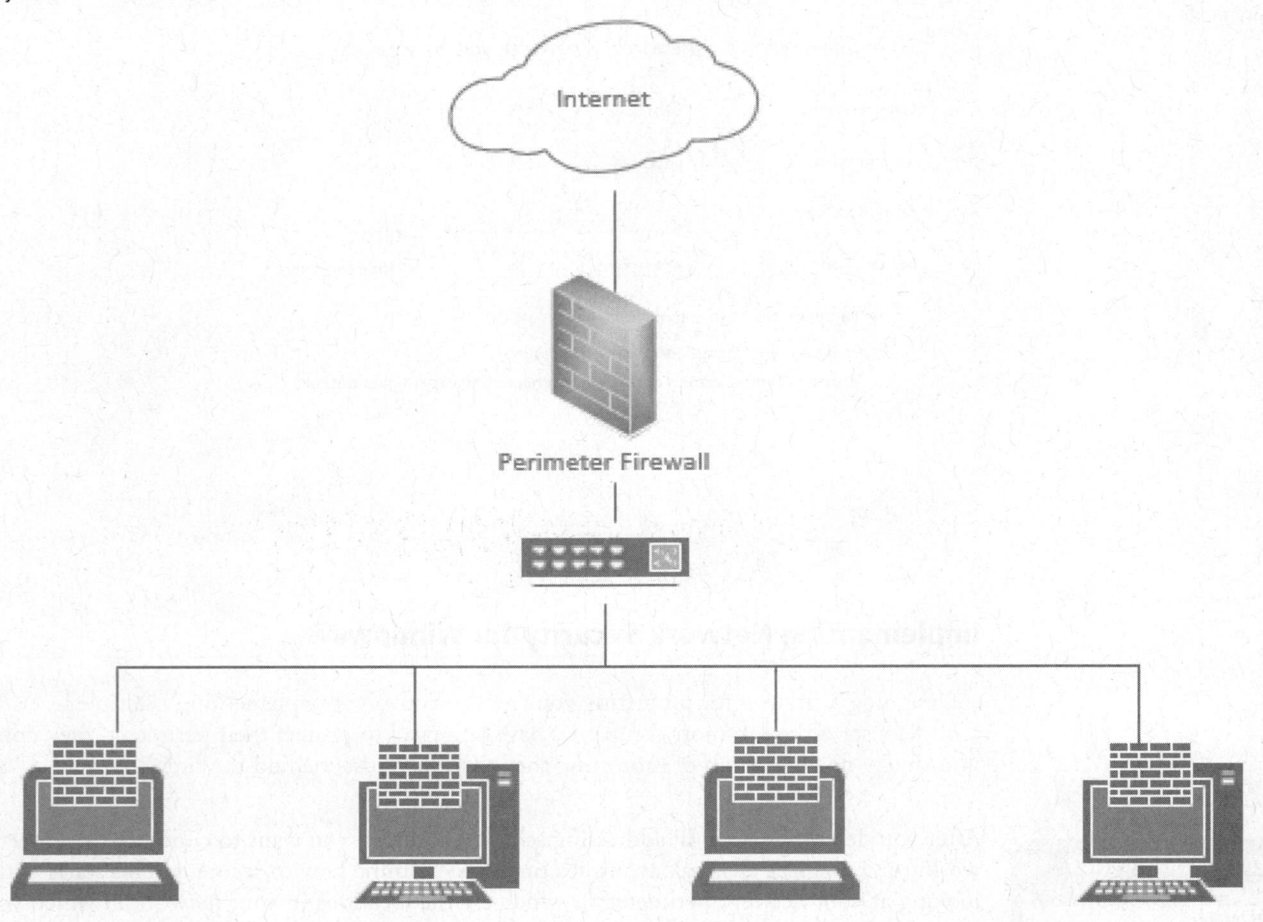

- ***Network perimeter firewalls:*** These types of firewall are found on the boundary between an internal and external network. They can be hardware- or software-based, and provide several types of functionality including managing and monitoring traffic through stateful connection analysis, providing Internet Protocol Security (IPsec) authentication and encryption, and providing NAT.
- ***Host-based firewalls:*** These firewalls run on individual computers (hosts) within the local network. They are designed to provide a second layer of defense, protect the computer from attacks and unauthorized access, and block specific types of traffic.

Because a network perimeter firewall monitors only traffic coming in and out of the network, it represents a single point of failure and does very little to protect against attacks that occur from within the private network. Without an additional layer of defense, using just a network perimeter firewall can put your entire network at risk. To create an additional level of protection, consider using a host-based firewall such as the Windows Firewall with Advanced Security (WFAS).

Windows Firewall with Advanced Security (WFAS) combines a stateful host-based firewall with IPsec. It is designed to protect against attacks that originate from within your network or those that might bypass the network perimeter firewall(s). WFAS inspects both IPv4 and IPv6 packets that enter and leave your computer and then compares them against the criteria contained in the firewall's rules. If the packet matches a rule, the action configured in the rule is applied. If the packet does not match a rule, the firewall will discard it and record an entry in its log files.

EXPLORING THE WFAS PROFILES

WFAS is network location–aware, so it can determine the type of network you are connecting to. After it identifies the type of network, it applies the appropriate profile to provide protection against attacks that can originate from inside and outside of your network. The following WFAS profiles (see Figure 5-14) can be used to apply settings to your computer:

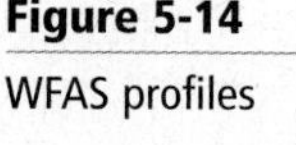

Figure 5-14
WFAS profiles

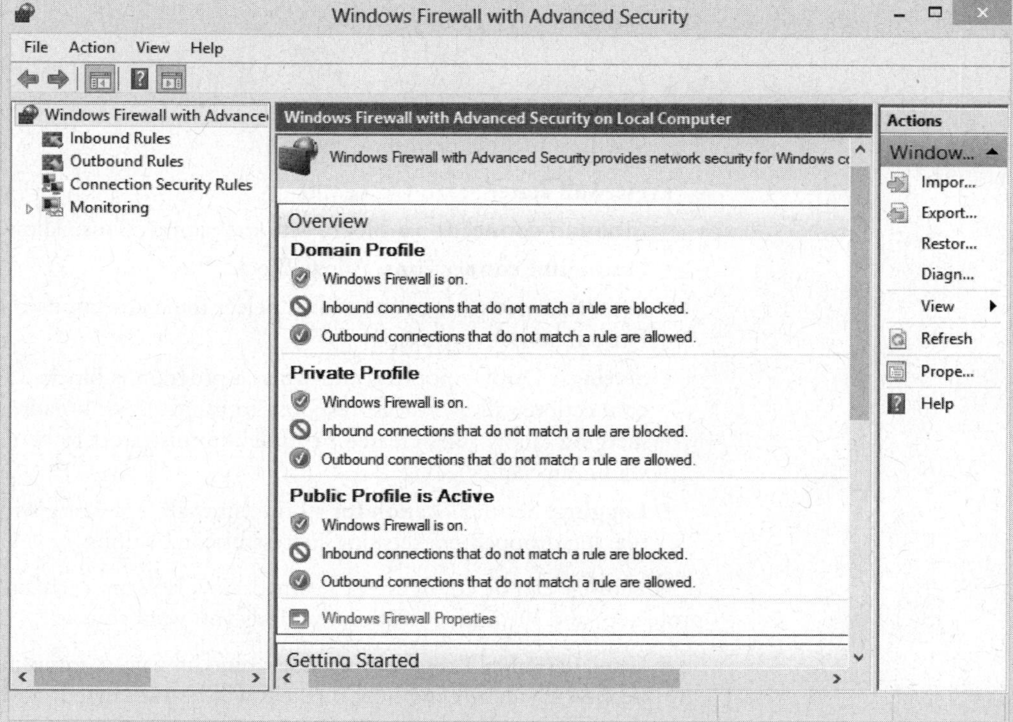

- A ***domain profile*** is used when your computer is connected to its corporate domain and can authenticate to the domain controller through one of its connections.
- A ***private profile*** is used when your computer is connected to a private network location (home or small office network) and is located behind a firewall and/or a device that performs NAT. If you are using this profile with a wireless network, you should implement encryption (WPA v2).
- A ***public profile*** is used when your computer is connected to a public network (for example, directly connected to the Internet). It is assigned to the computer when it is first connected to a new network; rules associated with this profile are the most restrictive.

You can click the Windows Firewall Properties link to see the range of settings available within each of the three profiles (see Figure 5-15).

Figure 5-15

Understanding WFAS profile property settings

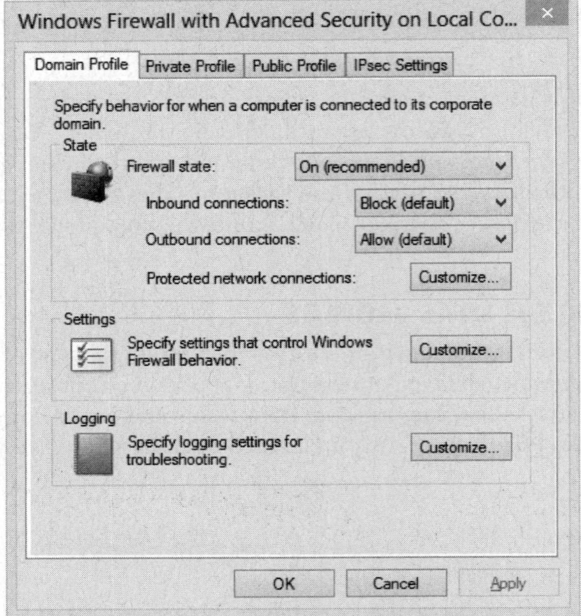

These settings include the following:

- **Firewall state:** Set to On or Off.
- **Inbound connections:** Block, Block all connections, Allow.
- **Outbound connections:** Allow, Block.
- **Protected network connections:** Select the connections/interfaces you want Windows Firewall to help protect.
- **Settings:** Display notifications when a program is blocked from receiving inbound connections; allow unicast response to multicast or broadcast network traffic; rule merging (allow rules created by local administrators to be merged with rules distributed via Group Policy).
- **Logging:** Set the location for storing firewall logs along with the size limit for the log file; log dropped packets; log successful connections.

IPsec settings can be configured to control how keys are exchanged, how your data is protected, and the authentication methods you want to use.

- **IPsec defaults:** These settings determine how your computer will establish a secure connection by identifying how the keys will be exchanged, how data will be protected, and the authentication method to use.

- **IPsec exemptions:** This setting enables you to exempt Internet Control Message Protocol (ICMP) to simplify the troubleshooting process; ICMP is designed to detect and report error conditions.
- **IPsec tunnel authorization:** This setting enables you to specify the users and computers that are authorized to establish IPsec tunnel connections with your computer.

UNDERSTANDING INBOUND RULES, OUTBOUND RULES, AND CONNECTION SECURITY RULES

WFAS enables you to configure three types of firewall rules (inbound, outbound, and connection security) that can be applied to one or more of the profiles (domain, private, public). These rules govern how the computer sends and/or receives traffic from users, computers, applications, and services. When a packet matches the rule's criteria, it will allow the connection, explicitly block the connection, or allow it only if the connection is using IPsec to secure it.

When configuring inbound/outbound rules, you have the option of selecting criteria that include a program name, TCP/UDP port number, system service name, local and remote interfaces, interface types, users/groups, computers/computer groups, and protocols.

TAKE NOTE*

Connection security rules specify how and when authentication occurs, but they do not allow connections. You need to create an inbound or outbound rule to allow the connection.

- ***Inbound rules:*** These rules explicitly allow or block inbound traffic that matches the criteria set in the rule. To set up an inbound rule, select the type (program, port, predefined, or custom), select the entity to which the rule applies (for example, program [all or path to specific .exe], port name/number), determine the action (allow, block, or allow if it is secure), select the profile it applies to (domain, private, public), and provide a name for the rule. When your system is set up, it is automatically configured to not allow unsolicited inbound traffic. If you decide to set up a service on your computer (a test website) and want others to connect to it, configure an inbound rule that allows traffic to the web service (typically running on TCP port 80).
- ***Outbound rules:*** These rules explicitly allow or deny outbound traffic that originates from the computer when it matches the criteria set in the rule. The setup for an outbound rule is identical to the options discussed in the inbound rule. Because outbound traffic is allowed by default, you create an outbound rule to block traffic that you did not want.
- ***Connection security rules:*** These rules secure the connection with both authentication (Kerberos, digital certificates, preshared keys) and encryption protocols. Connection security rules are used to determine how the traffic between the computer and others is secured. The process for creating a connection security rule involves setting the type of connection security you want to create (isolation, authentication encryption, server-to-server, tunnel), when you want authentication to occur on inbound/outbound connections (request but don't require it, require it for inbound but request for outbound, require for both), select the authentication method to use, which profile to apply the rule to (domain, private, public), and then provide a name for the rule.

ADDRESSING CONFLICTS WITH FIREWALL RULES

TAKE NOTE*

Before performing the following steps, close Internet Explorer.

When firewall rules conflict, they are applied in the following order (as soon as an incoming packet matches a rule, that rule is applied and processing stops):

1. Authenticated bypass rules: These are rules that allow a connection even if the existing firewall rules would block it. For example, you may be blocking a specific type of traffic but then want to allow a certain group of users and computers to bypass the block. These types of rules require that the authenticated computers utilize IPsec to prove their identity.
2. Block connection: Rules block matching inbound traffic.
3. Allow connection: Rules allow matching inbound traffic.
4. Default profile behavior: Block unsolicited inbound traffic; allow all outbound traffic.

CREATE AN OUTBOUND RULE

GET READY. To create an outbound rule, perform the following steps.

1. From the Windows 8 Start menu, type **Windows Advanced**. From *Results*, choose **Windows Firewall with Advanced Security**.
2. Right-click **Outbound Rules** and then choose **New Rule**.
3. Select **Program** and then click **Next**.
4. Click **Browse** and then navigate to the location of your installation of Internet Explorer. This can usually be found at c:*%ProgramFiles%\Internet Explorer\iexplore.exe*.
5. Click **iexplore.exe** and then click **Open**.
6. In the *New Outbound Rule Wizard* dialog box, click **Next**.
7. Select **Block the connection** and then click **Next**.
8. Select **Domain**, **Private**, and **Public**; then click **Next**.
9. For the name of the profile, type **IE Restriction**; for the description, type **Restricts IE from connecting to the Internet.**
10. Click **Finish**.

    Do not close the *Windows Firewall with Advanced Security* dialog box.
11. Attempt to access the Internet using Internet Explorer. You should see the message shown in Figure 5-16.

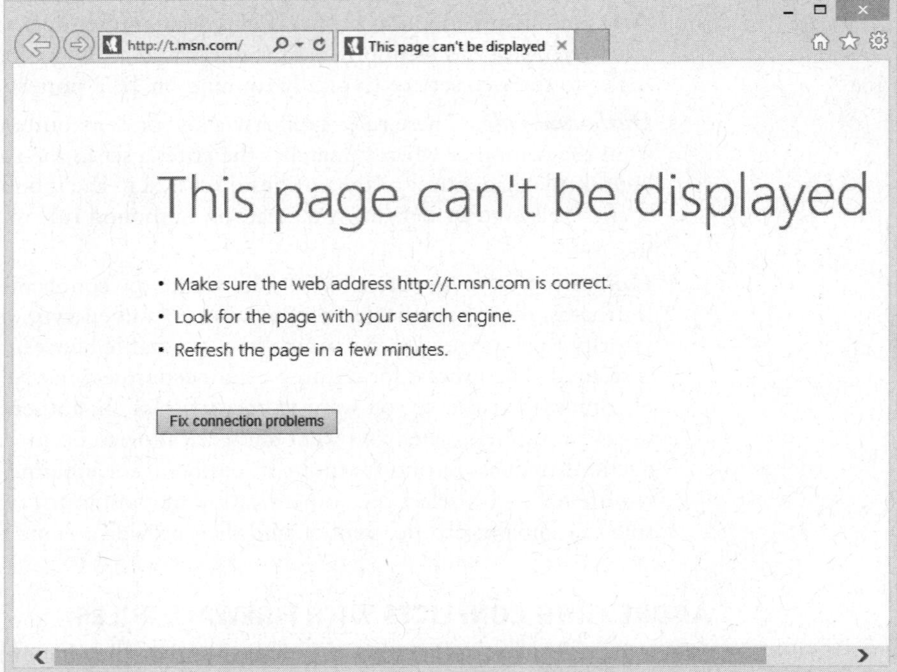

Figure 5-16

Enforcing restrictions on using Internet Explorer to access the Internet

12. Close the *Internet Explorer* window.
13. In the *Windows Firewall with Advanced Security* window, from the top menu, click **Action** and then choose **Export Policy**.
14. Navigate to a folder that you can access from your Windows Server 2012 domain controller. In the *File name* field, type **IE Restriction** and then click **Save**.

    Make a note of where you stored this policy; you will use it in the next exercise.

15. When *Policy successfully exported* is displayed, click **OK**.
16. Return to the *Windows Firewall with Advanced Security* dialog box and click **Outbound Rules**.
17. Locate the IE restriction rule you created earlier, right-click it, and then choose **Delete**. Click **Yes** to confirm you want to delete the rule.
18. Attempt to access the Internet using Internet Explorer. You should be successful.
19. Close the *Internet Explorer* window and close the *Windows Firewall with Advanced Security* window.

EXPORTING FIREWALL CONFIGURATION RULES

After you export the current firewall configuration from the *Action* menu in the *Windows Firewall with Advanced Security* window, you can then import it on another standalone system or copy it to a folder to use as a backup in case you make changes to the policy and need to return it to a known state. Policy files are exported as (*.wfw) files.

If you want to deploy the firewall configuration to multiple computers in your domain, create a Group Policy Object (GPO) and import the firewall settings into the policy.

IMPORT A WINDOW FIREWALL RULE INTO A GROUP POLICY OBJECT

GET READY. To import the firewall policy you created earlier into a GPO and restrict the use of Internet Explorer for your domain, log in with Administrative privileges to your domain controller and then perform the following steps:

1. If Server Manager does not open automatically, click the **Server Manager** icon on the task bar.
2. Click **Tools** > **Group Policy Management**.
3. Expand the *contoso.com* domain folder, right-click **Group Policy Objects**, and then choose **New**.
4. For the name, type **IE Restriction** and then click **OK**.
5. Double-click the *Group Policy Objects* folder and click **IE Restriction**.
6. Right-click and choose **Edit**.
7. Expand **Computer Configuration** > **Policies** > **Windows Settings** > **Security Settings** > **Windows Firewall with Advanced Security**.
8. Right-click the **Windows Firewall with Advanced Security** policy and choose **Import Policy** (see Figure 5-17).
9. When asked *Do you want to import a policy now?*, click **Yes**.
10. Browse to the folder where you saved the IE Restriction policy in the previous exercise. Click the **IE Restriction** policy and then click **Open**.
11. When you see *Policy successfully imported*, click **OK.**
12. Click the **Outbound Rules** folder.

    The IE Restriction policy is now listed in the GPO.
13. Close the *Group Policy Management Editor* window.
14. In the *Group Policy Management* console, right-click the **contoso.com** domain and choose **Link an Existing GPO**.
15. Click **IE Restriction** and then click **OK**.
16. Close the *Group Policy Management* console window.

    The GPO is now applied to your domain.

Figure 5-17

Importing WFAS settings

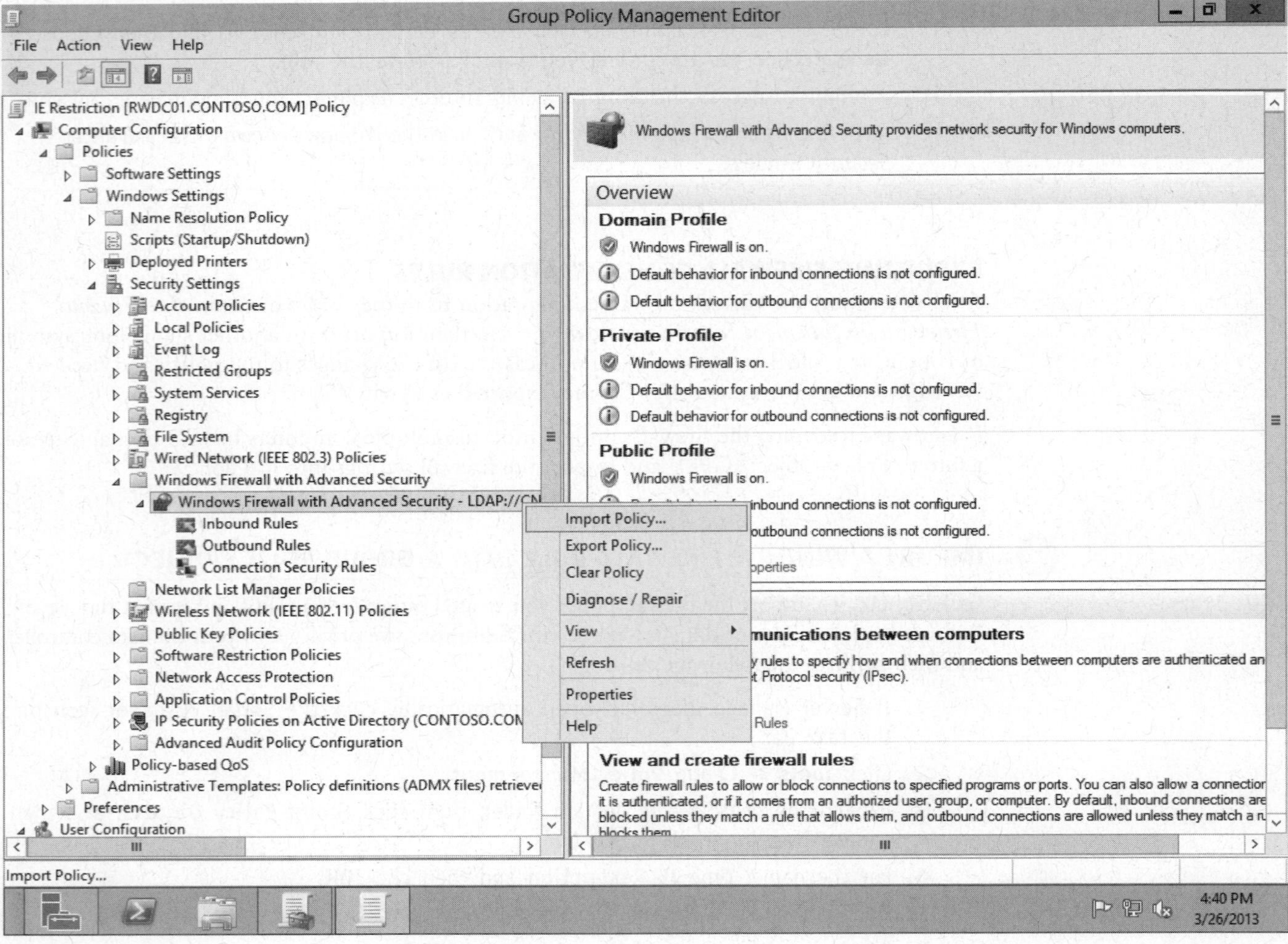

SKILL SUMMARY

IN THIS LESSON YOU LEARNED:

- The goal of IPv6 was to address the exhaustion of the IPv4 address space (IPv4 addresses are 32 bits long, and IPv6 addresses are 128 bits long). The transition to IPv6 is expected to take several years; expect to see a mix of IPv4, IPv4/IPv6 (dual stack), and IPv6-only networks.
- Name resolution is the process of associating host names to IP addresses. Windows operating systems support three name resolution systems: DNS, WINS, and LLMNR.
- In its original configuration, DNS was not designed with security in mind. DNSSEC was implemented to provide a way to confirm the identity of DNS servers that respond to queries.
- IPv4 and IPv6 addresses can be configured manually or automatically by using DHCP. When configured manually, you introduce the chance for misconfigurations that can affect the computer's ability to communicate.

- DHCP and DHCP relay agents can be used both in IPv4 and IPv6 networks to manage IP address/IP configuration assignments. There are two ways to configure DHCP when using it for IPv6 implementations: stateless address configuration and stateful address configuration.
- When working with wireless networks, you need to have a strategy that addresses compatibility issues, identifies encryption capabilities for protecting your data, and determines when to use ad-hoc versus infrastructure mode.
- Host-based firewalls add a second level of protection in case perimeter firewalls are bypassed. WFAS combines a stateful host-based firewall with IPsec that can help protect your individual computers.
- WFAS provides three profiles: domain, private, and public. It uses inbound, outbound, and connection security rules to provide custom security solutions that can block traffic based on a program, a TCP/UDP port number, a system service, local and remote interfaces, an interface type, users/groups, computers/computer groups, and/or protocols.

Knowledge Assessment

Multiple Choice

Select the correct answer for each of the following questions.

1. Which of the following are true regarding IPv4?
   a. 32-bit address
   b. 128-bit address
   c. Consists of a network ID and MAC address
   d. Consists of a host ID and MAC address

2. How many bits does a standard IPv6 unicast address use to represent the network ID?
   a. 32
   b. 64
   c. 128
   d. 10

3. Which of the following Windows PowerShell commands performs a DNS name query for www.contoso.com?
   a. `ping www.contoso.com`
   b. `dnsquery www.contoso.com`
   c. `resolve DNSName www.contoso.com`
   d. `resolve-DNSquery www.comcast.net`

4. Which of the following DNSSEC records stores the information used to validate signatures?
   a. RRSIG
   b. DNSKEY
   c. NSEC
   d. DS

5. Which of the following is a name resolution mechanism supported in Windows? (Select all that apply.)
   a. EFS
   b. WINS
   c. LLMNR
   d. DNS

6. Which of the following converts a DHCP client's broadcast into a unicast message that can be forwarded to a DHCP server located on another subnet?
   a. DHCP forwarder
   b. DNS forwarder
   c. DHCP
   d. DHCP relay agent

7. Which type of wireless network enables clients to connect to a wireless AP?
   a. ad-hoc
   b. WAN
   c. LAN
   d. infrastructure mode

8. Which of the following WFAS profiles is assigned to a computer when it is first connected to a new network?
   a. public profile
   b. domain profile
   c. private profile
   d. WFAS new profile

9. Which of the following rules specifies how and when authentication occurs?
   a. public rule
   b. inbound rule
   c. connection security rule
   d. outbound rule

10. Which of the following is true regarding WFAS rules? (Select all that apply.)
    a. Outbound traffic is allowed by default.
    b. Unsolicited inbound traffic is not allowed.
    c. Solicited inbound traffic is allowed.
    d. Connection security rules require inbound/outbound rules to allow connections.

Best Answer

Choose the letter that corresponds to the best answer. More than one answer choice may achieve the goal. Select the BEST answer.

1. Which of the following provides automatic IP addresses for clients located on a subnet without a DHCP server?
   a. DHCP server
   b. static IP address
   c. DHCP relay agent
   d. resolver

2. Which configuration can a DHCPv6 server setup running in stateless mode provide to clients?
   a. IP address
   b. subnet mask
   c. default gateway
   d. DNS recursive name servers

3. Which TCP/IP setting should be configured when you want to specify DNS suffixes to use other than resolving names through your parent domain?
   a. DNS suffix for this connection
   b. Append these DNS suffixes (in order)
   c. Append primary and connection specific DNS suffixes
   d. DNS server address, in order of use

4. When connecting a Windows 8 computer to a wireless AP, which of the following Wi-Fi encryption protocols provides the highest level of security?
   a. WPA
   b. WEP
   c. WPA v2
   d. IPsec
5. Which of the following should be used to protect clients from being redirected to a rogue host when using DNS?
   a. IPsec
   b. TLS/EAP
   c. DNSSEC
   d. Cache poisoning

Matching and Identification

1. Match the following terms with the related description or usage.

   _______ a) DNSSEC
   _______ b) AAAA record
   _______ c) DNS server
   _______ d) LLMNR
   _______ e) subnet mask
   _______ f) ANDing
   _______ g) domain profile
   _______ h) WPA enterprise mode
   _______ i) stateful
   _______ j) connection security rule

   1. A feature in WFAS that is used to determine how the traffic between two computers is authenticated and encrypted.
   2. The process a computer uses to determine whether another computer is on the same network.
   3. Used to associate a computer name to an IP address. Stores host to IP address mappings in a zone file.
   4. Used to determine the bits associated with the network ID and host ID.
   5. Uses two sets of keys: a session key that is changed each time the client communicates with an AP and a master key.
   6. An IPv6 address (host name) mapping to its IP address.
   7. A fallback name resolution technique when DNS and WINS are not available.
   8. Used when a computer is connected to its corporate domain and can authenticate to a domain controller.
   9. One of the ways you can configure a DHCP IPv6 server; provides IP address configuration to DHCP clients.
   10. Uses public key cryptography to digitally a zone.

Build a List

1. Specify the correct order of the steps that must be completed for a DHCP-enabled client to obtain IPv4 addressing information. Not all steps will be used.

   _______ Client receives offers of an IP address from a DHCP server.
   _______ DHCP server selects an IP address from the available address pool.
   _______ Client broadcasts request for an IP address.
   _______ Client sends broadcast message letting other DHCP servers know it has accepted an IP address offer.

_______ Client requests additional IP configuration from a selected DHCP server (DNS, default gateway)
_______ Client sends a recursive query to a DHCP server.

2. Specify the correct order of the steps in which WFAS rules are applied.
_______ Allow connections
_______ Default profile behavior
_______ Block connections
_______ Authenticated bypass rules

3. Specify the correct order of the steps that must be completed to create an outbound rule that blocks a program.
_______ Browse to the program's install location, select the program's executable, and then click **Open**.
_______ Open the *Windows Firewall with Advanced Security* console.
_______ Select the program to block and then click **Next**.
_______ Right-click **Outbound Rules** and then choose **New Rules**.
_______ Select **Block the connection**.
_______ Type a name and description for the rule and then click **Finish**.
_______ Select **Domain, Private, and/or Public profile**.

Choose an Option

1. Identify the option that automatically enters the FQDN of the computer into the DNS records.

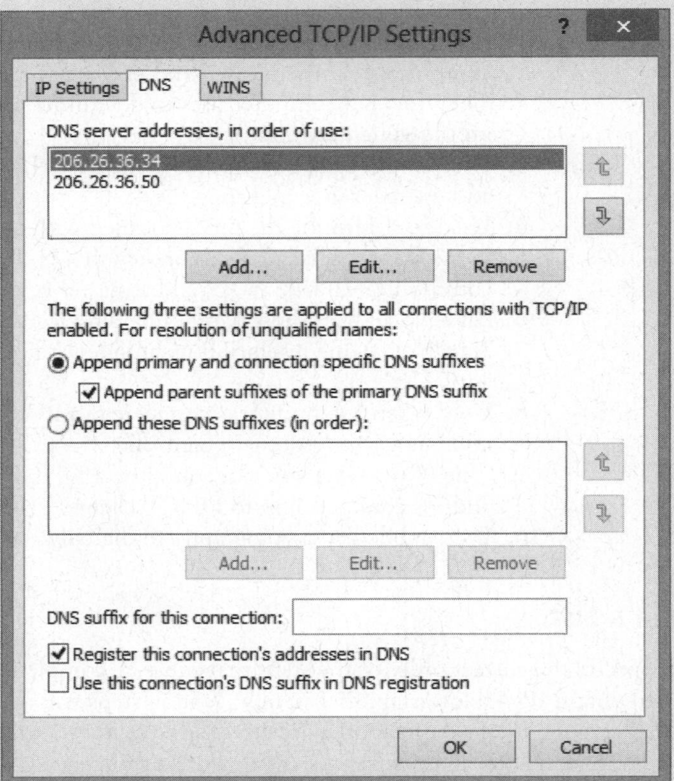

Business Case Scenarios

Scenario 5-1: Assigning IP Addresses

You have a network broken into six subnets and have placed a DHCP server on subnets 1, 3, and 5. Computers on subnets 2, 4, and 6 are not receiving IP addresses. How should you address the issue without having to enter static IP addresses on each of those systems?

Scenario 5-2: Configuring WFAS Security Rules

You have Windows 8 clients that are configured to use WFAS. You create a new connection security rule and apply it to the computers. What else do you need to do to complete the setup?

LESSON 6 Designing for Remote Access

70-688 EXAM OBJECTIVE

Objective 2.2 – Design for Remote Access. This objective may include but is not limited to the following design considerations: Off-network use and management, metered networks, VPN, RDP, DirectAccess, Remote Administration.

LESSON HEADING	EXAM OBJECTIVE
Providing Off-Network Use and Management	Off-network use and management
Exploring Virtual Private Networks	VPN, DirectAccess
Planning for Remote Access	RDP
Exploring Remote Access using Direct Access and Routing and Remote Access (RRAS)	VPN, DirectAccess
Using Connection Manager and the Connection Manager Administration Kit (CMAK)	VPN, Remote Administration
Using the Getting Started Wizard in Windows 8	VPN
Managing VPN Clients using Windows PowerShell	VPN
Performing Remote Administration	Remote Administration
Exploring Metered Networks	Metered networks

KEY TERMS

Connection Manager Administration Kit (CMAK)
DirectAccess
L2TP/IPsec
Metered internet connections
Network Access Protection (NAP)
Network Location Server (NLS)
Point to Point Tunneling Protocol (PPTP)
Windows PowerShell Remoting
Remote Server Administration Tools (RSAT)
Secure Socket Tunneling Protocol (SSTP)
Virtual Private Network (VPN)
VPN Reconnect (IKEv2)
WMI Filter

■ Providing Off-Network Use and Management

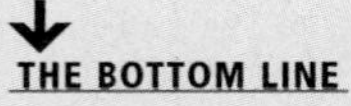

THE BOTTOM LINE

To manage off-network systems and devices you need to assess their current health, provide remote assistance and apply remediation steps.

CERTIFICATION READY
Off-network use and management
Objective 2.2

To be able to monitor and manage off-network systems effectively, you need to be able to assess their current health, provide remote assistance when necessary, and apply the appropriate remediation steps in order to get them back into compliance even when they are outside of your corporate network.

Microsoft offers several ways to manage and protect your off-network computers and devices.

- Windows Intune, discussed in Lesson 14, provides a cloud-based management solution that helps you manage your computers and mobile devices through a Web console. It provides the tools, reports, and licenses to ensure your computers are always current and protected. From a mobile device perspective, it allows you to work through Exchange ActiveSync or directly through Windows Intune to manage your remote workforce. Since Windows Intune is cloud-based, your users will not have to be attached to your corporate network in order to receive updates, patches or receive help removing malware.
- Remote Access Servers with Network Access Protection, discussed later in this lesson, allows you to create and enforce health requirement policies that specify the required software and system configurations the clients must have when connecting to your corporate network. In situations where a remote user has been off-network for a period of time, when they do reconnect, NAP will inspect the system and if not in compliance, redirect it for remediation to an isolated network segment where it can be updated with the latest service packs, updates, and virus definitions before being allowed to reconnect to the rest of the network.
- DirectAccess (discussed in this lesson) allows users to initiate connections with management servers which provide services such as Windows Update, Network Access Protection and antivirus support. Management servers can also be setup to communicate with DirectAccess clients to perform software and hardware inventory assessments.

Exploring Virtual Private Networks

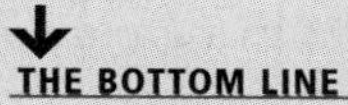

A VPN is a private network that uses tunneling, authentication and encryption protocols to allow users to access a private network over the public Internet.

CERTIFICATION READY
VPN, DirectAccess
Objective 2.2

A ***Virtual Private Network (VPN)*** is a private network that uses a public network (e.g., the Internet) to connect remote sites and users. The VPN makes it appear to computers, on each end of the connection, as if they are actually connected to the same network. This point to point connection is emulated by encapsulating the packet in an IP Header. The information in the header is used to route the information between the two VPN endpoints.

Tunneling protocols, authentication protocols and encryption levels applied to the VPN connections determine the level of VPN security you have available. In order for a VPN to work both the client and server will need to utilize the same protocols. Overall, VPNs can provide the following capabilities:

- Data encryption (confidentiality)
- Authentication
- Data Integrity: Ensure the packets are not modified while in transit
- Non-Repudiation: Guarantee the packets came from the source at a specific time

The VPN uses the concept of tunneling to establish and maintain a logical network connection (see Figure 6-1).

There are four types of VPN Tunneling protocols you will encounter:

- Point to Point Tunneling Protocol (PPTP)
- Layer 2 Tunneling Protocol over IPsec (L2TP/IPsec)
- Secure Socket Tunneling Protocol (SSTP)
- VPN Reconnect (or IKEv2)

Figure 6-1
VPN tunnel

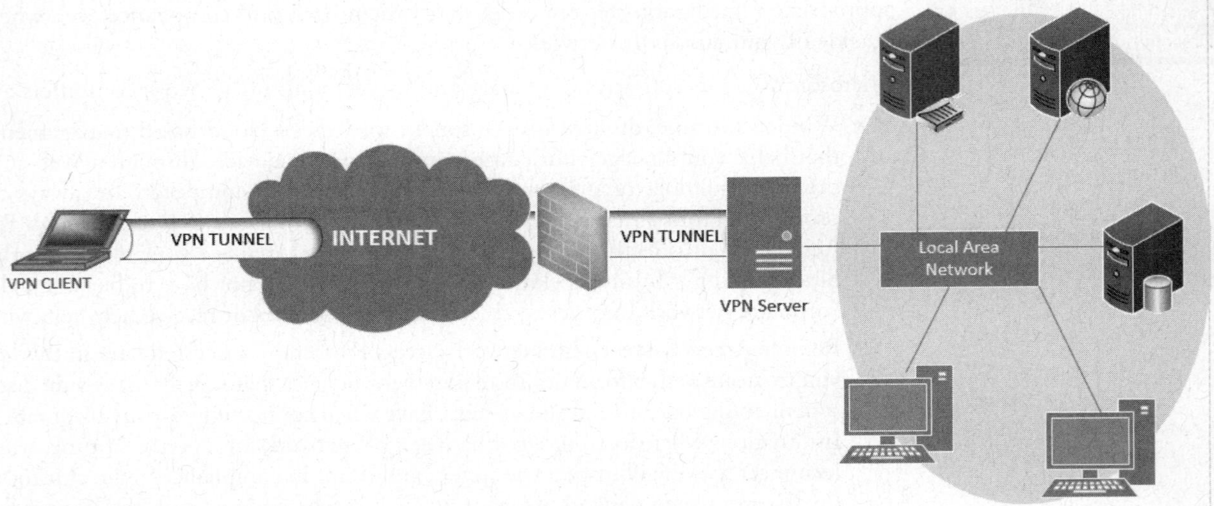

UNDERSTANDING PPTP

Point to Point Tunneling Protocol (PPTP) has widespread support with nearly all versions of Windows. It uses the Microsoft Point to Point Encryption (MPPE) protocol with RC4 (128 bit key) to protect data that is in transit. Although not as secure as L2TP/IPsec (discussed later) it can provide a reasonably secure option for remote access and site-to-site VPNs when used on combination with an authentication protocol such as MS-CHAPv2.

PPTP provides confidentiality meaning that it prevents the data from being viewed but it does not provide data integrity. In other words, it does not protect the packet from being intercepted and modified. PPTP does not implement any mechanisms that ensure the data is actually sent by the authorized person.

MORE INFORMATION

You can only encrypt data with PPTP if you use MS-CHAPv2 and EAP-TLS as the authentication protocol. PPTP is supported natively by Windows XP and later client operating systems, Windows Server 2003, 2008, 2008R2 and Windows Server 2012 server operating systems. It is typically used for remote access and site-to-site VPNs; works with IPv4; uses Network Address Translation (NAT) which is supported via PPTP enabled NAT routers. It uses PPP for user authentication and RC4 for data confidentiality.

UNDERSTANDING L2TP/IPSEC

While PPTP supports authentication of the user only, ***L2TP/IPsec*** requires that the computers mutually authenticate themselves to each other. The computer to computer authentication takes place before the user is authenticated.

L2TP provides a support mechanism for pre-shared keys, digital certificates or Kerberos for mutual authentication. Pre-shared keys are basically passwords and should only be used in test networks when you don't want to setup a Public Key Infrastructure (PKI). Digital certificates, which are stored in a format that cannot be modified, offer a more secure option. They are issued by Certificate Authorities that you trust. Kerberos is the native authentication protocol for Windows Server 2003 and later and provides the easiest way to secure VPN connections in a domain-based environment. It provides mutual authentication, anti-replay, and non-repudiation just like digital certificates.

Kerberos can only be used when both computers involved in the L2TP tunnel are in the same forest. L2TP uses IPsec to encrypt the Point to Point Protocol (PPP) packets. L2TP/IPsec provides data confidentiality and data integrity as well as proof that an authorized individual sent the message.

MORE INFORMATION

L2TP/IPsec is supported by Windows XP and later operating systems, Windows Server 2003, Windows Server 2008, Windows Server 2008R2, and Windows Server 2012 server operating systems. It is typically used for remote access and site-to-site VPNs; works over IPv4 and IPv6; supports Network Address Translation. It uses IPsec with 3DES (168bit key) and uses UDP Ports (500, 1701, 5500). It uses IPsec for machine authentication followed by PPP for user authentication.

UNDERSTANDING SECURE SOCKET TUNNELING PROTOCOL (SSTP)

Secure Socket Tunneling Protocol (SSTP) improved upon the PPTP and L2TP/IPsec VPN tunneling protocols. It works by sending PPP or L2TP traffic through an SSL 3.0 channel. The SSTP protocol uses SSL and TCP port 443 to relay traffic. By using TCP port 443, it will work in network environments where other VPN protocols might be blocked when traversing firewalls, network address translation (NAT) devices, and web proxies. SSTP uses a 2048-bit certificate for authentication and implements stronger encryption which makes it the most secure VPN protocol.

IKEv2 consists of the following protocols: IPsec Tunnel Mode, IKEv2, Encapsulating Security Payload (ESP), and MOBIKE. IKEv2 is used by IPsec for key negotiations, ESP for securing the packet transmissions, and MOBIKE (Mobility and Multi-homing Protocol) is used for switching tunnel endpoints. MOBIKE ensures that if there is a break in connectivity, the user can continue without restarting the connection.

MORE INFORMATION

SSTP is supported by Windows Vista SP1, Windows 7, Windows 8 client operating systems, Windows Server 2008, Windows Server 2008 R2, and Windows Server 2012 server operating systems. It is designed for remote access VPN and works over IPv4 and IPv6 networks, and traverses NAT, Firewalls and Web proxies. It uses a generic port that is rarely blocked by firewalls. It uses PPP for user authentication and RC4/AES for data confidentiality.

UNDERSTANDING VPN RECONNECT (IKEV2)

VPN Reconnect (IKEv2) is a feature introduced with Routing and Remote Access Services (RRAS) in Windows Server 2008 R2 and Windows 7. It is designed to provide users with consistent VPN connectivity and automatically reestablish a VPN when users temporarily lose their Internet connection. VPN Reconnect was designed for those remote workers who are sitting in the coffee shop, waiting at the airport for their next plane to arrive, trying to submit that last expense report from their hotel room or working anywhere Internet connections are less then optimal.

It differs from other VPN protocols in that it will not drop the VPN tunnel that is associated with the session. Instead, it keeps the connection alive for 30 minutes by default after it's been dropped. This allows you to reconnect automatically without having to go through the process of selecting your VPN connection and re-authenticating yourself all over again.

MORE INFORMATION

The IKEv2 setting (network outage) can be found in the RRAS console by right-clicking the RRAS server selecting Properties > IKEv2 tab.

VPN Reconnect is supported by Windows 7 and Windows 8 client operating systems, Windows Server 2008 R2 and Windows Server 2012 server operating systems, and is designed for remote access VPN. It works well over IPv4 and IPv6 networks and traverses NAT. It also supports user or machine authentication via IKEv2 and uses 3DES and AES for data confidentiality.

SELECTING THE RIGHT VPN

When selecting the appropriate VPN protocol to use, you must take into consideration the following:

- Operating systems you will be using, and their ability to traverse firewalls, NAT devices and web proxies.
- Authentication requirements; computers as well as the users.
- Implementations: Site-to-site VPN or a remote access VPN.

In most situations, using VPN Reconnect (IKEv2) will provide you the best option for security and uninterrupted VPN connectivity. You can then use SSTP for your VPN solution as a fall back mechanism.

■ Planning for Remote Access

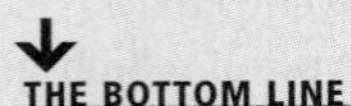

As part of your remote access design strategy, you must consider not only the user's experience but the bandwidth available, the redundancy of your network connections, the need to protect data passed between the remote clients and servers, and your ability to support the traffic that will cross your network links.

When planning for remote access, you must deliver a consistent experience to your users whether they connect over the local network or they connect across low-bandwidth networks when working from remote locations. In order for users to be productive while working remotely, they must have access to their remote resources at all times. As part of your remote access design, review your current topology and ensure you have redundancy built in not only to your devices (routers and switches) but to your network links as well.

CERTIFICATION READY
RDP
Objective 2.2

Although the Remote Desktop Protocol (RDP) uses compression and caching mechanisms to limit the amount of traffic transmitted over network links, consider the different types of traffic that will traverse the network links. For example, if you are using virtualization for your operating systems and applications to support your remote users, expect to see large bursts of data when the operating system and applications are sent to the remote client. Make sure your core infrastructure is capable of providing the bandwidth needed by your users.

If you are concerned about protecting sensitive data sent between remote users and your servers, configure group policies to require the use of a specific security layer to secure communications during RDP connections. RDP connections can be configured to support 128-bit encryption (the maximum level of encryption supported by the client) or 52-bit encryption mechanisms. The option you choose for your design is dependent on the capabilities of your remote clients and the level of encryption needed to meet your specific data protection needs. In general, your design should use the strongest encryption supported by your remote clients.

RDP 8.0 is integrated with Windows 2012 and Windows 8. With RDP 8.0, you can deploy remote clients (laptops, desktops, and/or virtual machines hosted in a data center) as part of your remote access strategy. If your remote access needs include supporting Windows 7 Service Pack 1 or Windows Server 2008 R2 Service Pack 1 systems, you should upgrade to RDP 8.0. This enables your older remote clients to gain access to the newer features. These features include an improved video conferencing experience, the ability to run a remote session from within another remote session, improved media streaming over slower public network links, and the ability for the remote client to automatically detect the characteristics of the network connection and optimize the connection accordingly.

■ Exploring Remote Access Using Direct Access and Routing and Remote Access (RRAS)

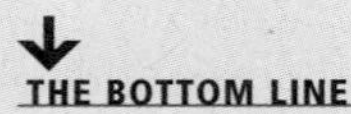

DirectAccess allows your remote users to connect automatically whenever their clients detect an Internet connection. RRAS is used to provide support for legacy VPN clients.

CERTIFICATION READY
VPN, DirectAccess
Objective 2.2

With the release of Windows Server 2012, Direct Access and Routing and Remote Access have now been combined into a single Remote Access role. You can configure both from within a single console that allows you to configure, manage, and monitor the DirectAccess and VPN remote access servers in your organization. Using the built-in dashboard, you can view server and client activity, generate detailed reports and even monitor the resources being accessed by the clients. Windows PowerShell can also be used to create automate scripts for remote access setup, configuration, troubleshooting and management tasks.

REVIEWING ENHANCEMENTS IN DIRECTACCESS WITH WINDOWS SERVER 2012

DirectAccess is designed for use by domain-based clients (Windows 7 (Enterprise and Ultimate), Windows 8 (Enterprise), Windows Server 2008 R2, and Windows Server 2012) while Routing and Remote Access Services (RRAS) provides traditional VPN access for legacy clients, non-domain clients, third party VPN clients and site-to-site connections between servers.

In previous releases (Windows Server 2008 R2), you had to deploy Direct Access and RRAS separately. RRAS implements IKEv2 and configures incoming and outgoing packet filters to drop all packets using transition technologies. On the other hand, Direct Access uses IPv6 transition technologies to establish client connections and IPsec Denial of Service (DoSP) to drop all IPv4 traffic and IPv6 traffic not protected with IPsec. In Windows Server 2012, Microsoft resolved these issues by modifying the IKEv2 policies to allow IPv6 transition technology traffic and modified the DSoP to allow VPN traffic.

Windows Server 2012 also removes the need to use Public Key Infrastructure which was a major obstacle to deploying Direct Access in Windows Server 2008 R2/Windows 7. It does this configuring the clients to send authentication requests to a Kerberos proxy service that runs on the Direct Access server. The Kerberos proxy service sends the requests to a domain controller for authentication.

Direct Access doesn't use a traditional VPN connection. While a traditional VPN required the user to manually initiate and disconnect a VPN connection when they wanted to connect to their corporate office. Direct Access is designed to establish connectivity whenever an internet connection is available. This occurs whether the user is logged on or not. From an administrator perspective, this allows you to manage and monitor the remote computer to apply patches and check for compliance enforcement.

Additional Features in Windows Server 2012 include:

- Force tunneling (sends all traffic through the Direct Access connection)
- Network Access Protection (NAP) compliance
- Support for locating the nearest Remote Access server from DirectAccess clients distributed across different geographical locations.
- Deploying DirectAccess for only remote management.
- You can configure the DirectAccess server with two network adapters at the network edge or behind an edge device, or with a single network adapter running behind a firewall or NAT device. By using a single adapter, you remove the requirement of needing dedicated public IPv4 addresses for DirectAccess deployments. Clients connect with the DirectAccess server by using IP-HTTPS.

UNDERSTANDING HOW DIRECT ACCESS WORKS

DirectAccess works by establishing two IPsec tunnels from the client to the DirectAccess server. The IPv6 packets, protected using IPsec, are encapsulated inside IPv4 packets to make the transition across the Internet (see Figure 6-2).

CERTIFICATION READY
DirectAccess
Objective 2.2

The first is an infrastructure tunnel that is used to communicate with the DNS server and domain controller to obtain group policy and to request authentication. The second tunnel is used to authenticate the user and provide access to resources inside the network.

Figure 6-2
DirectAccess tunnels

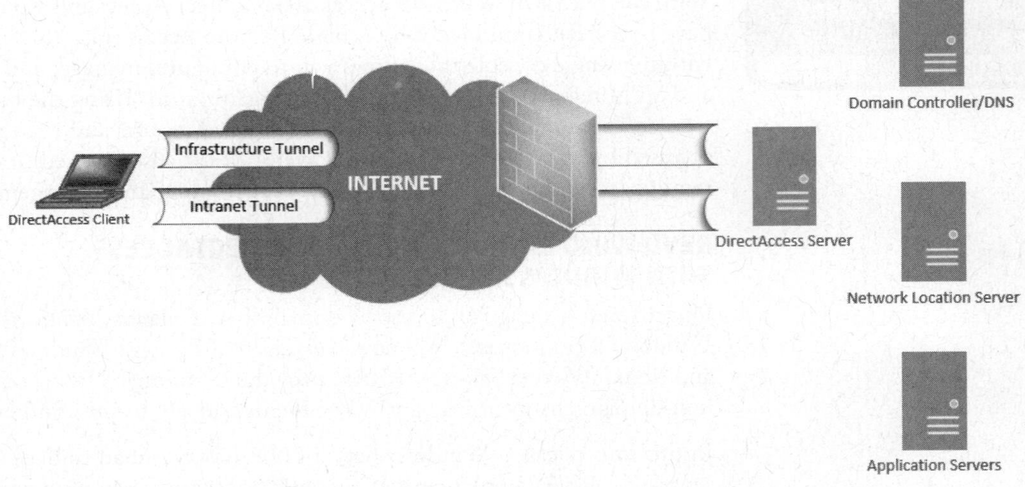

In Figure 6-2, you will see a ***Network Location Server (NLS)***. This can be installed directly on the Remote Access server or on another server in the network. NLS plays a critical role in whether the DirectAccess client components are enabled. In fact, NLS is basically a web server used by the client to determine if it is on the corporate network. If it detects that it is on the corporate network, the DA client components are not enabled. If it cannot connect to the NLS, it assumes it is not on the corporate network and enables DirectAccess. The secret to how this works is a URL written into the client's registry by way of a group policy created during the deployment of the Remote Access Server. The client uses the URL and DNS to attempt to locate the NLS.

The DA clients use IPv6 to connect to resources on the intranet or to other DA clients. In situations where you have servers providing resources running on the intranet that do not support IPv6, or you have disabled IPv6, or you use applications that do not work natively with IPv6, you will need to provide access to these devices for the DirectAccess clients. This is accomplished by Windows Server 2012 through the implementation of a protocol translation and name resolution gateway that supports NAT64 and DNS64.

NAT 64 will receive packets from the DA client and convert them into IPv4 before sending it to the resource on the intranet. It will convert IPv4 packets to IPv6 packets before sending the information back to the DA client. DNS64 handles the client's DNS query by converting the IPv4 answers into an associated IPv6 mapping on NAT64.

PLANNING YOUR SERVER DEPLOYMENT

When deploying Remote Access on the server, there are several decisions you will need to make. These include the topology you will use, whether or not you will support Windows 7 clients, and if you will implement a VPN for clients that do not support DirectAccess. You will also need to identify your IP addressing requirements, review your firewall settings, certificate requirements, DNS server information and address Network Location Service information issues.

- Microsoft's Remote Access supports one and two adapter topologies. When a single adapter is used the server should be installed behind a device such as a firewall or router. If you setup a remote access server with two adapters, one adapter is connected to the internal network and the other to either a perimeter network or directly to the Internet. If two adapters are used, you will need to make sure they are detected appropriately during the setup process. To make this process easier, name one of the internal and the other external prior to starting the installation of Remote Access.
- If you will be supporting Windows 7 remote clients, you will need to perform additional advanced configuration steps to enable them to connect via DirectAccess.

- If you will be supporting remote clients that do not support DirectAccess or will be unmanaged, you will need to provide VPN access. Using the Getting Started Wizard configures VPN IP addresses to be distributed by a DHCP Server and also configures the VPN clients to be authenticated using Active Directory.
- Firewall settings will need to be reviewed if you will be placing the RAS on an IPv4 subnet to ensure traffic is allowed to pass through: 6to4 traffic requires IP protocol 41 both inbound and outbound, IP-HTTPS requires TCP destination port 443 and TCP source port 443 outbound; If RAS is deployed with a single adapter and you install the network location service functionality, you will need to exempt TCP port 62000.
- During the setup of Remote Access, you will need to specify and IP address or fully qualified domain. This information, called the ConnectTo address is matched with the self-signed certificate used in IP-HTTPS connections and must be available via the public DNS. It is also used by the remote clients to connect to the server.
- If you configure your remote access server to use SSTP VPN, the wizard will integrate the certificate used by SSTP for IP-HTTPS. If SSTP VPN is not configured, the wizard will check to see if one has been configured for IP-HTTPS. If it can't find one, the wizard will provision a self-signed certificate and automatically enable Kerberos for authentication.
- DNS is used by DirectAccess clients to locate the Network Location Server. If they can reach the NLS, the clients assume they are on the local network and will not use DirectAccess and will rely on the DNS server configured on their local adapter for name resolution. If the client cannot locate the NLS, it will assume it is on the Internet and will use DirectAccess. This means it will consult its name resolution policy table (NRPT) to select a DNS server to use when resolving names. The Network Location Server is basically a website. Using the Getting Started Wizard to setup RAS will result in the NLS being setup on the server itself and a self-signed certificate will be generated.

PLANNING YOUR DIRECT ACCESS CLIENT DEPLOYMENT

When planning your client deployment, you will need to make decisions regarding whether you want to make DirectAccess available to mobile computers only or to any computer. The Getting Started Wizard, which can be run after installing the Remote Server role, will by default, configure DirectAccess for mobile computers that are members of the Domain Computers security group only. It does this by creating a WMI filter for the DirectAccess Client Settings GPO.

CERTIFICATION READY
DirectAccess
Objective 2.2

A ***WMI filter*** is used to control the application of the GPO. The WMI filter is evaluated on the target computer during the processing of the Group Policy. The GPO will only be applied if the WMI filter evaluates as true. In this case, even though there are other computers that are members of the Domain Computers security group, they will not receive the DirectAccess policy because they are not considered to be mobile computers.

USING THE GETTING STARTED WIZARD TO SETUP A REMOTE ACCESS SERVER

When setting up the Remote Access Server, you will have the option to use the Getting Started Wizard to complete the post installation setup. The Wizard backs up existing GPOs and then creates two group policy objects (GPOs) that are used by the server and the clients.

- DAServerSettings: This GPO is filtered to apply to the DirectAccess server computer account only (See Figure 6-3).
- DAClientSettings: This GPO is filtered to apply to **mobile computers** in the Domain Computers global security group. If you decide to change this default behavior, you will need to create a new security group for your DirectAccess clients (see Figure 6-4).

These policies are linked to the root of your Active Directory domain automatically if the install is run under the Domain Administrator's account.

The Getting Started Wizard also performs the following tasks:

Figure 6-3

DirectAccess server settings GPO

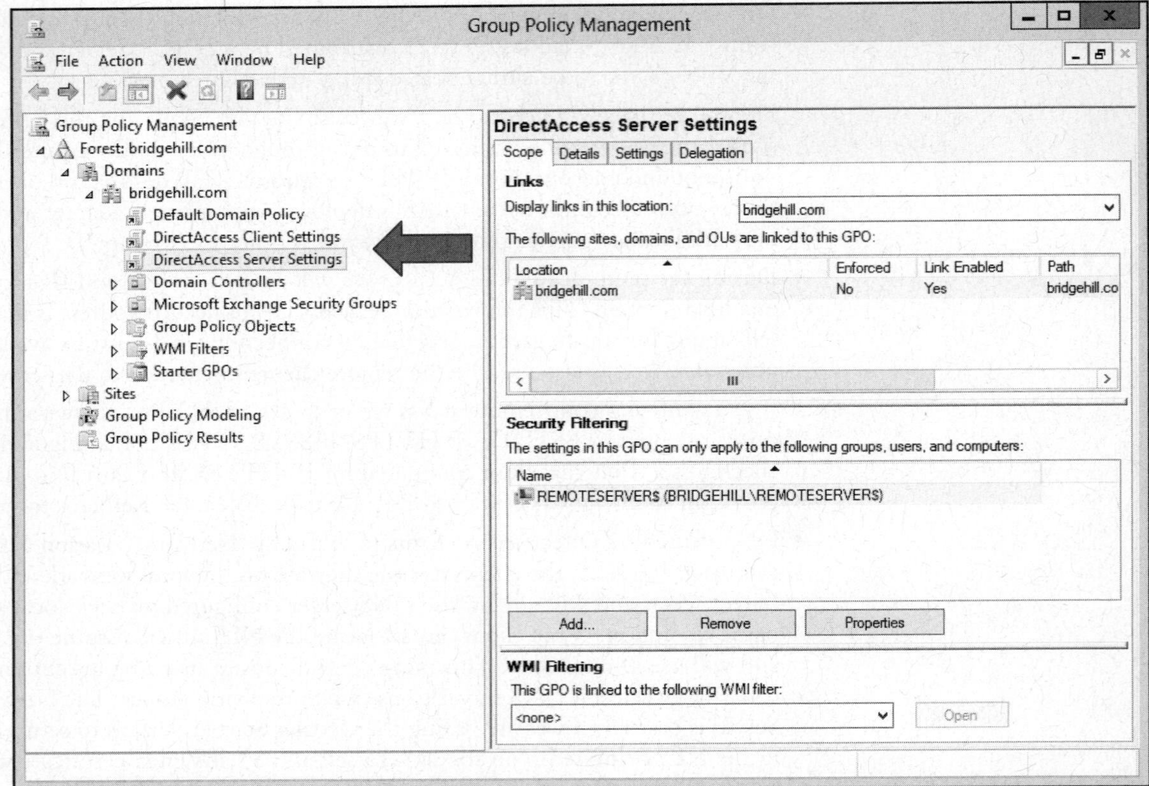

Figure 6-4

WMI filter applied for DirectAccess Client settings GPO

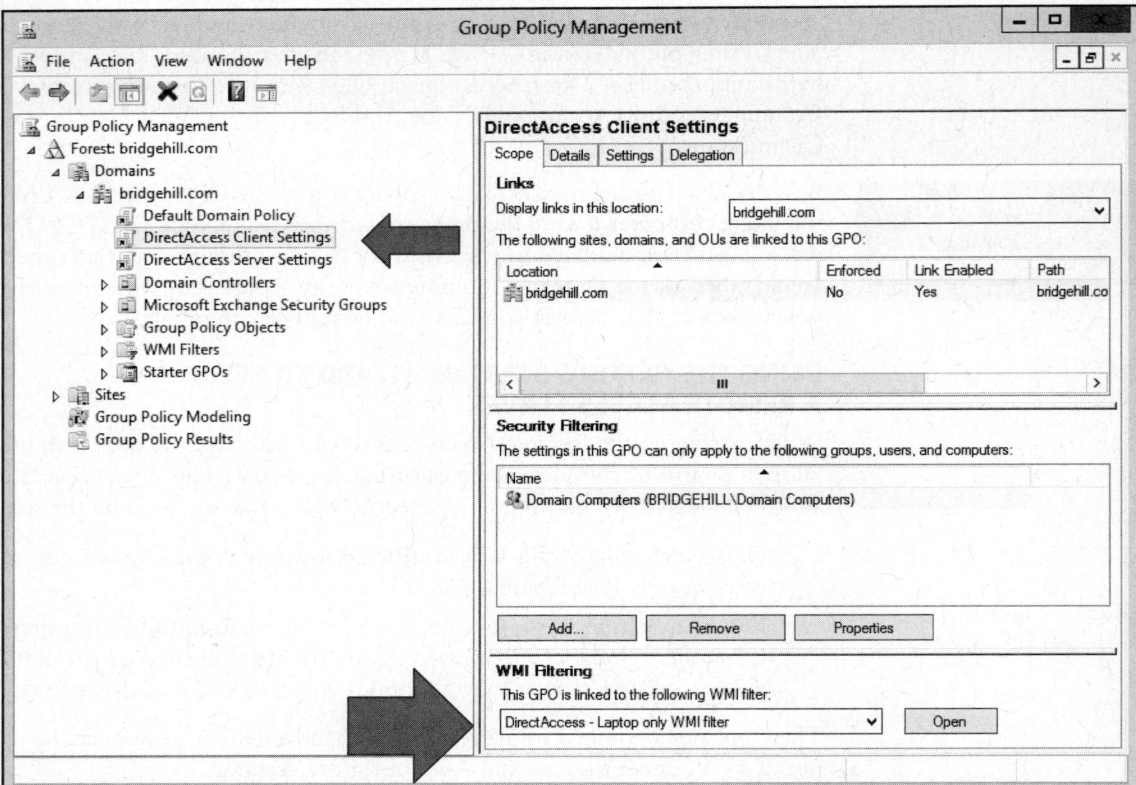

- Configures the Kerberos proxy which eliminates the need for you to setup a Public Key Infrastructure. You can also configure DirectAccess to use certificates issued by a PKI Certificate Authority.
- Enables NAT64 and DNS64 which are used for protocol translation in IPv4-only network environments.
- Generates, self-signs and verifies an IP-HTTPS certificate on the DirectAccess Server.
- Identifies the infrastructure servers in the domain
- Registers DNS entries used to check client connectivity.
- Creates client policies
- Applies GPOs to remote access servers

DEPLOY RRAS/DIRECTACCESS USING THE GETTING STARTED WIZARD

GET READY. To setup RRAS/DirectAccess with the Getting Started Wizard, perform the following steps. This requires a Windows Server 2012 member server, a domain controller and a DNS server present on the network

1. Login with domain administrative credentials to a Windows Server 2012 member server.
2. Open Server Manager.
3. Select Manage > **Add Roles and Features** (see Figure 6-5).

Figure 6-5

Add Roles and Features Wizard for Remote Access

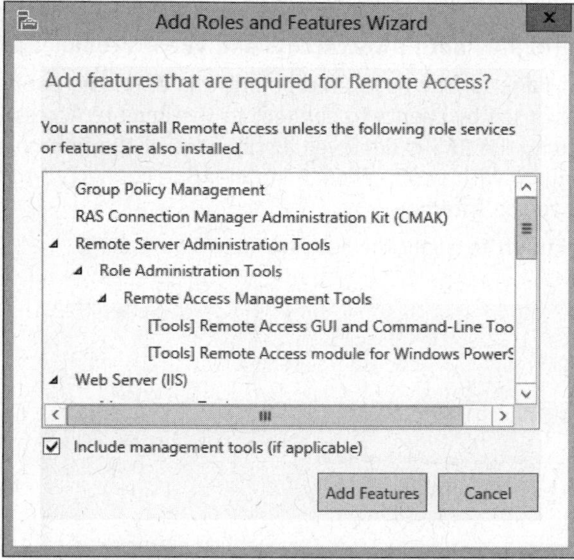

4. Click **Next.**
5. Select Role-based or featured-based installation and click **Next.**
6. Select the member server from the Server pool and click **Next.**
7. Select the **Remote Access** Role and then click **Add Features.**
8. Click **Next.**
9. Read the information regarding Remote Access and click **Next.**
10. Select **DirectAccess and VPN (RAS)** and click **Next.**
11. Read the Web Server role and click **Next.**
12. Click **Next.**
13. Click Install after confirming your installation selections.

14. Click the **Getting Started Wizard** after the installation completes (see Figure 6-6). **Note:** You can also start this wizard from within the Remote Access Management Console by clicking the Run the Getting Started Wizard link.

Figure 6-6

Remote Access Getting Started Wizard

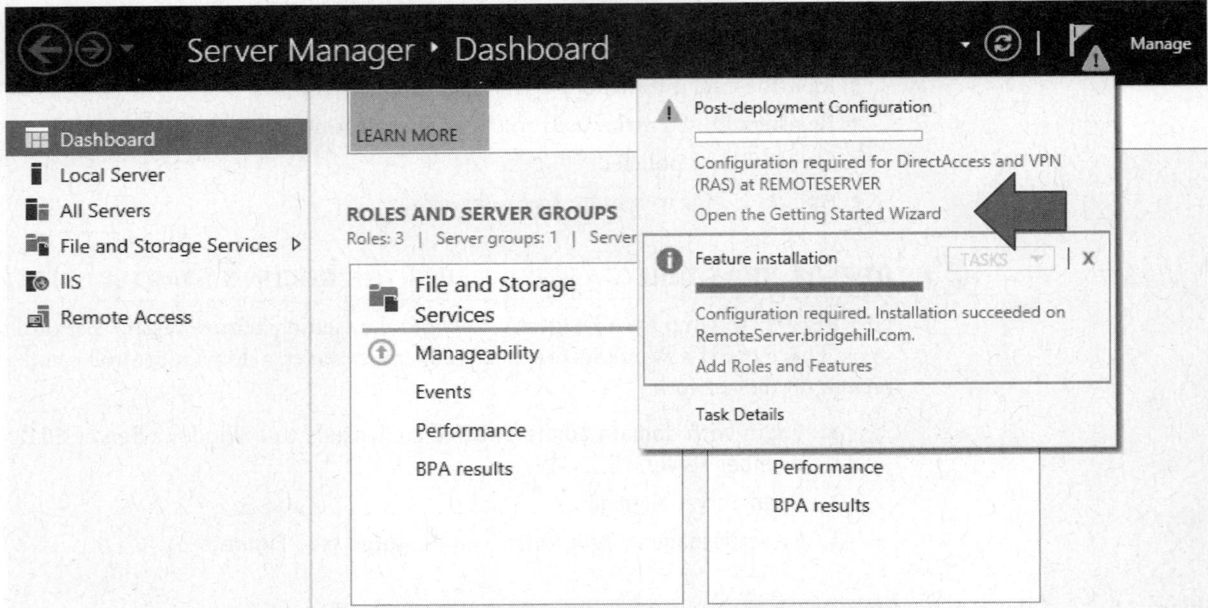

15. Select **Deploy both DirectAccess and VPN (recommended)**.
16. Select **Edge** for the network topology and enter the public name (FQDN) or IPv4 address used by clients to connect to the Remote Access Server. Click **Next.** In this topology, the RAS is deployed at the edge of the internal corporate network and is configured with two network adapters. One connected to the internal network, the other to the Internet.
17. Click **Finish** to apply the settings (see Figure 6-7).

Figure 6-7

Applying Getting Started Wizard settings

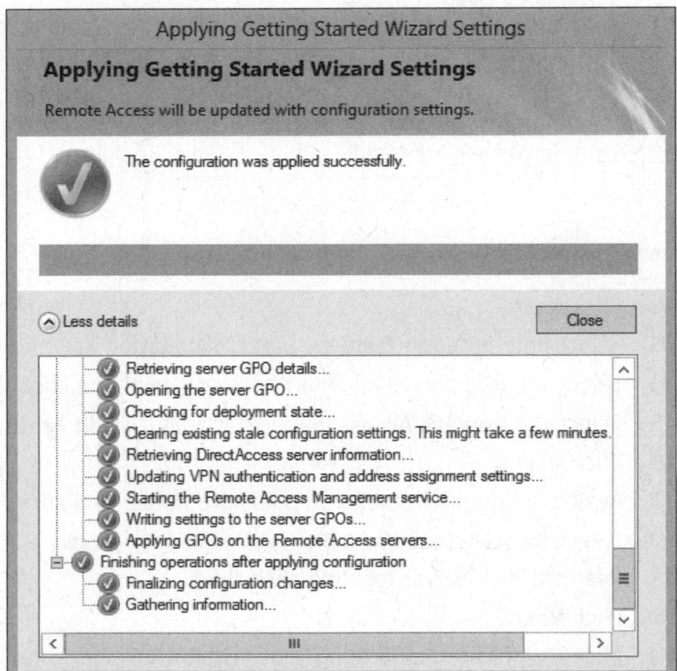

18. Select **More details** to monitor the tasks performed by the Wizard.
19. Click **Close** when process is completed.
20. Click **Finish.**
21. Select the **Operations Status** in the Remote Access Management Console that opens to confirm the server is working properly (see Figure 6-8).

Figure 6-8

Confirming Operations Status Post Installation

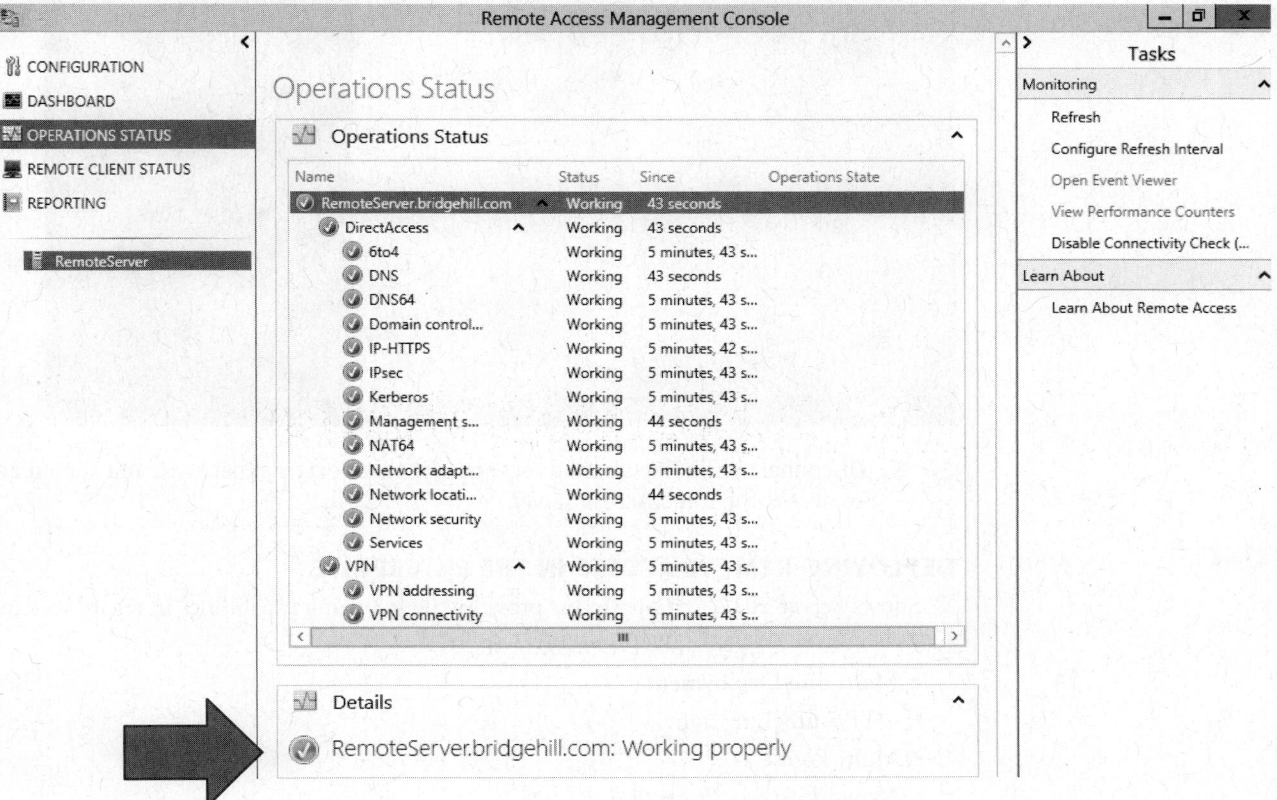

 VERIFY YOUR DIRECTACCESS DEPLOYMENT ON A MOBILE COMPUTER

GET READY. To verify that DirectAccess was deployed to a Windows 8 mobile computer, perform the following steps while connected to the domain.

1. Connect the DirectAccess mobile client to your corporate network and obtain the DAClientSettings GPO.
2. Open Windows PowerShell with administrative privileges.
3. Enter **gpresult/r** and press Enter.
4. Confirm the DirectAccess Client Settings GPO has been applied under the COMPUTER SETTINGS section of the output.
5. Exit from Windows PowerShell.
6. Click the Network connection icon in the notification area.
7. Click the **Workplace Connection** option and you will see you are connected to the network locally (see Figure 6-9).

Figure 6-9
Workplace Connection

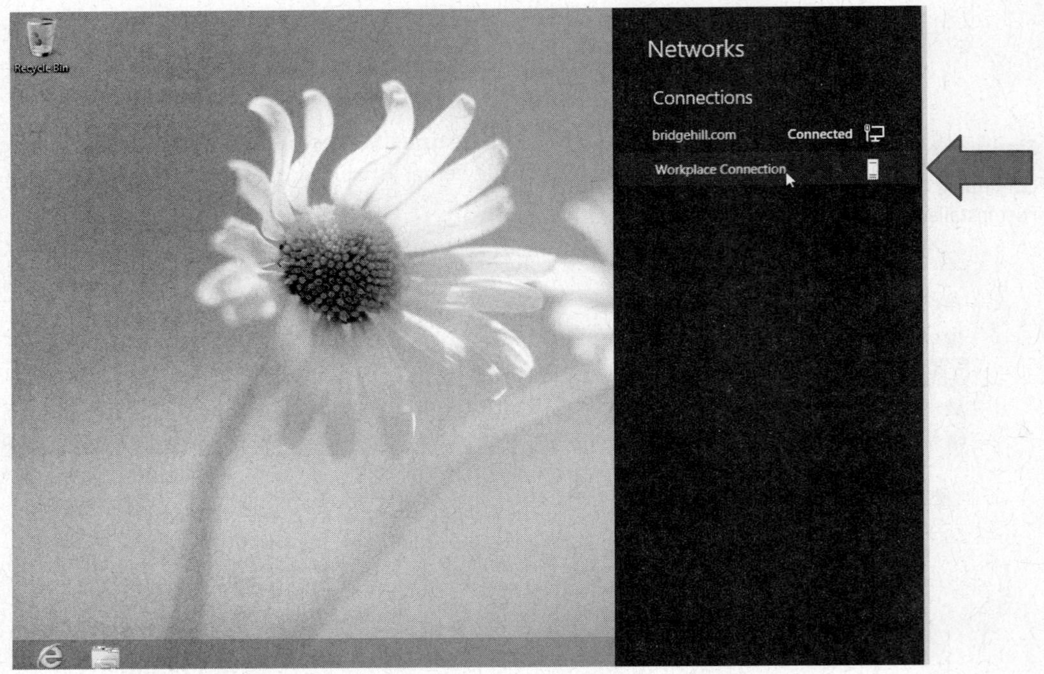

8. Disconnect the computer and reconnect it to an external network. You should be able to access the DirectAccess server.

DEPLOYING REMOTE ACCESS IN THE ENTERPRISE

Windows Server 2012 Remote Access provides the following capabilities in regard to deploying Remote Access in larger organizations:

- Multi-Site Deployment
- OTP Authentication
- Multi-Forest
- Network Access Protection

Deploying Remote Access servers (Multi-Site) with Clustering

In some situations, you may want to deploy multiple remote access servers or clusters to provide both redundancy and load balancing. This is especially true in situations where your employees are dispersed across geographical locations. This allows remote users to connect to a remote access server that is closest to their physical location and use it as an entry point into the network. While Windows 8 computers can automatically identify an entry point or the user can manually select one, Windows 7 requires that you manually enable support for Windows 7 on each entry point.

Cluster Deployments provide the following benefits:

- Grouping two or more remote access servers improves reliability and increases throughput.
- Provides always-on access. If one remote access server fails, users can continue to access the network using one of the other servers in the cluster.
- Clusters can be managed as a single entity. You can configure and manage settings from any server in the cluster or remotely by using the Remote Server Administration Tools (RSAT) for Windows 8. You can also monitor the entire cluster from a single console.

Deploying a single RAS in a clustered environment involves the following steps:

1. Implement a single remote access deployment. This involves configuring the remote access infrastructure, configuring the remote access server settings, and verifying the deployment.

2. Prepare cluster servers. This involves configuring each of the servers that will be in the cluster with the same topology as the first RAS server, configuring each of the servers with the appropriate IP address, routing and forwarding based on the configuration of the first server (all must be on the same subnet), and then joining each of the servers to the same domain as the first RAS server.
3. Configure a load-balanced cluster. This requires enabling load balancing, selecting the method (Windows NLB or External Load Balancing), and configuring the virtual IP address of the load-balanced cluster. You will also install the IP-HTTPS certificate and the network location server certificate and then add the servers to the cluster.
4. Verify the cluster. To make sure the cluster is operating appropriately, you will need to connect a DirectAccess client to the corporate network to obtain the policy, connect the client to the external network and attempt to access internal resources. You can then test connectivity through each server in the cluster by disconnecting all but one and then repeat for each cluster member.

Deploying Remote Access servers with OTP Authentication

In addition to configuring Remote Access to authenticate using standard Active Directory credentials, you can also use one-time password (OTP) user authentication. In order to use this option, the Remote Access server must already be deployed. For OTP authentication, you will need a RADIUS-enabled OTP server that supports the password authentication protocol (PAP). This requires that you configure the Remote Access server as a RADIUS agent, synchronize your Active Directory with the RADIUS server, and configure a shared secret and the port number for RADIUS traffic.

To support OTP, you will also need to plan how you will handle certificate authority requirements. DirectAccess clients obtain their OTP certificate by first requesting it from the Remote Access Server (RAS). The RAS server then verifies the credentials to make sure they are valid, signs a signing certificate using the registration authority certificate and then passes the enrollment request back to the DirectAccess client. The client enrolls the OTP certificate from the CA which also verifies the credentials and the actual request. The CA will only issue the certificate if it has been signed the Remote Access server's registration authority certificate.

+ MORE INFORMATION

The same internal CA that handles your IPsec certificates can be configured to handle DirectAccess OTP certificates

Deploying Remote Access servers in Multi-Forest Environments

To allow remote access between forests, you will need to make sure you configure a two-way transitive trust between the two forests. This will make it possible for administrators to edit the DirectAccess GPOs and use security groups for the other forest when setting up remote access. You will also need to make the Remote Access administrator a local administrator on all Remote Access servers in the new forest. In addition to these changes, you will need to configure at least one security group for the DirectAccess client machines in the new forest. If you have Windows 8 clients, you will need at least one security group for each forest but best practice dictates having one for each domain that has Windows 8 clients. You should also have the same setup in place for Windows 7 clients. Client GPOs will need to be created for each additional domain where DirectAccess will be applied.

Deploying Remote Access servers with Network Access Protection

Network Access Protection (NAP) is a feature that combines client and server elements. NAP allows you to create and enforce health requirement polices that specify the required software and system configurations that computers must have to connect to your network. NAP works by inspecting and assessing the health of computers and limiting their access when they are identified as being noncompliant. If a system is identified as non-compliant, NAP can automatically bring the client into compliance through a process called remediation.

Before deploying NAP, you need to determine what constitutes a compliant system and what you consider to be a non-compliant system. For example, you may consider a system to be compliant if it has the firewall running, has updated antivirus and malware definitions and is completely patched. Systems that are assessed as healthy will be allowed to gain access to your entire network while those that are not will be restricted to an area of the network (e.g. subnet) for additional remediation services. This subnet may have basic DNS and IP services as well as the ability to provide Microsoft Updates to bring the system into compliance. Once under compliance, the system will be able to access the rest of the network.

There are five enforcement options you can use for clients running the NAP agent:

MORE INFORMATION

NAP client capable systems include Windows XP SP3 and later operating system as well as Windows Server 2008 and later systems. All enforcement methods can be implemented using a minimum of one server running Windows Serve 2008, Windows Server 2008 R2 or Windows Server 2012. The additional services you will require are dependent upon the enforcement method you use.

- NAP with IPsec enforcement: Requires AD domain controller, Network Policy Server (NPS), Certification Authority (AD or Third Party) and Health Registration Authority role with Internet Information Services; client must first obtain an IPsec certificate to get access to the network. If the computer is not compliant, it may be allowed to communicate with selected resources on the network. For example, a Microsoft Update Server until it gets the certificate.
- NAP with 802.1x enforcement: Relies on the routers and switches that support your underlying network; regardless of how the client connects it will be checked for compliance against an NPS. If it doesn't meet compliance, it can be restricted to the remediation subnet.
- NAP with VPN enforcement: Requires RRAS server; running Network Policy Server role or configured to communicate with an NPS; clients that are healthy are let in; noncompliant systems are restricted to the remediation subnet. This does not protect against clients accessing in some other way.
- NAP with DHCP enforcement: Requires MS DHCP server; clients attempt to get IP address and the DHCP server will either have policies or check with a Network Policy Server (NPS). If the client meets those requirements, it gets an IP address; otherwise it will be assigned an IP address that lets it gain access to the remediation subnet. This does not protect against a client using a static IP address.

You can implement any of the enforcement methods without restricting the access of computers that are identified as noncompliant. This provides the benefit of automatic remediation and compliance monitoring. You will not have to setup a restricted area to isolate computers that need remediation, but can still generate the same NAP reports.

The option you choose to implement will depend upon what your overall design goal is for your computers, the infrastructure, cost, security needs and overall complexity.

DEPLOY REMOTE ACCESS IN THE ENTERPRISE FOR DIRECTACCESS CLIENTS ONLY

GET READY. To deploy Remote Access in the Enterprise, perform the following steps on a Windows Server 2012 member server:

1. Install the Remote Access Role You can streamline this by using the following Windows PowerShell command:

```
Install-WindowsFeature RemoteAccess - IncludeManagementTools
```

2. Select Tools > Remote Access Management from the Server manager console (see Figure 6-10).

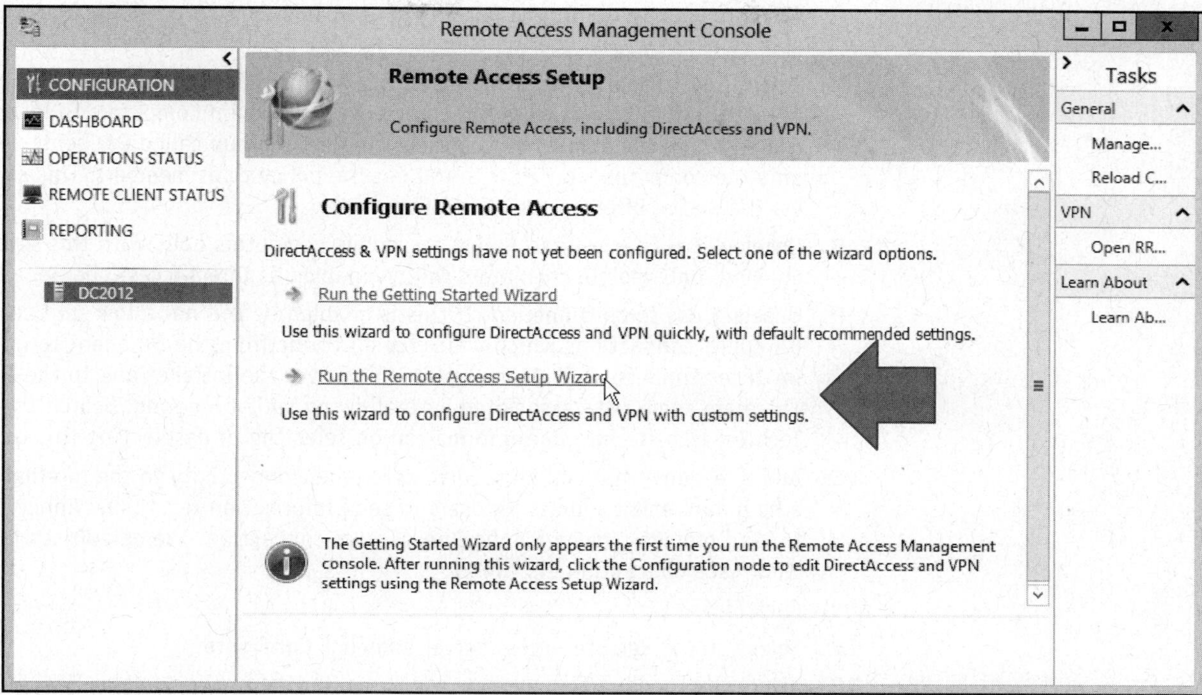

Figure 6-10
Advanced setup of Remote Access server

3. Click the **Run the Remote Access Setup Wizard** link.
4. Select Deploy DirectAccess only (see Figure 6-11).

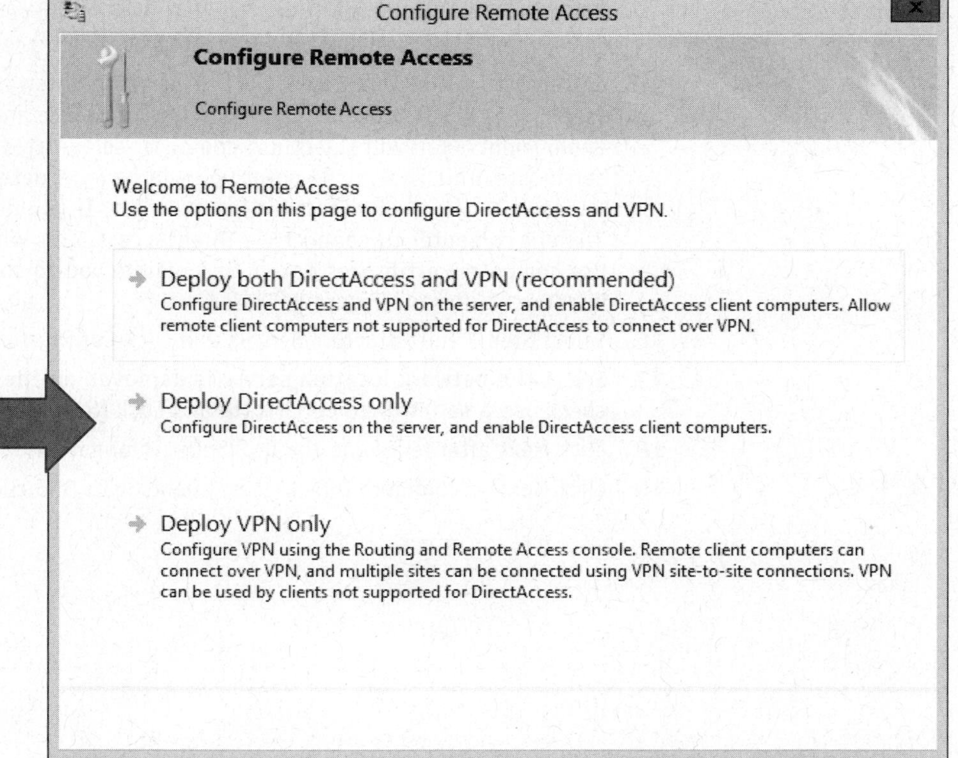

Figure 6-11
Configure deployment type

5. Select Step 1 Remote Clients and click **Configure**.
6. Select **Deploy full DirectAccess for client access and remote management** and click **Next.** Using this setting, DirectAccess client computers located on the internet can connect to the internal network via the Remote Access server. You will also be able to remotely manage the clients.
7. Select **Add** to select one or more security groups that contain the clients that you want to enable DirectAccess for. You can select Domain Computers to incorporate all computers in the domain but consider creating a group called DAClients and making only the computers you want to roll out the policy to as members. This can be done via the Active Directory Users and Computers.
8. Unselect the Enable DirectAccess for mobile computers only. With this setting enabled, only mobile computers will be enabled as DirectAccess clients.
9. Unselect use force tunneling. If this is enabled, it will not allow split tunneling for DA client connections which will force all traffic from the DA client to go over the DA IPsec tunnels. This means traffic going over the intranet and to the Internet. There are some risks associated with allowing split-tunneling. Search the Microsoft TechNet website for more information on selecting or deselecting this option.
10. Add a resource that will be used to determine connectivity to the internal network, a help desk email address for users to send information regarding connectivity issues to, and provide a name for the DirectAccess connection. The default setting is WorkPlace Connection Click **Next**.
11. Click **Finish**.
12. Select Step 2 Remote Access Server and click **Configure**.
13. Select the topology you want to use and enter the public name or IPv4 address that will be used by clients to connect to this server and click **Next.**
14. Identify the Internal network adapter that you want to use and select **use a self-signed certificate created Automatically by DirectAccess** and click **Next**.
This certificate will be used to authenticate IP-HTTPS connection. You can either browse to the certificate if you purchased a public certificate or you can use a self-signed certificate that can be created by DirectAccess automatically.
15. Select Active Directory credentials (user name/password) for user authentication (see Figure 6-12). Note: If you are using multi-site and two-factor authentication deployments, you will select use computer certificates and select the IPsec root certificate. This is also the point you will have to determine if you want to support Windows 7 client computers for DirectAccess. If you do, select the Enable Windows 7 client computer to connect via DirectAccess. This will automatically enable the use computer certificates option and require you to complete it to support Windows 7 clients. (Figure 6-12)
16. Select Step 3 Infrastructure Servers and click **Configure**.
17. Select **the network location server is deployed on the Remote Access server** and check **use a self-signed certificate** and click **Next.**
18. Click **Next** after reviewing the DNS Suffix information.
19. Click **Next** to configure DirectAccess clients with DNS client suffix search list.

Figure 6-12

Enabling authentication for DirectAccess clients

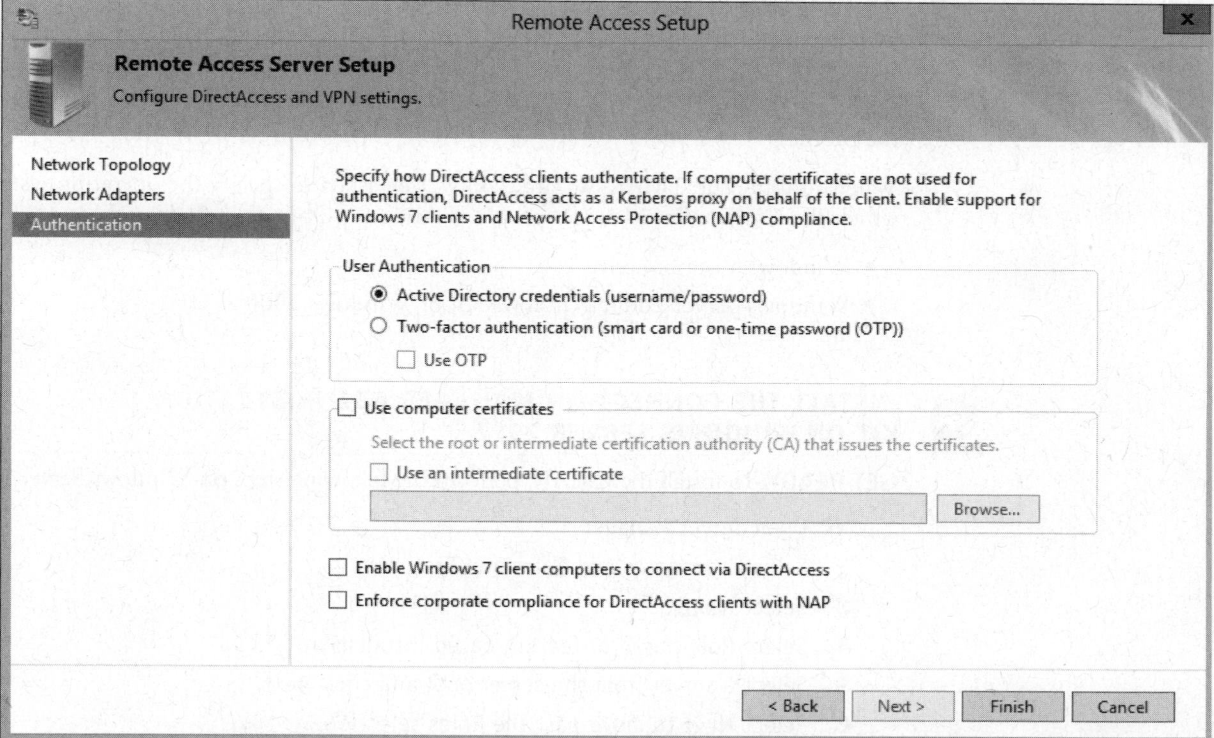

20. Click **Finish**.
21. Review the Configuration Settings and click **Apply**.

MORE INFORMATION

Configuring application servers is an optional task. This can be done if you require remote access clients to require authentication to selected application servers. This is controlled based on their inclusion into a security group. Traffic to these application servers will also be encrypted by default but you can decide to not encrypt if it makes sense for your environment.

Using Connection Manager and the Connection Manager Administration Kit (CMAK)

THE BOTTOM LINE

Connection Manager is a client network connection tool that helps administrators to simplify the management of their remote connections.

Connection Manager is a client network connection tool that helps administrators to simplify the management of remote connections. CM uses profiles that consist of settings that allow connections from the local computer to a remote network.

CERTIFICATION READY
VPN, Remote Administration
Objective 2.2

You use the ***Connection Manager Administration Kit (CMAK)*** to create and customize the profiles for Connection Manager and to distribute them to users. The profile, once completed, contains all the settings necessary for the user to connect including the IP address of the VPN server.

Connection Manager supports different features in a profile depending upon the operating system that is running on the client computer. You must create a connection profile on a computer that uses the same architecture (32/64-bit) as the clients on which you will install the profile.

When running the CMAK Wizard, you will be asked to specify the operating system on which the Connection Manager profile will be run. Options include:

- Windows Vista or above
- Windows Server 2003, Windows XP, or Windows 2000

INSTALL THE CONNECTION MANAGER ADMINISTRATION KIT ON WINDOWS SERVER 2012

GET READY. To install the CMAK, perform the following steps on Windows Server 2012:

1. Open Server Manager
2. Select Manage > Add Roles and Features
3. Select **Next.**
4. Select Role-based or feature-based installation.
5. Select a server from the server pool and click **Next.**
6. Select **Next** to move past the Roles selection.
7. Select RAS Connection Manager Administration Kit (CMAK).
8. Confirm Installation selections and click **Install.**
9. Confirm installation completes and click **Close.**
10. Select Tools > Connection Manager Administration Kit (see Figure 6-13).

Figure 6-13

Starting the Connection Manager Administration Kit (CMAK)

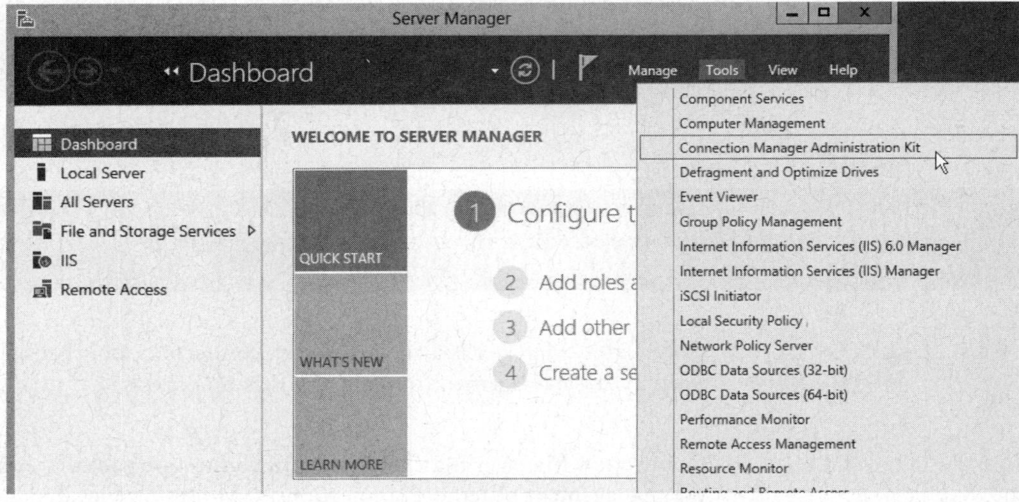

SETUP A SIMPLE VPN ONLY PROFILE USING CMAK

GET READY. To setup a simple VPN Profile using CMAK, perform the following steps. This activity is designed to expose the features and options available when creating a Connection Manager profile using CMAK from Windows Server 2012. As you walk through each step, be sure to read the explanation behind it to gain more insight into how CMAK could be used in your specific network environment. Note: The following creates a VPN only profile:

1. Start Connection Manager (Server Manager > Tools > Connection Manager Administration Kit.
2. Click **Next** after reading the Welcome message.
3. Select **Windows Vista or above** and click **Next**.
   This is where you need to match the architecture of the clients that will be installing and using the profile.
4. Select **New Profile** and click **Next**.
   Notice that you can modify an existing profile if one exists.
5. Read the information below and then Enter **MyVPN** for the service name and for the file name and click **Next**. The service name is used to identify the profile in Connection Manager and is also the name the users will see. The final executable file will also appear a MyVPN.exe.
6. Read the information below and then select **Do not add a realm name to the user name** and click **Next**.
   This is optional. Realm names, only used for dial up connections, provide the information necessary to forward authentication requests to the server that holds the user's credential information (e.g., Active Directory Domain Services). By selecting to not add a realm name, the connection profile will send the user name to the remote server exactly as it is typed. If a realm name was entered, the realm name would be added to the user name before it is sent to the remote server for authentication.
7. Select **Next** when prompted to merge information with another profile. If you had an additional profile, you could merge phone book information, access numbers and VPN host address information.
8. Read the information below and then select **Phone book from this profile** and specify a VPN server: **RemoteServer.bridgehill.com** and click **Next**. To gain access to the private network through the public Internet, a user establishes their connection by using a tunneling protocol. The user can connect directly to this private network through the tunnel by either dialing in to their local Internet Service Provider (ISP) or by using a direct connection to the Internet such as through a cable modem. In this area of profile setup, we are creating a VPN only profile by choosing these specific settings.

   The "Allow the user to choose a VPN server before connecting option" will require you to provide a text file that lists the VPN servers from which the user can choose. The following provides you with an example that can be created and modified within Notepad.

   ```
   [Settings]
   default=BridgeHill CorpHQ
   UpdateURL=http://remoteusers.bridgehill.com/MyVPNfile.txt
   Message=Select a server that is closest to your location.
   [BridgeHill VPN Servers]
   BridgeHill Computers CorpHQ=remoteusers.bridgehill.com
   BridgeHill Computers Los Angeles=LA.remoteusers.bridgehill.com
   BridgeHill Computers Austin=Austin.remoteusers.bridgehill.com
   ```

9. Select **Edit** to view the settings that can be configured for this VPN profile.

   In the General tab, you have the option to disable file and printer sharing and enable clients to connect using only IPv4, IPv6 or use both. On the IPv4 and IPv6 tabs you can configure how the VPN client will receive its IP address as well as the DNS and WINS address information. The Security tab provides options for selecting the tunneling, data encryption and authentication methods that will be used to communicate with the VPN server. Under the Advanced tabs, you can configure and register the connection's address and DNS suffice information (see Figure 6-14).

Figure 6-14

VPN settings

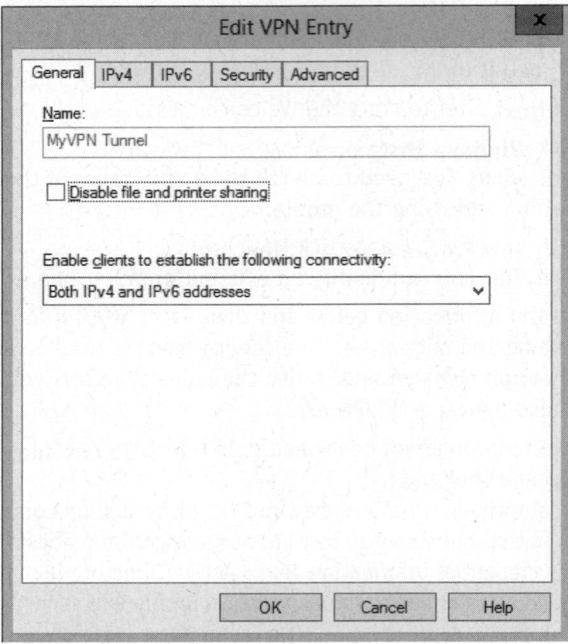

10. Clear the Automatically download phone book updates and click **Next**. By using Phone Book Administrator, included with Connection Point Services (CPS), you can create a phone book file that contains a list of multiple access numbers that can be used to connect to a remote dial-up network. CPS consists of a Phone Book Service (PBS) and the Phone Book Administrator (PBA). PBS is an extension to Internet Information Services extension. The PBA allows you to create and edit up to 100 unique phone books. Each phone book is a collection of Points of Presence (POPs) or dial up entries. The PBA allows you to associate POPs with the network configurations you define in the Connection Manager profile.
11. Click **Next**.
12. Make sure **Do not change the routing tables** is selected and click **Next**. Entries in a routing table control how client computers exchange data with other networks. You can define a routing table update via a file or use a URL that points to a route file.
13. Make sure **Do not configure proxy setting** is selected and click **Next**. Use this page to configure proxy server settings either by copying them from the Internet Explorer settings on the current user or use a Proxy settings file.
14. Select **Next** to not add any custom actions. These represent pre or post connect tasks you want to include.
15. Select **Next** to display a default graphic or select one of your own.
16. Select **Next** to display a default graphic for a custom phone book.
17. Select **Next** to use a default icon for the Connection Manager user interface.
18. Select **Next** to use the default help file. This will be displayed when the user clicks Help in the Connection Manager window.
19. Add any text you want to appear in the logon dialog box and click **Next**. (Example: Contact Support at 800-123-1234)

20. Select **Next** when prompted to display a custom license agreement. If selected, this would appear when the Connection Manager profile is installed on the client computer.
21. Specify any additional files that the Connection Manager profile will require and click **Next**.
22. Select the **Advanced customization** option and click **Next**.
23. Set the following values as shown in Figure 6-15 and click **Apply**.

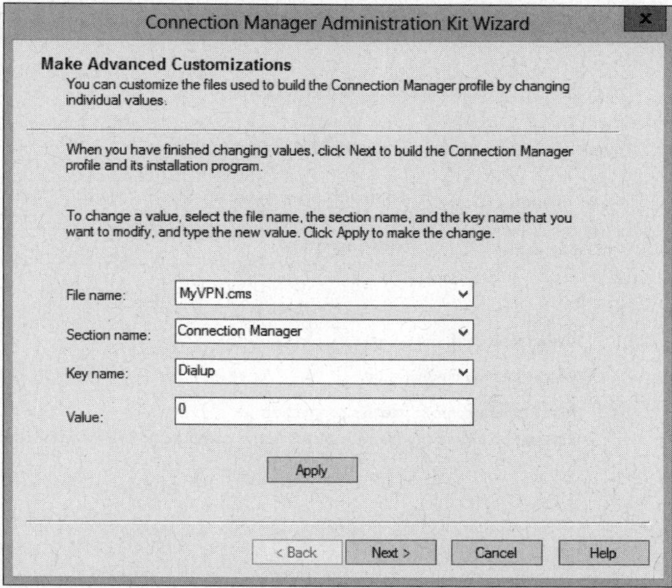

Figure 6-15

Advanced customization option to disable dial-up tab

24. Click **Next**.
25. Make a note of the location where the profile will be saved to. By default this will be the c:\Program Files\CMAK\Profiles\Windows Vista and above\MyVPN\MyVPN.exe
26. Click **Finish**.

Using the Getting Started Wizard in Windows 8

THE BOTTOM LINE

Windows 8 provides a simple Getting Started Wizard that helps make the setup and configuration of a VPN connection quick and simple for end users.

CERTIFICATION READY
VPN
Objective 2.2

To make the process of setting up a VPN profile and connecting to a VPN much simpler in Windows 8, you can use the **Get Connected Wizard**.

The GCW requires that you enter the server information and then it auto-discovers the authentication methods and tunneling protocols during the initial connection process.

CREATE A VPN CONNECTION USING THE GETTING STARTED WIZARD IN WINDOWS 8

GET READY. To create a VPN using the Windows 8 Getting Started Wizard, perform the following steps:

1. Select the Windows logo key + Q
2. Type **VPN** and set the context to **Settings**
3. Select **setup a virtual private network (VPN) connection** from the Results list.

4. Enter the Internet address of the Remote Access server and a destination name. Click **Create**. Authentication and Tunneling protocols will be negotiated and configured during the first successful connection attempt using the user name and password (see Figure 6-16).

Figure 6-16

Create a VPN Connection

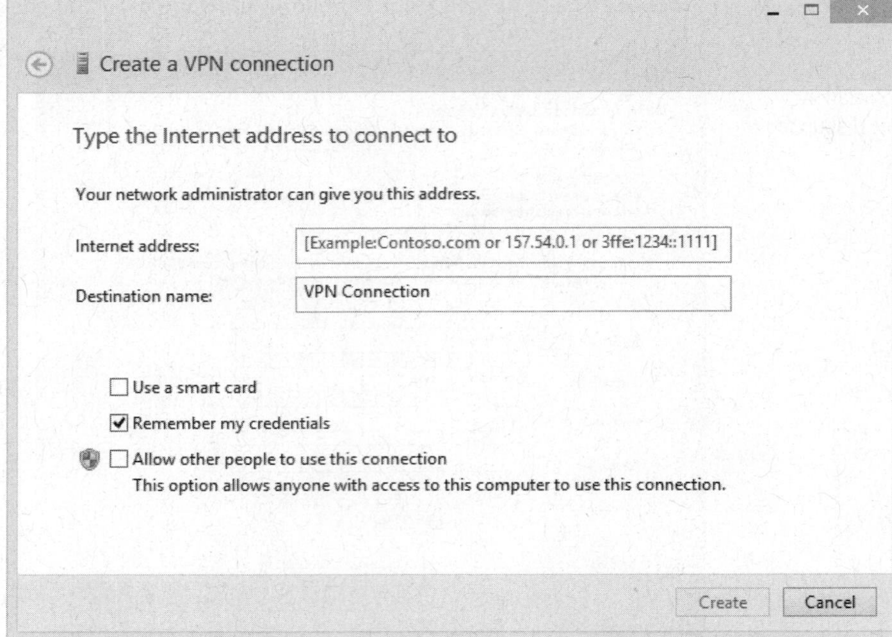

5. Select the Windows logo key + C to open the Charms bar.
6. Click Settings and then select the Internet access icon.
7. Select the VPN connection you created and click **Connect**.
8. Enter your credentials and click **OK**.

If you selected "remember my credentials" after making the initial connection, you can clear them by right-clicking the connection and select Clear cached credentials (see Figure 6-17).

Figure 6-17

Viewing connection Properties/clearing cached credentials

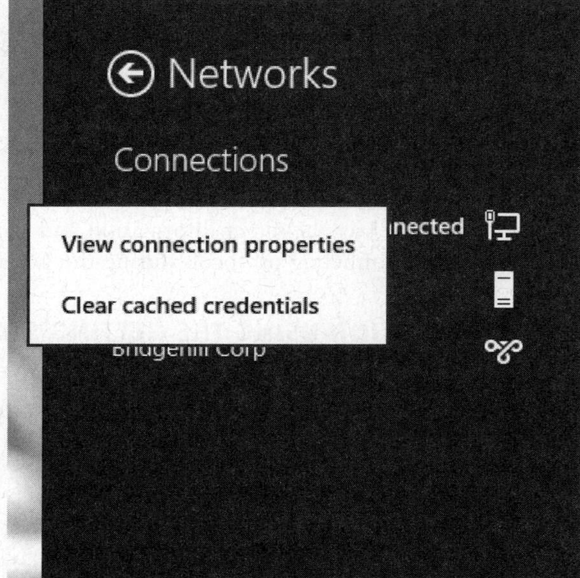

You can also view and edit your connection by selecting the View connection properties option (see Figure 6-18).

Figure 6-18

VPN connection properties

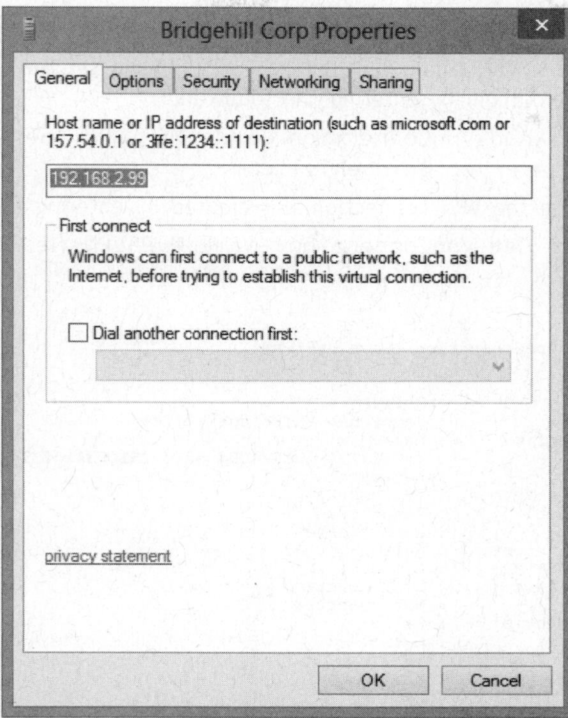

The following provides a brief explanation for each tab:

- General Tab: Provides host name and IP address of VPN server.
- Options Tab: Enable and disable your credentials, set idle time before hanging up, and configure PPP settings.
- Security Tab: Configure Data encryption settings, authentication and tunneling protocols.
- Networking Tab: Configure transports (IPv6, IPv4, File and Printer Sharing, and Client for Microsoft Networks).
- Sharing: Enable settings that allow others to connect through this computer's network connection.

MORE INFORMATION

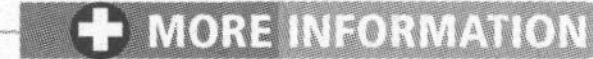

You can delete the VPN connection through the Control Panel > Network and Internet > Network Connections

Managing VPN Clients Using Windows PowerShell

THE BOTTOM LINE

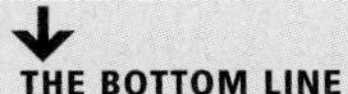

Windows PowerShell cmdlets can streamline the setup of VPN connections

CERTIFICATION READY
VPN
Objective 2.2

As you learned in earlier lessons, Windows PowerShell cmdlets allow you to streamline the setup of roles and features during installation and confirm settings on your computer.

You can also use them to view, create, configure and remove VPN connections on Windows 8 clients. Let's take a closer look at how to use Windows PowerShell to perform these common administrative tasks:

CREATE A VPN CONNECTION USING WINDOWS POWERSHELL

GET READY. To create a VPN Connection using Windows PowerShell, perform the following steps:

1. Open Windows PowerShell with Administrator permissions.
2. Create a VPN connection named MyPSVPN and set the server to RemoteServer.Bridgehill.com by entering the following:

   PS C:\Add-VpnConnection -Name MyPSVPN -ServerAddress RemoteServer.Bridgehill.com
3. Confirm the VPN connection was created by entering the following:

   PS C:\Get-VpnConnection -Name MyPSVPN (see Figure 6-19.)

Figure 6-19

Obtaining the VPN Connection information with Windows PowerShell Cmdlet

```
PS C:\> Get-VpnConnection -Name MyPSVPN


Name                   : MyPSVPN
ServerAddress          : RemoteServer.Bridgehill.com
AllUserConnection      : False
Guid                   : {AC3C7786-4D65-40D4-8274-251DC38E4835}
TunnelType             : Automatic
AuthenticationMethod   : {MsChapv2}
EncryptionLevel        : Required
L2tpIPsecAuth          : Certificate
UseWinlogonCredential  : False
EapConfigXmlStream     :
ConnectionStatus       : Disconnected
NapState               : NotConnected
RememberCredential     : False
SplitTunneling         : False
```

4. Create another VPN connection called VPNInt that uses split tunneling. Note: Setting the -splittunneling value to 1 is the equivalent to True which enables the setting.

   PS C:\Add-VpnConnection -name VPNInt -Server RemoteServer.Bridgehill.com -splittunneling 1
5. Review the VPN connection currently configured on the client by entering the following:

   PS C:\Get-VpnConnection (see Figure 6-20.)

Figure 6-20

Viewing two connections using Windows PowerShell Cmdlet

```
Name                   : MyPSVPN
ServerAddress          : RemoteServer.Bridgehill.com
AllUserConnection      : False
Guid                   : {AC3C7786-4D65-40D4-8274-251DC38E4835}
TunnelType             : Automatic
AuthenticationMethod   : {MsChapv2}
EncryptionLevel        : Required
L2tpIPsecAuth          : Certificate
UseWinlogonCredential  : False
EapConfigXmlStream     :
ConnectionStatus       : Disconnected
NapState               : NotConnected
RememberCredential     : False
SplitTunneling         : False

Name                   : VPNInt
ServerAddress          : RemoteServer.Bridgehill.com
AllUserConnection      : False
Guid                   : {2EF4D169-8380-4ECE-A761-A2BCE7646E86}
TunnelType             : Automatic
AuthenticationMethod   : {MsChapv2}
EncryptionLevel        : Required
L2tpIPsecAuth          : Certificate
UseWinlogonCredential  : False
EapConfigXmlStream     :
ConnectionStatus       : Disconnected
NapState               : NotConnected
RememberCredential     : False
SplitTunneling         : True
```

When viewing the second connection, you see that split-tunneling is enabled. After performing a little research you learn that split-tunneling allows the remote access VPN client to connect to your corporate network via the VPN link and also connect to the Internet via the interface established by the VPN itself. At this point, the client can connect to the file servers, database servers, mail servers and other corporate resources using its VPN connection. When the user attempts to connect to an Internet resource (FTP site or Web site) while working on the wireless network provided by their local coffee shop, their connection request does not go through the VPN link but instead goes through the gateway provided by the coffee shop's network. This opens up the possibility that someone could use the VPN client's authenticated connection to gain access to the corporate network. You decide this is too much of a security risk and decide to delete the setting.

6. Remove split-tunneling from this configuration by entering the following: Note: Setting the -splittunneling to 0 is the equivalent to False which disables the setting.

```
PS C:\Set-VpnConnection -name VPNInt -Server RemoteServer.
Bridgehill.com -splittunneling 0
```

7. Confirm the split tunneling setting was changed from True to False by running the following command:

```
PS C:\Get-VpnConnection
```

8. Remove the VPNInt and MyPSVPN connections using the following command. Note: the -force switch bypasses the need to confirm the deletion.

```
PS C:\Remove-VpnConnection -Name MyPSVPN,VPNInt -force
```

9. Confirm the deletion by typing:

```
PS C:\Get-VpnConnection
```

Performing Remote Administration

Remote administration tools such as RSAT and Windows PowerShell Remoting allow you to manage your clients and servers from anywhere on the network.

CERTIFICATION READY
Remote Administration
Objective 2.2

At one point in the evolution of servers, it was common to have to walk into the server room to add a user account or perform a specific administrative task. Over the years, that has changed dramatically through the use of remote administration tools. These tools, installed on the client, allow you to perform most high-level administration tasks directly from your desktop. With the release of Windows 8/Windows Server 2012, you can now use the ***Remote Server Administration Tools (RSAT)*** and ***Windows PowerShell Remoting*** to manage your server administration tasks. Let's take a closer look at each of these resources.

REMOTE SERVER ADMINISTRATION TOOLS (RSAT) FOR WINDOWS 8

The **Remote Server Administration Tools (RSAT)** allow you to manage roles and features installed on Windows Server 2012 from a PC running Windows 8. The tools included with RSAT include:

- Server Manager
- Microsoft Management Console (MMC) snap-ins consoles
- Windows PowerShell cmdlets and providers
- Command line tools for managing roles and features running on Windows Server 2012

The tools are designed to remotely manage Windows Server 2012 running the Server Core installation option and the minimal server graphical interface configuration. In some limited cases, RSAT will work with Windows Server 2008, Windows Server 2008 R2 and Windows Server 2003.

MORE INFORMATION

RSAT can only be installed on computers running Windows 8 and provides package files that run on both x86 and x64-based editions of Windows 8. It is available at Microsoft's Download Website.

INSTALL RSAT ON A WINDOWS 8 CLIENT AND CONNECT TO SERVER

GET READY. To install RSAT and connect to a server, perform the following steps:

1. Log in with Administrative credentials.
2. Download the Remote Server Administration Tools for Windows 8 64-bit package from Microsoft's Download Website.
3. Double-click the installation file **Windows6.2-KB2693643-x64.msu**.
4. Select **Open** if prompted by the Open File-Security Warning dialog box.
5. Click **Yes** when prompted by the Windows Update Standalone Installer dialog box to install the update.
6. Read and accept the license terms. Click **I accept**.
7. Press the Windows logo key + Q and search for Administrative Tools using the Settings context.
8. Select **Administrative Tools** to open and view (see Figure 6-21).

Figure 6-21

RSAT for Windows 8

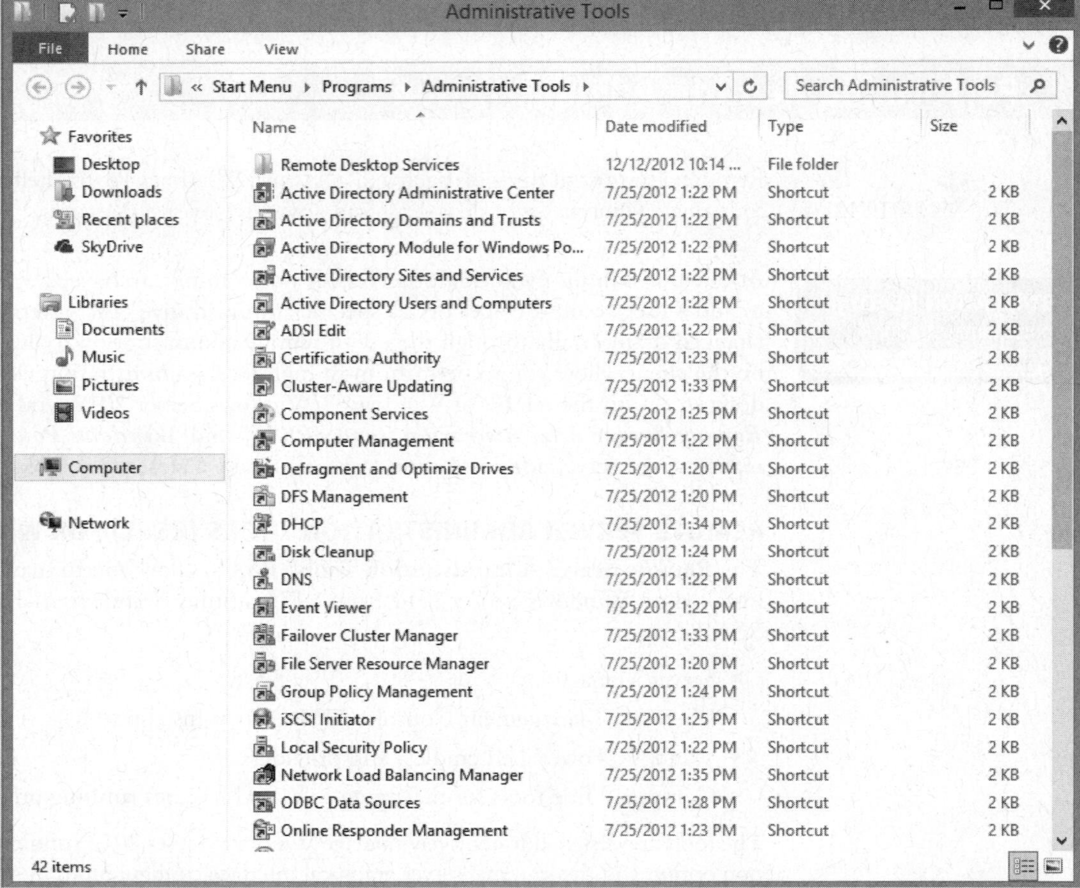

9. Click **Server Manager**.
10. Select **Dashboard**.
11. Select **Add other Servers to manage** (see Figure 6-22).

Figure 6-22

Add other servers to manage

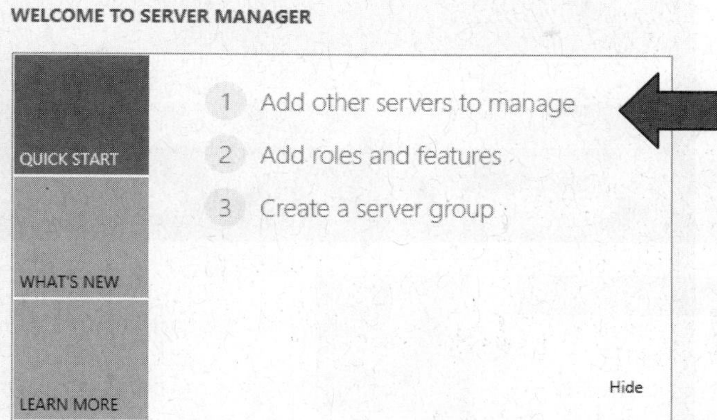

12. Confirm location is set to your domain and click **Find Now**.
13. Select the server you want to manage and click the **right arrow** (see Figure 6-23).

Figure 6-23

Adding server to manage

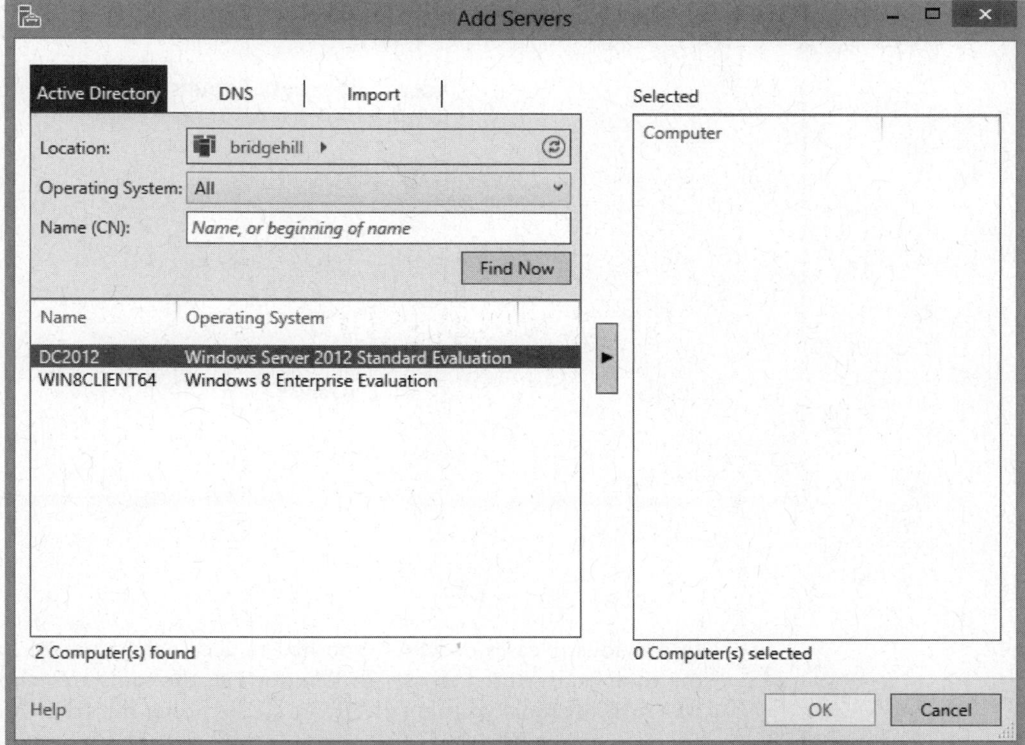

14. Select **OK**.
15. Review the roles currently handled by the server you connected to.

In the example in Figure 6-24, you can see the server is supporting six roles (AD DS, App Server, DNS, File and Storage Services, IIS, and WSUS). Scrolling down the page, you will be able to see the overall information and health of each service.

Figure 6-24

Viewing server roles/features via Server Manager Console

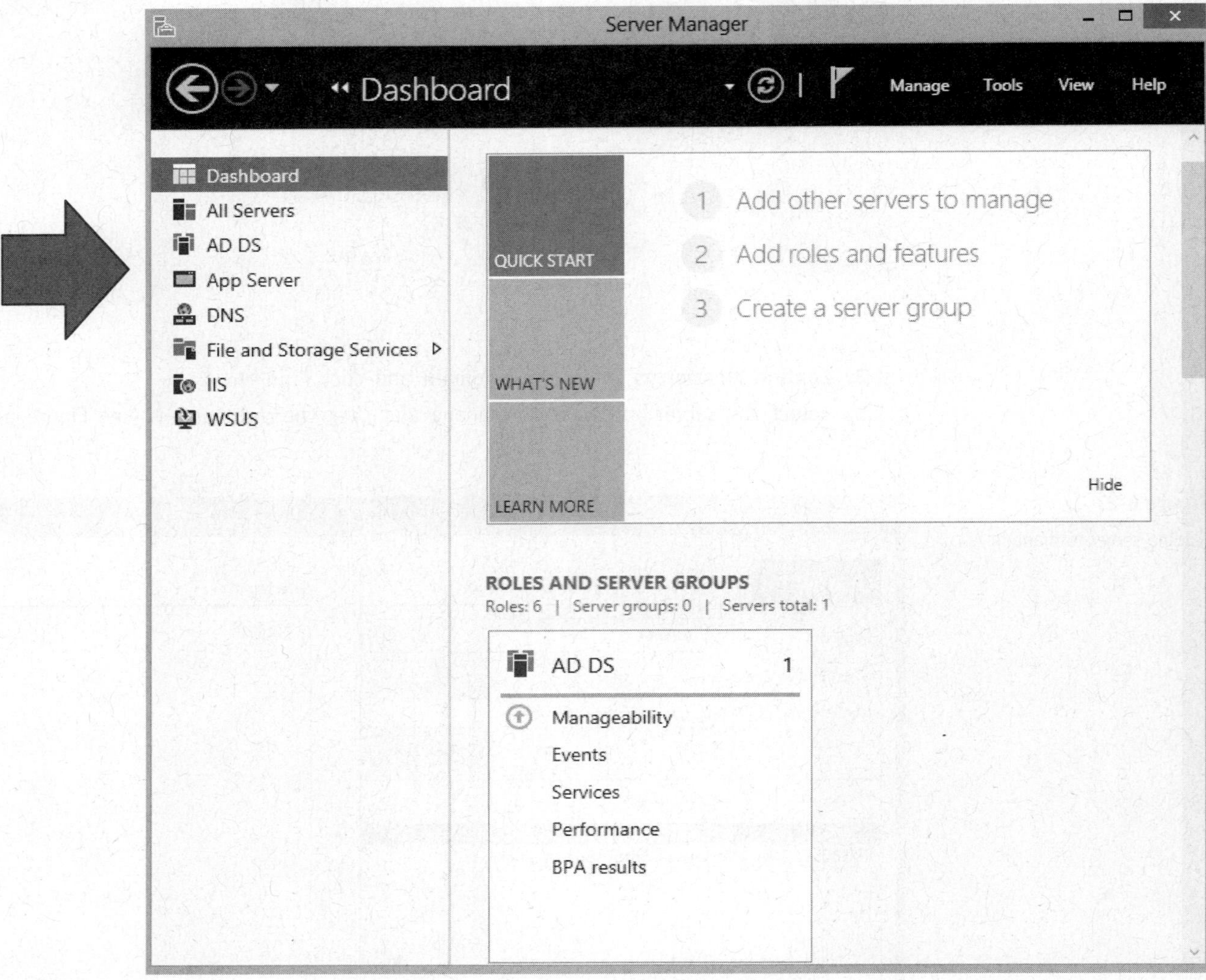

In previous releases of RSAT, you had to access the Control Panel > Programs to enable the tools you wanted to use. In Windows 8, the tools are enabled by default. You can still turn off tools you don't want to use by going into the Control Panel>Programs and Features>Turn Windows features on or off and then select the tools that you don't intend to use.

You can also access the GUI-based tools from within the Server Manager console by selecting the Tools menu (see Figure 6-25).

Figure 6-25

Accessing GUI-based tools via the Server Manager Console

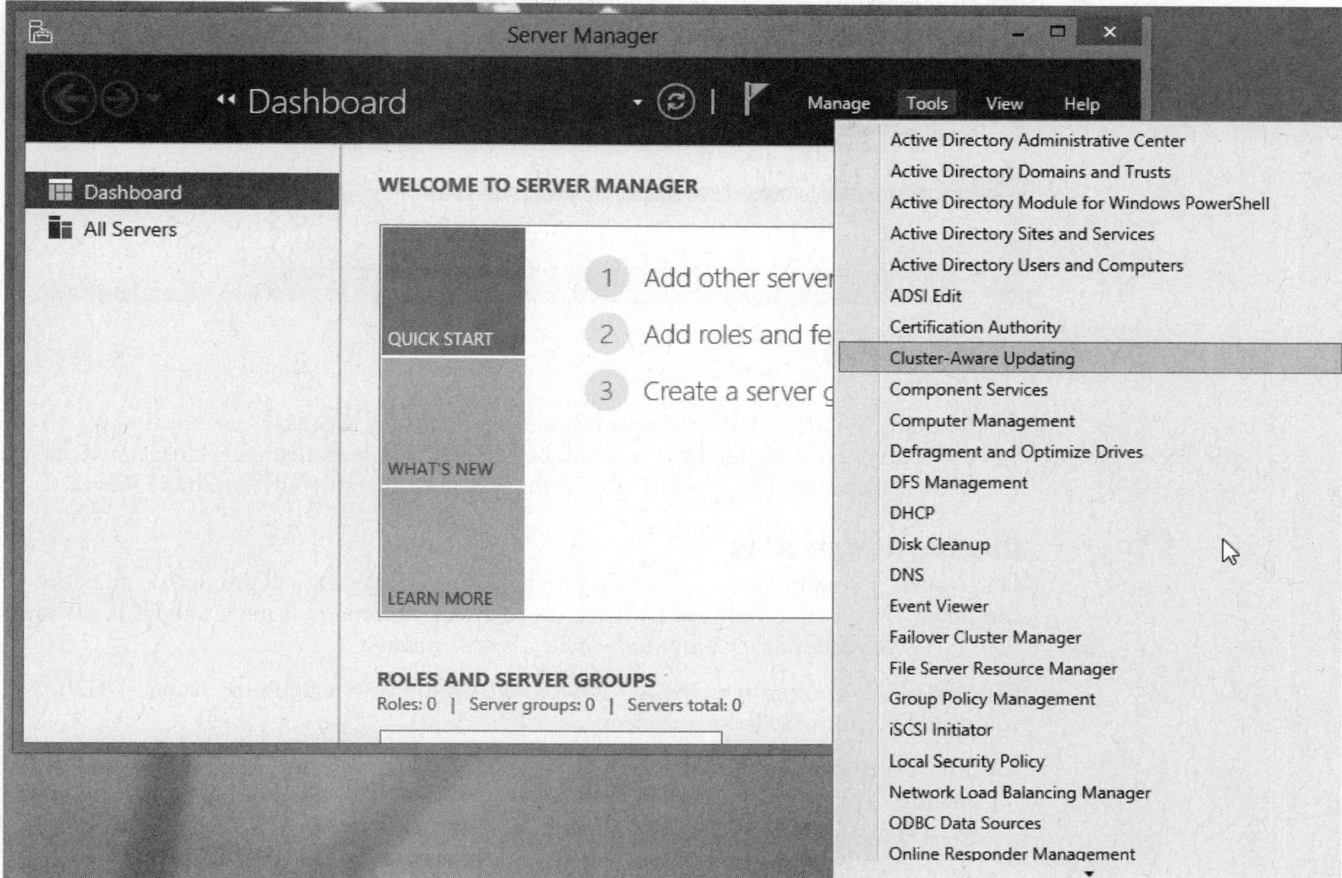

INTRODUCING WINDOWS POWERSHELL REMOTING

CERTIFICATION READY
Remote Administration
Objective 2.2

Windows PowerShell Remoting is a server-client application that allows you to securely connect to a remote Windows PowerShell host and run script interactively. It allows you to run commands on a remote system as though you were sitting physically at its console. Windows PowerShell Remoting is built upon the Web Services for Management protocol and uses Windows Remote Management service to handle the authentication and communication elements.

Windows Remote Management is responsible for routing the packets to the right location while Web Services for Management requires a port to be made accessible via your firewall. The commands that you enter and send to the remote computer are executed on the local server and the information and results are sent back to the client.

You run the Enable-PSRemoting command which enables remote management of the computer by using the Windows Management (WinRM) Service. This includes the following tasks as shown in Figure 6-26:

- Starting or restarting (if already started) the WinRM service.
- Setting the WinRM service startup type to automatic.
- Creating a listener to accept requests on any IP address.

Figure 6-26

Enabling PS Remoting

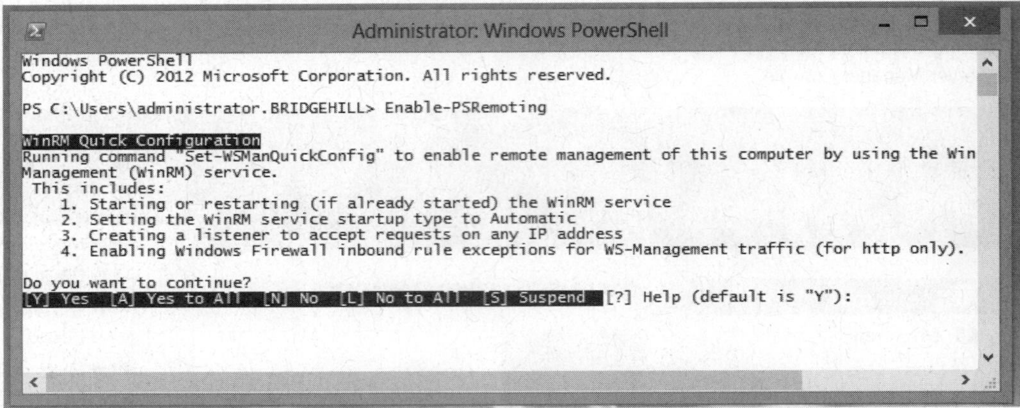

- Enabling Windows Firewall inbound rule exceptions for WS-Management traffic (for http only). This inbound rule will be listed as Windows Remote Management via WS-Management (TCP port 5985) in the inbound rules of your Windows Firewall.

One-to-one Remoting

One-to-One Remoting involves bringing up the Windows PowerShell prompt on a remote computer. This is accomplished by using the following command from Windows PowerShell: PS C:\> enter-pssession –ComputerName <*computername*>

For example, to enter into a One-to-One Remote session with a computer named DC2012, you would perform the following steps:

- Run the enable-psremoting common on DC2012 to allow it to receive remote commands.
- Start Windows PowerShell on your computer
- PS C:\> enter-pssession –ComputerName DC2012

Once connected, you will see that Windows PowerShell includes the name of the computer you are now connected to.

[DC2012]: PS C:\>

To exit from the remote machine, you would enter:

PS C:\> exit-pssession

One-to-Many Remoting

One-to-many remoting allows you to send one or more commands to multiple computers. Each of these computers will run the command, produce the results in an XML file and return them to you. This information is then categorized and presented on your client machine.

CONNECT TO REMOTE SERVER USING WINDOWS POWERSHELL (ONE TO ONE)

GET READY. To connect to a remote server using Windows PowerShell, perform the following steps:

1. Open a Windows PowerShell window on your Windows 8 Computer.
2. Run the following command to enable remoting on your computer and select **A** to continue (see Figure 6-27).

Figure 6-27
Enable PS remoting

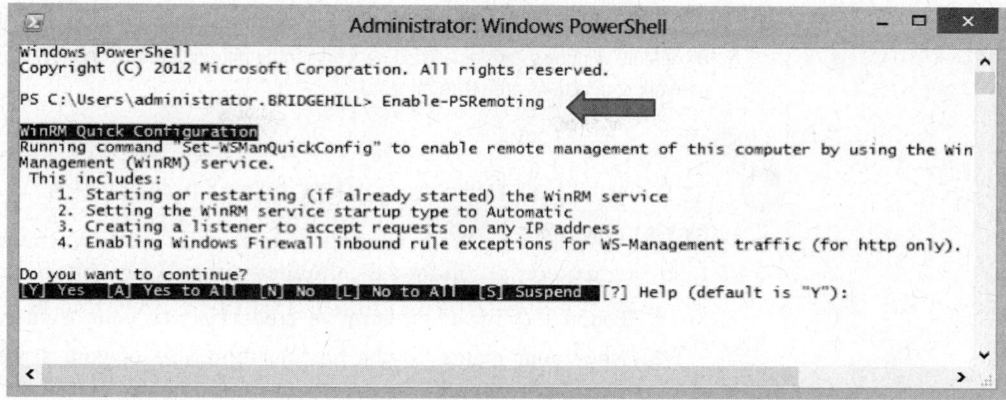

3. Enter the following command to create an interactive remote connection:

   PS C:\> **enter-pssession-ComputerName <computername>**

   where <computername> is another computer on your network
4. Enter the following command to see a list of all services running on the computer:

   [RemoteComputerName] PS C:\> **Get-Service**
5. Enter the following command to see a list of all processes running on the computer:

   [RemoteComputerName] PS C:\> **Get-Process**
6. Enter the following command to see the access control list applied via NTFS for the c: drive:

   [RemoteComputerName] PS C:\> **Get-acl c:**
7. Enter the following command to exit from Windows PowerShell:

   [RemoteComputerName] PS C:\> **Exit-PSSession**

Exploring Metered Networks

THE BOTTOM LINE

Metered connections can result in high costs when it comes to transferring and synching your computers. Windows 8 provides a mechanism to help you configure your system to recognize them and reconfigures itself to reduce costs.

CERTIFICATION READY
Metered networks
Objective 2.2

The days of unlimited broadband networks are quickly coming to a close as more broadband companies adopt metered plans similar to what they now have in place for your mobile devices. The premise behind metering is that a small percentage of users are consuming the majority of the bandwidth streaming videos, playing online games, or downloading large files from torrents. To protect against exhausting the available bandwidth, Internet Service Providers (ISPs) are rolling out plans that have a data limit that once exceeded, will result in additional billing. These are known as ***metered internet connections.***

Windows 8 provides you with a way to reduce the amount of data you send and receive over a metered connection. When a connection is metered, Microsoft indicates you may see the following effects:

- Automatic sync of Offline Files may be disabled.
- Updating of the start screen may be stopped.
- Windows Store app downloads may be paused.
- Only Priority updates will be downloaded from Windows Update.
- Tile Updates are limited to 50MB/month.

MORE INFORMATION

By default, Windows considers Wi-Fi networks to be non-metered while mobile broadband networks and Ethernet network connections are set to metered.

SET A WI-FI NETWORK CONNECTION TO METERED

GET READY. To set a Wi-Fi connection to metered, perform the following steps. Note: The following requires a Windows 8 computer with a Wi-Fi connection:

1. Logon in with administrative credentials to your Windows 8 PC.
2. Move your mouse to the bottom right side of your screen and select **Settings** from the Charms bar.
3. Select the **Internet Access Icon** (see Figure 6-28).

Figure 6-28
Internet Access icon

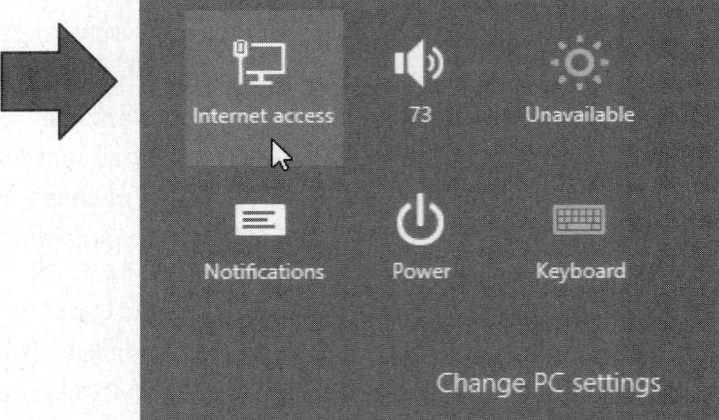

4. Right-click your wireless network connection and select **Set as metered connection** (see Figure 6-29). At this point, Windows will keep track of the amount of data you are using.

Figure 6-29
Setting a metered connection

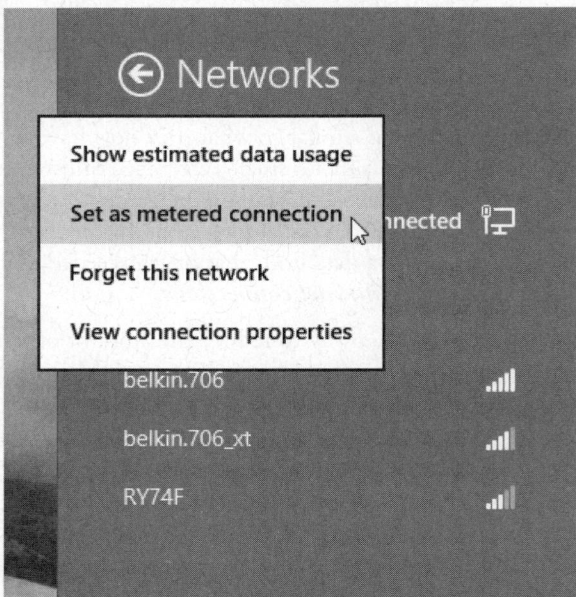

5. Right-click the wireless network connection and select **Show estimated data usage** to monitor how much data you are using.

   Note: Clicking Reset will set your data usage counter to zero. This only resets your information. Your ISP will still maintain information regarding your total data usage.

6. Open Task Manager and select the App History tab to view which applications are using the most data over the metered connection (see Figure 6-30).

Figure 6-30

Identifying apps using data over the metered connection

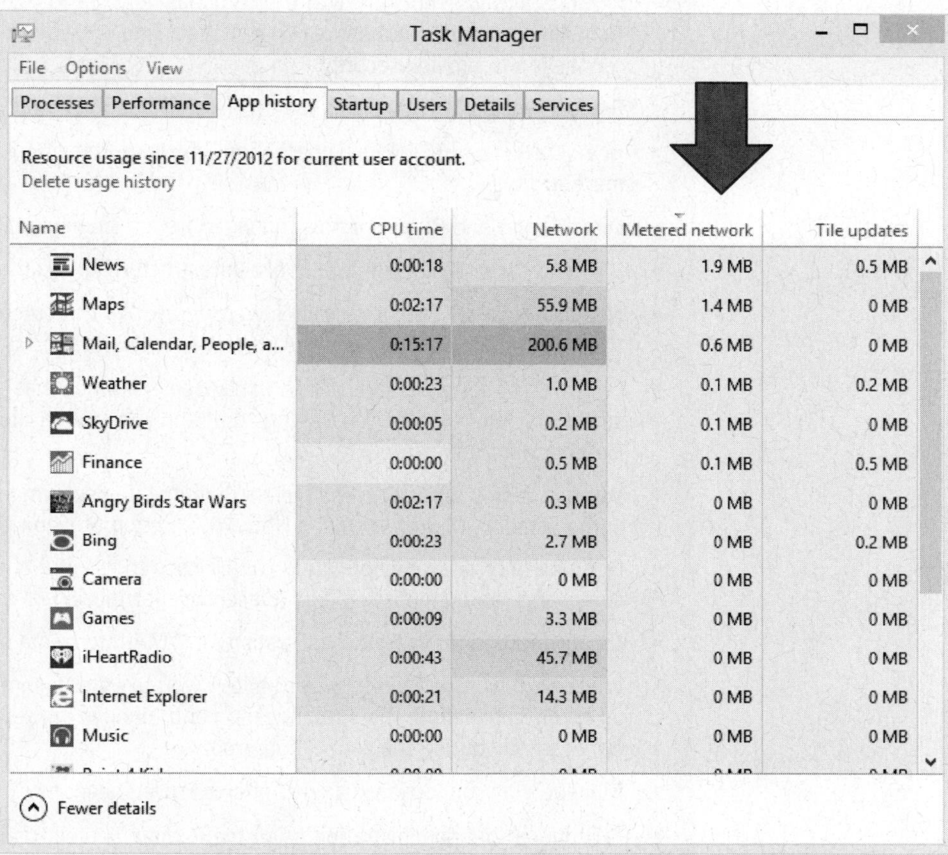

Name	CPU time	Network	Metered network	Tile updates
News	0:00:18	5.8 MB	1.9 MB	0.5 MB
Maps	0:02:17	55.9 MB	1.4 MB	0 MB
Mail, Calendar, People, a...	0:15:17	200.6 MB	0.6 MB	0 MB
Weather	0:00:23	1.0 MB	0.1 MB	0.2 MB
SkyDrive	0:00:05	0.2 MB	0.1 MB	0 MB
Finance	0:00:00	0.5 MB	0.1 MB	0.5 MB
Angry Birds Star Wars	0:02:17	0.3 MB	0 MB	0 MB
Bing	0:00:23	2.7 MB	0 MB	0.2 MB
Camera	0:00:00	0 MB	0 MB	0 MB
Games	0:00:09	3.3 MB	0 MB	0 MB
iHeartRadio	0:00:43	45.7 MB	0 MB	0 MB
Internet Explorer	0:00:21	14.3 MB	0 MB	0 MB
Music	0:00:00	0 MB	0 MB	0 MB

You can also lower your data usage costs by performing the following additional tasks on a metered connection:

7. Go to Settings and select **Change PC Settings**.
8. Select **Devices** under PC Settings menu.
9. Drag the slider to **Off** under Download over metered connections. This will block the download of device drivers from Windows Update and device info while you are working over a metered connection.
10. Select **Sync your settings** under the PC Settings menu.
11. Drag the slider to **Off** for Sync settings over metered connections.

    To returned your setting to non-metered:

12. Go to **Settings**.
13. Select the **Network Icon**.
14. Right-click your metered connection.
15. Select **Set as non-metered connection**.

SKILL SUMMARY

IN THIS LESSON YOU LEARNED:

- To be able to monitor and manage off-network systems, you need to be able to assess their currently health, provide remote assistance, and apply the appropriate remediation steps to get them back into compliance.
- A VPN is a private network that uses a public network to connect remote users and sites. Tunneling protocols, authentication protocols, and encryption levels are applied to the VPN connection to provide security.
- The four types of VPN tunneling protocols are: PPTP, L2TP/IPsec, SSTP and VPN Reconnect/IKEv2.
- In most situations, VPN Reconnect should be your first choice with SSTP as a fall back mechanism.
- DirectAccess and RRAS are now managed from a single console in Windows Server 2012.
- DirectAccess clients use two tunnels: Infrastructure and Authentication.
- Network Location Server is really a website used to DirectAccess clients to determine if they are connected directly to the corporate network.
- DirectAccess setup creates two GPOs: DAServersettings that apply to the DirectAccess server only and the DAClientSettings that apply to mobile clients only if installed via the Getting Started Wizard.
- You can deploy remote access servers in multi-site deployment/clusters, OTP authentication, Multi-forest, and Network Access protection configurations.
- Network Access Protection (NAP) can be used to monitor and assess clients for compliance and provide remediation services for those who fall short.
- Use Connection Manager Administration Kit (CMAK) to create profiles for remote connections.
- Windows 8 Getting Started Wizard allows you to enter minimal information when setting up a VPN connection. The authentication and tunneling protocols are managed transparently during the connection process.
- Manage VPN connections using Windows PowerShell.
- Perform remote administration using the Remote Server Administration Tools and Windows PowerShell Remoting.
- Widows 8 can be configured to recognize and use metered connections more efficiently. When it recognizes a meter connection, it will disable the sync of offline files, pause download of Windows Store Apps, and download only priority updates from Windows Update to reduce costs associated with transferring data across metered connections.

■ Knowledge Assessment

Multiple Choice

Select the correct answer for each of the following questions.

1. Which of the following should you take into consideration when selecting a protocol to use with VPN?
   a. Operating systems
   b. Authentication requirements

c. Implementation requirements
d. TPA-chip support on clients

2. When using DirectAccess how many IPsec tunnels are created?
   a. 1
   b. 2
   c. 3
   d. 4
3. The WMI filter, used when setting up the DAClientSettings GPO does what?
   a. Allows all computers in the Domain Computers global group to receive the policy settings
   b. Allows all mobile computers in the Domain Computers global group to receive the policy settings
   c. Individuals, Organizations, Servers, Devices and Administrators
   d. Evaluates as true on the DirectAccess server computer.
4. Which statements are true regarding using the Getting Started Wizard to automate the installation of the DirectAccess server?
   a. Configures the Kerberos proxy; eliminates need to setup PKI
   b. Enables NAT64 and DNS64
   c. Generates and self-signs an IP-HTTPS certificate
   d. Creates two client policies
5. Which of the following represents a NAP enforcement policy that relies on your routers and switches?
   a. NAP with IPsec enforcement
   b. NAP with VPN enforcement
   c. NAP with Infrastructure enforcement
   d. NAP with 802.1x enforcement
6. Which of the following are true regarding CMAK?
   a. Used to create and customize profiles for Connection Manager
   b. Requires that you create the connection profile on a computer that uses the same operating system
   c. Requires that you create the connection profile on a computer that uses the same architecture.
   d. Creates a Microsoft installer (.msi) file for distribution.
7. What are the two requirements for setting up a VPN connection using the Getting Started Wizard in Windows 8?
   a. Address of the remote server
   b. Destination Name
   c. Authentication protocol to use
   d. VPN tunneling protocol to use
8. What Windows PowerShell command is used to view VPN connections on a client computer?
   a. Get-VpnConnection
   b. Set-VpnConnection
   c. View-VpnConnection
   d. Add-VpnConnection
9. This tool is used to manage roles and features installed on a Windows Server 2012 computer from a Windows 8 client.
   a. Server Manager
   b. MMC
   c. RSAT
   d. CMAK

10. When setting up Windows 8 for metered connection, which of the following may be happen?
    a. Automatic sync of Offline Files may be disabled
    b. Only Priority updates will be downloaded from Windows Update
    c. Updating of the start screen will not be disabled
    d. Windows Store app downloads may be paused.

Best Answer

Choose the letter that corresponds to the best answer. More than one answer choice may achieve the goal. Select the BEST answer.

1. You want to use a VPN tunneling protocol that will provide you with the best option for security and uninterrupted VPN connectivity while at the same time having a fall back mechanism? What protocol pair will best fit your needs?
   a. VPN Reconnect and PPTP
   b. VPN Reconnect and SSTP
   c. VPN Reconnect and L2TP/IPsec
   d. SSTP and L2TP/IPsec
2. You want to setup a VPN on a Windows 8 computer. What tool would require the least amount of effort to complete the job?
   a. Windows PowerShell
   b. Getting Started Wizard in Windows 8
   c. CMAK
   d. Manually creating the VPN connection on the client computer
3. You need a tool that allows you to remotely manage Windows Server 2012 running the Server Core installation option from a Windows 8 computer. Which of the following would consider the best to handle the majority of the tasks you will need to perform on a daily basis?
   a. Windows PowerShell Remoting
   b. RRAS console
   c. RSAT
   d. Active Directory Users and Computer snap-in
4. You are running Windows 7 and Windows 8 clients over a VPN. You need a tunneling protocol that will support both IPv4 and IPv6 protocols? Which would you recommend?
   a. SSTP
   b. VPN Reconnect (IKEv2)
   c. L2TP/IPsec
   d. PPTP
5. You are considering setting up DirectAccess in your network which consists of a Windows Server 2008R2 and a Windows Server 2012 computer. Your clients are running Windows 7 and Windows 8. You don't currently have a PKI in place. Which option would provide you with a solution with the least amount of configurations/ infrastructure modifications?
   a. Setup DirectAccess on the Windows 2008R2 and create a PKI infrastructure.
   b. Setup DirectAccess on the Windows Server 2012 and create a PKI infrastructure.
   c. Setup a DirectAccess on the Windows Server 2012 and use self-signed certificates.
   d. Setup DirectAccess on the Windows Server 2012 system and the Windows Server 2008R2 system.

Matching and Identification

1. Match the following terms with the related description or usage.
   _________ a) Connection Manager Administration Kit (CMAK)
   _________ b) DirectAccess

________ **c)** L2TP/IPsec
________ **d)** PPTP
________ **e)** Network Access Protection
________ **f)** RSAT
________ **g)** SSTP
________ **h)** VPN Reconnect
________ **i)** WMI Filter
________ **j)** Metered connection

1. Works by establishing two IPsec tunnels from the client to the server.
2. Uses the Microsoft Point to Point Encryption (MPPE) protocol with RC4 to protect data.
3. Designed to provide users with consistent VPN connectivity and re-establish a VPN when users temporarily lose their Internet connection.
4. Allows you to create and enforce health requirement policies that specify the required software and system configurations that computers must have to connect to the network.
5. Can result in high costs when transferring and synching computers over them.
6. Requires computers mutually authenticate themselves. The computer to computer authentication takes place before the user is authenticated.
7. Used to control the application of a GPO; evaluated on the target computer during the processing of the Group Policy.
8. Allows you to manage roles and features on Windows Server 2012 from a PC running Windows 8.
9. Approved upon PPTP and L2TP/IPsec; works by sending PPP or L2TP traffic through an SSL 3.0 channel.
10. Used to create and customize profiles that contain settings necessary for a user to connect including the IP address of the VPN server.

Build a List

1. Identify the four basic steps, in order to set a Wi-Fi connection to metered on a Windows 8 computer.
________ Select the Internet Access icon
________ Logon with administrative credentials
________ Right-click the wireless connection as select Set as Metered
________ Select Settings from the Charms bar

2. Identify the five steps, in order, to use Windows PowerShell Remoting to connect and manage a remote server named Orion:
________ Start Windows PowerShell on your computer
________ Perform any remote commands on Orion to complete the administration task
________ enter-pssession –ComputerName Orion
________ Run the enable-psremoting command to configure Orion to receive remote commands.
________ Enter exit-pssession to close the remote session

3. Identify the eight basic steps, in order, to validate a DirectAccess deployment on a Windows 8 mobile computer
________ Exit Windows PowerShell on the mobile client computer
________ Confirm the DirectAccess Client Settings GPO has been applied under the COMPUTER SETTINGS section of the output on the mobile client
________ Click the Network connection icon in the notification area on the mobile client
________ Click the Workplace Connection option, on the mobile client, and you will see you are connected to the network locally.
________ Disconnect the mobile client computer and reconnect it to an external network. You should be able to access the DirectAccess server.

_________ Open Windows PowerShell with administrative privileges on the mobile client computer

_________ Enter gpresult /r and press enter on the mobile client

_________ Connect the DirectAccess mobile client to the corporate network to obtain DAClientSettings GPO

Choose an Option

1. Which option in the VPN output could potentially introduce a security risk for this VPN client?

```
Name                    : MyPSVPN
ServerAddress           : RemoteServer.Bridgehill.com
AllUserConnection       : False
Guid                    : {AC3C7786-4D65-40D4-8274-251DC38E4835}
TunnelType              : Automatic
AuthenticationMethod    : {MsChapv2}
EncryptionLevel         : Required
L2tpIPsecAuth           : Certificate
UseWinlogonCredential   : False
EapConfigXmlStream      :
ConnectionStatus        : Disconnected
NapState                : NotConnected
RememberCredential      : False
SplitTunneling          : False

Name                    : VPNInt
ServerAddress           : RemoteServer.Bridgehill.com
AllUserConnection       : False
Guid                    : {2EF4D169-8380-4ECE-A761-A2BCE7646E86}
TunnelType              : Automatic
AuthenticationMethod    : {MsChapv2}
EncryptionLevel         : Required
L2tpIPsecAuth           : Certificate
UseWinlogonCredential   : False
EapConfigXmlStream      :
ConnectionStatus        : Disconnected
NapState                : NotConnected
RememberCredential      : False
SplitTunneling          : True
```

■ Business Case Scenarios

Scenario 6-1: DirectAccess

You have setup a Windows Server for DirectAccess using the Getting Started Wizard. You log on to a Windows 8 computer in the domain and run the gpresult /r command. After reviewing the output, you notice that the client did not receive the DirectAccess Client GPO. What could be causing the problem?

Scenario 6-2: Network Access Protection

You have configured NAP using the NAP with DHCP enforcement policy yet one user's computer seems to be able to access the network even when it should be directed to remediation. How is this possible?

Design for Authentication and Authorization

LESSON 7

70-412 EXAM OBJECTIVE

Objective 2.3 – Design for authentication and authorization. This objective may include but is not limited to the following design considerations: Two-factor authentication including certificates, smart cards, picture passwords, and biometrics; workgroup vs. domain; trust relationships; local account vs. Microsoft account.

Lesson Heading	Exam Objective
Designing for Authentication and Authorization	
Using Two-Factor Authentication	Two-factor authentication, including certificates, smart cards, picture passwords, and biometrics
Using Local Accounts vs. Microsoft Accounts	Local account vs. Microsoft account
Authenticating Using Workgroups and Domains	Workgroup vs. domain
Understanding Trust Relationships	Trust relationships

KEY TERMS

authentication
authentication factors
authorization
biometrics
Certificate Authority (CA)
confidentiality
digital certificate
external trusts
forest trusts
Global Catalog
integrity
Kerberos v5
Key Distribution Center (KDC)
Local Security Authority (LSA)
NTLM
nonrepudiation
non-transitive trust relationship
one-way trust
picture password
public key infrastructure (PKI)
realm trusts
Security Accounts Manager (SAM)
SSL
Server Name Indication (SNI) extensions
shortcut trusts
smart cards
TLS Handshake protocol
TLS Record protocol
transitive trust relationship
TLS
trusted domain
Trusted Platform Module (TPM) chip
trusting domain
trusts
two-factor authentication
two-way trust

■ Designing for Authentication and Authorization

THE BOTTOM LINE

Today's network administrators are faced with securing network resources that are being accessed by employees both inside and outside of the organization. Having a well-designed authentication and authorization strategy is the key to ensuring resource availability and integrity.

Network administrators are often faced with the task of securing network resources that are being accessed by employees from both inside and outside of the company. When designing a strategy to secure these resources, you need to keep in mind these key pillars of information security:

- ***Authentication:*** Represents the way that security principals (users, computers, and processes) prove their identity before they are allowed to connect to your network. In the past, authentication was handled through the use of passwords. Today, additional authentication tools, including digital certificates, smart cards, picture passwords, and biometrics, are used.
- ***Authorization:*** After security principals prove their identity, authorization determines what they can do. This is determined through the use of access control lists (ACLs) that are attached to each resource.
- ***Confidentiality:*** This process is about preventing people from reading information they are not authorized to read. Confidentiality is handled through the use of encryption technologies.
- ***Integrity:*** This is the ability to guarantee that the information has not been arbitrarily changed from the time it was sent from the original source and received by the other party.
- ***Nonrepudiation:*** This is a method used to provide proof that a security principal (user, computer, process) is the source of data, an action, or a communication. This is usually provided through the use of public key/private key technologies.

Each of these pillars of security should become part of your overall security design. This lesson focuses on two of them specifically: authentication and authorization.

Using Two-Factor Authentication

Authentication is the process of verifying you are who you say you are. Two-factor authentication involves proving your identity using at least two authentication factors.

CERTIFICATION READY
Two-Factor authentication
Objective 2.3

Authentication is the process of verifying that security principals (users, computers, or processes) are who they say they are. To prove their identity, security principals can use one or more authentication factors, which are basically pieces of information. For example, you could use something you know (a password or PIN); something you have (a smart card); or something that is unique to you (a biometric), such as your fingerprint or iris scan. These three pieces of information are called ***authentication factors*** (see Figure 7-1). When only one of these pieces of information is used (e.g., a password), it's called one-factor authentication. ***Two-factor authentication*** requires the use of two of the three authentication factors. Windows 8 supports the following methods of authentication: passwords, picture passwords, digital certificates, smart cards, and biometrics.

Figure 7-1
Authentication factors

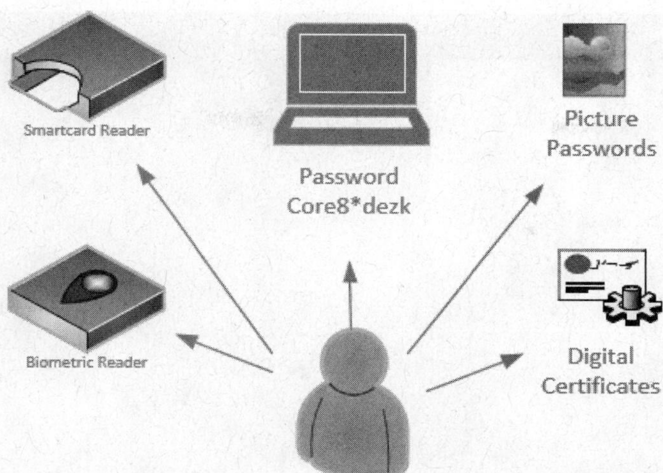

PASSWORDS

Traditional passwords have been used for years to authenticate users. Although they are the most common method, they are also the weakest. Users will typically choose a very simple password, write it down, and store it in a very insecure place. There are also several different ways for someone to discover your password and assume your identity. Through brute force attacks, social engineering, and eavesdropping, even strong passwords can be compromised.

You can strengthen passwords by instituting the use of strong passwords in your organization and use Group Policy to enforce those policies. A strong password has the following characteristics:

- At least eight characters long
- Uses at least one character from the following: upper- and lowercase letters, punctuation marks, numbers
- Does not include your login name, your real name, or your company name
- Does not include a complete word that can be found in the dictionary
- Should not be the same password that you have used in the past or used on other website accounts

PICTURE PASSWORDS

CERTIFICATION READY
Picture passwords
Objective 2.3

A ***picture password*** (see Figure 7-2) consists of two components: a picture and a gesture that you draw on it. You can pick the image from a default set included with the Windows 8 installation or select your own. After the picture is selected, you can then place your gestures. A picture password is limited to three gestures (circles, straight lines, and taps). Because the combination of the three is infinite, a picture password offers more security than a traditional password. When you sign on, the gestures you use are compared with those that you created when the password was set. If they are correct, you are authenticated. If they are wrong (for example, if you used circle instead of a line), authentication fails.

CREATE A WINDOWS 8 PICTURE PASSWORD

GET READY. To create a picture password, perform the following steps:

1. On the *Settings* charm, click **Change PC Settings.**
2. Click **Users.**
3. Click **Create a picture password.**
4. Confirm your password if prompted and click **OK.**
5. Click **Choose Picture.**
6. Navigate to the picture you want to use.

Figure 7-2
Picture passwords

7. Choose the picture and click **Open**.
8. Click **Use this Picture**.
9. Draw three gestures on your picture. You can use any combination of circles, straight lines, and taps. Be sure to remember the order in which you use the gestures.
10. Repeat the same three gestures to confirm.
11. Click **Finish**.
12. Sign out with the user account.
13. Choose the user account to log in with.
14. Repeat the gestures you used when setting up the picture password.

DIGITAL CERTIFICATES

CERTIFICATION READY
Certificates
Objective 2.3

A ***digital certificate*** is a collection of data that binds an identity to a key pair. In addition to authentication, these certificates can be used for authorization, non-repudiation, and other types of security control. A digital certificate contains a name that indicates who or what owns the certificate, a public key, the name of the ***Certificate Authority (CA)*** that issued it, and the digital signature of the CA that issued it. A CA is the computer that creates and manages the distribution and revocation of certificates.

SMART CARDS

CERTIFICATION READY
Smart cards
Objective 2.3

Smart cards, used with a smart card reader attached to a computer, contain an embedded processor that is used to communicate with the host computer and the card reader. They can be used to authenticate users, ensure data integrity when signing documents, and provide confidentiality when you need encryption. In order to authenticate, users insert their card into a reader connected to their computer and then enter their PIN. The smart card holds the users' logon information, private key, digital certificate, and other private information.

To deploy smart cards, you need a ***public key infrastructure (PKI)***, which includes digital certificates, CAs, and other components that are used to create, distribute, validate, and revoke certificates. Smart cards can be credit card–sized devices or a token style (USB device). Information stored on the cards cannot be extracted from the device, all communication with the card is encrypted to protect against malicious software intercepting it, and brute force attempts to hack the PIN will result in the card being blocked until an administrator can unlock it. Because both the smart card and a PIN are required, it is much less likely that someone will be able to steal both.

Windows 8 introduces a new feature called virtual smart cards (VSCs), which makes additional hardware (smart card readers and smart cards) unnecessary. These cards emulate the functionality of regular smart cards but require a ***Trusted Platform Module (TPM) chip*** to protect the private keys. The TPM is used to encrypt the information, which is then stored on the computer's hard drive. If the user will need to access multiple computers using the VSC, one will have to be created and issued to the user for each system. It is also possible to have multiple VSCs (one for each user) on multi-use computers. If a computer is lost or stolen, the user can contact an administrator who can revoke the certificate associated with the VSC on the user's computer.

SET UP A VIRTUAL TPM SMART CARD ENVIRONMENT

GET READY. To set up a virtual TPM smart card environment, you must have a computer running Windows 8 (TPM supported), you must be connected to a domain, and you must have access to a domain server with a functional CA in place. Then perform the following steps:

1. Create a certificate template (on the domain controller): This is the certificate you request in Step 3 on the client.
2. Create the VSC on the Windows 8 client machine using the TPM VSC Manager and then type a PIN.
3. Use the Certificate console on the Windows 8 client machine, to request a new certificate and then select the one you created in Step 1.

After these steps are complete, you can use the VSC next time you boot your system.

BIOMETRICS

CERTIFICATION READY
Biometrics
Objective 2.3

Biometrics takes advantage of the uniqueness of every individual. By using a person's fingerprint, face, voice, or retina, biometrics offers advantages over other methods. For example, the user has to physically be present at the point of identification, does not need to remember passwords or a PIN, and does not have to carry smart cards that can be lost or stolen. Instead of using biometrics to replace other methods, consider using them as an additional layer of security.

In the past, administrators had to struggle with managing third-party software and hardware to support biometrics. With each vendor providing different drivers, software, and management tools, it became very labor-intensive to support. Fortunately, Microsoft introduced native support for biometric technologies through its Windows Biometric Framework (WBF). WBF enables users to manage device settings for biometric devices through the Control Panel, provides support for managing device drivers; and manages Group Policy settings that can be used to enable, disable, or limit use of biometric data for a local computer or domain. A fingerprint reader is the most commonly used biometric device in corporate networks. These devices can be purchased separately or can be built into new laptops. The reader captures an image of your fingerprint and then saves it to the computer. The process is called enrolling. When you log on, the reader will scan your fingerprint and compare it with the one on file.

Using Local Accounts vs. Microsoft Accounts

User accounts allow employees to participate on the network and to gain access to the resources that are made available. Understanding which account to use and its limitations in regard to user experience, access to Windows apps, and password management will be important considerations when designing your authentication strategy.

CERTIFICATION READY
Local account vs. Microsoft account
Objective 2.3

In Lesson 4, you learned how to set up and configure both local accounts and Microsoft user accounts on your Windows 8 computer. In this section, we look at what to consider when determining the type of account to use as part of your authentication strategy.

A Microsoft user account is required in order to provide users with the ability to download apps from the Windows Store, synchronize their settings between Windows 8 computers and mobile devices, and run Windows 8 apps such as Mail, People, SkyDrive, and Messaging. Although you can browse the Store with a local user account, you cannot download Windows apps. If your strategy is to continue to use traditional applications (installed from DVDs or websites) and only download Microsoft updates, a local account would suffice.

If your strategy includes setting up multiple Windows 8 computers on a network without Active Directory, Microsoft user accounts can reduce the administration overhead that is necessary when implementing local user accounts. Using local user accounts requires that you create the same account on each computer the user needs to access resources. Any changes the user makes to personalize her desktop will not follow her to other Windows 8 computers or devices. Using a Microsoft user account allows the user to access any of the Windows 8 computers and devices while maintaining a consistent desktop experience across each computer. On each computer or device, she can access her Windows Store apps, browse her favorites, review her history, and use many other settings stored in the cloud.

Implementing Microsoft user accounts can also simplify the process of recovering lost passwords. When you lose the password to a local user account, you must have access to the local administrator account to reset it, you must have created a password reset disk beforehand, or you must use a third-party software program. On the other hand, if you use Microsoft user accounts, you can recover from a lost password by using a previously assigned hint or by resetting you password from Microsoft's website.

If you are considering working with Microsoft accounts in combination with domain-based accounts, there are two options:

- Sign in with your Microsoft user account when you need to run a Windows app.
- Connect your domain account to your Microsoft user account.

If you choose the first option, each time a user logs in with his domain account and then attempts to open a Windows app (Mail, People, SkyDrive, or Messaging), he must enter his Microsoft user account credentials. This can become very time consuming because the process is repeated each time he opens another Windows app.

The second option is to connect your Microsoft user accounts to your domain accounts. For enterprise environments, Group Policy can be used to control whether users can link their Microsoft user account to their domain account as well as what can and cannot be synchronized. If linking your domain credentials to your Microsoft user account fits your authentication strategy, keep in mind that the domain credentials will not be uploaded to the cloud and are never synchronized with other computers.

Authenticating Using Workgroups and Domains

When designing an authentication strategy, you can choose between a workgroup and a domain. Workgroups provide a distributed authentication mechanism, whereas domains provide a central authentication mechanism that can support scalability.

CERTIFICATION READY
Workgroup vs. domain
Objective 2.3

In Lesson 4, you learned that workgroups are a collection of computers that interact with each other but without any centralized authority. Workgroup computers must be on the same network segment and will maintain their own local security database to store user accounts (see Figure 7-3). This database, also called the ***Security Accounts Manager (SAM)***, contains user accounts and their associated passwords. When you enter your user name and password on a Windows computer, a process called the ***Local Security Authority (LSA)*** queries the SAM database to determine whether an account with the user name and password you used exists. If it does, you will be granted access to the system. If the same user needs access to another computer in the workgroup, they must have a separate account stored in that computer's SAM. In addition to verifying users who log on, LSA also handles any password changes and enforces overall security policy on the system.

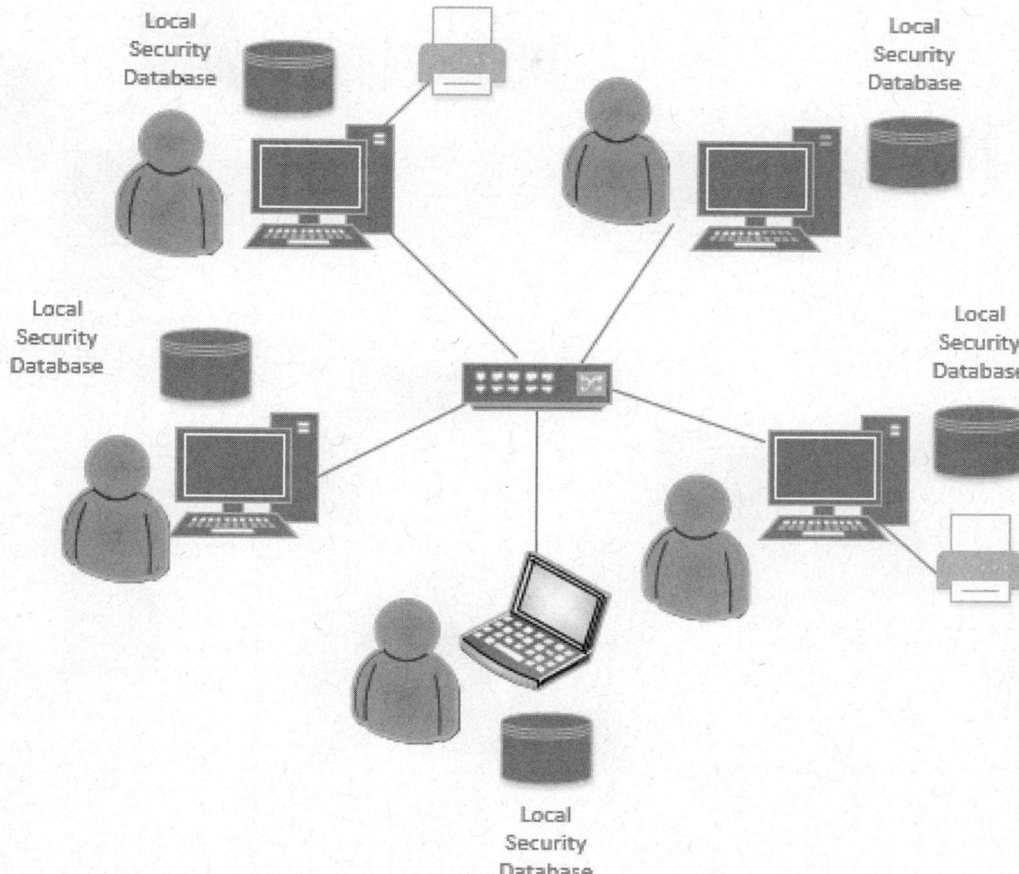

Figure 7-3
Authenticating in the workgroup model

TAKE NOTE*
It is best practice to have at least two domain controllers on your network at any given time in case one fails or you need to take it down for maintenance.

As you can imagine, as the number of computers increases, maintaining accounts for each user on multiple machines can become very labor-intensive. If an account is present on the other computer, users will not have to enter their user name and password again to connect and use the resource; it will be handled automatically in the background. If they attempt to access a resource on another computer and do not have an account, they will be prompted to enter a user name and password before connecting and using the resource. The user name and password must be stored in the computer's local SAM to gain access to its resources. Workgroups are very simple to design and don't require a Windows server to implement. On the other hand, they are designed for small groups of computers and provide very limited scalability.

DOMAINS

When users log on to a computer that is a member of a domain, they are not being authenticated by the computer on which they are working. Instead, their credentials (user name/password) are sent to a special computer that manages Active Directory. Active Directory is a database along with collection of supporting components that are installed on one or more computers in the domain. These computers, called domain controllers, maintain a copy of the Active Directory that stores user accounts in the form of objects. These objects are then replicated between domain controllers. When using a domain model (see Figure 7-4), you have to create only a single user account for each users to provide access to all resources in the domain. When running Windows 8, you must have either the Professional or Enterprise edition to join a domain.

Figure 7-4
Authenticating in the domain model

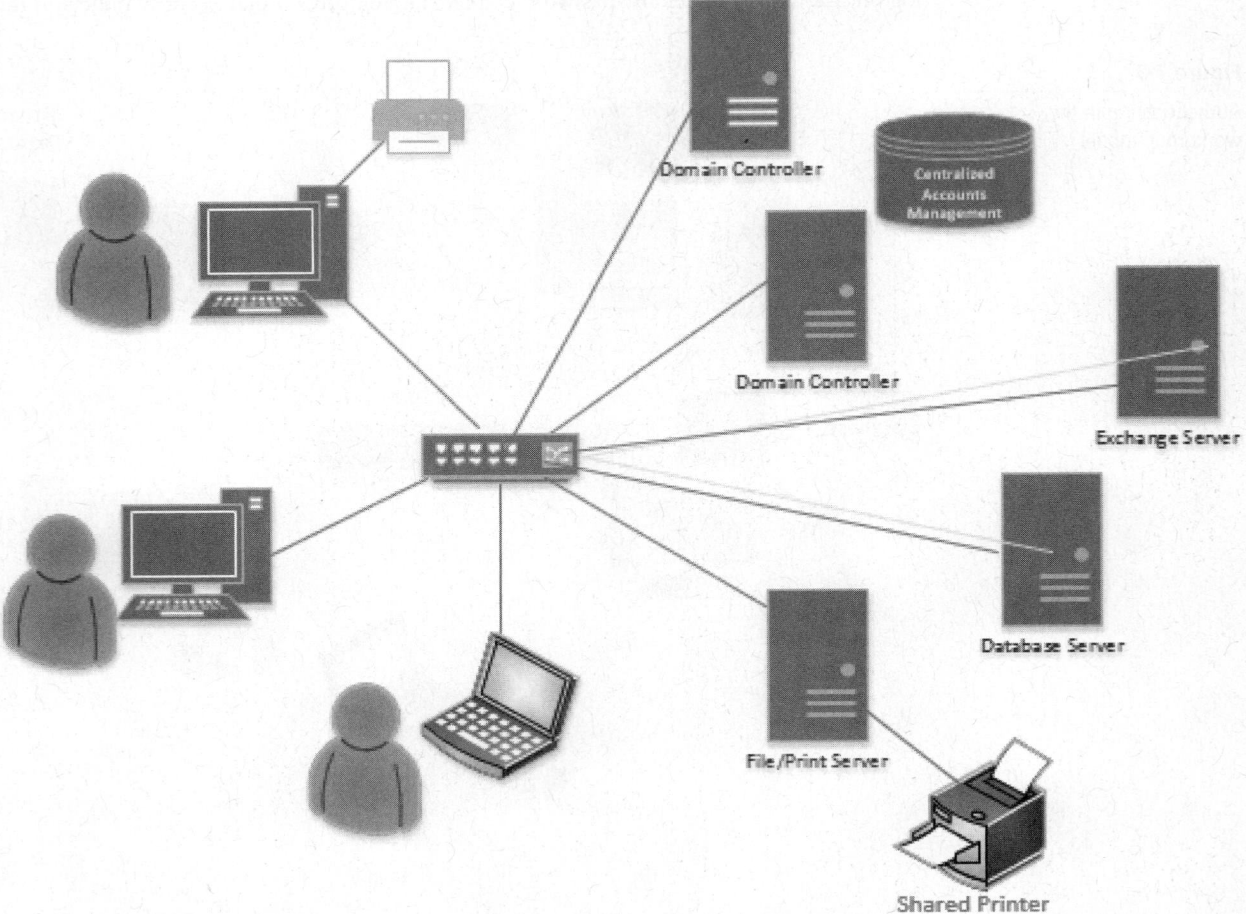

It is possible that a company will have more than one domain as part of its Active Directory implementation. Multiple domains are connected to create trees, and multiple trees can be connected to create a forest. When you implement multiple domains, a feature called the ***Global Catalog*** is used to find users, computers, and resources throughout the other domains.

KERBEROS AUTHENTICATION

When authenticating and using resources in a domain, you will use ***Kerberos v5***. Kerberos v5 is a protocol that defines how clients interact with a network authentication service. Figure 7-5 provides a simplified explanation of what happens between a user/computer, a domain controller (running the ***Key Distribution Center or KDC***), and a file server containing the resource the user wants to access. The Key Distribution Center is the network authentication service that supplies ticket-granting tickets (TGTs) used by the Kerberos v5 protocol.

1. When a user logs on to a computer in a domain with the domain account, the LSA takes the information and creates an authentication package. This package is sent by the user's computer to the Key Distribution Center (KDC), which is a service running on a domain controller.
2. The KDC validates the authentication package and sends a ticket-granting ticket (TGT) to the user. The TGT contains information about the user's computer as well as a list of Security Identifiers (SIDS) for the user account and any group accounts the user belongs to.
3. When the user attempts to access a resource (e.g., a folder or file) on a file server named FS1, she will need a session ticket.

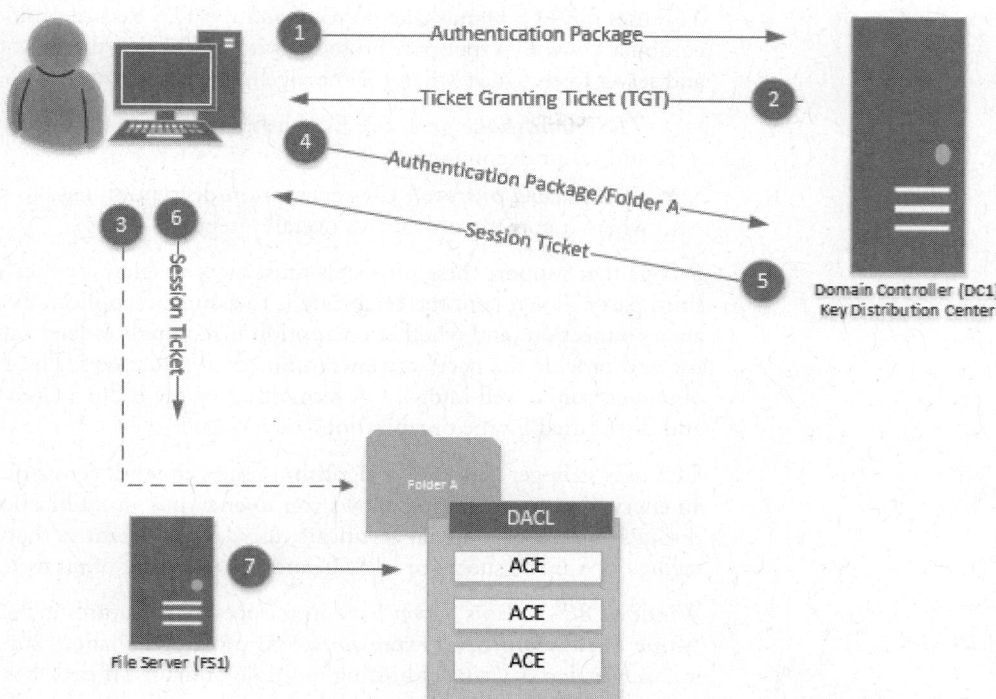

Figure 7-5
The Kerberos authentication process

4. To get the session ticket, the client will create another authentication package and send it back to the KDC along with a request for that resource.
5. The KDC validates the authentication package and sends the user a session ticket.
6. The session ticket is then used to authenticate to FS1. FS1 will decrypt the ticket and validate it.
7. FS1 will then compare the ticket to a discretionary access control list (DACL) that is attached to the resource. The DACL consists of one or more access control entries (ACEs). Each ACE contains a SID for a user account or group and the permissions applied to it for the resource. If the ACE contains one or more SIDs that matches those in the user's ticket, they are granted the permissions provided for that SID.

WINDOWS NT LAN MANAGER (NTLM) v2

NTLM is a family of authentication protocols first introduced with Windows NT. It is a based on a challenge/response mechanism used to authenticate users and computers. Although Kerberos v5 is the preferred authentication protocol for Active Directory–based environments, NTLM is used for systems running Windows NT 4.0 and earlier and for computers that are members of a workgroup. It is also used when authenticating to a server that belongs to a different Active Directory forest.

TRANSPORT LAYER SECURITY (TLS)/SECURE SOCKETS LAYER (SSL)

When communicating across untrusted networks, you need to know that you are connecting to the right servers and that your data is safe during transit. Transport Layer Security (TLS) and Secure Sockets Layer (SSL) are two different communication protocols that can securely authenticate servers and clients and protect you from eavesdropping and tampering. Windows implements TLS and SSL through the SChannel security support provider.

TLS is actually based on SSL, but uses a different handshake protocol. Although both can protect your systems, they are not interoperable.

TLS uses the TLS Handshake protocol and the TLS Record protocol. Both must be used in combination with a transport protocol, with TCP being the most obvious. TLS allows the client and server to recognize when the message has been interfered with, intercepted, or modified.

- ***TLS Handshake protocol:*** Establishes the encryption/decryption keys and algorithm, and resumes connections
- ***TLS Record protocol:*** Uses encryption/decryption keys to secure the data, and validate where it comes from and its overall integrity

Servers that support these protocols must have a digital certificate issued to them by a trusted third party. The role of the certificate is to assure an application or user that it is safe to initiate a connection, and whether encryption is required to determine the shared algorithm to use and provide the necessary encryption/decryption keys. The digital certificates are usually obtained from a well-known CA recognized by the industry as a whole; they are not created and distributed by the organization's own CAs.

TLS uses stronger encryption algorithms and can work across different ports, whereas ***SSL***, an encryption protocol that allows you to encrypt communications between users and servers through the use of a digital certificate, uses security features that require a specific port to be secure. TLS is the successor to SSL, and the terms are often used interchangeably.

Windows 8/Windows Server have introduced new features including TLS support for ***Server Name Indication (SNI) extensions***. SNI provides enhanced support when a client connects to a server that is virtually hosting multiple domains. If each has its own digital certificate, the server needs to be able to provide the correct certificate to the client computer. SNI allows the client to inform the target domain earlier in the process, enabling it to select the appropriate certificate. By providing this enhancement, you can host multiple SSL websites using a single IP and port combination, allow multiple simultaneous connections to the SSL websites, and help clients determine the appropriate certificate to select during authentication.

Understanding Trust Relationships

When building an enterprise network that spans multiple domains and Active Directory forests, you must plan for access to resources across the entire organization and look for ways to optimize the authentication process. Trusts provide the foundation upon which authorization to resources can be built.

CERTIFICATION READY
Trust relationships
Objective 2.3

Trusts are relationships between domains or forests that enable a user to be authenticated by domain controllers from another domain. Through trusts, users can access and share resources across security boundaries. Domain controllers authenticate users using either Kerberos v5 or NTLM. Kerberos v5 is the default protocol, but NTLM is used when authenticating to a server that belongs to a different Active Directory forest. Clients using Kerberos v5 must obtain their TGT from a domain controller in their domain and present it to the domain controller in the trusting domain. If the client uses NTLM, the server that contains the resource has to contact the domain controller in the user's domain to validate their credentials.

Here are a few terms you will need to understand when discussing trust relationships.

- ***One-way trust:*** A trust that goes in one direction. Domain A is trusted by Domain B; therefore, users in Domain A can access resources in Domain B, but Domain B users cannot access resources in Domain A.
- ***Two-way trust:*** A trust that goes in both directions. Domain A is trusted by Domain B, and Domain B is trusted by Domain A. Users in each domain can access resources in each other's domains.
- ***Trusted domain:*** The domain that contains the user accounts that want to gain access to the other domain.

- ***Trusting domain:*** The domain that contains the resources that can be accessed by user accounts in the trusted domain.
- ***Transitive trust relationship:*** Trust extends between all trusted and trusting domains. All domains trust all other domains.
- ***Non-transitive trust relationship:*** Trust does not extend across domains. Domain A trusts Domain B, and Domain B trusts Domain C. Domain A does not trust Domain C.

The following section covers the types of trust relationships that can be configured.

EXTERNAL TRUSTS

External trusts (see Figure 7-6) can be created between a domain in a forest and a Windows NT 4.0 (or later) domain or a domain in another forest that is not joined by a forest trust. For example, if Contoso acquires Acme, and you want Contoso employees located in the east.contoso.com domain to be able to access resources in the west.acme.com domain, you can create an external trust relationship between those two domains. If it is configured as a one-way trust, employees located in the west.acme.com domain would not have access to resources in the east.contoso.com domain.

- Direction: One-way or two-way. In a one-way trust, the trusted domain is the domain whose accounts can be given access to resources in the trusting domain. If you want the trust to extend both ways, you have to create two one-way external trusts.
- Transitivity: Non-transitive. This trust does not extend to other domains.

Figure 7-6

Accessing resources using an external trust (one-way)

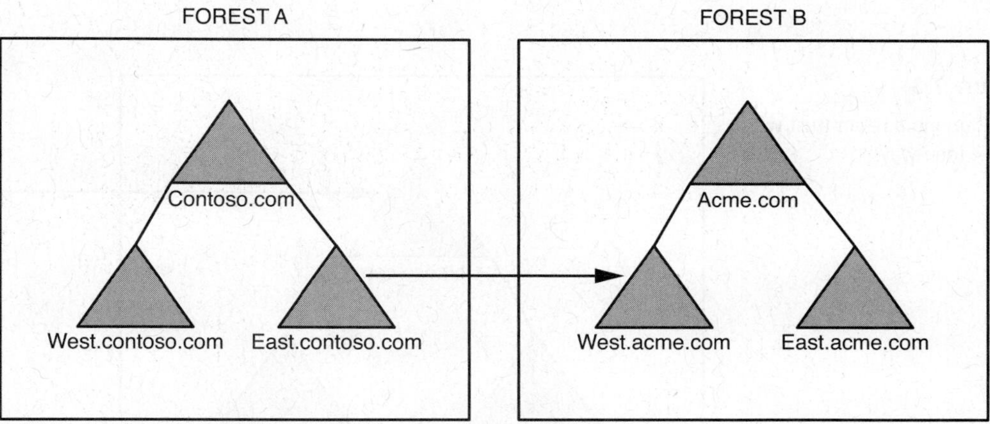

FOREST TRUSTS

Forest trusts (see Figure 7-7) can be created between two forest root domains if the forest functional level is Windows Server 2003 or later. For example, if Contoso acquires Acme and both are running Windows Server 2003 or later forests, you can create a forest trust to allow access for users in both forests. The access will depend on whether it is a one-way or two-way trust.

- Direction: One-way or two-way
  - o In a one-way forest trust, members of the trusted forest can use resources that are located in the trusting forest. Example: Forest A (trusted) and Forest B (trusting). Members of Forest A can access resources located in Forest B, but Forest B members cannot access resources in Forest A.
  - o If a two-way trust is set up between Forest A and Forest B, members from Forest A can access Forest B, and vice versa.
- Transitivity: Transitive
  - o This trust extends to other domains.

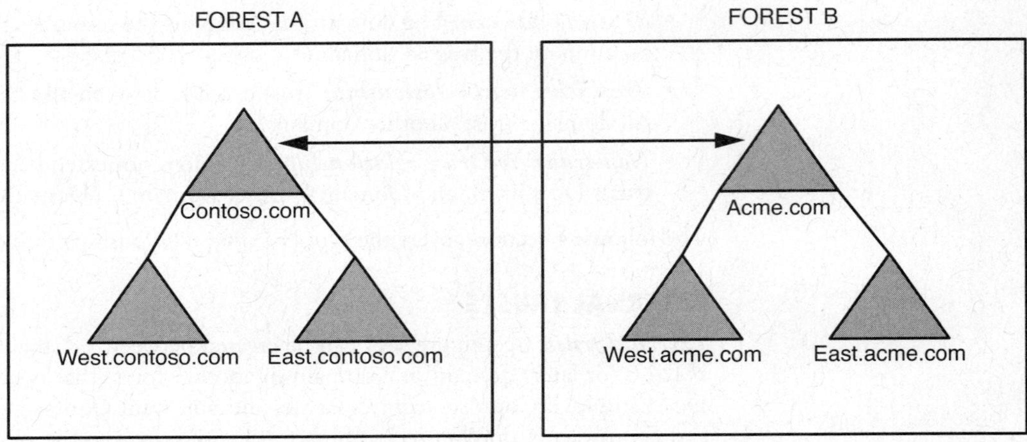

Figure 7-7

Accessing resources using a forest trust (two-way)

REALM TRUSTS

Realm trusts (see Figure 7-8) are used to form relationships between an Active Directory domain and a non–Windows Kerberos realm. For example, if Contoso acquired another company that was running a UNIX network, you could create a realm trust to provide users at Company B with access to Contoso resources.

- Direction: One-way or two-way
- Transitivity: Transitive or non-transitive

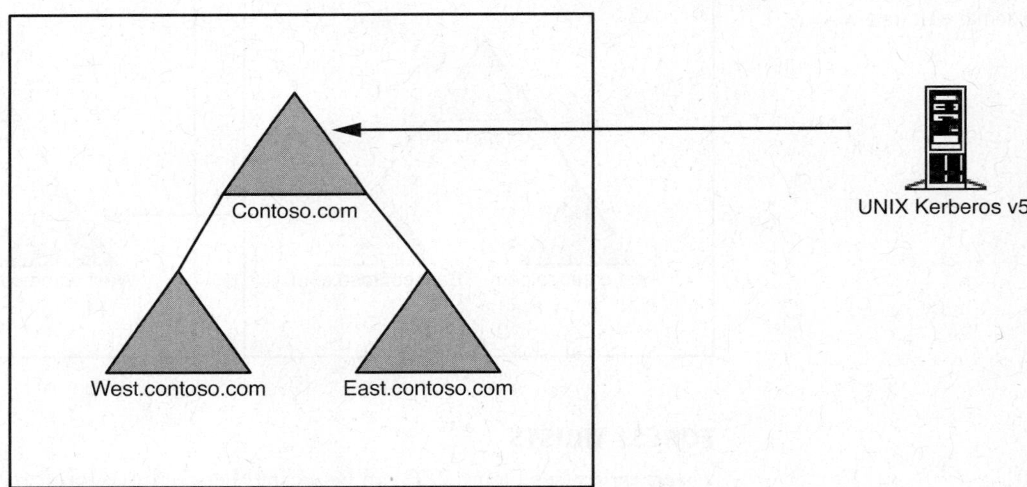

Figure 7-8

Configuring a realm trust with UNIX (one-way)

SHORTCUT TRUSTS

Shortcut trusts (see Figure 7-9) can be used to optimize the authentication process. Even if domains within a forest trust each other, authentication has to walk a trust path from the child domain to the parent domain. A shortcut trust can be made between two domains within the forest to optimize this process. This works well when users have to cross multiple domains to access resources or if a parent domain is located across a slower wide area network (WAN) link.

For example, if employees in the sales.east.contoso.com domain and employees in the sales.west.contoso.com domain are heavy users of resources in each other's domain, a two-way shortcut trust between the two optimizes the authentication process.

Without a shortcut trust in place, the following occurs. When a user in the sales.west.contoso.com domain wants to access a resource in the sales.east.contoso.com domain, the user has to request a session ticket from the sales.west.contoso.com domain controller. This domain controller has to make the request with a domain controller in the west.contoso.com domain, which then makes a request of a domain controller in the contoso.com domain, and so on. This process continues until the request reaches a domain controller in the sales.east.contoso.com domain. This domain controller, located in the same domain as the resource computer, issues the session ticket and passes it back to the user in the sales.west.contoso.com domain.

- Direction: One-way or two-way
- Transitivity: Transitive

Figure 7-9

Optimizing authentication using a shortcut trust (two-way)

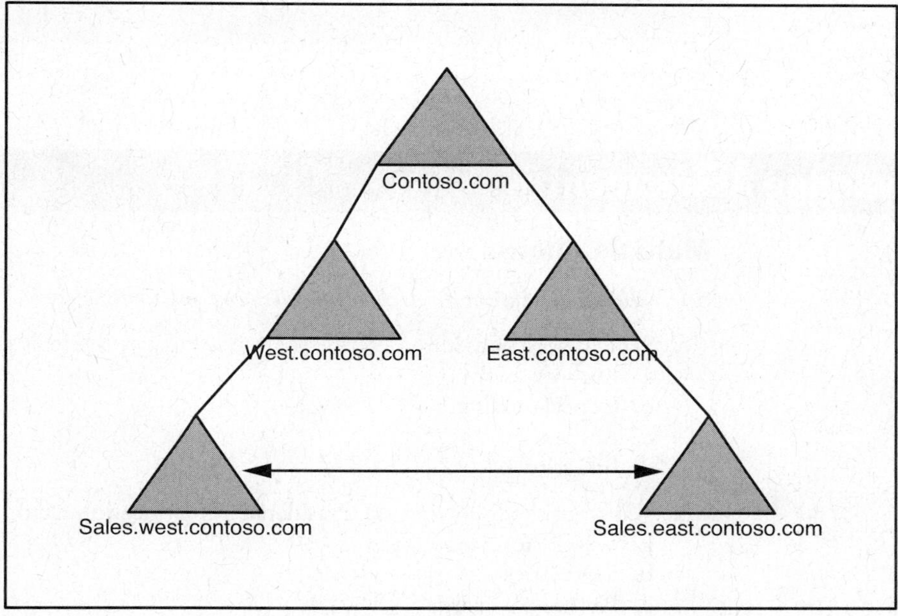

TAKE NOTE* Trusts are set up using the Active Directory Domains and Trusts snap-in. To create and manage trusts, you must be a member of the Domain Admins or the Enterprise Admins group. Trusts can also be set up from a command line using the NetDom utility.

SKILL SUMMARY

In this lesson you learned:

- When designing a strategy to secure resources, you need to keep in mind the pillars of security: authentication, authorization, confidentiality, integrity, and non-repudiation.
- Authentication is the process of verifying that users, computers, or processes are who they say they are. This is accomplished through the use of one or more authentication factors: passwords, picture passwords, digital certificates, smart cards, and biometrics. When two are used in combination, it's called two-factor authentication.

- Workgroups provide a decentralized approach to authenticating users in that each computer's SAM database handles its own account management. On the other hand, domains provide a centralized database called Active Directory that enables you to create a single account and access resources throughout the enterprise.
- When authenticating in domains, you use the Kerberos v5 protocol. This protocol uses a KDC, which provides TGTs and session tickets used to validate the user/computer when it attempts to access resources in the domain.
- When building networks that span multiple domains and Active Directory forests, you must plan for access to resources between domains. This is accomplished through the use of external trusts, forest trusts, realm trusts, and shortcut trusts.
- Shortcut trusts enable you to optimize authentication between domains by enabling computers/users to bypass the trust path that is typically used between parent and child domains.

Knowledge Assessment

Multiple Choice

Select the correct answer for each of the following questions.

1. Which word is used to describe the way security principals prove their identity?
   a. Authorization
   b. Confidentiality
   c. Authentication
   d. Integrity
2. Which of the following are considered authentication factors? (Select all that apply.)
   a. Wi-Fi Protected Access
   b. Biometrics
   c. Picture passwords
   d. Smart cards
3. Which types of gestures do picture passwords support? (Select all that apply.)
   a. Straight lines
   b. Circles
   c. Taps
   d. Angles
4. Which of the following statements describe a characteristic of a trust? (Select all that apply.)
   a. Trusts can be one way.
   b. A trusting domain contains the user accounts that want to gain access to the trusted domain.
   c. Transitive trust relationships extend between all trusted and trusting domains.
   d. Trusts can be two-way.
5. Which of the following authentication protocols is based on a challenge/response mechanism?
   a. NTLM
   b. Kerberos
   c. TLS/SLS
   d. File Replication Service

6. Which of the following characteristics describe the characteristics of a workgroup? (Select all that apply.)
   a. All computers are located on same network segment.
   b. Provides centralized management of user accounts.
   c. Is scalable.
   d. Uses the SAM database.
7. Which authentication protocol is used in Windows Active Directory domains?
   a. Kerberos
   b. TGT
   c. KDC
   d. TLS/SSL
8. Which of the following protocols can be used to communicate safely across untrusted networks? (Select two.)
   a. TLS
   b. NTLM
   c. Kerberos
   d. SSL
9. Which of the following trusts is created to optimize authentication?
   a. Forest trust
   b. Realm trust
   c. Shortcut trust
   d. Domain trust
10. Which of the following tools is used to set up a trust?
    a. Active Directory Trusts tool
    b. Active Directory Domains tool
    c. Active Directory Users and Computers tool
    d. Active Directory Domains and Trusts tool

Best Answer

Choose the letter that corresponds to the best answer. More than one answer choice may achieve the goal. Select the BEST answer.

1. You currently have 10 computers on your network that are configured to share a few printers and a single document folder. Your company is not expected to add more computers or users over the next year. You also don't have an IT staff to support your network. Which of the following models is the best fit your needs?
   a. Domain model
   b. Workgroup model
   c. Ad-hoc model
   d. Infrastructure model
2. Which of the following authentication factors offers the most security?
   a. Password
   b. Picture password
   c. Smart card
   d. Smart card with a PIN
3. Which of the following authentication types is the least secure?
   a. Password (20 characters, mixed with upper- and lowercase, numbers, and symbols)
   b. Smart card
   c. Smart card with a PIN
   d. VSC

4. Which of the following trusts should be used with a UNIX network whose users need access to resources in your Windows 2012 Active Directory forest after a recent merger?
   a. Forest trust
   b. Shortcut trust
   c. Realm trust
   d. Domain trust

5. Which of the following authentication protocols is best designed to support today's Active Directory-based networks?
   a. NTLMv2
   b. NTLMv1
   c. Kerberosv1
   d. Kerberosv5

Matching and Identification

1. Match the following terms with the related description or usage.

   _______ a) Authentication
   _______ b) SAM
   _______ c) Two-factor authentication
   _______ d) Trust
   _______ e) Shortcut trust
   _______ f) Authorization
   _______ g) Workgroup
   _______ h) Domain
   _______ i) TGT
   _______ j) Digital certificate

   1. Is a type of relationship between domains or forests that enable a user to be authenticated by domain controllers from another domain.
   2. Contains user accounts and their associated passwords in a workgroup model.
   3. Determines what a security principal can do after being authenticated.
   4. Requires the use of two of the three authentication factors.
   5. Provides centralized account management.
   6. Is a collection of computers that interact with each other without any centralized authority.
   7. Contains information about the user's computer, a list of SIDs for the user account, and any group account memberships.
   8. Represents the way that security principals prove their identity.
   9. Is a collection of data that binds an identity to a key pair.
   10. Is used to optimize the authentication process.

Build a List

1. Specify the correct order of the steps that must be completed to use Kerberos for authentication.

   _______ An authentication package is created and sent to the KDC.
   _______ The user attempts to access a resource and needs a session ticket.
   _______ The KDC validates the authentication package and sends the user a session ticket.
   _______ The KDC validates the authentication package and sends the user a TGT.
   _______ The client creates an authentication package (to get a session ticket) and sends it to the KDC along with a request for the resource.
   _______ A session ticket is used to authenticate to the file server that contains the resource the user wants.
   _______ The file server compares the ticket to a DACL.

2. Specify the correct order of the steps that must be completed to create a picture password.

    _________ Choose **Picture**.
    _________ Click **Create a picture password**.
    _________ Draw three gestures.
    _________ Confirm the gestures.
    _________ Log in using the picture password.

Choose an Option

1. Identify the trust type shown in the following figure.

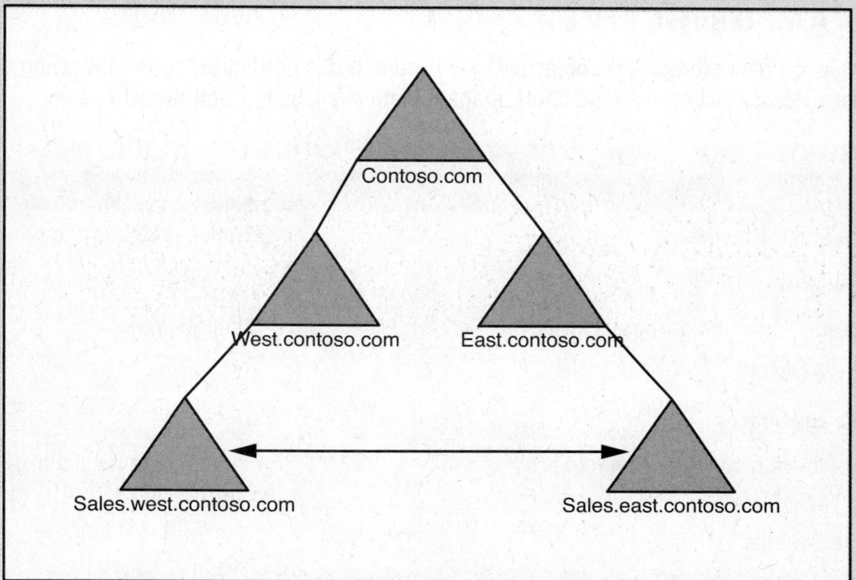

Business Case Scenarios

Scenario 7-1: Troubleshooting Authentication Problems

You have a network that includes the following domains:

- blueridge.com
- east.blueridge.com
- west.blueridge.com
- sales.west.blueridge.com

The users in the sales.west.blueridge.com domain are complaining that authenticating to access resources in the east.blueridge.com domain is taking a long time. What type of trust would you recommend to address the issue?

Scenario 7-2: Troubleshooting Trust Relationships

You have been tasked with providing access to resources in your Active Directory forest from users working in an NT 4.0 domain due to a recent merger. You want to slowly migrate the NT 4.0 domain to a Windows Server 2012 domain, but you do not want users from your company accessing or adding additional resources into the NT 4.0 domain in the meantime. How would you establish your trust and in what direction(s)?

Managing Data Storage

70-412 EXAM OBJECTIVE

Objective 2.4 – Manage data storage. This objective may include but is not limited to the following data storage issues: Resolve data storage issues; manage pools; manage data availability using BranchCache.

Lesson Heading	Exam Objective
Resolving Data Storage Issues	Resolve data storage issues
Using Disk Quotas	
Managing Storage Pools and Storage Spaces	Manage pools
Creating Storage Pools	
Creating Storage Spaces	
Managing Data Availability Using BranchCache	Manage data availability using BranchCache
BranchCache Benefits	
Understanding Content Servers	
Understanding BranchCache Operating Modes: Hosted-Cache Mode and Distributed-Cache Mode	

KEY TERMS

BranchCache
BranchCache-enabled server (content server)
disk quotas
distributed-cache mode
External SATA (eSATA)
File Server Resource Manager
hosted-cache mode
parity
Serial Advanced Technology Attachment (SATA)
simple (no resiliency)
Small Computer System Interface (SCSI)
storage spaces
storage pool
thin provisioning
three-way mirror
two-way mirror
Universal Serial Bus (USB)

Resolving Data Storage Issues

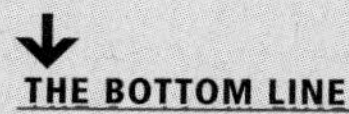

THE BOTTOM LINE

Although the average disk capacity has increased dramatically over the years, there is one thing you can count on: Users will always find a way to store enormous amounts of data on volumes they have access to. Disk quotas, storage spaces and BranchCache are features that can be used to resolve data storage issues within your organization.

CERTIFICATION READY
Resolve data storage issues
Objective 2.4

User data typically includes multiple versions of their documents, copies of other users' documents, high-definition videos downloaded from the Internet, or just about anything else they're not ready to delete. As users' appetites for more storage continue to increase, administrators find themselves purchasing and using a wide variety of drives with different capacities (100 GB, 500 GB, 10 TB) and different drive interfaces to fit their data storage needs. The type of interface you select depends a lot on the connections available with your motherboard and the performance you need out of the drive. Examples of drive interfaces include:

- ***Small Computer System Interface (SCSI)*** is a set of standards for interfaces designed to connect and transfer information between high-speed hardware devices and a motherboard. Devices are connected together in a chain. Each device in the chain gets a SCSI ID and the last device in the chain must be terminated. SATA has replaced SCSI on most modern computers.
- ***Serial Advanced Technology Attachment (SATA)*** is a serial interface that transfers data in bursts instead of parallel. It comes in three varieties: 1.5 Gbps (SATA-1.0), 3 Gbps (SATA-2.0), and 6 Gbps (SATA 3.0). These have maximum throughputs of 150 Mbps, 300 Mbps and 600 Mbps. ***External SATA (eSATA)*** extends the SATA bus to external devices.
- ***Universal Serial Bus (USB)*** is a serial interface that is used to connect keyboards, mice, printers, scanners, and removable media drives. Up to 127 peripherals can be connected to a single USB port. USB 2.0 has a maximum transfer rate of 480 Mbps while USB 3.0, released in 2008, claims a theoretical maximum transmission speed of up to 5 Gbps.

In addition to controlling how much data users can store on the network and managing their need for additional storage space, administrators also have to deal with helping users who work in branch offices. These users must traverse slow wide area network (WAN) links to download content from their main office. This is not only frustrating but also affects their overall productivity.

Fortunately, Windows 8 provides several options for resolving these types of data storage issues:

- Disk quotas
- Storage spaces
- BranchCache

Using Disk Quotas

Letting users store their files and folders on the network can result in a select few abusing the process. As an administrator, your goal is to provide storage space while at the same time minimizing the costs of adding more storage. ***Disk quotas*** enable you to maintain a balance between the two by limiting the amount of storage space allocated to your users.

Disk quotas, a feature first introduced in Windows 2000, are available in Windows 8 and Windows Server 2012 editions. They enable you to set the amount of storage space available to each user. When enabled, the Disk Quota Manager monitors and tracks the files that are owned by a specific user. It then compares the amount of disk space being consumed by the user to the limit set by the administrator. When users reach their limit, the Disk Quota

Manager will notify them and/or restrict them from adding more data to the disk.

Here are a few key things to know about using disk quotas:

- Quotas can be configured only on NTFS volumes.
- Users are charged only for the files they own.
- Quotas must be enabled separately on each volume and are applied on a per-user basis.
- Quotas do not apply to administrators.
- Only domain administrators or local administrators can enable the feature.

Configuring disk quotas involves three steps:

1. Enable quotas on the volume.
2. Configure the quota settings.
3. Create quota entries for specific users.

ENABLING QUOTAS ON INDIVIDUAL COMPUTERS

To enable quota management, you can use Disk Management (diskmgmt.msc) or File Explorer to locate the volume on which you want to enable the feature. Right-click it and choose Properties. Click the Quota tab, which displays the *Enable quota management* option (see Figure 8-1). From the Quota tab, you can also deny disk space to users who exceed their quota limit, set the amount of disk space available to users along with their warning levels, and log events. Logging identifies the user and what triggered the event (for example, a warning or an exceeded quota limit).

Figure 8-1

Reviewing disk quota settings

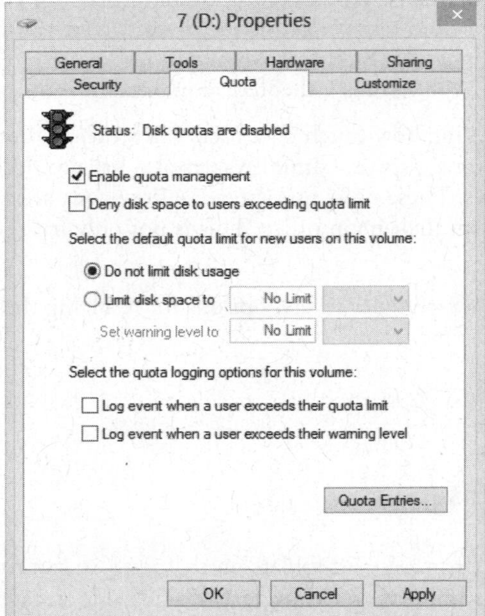

If you enable the *Deny Disk Space to users exceeding quota limit* option, users who reach the limits you set will be denied additional storage space on the volume. Users will receive an "insufficient disk space" error on their screens. If the check box is not selected, users are warned when they reach their limits, but not restricted from adding more data to the volume. By not restricting users initially, you can get a better picture of who is consuming the volume to store data and how much space they are actually using. This information can then be analyzed to determine effective quota policies.

TAKE NOTE*

When you enable disk quotas for a volume, they apply only to new users who have yet to place data on the volume. If existing users already have files/folders on the volume, you have to add them as new quota entries.

When you configure quotas, you apply a default setting for all users and then click the *Quota Entries* button to configure exceptions for specific users/groups. In other words, when you create a quota entry for a user, the default setting no longer applies to that user. Because quotas are enabled on a per-volume basis, you may decide that you want to configure the exact same quota entries for another volume. You can do this by clicking Quota Entries, choosing the entries you want to use on the other volume, and then clicking Quota > Export. You can then enable quota management on the other volume and import the quota entries.

When planning your quota strategy, consider grouping your users based on the amount of disk space you think they will require. For example, your marketing and graphic design staff typically needs more space than other groups. Set default limits that are not too restrictive for all users' accounts and then modify them for users who need more disk space. Consider growth requirements and increase as needed.

ENABLING QUOTAS USING GROUP POLICY

Group Policy can also be used to manage disk quotas on selected computers at the site, domain, or organizational unit (OU) level. This policy can be found in the Computer Configuration\Administrative Templates\System\Disk Quotas section of a Group Policy. On Windows Server 2012, there are six disk quota settings you can use:

- **Enable disk quotas:** Enabling this setting turns on disk quota management on all NTFS volumes of the computer and users cannot turn it off.
- **Enforce disk quota limit:** Enabling this policy determines whether disk quota limits are enforced and prevents the user from changing the setting.
- **Specify default quota limit and warning level:** This policy setting specifies the default disk quota limit and warning level for all new users as soon as they write to the volume. It does not affect disk-quota limits for current users. The policy settings here determine how much disk space can be used by each user on each of the NTFS file system volumes on a computer. It also specifies a warning level.
- **Log event when quote limit is exceeded:** This setting determines whether the system records an event in the local Application log when users reach their disk quota limit.
- **Log event when quota warning level is exceeded:** This setting determines whether the system records an event in the Application log when users reach their disk quota warning limit.
- **Apply policy to removable media:** This policy extends the disk quota policies in this folder to NTFS file system volumes or other removable media.

ENABLE DISK QUOTAS ON WINDOWS 8

GET READY. To enable a disk quota, perform the following steps:

1. Press the **Windows logo key + r**, type **diskmgmt.msc**, and then click **OK**.
2. Right-click the volume you want to enable quota management on and choose **Properties**.
3. Click the Quota tab (see Figure 8-2) and then click **Enable Quota management**.

   Do not click the *Deny disk space to users exceeding quota limit* option. By not selecting this option, you will be able to audit how the volume is being consumed without restricting access to users who exceed the quota limit.

Figure 8-2

Enabling quota management and setting default quota limits

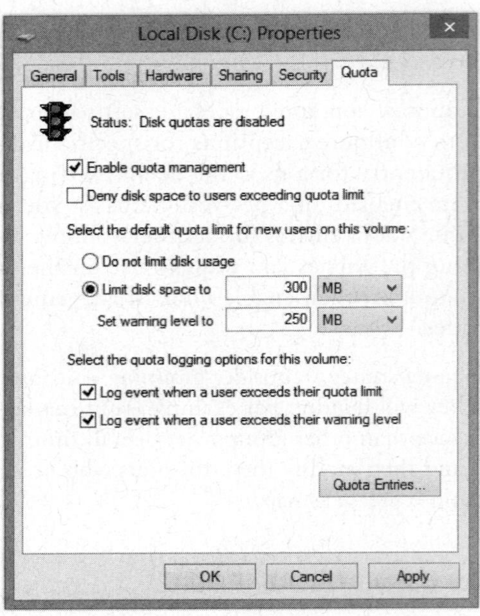

4. Select **Limit disk space to** and type **300** in the field provided. Click the arrow to select **MB**.
5. For the *Set warning level to* setting, type **250** in the field provided. Click the arrow to select **MB**.
6. In the *Select the quota logging options for this volume* section, select both **Log event when a user exceeds their quota limit** and **Log event when a user exceeds their warning level**.
7. Click **OK**.
8. After reading the disk quota message, click **OK**.
9. Right-click the volume you enabled quota management on and choose **Properties**.
10. Click the **Quota** tab and then click **Quota Entries** to see whether any user accounts are currently reaching their limits.
11. On the top menu, click **Quota**. (The *Export* option can be used to export your quota settings to another NTFS volume; do *not* export at this time, however.)
12. Click **Quota** > **Close** to exit the *Quota Entries* screen.
13. Remove the check mark next to *Enable quota management* to return your system to its original setting. Click **OK** to close.
14. After reading the message indicating the volume will be rescanned, click **OK**.

The ***File Server Resource Manager***, a feature in Windows Server 2012, provides a more enhanced approach to quota management. This tool enables you to configure disk quotas on a per-volume and per-folder basis and comes with several templates to work from.

These templates are categorized as hard and soft. Hard means the user cannot store files after reaching the defined limit; soft means the user can continue to store files. These templates are entirely separate from the NTFS quota management discussed earlier and in most cases should not be used together with NTFS quota management.

Managing Storage Pools and Storage Spaces

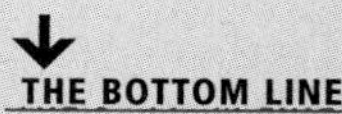

THE BOTTOM LINE

Storage Spaces is a feature in Windows 8/Windows Server 2012 that allows you to combine multiple disks into a single logical volume that can be mirrored to protect against one or more drive failures.

CERTIFICATION READY
Manage pools
Objective 2.4

The Storage Spaces feature in Windows 8 allows you to combine several physical drives, which the operating system will see as one large drive. The drives can be of any capacity and can consist of a variety of different drive interfaces—Small Computer System Interface (SCSI), Universal Serial Bus (USB), and Serial ATA (SATA).

When the drives are combined, Windows places them into a ***storage pool***. These storage pools can then be segmented into multiple storage spaces, which are then formatted with a file system and can be used just like any other regular disk on your computer. New disks (internal/external) can be added to the storage pool as space requirements increase over time.

Although data can be stored on the drives, you cannot use storage spaces to host the Windows operating system files.

TAKE NOTE*

On Windows Server 2012, you can use storage spaces with failover clusters, which are groups of computers connected via physical cables and by clustering software. When one fails, another member of the cluster takes over. To use storage spaces with this type of configuration, you are restricted to using Serial Attached SCSI (SAS) devices. You can manage storage spaces from the Control Panel on Windows 8 clients and through the File and Storage Services role in Server Manager. You can also configure it using Windows PowerShell.

Storage spaces offer two key benefits:

- By spreading data across multiple disks you achieve data resiliency, which can protect your data against hard disk failure.
- Volume sizes can be larger than the actual physical size of your drives in the storage pool. This is accomplished through a process called thin provisioning.

Creating Storage Pools

Creating a storage pool allows you to combine multiple smaller drives that you might not otherwise be able to use by themselves into a larger single logical volume.

To create a storage pool on a Windows 8 client, you access the Manage Storage Spaces tool found in the Control Panel. The Wizard prompts you to select the disks that you want to use and then add them to the storage pool. For example, if you have two physical disks with capacities of 200 GB and 300 GB, it creates a pool that has a total capacity of 500 GB (see Figure 8-3).

Figure 8-3

Creating a storage pool with two disks

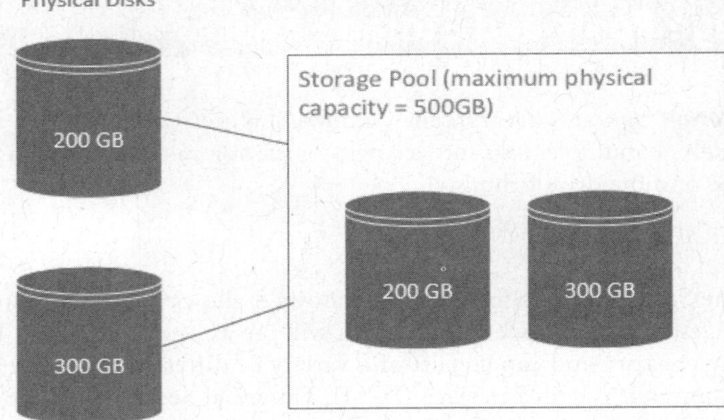

Creating Storage Spaces

After selecting the drives to include in your storage pool, you will be prompted to create the storage space. This involves entering a name, selecting a drive letter, identifying the type of resiliency you want to configure, and setting the maximum size you want to assign to the storage space.

When creating storage spaces, there are four resiliency types to select from (see Figure 8-4). Only three of them provide real fault-tolerance.

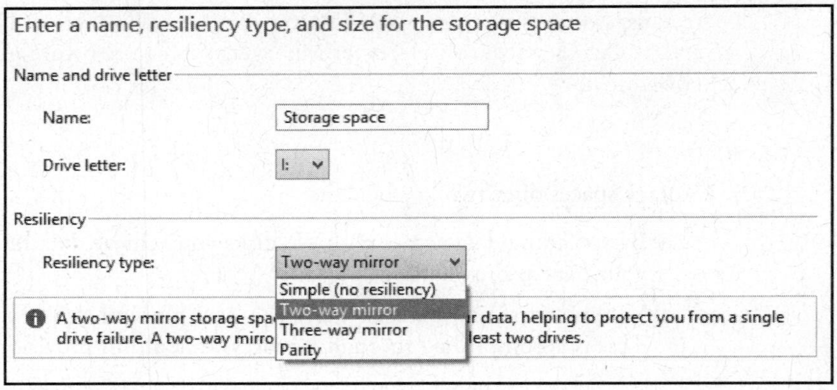

Figure 8-4

Configuring resiliency settings

Enter a name, resiliency type, and size for the storage space

Name and drive letter

Name: Storage space

Drive letter: I:

Resiliency

Resiliency type: Two-way mirror

Simple (no resiliency)
Two-way mirror
Three-way mirror
Parity

A two-way mirror storage spa... r data, helping to protect you from a single drive failure. A two-way mirro... least two drives.

- ***Simple (no resiliency):*** Writes one copy of your data but doesn't protect against drive failures; requires at least one drive.
- ***Two-way mirror:*** Writes two copies of your data to protect against a single drive failure; requires at least two drives.
- ***Three-way mirror:*** Writes three copies of your data to protect against two simultaneous drive failures; requires at least five drives.
- ***Parity:*** Writes data with parity information to protect against single drive failures; requires at least three drives.

You also need to decide how much of the total storage pool capacity you want to use for your new storage space. In Figure 8-3, you saw the total pool capacity is 500 GB. By using a process called ***thin provisioning*** (see Figure 8-5), you can create a storage space that is larger than the available capacity of the storage pool. After setting the size, the Wizard will create the storage space based on the parameters you provided.

Figure 8-5

An example of thin provisioning

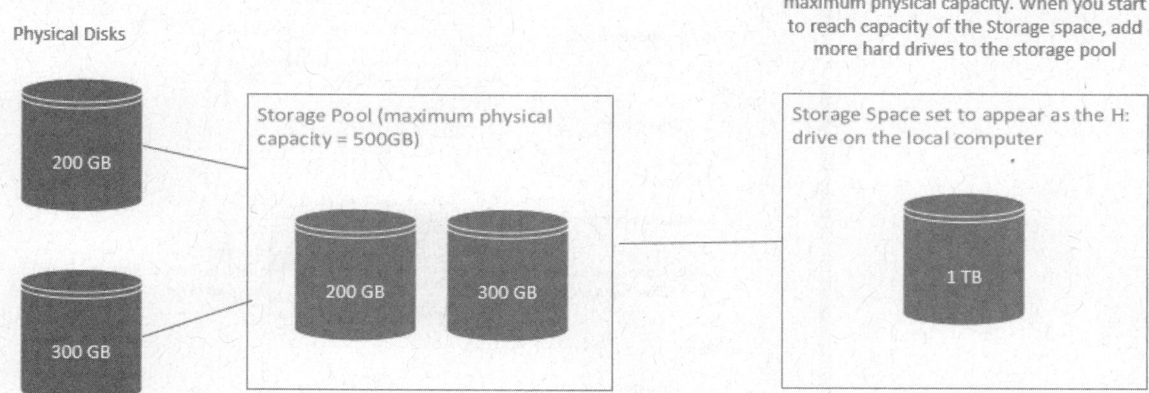

Thin provisioning reserves the space for future use. For example, in Figure 8-5, you can see there are two physical drives being added to the storage pool to create a total capacity of 500 GB. Even though you have a total capacity of only 500 GB, you can configure the storage space that uses this pool to be 1 TB or greater capacity. When the storage pool approaches capacity, you will receive a warning and need to add more disks to the pool. This approach works well in situations in which you expect your data storage needs will grow, but you don't want to purchase additional disks immediately.

After the storage space is created, it will appear as a drive in File Explorer. The drive can be protected using BitLocker and NTFS permissions, just like any other drive in Windows 8.

CREATE A STORAGE POOL AND A STORAGE SPACE IN WINDOWS 8

GET READY. To create a storage pool and storage space, perform the following steps:

1. Log on with administrative credentials.
2. Connect the drives you want to use to your computer.
3. Press the **Windows logo key + w** and then type **Storage Spaces**.
4. From the *Results* list, click **Storage Spaces**.
5. Click **Create a new pool and storage space**.
6. Select the drive(s) you want to include in the new storage pool. (Warning: Any data on these drives will be deleted.)
7. Click **Create pool**.

Once the pool is created, you will be taken automatically to the *Create a storage space screen* shown in Figure 8-6.

Figure 8-6

Creating a storage space

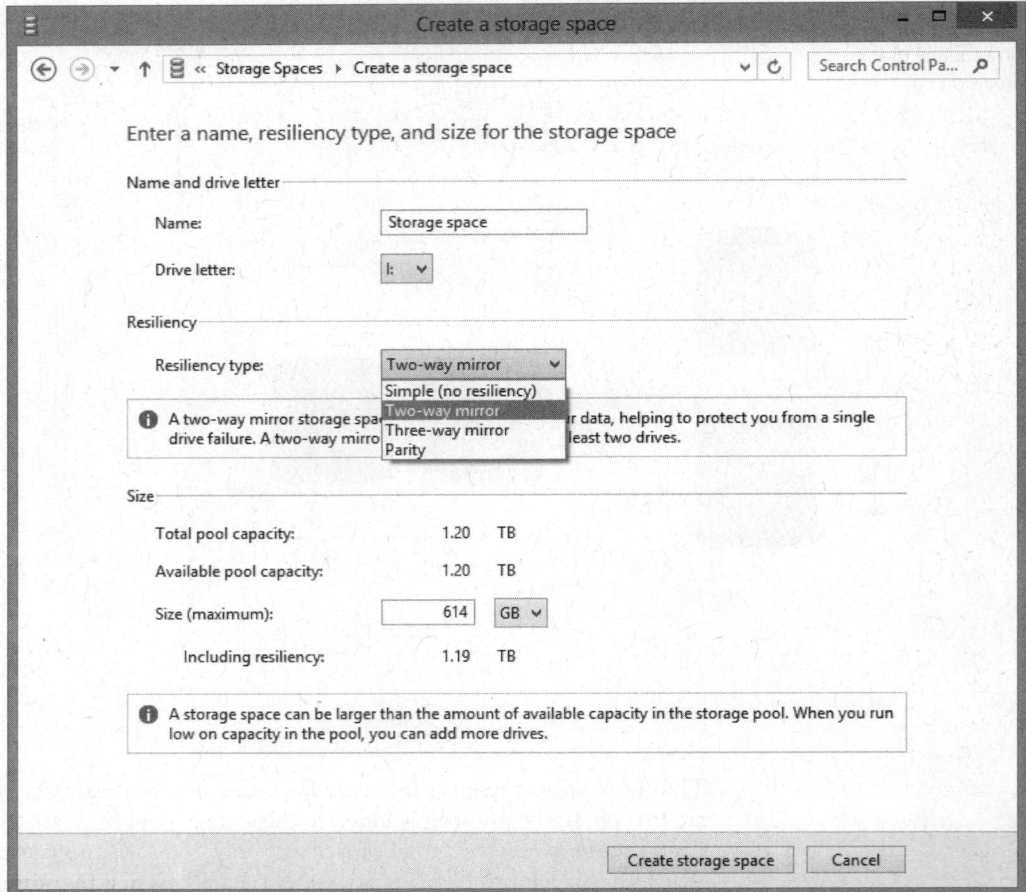

8. In the *Name* field, type a name for your storage space.
9. In the *Drive letter* field, click the down arrow and then choose a driver letter for the storage space.
10. In the *Resiliency type* field, click the down arrow and then choose the resiliency type.
11. In the *Size (maximum)* field, type the maximum size that you want for your storage space.
12. Click **Create storage space**.
13. Open File Explorer and confirm that the new storage space appears under the drive letter you assigned in Step 9.

After completing the setup of your storage space, you can continue to monitor and manage it from the Manage Storage Space tool. You can perform the following tasks:

- View your storage pool(s).
- View the storage spaces in the pools.
- View the physical drives included in the pool(s).
- Identify how much pool capacity is currently being used.
- Add more drives to the pool.

- Rename the pool.
- Change the size of storage spaces.
- View files stored in storage spaces.
- Delete storage spaces.

Managing Data Availability Using BranchCache

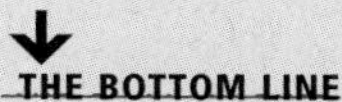

THE BOTTOM LINE

BranchCaching is designed to optimize the link between branch offices and main offices by caching information from content servers on local computers within the branch. This reduces traffic on the wide area network links, reduces response time for opening files, and improves the experience for users connecting over slow links.

CERTIFICATION READY
Manage data availability using BranchCache
Objective 2.4

BranchCache, a feature available in Windows 8 and Windows Server 2012, is designed to improve the overall experience for companies that have employees working in branch offices. In the past, most companies would set up a dedicated WAN link or a Virtual Private Network (VPN) to provide access to resources located at their main office. In either case, when large files were downloaded by one employee or when multiple employees needed access to resources at the main office concurrently, the available bandwidth would be consumed quickly.

BranchCache Benefits

BranchCache provides a better approach to managing and optimizing the WAN link. By copying data from content servers and caching it on a server physically located in the branch office, users can access their files over the much faster local area network (LAN) connection. If you do not have a server, you can also configure Windows 8 clients to support caching.

BranchCache provides the following additional benefits:

- All data stored in the cache is encrypted.
- By using metadata, you reduce the amount of data traffic traversing the WAN link.
- Users always have access to the current version of the data.

Understanding Content Servers

Content obtained from a ***BranchCache-enabled server***, also called a ***content server***, can be cached on the client systems at the branch office or on BranchCache servers at the branch office. Future requests for the same content can be delivered from the client system or the BranchCache server without having to cross the slower WAN link.

The following represent the types of BranchCache enabled servers (content servers) that can be configured. You must deploy at least one or more of these types of servers at your main office:

- Web servers: Windows Server 2008 R2/2012 running Internet Information Services (IIS) with BranchCache enabled. These servers use the Hypertext Transfer Protocol (HTTP) and Hypertext Transfer Protocol Secure (HTTPS) protocols.
- Application (BITS) servers: Windows Server 2012 running the Background Intelligent Transfer Service (BITS) with BranchCache enabled.

- File servers: Windows Server 2008 R2/2012 running the File Service server role and the BranchCache for Network Files role service. These servers use the Server Message Block (SMB) protocol to send content.

Understanding BranchCache Operating Modes: Hosted-Cache Mode and Distributed-Cache Mode

There are two operating modes for BranchCache: hosted-cache mode and distributed-cache mode. You typically use hosted-cache mode when you have more than 50 systems at the branch office. If you have fewer than 50, distributed-cache mode may be a more viable option.

With ***hosted-cache mode*** (see Figure 8-7), you deploy a computer running Windows Server 2012 at the branch office. The clients are configured with the name of the server and can retrieve content from it. If the content is not available in the cache on the local server, the client will traverse the WAN link, download the data, and then make it available to the hosted cache server for other clients to use. By using the fully qualified domain name (FQDN), the clients can use DNS and thus communicate with the server across subnets.

Figure 8-7

An example of hosted-cache mode

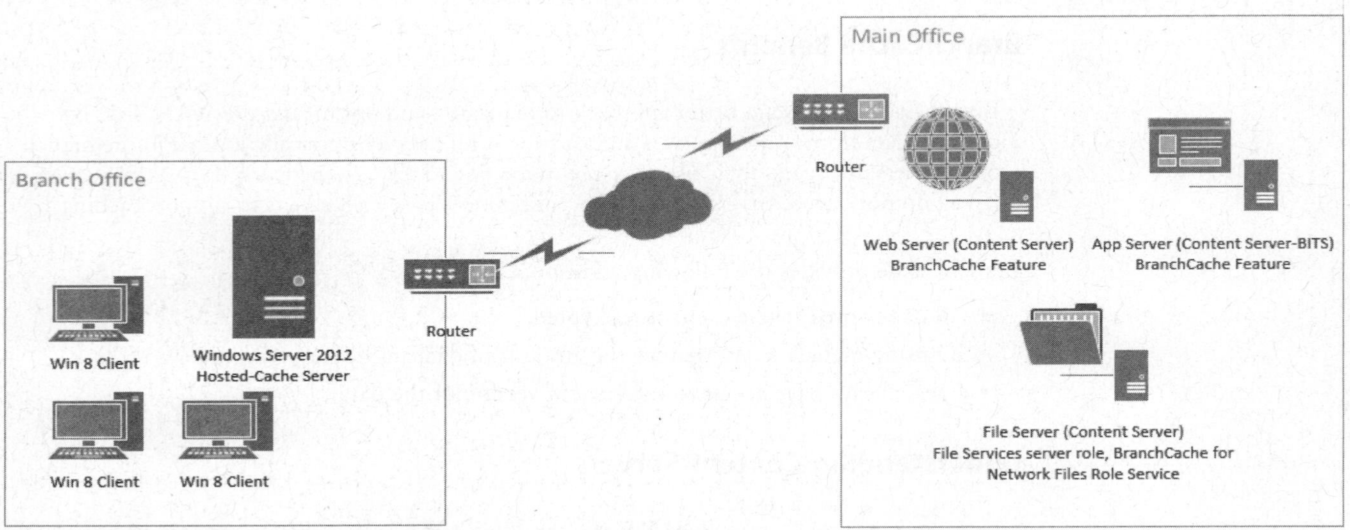

TAKE NOTE*

A Windows Server 2012 can support Windows 7 clients, but must have a certificate compatible with Transport Layer Security (TLS). To obtain the best performance and use the new features in BranchCache, use Windows 8 clients.

When a Windows 8 client connects to a main office File Server and requests a file, the server first authenticates and authorizes the client. If successful, the server returns content metadata (identifiers) to the Windows 8 client, which then uses the hash information to search for the file on the hosted-cache server. If this is the first time the file has ever been requested, the Windows 8 client will contact the main office file server and retrieve the file. The Windows 8 client will then contact the hosted-cache server located at its branch office and offer the content to the server. The hosted-cache server will then retrieve the content and cache it. When another Windows 8 client at the branch office requests the same file from the main office file server, the server authenticates and authorizes the client. After the process is complete, the file server returns metadata and the Windows 8 client obtains the information from the hosted-cache server at its local branch office.

With ***distributed-cache mode*** (see Figure 8-8), Windows 8 client computers request data from the main office and then cache it locally themselves. This content is then made available to other clients on the same branch office network.

Figure 8-8

An example of distributed-cache mode

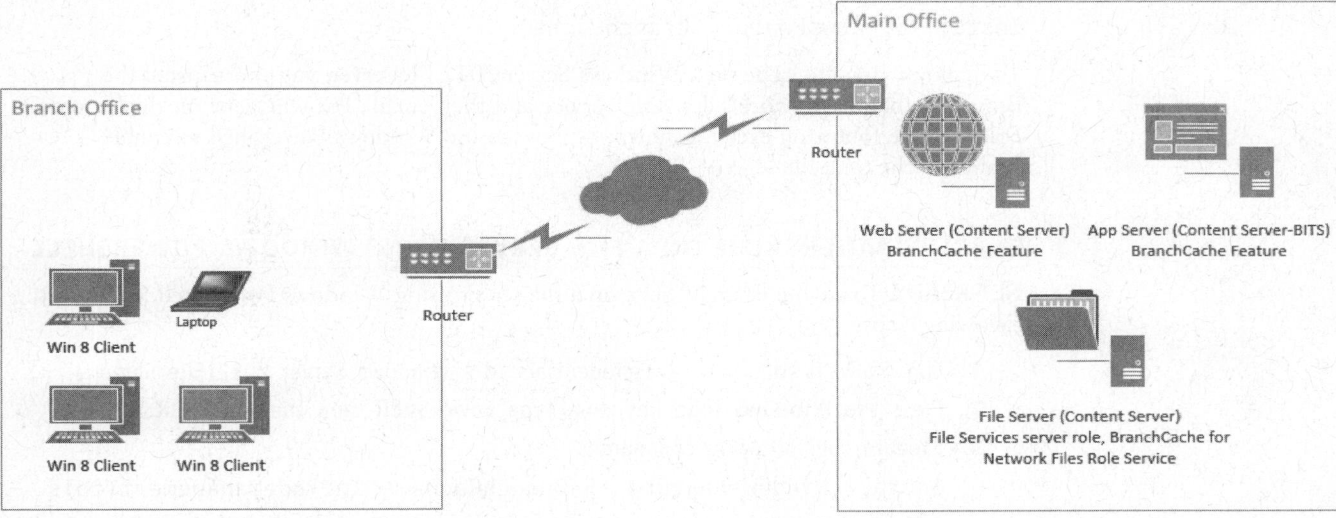

When the first Windows 8 client connects and downloads a specific set of files from the main office file server it becomes the source for that content at the local branch office. When another Windows 8 client connects to the main office file server to download the same file, it is authenticated and authorized. The content metadata is then sent from the file server to this client. The Windows 8 client then sends a request for the segment hashes on the local network to determine if another computer on the same local network has the data cached This is done using a special multicast packet. Because the first Windows 8 client that connected and downloaded the file already has the content, the second Windows 8 client retrieves it directly from that computer.

Distributed-cache mode allows you to take advantage of BranchCache with minimal hardware requirements at the branch office. Although this mode works well in small offices with 50 or fewer computers without a server, it can produce situations in which content has to be retrieved from the main office because the computer that has the data is not currently available on the local network.

You can use a combination of these modes across your branch offices. For example, you can have one branch office that uses distributed-cache mode and another that uses the hosted-cache mode.

In both modes, the client will traverse the slower WAN link to communicate with the BranchCache-enabled server located in the main office. After the client is authenticated, content metadata is sent instead of the actual data files. Content metadata is much smaller in size and reduces the bandwidth requirements. It also ensures the clients receive hashes for the most current content. The content itself is broken into blocks (block hashes), each receiving its own hash. The blocks are organized into collections called segments (segment hashes). The content metadata includes both the block and segment hash information. It is the content metadata that the client uses to search for the file in both the hosted and distributed cache modes.

ENABLING BRANCHCACHE ON CONTENT SERVERS

BranchCache is installed and enabled for web servers and application servers by clicking Server Manager > Manager > Add Roles and Features. After selecting the server, you enable the BranchCache feature, confirm the installation, and then click Install. You can also enable BranchCache using the following Windows PowerShell command:

```
Install-WindowsFeature BranchCache
```

To deploy a BranchCache on a Windows Server 2012 file server, you must install the BranchCache for Network Files Role Service and then enable BranchCache on the Shared Folders. The following exercise shows you how to use Windows PowerShell to enable BranchCache on a file server.

ENABLE BRANCHCACHE ON A FILE SERVER USING WINDOWS POWERSHELL

GET READY. To enable BranchCache on a file server using Windows PowerShell, perform the following steps:

1. Log on with administrative credentials to a Windows Server 2012 File Server.
2. Press the **Windows logo key + r**, type **PowerShell**, and then click **OK.**
3. Execute the following command:

   ```
   Install-WindowsFeature FS-BranchCache - IncludeManagementTools
   ```

   After the install is complete, continue to Step 4. Do not exit Windows PowerShell.
4. Execute the following command:

   ```
   Install-WindowsFeature FS-Data-Deduplication
   -IncludeManagementTools
   ```
5. After the install is complete, close the Windows PowerShell window.

After completing the installation of the BranchCache for Network Files Feature, you must create and share a folder.

CREATE AND SHARE A FOLDER

GET READY. To create and share a folder, perform the following steps:

1. Click the Server Manager icon on the task bar to open the Server Manager console.
2. Click **File and Storage Services > Shares.**
3. Click **Tasks > New Share.**
4. Click **SMB Share-Quick** and then click **Next.**
5. Select the volume that will be used to store your share and then click **Next.**
6. Type a share name (for example, **BranchCacheShare**) and then click **Next.**
7. Select **Enable BranchCache on the file share** (see Figure 8-9) and then click **Next.**

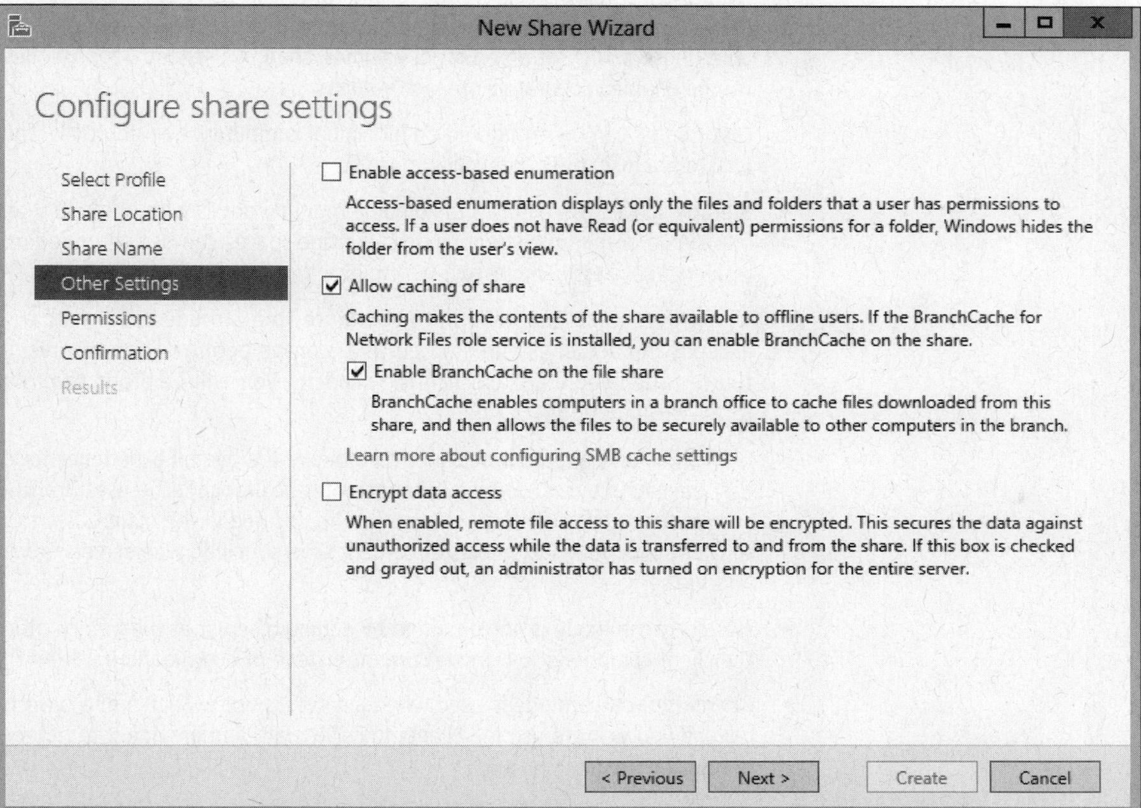

Figure 8-9

Enabling BranchCache on the file share

8. Accept the default permissions for the share and then click **Next**.
9. Review your settings and click **Create**.
10. Click **Close** after the share is created.
11. Close the Server Manager tool.

ENABLE BRANCHCACHE ON A WINDOWS 8 CLIENT USING WINDOWS POWERSHELL

GET READY. To enable BranchCache on a Windows 8 client using Windows PowerShell, log on with administrative credentials to a Windows 8 client connected to a domain and then perform the following steps:

1. Press the **Windows logo key** + r, type **PowerShell**, and then click **OK**.
2. Execute the following Windows PowerShell command:
   ```
   Enable-BCHostedClient
   ```
3. Type the FQDN of the file server on which you enabled BranchCache earlier and then click **Enter**.
4. Confirm the configuration by typing **Get-BCStatus** and then clicking **Enter**.
5. Review the output to confirm that BranchCacheEnabled is set to True, BranchCache-ServiceStatus is set to Running, and BranchCacheServiceStartType is manual.
6. Close the Windows PowerShell window.

SKILL SUMMARY

IN THIS LESSON, YOU LEARNED:

- Using the disk quota management enables you to set the amount of storage space available to users. It is set up on NTFS volumes, charges users only for the files they own, and can be enabled separately on each volume.
- Disk quotas can be configured on individual computers by using Disk Management (diskmgmt.msc) or Group Policy.
- Storage spaces can be used to combine multiple drives with different interfaces/capacities into single or multiple storage pools. Storage spaces can be configured using one of four resiliency settings: Simple, two-way mirror, three-way mirror, and Parity.
- Thin provisioning enables you to configure your storage space with a size that exceeds the actual size of your current storage pool. You can reserve space for the future; when you start to reach the capacity, you will be prompted to add more disks to the storage pool.
- BranchCache is a feature designed to improve the overall experience for companies that have employees working in branch offices. BranchCache uses BranchCache enabled servers (also called content servers) that are located in the main office to provide resources to client comptuers: Examples of content severs include web servers, application servers, and file servers.
- Hosted-cache mode is implemented by adding a server at the branch office that is used by the client computers to retrieve content instead of downloading it from the main office.
- Distributed-cache mode is used when a server is not available at a branch office, but instead you want to use the clients to cache data and provide it to other computers on the local network.
- In hosted-cache and distributed-cache modes, the clients will still traverse the WAN link to communicate with a BranchCache-enabled server. Instead of transferring over the entire file, content metadata is used to reduce the bandwidth requirements and optimize use of the link. The content metadata is used by the client to search for the actual data file, which can be on a local server or on another client on their local network segment.

■ Knowledge Assessment

Multiple Choice

Select the correct answer for each of the following questions.

1. Which of the following are true characteristics of disk quotas? (Select all that apply.)
   a. They can be configured only on NTFS volumes.
   b. They do not apply to administrators.
   c. Users are charged for files they own.
   d. They cannot be implemented on Windows 7/8 computers.
2. Which of the following tools is used to enable Disk Quotas on a FAT 32 volume?
   a. diskmgmt.msc
   b. discmgmt.msc
   c. Disk Quota Manager
   d. None of the above

3. Which of the following drives can be added to a storage pool? (Select all that apply.)
   a. SATA
   b. eSATA
   c. USB
   d. SCSI
4. Which of the following resiliency settings requires at least five drives?
   a. Parity
   b. Three-way mirror
   c. Two-way mirror
   d. Simple
5. Which of the following content servers can be used with BranchCache? (Select all that apply.)
   a. Web servers
   b. File servers
   c. Application (BITS) servers
   d. RADIUS servers
6. Which of the following commands can be used to enable BranchCache on a File server using Windows PowerShell?
   a. `Install-Windows Feature FS_Branch Cache`
   b. `Install-WindowsFeature FS-BranchCache -IncludeManagementTools`
   c. `Install-WindowsFeature -Branch Cache`
   d. `Install-WindowsFeature BranchCache`
7. Which BranchCache mode enables clients to cache information and share it with each other?
   a. Client-cache mode
   b. Hosted-cache mode
   c. Distributed-cache mode
   d. Client distribution mode
8. Which of the following terms best describes the information returned by content servers when requests are made by clients?
   a. Hashes
   b. Content metadata
   c. Streamed content
   d. Replicated metadata
9. Which process reserves space for future use when working with storage spaces/storage pools?
   a. Partitions
   b. Thin provisioning
   c. SMB blocks
   d. Provisioned storage blocks
10. How many disks are needed when setting up parity for your resiliency settings in a storage pool?
   a. 2
   b. 3
   c. 5
   d. 4

Best Answer

Choose the letter that corresponds to the best answer. More than one answer choice may achieve the goal. Select the BEST answer.

1. Which type of resiliency works best for protecting yourself from two drives failing simultaneously while setting up your storage space?
   a. Three-way mirror
   b. Two-way mirror

c. Parity
d. Simple

2. Which of the following solutions enables you to reduce the traffic load originating from your branch office for files and folders at the main office while still not requiring you to add any servers at your branch office location?
   a. Setting up an existing Windows 8 computer to run in hosted-cache mode.
   b. Setting up an existing server to use hosted-cache mode.
   c. Setting up Windows 8 computers to use distributed-cache mode.
   d. Increasing the bandwidth available over the WAN link.

3. Which of the following solutions is best for applying disk quotas on a volume in which existing users have files/folders already in place?
   a. Moving the user's data to another volume and then copying it back after setting the new quota.
   b. Requesting that users move their data.
   c. Adding them as new quota entries.
   d. Excluding the users from disk quotas.

4. Which of the following approaches is best when you would like to reserve at least 500 GB of space for a new storage space yet you have only 100 GB of actual physical disk space?
   a. Wait until you have enough physical disk capacity to create the 500 GB storage space.
   b. Purchase new drives before creating the space.
   c. Use thin provisioning and go ahead and create the space. You can purchase drives later when you need them.
   d. Configure one pool now and another when you have the drives.

5. Which of the following tools is the best solution for adding more drives to your storage pool and also renaming the pool?
   a. Windows PowerShell
   b. Disk Manager
   c. Manage Storage Space
   d. You cannot add additional drives to the pool without re-creating it

Matching and Identification

1. Match the following terms with the related description or usage.
   _______ a) BranchCache
   _______ b) Hosted-cache mode
   _______ c) Disk quota
   _______ d) Storage space
   _______ e) Storage pool
   _______ f) Thin provisioning
   _______ g) Content server
   _______ h) three-way mirror
   _______ i) Parity
   _______ j) two-way mirror
   1. Clients are configured with the name of a server from which they retrieve content.
   2. Enables you to set the amount of storage space available for each user.
   3. Writes three copies of your data to protect against the simultaneous failure of two drives; requires at least five drives to implement.
   4. Writes data with parity information to protect against single drive failures; requires at least three drives.
   5. Contains source content downloaded by the branch office computers.

6. A feature designed to improve the overall experience for branch office employees connecting over slow WAN links.
7. A collection of disks that are combined to create one or more storage spaces.
8. Enables you to create a storage space that is larger than the available capacity of the storage pool.
9. Writes two copies of your data to protect against a single drive failure; requires at least two drives.
10. Enables you to take multiple drives and combine them into a storage pool.

Build a List

1. Identify the basic steps, in order, to create a Storage pool.
   _______ Click **Create pool**.
   _______ Log on with administrative credentials.
   _______ Select the drive(s) you want to include in the new storage pool.
   _______ Click *Create a new pool and storage space.*
   _______ Connect the drives to your computer.
   _______ Press the **Windows logo key + r**, type **Storage Spaces**, and then select it from the *Results* list.
   _______ From the *Results* list, click **Storage Spaces**.

2. Specify the correct order of the steps that must be completed to create a storage space.
   _______ Choose a drive letter.
   _______ Type a name for the storage space.
   _______ Choose the resiliency type.
   _______ Click *Create storage space.*
   _______ Type the maximum size for your storage space.

Choose an Option

1. Identify the setting that restricts a user's access to the volume if they exceed their quota limit.

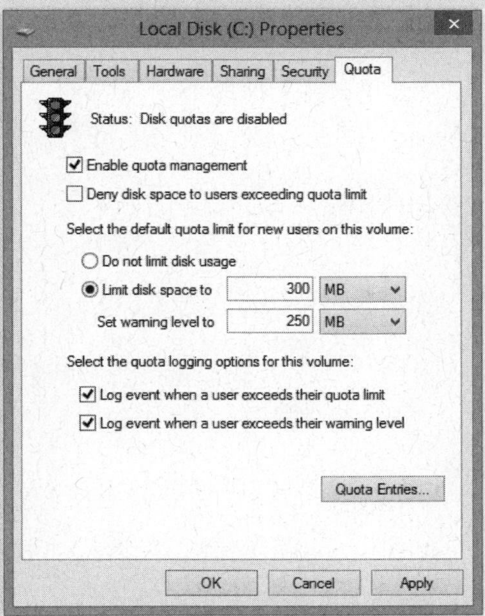

■ Business Case Scenarios

Scenario 8-1: Configuring BranchCache

You have 10 computers running Windows 8 at a branch office. After setting up BranchCache in distributed mode, you notice they are still using the slow WAN link to attempt to access files/folders. Is that a normal operation? If not, what could be causing it?

Scenario 8-2: Configuring Storage Space/Storage Pools

You create a new storage pool for the following disks on your Windows 8 computer:

- SATA: 1 TB
- SAS: 1 TB

What is the maximum size you can allocate for your new storage space?

Managing Data Security

LESSON 9

70-688 EXAM OBJECTIVE

Objective 2.5 – Manage data security. This objective may include but is not limited to the following data security considerations: Manage share/NTFS permissions for storage spaces; configure EFS; configure security for removable media; manage BitLocker and BitLocker To Go.

LESSON HEADING	EXAM OBJECTIVE
Managing Share Permissions and NTFS Permissions for Storage Spaces	Manage share/NTFS permissions for storage spaces
Configuring Share Permissions	
Configuring NTFS Permissions	
Combining NTFS and Share Permissions	
Configuring the Encrypting File System (EFS)	Configure EFS
Configuring Security for Removable Media	Configure security for removable media
Managing BitLocker and BitLocker To Go	Manage BitLocker and BitLocker To Go
Using BitLocker Drive Encryption	
Using BitLocker To Go on Workspace Drives	
Using BitLocker To Go on Removable Media	
Managing BitLocker To Go	
Using Microsoft BitLocker Administration and Monitoring (MBAM) 1.0	

KEY TERMS

BitLocker Drive Encryption
BitLocker To Go
EFS recovery agent (ERA)
Encrypting File System (EFS)
Group Policy
Group Policy Management Console (GPMC)
Group Policy Objects (GPOs)
Local Group Policy Editor (LGPE)
Microsoft BitLocker Administration and Monitoring (MBAM)
NTFS permissions
recovery key
Remote Server Administration Tools (RSAT) for Windows 8
Secure Digital (SD) cards
share permissions
Trusted Platform Module (TPM)

■ Managing Share Permissions and NTFS Permissions for Storage Spaces

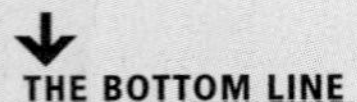

THE BOTTOM LINE

Share permissions and NTFS permissions are used to control access to resources located in your storage space.

CERTIFICATION READY
Manage Share/NTFS Permissions for Storage Spaces
Objective 2.5

As you learned in Lesson 8, storage spaces appear just like any other drive in File Explorer, so you can apply permissions to the files and folders it contains.

The format of your disk (FAT16, FAT32, exFAT, NTFS) determines the type of security available to you. Windows 8 and Windows Server 2012 still rely on the basic approach to securing resources used by previous versions, but they do introduce new features. Before we review those changes, let's take a quick look at share and NTFS permissions and how they work.

Configuring Share Permissions

Share permissions are the permissions you set for folders when you share them either on a workgroup or domain-based network. The permissions you set determine the type of access users have to the folder and its contents.

Share permissions are set for folders when they are shared in workgroups and domain-based networks and are only associated with the folder. They determine the type of access that others will have to the folder when they connect to it over the network.

If they log on locally where the share is located, these permissions will not apply. Share permissions are not granular; therefore, the permission you assign to the share will automatically apply to the files and subfolders within the share itself.

For drives formatted with the FAT/FAT32 file system, share permissions are the only option available, as shown by the Sharing tab shown in Figure 9-1. Table 9-1 provides more information on share level permissions that are available.

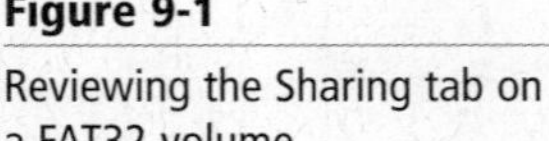

Figure 9-1

Reviewing the Sharing tab on a FAT32 volume

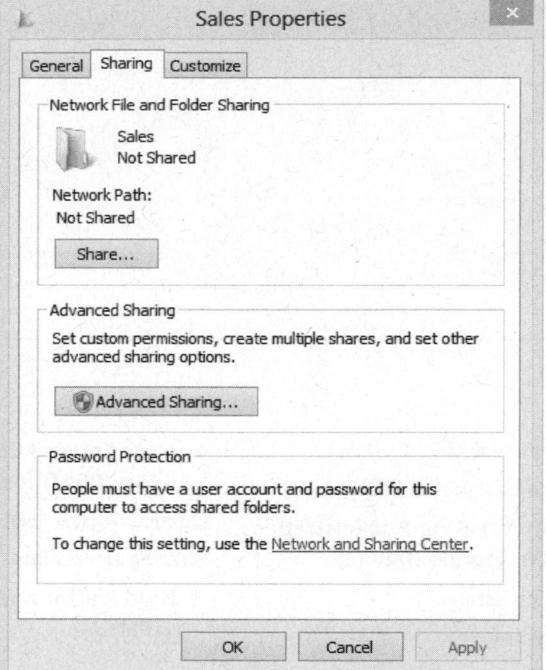

Table 9-1

Understanding Share Permissions

Permission	Description
Read	Enables user/group to view file and subfolder names, view data in files, and run programs
Change	Enables user/group to add files and subfolders to the shared folder, change data in files, delete subfolders and files, and change any permission associated with Read
Full Control	Enables user/group to change file permissions (NTFS only), take ownership of files (NTFS only), and perform tasks associated with Change/Read

Configuring NTFS Permissions

NTFS file permissions is a powerful tool that enables you to control access to your files and folders whether they are accessed across the network or by someone logging on to the computer locally.

CERTIFICATION READY
Manage Share/NTFS Permissions for Storage Spaces
Objective 2.5

In addition to the permissions you set when sharing a folder, Windows offers a more comprehensive set of permissions called ***NTFS permissions***. These permissions are available on volumes formatted with the NTFS file system.

NTFS permissions differ from share permissions in two ways.

- They apply to files and folders on NTFS volumes.
- They apply whether the user attempts to access them over the network or locally.

In Figure 9-2, an additional Security tab is present because the folder is located on an NTFS volume. As you can see, there are a number of different permissions available for selected users and groups (see Table 9-2).

Figure 9-2

Reviewing the Security tab on an NTFS volume

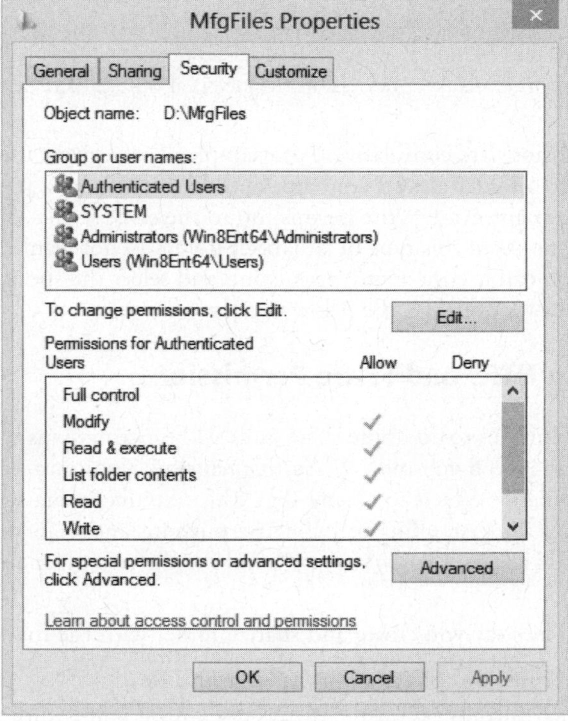

Table 9-2

NTFS Permissions

Permission	Description
Read	Folder: Enables user/group to read the contents of the folder. File: Enables user/group to read the contents of the file.
Read & Execute	Folder: Enables user/group to read the contents of the folder and execute programs in the folder. File: Enables user/group to read the contents of the file and execute the program.
Write	Folder: Enables user/group to create files and folders. File: Enables user/group to create a file.
Modify	Folder: Enables user/group to read and write permissions. User can delete files within the folder and view the contents of subfolders. File: Enables user/group to read and write permissions. User can modify the contents of the file.
List Folder Contents	Folder: Enables user/group to view a list of files in the selected folder; user is not allowed to read the contents of a file or execute a file. File: There is no equivalent permission for files.
Full Control	Folder: Enables user/group to add, change, move, and delete items. User can also add and remove permissions on the folder and its subfolders. File: Enables user/group to change, move, delete, and manage permissions. User can also add, change, and remove permissions on the file.

TAKE NOTE* In Windows 8 and Windows Server 2012, a new Share tab can be found by clicking the Advanced button. This tab provides information about security settings on a remote file share.

NTFS permissions are cumulative. For example, if you give a user in the sales group Read permissions to a folder and its contents, and the user is also a member of the marketing group, which has been given the Write permission to the same folder, the user will have Read + Write permissions. In this type of situation, if you do not want the user to be able to write to the folder, you can use the Deny permission and select the specific user account. The Deny permission always overrides the Allow permission.

Combining NTFS and Share Permissions

It is very common to combine share and NTFS permissions when providing access to resources on NTFS volumes. When this happens, you must have a good understanding of the cumulative effects to ensure that your resources remain protected. Now that you have a better understanding of NTFS permissions and share permissions, you need to understand what happens when you combine the two on the same resource.

For example, let's say you create and share a folder with the following settings:

- Share permission (Share tab)—Sales group: Read
- NTFS permission (Security tab)—Sales group: Full Control

When users connect to the share over the network, both the share and NTFS permissions combine, and the most restrictive set is applied. In the preceding example, the share permission of Read is more restrictive then the NTFS permission, so users could read the folder and its contents. If the same users were to log on locally to the computer in which this share is located, they would bypass the share permissions, and their level of access would be based on the NTFS permission. In this example, they would have Full Control.

VIEWING EFFECTIVE PERMISSIONS ON A RESOURCE

In Windows 8, the Effective Access tab has been added to enable you to view the effective permissions for a user, group, or device account on a resource. You can access this tab by right-clicking the file or folder, choosing Properties, clicking the Security tab, and then clicking Advanced.

For example, let's say you create a folder called *MyPubFiles* and then share the folder, allowing the Sales group Full Control. You also configure the NTFS permissions for Matthew, a member of the group, with the following settings: Read & Execute, List Folder Contents, and Read. What would Matthew's effective permission be?

To determine Matthew's effective permissions, you would right-click the MyPubFiles folder and choose Properties. You can then click the *Security* tab and then click *Advanced*. Once you are in the Advanced Security Settings for *MyPubFiles* dialog box, click *Select a user* and then search for Matthew's account. Once it's located, click *View effective access* to see what permissions he has for the folder.

As shown in Figure 9-3, even though Matthew has Full Control to the share due to his membership in the Sales group, NTFS permissions are restricting him to only reading, listing folder contents, and executing files within the folder. He cannot create files, folders, or make any changes to the documents.

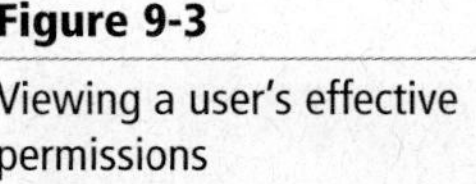

Figure 9-3

Viewing a user's effective permissions

REVIEW PERMISSIONS USING THE EFFECTIVE ACCESS TAB

GET READY. To view the effective permissions for the local Administrator account, log on to your computer with Administrative credentials and then perform the following steps:

1. Press the **Windows logo key + q** and then type **File Explorer**.
2. Click **Local Disk (C:)** and browse to the *C:\Windows* folder.
3. Right-click the **Windows** folder and choose **Properties**.
4. Click the **Security** tab and then click **Advanced**.
5. Click the **Effective Access** tab.
6. Click **Select a user**.
7. In the *Enter the object name to select* field, type **Administrator** and then click **OK**.
8. Click **View effective access**.
9. Review the current permissions for the local Administrator account on C:\Windows and then click **OK**.
10. Click **OK** to accept your changes and to close the *Windows Properties* dialog box.

When planning your NTFS/Share permissions on storage spaces or any volumes in which files/folders are shared, the best approach is to set the Share permissions to provide Full Control to the appropriate user group and then use NTFS permissions to further lock down access to the resource. This process ensures that resources are secured regardless of how they are accessed (remotely or locally).

■ Configuring The Encrypting File System (EFS)

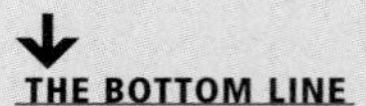

THE BOTTOM LINE

Encrypting File System (EFS) is an encryption service built into Windows 8 that has been around since the release of Windows XP. EFS is designed to provide file level encryption to protect your confidential files when others have physical access to your computer.

Using EFS, users can encrypt and decrypt their files/folders to protect sensitive data on their computer in case it's lost or stolen. The encryption key is associated with the user's logon account and is stored as part of the user profile.

CERTIFICATION READY
Configure EFS
Objective 2.5

To use EFS, you must store your files on an NTFS volume. If you are using Windows compression on the file/folder, you have to uncompress it before you can encrypt it.

Encrypting a folder or file is as simple as right-clicking the object, choosing Properties, clicking the General tab, and then clicking Advanced. The Advanced Attributes dialog box appears (see Figure 9-4). To enable encryption, select the *Encrypt contents to secure data* option. If the folder contains files and subfolders, you will be prompted to apply encryption to just the folder or to apply changes to the folder, subfolder, and files.

The first time you encrypt a file or folder in Windows 8, you will be prompted to back up your file encryption certificate and key. Doing so will launch the Certificate Export Wizard, in which you can apply a password to the exported file, provide a name, and then determine a location to store the file. You should always make a backup of the key to make sure you can recover your encrypted information if you lose the key. Consider placing it somewhere other than your computer, such as in a shared folder on the network or on a USB flash drive.

Figure 9-4
Enabling encryption

Files and folders that you encrypt will display in green color in File Explorer (see Figure 9-5).

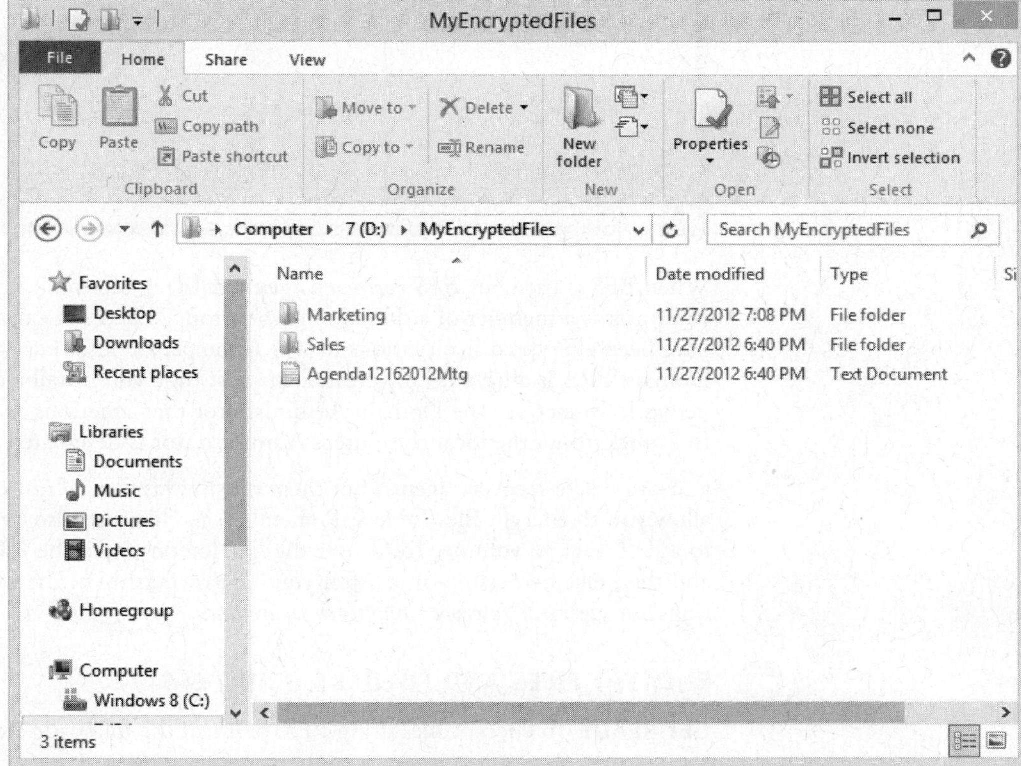

Figure 9-5
Displaying encrypted folders and files

Encrypted files/folders can be moved and copied, but you should keep the following in mind:

- Moving an encrypted file from an NTFS volume to a FAT/FAT32 volume will decrypt it. FAT/FAT32 does not support encryption. It will also remove any NTFS permissions configured on the file.
- Moving an encrypted file between NTFS volumes on the same computer will maintain the encryption. NTFS permissions will also be maintained when the file is moved.

If you want to use your encrypted files on another computer, you need to export the EFS certificate and key from your computer and then import it at the other computer. If you want to share your encrypted files with another user, the other person has to export the EFS certificate and then import it on your computer. After it is imported, you will add the certificate to the file you want to share through the file's property settings. Exporting and importing are done via the Certification snap-in (certmgr.msc), as shown in Figure 9-6.

Figure 9-6

Exporting an EFS certificate

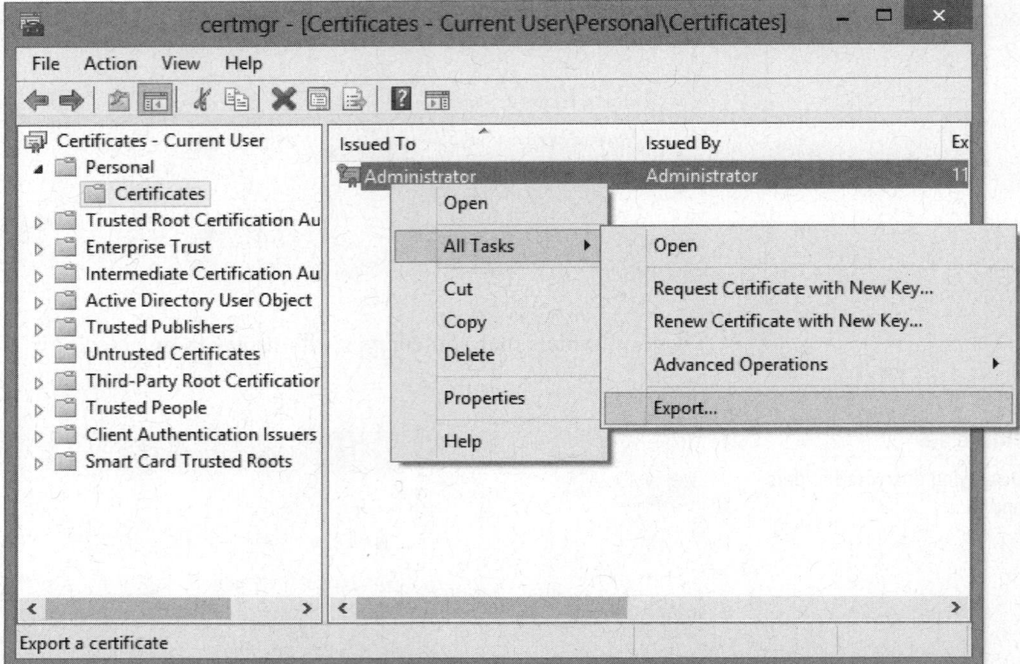

When EFS is used, an ***EFS recovery agent (ERA)*** is automatically created, whether the computer is a member of a domain or workgroup. The ERA can recover files/folders that have been encrypted in situations in which the person loses keys or leaves the company. The Domain ERA is automatically created the first time you install a domain controller on the network. In fact, it's the Domain Administrator that functions as the recovery agent account. In a workgroup, the local computer's Administrator is designated as the recovery agent.

You can delete recovery agents, but there must always be at least one, or else EFS will not allow you to encrypt files/folders. Remember, the files can also be decrypted by moving them to a FAT/FAT32 volume. To recover the file, log on under the ERA account, locate the file, and then take ownership of it. After you have ownership of the file, go into its property settings and deselect *Encrypt contents to secure data.*

ENCRYPT FILES AND FOLDERS USING EFS

GET READY. To encrypt files using EFS, perform the following steps:

1. Press the **Windows logo key + q** and then type **File Explorer**.
2. Choose **File Explorer** from the *Results* list.
3. Right-click the Local Disk (C:) and choose **New > Folder**.
4. Right-click the new folder and select **Rename**. Type **MyEncryptedFiles** and then press **Enter**.
5. Double-click the **MyEncryptedFiles** folder to open it.
6. In the MyEncryptedFiles folder, right-click and choose **New > Folder**. Type **Marketing** and then press **Enter**.

7. Right-click and choose **New > Folder**. Type **Sales** and then press **Enter**.
8. Right click and choose **New > Text Document**. Type **Agenda12162012** and then press **Enter**.
9. Press the **Backspace** to navigate back to the Local Disk (C:). Right-click the **MyEncryptedFiles** folder and choose **Properties**.
10. Click **Advanced**.
11. Select the **Encrypt contents to secure data** check box and then click **OK**.
12. When the *MyEncryptedFiles* dialog box appears, click **OK** to close it.
13. Select **Apply changes to this folder, subfolders, and files** and click **OK**. The *MyEncryptedFiles* folder will display as green to indicate it has been encrypted.
14. Double-click the **MyEncryptedFiles** folder and review the files and subfolders to confirm that they are also encrypted (they display in green). Minimize the **MyEncryptedFiles** window to return to your desktop.
15. Right-click anywhere on your desktop and choose **New > Text Document**. Type **SalesFigures** and then press **Enter**.
16. Right-click the **SalesFigures.txt** document and choose **Copy**.
17. Maximize the *MyEncryptedFiles* window and double-click the **Sales** folder to open it. Right-click and choose **Paste** to copy the *SalesFigure.txt* document into the *Sales* folder. The file will be encrypted (turn green) automatically.
18. Right-click the **SalesFigures.txt** file that is now encrypted and then choose **Copy**.
19. Minimize the *MyEncryptedFiles* window.
20. Right-click anywhere on your desktop and choose **New > Folder**. Type **Transfer** and then press **Enter**.
21. Double-click the **Transfer** folder to open it.
22. Right-click and choose **Paste** to copy the *SalesFigures.txt* file into the *Transfer* folder. The file will remain encrypted (green).
23. (Optional) If you have a USB drive formatted with FAT32, drag the file to the USB drive. (You will receive a message that indicates the file is being copied to a destination that does not support encryption. Click **Yes** to continue.)
24. Open the USB drive and confirm the file is not decrypted.

Configuring Security for Removable Media

In today's networks, the biggest concern of administrators has been the arrival of removable storage devices. With Windows 8 and Windows Server 2012, you fortunately have several options for monitoring and securing these types of devices. Controlling the use of removable media is critical to the overall security of your network.

CERTIFICATION READY
Configure security for removable media
Objective 2.5

Monitoring and securing removable media include using Group Policy to control whether users are allowed to use removable media on your network or on specific computers; and whether they can deploy BitLocker/BitLocker To Go to encrypt and protect removable media that is lost or stolen.

Using Group Policy

Group Policy provides control over users and computers in the network. It can be used to define the state of the user and/or computer environment and then continually enforce it over specific groups of users or computers or across the entire organization.

Group Policy allows you to implement specific configurations (security and networking policies) for users and computers that define what they can and cannot do on the network. These collections of user and computer configurations are called ***Group Policy Objects (GPOs)***. GPOs are associated with Active Directory containers (sites, domains, and organizational units [OUs]) and are managed from the ***Group Policy Management Console (GPMC)***. The GPMC (gpmc.msc) provides a single interface for managing GPOs across your entire organization. To use GPMC on a Windows 8 computer that is a member of a domain, you will need to install the ***Remote Server Administration Tools (RSAT) for Windows 8*** from Microsoft's website. RSAT allows you to remotely manage roles and features in Windows Server 2012 from a computer running Windows 8. To access GPMC on a Windows 2012 server, you can press the *Windows logo key* + *r* and type *gpmc.msc* or access it from the Server Manager console (*Tools* > *Group Policy Management*).

There are also local GPOs that can be configured on individual computers. To manage the local settings, you can use the ***Local Group Policy Editor*** (***LGPE***; gpedit.msc). The LGPE is commonly used in situations where you have computers that are not members of an Active Directory domain. To locate LGPE, press the *Windows logo key* + *w* and type *edit group policy*. You can also access it by pressing the *Windows logo key* + *r* and typing *gpedit.msc*.

GPOs are separated into two sections: Computer Configuration and User Configuration, as shown in Figure 9-7. You would configure the Computer Configuration section to set policies that are applied to the computer regardless of who logs on to it. The User Configuration is used to set policies that apply to users, regardless of which computer they log on to.

Figure 9-7

Reviewing the Computer Configuration section and the User Configuration section of a GPO

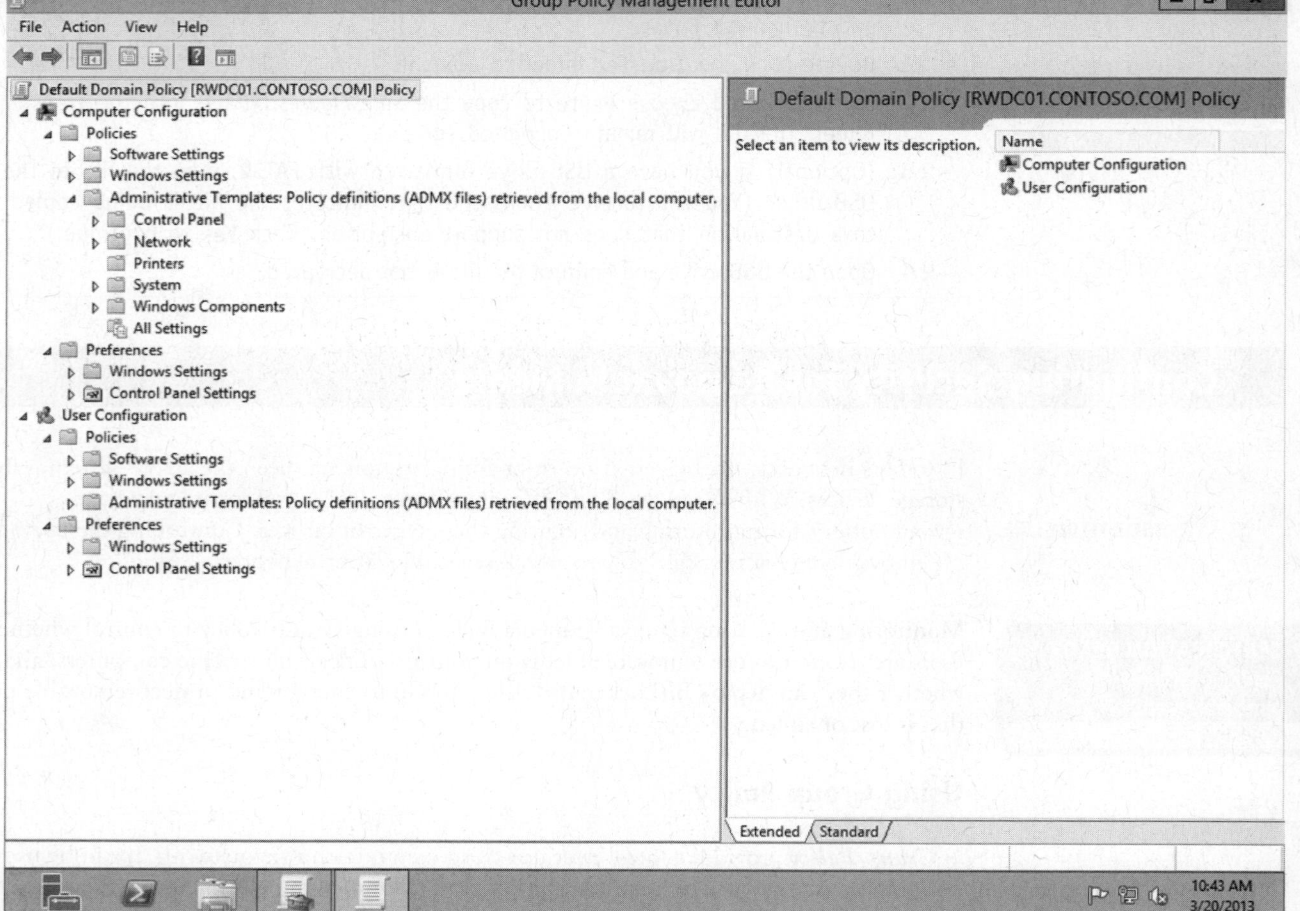

You can configure GPOs to monitor the use of removable storage devices on your network. The setting can be found in the following location using the GPMC:

- **Computer Configuration\Policies\Windows Settings\Security Settings\Advanced Audit Policy Configuration\Audit Policies.** The Audit Removable Storage setting enables you to audit user attempts to access file system objects on a removable storage device. If you enable this policy, a security audit event is generated each time an account accesses the removable storage device.

You can also configure GPOs to prevent the use of removable media on your network for computers and/or users.

The settings can be found in both Computer and User locations in the GPMC:

- **Computer Configuration\Policies\Administrative Templates\System\Removable Storage Access**. These settings will be applied to the computer and every user who logs on to it.
- **User Configuration\Policies\Administrative Templates\System\Removable Storage Access.** These settings will be applied only to users/groups that are included in an Active Directory container to which you link the GPO.

On Windows 8 clients, you can configure similar settings using the LGPE (gpedit.msc). When enabled and applied, the *Prevent installation of removable devices* setting (see Figure 9-8) prevents Windows from installing removable devices. A device is considered removable when the driver for the device to which it is connected indicates the device is removable. For example, a USB device is reported removable by the drivers for the USB hub to which it is connected.

Figure 9-8

Preventing the installation of removable devices using a local GPO

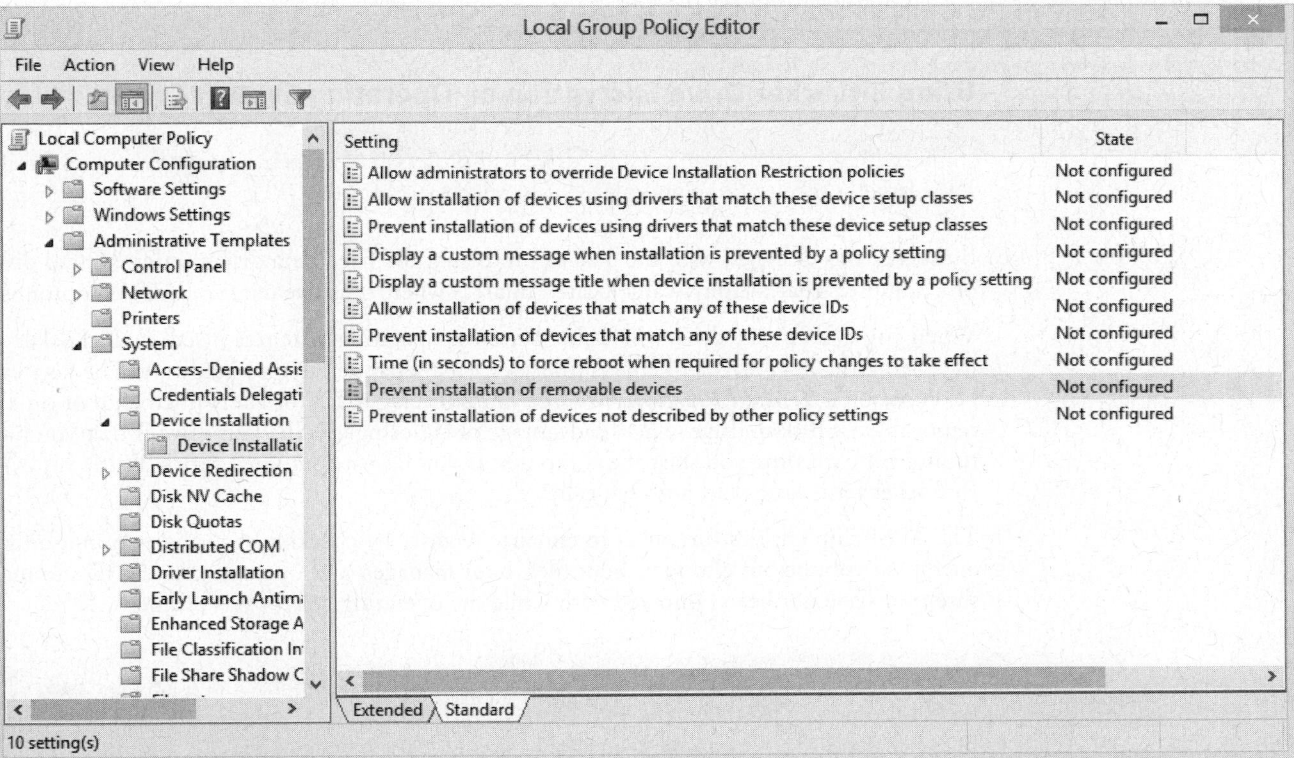

Managing BitLocker and BitLocker To Go

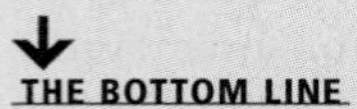

THE BOTTOM LINE

BitLocker Drive Encryption and BitLocker To Go are designed to protect sensitive data stored on fixed and removable drives even in situations where they are lost, stolen or moved to another computer.

BitLocker Drive Encryption is designed to protect against brute force attacks to gain access to your fixed drive or situations in which someone tries to install and access your fixed drive from another computer. It provides full disk encryption capabilities for fixed drives (including storage pools) and operating system drives. You can further enhance security by checking the integrity of boot files if a ***Trusted Platform Module (TPM)*** chip is available on your computer. The TPM is a dedicated cryptographic processor chip that the computer uses to store the BitLocker encryption keys.

CERTIFICATION READY
Manage BitLocker and BitLocker To Go
Objective 2.5

BitLocker To Go is BitLocker Drive Encryption on removable media drives. This includes ***Secure Digital (SD) cards***, USB flash drives, and external hard disk drives. SD cards are nonvolatile memory cards used in mobile phones, digital cameras, and tablet computers.

BitLocker Drive Encryption and BitLocker To Go are available in Windows 8 Professional/ Enterprise operating systems and Windows Server 2012. They are not designed to replace EFS or NTFS permissions. Instead, they are designed to add an additional layer of security and protection.

TAKE NOTE*
In order to encrypt a drive, the drive must be formatted using FAT, FAT32, or NTFS; and must have at least 64 MB of space available.

When encrypting affixed disk, storage pool, or removable media, there are two options:

- **Encrypt used disk space only:** This option encrypts only the part of the drive that currently has data stored on it.
- **Encrypt entire drive:** This option encrypts the full volume and offers more security because it will encrypt areas that contain data that has been deleted but still may be retrievable from the drive.

Using BitLocker Drive Encryption on Operating System Drives

Encrypting your operating system drive will protect it from being tampered with even if the drive is taken offline and placed into another computer.

BitLocker was designed with the goal of protecting the fixed data drives (internal hard disks) on computers that are physically located in areas where sensitive data could be compromised.

When you encrypt the drive where the Windows operating system is installed, BitLocker must store the keys it uses to encrypt/decrypt on a separate piece of hardware. The keys can be stored on a ***Trusted Platform Module (TPM)*** version 1.2 (or later) microchip or on a removable USB flash drive. The disadvantage of choosing a USB flash drive is that you have to insert it each time you start the computer. If you have a computer with a TPM chip, BitLocker retrieves its key automatically.

The TPM chip enables BitLocker to enhance security by checking the validity of not only the encrypted volume but also your boot files, boot manager, and operating system files to make sure they have not been tampered with while the operating system was offline.

TAKE NOTE*
You can determine if you have a TPM chip by pressing the Windows logo key + r and typing tpm.msc. This opens the TPM console on a Windows 8 computer. If the TPM chip does not appear in the console, you should make sure it is enabled via the computer's BIOS.

To support BitLocker Drive Encryption on the drive that contains your operating system, you need the following:

- Two partitions: BitLocker will hold files needed to start your computer on one partition. This is called the system partition and needs to be a minimum of 100 MB in size. This partition is not encrypted. The second partition, encrypted by BitLocker, will hold the operating system. This allows BitLocker to protect the operating system and the information in the encrypted drive and to perform its pre–startup authentication steps and verify system integrity.
- NTFS file system: The partitions have to be formatted using the NTFS file system.
- TPM-compatible BIOS: Your basic input/output system (BIOS) must be compatible with TPM version 1.2 or 2.0; otherwise, the BIOS firmware must be able to read from a USB drive that contains the startup key on boot to enable BitLocker on an operating system drive. BitLocker needs the startup key from either the TPM or the USB flash drive before it can unlock the protected drive. If a USB drive is used on a non-TPM system, BitLocker cannot verify the integrity of the system.

UNDERSTANDING TPM MODES

When using TPM with BitLocker, you can select from the following modes; each provides a different level of security:

- TPM-Only mode: Validates boot files, operating system files, and any BitLocker-encrypted volumes. The user doesn't have to enter a key when the computer boots into Windows. Using this mode enables someone to hard-boot your system and gain access to the system if the hardware has not been tampered with.
- TPM-PIN mode: Validates boot files, operating system files, and any BitLocker-encrypted volumes. The user must enter a PIN before the computer can boot into Windows. A GPO can be configured to require a more stringent password instead of using simple numbers for the PIN.
- TPM-Startup Key mode: Validates boot files, operating system files, and any BitLocker-encrypted volumes. The user must use a USB flash drive with the keys before the computer can boot into Windows.
- TPM-SmartCard mode: Validates boot files, operating system files, and any BitLocker-encrypted volumes. The users must insert a smart card that includes a valid certificate before the computer can boot into Windows.
- No TPM mode: Validates BitLocker-encrypted volumes, but does not protect the boot environment. Used in computers without a TPM v1.2 or later chip. The user requires a USB flash drive, used during boot, to read the keys when the computer starts.

In each case, if the TPM is missing or the integrity of the files is in question, BitLocker will go into Recover mode, which requires you to enter a key or password to regain access. If you can't remember the password, you can use a recovery key. If the recovery key is stored on a USB flash drive, you can insert the USB when prompted and press Enter. You do not have to enter a recovery key; the computer will reboot and unlock automatically. However, if the key was saved to another computer or in another location, you need to retrieve the recovery key and enter it to continue.

TAKE NOTE*

If the computer halts earlier in the process due to a problem with TPM or boot data corruption, you do not have access to enter the information from the keyboard. Instead, use the F1–F9 function keys that represent the digits 1–9. F10 represents 0.

Here are a few scenarios that cause BitLocker To Go into recovery mode:

- Changing the boot order to another fixed drive in an attempt to access the lost/stolen hard drive protected by BitLocker
- Setting the CD/DVD drive before the hard drive in the boot order and then inserting or removing a CD/DVD
- Entering a PIN too many times
- Adding or removing hardware (PCMCIA wireless cards, video cards, network cards)
- Moving the BitLocker-protected drive to another computer
- Using a BIOS hot key during the boot process to change the boot order to another drive
- Pressing the F8 or F10 key during the boot process

When using BitLocker on domain-based computers that use the TPM-PIN mode, the system volume will automatically unlock without needing the user to enter a PIN if the following conditions are met:

- TPM is enabled.
- The computer is a member of the domain and is currently connected to it over a wired connection.
- A Network Unlock server (used to distribute the Network Unlock certificates to clients, which then use them to create the network unlock keys) is installed on a Windows Deployment Services server.

If the computer is a member of a domain but does not meet these conditions, the users have to enter their PIN during the boot process.

If you attempt to enable BitLocker using the BitLocker Drive Encryption Control Panel for your operating system drive and you do not have a compatible TPM, the warning message shown in Figure 9-9 is displayed.

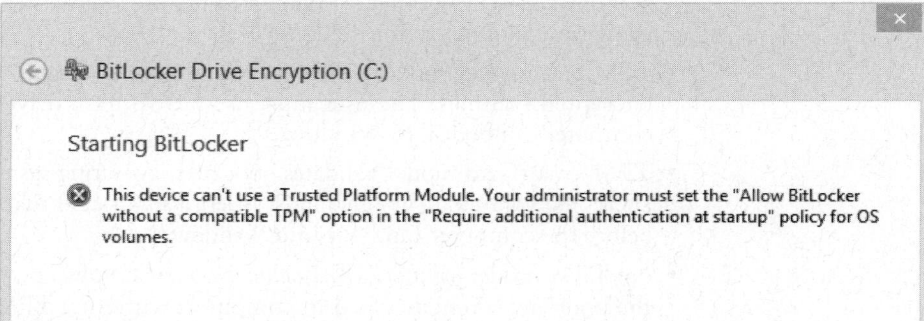

Figure 9-9
Viewing the TPM warning message

If this happens, you need to make the changes to Group Policy, as indicated in the message, and set your system to boot from a USB drive. These settings can be found in the LGPE if you want to configure the policy on a computer that is not a member of a domain. If you want to configure and apply the policy to multiple computers across your domain, use the GPMC. These settings can be found in the following locations:

- **LGPE:** The settings are located in Computer Configuration\Administrative Templates\Windows Components\BitLocker Drive Encryption\Operating System Drives. Select *Require additional authentication at startup.* Under the Options section, make sure *Allow BitLocker without a compatible TPM (requires a password or a startup key on a USB flash drive)* is checked.
- **Group Policy Management Console:** The settings are located in Computer Configuration\Policies\Administrative Templates\Windows Components\BitLocker Drive Encryption\Operating System Drives. Select *Require additional authentication at startup.* Under the Options section, make sure *Allow BitLocker without a compatible TPM (requires a password or a startup key on a USB flash drive)* is checked.

After configuring the appropriate policy settings, you can go back to the hard drive and turn on BitLocker. After BitLocker has prepared the drive, you will be asked to restart the system. After the computer boots, you will be prompted to set your BitLocker startup preferences. Your options include these:

- **Use BitLocker without additional keys**
- **Require a PIN at every startup**
- **Require a Startup key at every startup**

After selecting *Require a Startup key at every startup* option, you will be asked to save your Startup key. Insert the USB drive, and the keys will be copied to the device. From this point on, each time you boot the system, you will need to use the USB drive to provide the BitLocker keys.

Using BitLocker To Go on Workspace Drives

Enabling BitLocker To Go on a Windows To Go workspace drive ensures that the data is protected, and unauthorized users cannot access your data or use the workspace drive if it is lost or stolen.

In Lesson 1, you learned that you can configure encryption on Windows To Go workspace drives during the initial setup of the workspace. These types of drives are designed for roaming (using multiple computers); therefore, the TPM chip cannot be used by BitLocker to protect the drive. Instead, you provide a recovery password to unlock the drive and boot into the workspace. By default, the password must be at least eight characters long unless you have configured stronger password policies on your network using Group Policy.

The recovery password is saved in the documents library of the computer used to create the workspace.

If the computer was a member of an Active Directory domain, and you are using Active Directory Domain Services (AD DS) to store recovery passwords, it may also be saved under the computer account of the computer used to create the workspace. You can use this recovery password if the password you created earlier is lost or stolen.

Using BitLocker To Go on Removable Media

In addition to using BitLocker to protect a Windows To Go Workspace drive, you can also use it to protect removable media containing your data files.

Using BitLocker To Go on removable media involves the following steps:

1. Connecting the drive
2. Enabling BitLocker To Go Encryption
3. Setting a password or using a smart card for authentication
4. Backing up the recovery key
5. Encrypting the drive (entire drive or used space only)

A ***recovery key*** is a string of 48 random numbers (for example, 031449-152141-040282-547360-281974-173019-554092-404162) that enables you to access the encrypted drive if you forget the password. If you are using a removable data drive, the key cannot be stored on the removable media you are encrypting. You can back up the recovery key to your Microsoft user account, save it to a file, or print the recovery key.

When saving the key initially, you will be prompted to store the key in more than one place. If you select Yes, you will be asked to select a second location for the keys. Although not required, it is best practice to have the recovery key stored in more than one place to provide a second level of back up.

ENABLE ENCRYPTION ON A REMOVABLE DATA DRIVE

GET READY. To enable encryption on a removable drive, log on to a Windows 8 computer as an administrator and then perform the following steps:

1. Insert a USB drive into a USB port on your computer.
2. Press the **Windows logo key + w** and then type **BitLocker**.
3. From the *Results* list, click **Manage BitLocker**.
4. Under *Removable data drives – BitLocker to Go,* click **Turn on BitLocker**.
5. Select **Use a password to unlock the drive**.
6. In the *Enter your password* field and *Reenter your password* field, type the same password and then click **Next**.
7. In the *How do you want to back up your recovery key* dialog box, click **Save to a file**.
8. In the *Save BitLocker recovery key as* dialog box, choose **Desktop** and then click in the *File name* field and type **MyBitLockerRecoveryKey**.
9. Click **Save** and then click **Next** to continue.
10. Select **Encrypt entire drive (slower but best for PCs and drives already in use)** and then click **Next**.
11. Click **Start encrypting**.
12. Click **Manage BitLocker**.
    During the encryption process, *BitLocker Encrypting* will be shown next to the removable drive. After encryption has completed, this will change to *BitLocker on*.
13. Close the *BitLocker Drive Encryption* Control Panel.
14. Eject the USB drive, wait for a few seconds, and then insert the drive back into the system.
15. Open File Explorer and then locate the USB drive that is being protected by BitLocker To Go (see Figure 9-10).

Figure 9-10

The padlock icon indicates BitLocker is protecting the removable disk

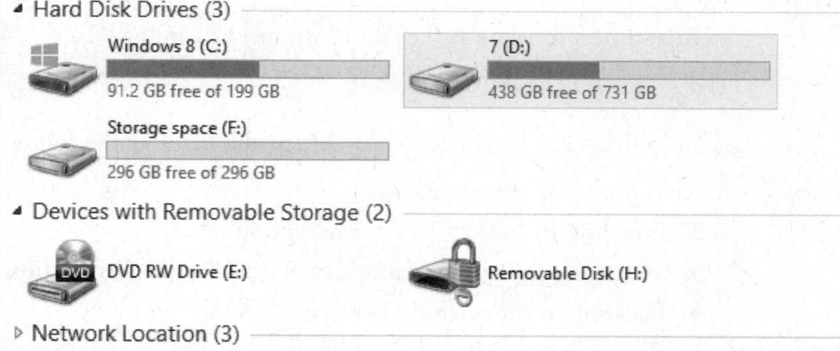

16. Double-click **Removable Disk**.
17. In the *Enter password to unlock this drive* field, type your BitLocker password to access the disk and then click **Unlock**.

18. Browse the files on the removable disk to confirm you can now access the data.
19. After you have confirmed access, close the dialog box.

Managing BitLocker To Go

After BitLocker to Go is configured on your removable media drives, there are several administrative tasks that can be performed from the BitLocker Drive Encryption Control Panel. For example, you may need to change your password if it is compromised, create an additional backup of your recovery key, or turn off encryption on the drive so you can install additional applications.

After completing the encryption of the USB drive, any new files added to it will automatically be encrypted. If you copy these files to another drive or to a different PC, they will be decrypted. If you share the files with others over a network, they will be encrypted as long as they are on the drive.

You can perform the following tasks from the Manage BitLocker tool on this encrypted USB data drive:

- **Back up recovery key:** This option enables you to back up the recovery key by saving it to your Microsoft user account, saving it to a file, or printing the recovery key.
- **Change password:** This option enables you to change the password. You have to enter the old password and then input and confirm a new password.
- **Remove password:** This option enables you to remove the current password, but requires that you add another unlocking method before removing it.
- **Add smart card:** This option prompts you to insert a smart card to use.
- **Turn on auto-unlock:** This option (available for data drives) can be set to automatically unlock when you sign in to the PC.
- **Turn off BitLocker:** This option enables you to turn off BitLocker temporarily to install an application or decrypt the drive.

RECOVERING ENCRYPTED DATA FROM A REMOVABLE DRIVE

One of the most common problems administrators face is a user who loses a PIN. In this case, you must recover it in order to gain access to the BitLocker-encrypted drive. For example, let's say you misplaced the password that you used when completing the previous activity, "Enable Encryption on a Removable Data Drive." How can you regain access to the drive?

If you backed up the recovery keys to a USB drive, saved it to a file, or printed it out, you can use the information to regain access. When the BitLocker password screen appears, click the *More options* link (see Figure 9-11) and then click the *Enter recovery key* link.

Figure 9-11

Entering your BitLocker recovery key

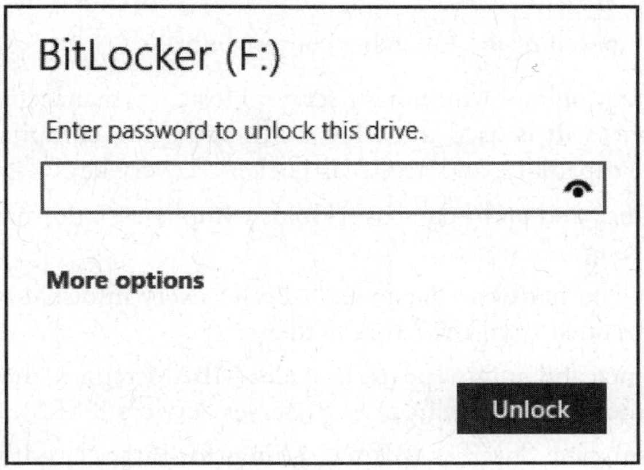

BitLocker (F:)

Enter password to unlock this drive.

More options

Unlock

To make sure you are using the correct recovery key, the prompt provides a Key ID (see Figure 9-12), which is included in the file you saved earlier. Enter the 48-digit key and you will regain access to the drive.

Figure 9-12

Entering your BitLocker recovery key ID

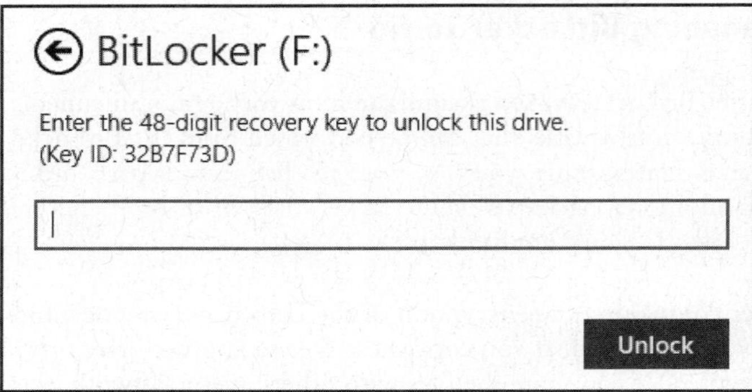

Obviously, allowing your users to manage their own BitLocker can result in lost startup keys and PINs. A better approach is to store the BitLocker recovery information in Active Directory. In Windows Server 2003 (SP1), the Active Directory schema has to be extended to support storing BitLocker recovery information. In Windows Server 2008, 2008R2, and Windows Server 2012, the schema already contains the attributes required. The recovery information is stored in plain text and can be found on the BitLocker Recovery tab for each computer container in Active Directory; only domain administrators have access to it.

MORE INFORMATION

For more information on adding recovery keys to Active Directory, go to the Microsoft website and search on "BitLocker Recovery Keys Active Directory."

Using Microsoft BitLocker Administration and Monitoring (MBAM) 1.0

As the number of computers using BitLocker on your network increases, you will find that tasks such as recovering lost PINs, making sure critical systems have BitLocker enabled, and controlling what can be encrypted (used disk space, entire drive) can become very labor-intensive. Microsoft BitLocker Administration and Monitoring (MBAM) can help.

Microsoft BitLocker Administration and Monitoring (MBAM) is a simple administrative interface for setting encryption policies, monitoring computers against those policies, and reporting the encryption status across your organization. It can also be used to access recovery information when users forget their passwords, lose their PINs, or when a computer enters into recovery mode when its BIOS or boot record is changed.

MBAM is composed of the following components:

- Administration and Monitoring server: Hosts the management console and monitors web services. It is used to review audit activities, compliance, and status; manage hardware capability; and access BitLocker recovery keys.
- Compliance and audit database: Holds compliance information for MBAM clients; used for reporting functions.
- Recovery and hardware database: Stores recovery information and hardware information that is obtained from the MBAM clients.
- Compliance and audit reports: Provides MBAM reports that can be viewed from the Management console or from SQL Server Services (SSRS).
- Policy template: Specifies MBAM settings for BitLocker drive encryption.

- MBAM client agent: Uses Group Policy to enforce encryption settings; collects recovery keys, recovery, and hardware information from MBAM clients and compliance data that is passed to the reporting system. The client software can be installed on Windows 7 (Enterprise/Ultimate Editions) and Windows 8 (Professional/Enterprise Editions). The clients must be TPM v 1.2–capable, and the chip must be enabled in the BIOS.

SKILL SUMMARY

IN THIS LESSON YOU LEARNED:

- Share permissions are applied only when accessing a folder over the network. NTFS permissions are applied to files and folders, and are enforced both locally and remotely.
- When you combine share and NTFS permissions, the more restrictive of the two wins. Use the Effective Access tab to see the permissions (share and NTFS) applied to a specific resource.
- The Encrypting File System (EFS) can be used to protect sensitive data from others who may use your system, or to offer protection in the case of loss or theft. To encrypt a file/folder, it must be on an NTFS volume and not be compressed. Encrypted files/folders appear green in File Explorer.
- Moving an encrypted file/folder from an NTFS volume to a FAT/FAT32 volume will decrypt it; moving it between NTFS volumes will maintain encryption.
- Using the GPMC and the LGPE enables you to create policies to restrict users' access to removable media.
- BitLocker Drive Encryption and BitLocker To Go provide encryption for hard drives. Neither is a replacement for EFS; they are additional layers of defense you can add to protect your computer.
- You can encrypt the entire hard drive or used space only. Encrypting the entire hard drive ensures that "deleted" areas on the disk are also encrypted.
- Trusted Platform Module (TPM) v 1.2 or later chips are required to provide enhanced security by checking the validity of not only the encrypted volume but also your boot files, boot manager, and operating system files.
- Recovery keys are used to gain access to encrypted drives. They can be backed up to a USB drive, saved to a file, or printed out.
- MBAM provides a simple administrative interface for setting encrypting policies, monitoring computers against those policies, and reporting the encryption status across your organization.

■ Knowledge Assessment

Multiple Choice

Select the correct answer for each of the following questions.

1. Which of the following share permissions on a FAT32 volume enable you to add files and folders to a shared folder? (Select all that apply.)
   - **a.** Read
   - **b.** Write
   - **c.** Change
   - **d.** Full Control

2. Which of the following decrypts a file that has been encrypted using EFS? (Select all that apply.)
   a. Using ERA
   b. Moving it to another NTFS volume
   c. Moving it to a FAT32 volume
   d. Moving it to another NTFS volume on another computer

3. Which of the following tools prevents the installation of removable devices on a standalone Windows 8 computer?
   a. GPMC
   b. LGPE
   c. BitLocker Group Policy
   d. BitLocker To Go Group Policy

4. Which of the following statements best describes a characteristic of a folder that is encrypted with EFS? (Select all that apply.)
   a. The color of the folder appears as green in File Explorer.
   b. The color of the folder appears as blue in File Explorer.
   c. The *Encrypt contents to secure data* attribute is checked in the folder's Advanced attributes dialog box.
   d. The folder appears in italic font.

5. Which of the following statements is true of BitLocker Drive Encryption? (Select all that apply.)
   a. BitLocker encrypts used disk space only
   b. BitLocker encrypts files only
   c. BitLocker encrypts folders only
   d. BitLocker encrypts entire drive

6. Which of the following versions of TPM is required in order to enhance security by checking the validity of not only the encrypted volume but also boot files, boot manager, and operating system files?
   a. TPM v1
   b. TPM v1.2
   c. TPM v1.1
   d. TPM

7. Which of the following scenarios could cause BitLocker to go into recovery mode? (Select all that apply.)
   a. Adding a video card
   b. Changing the boot order to another drive
   c. Moving the BitLocker drive to another computer
   d. Entering your PIN too many times

8. A recovery key is a string of how many random numbers?
   a. 128
   b. 64
   c. 48
   d. 6

9. Which of the following are options for backing up a BitLocker recovery key when encrypting your removable media? (Select all that apply.)
   a. Print it
   b. Save it to a file
   c. Store it on the removable media you are encrypting
   d. Back it up to your Microsoft user account

10. To encrypt a drive, what is the minimal amount of space that must be available?
    a. 60 MB
    b. 1 GB
    c. 64 MB
    d. 50 MB

Best Answer

Choose the letter that corresponds to the best answer. Select the BEST answer. You might need to choose more than one answer choice to achieve the goal.

1. Which of the following is the best solution to protecting files and folders on your hard drive when multiple users are provided access to the same computer?
   a. BitLocker Drive Encryption
   b. EFS
   c. BitLocker To Go
   d. NTFS
2. Which of the following methods is the fastest way to decrypt a file stored on a computer that has both NTFS and FAT32 volumes?
   a. Use EFS Recovery agent.
   b. Move it to a FAT32 volume.
   c. Move it to another NTFS volume.
   d. Move it to another NTFS volume on another computer.
3. Which of the following methods is most effective for disabling the use of removable media across your entire network?
   a. Use LGPE on each computer.
   b. Use GPMC to create a GPO and apply it across your domain.
   c. Develop a written policy and distribute it to all employees.
   d. Disable the USB ports on each computer using Device manager.
4. Which of the following methods is most effective for confirming that you have a TPM chip in your computer?
   a. Press the Windows logo key + q and then type tpm.msc.
   b. Consult the manual that came with your motherboard.
   c. Research the manufacturer's website.
   d. Open the computer and locate the TPM chip.
5. Which of the following TPM modes provides the strongest protection?
   a. TPM-Smart Card mode
   b. TPM-Only mode
   c. TPM-Startup key
   d. No TPM

Matching and Identification

1. Match the following terms with the related description or usage.
   _______ a) EFS
   _______ b) MBAM
   _______ c) NTFS permissions
   _______ d) Recovery key
   _______ e) ERA
   _______ f) TPM-Startup key
   _______ g) Share permission
   _______ h) Recover mode

________ **i)** TPM v1.2 chip
________ **j)** Effective Access tab

1. Apply whether a resource is accessed locally or across the network.
2. A system response to BitLocker, detecting that the boot files have been tampered with.
3. Encrypts files and folders to protect sensitive data.
4. Provides 48 random numbers that enable you to access a BitLocker-encrypted drive.
5. Permissions set for folders when you share them in workgroups and domains.
6. Simple administrative interface for setting encryption policies across your organization.
7. A microchip in which BitLocker stores its keys.
8. Additional tab added in Windows 8 to enable you to view the effective permissions on a resource.
9. Validates boot files, operating system files, and any BitLocker-encrypted volumes; user must have a USB flash drive before the computer can boot into Windows.
10. Automatically created by EFS. You can recover files/folders when people lose their keys or leave the company.

Build a List

1. Specify the correct order of the steps that must be completed to use BitLocker To Go on removable media.
________ Back up your recovery key.
________ Connect the drive.
________ Encrypt the drive.
________ Set a password for authentication.
________ Enable BitLocker To Go encryption.

2. Specify the correct order of the steps that must be completed to use EFS to encrypt a compressed folder with its subfolders and files.
________ Check **Encrypt contents to secure data** and then click **OK**.
________ Right-click the folder, select **Properties**, and then click **Advanced**.
________ Deselect **Compress contents to save disk space**.
________ Click **Apply changes to this folder, subfolders, and files**.

3. Specify the correct order of the steps that must be completed to access a BitLocker drive that has gone into Recover mode. You have multiple recovery keys printed out in a document you carry with you.
________ Turn on your computer.
________ Type the recovery key and press **Enter**.
________ Computer boots into Recover mode.
________ Compare the printed password file with the password ID on the Recovery console display.
________ Computer boots into system.

Choose an Option

1. Identify the option that, when enabled, prevents you from encrypting the folder.

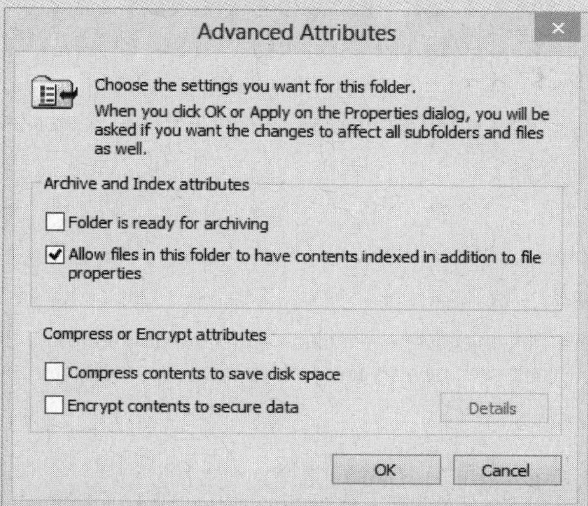

Business Case Scenarios

Scenario 9-1: Configuring Permissions

You have set up a shared folder on a FAT32 volume that is set with the following permissions:

Share name: **MyDocs**

Share Permission: **Read**

Group: **Everyone**

After configuring the share, you notice that multiple people have added files to it. What is the problem and how should you address it?

Scenario 9-2: Encrypting Files

You have a computer that is shared by multiple users. You want to make sure the files you have on the system are protected from prying eyes. You are considering using BitLocker Drive Encryption. Is that a viable solution? Explain.

Managing Hardware and Printers

70-688 EXAM OBJECTIVE

Objective 3.1 – Manage hardware and printers. This objective may include but is not limited to the following considerations: Resolve hardware and device issues; sync devices and resolve sync issues; monitor and manage print servers.

Lesson Heading	Exam Objective
Resolving Hardware and Device Issues	Resolve hardware and device issues
Using Device Manager	
Exploring Driver Signing	
Performing Driver Roll Backs	
Identifying Problem Devices	
Troubleshooting a Problem Device	
Syncing Devices and Resolving Sync Issues	Sync devices and resolve sync issues
Synchronizing Your PC Settings	
Using Sync Center	
Managing Offline Files	
Resolving Sync Conflicts	
Monitoring and Managing Print Servers	Monitor and manage print servers
Exploring the v4 Print Driver Model	
Managing Print Servers	

KEY TERMS

Action Center
Device Manager
distributed scan server
driver signing
Internet Printing
print device
print driver
printer
Print and Document services role
Print Management snap-in
print queue
print server
Print Spooler service
Roll Back Driver
Server Manager
spooling
Sync Center
sync conflict
Windows Hardware Quality Labs (WHQL)

Resolving Hardware and Device Issues

In combination with Windows Server 2012, Windows 8 provides several tools you can use to manage hardware and printers on your network.

CERTIFICATION READY
Resolve hardware and device issues
Objective 3.1

On a Windows 8 computer, you use Device Manager to identify and resolve hardware and device issues. You can use the ***Roll Back Driver*** recovery feature to reinstall device drivers after a newer driver fails.

Using Device Manager

Device Manager enables you to install and update drivers for your hardware devices, make changes to the hardware settings on a device, and troubleshoot hardware configuration problems.

Device Manager can be found in the Control Panel in Windows 8. The easiest way to access the tool is to press the *Windows logo key* + *w*, type *Device Manager*, and then select it from *Results*.

After you open the tool, drill down to Device Manager, which provides you with a detailed listing of all devices installed on the computer.

MORE INFORMATION

When you install a device, Windows Update checks for the latest drivers if you have Automatic Updates enabled. You will learn more about Windows Update in Lesson 13.

By default, devices are listed alphabetically by device type, but you can adjust them (select View from the menu) to Device by type or connection, and Resource by type or connection.

To update a driver for a device, scan for hardware changes, view the device's properties, or disable or uninstall a device, right-click and select the option from the menu (see Figure 10-1). To view a device's properties, double-click the device.

Exploring Driver Signing

Driver signing ensures the device drivers used by Windows include a digital signature. This digital signature indicates who the publisher of the software is and can alert you if the driver has been altered from its original contents.

For each piece of hardware in your computer, there is a device driver. Windows 8 interacts with the device driver rather than the device itself by calling functions in the drivers that carry out the actions on the device. The driver files provided with Windows 8 have been digitally signed. This means they have been tested and verified for compatibility, reliability, and functionality with Windows 8. These tests, conducted by the ***Windows Hardware Quality Labs (WHQL)***, are designed to ensure that your system maintains stability. The signature is also designed to ensure that the file has not been overwritten by another program as part of its installation process or has been altered from its original package contents.

When you install a driver, Windows checks the driver's digital signature. When the driver is not signed by Microsoft, a message appears alerting you to the fact that *Windows cannot verify the digital signature for the drivers required for this device...* You can then choose to install the

Figure 10-1

Reviewing options for configuring devices

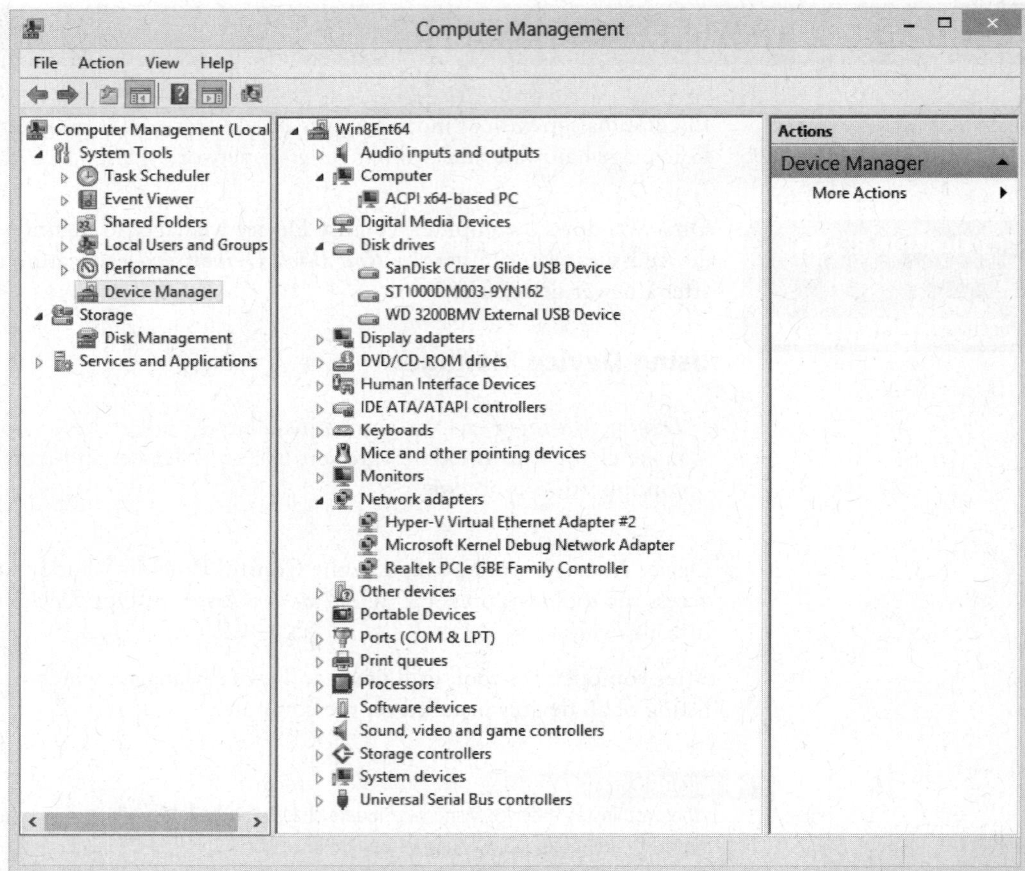

driver anyway or stop the installation and check for updated driver software from the manufacturer's website. Although this is the default behavior, you can use Group Policy to control how you want to manage unsigned drivers across your organization.

Group Policy can be configured to control whether unsigned drivers are allowed. To apply the policy to a single computer, use the Local Group Policy Editor. To apply to multiple systems, use the Group Policy Management Console (GPMC). The setting can be found here: User Configuration\Administrative Templates\System\Driver Installation\Code signing for device drivers.

After you enable the policy, you can determine how the computer will respond when a user tries to install device drivers that are not digitally signed. The options include the following:

- Ignore: Directs the system to proceed with the installation even if it includes unsigned files.
- Warn: Notifies the user that the files are not digitally signed, and enables them to decide whether to stop or to proceed with the installation and whether to permit unsigned files to be installed.
- Block: Directs the system to refuse to install unsigned files.

TAKE NOTE*

Certified drivers are stored in the Windows 8 driver store. This store can be found in the %systemroot%\system23\driverstore. When you install a new plug-and-play (PnP) device, Windows 8 checks this store for compatible drivers.

Performing Driver Roll Backs

Driver Roll Back is a system recovery feature in Windows 8 that enables you to reinstall the last device driver that was functioning.

While updating an existing device driver can add new functionality to your system, there may be times when it can cause the device to stop working. Fortunately, when you update a device driver the previous driver package is automatically saved and information is added into the registry. This allows you to roll back one prior driver version.

If the current driver is the only one that was ever installed, the Roll Back feature is not available. Roll Back is not available if you have not updated the driver in the past.

ROLL BACK A DEVICE DRIVER

GET READY. To roll back a device driver, log in with local Administrative privileges and then perform the following steps:

1. Press the **Windows logo key + w** and then type **Device Manager**.
2. Choose **Device Manager** from the *Results*.
3. Expand **Network Adapters**.
4. Right-click the adapter and choose **Update Driver Software**.
5. Click **Browse my computer for driver software.**
6. Click **Let me pick from a list of device drivers on my computer.**
7. Deselect **Show compatible hardware.**
8. Click **Marvel** for the manufacturer and then **Marvel 3COM 3C2000-T Gigabit Adapter** for the network adapter and click **Next.**
9. When the *Update Driver Warning* message appears, click **Yes.**
10. When the *Windows has successfully updated your driver software* message appears, click **Close.**
11. Click **Yes** to restart the computer and then log back in.
12. Press the **Windows logo key + w**, type **Device Manager**, and then choose it from *Results*.
13. Expand **Network Adapters** and then locate the network adapter you updated the driver for.
14. Right-click the adapter and choose **Properties.**
15. Click the **Driver** tab and then click **Roll Back Driver.**
16. When prompted to roll back the driver, click **Yes.**
17. Click **Close** to exit out of the *Adapter Properties* dialog box and then close the *Device Manager* window.

Identifying Problem Devices

Device Manager also displays all of the devices installed on your computer. When a device is experiencing problems, Device Manager uses symbols to provide information about the particular error condition.

When there is an issue with a device, you will see one of the following symbols (each symbol represents a specific type of problem):

- Blue question mark inside white circle: Driver installed; may not provide full functionality.
- Red "X": Disabled device; device is installed in computer and is consuming resources; protected mode driver not loaded; device installed improperly.
- Black exclamation point on yellow field: Device in problem state; the device might be functioning; problem code will be displayed with device.
- Blue "I" on white field: Use automatic settings not selected for device; resource was manually selected; does not indicate a problem or disabled state.

- Problem code: Code explaining the problem with the device.
- White circle with down arrow: Device was disabled by an administrator or user.
- Yellow warning symbol with exclamation point: There is a problem with the device.

Troubleshooting a Problem Device

TAKE NOTE*

To disable a problem device in Device Manager, right-click it and choose Disable.

The ***Action Center*** shows important notifications related to the security and maintenance of your computer. When problems occur, you will be alerted to investigate them further.

Windows 8 uses built-in hardware diagnostics to detect hardware problems on your computer. When problems are identified, a message appears that lets you know about the problem. If you select the message, you will be taken to the Action Center, which provides a central location to view any problems with your hardware or software.

When there is a problem, you will see two types of messages in the notification area (bottom-right corner of your desktop):

- Red items (white flag, red circle with white x): These are important messages that indicate a significant problem that needs to be addressed. For example, your firewall is turned off, or spyware or antivirus applications need to be updated.
- Yellow items: These are messages that suggest tasks that can make your computer run better. For example, updating an application or configuring Windows Update to automatically download and install updates rather than checking with you beforehand.

How you troubleshoot a device depends upon the type of problem you encounter. For example, let's say you notice a USB printer device under Other Devices that has a white circle with a blue question mark. Windows places devices that don't have a device driver available under this folder. If you double-click the device and navigate to the Driver tab, you can gain more information about the problem with the device.

Figure 10-2 shows that the driver provider is unknown and there is no information on a driver at all. If you click the Driver Details button, you will receive a message indicating there are no driver files loaded for the device.

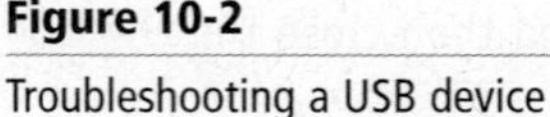

Figure 10-2

Troubleshooting a USB device

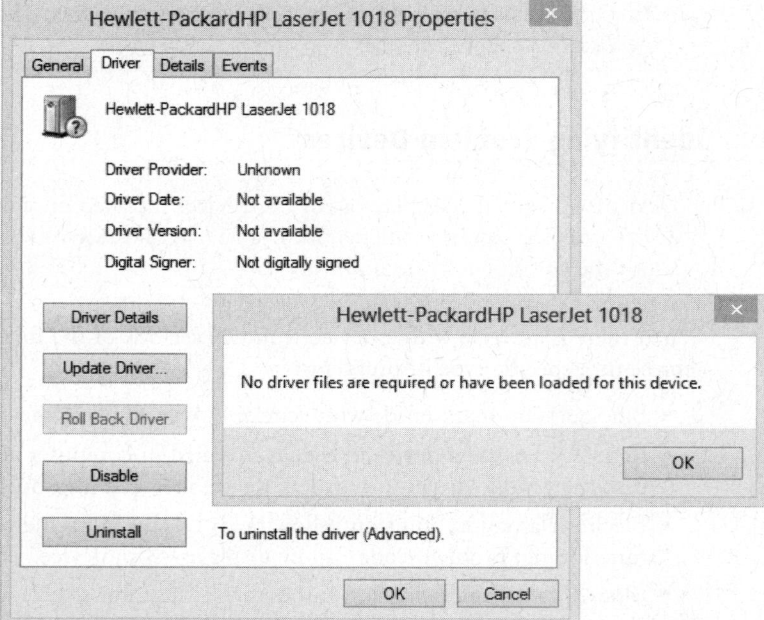

At this point, you can click Update Driver and allow Windows 8 to search automatically for an updated driver, or browse your computer for the device driver. If you allow Windows 8 to search automatically, and it does not locate a device, you will be prompted to visit the manufacturer's website to check for updated drivers.

In this situation, the USB device is an HP LaserJet 1018 printer that is not supported on Windows 8.

■ Syncing Devices and Resolving Sync Issues

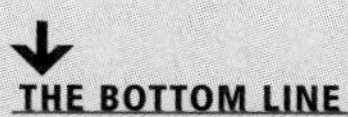

Users who work across multiple devices want to be able to keep their address books, music, and document files in sync and accessible, regardless of the device they are using at the time. Windows 8 provides several ways to ensure that the user has a consistent experience.

CERTIFICATION READY
Sync devices and resolve sync issues
Objective 3.1

You can use your Microsoft user account, PC settings, and Sync Center to ensure a consistent experience for users who move between devices. Solutions include synchronizing your PC settings across your desktop, laptop, and smartphone using your Microsoft user account; and configuring Sync Center to maintain access to files and folders stored on a network file share when you are offline.

Synchronizing Your PC Settings

Using your Microsoft user account, you can select the PC settings you want to sync and make available across all your trusted computers running Windows 8.

When you sign into the Windows 8 computer with your Microsoft User account, the system will automatically sync most of the settings for you. Only passwords, which require the PC to be trusted, are not synchronized automatically.

Information that can be synchronized includes the following:

- General (colors, background, lock screen, and your account picture)
- Desktop personalization (themes, taskbar)
- Passwords (local password, passwords used on websites via Internet Explorer, network passwords)
- Ease of access (customizations made to magnifier, narrator, and the onscreen keyboard)
- Language preferences
- App settings (app settings, app purchases made)
- Browser (history, bookmarks, and favorites)
- Other Windows settings (File Explorer, mouse)

SYNC YOUR PC SETTINGS

GET READY. To sync your PC Settings, log into a Windows 8 computer using your Microsoft User Account and then perform the following steps:

1. Press the **Windows logo key + i.**
2. Click **Change PC settings.**
3. Under *PC settings,* click **Sync your settings** and then confirm that **Sync settings on this PC** is set to **On** (see Figure 10-3).

Figure 10-3

Synchronizing via PC Settings

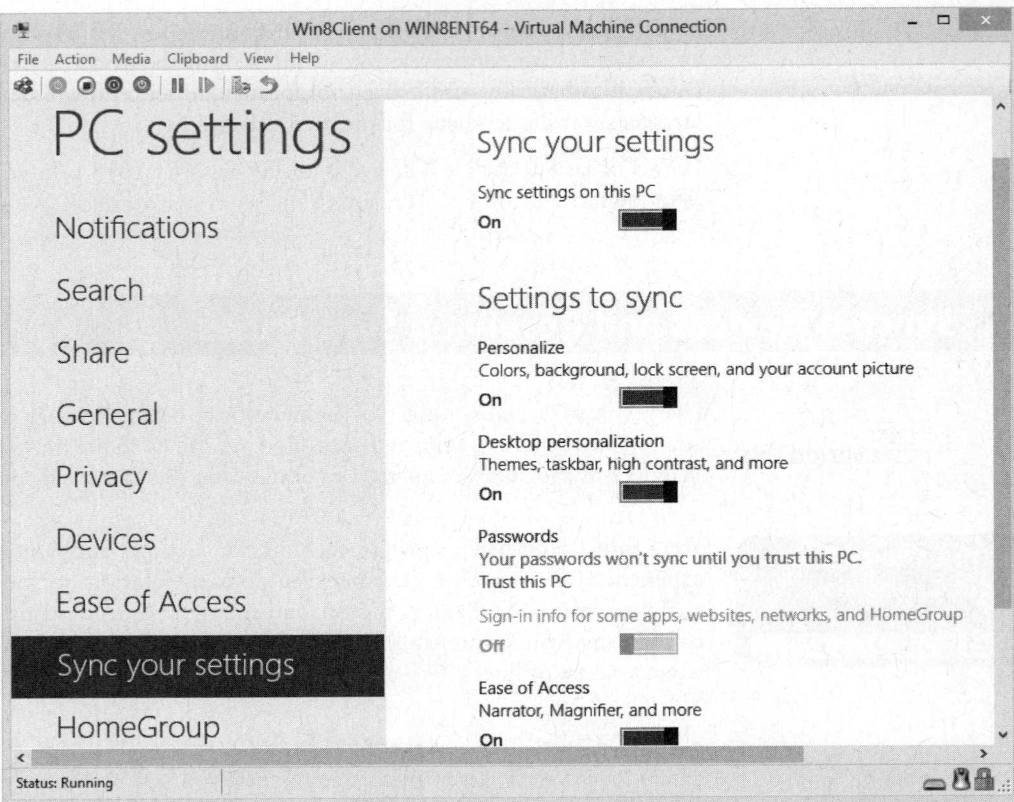

4. Under *Settings to Sync,* drag the slider bar all the way to the left to turn off sync for each item that you do not want to synchronize between your devices.
5. After configuring your sync settings, press the **Windows logo key** to return to the Windows 8 start screen.

To sync passwords, you will need to trust the PC. You can do this by clicking the *Trust this PC* link, which takes you to Microsoft's Account settings web page. From there, you will login with your Microsoft User Account and select how you want to receive the security code (email, phone, or text message). Once you have the security code, you can type it to complete the trust process. After the PC has been trusted, you will be able to sync your password settings.

You can also determine if you want to sync over metered connections. Metered connections are those where the provider charges a certain fee based on the data sent and received from your computer. In most cases, you will turn off sync when working over metered connections and wait until you are on a non-metered connection to enable it.

Using Sync Center

Sync Center enables you to sync certain mobile devices as well as files stored in folders on network servers (offline files).

Sync Center offers two ways to sync your data:

- **One-way sync:** Data kept in a primary location is synchronized with data in another location. For example, if you have a portable mp3 device, you can configure a one-way sync so that you maintain the music files on your computer and the mp3 player holds only a copy of the files. When it comes time to sync, only data on the computer will be transferred to the mp3 player, not vice versa.

- **Two-way sync:** Data is transferred in both directions. This works well when you want to make sure key files you work with on the network and on your device are always in sync (offline files).

When working with mobile devices, Microsoft recommends using the software that comes with your device (mobile phone, music device, and so on) to perform synchronization. If your device is compatible with Sync Center, you can perform the next exercise to sync your device.

SYNC A DEVICE

GET READY. If your device is compatible with Sync Center, sync your device by performing the following steps:

1. Turn on the device and then connect it to your PC.
2. Open Sync Center and then click **Set up new sync partnerships**.
3. Click **Set Up**.
4. Configure the settings and schedule for how and when you want to sync with the device.

Managing Offline Files

Sync Center's primary purpose is to synchronize files available on your network. When you set up an offline files sync partnership with a folder, any time you disconnect from the network, you can continue to work on the files.

Changes you make to the files while offline will be made to the files in the network folder when you reconnect. Sync Center tracks the version number for a file. If the file has changed, it copies the updated version to the other location to keep both locations in sync. In case of conflicts, Sync Center will notify you and you can choose to address the conflict.

If you select the Manage Offline Files link within Sync Center (see Figure 10-4), you will see the following tabs:

Figure 10-4

Reviewing Offline Files property settings

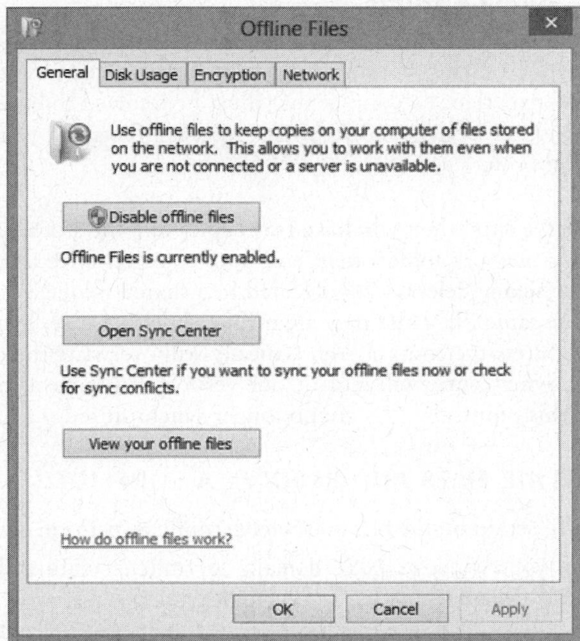

- **General**
  - o **Disable Offline Files:** Enables and disables the Offline Files feature.
  - o **Open Sync Center:** Opens Sync Center, checks for conflicts.
  - o **View Your Offline File:** Provides access to your offline files.
- **Disk Usage:** Provides information on how much disk space is currently used and is available for storing offline files; enables you to change the maximum amount of space offline files and temporary files can use on your computer.
- **Encryption:** Enables you to encrypt and unencrypt your offline files.
- **Network:** Settings here determine how often the computer will check for a slow connection. By default, it is set to 5 minutes.

SCHEDULING FOR OFFLINE FILES

To set a schedule for the items you want to synchronize along with the date/time or the event that triggers the synchronization, simply right-click the Offline Files icon and choose Schedule for Offline Files. The options are as follows:

- **At a scheduled time:** This option enables you to set a start date and time, and determine the frequency you want to repeat the schedule (minutes, hours, days, weeks, or months).
- **When an event occurs:** This option configures synchronization to occur when one of the following events occurs:
  - o You log on to your computer.
  - o Your computer is idle for *x* minutes/hours.
  - o You lock Windows.
  - o You unlock Windows.

Additional start-and-stop scheduling options include the following:

- Start sync only if the computer is awake, has been idle for *x* minutes, and/or the computer is running on external power.
- Stop sync if the computer wakes up from being idle or the computer is no longer running on external power.

Resolving Sync Conflicts

Although synchronizing can help keep your files in a consistent state, there will be times that you will experience a conflict that must be resolved to ensure you have the right file in the right place. Understanding what causes conflicts and your options to resolve them will help you protect your files.

A ***sync conflict*** occurs when you have two copies of a file stored in different locations (e.g., locally and in a network folder) that have both changed since the last sync. A conflict can also occur if someone deletes a file (located in a shared folder) while another person makes a change to the same file while they are offline. In either case, Sync Center will ask you how you want to address the conflict. You typically will overwrite the older file, but if you choose to keep both, Sync Center will rename one version and make a copy of both files in both locations. At this point, the files are no longer synchronized.

SET UP OFFLINE FILES AND RESOLVE A CONFLICT

GET READY. To set up offline files and resolve conflicts, perform the following steps:

First, from your Windows 2012 domain controller, create a folder, share it, and then create a file called *MyFile.txt* in the folder.

1. Log on to your domain controller with administrative credentials.
2. Press the **Windows logo key + e**.

> **TAKE NOTE***
> The following activity requires a domain controller and a Windows 8 client computer connected to the domain.

3. Double click the **C: drive** on your computer to open it.
4. Right-click and choose **New > Folder** and then type **Harmony**.
5. After the folder is created, right click and choose **Share with > Specific people**.
6. In the *File Sharing* dialog box, type **Everyone** and then click **Add**.
7. Under the Permission Level column, click the **Read** permission for **Everyone** and then change it to **Read/Write**.
8. Click **Share** and then click **Done** to complete the setup of the shared folder.
9. Double-click the **Harmony** folder to open it.
10. Right-click and choose **New > Text Document**.
11. Type **MyFile** for the name and then press **Enter**.

Now, from a Windows 8 client computer, connect to the shared folder on the domain controller.

1. Log on to the Windows 8 client computer with a regular domain user account.
2. Press the **Windows logo key + r**, type ***servername*\harmony**, and then press **Enter**. (Replace *servername* with the name of your domain controller.)
3. Double-click **Myfile.txt** to open it and then type **Connected over network** into the file.
4. Click **File > Save**.
5. Right-click the file and choose **Always available offline** (see Figure 10-5).

Figure 10-5
Configuring a folder to be available offline

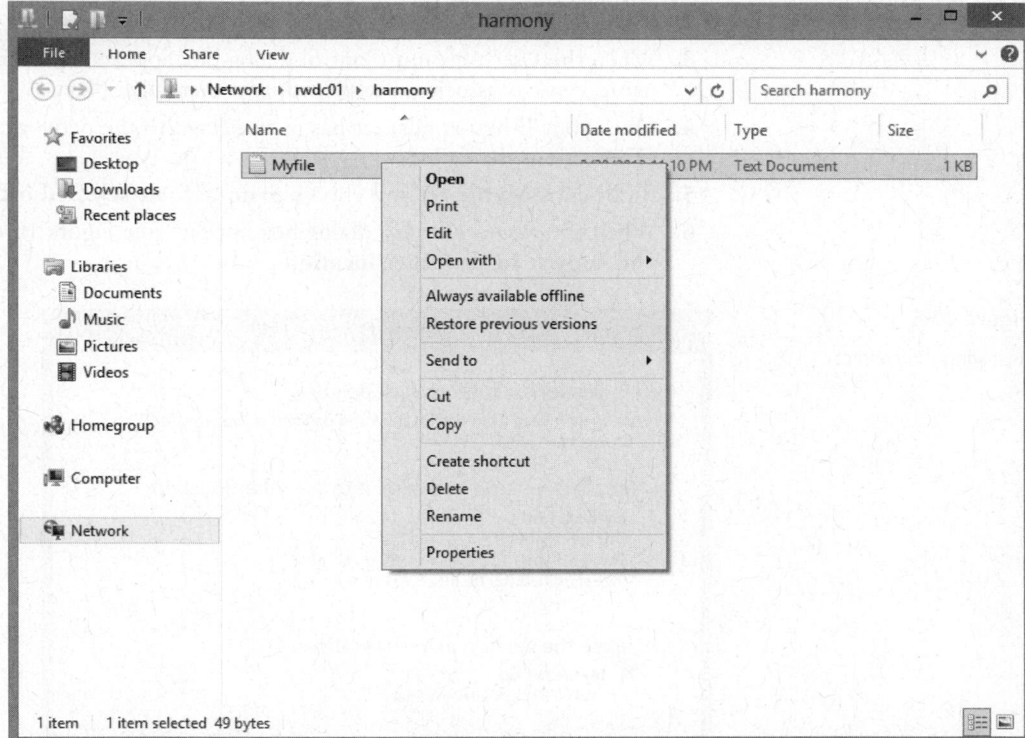

6. Close the dialog box and then close the Harmony dialog box.
7. Press the **Windows logo key + w**, type **View network connections**, and then choose it from *Results*.
8. Right-click your Ethernet adapter and choose **Disable**.
9. When the User Account Control dialog box appears, type **Administrator** for the user name, type its associated password, and then click **Next**.

Your Ethernet adapter is now disabled which simulates an offline environment for this computer.

10. From the Windows domain controller, delete the file while the Windows 8 client computer is disconnected from the network.

This creates a conflict that you will need to resolve later.

1. Log on to your domain controller with administrative credentials.
2. Press the **Windows logo key + e**.
3. Double-click the **C: drive** on your computer to open it.
4. Double-click the **Harmony** folder on your computer to open it.
5. Right-click **Myfile** and choose **Delete**.

From the Windows 8 client computer, make a change to the file while you are still offline.

1. Press the **Windows logo key + r**, type ***servername*\harmony**, and then press **Enter**. (Replace *servername* with the name of your domain controller.)
2. Double-click **Myfile.txt** to open it and then type **Changes made while offline** into the file.
3. Click **File > Save**.
4. Close the *Myfile.txt* dialog box.

From the Windows 8 client computer, enable your Ethernet adapter and reconnect to the network.

1. Press the **Windows logo key + w**, type **View network connections**, and then choose it from *Results*.
2. Right-click your Ethernet adapter and choose **Enable**.
3. When the User Account Control dialog box appears, type **Administrator** for the user name, type its associated password, and then click **Next**.
4. Once your Ethernet adapter has reconnected to the network, close the Network Connections dialog box.
5. Right-click **Myfile.txt** and choose **Sync > Sync selected offline files**.
6. When the *Resolve Conflict* dialog box appears (see Figure 10-6), select **Keep this version and copy it to the other location**.

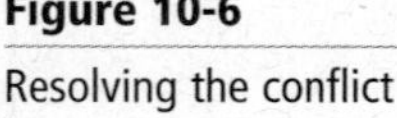
Figure 10-6
Resolving the conflict

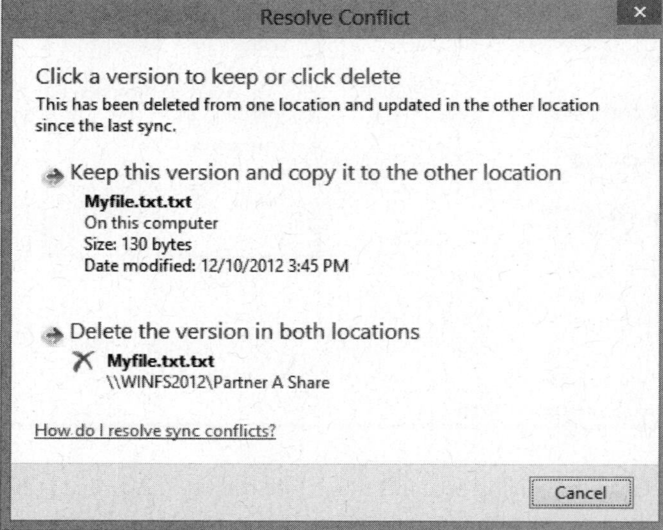

7. Close the dialog box.

The file has now been restored on the domain controller.

Monitoring and Managing Print Servers

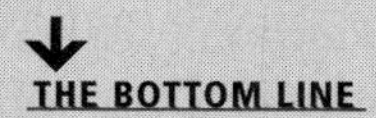

Windows Server 2012 provides the Server Manager and the Print Management snap-in to manage printers and print servers in your organization. Windows 8 and Windows Server 2012 have also introduced new features that will make the process of monitoring and managing print servers much easier.

CERTIFICATION READY
Monitor and manage print servers
Objective 3.1

Before we review these new features, let's cover a few terms that you need to be familiar with:

- ***Print device:*** The actual physical hardware that prints the data.
- ***Printer:*** The software interface that is used by your operating system to deliver requests to the physical print device.
- ***Print server:*** A computer that is connected to and shares one or more print devices.
- ***Print driver:*** The software used by the operating system to convert your print commands into a printer language (Printer Control Language (PCL)/PostScript). It also tells the operating system about the attributes or capabilities of the printer.
- ***Spooling:*** The process of caching your print request to a hard disk. By spooling the print job, the operating system sends the print job to the background, enabling the application to resume rather than waiting for the job to finish.
- ***Print queue:*** A representation of a print device (physical printer) in Windows. Opening a print queue displays active print jobs and their status.
- ***Print Spooler service:*** A service that manages all the print jobs and print queues on a server.

Exploring the v4 Print Driver Model

The v4 print driver model includes changes to printer sharing known as enhanced Point and Print which eliminates the need to install cross platform drivers and removes the need to use the Print Server as a single distribution point for print drivers.

For Windows 8/Windows Server 2012, Microsoft redesigned the print driver architecture used in previous releases of its operating systems. This new version (v4) offers several advantages over the previous release (v3). With v3 (available from Windows 2000 through Windows 7), you had to install specific drivers provided by the original equipment manufacturers (OEMs) for each printer, make sure the client and server used the same driver, and install separate drivers based on the client's architecture (32 vs. 64-bit). In v3, the print server also provided a central software distribution point to distribute printer drivers to clients who wanted to print to its shared printers.

As you can imagine, this accounted for a large number of drivers required to manage printers on the average network. It also forced Microsoft to include multiple printer drivers in the Windows installation media to ensure that users always had the appropriate drivers for any printer they were using. Thousands of other printer drivers were accessible via Windows Update.

TAKE NOTE*

Prior to Windows 8 and Windows Server 2012, a large percentage of the Windows installation files consisted of driver files for printers that would never be used by the client. Windows 7 currently allocates about 450 MB of space for print drivers. Windows 8 uses about 185 MB.

To address these issues, Microsoft worked with OEMs to develop a new printer driver model (v4) that provides the following benefits:

- Separate drivers for client architecture (32/64-bit) are no longer required.
- Drivers are isolated to eliminate conflicts. These drivers are isolated from the print spooler process and loaded into a shared area with other isolated drivers. This keeps drivers that have a problem from affecting the print spooler process and other printers and drivers that are loaded. An administrator can also configure the drivers to run in a process that is separate from the spooler process and not shared with other printer drivers.
- Print class drivers that support a wide set of devices that use the same printer description language (PCL, PS, XPS) result in fewer drivers along with smaller drivers' files.
- The print server no longer serves as a software distribution point. Instead, the printer configuration and its capabilities are sent to the client who uses them without needing a specific printer driver.

Windows 8 and Windows Server 2012 also use the new enhanced Point and Print feature. This feature allows users to connect to a shared printer without having to install the printer driver software. When the user connects to a print queue using a v4 driver from a client computer, the user's computer installs the print queue using the enhanced Point and Print process.

If the computer is running Windows 8, the driver will be downloaded from the local driver store, Windows Update, or Windows Server Update Services (WSUS). Users will not be prompted to provide credentials to install the driver but will see a printer installation indicator in their status bar. After the install is completed, the printer is ready to use.

TAKE NOTE*

Systems prior to Windows 8 do not support the v4 print model, but can print to a v4 queue shared from a Windows Server 2012 print server by using the enhanced Point and Print compatibility driver found on any print server running Windows Server 2012.

Managing Print Servers

The ***Print and Document services role*** in Windows Server 2012 allows you to centralize Print Server and network printer tasks. You can use it to monitor print queues and receive notifications when print jobs stop processing. You can also use it to migrate Print Servers and deploy printer connections using Group Policy.

In Windows Server 2012, you can manage printers using one of the following:

- ***Server Manager:*** Displays print-related events from Event Viewer and includes an instance of the Print Management snap-in, but can only manage the local server.
- ***Print Management snap-in*** (included as part of the Print and Document Services/Print Server role): Manages multiple printers and print servers across your organization and migrates printers to and from other Windows print servers. This tool provides a single interface, enabling you to manage printers and printer servers running on Windows 2000, Windows XP, Windows Server 2003, Windows Server 2008, and Windows Server 2012.

INSTALL THE PRINT AND DOCUMENT SERVICES ROLE ON A DOMAIN CONTROLLER

TAKE NOTE*

The following exercise requires a Windows Server 2012 computer that is part of an Active Directory domain.

GET READY. To set up the Print Management snap-in, perform the following steps:

1. Log on to your domain controller with administrative privileges. The Server Manager will start automatically. If it does not start, select the Server Manager icon from the task bar.
2. Click **Manage > Add Roles and Features.**

3. When the *Before you begin* screen appears, click **Next**.
4. Click **Next** to accept the default setting *Role-based or feature-based installation*.
5. Choose your domain controller form the Server Pool and click **Next**.
6. On the *Select server roles* screen, select **Print and Document Services**.
7. Click **Add Features** when the *Add Roles and Features Wizard* dialog box appears and then click **Next**.
8. On the *Select server roles* screen, click **Next**.
9. On the *Select features* screen, click **Next**.
10. On the *Print and Document Services* screen, click **Next**.
11. Select **Print Server** and then click **Next**.
12. Select **Restart the destination server automatically if required** and then, when asked if you want to allow automatic restarts, click **Yes**.
13. Click **Install**.
14. When the installation is completed, click **Close**.

During the installation, you selected Print Server as the role service. This adds the Print Management console (see Figure 10-7), which is used to manage multiple printers/print servers and can be used to move printers to and from other Windows print servers.

Figure 10-7

The Print Management console

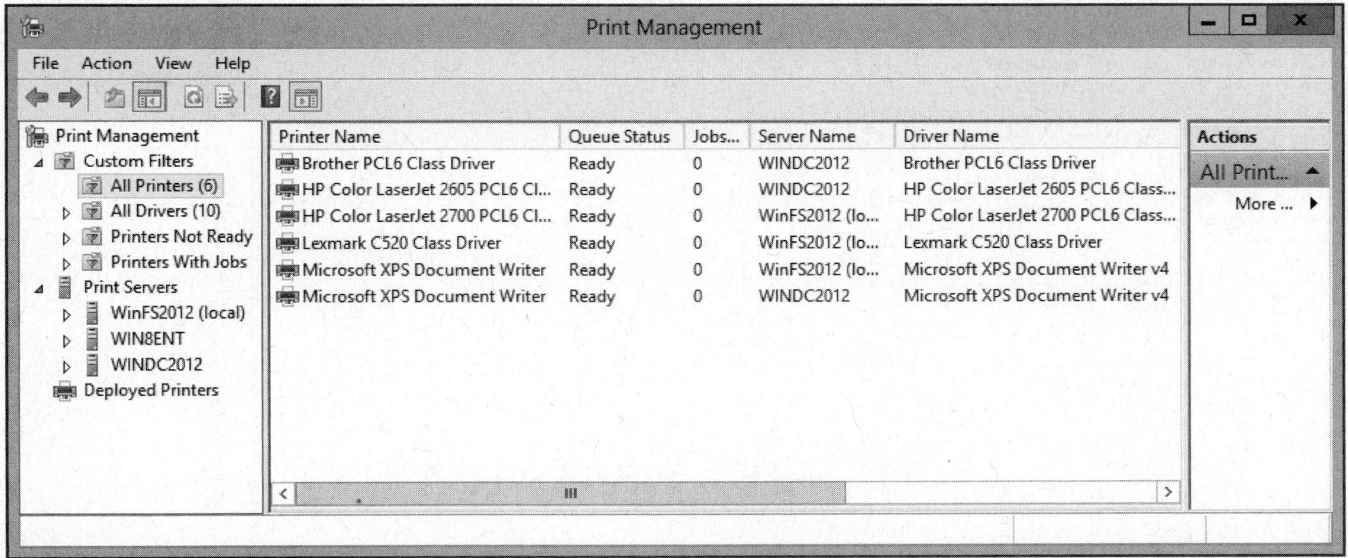

There are other role services included in Print and Document Services.

Here is a brief overview of what each service provides:

- ***Distributed scan server:*** Provides a service that receives scanned documents from network scanners and routes them to the correct destinations. It also includes the Scan Management snap-in that you can use to manage network scanners and configure scan processes.
- ***Internet printing:*** Creates a website in which users can manage print jobs on the server. Also enables users to use a web browser to connect and print to shared printers on the server using the Internet Printing Protocol.
- ***Line Printer Daemon (LPD) service:*** Enables UNIX-based computers using the Line Printer Remote (LPR) service to print to shared printers available on this server.

MORE INFORMATION

You can remotely manage printers from your Windows 8 computer by downloading the Remote Server Administration Tools (RSAT) for Windows 8. You can find the tools on the Microsoft website by searching for "RSAT for Windows 8."

ADD A PRINTER TO THE LOCAL PRINT SERVER

GET READY. To add a printer to the local print server, perform the following steps:

TAKE NOTE*

The following should be performed on the same Windows Server 2012 computer you set up Print Management for in the previous activity.

1. Log on to your domain controller with administrative privileges.

   The Server Manager starts automatically. If it does not start, go to the task bar and click the **Server Manager** icon.
2. Click **Tools > Print Management.**
3. Expand the Print Servers node and locate the server on which you installed Print and Document Services.
4. Right-click the server and then choose **Add Printer** (see Figure 10-8).

Figure 10-8

Adding a printer

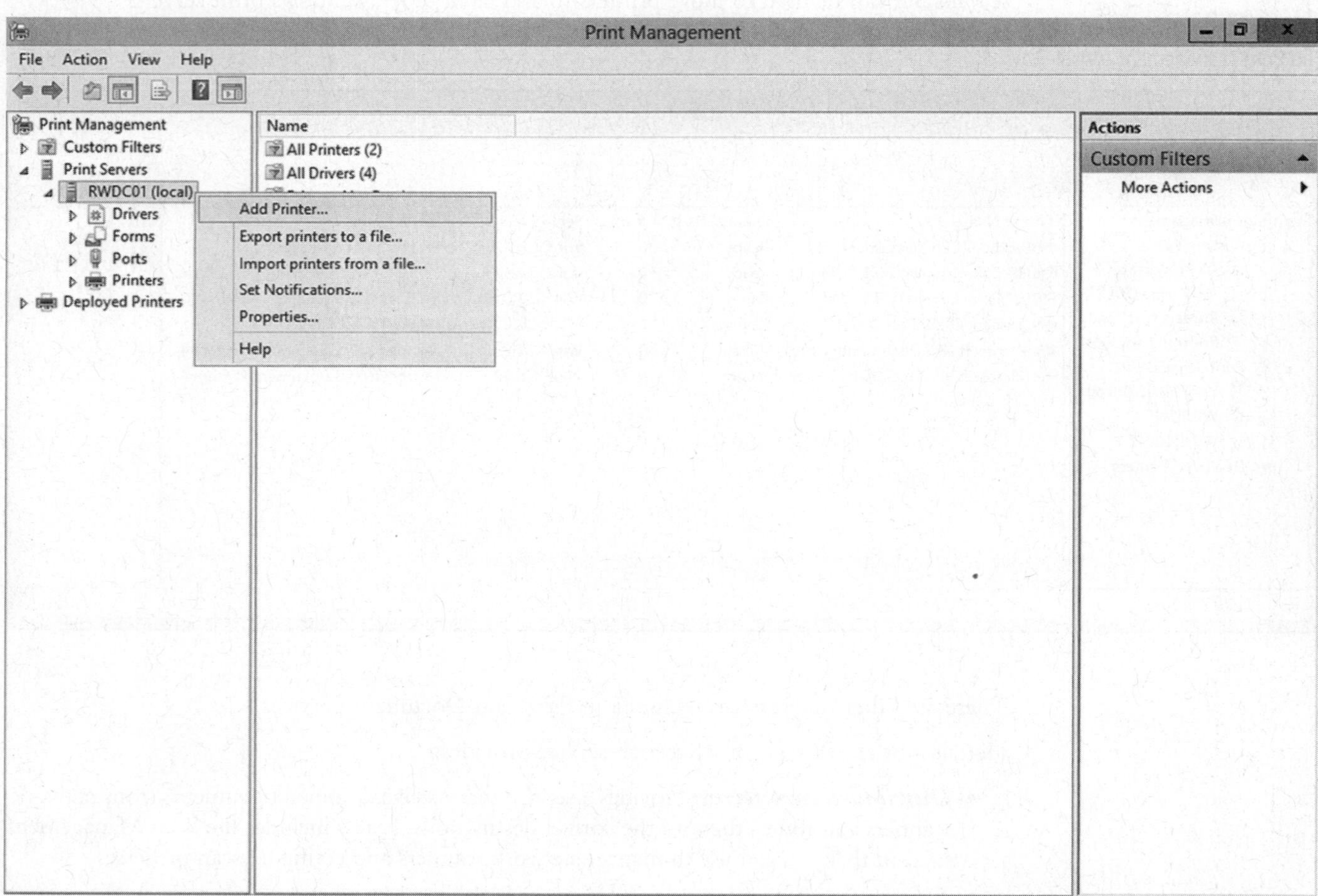

5. Select **Add a new printer using an existing port: LPT1: (Printer Port)** and then click **Next.**
6. To accept the default settings, click **Next.**

7. Click **Windows Update.**

   This allows Windows to update the list of printers.

8. Select **HP** as the manufacturer and select the model **HP Color LaserJet 2550 PS**. Click **Next.**
9. To accept the default settings for the printer name and share name, click **Next.**
10. Review your settings and then click **Next.**
11. After the driver installs successfully, click **Finish.**
12. Click the **All Printers folder** and then confirm the new printer appears under the *Printer name* column.
13. Right-click the printer and select **List in Directory** (see Figure 10-9).

    Listing printers in Active Directory helps users to locate and install them more efficiently.

Figure 10-9

Listing a printer in the directory

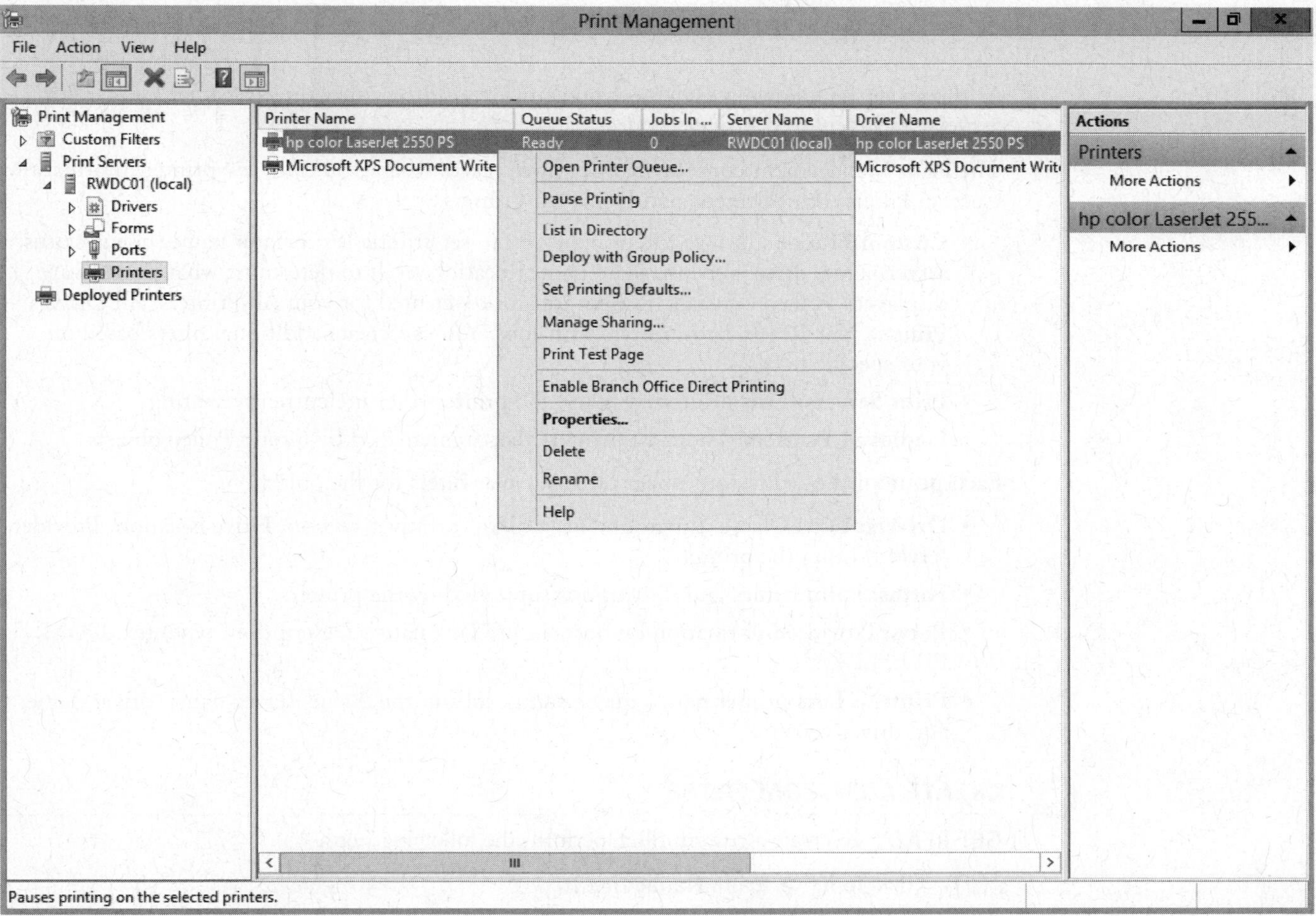

Your printer is now available for users to select as a resource.

14. Close the Print Management console.

The following exercises show you how to do a few others things with Print Manager.

ADD A PRINT SERVER

GET READY. To add a print server, perform the following steps:

1. Click **Tools > Printer Management**.
2. Right-click the **Print Servers** node and then choose **Add/Remove Servers**.
3. Type the name of the print server or click **Browse** to locate the server you want to add.
4. Click **Add to List**.
5. Click **OK**.

REMOVE A PRINT SERVER

GET READY. To remove a print server, perform the following steps:

1. Click **Tools > Printer Management**.
2. Right-click **Print Servers** node and then choose **Add/Remove Servers**.
3. Under *Print servers*, choose the print server you want to remove.
4. Click **Remove**.
5. Click **OK**.

As shown in the following exercises, you can view printers using the Customer Filters, Print Servers, and Deployed Printers nodes.

The Print Management console provides three places where you can view printer information: Custom Filters, Print Servers, and Deployed Printers.

- **Custom Filters:** Custom filters allow you to set criteria (ex: printer name, queue status, server name, driver version, share name, location, etc.) to determine what printers are displayed. Four pre-installed filters are already created for you: All Printers, All Drivers, Printers Not Ready, and Printers with Jobs. You can create additional filters based on your specific needs.
- **Print Servers:** Lists print servers and the printers they are currently sharing.
- **Deployed Printers:** These are printers that are managed by Group Policy objects.

Each printer is linked to four objects that serve as filters for the object:

- **Drivers:** Drive Name, Environment (x86/x64), Driver version, Drive isolation, Provider, server hosting the printer.
- **Forms:** Form names and dimensions supported by the printer.
- **Ports:** Provides information on ports in use Port name, Description, type) (ex: COM, FILE, LPT).
- **Printers:** Lists printer name, queue status, jobs in the queue, server name, driver name, and driver version.

CREATE A CUSTOM FILTER

GET READY. To create a custom filter, perform the following steps:

1. Click **Tools > Print Management**.
2. Right-click **Custom Filters** and choose **Add New Printer Filter**.
3. In the Name field, type: **HP Printers** and then click **Next**.
4. On the *Define a filter* page (see Figure 10-10), click the arrow under the *Field* column and choose **Printer Name**. Under the *Condition* column, choose **contains**. In the *Value* field, type **HP**.
5. Click **Next** to continue.
6. On the *Set Notifications (Optional)* page, click **Finish**.

Figure 10-10

Creating a custom filter

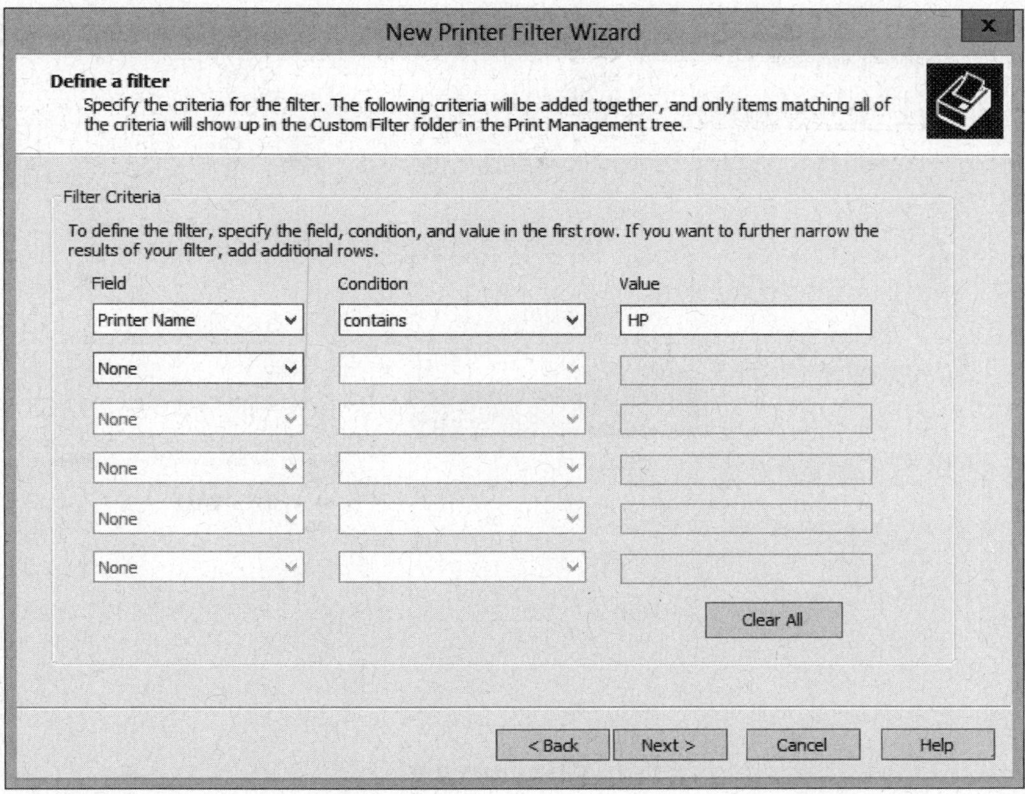

7. Under Custom Filters, click **HP Printers** (the custom filter you just created). You will see the HP Color LasetJet 2550 PS printer that you installed earlier. It is the only HP printer currently in operation.

Now that you have a better understanding of how to perform basic printer administrative tasks using the Print Management console, you can now turn your attention to installing a printer on a Windows 8 client computer.

INSTALL A PRINTER FOR A WINDOWS 8 CLIENT

GET READY. To install a printer on a Windows 8 client, perform the following steps:

TAKE NOTE*

The Windows 8 client should be connected to the same domain as the print server.

1. Log on to the Windows 8 client computer with a domain user account.
2. Press the **Windows logo key + c** to activate the Charms bar.
3. Click **Settings > Change PC Settings**.
4. Under *PC settings*, click **Devices** (see Figure 10-11).
5. Click **Add a device**.

   Windows scans the network for devices. Because the printer was published to Active Directory earlier, it should show up at the top of the list.
6. Click **HP Color Laserjet 2550 PS**.

   Once the installation completes, the printer will appear under *Devices*.
7. Press the **Windows logo key** to return to the Windows 8 start menu.
8. Type **Notepad** and then select it from *Results*.
9. Type a few characters into the Notepad application and then click **File > Print**.
10. Choose the **HP Color Laserjet 2550 PS** printer and then click **Print**.
11. Close the Notepad document. You do not have to save the file.

Figure 10-11

Adding a device in Windows 8

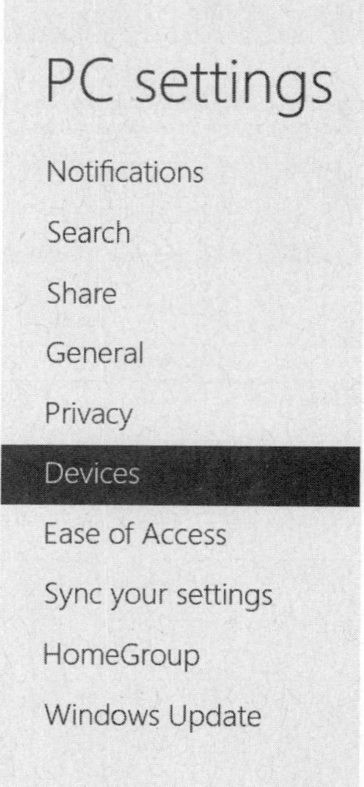

SKILL SUMMARY

IN THIS LESSON, YOU LEARNED:

- You can use the Device Manager to resolve hardware and device issues by updating drivers, scanning for hardware changes, viewing device properties, and disabling or uninstalling a device.
- The driver files provided with Windows 8 have been digitally signed and tested for compatibility, reliability, and functionality with Windows 8.
- You can control how Windows 8 handles unsigned device drivers by using the Local Group Policy Editor or the GPMC. Options include ignore, warn, and block.
- Driver Roll Back is a system recovery feature in Windows 8 that enables you to reinstall the last device driver that was functioning.
- Windows 8 uses built-in hardware diagnostics to detect hardware problems on your computer. If problems are detected, Action Center displays messages to alert you to the problem.
- Using your Microsoft user account, you can select the PC settings you want to sync and make them available across trusted computers. These settings include general, desktop personalization, passwords, customizations, language preferences, app settings, and other Windows settings. To sync password settings, you have to trust the PC.
- Sync Center enables you to sync certain mobile devices using both one-way and two-way sync. Its primary purpose is to sync files available on network shares.
- Sync conflicts occur when you have a file stored in two different locations that have both changed since the last sync. Windows Sync Center asks you how you want to address the conflict.
- Windows 2012 and Windows 8 have been designed to use new print driver architecture (v4), which reduced the number of separate drivers that have to be installed and removed the need for a central distribution point for printer drivers required in previous releases.

- The Print Management snap-in, included as part of the Print and Document Services/Print Server role, is used to manage multiple printers or print servers across your organization. Server Manager is designed to manage only the local print server.
- You understand the process needed to add/remove print servers, view printers, list printers in Active Directory; and how to install a network printer on a Windows 8 client.

Knowledge Assessment

Multiple Choice

Select the correct answer for each of the following questions.

1. Which of the following can be used to roll back a faulty print driver?
   a. Print Management Console
   b. Device Manager
   c. Activity Center
   d. Rollback.exe
2. Driver signing ensures that the driver files provided for Windows 8 are compatible, reliable, and function appropriately with the operating system. What is responsible for managing how unsigned drivers are handled?
   a. Windows Hardware Quality Labs (WHQLs)
   b. Network administrators
   c. Windows Device Quality Labs (WDQLs)
   d. Windows Device Signature Labs (WDSLs)
3. Which of the following are options for how the computer will respond when a user tries to install device drivers that are not digitally signed? (Select all that apply.)
   a. Block
   b. Ignore
   c. Warn
   d. Alert
4. When a device has been disabled, which of the following symbols appear?
   a. Blue "I" on a white field
   b. Red "X"
   c. Black exclamation point on a yellow field
   d. Blue "X"
5. Which information can be synched on an untrusted PC? (Select all that apply.)
   a. Lock screen and your account picture
   b. Local password, passwords used on websites via Internet Explorer
   c. Browser history, bookmarks, and favorites
   d. App settings
6. Which of the following are ways in which Sync Center syncs your mobile devices and offline files? (Select all that apply.)
   a. One-way
   b. Peer-to-peer
   c. Three-way
   d. Two-way

7. When scheduling for offline file sync, which of the following are examples of event triggers that can be configured? (Select all that apply.)
   a. Logging on to your computer
   b. Shutting down the computer
   c. Locking Windows
   d. Unlocking Windows

8. Which of the following causes a sync conflict? (Select all that apply.)
   a. You delete a file in a shared folder after another person makes a change to the same file while they are offline.
   b. You have a file stored locally and in a network folder, and both have changed since the last sync.
   c. You open a file while offline.
   d. You open a file from a network share while connected to the network.

9. Which term best describes the actual physical hardware that prints data?
   a. Print server
   b. Printer
   c. Print device
   d. Print spooler

10. Which of the following tools can be used to manage a local print server? (Select all that apply.)
   a. Server Manager
   b. Print Management snap-in
   c. Device Manager
   d. Action Center

Best Answer

Choose the letter that corresponds to the best answer. More than one answer choice may achieve the goal. Select the BEST answer.

1. When setting up a policy that determines how to best manage device drivers that are not digitally signed in your organization, which of the following options provide the best stability for your Windows 8 systems?
   a. Ignore
   b. Warn
   c. Block
   d. Alert

2. Which of the following tools is best to use when you have bookmarked your favorite sites and want to make sure they are available across multiple PCs?
   a. Export your favorites to a network folder and use Sync Center to sync them across your PCs.
   b. Configure them to sync via PC Settings.
   c. Make them part of your roaming profile.
   d. Store your favorites in Sky Drive.

3. Which of the following tools provides a central location from which the print services can be managed for the entire network?
   a. Event Viewer
   b. Server Manager
   c. Print Management snap-in
   d. Computer Management

4. You currently cannot print to a USB print device after updating its driver files. Which of the following tasks is the quickest way to return your print device back to normal operation?
   a. Reinstalling the driver
   b. Rolling back the driver
   c. Researching the manufacturer's website for current driver information
   d. Installing a generic driver

5. While running Windows 8 and connecting to a shared print queue using a v4 driver, which of the following locations is the *least* likely location from which the driver will be downloaded?
   a. WSUS server
   b. Windows Update
   c. Windows 8 local driver store
   d. From the print server itself

Matching and Identification

1. Match the following terms with the related description or usage.

   _______ a) Action Center
   _______ b) Device Manager
   _______ c) Driver Roll Back
   _______ d) Sync Center
   _______ e) Sync conflict
   _______ f) Printer
   _______ g) Print server
   _______ h) Print device
   _______ i) WHQL
   _______ j) PC settings

   1. Enables you to sync certain mobile devices as well as files stored in folders on network servers
   2. Provides a detailed listing of all devices on your computer
   3. Provides a central location to view any problems with hardware or software
   4. A system recovery feature in Windows 8 that enables you to reinstall the last device driver that was functioning
   5. Responsible for driver signing
   6. The software interface that is used by your operating system to deliver request to the physical print device
   7. Occurs when you have a file stored in two different locations that have both changed since the last sync
   8. Used with your Microsoft user account to sync PC settings across multiple Windows 8 devices
   9. A computer that is connected to and sharing one or more print devices
   10. The actual physical hardware that prints the data

Build a List

1. Specify the correct order of the steps that must be completed to remove a print server.

   _______ Choose **Tools < Print Management**.
   _______ Choose the print server you want to remove.
   _______ Click **OK**.
   _______ Right-click the **Print Servers** node and choose **Add/Remove Servers**.
   _______ Click **Remove**.

2. Specify the correct order of the steps that must be completed to synchronize your PC settings.
   _______ Click **Change PC Settings**.
   _______ Log in with your Microsoft User Account and press the **Windows logo key + i**.
   _______ Under *Settings to Sync*, drag the slider bar to the right to turn on sync for the item.
   _______ Select **Sync Your Settings**.
   _______ Set **Sync your settings on this PC** to **On**.

3. Specify the correct order of the steps that must be completed to roll back a device driver.
   _______ Click **Roll Back Driver**.
   _______ Open **Device Manager**.
   _______ Right-click the device and select **Properties**.
   _______ When prompted to roll back the driver, click **Yes**.
   _______ Click the **Driver** tab.

Choose an Option

1. Which option helps users find their printers in Active Directory?

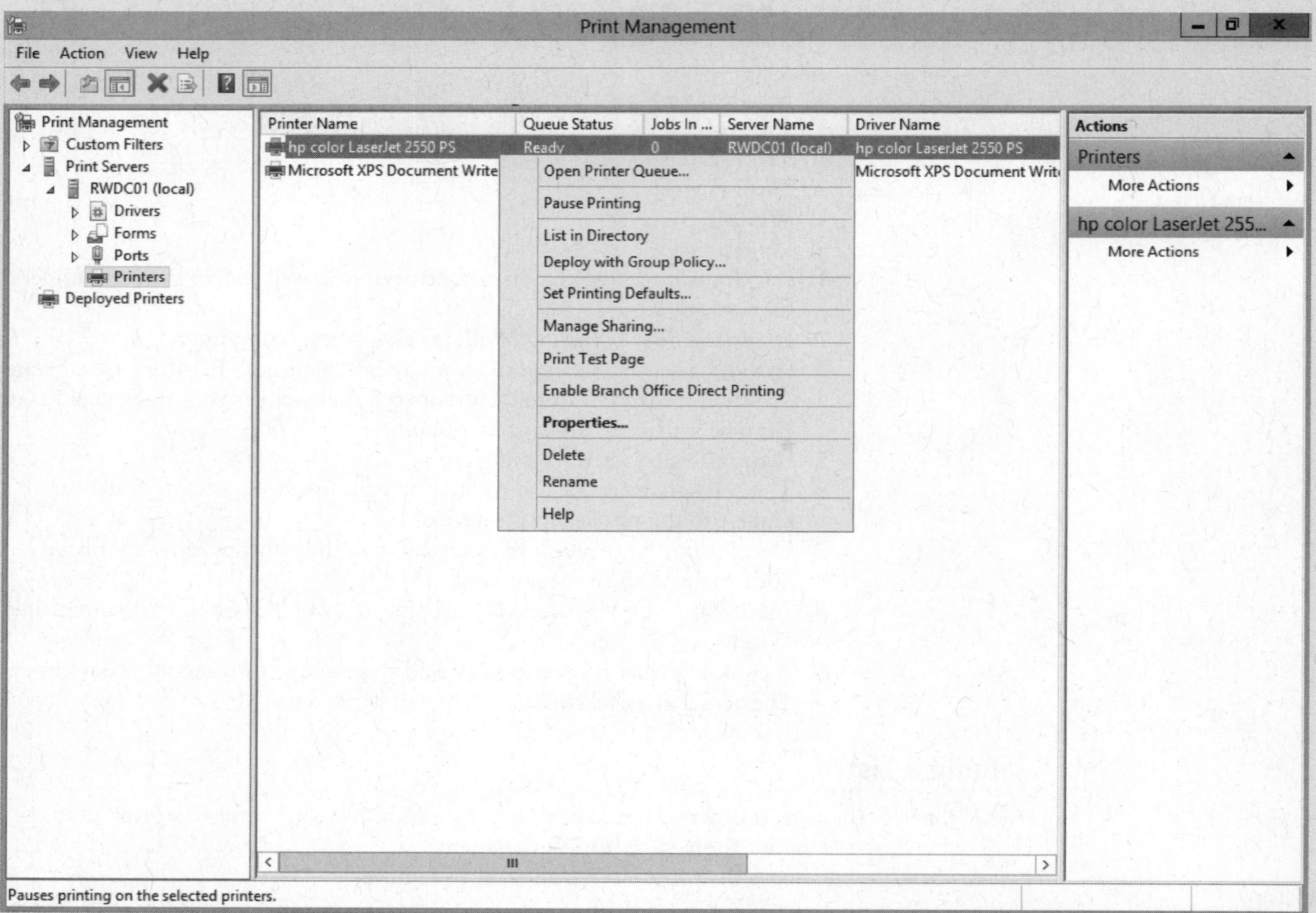

Business Case Scenarios

Scenario 10-1: Troubleshooting Print Devices

A user has contacted you because he cannot print documents to a device that is directly connected to a USB port. After talking to him, you discover that he updated the driver before leaving the office yesterday. What is the problem and how should you address it?

Scenario 10-2: Controlling Driver Signing

You are concerned that users will install device drivers in your organization that are not tested with Windows 8. You currently have 200 Windows 8 computers in an Active Directory–based network and have only two people working on your help desk. What is the best way to maintain the stability of your Windows 8 systems?

Managing Mobile Devices

70-688 EXAM OBJECTIVE

Objective 3.2 – Manage mobile devices. This objective may include but is not limited to the following: Resolve mobility issues; manage mobile device policies, including security policies, NFC, secure SIM, and remote access; manage mobile access; manage Microsoft Exchange ActiveSync in mobile devices.

Lesson Heading	Exam Objective
Managing Mobile Access to Your Network	Manage mobile devices
Exploring Exchange Active Sync/Mobile Device Policies in Exchange Server 2013	Manage Microsoft Exchange ActiveSync in mobile devices
Exploring Mobile Policy Settings in Exchange Server 2013	Security policies, remote access
Securing Your Communications Using SSL	
Exploring System Center Configuration Manager (SCCM) 2012 Mobile Device Management	Manage mobile access
Light Mobile Device Management	
In-Depth Mobile Device Management	
Managing Mobile Device Policies	Manage mobile device policies
Using Near Field Communication (NFC) Using Secure SIMs Using the Windows Phone 8 Wallet	NFC Secure SIM
Resolving Mobility Issues	Resolve mobility issues

KEY TERMS

Active Directory Certificate Services (AD CS)
Bring Your Own Device (BYOD)
card emulation mode
Certification Authority (CA)
Exchange ActiveSync
Exchange Server connector
near field communication (NFC)
peer-to-peer mode
public key infrastructure (PKI)
reader/writer mode
remote wipe command
Secure Sockets Layer (SSL)
subscriber identity module (SIM)
System Center Configuration Manager (SCCM) 2012
Tap and Do
Windows Phone 8 wallet

Managing Mobile Access to Your Network

Employees who bring their own smartphones, laptops, and tablets to work are quickly becoming the norm in most businesses. In fact, the term ***Bring Your Own Device (BYOD)*** has already been coined to identify this group. Today's employees expect to be able to use their mobile devices at work, making security a major concern for IT staff.

Preparing a BYOD policy is critical to protecting your network from users who want to connect their personal devices to your network. This means you need to develop an acceptable use policy, gain management support, and then communicate the policy to your end users. The policy has to describe the expectations and consequences of mobile devices usage across your organization. After you have a policy in place, you can select the appropriate software and infrastructure to design and implement.

CERTIFICATION READY
Manage mobile devices
Objective 3.2

When creating a BYOD policy, your questions usually revolve around how the mobile devices are protected, what users can and cannot access, and what happens when they leave the company. Here are a few questions to ask when developing your own BYOD acceptable use policy:

- How can you identify the BYOD devices used on your network?
- Who are the owners of the devices that are being used?
- Should you require that the entire device be encrypted?
- What type of password requirements should employees use?
- What activity will you allow with the devices?
- What happens in case the devices are lost or stolen?
- What services can employees use with the mobile device?
- Will employees only be able to use e-mail? Should e-mail access be limited to corporate e-mail accounts?
- How frequently should you audit employees' devices against your corporate policy?

A failure to establish a BYOD policy means that you allow employees to access your corporate network, with or without your knowledge. If not done securely, this access can affect your company's reputation and bottom line in case of a security breach.

Microsoft offers several methods for protecting your mobile devices. We look at the following two options in this lesson:

- Exchange ActiveSync: Exchange Server 2013 enables you to manage which mobile devices are allowed to connect to your network; and to control encryption, password and access requirements. You can also remotely wipe a device if it is lost or stolen.
- System Center Configuration Manager (SCCM) 2012: SCCM 2012 comes with an ***Exchange Server connector*** that enables you to manage your mobile devices that are synced with your Exchange Server. You can collect inventory information, perform a remote wipe of devices, quarantine or block the device, and change and manage Exchange ActiveSync mailbox policies.

Exploring Exchange Active Sync/Mobile Device Policies In Exchange Server 2013

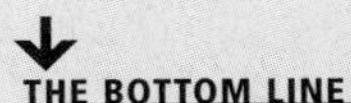

Exchange ActiveSync enables you to create mobile device policies that can increase security for your corporate network.

Exchange ActiveSync is a client synchronization protocol based on XML that enables you to connect your mobile device to your Exchange mailbox.

CERTIFICATION READY
Manage Microsoft Exchange ActiveSync in mobile devices
Objective 3.2

Exchange ActiveSync enables communications from ActiveSync–compliant mobile devices such as the Windows Phone, Apple iPhone, iPad, iPod, and Google Android phones. The features available with ActiveSync differ from device to device because it is up to the manufacturers to determine what features they want to support with the protocol. Exchange ActiveSync works over HTTP and HTTPS (see Figure 11-1), and supports offline access to messages, contacts, and calendar information.

Figure 11-1
Using Exchange ActiveSync over HTTP/HTTPS

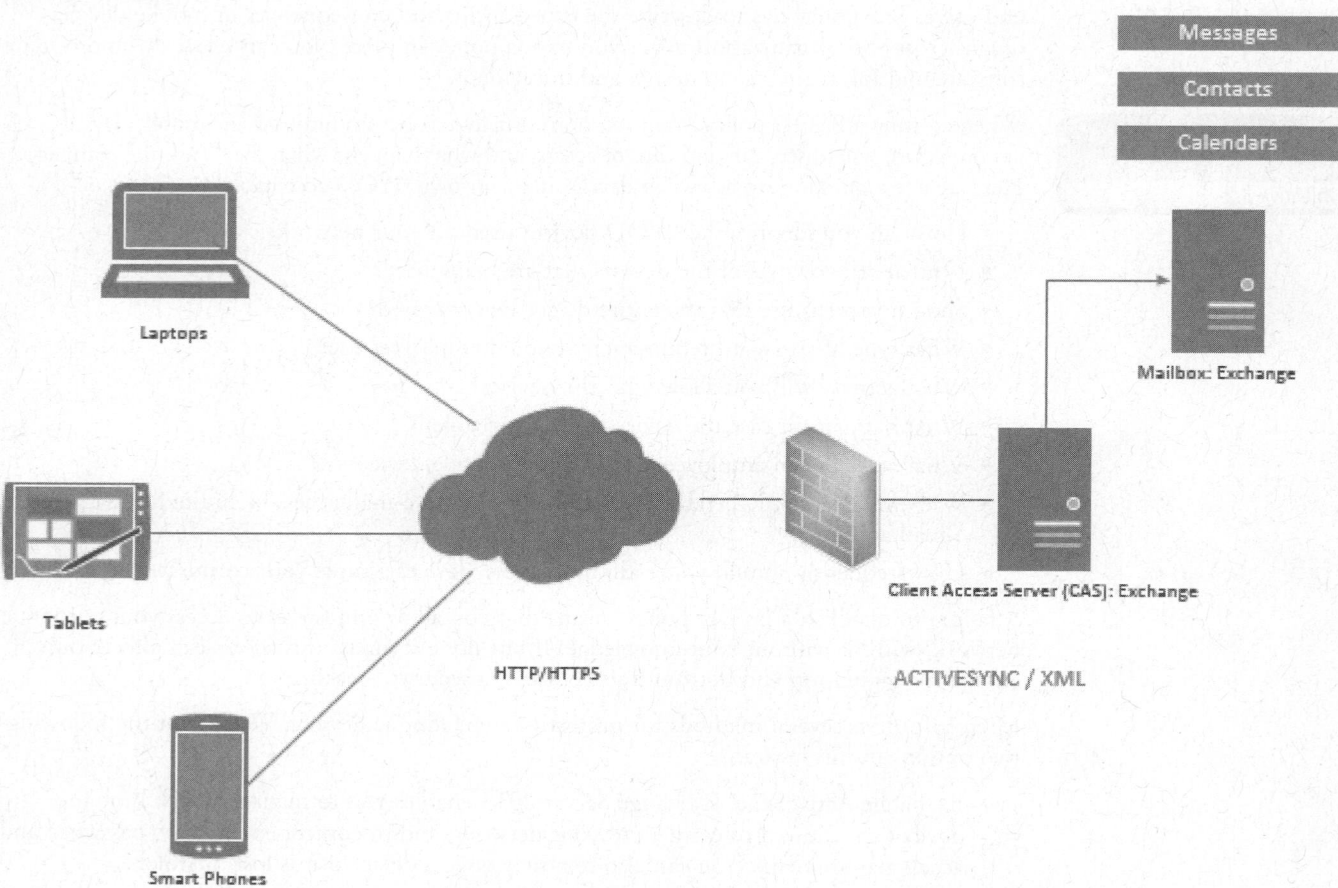

TAKE NOTE*
Exchange ActiveSync is enabled by default on Exchange Server 2013. If you have an Exchange mailbox, you can sync your mobile device with it.

Exchange ActiveSync provides you with tools to control policies and manage and secure your mobile devices. Here are just a few of the tasks you can perform with Exchange ActiveSync:

- Issue remote wipe commands in case the mobile device is lost or stolen. A ***remote wipe command*** clears all corporate and user information that is stored on the device.
- Specify the length and complexity of the password for the mobile device (4–18 character alphanumeric passwords), device locking, and number of password attempts.
- Require encryption on the mobile device and/or the devices removable storage card.
- Control which types of mobile devices/users are allowed to connect to your Exchange Server.
- Run, view, and export reports.

Exploring Mobile Policy Settings in Exchange Server 2013

Some of the built-in security features in mobile devices can be controlled from Exchange Server, so you can create security policies that are automatically sent to each device the next time the mobile device starts synchronizing. These settings can harden security on the devices by requiring stronger passwords, enabling encryption, and controlling which older devices are allowed to connect to your network.

You create Exchange ActiveSync mailbox policies to make management of mobile devices easier. These policies, which can be applied to each of your Exchange ActiveSync users, enable you to apply settings to a user's mobile device.

CERTIFICATION READY
Security policies, remote access
Objective 3.2

A new mobile device mailbox policy includes the following settings:

- **Name:** Displays the name of the mobile policy.
- **This is the default policy:** Sets the policy as the default.
- **Allow mobile devices that do not fully support these policies to synchronize:** Enables you to decide whether to allow mobile devices that do not support some or all of the selected policies.

Policies for Exchange ActiveSync:

- **Require a password:** This option enables you to configure additional password requirements, as follows:
  - o **Allow simple passwords:** Enables mobile devices to use simple passwords (e.g., 1234).
  - o **Require an alphanumeric password:** Requires lower- and uppercase letters, numbers, and symbols.
  - o **Password must include this many character sets:** Options include 1,2,3,4. Selecting 2 means you need to use at least 2 of the character sets (e.g., letters and numbers).
- **Require encryption on device:** Enables encryption on the mobile device.
- **Minimum password length:** Sets minimum length for password; specify the number in the space provided.
- **Number of sign-in failures before device is wiped:** If a user fails to sign in after the specified number of attempts, the device is wiped.
- **Require sign-in after the device has been inactive for (minutes):** Locks devices after they are idle for the number of minutes you specify, requiring users to sign in again.
- **Enforce password lifetime (days):** Specifies the number of days before the password must be changed. If you enable this feature, users are prompted to reset their password after the number of days you specify.
- **Password recycle count:** Enables you to determine the number of different passwords a user must use before they can reuse a password. You can specify from 0–50.

CREATE A MOBILE DEVICE MAILBOX POLICY

GET READY. To create a mobile device mailbox policy, perform the following steps.

1. Log in with local Administrative privileges to your computer.
2. In the Internet Explorer browser address field, type **https://<exchangeserver>/ecp** to open the Exchange administrator center (EAC). Replace *<exchangeserver>* with the actual name of your Exchange server.

TAKE NOTE*

The following exercise requires a Microsoft Exchange 2013 Server running the Mailbox and Client Access Server (CAS) roles.

3. In the Domain\user name and Password fields, type your Administrative credentials and then click **OK** to access the EAC.
4. From the menu on the left, click **mobile** and then, from the center pane, choose **mobile device mailbox policies.**
5. In the center pane, click the + symbol to create a new mobile device mailbox policy.
6. In the *Name* field, type a name for the policy (for example, **My Mobile Policy**).
7. Select **This is the default policy.**
8. Select **Require a password.**
9. Select **Require an alphanumeric password.**
10. Under the *Password must include this many character sets* section, click the drop-down box and then select **3**.
11. Select **Minimum password length** and, in the field that appears, type **6** (see Figure 11-2).

Figure 11-2

Configuring a mobile device policy

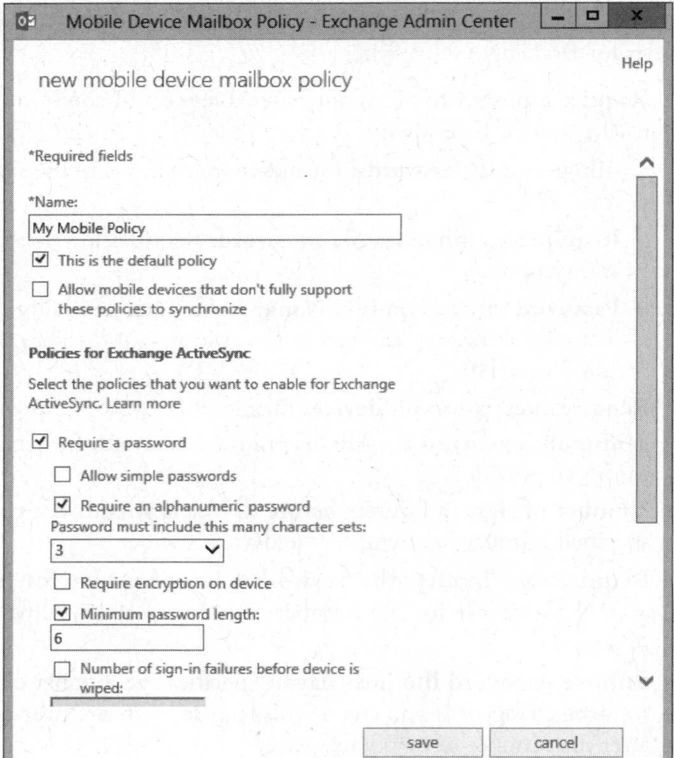

12. Select **Enforce password lifetime (days)** and, in the field that appears, type **60**.
13. Under *Password recycle count*, type **5**.
14. Click **Save**.

    The new policy appears in the middle pane.
15. Close the Exchange admin center browser window.

Having a strong mobile policy in place goes a long way toward protecting your user's mobile device, but when one of your users loses a phone or it is stolen, you need to rely on something more than just your mobile policy. In those situations, the best approach is to remotely wipe the device.

PERFORM A MOBILE DEVICE REMOTE WIPE

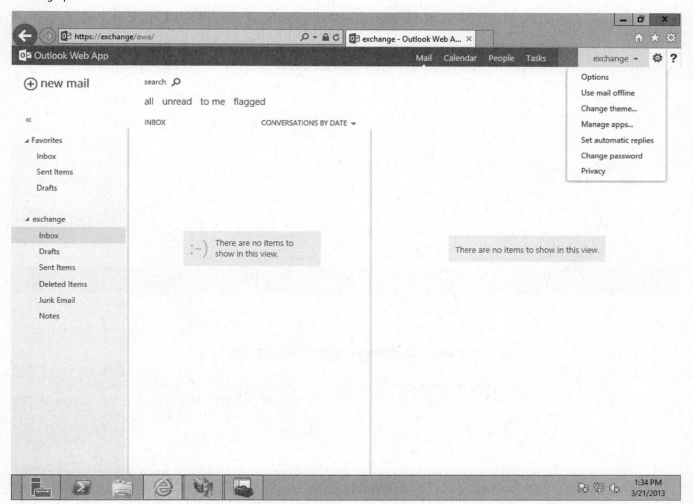

> **TAKE NOTE***
> The following exercise requires a Microsoft Exchange 2013 Server running the Mailbox and CAS roles.

GET READY. To wipe a mobile device, perform the following steps:

1. In the Internet Explorer browser address field, type your Outlook Web Access (OWA) web address: **https://<exchangeserver>/OWA**.
2. In the *Domain\user name* field and *Password* field, type your login information and then click **Sign-in**.
3. From the menu at the top, click **Exchange** and then choose **Options** (see Figure 11-3).

Figure 11-3

Selecting Options

4. From the options menu on the left, click **Phone**.
5. In the middle pane, click the **Wipe Device** button (see Figure 11-4).

   If the device is lost, the user can also remove it from the list by clicking the Delete (trashcan) icon.

Figure 11-4
Wiping a mobile device

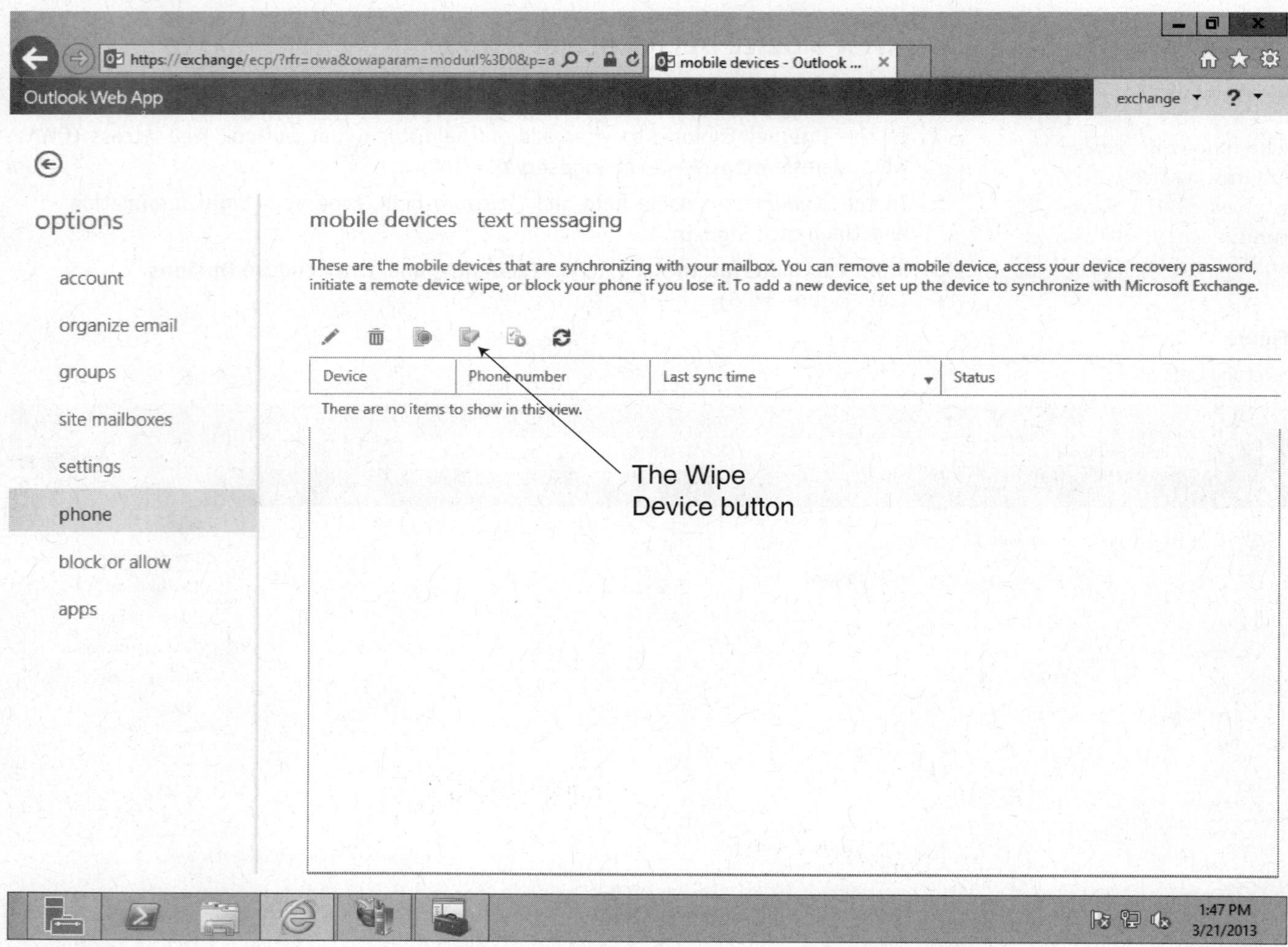

Securing Your Communications Using SSL

Secure Sockets Layer (SSL) is an encryption protocol that enables mobile devices to connect to Exchange ActiveSync over a secure encrypted link. It ensures that all data passed between the mobile devices and the server is private. A digital certificate is used to authenticate the server's identity to the mobile device.

When you set up Exchange Server 2013 to run the CAS role, a virtual directory is created for Exchange ActiveSync (see Figure 11-5). The virtual directory is used by Internet Information Services (IIS) to enable access to Exchange ActiveSync and the Outlook Web App. To manage authentication and enable the server to authenticate itself to the mobile device, an SSL certificate must be configured for the Exchange ActiveSync virtual directory.

You can obtain your SSL certificate by purchasing it from a third-party ***Certification Authority (CA)***. A CA creates and manages the distribution and revocation of certificates. An alternative approach is to use ***Active Directory Certificate Services (AD CS)*** to install your own CA. AD CS provides the certificate infrastructure and is used to create certification authorities that issue and manage certificates. Once you have obtained your certificate, you can configure SSL on your Exchange ActiveSync virtual directory.

CONFIGURE SSL ON THE EXCHANGE ACTIVESYNC VIRTUAL DIRECTORY

GET READY. To configure SSL on the Exchange ActiveSync virtual directory, perform the following steps.

1. Log in with local Administrative privileges on the server hosting the Exchange ActiveSync virtual directory.
2. Server Manager opens automatically. If it does not open, click the **Server Manager** icon on the task bar.
3. Click **Tools** > **Internet Information Services (IIS) Manager**.
4. Expand ***servername*** > **Sites** > **Exchange Back End**.
5. Click **Microsoft-Server-ActiveSync** and then double click **SSL Settings** (see Figure 11-5).

Figure 11-5

Configuring SSL

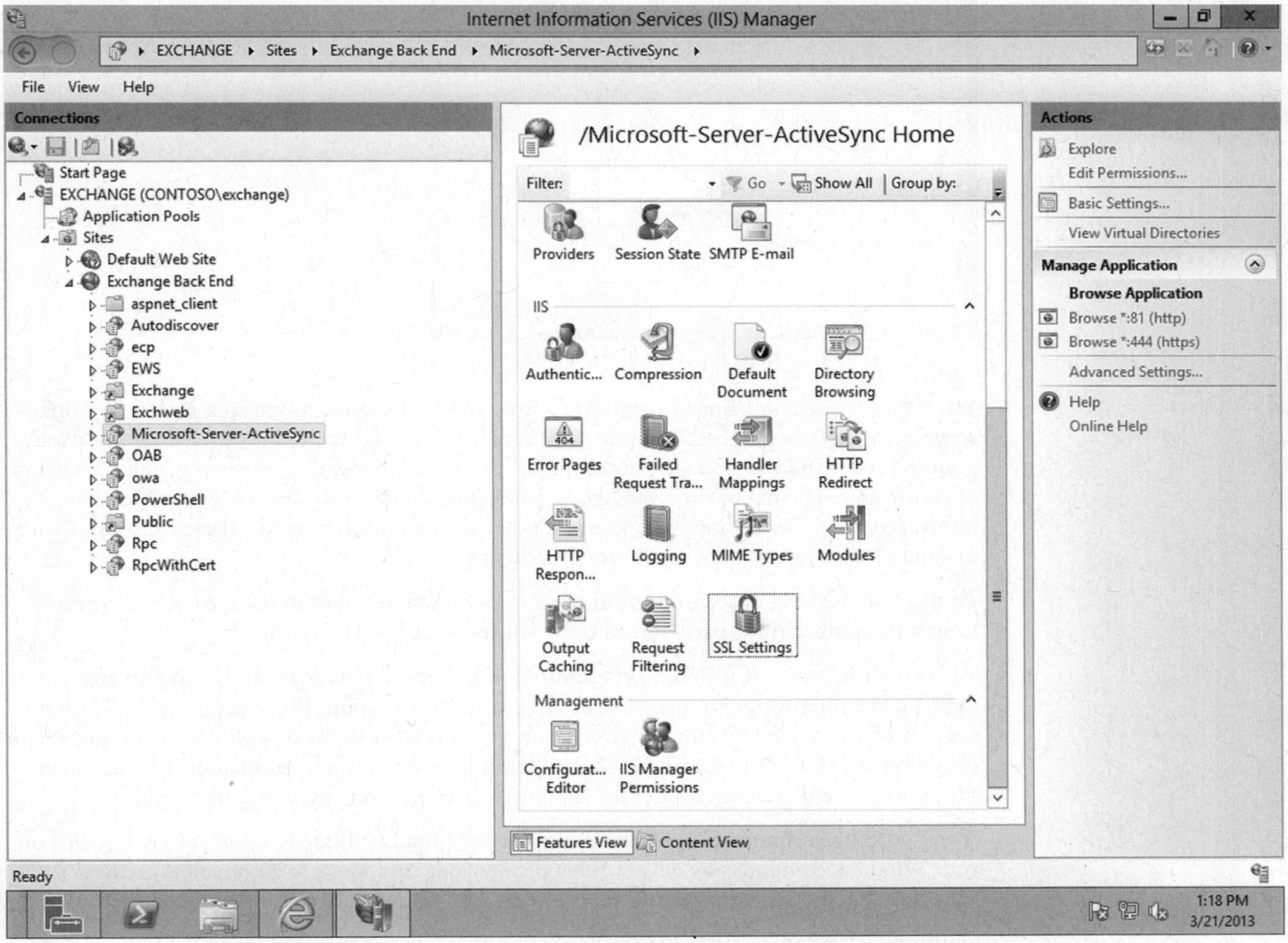

6. In the middle pane, under *SSL Settings*, confirm that *Require SSL* is selected.
7. Under *Client certificates*, select **Require**.
8. In the *Actions* pane, click **Apply** and then close the IIS Manager console.

MANAGING CLIENT AUTHENTICATION

When you install the CAS role on Exchange, you automatically install a default self-signed digital certificate. The certificate is used to authenticate that the computer is what it claims to be. The certificate also protects against someone tampering with data exchanged between the client and the server. Figure 11-6 shows the certificate created by default.

Figure 11-6

Reviewing the default self-signed certificate

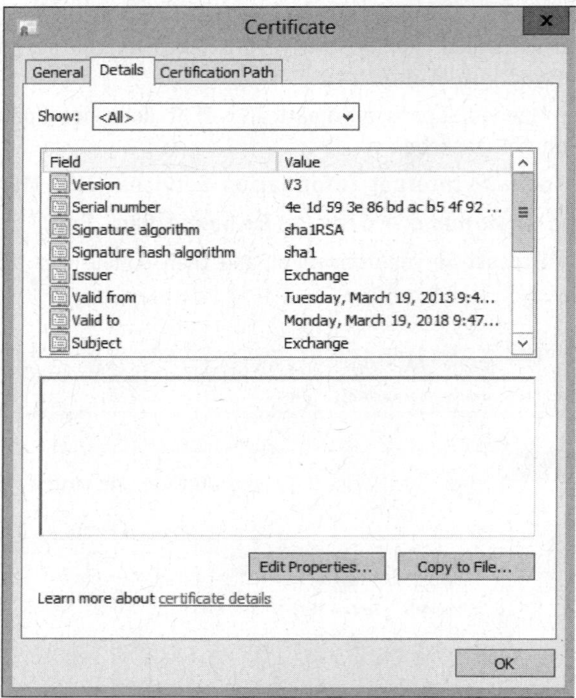

You typically use a self-signed certificate when you do not want to set up a ***public key infrastructure (PKI)*** to purchase a commercial certificate. A PKI includes the hardware, software, policies, and standards necessary to centrally administer the issuing, renewing, and revocation of certificates. The major disadvantage of self-signed digital certificates is you can exchange information only with those who know you personally. In other words, there is no third party to validate that your digital certificate is authentic.

To increase the level of security, consider configuring your server to use a trusted certificate from a recognized third-party CA or use a trusted Windows PKI CA.

You can set up your own PKI by configuring one or more CAs that can be used to create the digital certificates for computers and users in your organization. If the computers and users are part of an Active Directory environment, you can set it up so that all your computers have the company's CA chain installed. Users and computers can then automatically be assigned the appropriate digital certificates for signing documents and encrypting messages.

If you purchase a commercial certificate, the vendor's root certificate is automatically installed on your Windows computers by default. This enables your computers to automatically trust these CAs. You can also share the certificate with users who are not members of your organization.

Commercial organizations such as VeriSign and Thawte offer three types of commercial certificates:

- Class 1: These certificates are issued to individuals who have a valid e-mail address. They are designed to be used for digital signatures, access control, encryption, and noncommercial transactions in which proof of identity is not required.

- Class 2: These certificates are issued to individuals and devices. They are designed with the same features as Class 1, but for transactions in which identity is required and information in the validating database is sufficient. They are used for device authentication, messaging software, content integrity, and confidentiality encryption.
- Class 3: These certificates are used by individuals, organizations, servers, devices, and administrators for CAs. They are also used for root authorities. These certificates are designed for digital signatures, encryption, and access controls where proof of identity must be assured. They are appropriate for server authentication, messaging, software, integrity of content, and confidentiality encryption.

Exploring System Center Configuration Manager (SCCM) 2012 Mobile Device Management

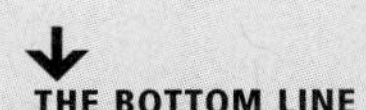

System Center Configuration Manager (SCCM) 2012 provides an Exchange connector that enables you to manage your mobile policies from a central point by pulling the mobile device details from Exchange into the SCCM database.

SCCM 2012 comes with an ***Exchange Server connector***, which enables you to manage your mobile devices that are synced with your Exchange Server. You can collect inventory information, perform remote wipe of devices, quarantine or block the devices, and change and manage Exchange ActiveSync mailbox policies. The Exchange connector establishes a connection with the Exchange Server and pulls the mobile device details into the SCCM database.

CERTIFICATION READY
Manage mobile access
Objective 3.2

SCCM service pack 1 (SP1), released in January 2013, provides the following enhancements: deployment and management of Windows 8 and Windows Server 2012; a distribution point for Windows Azure; automation of administrative tasks through Windows PowerShell support; and management of Mac OS X clients, Linux servers, and UNIX servers. Using SP1, you can deploy and update Windows 8 apps alongside your existing traditional and virtual applications. It also supports the deployment of Windows 8 USB Windows To Go drives; and supports Windows 8 folder redirection, roaming user profiles, and client-side caching features. SP1 also enables SCCM to detect 3G and 4G network connections prior to deploying software.

Two mobile device management types are available when using SCCM 2012:

- Light mobile device management
- In-depth mobile device management

Light Mobile Device Management

Using Exchange ActiveSync, you can leverage your existing Exchange device policies to handle light management of your mobile devices to perform tasks such as remote wipe and device lockdown.

This type of mobile device management works through the Exchange Server connector and uses the capabilities of ActiveSync available to Exchange Server (i.e., device policies). Because not all manufacturers incorporate all ActiveSync features, SCCM is limited to those available for managing the device.

Light mobile device management provides excellent inventory and reporting capabilities, enables you to define an organization-level ActiveSync policy; supports device wipe; and supports EAS devices including Windows Phone 7/8, iOS, Android, and Palm devices. It also supports Exchange 2010 and later installations as well as hosted Exchange environments.

When setting up light mobile device management, you need to make the following types of decisions:

- Determine whether to connect to an on-premise Exchange Server or a hosted Exchange Server.
- Determine which account to use when accessing the Exchange Server to find and manage your mobile devices. It can be the computer account of the site server or an account you specify.
- Specify when and how to find the mobile devices managed by the Exchange connector.
- Identify the policies that you want to manage with Exchange versus Configuration Manager 2012. These settings include the following:
  - General settings: Internet sharing from mobile devices, computer synchronization, and provisioning of mobile devices
  - Password settings: require passwords settings on mobile devices; password length, expiration, password history, number of failed login attempts before wiping the device, and password complexity
  - E-mail management settings: POP and IMAP e-mail, maximum time to keep e-mail and calendar entries, message formats, size limits for e-mail automatically downloaded, and e-mail attachments/size allowed
  - Security settings: Remote desktop, removable storage, camera, Bluetooth, wireless network connections, infrared, browser, storage card encryption, file encryption on the mobile device, and Systems Management Server (SMS) and Microsoft Metadirectory Services (MMS) messaging
  - Application management: Allowing or prohibiting unsigned file installation and unsigned applications
- Policy settings that you configure using the Exchange Server connector are applied to devices discovered by the connector. They appear under the Assets and Compliance > Overview > Devices > All Mobile Devices node.

In-Depth Mobile Device Management

In-depth mobile device management, handled through SCCM 2012, enables you to enroll and manage your mobile devices by installing the mobile device client.

- In-depth mobile device management requires a PKI. It establishes a trust between the device and the SMS, enables you to secure over-the-air enrollment; monitor and remediate out-of-compliance devices; inventory devices; deploy and remove applications, settings, and perform remote wipes. These additional functions are possible through the installation of the SCCM 2012 mobile device client when you enroll mobile devices. Other features of in-depth mobile device management include the following:
  - Supports Windows Phone 6.5x and WinCE
  - Increases reporting capabilities and information for mobile devices including installed apps, memory, operating system information, status, and so on
  - Supports binding the device to a specific user

CONFIGURE THE EXCHANGE SERVER CONNECTOR

GET READY. To set up an Exchange Server connector for light-device management, perform the following steps:

TAKE NOTE* The following exercise requires a Microsoft Exchange 2013 Server running the Mailbox and CAS roles and a server with SCCM 2012 installed.

1. Log in with local Administrative privileges to a Windows 8 computer with the Configuration Manager Console installed.
2. From the Windows 8 start menu type **configuration manager**, choose **Configuration Manager Console** from the *Results* list.
3. In the Administration workspace, expand the **Overview** > **Hierarchy** configuration folder.
4. Right-click **Exchange Server Connectors** and then choose **Add Exchange Server** (see Figure 11-7).

Figure 11-7

Adding an Exchange Server connector

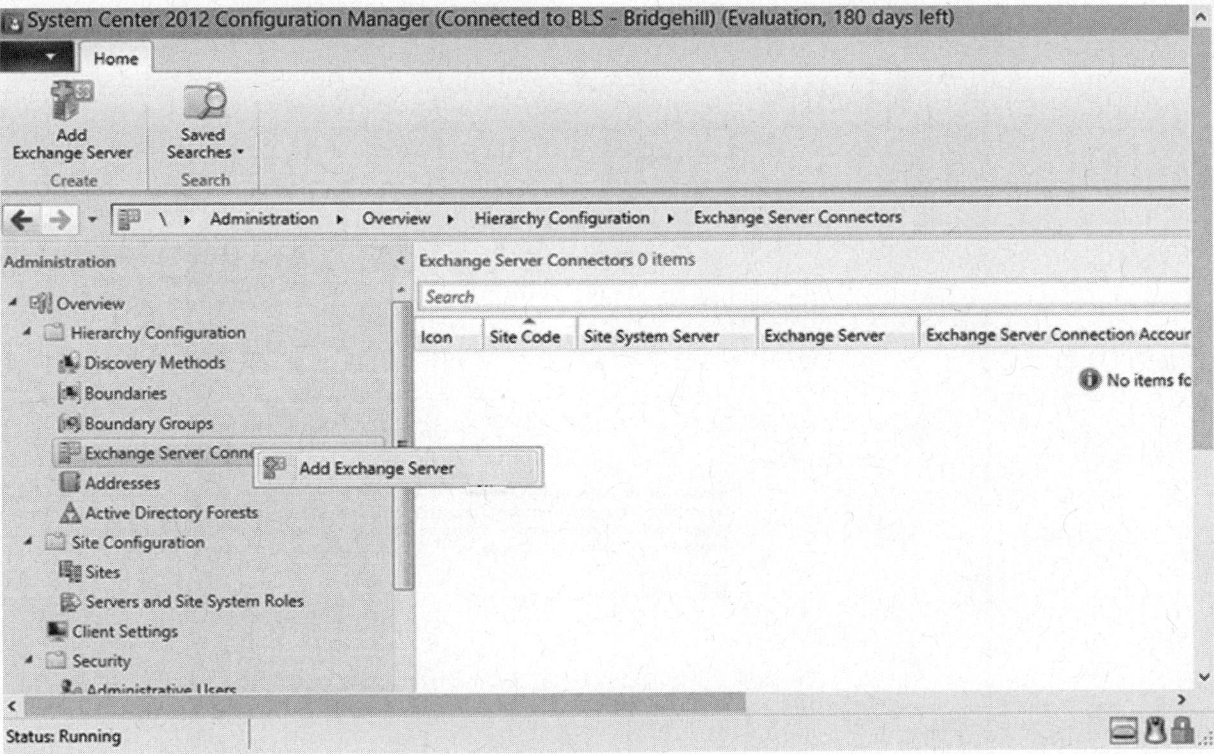

5. Under *Specify the Exchange Server environment*, select **On-premise Exchange Server**, in the *Server address (URL)* field, type the server's FQDN (for example, dc2012.contoso.com) and then click **Next**.

   If multiple Exchange Servers are running the Client Access server role, you need to select the Advanced Configuration option. It requires you to type the FQDN for each server as well as its Active Directory site location.

6. Under *Exchange Server Connection Account*, select **Use the computer account of the site server** and then click **Next**.
7. In the *Delta synchronization interval (minutes)* field, type **720** and then click **Next**.

   This setting identifies new mobile devices and limited changes for known mobile devices to twice per day.
8. On the *Configure mobile device settings* screen, review the settings that can be overridden and then click **Next**.

   These settings include *General*, *Password*, *Email Management*, *Security*, and *Applications* (see Figure 11-8). At this point, you need to decide whether Exchange or Configuration Manager 2012 should manage the policy settings. By default, Exchange will manage mobile device management.

Figure 11-8

Configuring mobile device settings using Exchange connector

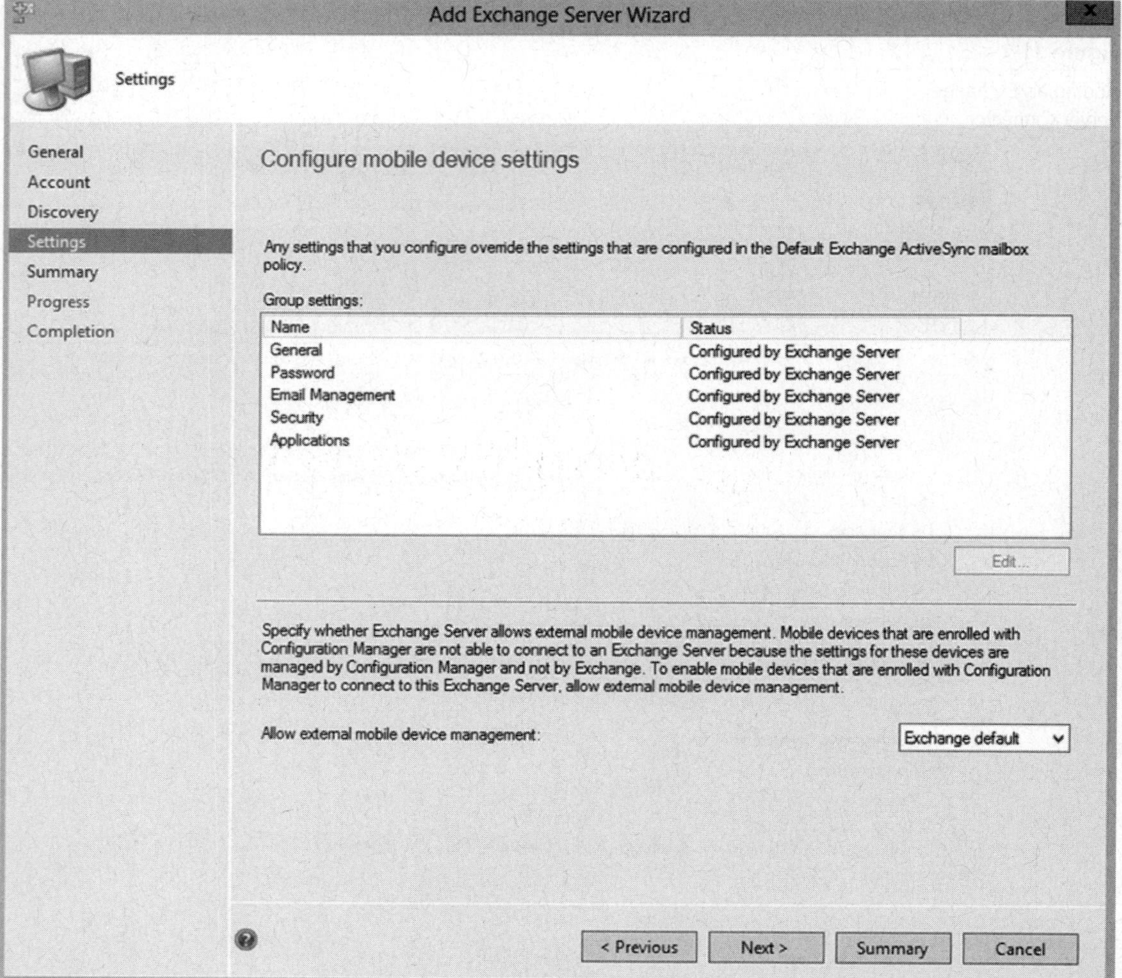

9. Under *Details*, confirm the settings and then click **Next**.
10. When the Add Exchange Server Wizard completed successfully message appears, click **Close** (see Figure 11-9).

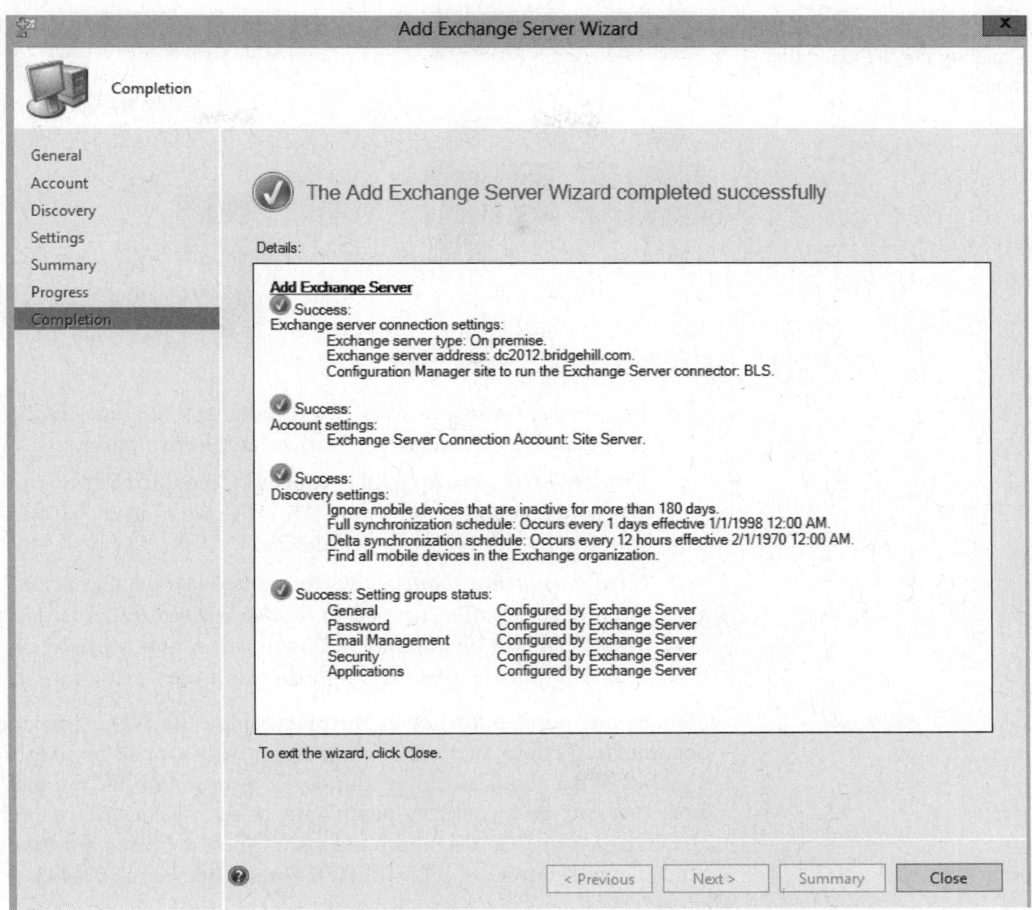

Figure 11-9

Reviewing the Exchange server wizard results

Managing Mobile Device Policies

THE BOTTOM LINE

Near field communication (NFC), secure SIMs, and the Windows 8 wallet all provide mechanisms that enable you to share information while maintaining a level of security.

CERTIFICATION READY
Manage mobile device policies
Objective 3.2

Exchanging information with other mobile devices; accessing your network securely; and storing and accessing your credit/debit card numbers, electronic cash, checks and coupons in a safe place are all important aspects to consider when managing mobile devices. Microsoft provides several technologies that are designed to make your mobile experience more enjoyable while keeping your information protected.

Using Near Field Communication (NFC)

CERTIFICATION READY
NFC
Objective 3.2

Near field communication (NFC) is a short-range wireless communication system supported natively in Windows 8. It enables NFC-capable devices that are in close proximity to each other (within 4 centimeters) to exchange information. It uses technology similar to radio frequency identification (RFID) tags and operates at 13.56 MHz, supporting data rates of 106 kbps, 212 kbps, and 424 kbps.

NFC-enabled devices can operate in the modes shown in Figure 11-10.

Figure 11-10

Exploring the NFC operating modes

- ***Peer-to-peer mode*** enables two devices to share data. For example, you can share your Wi-Fi settings or exchange your contact information.
- ***Reader/writer mode*** enables your NFC-enabled device to read NFC tags embedded in magazines, posters, and so on. An NFC tag is a passive element that stores data that can be ready by the NFS-enabled device.
- ***Card emulation mode*** allows for contactless payments and ticketing. For example, proof of registration needed to receive a travel discount can be stored on the phone; and tickets can also be purchased, downloaded, and accessed on the phone. NFC readers can help you quickly move through the gates with just a tap of your phone.

Sounds interesting, but what are the practical uses for NFC? Imagine being able to share URLs, documents, pictures, or contact information with a friend by simply touching your phones together. What about touching your device against an NFC tag that provides information about a product you are considering purchasing, using your device to purchase tickets to a movie or buy groceries at your local neighborhood store? These are just a few examples of how Microsoft envisions the integration of NFC with Windows 8 (see Figure 11-11).

Figure 11-11

Reviewing examples of NFC technology points

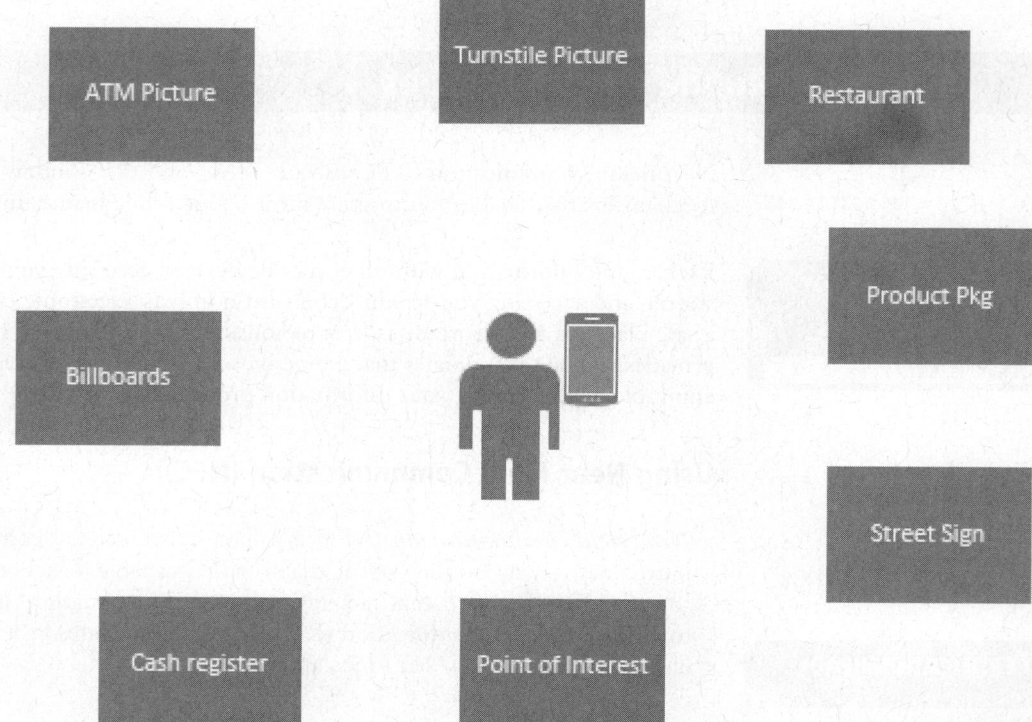

Microsoft's implementation of NFC has been coined ***Tap and Do***, which is described as a gesture that represents an interaction between two people that triggers an exchange of information between their devices (phones, tablets, laptops). The *Windows 8 Near Field Proximity Implementation Specification* whitepaper, located on Microsoft's website, provides an excellent review of their use cases:

- Tap and Setup: Set up peripheral wireless devices.
- Tap and Reconnect: Reconnect with previous paired devices.
- Tap and Use: Connect an app running on your phone with an app running on the other person's phone.
- Tap and Launch: Invite another person to start an app that you are running.
- Tap and Acquire: Invite other users to obtain an app that you are running.
- Tap and Send: Send content on your device to the other person's device.
- Tap and Receive: Receive content from another device or poster.

MORE INFORMATION

For a more detailed look at Microsoft's implementation of NFC, go to Microsoft's website and search for the whitepaper titled, *Windows 8 Near Field Proximity Implementation Specification*.

Using Secure SIMs

A ***subscriber identity module (SIM)*** is an integrated circuit on a small silicon chip. The SIM is embedded into a removable SIM card, which is used to identify and authenticate the user on mobile devices.

CERTIFICATION READY
Secure SIM
Objective 3.2

The SIM card contains a Mobile Subscriber Integrated Services Digital Network Number (MSISDN) and an International Mobile Subscriber Identity Number (IMSI). The MSISDN is your telephone number, and the IMSI is a unique identifier that the cell phone provider uses to identify you. You can also store contact information in your SIM, which enables you to move the information to another phone.

A secure SIM is designed to ensure that people cannot eavesdrop on your telephone calls and that smart devices can access a network securely. It exchanges information with the server on the network you are trying to connect to, exchanges key data, and provides access only if the server identifies and accepts your request. A personal identification number (PIN) is used to authenticate you. The service itself works independently of the operating system.

Using the Windows Phone 8 Wallet

A Windows Phone 8 wallet combines the features of NFC and a wallet feature that enables you to quickly access your personal financial data.

A ***Windows Phone 8 wallet*** is software that contains information about your payment methods for purchases (credit/debit card numbers, boarding passes, electronic cash, digital IDs, electronic checks, and coupons). You can think of it as a digital replacement for all those items that you usually store in a purse, put in a wallet, or carry around in your pocket. Although other vendors have created similar digital wallets, Microsoft has embedded a secure payment element into the SIM card rather than the phone. By not integrating with the device itself, you can move your "digital wallet" to a new phone when the time comes.

Using the digital wallet on your Windows 8 device, you can view your fast cards (used for NFC transactions), view cards in your wallet, see any coupons you've collected, and keep track of your card balances and transactions.

TAKE NOTE*

Not all Windows 8 phones support NFC transactions. To determine whether your phone does, go to your wallet settings. Click More and then click Settings + PIN. If your phone supports NFC transactions, you see the option here to turn it on.

To protect access to your wallet, you should set up a wallet PIN, which protects you against unwanted NFC payments and purchases from the Windows Store.

MORE INFORMATION

You can learn more about the Windows Phone 8 wallet by visiting the Microsoft website and searching for *Windows Phone 8 wallet.*

SET UP A WINDOWS PHONE 8 WALLET PIN

GET READY. To set up a wallet PIN to protect access to your Windows 8 Phone wallet, perform the following steps.

TAKE NOTE*

You need Windows Phone 8 to complete the following activity.

1. Turn on your phone and navigate to the App list.
2. Click **Wallet.**
3. Click **More** and then click **Settings + PIN.**
4. Turn on the **Wallet PIN** switch.
5. Type and confirm your PIN (at least four digits) and then click **Done.**
6. To require the PIN for purchases in the Windows Store, select the **Use Wallet PIN to protect music, app, and in-app purchases** check box.

Resolving Mobility Issues

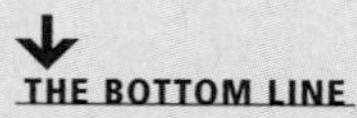

THE BOTTOM LINE

To successfully resolve mobility issues, you need to be familiar with the technology used and have a systematic approach to analyze and determine exactly what is wrong. It requires you to isolate the problem device(s), confirm basic connectivity, evaluate mobile device policies, and determine whether existing infrastructure devices (firewalls, routers) are potential sources of mobility problems.

CERTIFICATION READY
Resolve mobility issues
Objective 3.2

The process for resolving mobility issues depends upon what method you use to deploy and secure them. Here are a few things to consider when resolving mobility issues:

- Isolate it to the client or the server. If a single mobile device is experiencing the problem, the problem points to the device. If multiple devices are having problems, the server is most likely the culprit.
- Review the version of ActiveSync and the model of the mobile device. The features available with ActiveSync differ from device to device because it is up to manufacturers to determine what features they want to support with the protocol. It can be changed from one version of the operating system to another.
- Confirm basic connectivity and review the settings on the mobile device to make sure the server name and account are correct for the device.

- Log in to the EAC and select Mobile > Mobile Device Access to see whether the mobile device shows up. If you do not see the device, there is a connectivity problem.
- Review device policies to see whether any of them are blocking the device. If they are, you can create an exemption for the device, assign a less-restrictive policy, or adjust the policy to no longer block the device. You can also tell the user that current security policies prohibit the use of the device.
- Review device error messages on the mobile device. These errors can provide insight about where the problem may be located (client, server, or connections between the two).
- Review authentication settings. If SSL is configured, review the certificate and make sure it has been approved by a trusted CA.
- Review your personal and perimeter firewall rules and settings to make sure the traffic is not being blocked.

MORE INFORMATION

For additional troubleshooting tips when working with Microsoft Exchange ActiveSync, search Microsoft's website for *Troubleshooting Exchange ActiveSync*.

There are a variety of ways mobile clients can connect to an Exchange Server. Problems with connectivity can be the firewall (blocked ports), a corrupted DNS server, certificate issues, or proxy misconfiguration. To help determine where the problem is, you can use the Microsoft Remote Connectivity Analyzer website. This is a public website, outside of your public firewall, that enables you to run simulated connections using a test account from your network. The test simulates the client access method you choose. Tools on this site break down the progress and identify exactly where the communication fails. You can also access links to additional resources to help you resolve the problem.

SKILL SUMMARY

IN THIS LESSON, YOU LEARNED:

- It is important to establish a BYOD policy for your organization to support your mobile users and protect your network from security risks. This process involves creating an acceptable use policy, gaining management support, and communicating the policy to your end users.
- Exchange ActiveSync is a client synchronization protocol based on XML that helps you connect mobile devices to Exchange mailboxes.
- Exchange ActiveSync features vary from device to device, depending on which features the manufacturer wants to support with the protocol.
- When setting up Exchange Server, ActiveSync is enabled by default. If you have a mailbox set up, you can automatically sync your mobile device with it.
- Remote wipe can be used when a mobile device is lost or stolen.
- You can configure policies that control the types of mobile devices that can connect to the network, the complexity of the passwords required, and the number of password attempts allowed.
- Configuring a new mobile device mailbox policy involves setting password parameters (complexity, minimum length, password lifetime, and password recycle counts), enabling encryption on the mobile devices, and determining the number of sign-in failures allowed.

- Employees who use mobile devices can perform a remote wipe of their device by logging in to OWA.
- Commercial organizations such as VeriSign and Thawte offer three types of commercial certificates: Class 1 certificates are issued to individuals with a valid e-mail address; Class 2 certificates are issued to individuals and devices; and Class 3 certificates are issued to individuals, organizations, servers, devices, and administrators for CAs.
- You can use SCCM 2012 to pull mobile device policies and details into the SCCM database. You can then maintain a single management point for mobile policies across your entire organization while collecting inventory on mobile device assets, having software information, and running compliance reports.
- There are two mobile device management types available within SCCM 2012: light mobile device management and in-depth mobile device management. Light mobile device management works through Exchange Server connector and uses ActiveSync. In-depth mobile device management requires a PKI.
- NFC is a short-range wireless communication system natively supported in Windows 8 that operates in peer-to-peer mode, reader/writer mode, and card emulation mode.
- Windows Phone 8 supports secure SIMs that enable you to use the card emulation mode to conduct transactions such as purchasing tickets for a movie or buying groceries.
- Microsoft's implementation of NFC is coined Tap and Do. This is a gesture that represents an interaction between two people that triggers an exchange of information.
- Windows Phone 8 wallet is software that contains information about your payment methods for purchases (credit/debit card numbers, boarding passes, electronic cash, digital IDs, electronic checks, and coupons). The digital wallet included with Windows 8 can use a secure SIM.
- There are several ways to troubleshoot problems with mobile device connectivity. Some of the approaches include isolating client/server issues, reviewing versions of ActiveSync, confirming basic connectivity, using the EAC, reviewing device and firewall policies, reviewing error messages on the mobile device, and checking authentication settings.

Knowledge Assessment

Multiple Choice

Select the correct answer for each of the following questions.

1. Which of the following is *not* a question you would ask when developing a BYOD policy?
   - **a.** Who are the owners of mobile devices?
   - **b.** What services can mobile users access and use?
   - **c.** What happens if a mobile device is stolen?
   - **d.** What devices do an employee's family members use at home?
2. Which of the following is a client synchronization protocol based on XML that enables you to connect your mobile device to your Exchange mailbox?
   - **a.** HTML
   - **b.** HTTPS

c. Exchange Server connector protocol
d. Exchange ActiveSync

3. A Class 2 commercial certificate can be issued to which of the following?
   a. Individuals only
   b. Individuals and devices
   c. Individuals, organizations, servers, devices, and administrators
   d. Individuals, organizations, servers, and devices

4. Which of the following components is used to establish a connection with the Exchange Server and pull the mobile device details into SCCM 2012?
   a. Exchange Server connector
   b. Device Manager
   c. XML
   d. Exchange ActiveSync Server connector

5. Which of the following types of mobile device management works through the Exchange Server connector using the capabilities of ActiveSync and does not require a PKI?
   a. In-depth mobile device management
   b. Light mobile device management
   c. EAC device management
   d. Soft mobile device management

6. Which of the following is a short-range wireless communication system that is natively supported in Windows 8?
   a. RFID
   b. WPA
   c. WEP
   d. NFC

7. Which of the following NFC modes is used for contactless payments and ticketing?
   a. Peer-to-peer mode
   b. Card emulation mode
   c. Reader/writer mode
   d. Contactless payment mode

8. Which of the following is a unique identifier used by the cell phone provider to identify you?
   a. SIMID
   b. MSISDN
   c. IMSI
   d. SIMID

9. A digital wallet contains which of the following elements used for NFC transactions?
   a. Emulated card system
   b. Fast cards
   c. Quick cards
   d. Peer-to-peer cards

10. Windows 8 is designed to support which of the following elements designed to keep people from eavesdropping on your telephone calls and to make sure that smart devices can access a network securely?
    a. SIM
    b. Secure SIM
    c. MSISDN
    d. IMSI

Best Answer

Choose the letter that corresponds to the best answer. More than one answer choice may achieve the goal. Select the BEST answer.

1. Which of the following tools is used to manage your mobile device policy as well as deploy and inventory software installed on your mobile devices?
   a. Exchange Server with ActiveSync
   b. WSUS/Group Policy
   c. SCCM 2012 with Exchange Server connector
   d. Group Policy

2. Which of the following types of certificates provide the best way to identify users on your network while still enabling you to identify these same entities to others outside of your organization?
   a. Self-signed certificates
   b. Class 1 commercial certificates
   c. Class 2 commercial certificates
   d. Class 3 commercial certificates

3. Which of the following is the most important component for managing mobile device polices within your organization?
   a. BYOD (Acceptable Use Policy)
   b. SCCM 2012
   c. Exchange Server 2013 with ActiveSync
   d. IT support

4. Which of the following are Exchange ActiveSync policies that can be used to protect your remote device? (Select all that apply.)
   a. Require a password
   b. Require encryption on the device
   c. Enforce password lifetime
   d. Number of sign-in failures before device is wiped

5. Which of the following options provides the most efficient way for users to wipe their mobile devices when they know for sure they were stolen?
   a. Submit the request for their admin to wipe the device.
   b. Call their admin and ask him or her to wipe the device.
   c. Wait for the person who stole it to attempt to log in, which wipes the device based on existing mobile policies.
   d. Use the OWA web address to connect and wipe their mobile device.

Matching and Identification

1. Match the following terms with the related description or usage.
   ________ **a)** BYOD
   ________ **b)** Card emulation mode
   ________ **c)** Digital wallet
   ________ **d)** Exchange ActiveSync
   ________ **e)** Exchange Server connector
   ________ **f)** NFC
   ________ **g)** In-depth mobile device management
   ________ **h)** Light mobile device management

_______ i) SIM
_______ j) Tap and Do

1. Requires a PKI; enables you to secure over-the-air enrollment; monitor and remediate out-of-compliant devices; inventory devices; and deploy applications.
2. Software that contains information about your payment methods for purchases.
3. A client synchronization protocol based on XML.
4. A mobile device management type that works through the Exchange Server connector and uses the capabilities of ActiveSync available on the Exchange Server.
5. An integrated circuit on a small silicon chip that contains MSISDN and IMSI information.
6. Establishes a connection with the Exchange Server and pulls the mobile device details into the SCCM database.
7. A short-range wireless communication system supported natively in Windows 8.
8. Describes a gesture that represents an interaction between two people that triggers an exchange of information.
9. Enables contactless payments and ticketing.
10. Employees who bring their own devices to the workplace and expect to use and connect them to access corporate resources.

Build a List

1. Specify the correct order of the steps that must be completed to configure the Exchange ActiveSync virtual directory for SSL.
   _______ Confirm that *Require SSL* is selected.
   _______ Select **Require**.
   _______ Double-click **SSL Settings**.
   _______ Click the Microsoft Server-ActiveSync virtual directory.

2. Specify the correct order of the steps that must be completed to remotely wipe a mobile device.
   _______ Click the **Wipe Device** button.
   _______ From the menu at the top, click **Exchange** and then choose **Options**.
   _______ Type your login information and click **Sign-in**.
   _______ From the menu on the left, click **Phone**.
   _______ Open Internet Explorer and type your OWA web address.

3. Specify the correct order of the steps that must be completed to set up a Wallet PIN in Windows 8.
   _______ Click the **Use Wallet PIN** to protect music, app, and in-app purchase options.
   _______ Type and confirm your PIN and then click **Done**.
   _______ Turn on the **Wallet PIN** switch.
   _______ Click **More** and then click **Settings + PIN**.
   _______ Click **Wallet**.
   _______ Turn on your phone and navigate to the App list.

Choose an Option

1. Which mode enables you to share your Wi-Fi settings with another user?

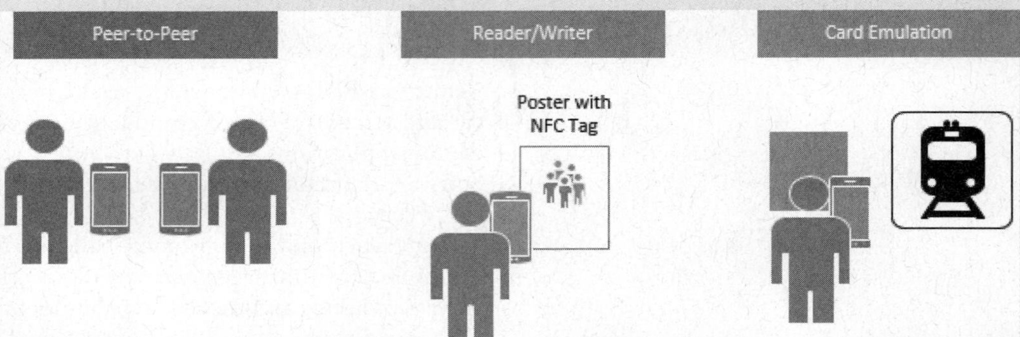

■ Business Case Scenarios

Scenario 11-1: Syncing your Mobile Users

Many of your users are bringing their smartphones and tablets to work. Once at work, they ask that you provide the wireless access key to gain access. You want to allow your Exchange Admins to continue to manage mailbox issues while transitioning the management of mobile devices and their associated policies to another small group within your IT department. Is this possible? If so, how should you approach it?

Scenario 11-2: Configuring Digital Certificates/Authentication

You set up Exchange Server 2013 on your network, which created a virtual directory. You want to make sure it is as secure as possible, so you decide to use the self-signed digital certificate created during the installation process. You make sure this certificate is trusted by all your internal users and computers. If you know you need to share the certificate with users who are not members of your organization, what should you do?

Designing a Recovery Solution

LESSON 12

70-688 EXAM OBJECTIVE

Objective 3.3 – Design a recovery solution. This objective may include but is not limited to the following design considerations: PC refresh/reset; Windows 7 file recovery; recovery drive; system Restore; user files including local files, SkyDrive, and File History; user profile settings; application settings.

Lesson Heading	Exam Objective
Designing a Recovery Solution	
Using PC Refresh and PC Reset	PC Refresh/PC Reset
Using PC Refresh	
Using PC Reset	
Scheduling a Windows 7 File Recovery	Windows 7 file recovery
Creating a Windows 8 File Recovery Drive	Recovery drive
Performing a System Restore	System restore
Using File History to Recover User Files/Local Files	User files including local files, SkyDrive, and File History
Understanding File History	
Using File History to Restore Files	
Exploring Third-Party Tools/Cloud Backup	
Recovering User Profile Settings	User profile settings
Recovering Application Settings	Application settings
Using recimg.exe	

KEY TERMS

File History
PC Refresh
PC Reset
recimg.exe
restore points
traditional desktop applications
user profiles
Windows 7 File Recovery
Windows 8 File Recovery drive
Windows 8 System Restore

Designing a Recovery Solution

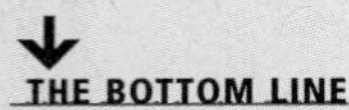

THE BOTTOM LINE

Windows 8 provides you with several ways to protect and recover your information. Some are designed to protect your user files; others are designed to incorporate applications and user settings.

"It will never happen to me!" How many times have you heard that statement?

In 1956, IBM released the 305 Random Access Method of Accounting and Control (RAMAC) computer, which was the first computer to use a hard drive. The drive had a capacity of 4.4 MB and sold for approximately $35,000. In 2012, you can purchase a 3 TB drive for about $250. As the physical size of drives continues to get smaller and their capacity grows larger, users are eagerly filling them with both personal and business data.

This data can be accidentally deleted or damaged by a malicious program or virus, or the drive can cease to function at any time. As a network administrator, it is critical that you have a recovery solution in place to protect your users' data. In this lesson, you explore several options that Windows 8 provides for protecting your users' critical information. Some options are designed to protect the users' files only; others provide a more robust approach to incorporate applications, user settings, and more.

Using PC Refresh and PC Reset

THE BOTTOM LINE

PC Refresh, PC Reset, and recimg.exe provide ways to recover your system when it is no longer functioning normally.

CERTIFICATION READY
PC Refresh/Reset
Objective 3.3

When a Windows 8 computer no longer functions normally, you must return it to a known good state. Windows 8 provides three options that can help recover the computer:

- PC Reset: Removes everything and reinstalls Windows.
- PC Refresh: Refreshes your PC without affecting your files.
- recimg.exe: Creates an image that can include traditional desktop applications. Traditional desktop applications are those installed from a website or installed from a CD/DVD.

Using PC Reset

A ***PC Reset*** is used when you want to return the computer back to its original state when it was purchased or when you first set it up. It removes all your personal data, applications (traditional and Windows Store apps), and custom settings.

A PC Reset works well when you are giving the computer to someone else or you want to send it to a computer recycler.

PERFORM A PC RESET

GET READY. To perform a PC Reset on Windows 8, log in with local Administrative privileges and then perform the following steps:

WARNING The following exercise removes everything on the computer.

1. Insert your Windows 8 installation media.
2. Press the **Windows logo key + w** and then type **Remove**.
3. From *Results*, choose **Remove everything and reinstall Windows**.

4. On the *Reset your* PC screen, click **Next**.
5. Click **Just remove my files** (see Figure 12-1).

   This process formats the drive; if the drive contains sensitive information, click **Fully clean the drive**. It writes random patterns to each sector on the drive, adding an additional level of protection.

Figure 12-1

Removing files

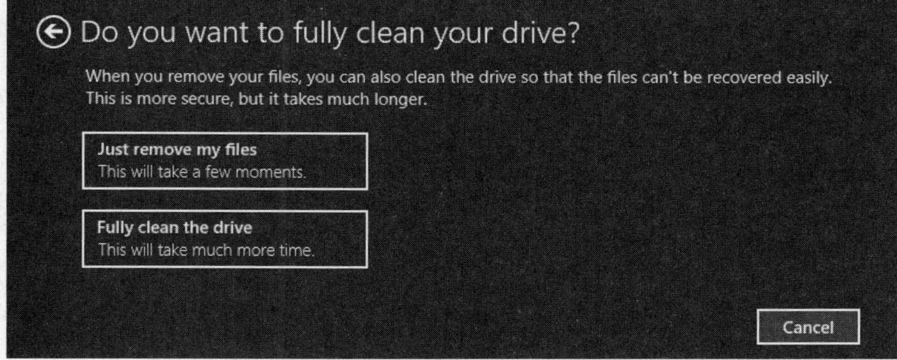

6. On the *Ready to reset your PC* screen, read the information and click **Reset**.

   The computer restarts.
7. Read and select **I accept the license terms for using Windows** and then click **Accept**.
8. On the *Personalize* screen, drag the slider to choose a color scheme, type a name for your PC, and then click **Next**.
9. Click **Use express settings**.
10. On the *Sign in to your PC* screen, type the e-mail address to use for your Microsoft account in the field provided and then click **Next**.
11. Type the password for your Microsoft account and click **Next**.
12. On the *Add security info* screen, type a phone number and an alternate e-mail address and then click **Next**.

    Your account is now created on the Windows 8 computer. When the reset finishes, you are automatically logged in and taken to the Windows 8 Start menu.

Using PC Refresh

A ***PC Refresh*** is a little less intrusive than a PC Reset. It enables you to keep your personal data, Windows Store apps, and basic settings: drive letter assignments (mapped drives), personalization settings, BitLocker or BitLocker To Go settings, and wireless network settings.

A PC Refresh does not preserve your PC settings, display settings, Windows firewall settings, or ***traditional desktop applications*** that were installed from a disc or a website. In the case of traditional desktop applications, an HTML file is placed on your desktop to assist you with reinstalling those apps after the refresh is complete.

PERFORM A PC REFRESH

WARNING A PC Refresh removes any traditional applications installed from a disc or website. You must reinstall them after the refresh has completed.

GET READY. To perform a PC Refresh, log in with local Administrative privileges and then perform the following steps:

1. Insert your Windows 8 installation media.
2. Press the **Windows logo key + w** and then type **Refresh**.

3. From *Results*, choose **Refresh your PC**.
4. On the *Refresh your PC* screen, click **Next**.
5. Click **Refresh**.

   The computer restarts.
6. When the *Windows 8 lock* screen appears, press the **space bar** and type your password to log in.
7. When asked, *Do you want to turn on sharing between PCs and connect to devices on this network?*, click **Yes, turn on sharing and connect to devices.**

   Your system has now been refreshed and should be operating normally.

If your Windows 8 computer has traditional applications that were installed from a disc or from other websites, they are removed from your computer during a PC Refresh. Windows puts a link to a list of the removed applications on your desktop. If you click the link, you see a list of the applications removed (see Figure 12-2). Clicking the application's name directs you to the manufacturer's website from which you can download and reinstall it.

Figure 12-2

Reviewing removed apps after refreshing your PC

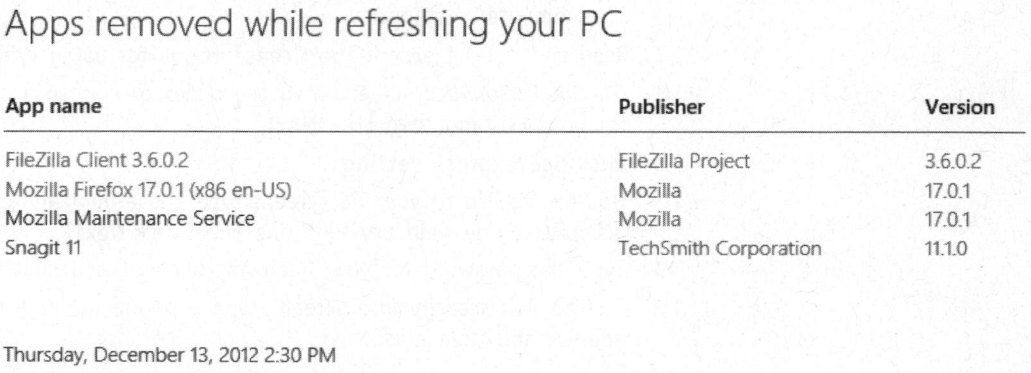

Apps removed while refreshing your PC

App name	Publisher	Version
FileZilla Client 3.6.0.2	FileZilla Project	3.6.0.2
Mozilla Firefox 17.0.1 (x86 en-US)	Mozilla	17.0.1
Mozilla Maintenance Service	Mozilla	17.0.1
Snagit 11	TechSmith Corporation	11.1.0

Thursday, December 13, 2012 2:30 PM

■ Scheduling a Windows 7 File Recovery

Windows 7 File Recovery was designed to protect your computer in the event of a system failure by storing your data in another medium (hard drive, network folder, or CD/DVD). It can also back up a system image of your computer, including applications.

Windows 7 File Recovery, previously named Windows Backup and Restore, is available in Windows 8. Because this feature has been superseded in favor of the new File History feature (discussed later), Microsoft does not recommend using both at the same time. File History has been designed to check for an existing Windows Backup schedule. If one exists, it disables itself. To use the File History feature, delete your Windows Backup schedule if one has been enabled.

CERTIFICATION READY
Windows 7 file recovery
Objective 3.3

File History is designed to only back up your personal files. If you need to back up your applications and system files, consider using either PC Reset or PC Refresh, discussed earlier. If these tools do not meet your needs for managing your system and application files, the Windows 7 File Recovery tool can be used in Windows 8 as an alternative to a third-party backup program.

In the exercise that follows, you learn how to use the Windows 7 File Recovery feature to make a full backup of your system, including a system image.

SCHEDULE A WINDOWS 8 BACKUP TO INCLUDE YOUR SYSTEM IMAGE

GET READY. To schedule a full Windows 8 backup to an external drive, log in with local Administrative privileges and then perform the following steps:

1. Connect your external drive. This drive must have enough capacity to store your data files and a system image.
2. Press the **Windows logo key** + w and then type **File Recovery**.
3. From *Results*, click **Windows 7 File Recovery**.
4. Click **Set up backup.**
5. In the *Select where you want to save your backup* screen, click your external drive, as shown in Figure 12-3.

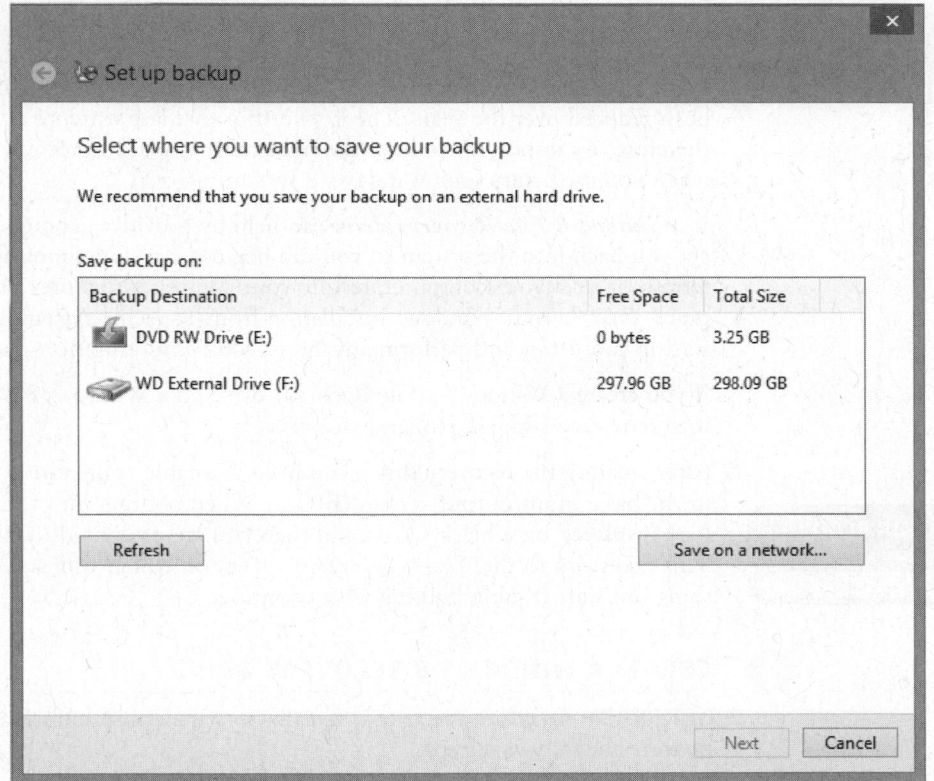

Figure 12-3

Setting a location for the backup

6. Click **Next.**
7. Select **Let Windows choose (recommended)** and click **Next.**

   Windows backs up data files saved in libraries, on the desktop, and in default Windows folders. It also creates a system image (only one per computer can be kept in the backup location), which can be used to restore your computer in case of failure.

   You can also select *Let me choose to select specific libraries and folders* and whether you want to include a system image as part of your backup.
8. Review the Backup Summary and then click **Change schedule.**

9. Select **Run backup on a schedule (recommended)** and click **OK** to accept the default settings.

   Your backup now runs every Sunday at 7:00 PM.

10. Click **Turn off schedule** to complete this exercise, ensuring that the backup does not attempt to run later.

You may need to create a system repair disk to restore a system image if you do not have your Windows 8 installation media. You can create this disk from within the Windows 7 File Recovery Control Panel by clicking *Create a system image*.

■ Creating a Windows 8 File Recovery Drive

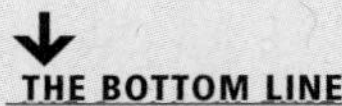

THE BOTTOM LINE

If your system fails to boot and you do not have access to the Windows 8 installation media, you can create a recovery drive that includes a boot environment and troubleshooting tools to regain access to your computer.

With improvements in operating system design, the chances of your system crashing have been reduced over the years. The keyword in that last sentence is *reduced*, not eliminated; therefore, it's important to have the right tools in place to recover from a system failure even when you can't start your Windows 8 system.

A ***Windows 8 File Recovery drive*** can help by providing enough of a boot environment to get you back into the system so you can begin the troubleshooting process It can be used to refresh or reset your computer, restore your computer to a previously created system restore point, recover your Windows installation from a specific system image file, automatically fix startup problems, and perform advanced troubleshooting from the command prompt.

If you create a Windows 8 File Recovery drive on a Windows 8 32-bit system, you cannot use it to repair a 64-bit system, and vice versa.

CERTIFICATION READY
Recovery drive
Objective 3.3

After creating the recovery drive, you need to enable your system to boot from a USB device in the basic input/output system (BIOS). When booting into the drive, you see the Windows logo displayed on a black screen and then you are prompted to choose your keyboard layout. This takes you to the *Choose an option* screen, on which you can access the troubleshooting tools and start troubleshooting your computer.

CREATE A WINDOWS 8 RECOVERY DRIVE

GET READY. To create a recovery drive, log in with local Administrative privileges and then perform the following steps:

1. Connect a USB drive to your computer. The drive must hold at least 256 MB and all data on the drive deleted.
2. Press the **Windows logo key + w** and then type **Create recovery drive**.
3. From *Results*, click **Create a Recovery Drive**.
4. Select **Yes** if prompted to *Allow the Recovery Media Center to make changes to the computer*.
5. Click **Next**. Windows 8 searches and displays the available drives.
6. Click **Next** to use the drive you inserted.
7. After reviewing the message that *Everything on the drive will be deleted*, click **Create**.
8. Click **Finish**.

Performing a System Restore

THE BOTTOM LINE

Windows 8 System Restore is another recovery option for your computer; it backs up your settings and registry, but does not back up your personal data.

Windows 8 System Restore saves information about your drivers, registry settings, programs, and system files in the form of ***restore points*** for drives with system protection turned on. You can then use the restore points to return these items to an earlier state without affecting your personal files. You should create restore points prior to performing any major system event such as the installation of a program or a new device driver.

CERTIFICATION READY
System restore
Objective 3.3

By default, Windows 8 automatically creates restore points every 7 days if you have not created one during that time period. You can also create restore points manually any time you want.

TAKE NOTE*

You can also access System Restore via the Control Panel > System and Security > System Protection.

CREATE A SYSTEM RESTORE POINT

GET READY. To create a system restore, log in with local Administrative privileges and then perform the following steps:

1. Press the **Windows logo key + w** and then type **System Restore.**
2. From *Results,* click **Create a Restore point.**
3. Click **Configure** and then make sure the option **Turn on system protection** is selected (see Figure 12-4).

Figure 12-4

Confirming system protection is enabled

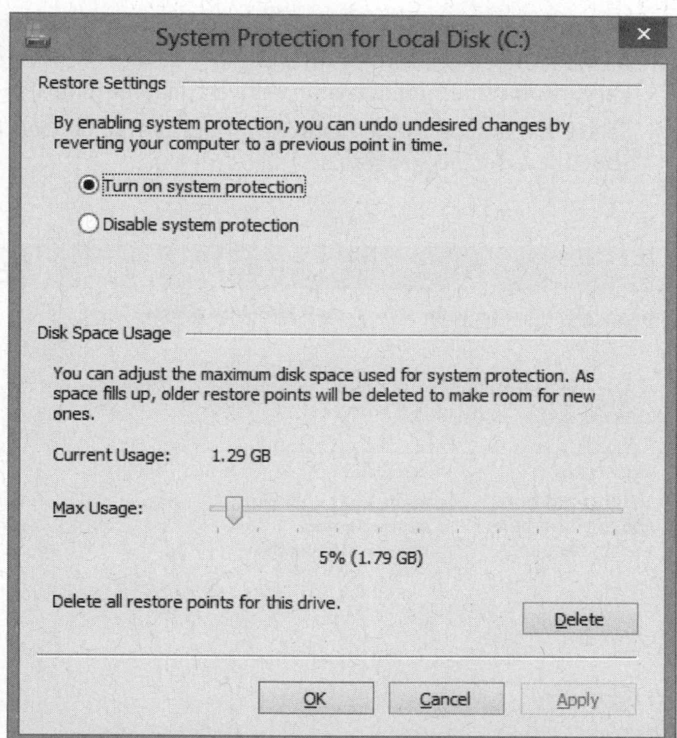

4. Drag the *Max Usage* slider to **10%.**

   This adjusts the disk space for system protection. When the space fills up, older restore points are deleted to make room for new ones.

5. Click **Apply** and then click **OK**.
6. Click **Create** to create a new restore point.
7. Type **Before AppX installation** as the description for the restore point.

   This helps you identify the restore point later.
8. Click **Create**.
9. When notified that the restore point was created successfully, click **Close**.
10. Click **OK** to accept your settings and to close the *System Properties* dialog box.

A restore point is a representation of the state of your computer's system files and settings. In most cases, you want to restore the most recent restore point, but you can choose from a list of restore points if you have more than one. The best approach is to use the restore point that was created just before you starting experiencing problems with your computer.

In the exercise that follows, assume that the installation of the application was completed, and your system is not functioning normally. To return your computer to a functioning state, use the restore point you just created.

PERFORM A SYSTEM RESTORE USING A RESTORE POINT

GET READY. To perform a system restore, log in with local Administrative privileges and then perform the following steps:

1. Press the **Windows logo key + w** and then type **system restore**.
2. From *Results*, click **Create a Restore point**.
3. Click **System Restore**.
4. Click **Next** to start the System Restore Wizard.

   A system restore does not affect your documents, pictures, or other personal data. Recently installed programs and drivers may be uninstalled.
5. Select the **Before AppX Installation** restore point (see Figure 12-5) and then click **Scan for affected programs**.

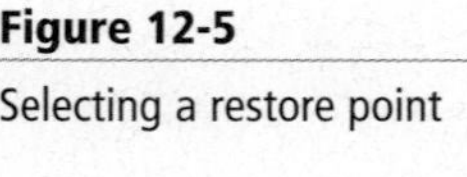

Figure 12-5

Selecting a restore point

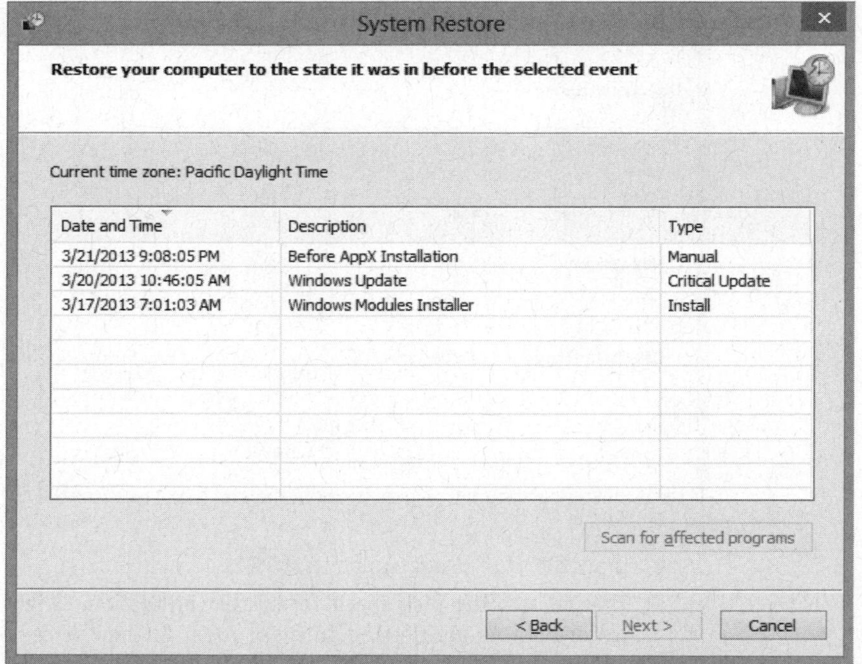

After the scan is completed, you see any programs and drivers that will be deleted, as well as programs and drivers that might be restored.

6. Click **Close** and then click **Next**.
7. Click **Finish**.
8. If you changed your Windows password, you should also create a password reset disk by selecting the **Windows logo key + w** and then searching for **Create a password reset disk**.
9. Click **Yes** to begin the system restore process.

   Windows restarts the computer, restores your files and settings, restores the registry, and removes temp files as part of the restore process.
10. When the restore process is completed, log back in to your system.

Using File History to Recover User Files/Local Files

File History provides options for backing up and recovering access to your personal files in case of a system problem.

CERTIFICATION READY
User Files, Including local files, SkyDrive, and File History
Objective 3.3

Folder Redirection and Roaming User Profiles, discussed in earlier lessons, are excellent ways to maintain your data if your system fails. These features store your user files and settings in a shared folder on a company server that is backed up as part of your organization's data-recovery strategies.

In the following section, you learn about an additional option that is available for protecting your data: File History.

Understanding File History

File History is a new feature in Windows 8 that is designed to keep your personal files safe. It enables users who are not administrators to select an external drive or a folder on the network, and automatically backs up and restores their personal files.

In Windows 8, File History simplifies the process of protecting your personal files. It eliminates the need to use a more complicated backup process included with previous releases of the operating system and introduces a process that is automatic and transparent to your user. It is disabled by default, so you need to enable it to take advantage of its features.

File History scans for changes to your personal files. When a change is detected, the file is moved to an external location you specify, so you can recover previous versions of files if necessary. To optimize performance, File History consults the NTFS change journal to determine whether a file has changed instead of scanning, opening, and reading directories on the volume. By default, File History backs up everything in your libraries, desktop, and favorites. The libraries contain items such as My Documents, My Music, My Pictures, and Public document folders. File History does not back up your system and application files.

File History does not require Administrative privileges to set up and run. The user can decide when to turn it on and off, select the external drive to use, and restore files without having to contact an administrator. Although File History does not back up your files to the cloud as SkyDrive does, it can be used to back up the SkyDrive folder if you are using the SkyDrive desktop app for Windows.

The following exercise describes the process to turn on File History, which automatically begins scanning and copying all your files to an external USB drive.

ENABLE FILE HISTORY

GET READY. To enable File History, log in with a domain user account and then perform the following steps:

1. Connect an external drive.
2. Press the **Windows logo key** + w and then type **File History.**
3. From *Results,* choose **File History.**
4. Click **Turn on** (see Figure 12-6).

   This option creates a folder named File History on the drive selected and automatically begins copying your files to the drive.

Figure 12-6

Turning on File History

File History

Control Panel ▸ System and Security ▸ File History

Search Co...

Control Panel Home

Restore personal files

Select drive

Exclude folders

Advanced settings

Keep a history of your files

File History saves copies of your files so you can get them back if they're lost or damaged.

File History is off

Copy files from: libraries, desktop, contacts, favorites and SkyDrive

Copy files to:

WD external drive (F:)

297 GB free of 298 GB

Turn on

See also

Recovery

Windows 7 File Recovery

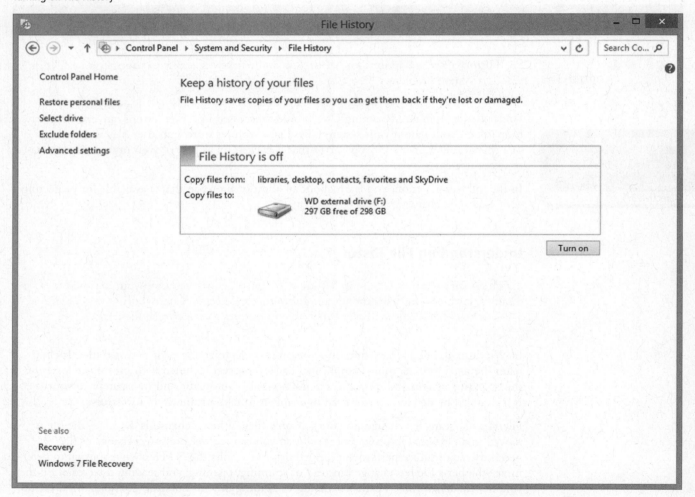

5. Close the *File History* dialog box.
6. Right-click your desktop and choose **New** > **Text Document.**
7. Type **FileHistoryTest** for the name and press **Enter.**

   This file is used in the exercise that follows.

The *File History* dialog box (see Figure 12-7) also includes the following two settings:

- **Exclude folders:** If you don't want to save copies of specific folders or libraries, you can specify them here.
- **Advanced settings:** You can identify the folders to exclude, the frequency for which they are backed up, and the amount of cache space you want to set aside for them.

When you click the *Advanced settings* link, the *Advanced Settings* dialog appears (see Figure 12-7).

Figure 12-7

Configuring advanced settings

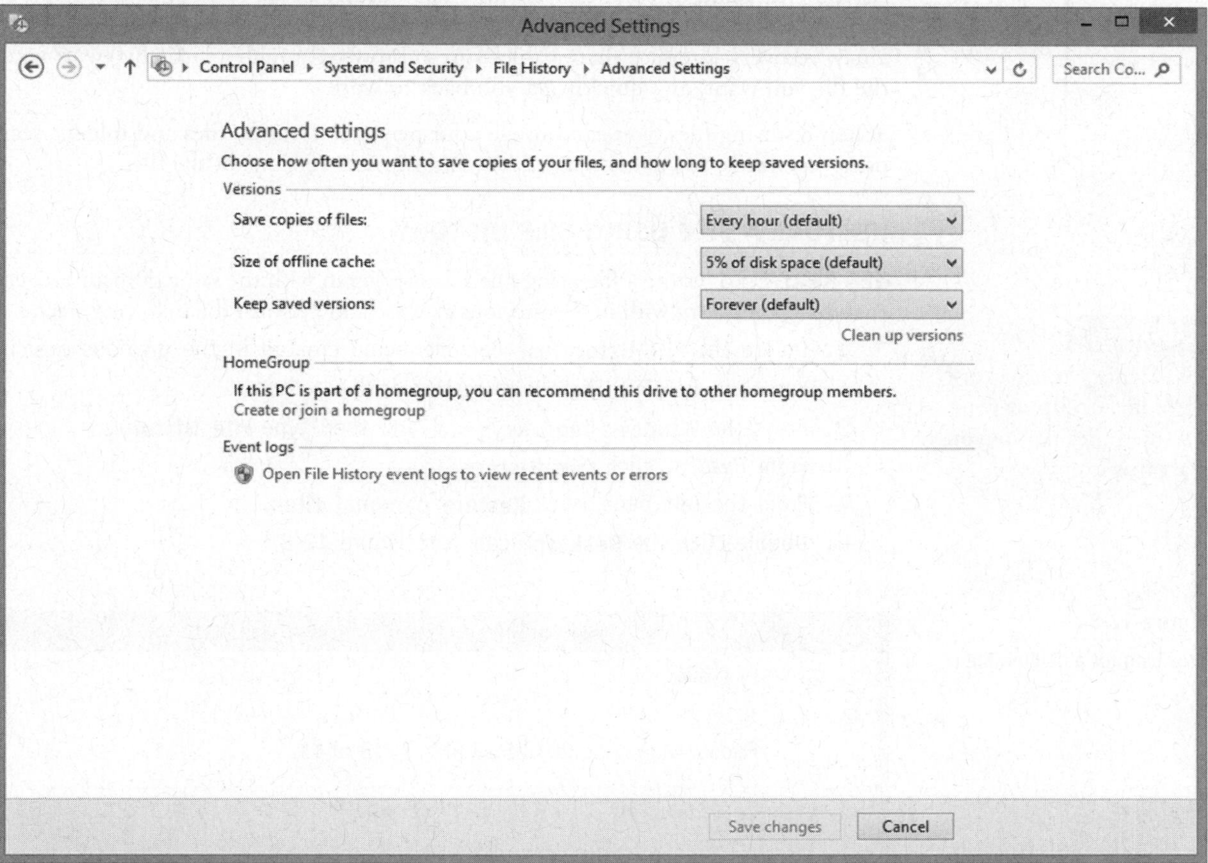

The *Versions* section includes the following settings:

- **Save copies of files:** The default is set to copy files every hour. Options include every 10, 15, 20, or 30 minutes; every 3, 6, or 12 hours; or daily.
- **Size of offline cache:** The default is set to 5%. Options include 2%, 10%, or 20% of disk space.
- **Keep saved versions:** The default is forever, but you can also set it to keep until space is needed; 1, 3, 6, or 9 months; or 1 or 2 years.
- **Clean up versions:** Settings here are used to configure when files and folders older than a certain age are deleted. Files and folders/versions that were excluded or removed from your libraries are also deleted. Options here include *All but the latest one, Older than 1, 3, 6 or 9 months, Older than 1 year (default), and Older than 2 years.*

If you have a HomeGroup, you can use the *HomeGroup* section to recommend the drive to other HomeGroup members. Each HomeGroup member can decide whether to accept the recommendation. If they do, their information is automatically backed up to the network share you set up.

Using File History to Restore Files

You can restore files through a familiar File Explorer interface after File History has copied all files to an external location.

As you create and delete files over time, File History keeps track of each version. If you accidentally delete a file that you need, the recovery process is very simple. File History provides a new recovery interface that enables you to browse through a virtual view of your files, select the file you want, and quickly get you back to work.

When restoring files, you can browse your personal libraries, files and folders; search for a file using keywords, file names, and dates; and preview versions of the files.

RESTORE A FILE USING FILE HISTORY

GET READY. To restore a file using File History, log in with the same domain account you enabled File History with in the previous exercise and perform the following steps:

TAKE NOTE*

File History must complete its backup of your personal files before you start this exercise.

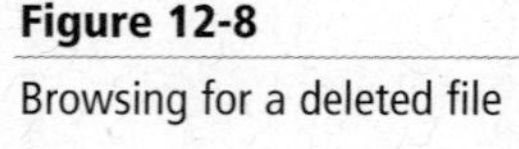

1. Delete the **FileHistoryTest** document you created in the previous exercise. You then use File History to restore it.
2. Press the **Windows logo key + w** and then type **File History**.
3. From *Results*, click **File History**.
4. From the left pane, click **Restore personal files**.
5. Double-click the **Desktop** icon (see Figure 12-8).

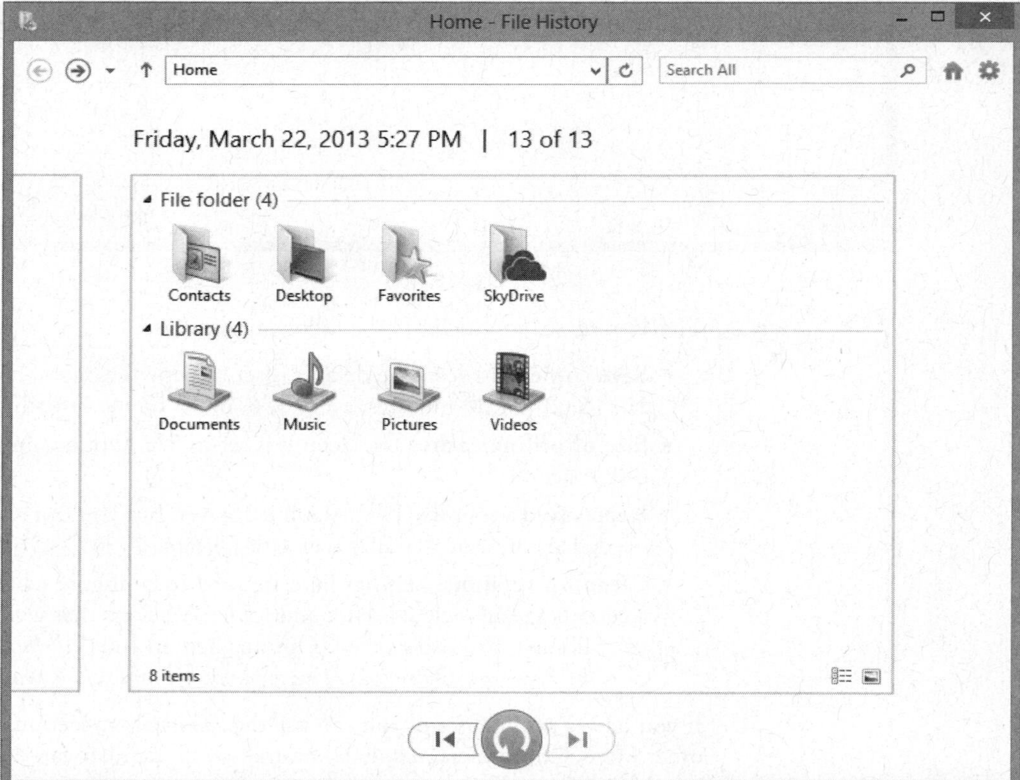

Figure 12-8

Browsing for a deleted file

6. Double-click the **FileHistoryTest** document.

   You can now view its contents. If there are multiple versions of the same file, use the left and right buttons to see each version before choosing to restore.

7. Click the **Restore to Original Location** button (see Figure 12-9).

Figure 12-9

Clicking the Restore to Original Location button

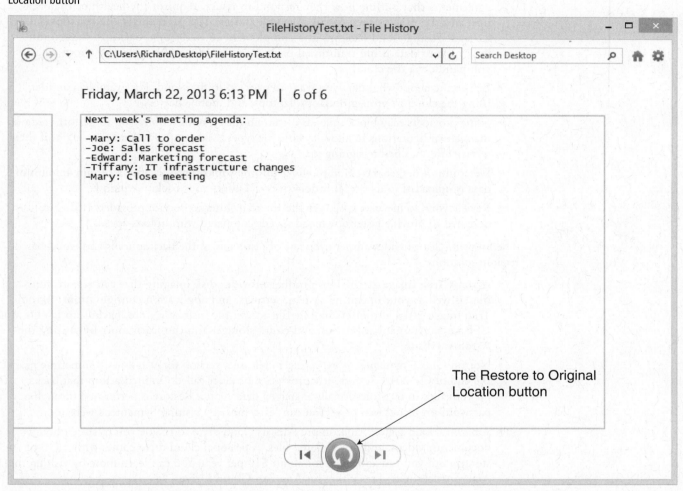

8. Confirm that the *FileHistoryTest.txt* document has been restored and then close the *Desktop* dialog box.

■ Exploring Third-Party Tools/Cloud Backup

Third parties offer additional software (local and in the cloud) that can protect and recover your critical information.

There are a variety of third-party tools and cloud backup solutions on the market that are designed to work with Windows 8. In general, when looking at cloud backup solutions as part of your overall strategy, keep the following in mind:

- **Cloud backup solutions** are not the same as **cloud storage solutions**. Cloud storage solutions involve obtaining an account and installing their software to enable you to back up files to the cloud. They also come with a monthly storage fee based on how many gigabytes you store. Some may even charge you based on how much you upload or download. A cloud backup service provides the same services, plus it adds software to automate the backups. These vendors also use a special data-compression technique called *Data Deduplication* to eliminate duplicate copies of repeating data to reduce the amount of traffic over the network. They also include service-level agreements that outline how they respond to issues, monitor the health of the backups, and the process they use to alert you and escalate problems if the backups fail. Consider using cloud backups as a complement to traditional backups. Back up the bulk of your data using traditional backup procedures and be selective about what you handle via the cloud.
- Be specific about what data you want to back up to the cloud. For example, consider using the cloud to protect desktops, laptops, and mobile devices.
- Some providers may block uploads of certain file types or require you to perform tedious manual configurations to allow specific file types. Make sure you read the details of their service offerings before signing up.
- Determine whether the cloud provider throttles upload speeds after a certain amount of data is uploaded to its site. If it does, it could affect your backup window.
- Review your connection speeds to the Internet. Internet service providers (ISPs) are designed to provide faster download speeds compared with upload speeds.

The following list provides a brief overview of just a few of the backup tools and cloud-based backup solutions:

- Acronis True Image 2013: This product provides disk imaging that can restore your files as well as your operating system, settings, and application configurations. Acronis True Image 2013 also offers mobile file access; file history/restore, backup to DVDs, USB keys, external hard drives, and cloud storage. You can learn more by visiting the Acronis website.
- Norton Ghost: Symantec is expecting to release a version for Windows 8 sometime near the end of Q1 2013. It currently provides a product called Online Backup that backs up your files to its professionally managed data center. Restore is performed through a password-protected web page. You can learn more by visiting Symantec's website.
- Amazon Cloud Drive: Amazon provides its cloud drive to enable you to store photos, documents, videos, and other digital files. A personal cloud drive comes with 5 GB of storage, but you can add more for about $10 per year. You can learn more by visiting the Amazon website and searching for **Amazon Cloud Drive**.
- Carbonite: Carbonite provides simple, browser-based admin dashboard, encrypted, offsite storage at its secure data centers, and HIPAA and private encryption key management. You can learn more by visiting Carbonite's website.
- Mozy: Mozy provides online backup solutions for personal use, small businesses, and enterprises. You can learn more by visiting Mozy's website.

■ Recovering User Profile Settings

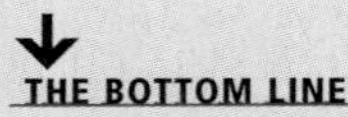

User profiles contain settings that control the look and feel of Windows. When a profile is corrupted, you need to know how to restore it in Windows 8.

User profiles are a collection of settings that enable you to customize how you want Windows 8 to look and function. Windows 8 stores user profile information in *%systemDrive%\users\%username%*, where *%systemDrive%* is the system path variable that refers to the location of critical operating system files (for example, *C:>*).

CERTIFICATION READY
User profile settings
Objective 3.3

%username% is the variable that represents a specific user (for example, *Matthew*). See Figure 12-10.

Figure 12-10

Reviewing contents of a user's profile folder

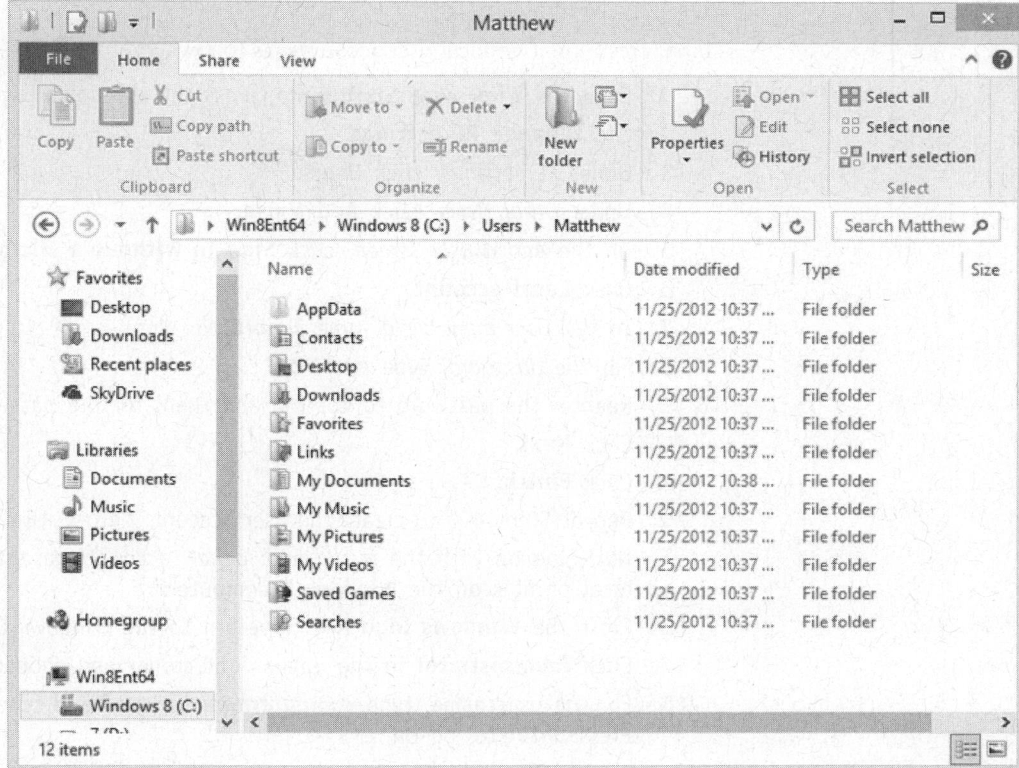

Within the user's profile, the following folders are displayed:

- **AppData:** User-specific application settings
- **Contacts:** Contacts and contact groups
- **Desktop:** User's desktop
- **Downloads:** Applications and data downloaded from the Internet
- **Favorites:** User's Internet favorites
- **Links:** User's Internet links
- **My Documents:** User's document folder
- **My Music:** User's music files
- **My Pictures:** User's picture files
- **My Videos:** User's video files
- **Saved Games:** User's saved game data
- **Searches:** User's saved searches

If your user profile becomes corrupted, you need to restore the data. The basic steps required depend upon whether the profile is local or roaming.

RECOVER A CORRUPTED LOCAL PROFILE IN WINDOWS 8

GET READY. To recover a corrupted local profile in Windows 8, log in with Administrative privileges and then perform the following steps:

TAKE NOTE* To complete this exercise, you must create two local accounts. *Joeold* is used to represent the account that has been corrupted. *Joenew* represents the account that you use to recover the corrupted account.

First, create the two local user accounts, as follows:

1. From the Windows 8 Start menu, press the **Windows logo key + I.**
2. Click **Change PC settings.**
3. Under *PC settings,* click **Users.**
4. Under *Other Users,* click **Add a user.**
5. On the *Add a user screen,* click **Sign in without a Microsoft account.**
6. Click **Local account.**
7. In the *User name field,* type **Joeold.**
8. For the *password,* type **pass123**.**
9. Reenter the password to confirm and then, for the password hint, type **123**.**
10. Click **Next.**
11. Click **Finish.**
12. Repeat Steps 4–8 to create the user account **joenew.** Use the same password and hint.

    Next, log on with the *joeold* and *joenew* accounts to automatically create their local profiles on the Windows 8 computer:
13. Press the **Windows logo key** to return to the Windows 8 Start menu.
14. Click **Administrator** in the upper-right corner and choose **Switch account.**
15. For the user name, type ***computername*\joeold** and type his password: **pass123**.** Press **Enter** to log on.

    This creates a profile folder for the *joeold* local account. Replace *computername* with the name of your Windows 8 computer.
16. Click **joeold** in the upper-right corner and choose **Sign out.**
17. Press the **space bar** and click **Other user.**
18. For the user name, type ***computername*\joenew** and type his password **pass123**.** Press **Enter** to log on.

    This creates a profile folder for the *joenew* local account. Replace *computername* with the name of your Windows 8 computer.
19. Click the user name **joenew** in the upper-right corner and choose **Sign out.**

    Next, assume that the *joeold* profile has been corrupted, and he can see only a few tiles on his Windows 8 start menu. You must copy the files from the corrupted user account (*joeold*) to the new user account (*joenew*) so he can retain his settings:
20. Press the **space bar** and click your **Administrator** account. Type your password and click **Enter.**
21. From the Windows 8 **Start** menu, type **Control Panel.** From *Results,* choose it.
22. From the menu at the top, click **Open Control Panel.**
23. Click **Appearance and Personalization.** Under *Folder Options,* click **Show hidden files and folders.**

24. In the *Folder Options* dialog box, deselect **Hide protected operating system files (recommended)**. When the *Warning* box appears, click **Yes** and then click **OK** to close the *Folder Options* dialog box.
25. Close the *Appearance and Personalization* dialog box.
26. Press the **Windows logo key + e** and then double-click **Local Disk (C:)**.
27. Double-click the **Users** folder and then double-click the **joeold** folder.

    This is where you find his profile information.
28. Select all the files in this folder except for NTUSER.DAT, ntuser.dat.LOG1, ntuser.dat.LOG2, and ntuser.ini, as shown in Figure 12-11.

Figure 12-11

Copying user profile files

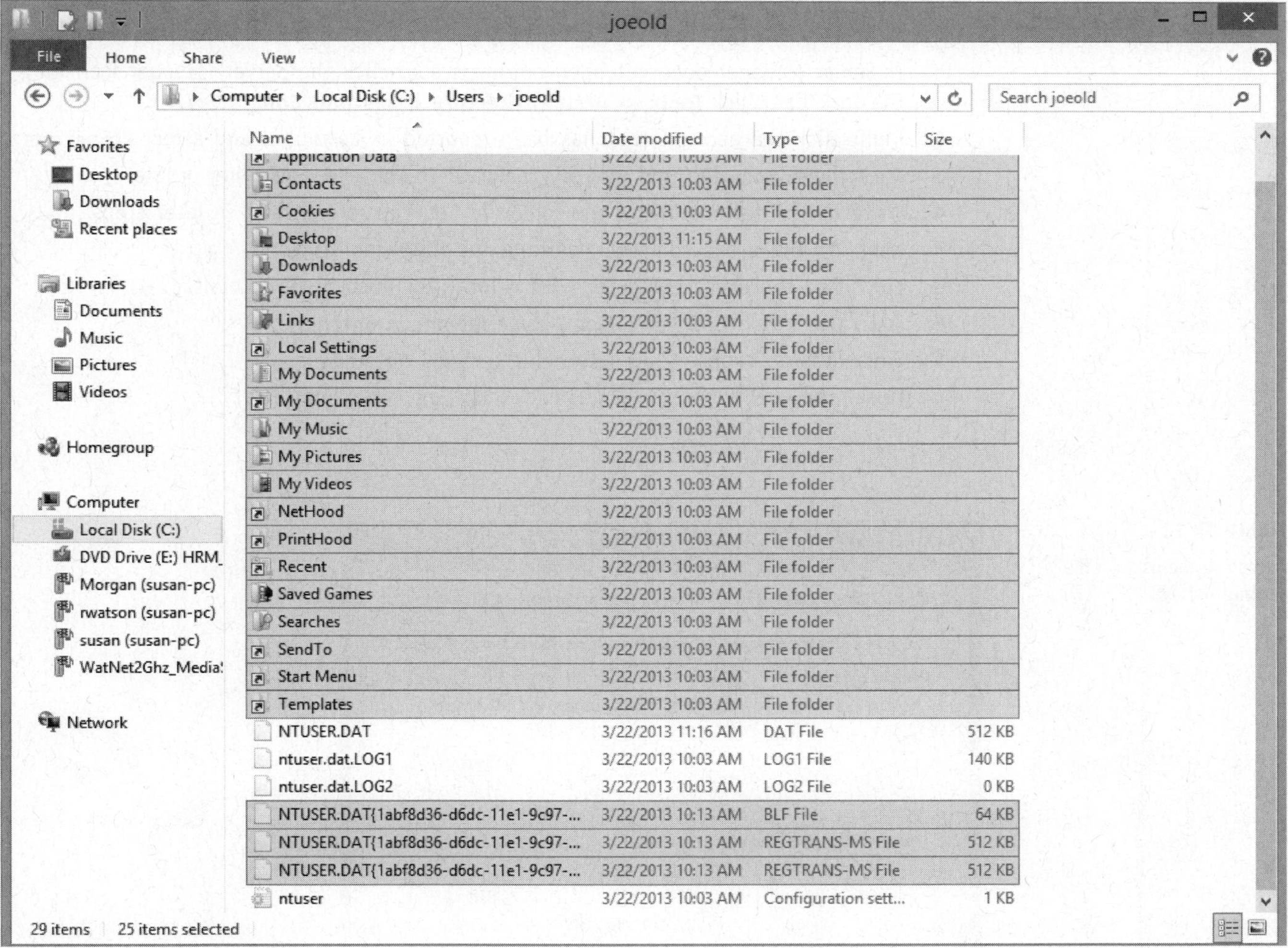

29. With the folders highlighted, right-click and choose **Copy**.
30. To move up one level in the directory structure, press the **Backspace** key. Double-click the **joenew** folder.
31. Right-click anywhere inside the white area of the *joenew* folder and choose **Paste**.
32. Log off and then log back on as **joenew**.

The user now has access to his profile and his Windows 8 Start menu.

RECOVER A CORRUPTED ROAMING PROFILE

TAKE NOTE* The following steps can be performed on the server or remotely from any computer that has access to a domain controller using the Active Directory Users and Computers tool.

GET READY. To recover a corrupted roaming profile, log in with Administrative privileges and then perform the following steps:

TAKE NOTE* Before assuming that you have a corrupted roaming profile, you should try to log on to the same computer with another roaming user account. If the other user's roaming account has the same problem, the problem is not related to the profile. Assuming that the corruption is limited to a specific user, perform the following steps to recover it.

1. If Server Manager does not open automatically, click the Server Manager icon on the task bar. Click **Tools** > **Active Directory Users and Computers**.
2. Right-click the account that has been reported as corrupted and select **Properties**.
3. Click the **Profile** tab and identify the path to the user's roaming profile.
4. Write down the location of the folder so you can reference it in later steps.

   Next, on the user's computer, perform the following steps:
5. Log in to the user's computer with a local administrator's account.
6. From the Windows 8 **Start** menu, type **Advanced Settings**.
7. From *Results*, choose **View advanced systems settings**.
8. Under the *User Profiles* section, click **Settings** (see Figure 12-12).

Figure 12-12

Accessing the user profile settings

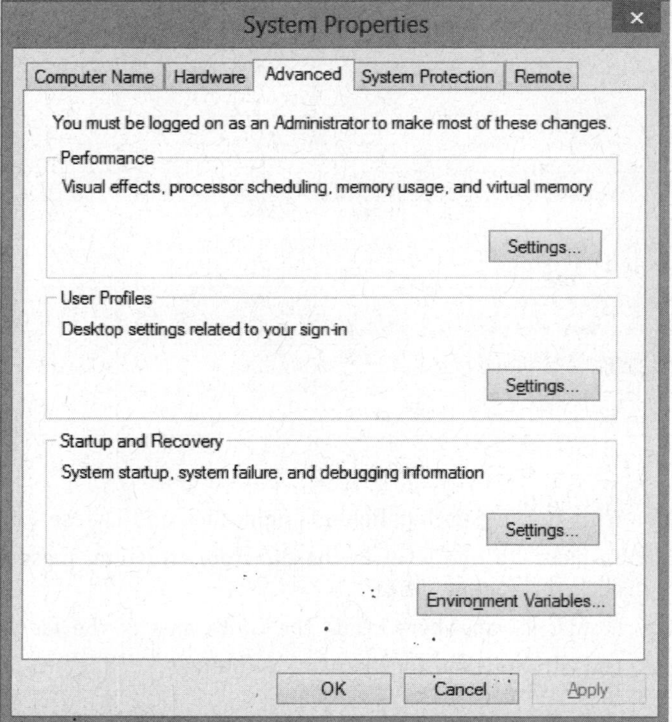

9. Select the user profile you want to delete and click **Delete**. This removes the *local copy* of the user's roaming profile.

   Now rename/delete the profile on the server:

10. Navigate to the user's roaming profile on the server using the information from Steps 1–3.
11. Rename the user's folder to ***<username>*old**. Replace *username* with the name of the actual user.
12. Ask the user to log on and then log off.

    This action creates a new profile on the local computer and the server. You can then restore any applicable information from the folder you renamed in the previous step.

13. Ask the user to log on and confirm that all her important settings are available to her.

Recovering Application Settings

THE BOTTOM LINE

Applications settings (traditional desktop applications and Windows apps from the Windows Store) should be considered in your recovery strategy. Users depend upon these programs, and in most cases have configured and personalized them to work the way they want. Having a backup of these programs and their settings ensure that you can restore them quickly.

In Lesson 10, you learned that by using your Microsoft user account, you can select the PC settings you want to sync and make available across all your trusted computers running Windows 8. One of those configurations was the App Settings option, which ensures that when you buy and download apps from the Windows store, you can use them on other computers running Windows 8. A PC Refresh, discussed earlier, can keep your Windows Store apps, but if you want to keep your settings and traditional desktop applications, use recimg.exe to make an image of everything on the computer.

CERTIFICATION READY
Application settings
Objective 3.3

Roaming profiles can also contain information about application settings and preferences in addition to user defined personal settings (desktop, color, drive mappings). Recovering these types of profiles was discussed earlier in this lesson.

Using recimg.exe

If you want to keep your settings and traditional desktop applications, use a utility called ***recimg.exe*** to make an image of the computer.

The secret of this technique is to first configure Windows 8 with the settings you want to use and remember to install applications such as Microsoft Office. The process involves creating a directory to store the image and then running the utility to capture an image of the computer and save it to the folder. The next time you perform a PC Refresh, the image is used to return your system to a known state.

CREATE AN IMAGE USING RECIMG.EXE

GET READY. To create an image using recimg.exe, log in with local Administrative privileges and then perform the following steps:

1. Set up the computer with the traditional applications and personal settings you want to use as your base system.
2. From the Windows 8 Start menu, type **cmd**.
3. Right-click the command prompt icon and select **Run as Administrator**.
4. When the *User Account Control* dialog box appears click **Yes**.
5. Create a new directory by typing the following and pressing **Enter**:

   `md c:\myrefreshimage`
6. Create the image by typing the following and pressing **Enter**:

   `recimg -CreateImage c:\myrefreshimage`
7. recimg initializes, creates the snapshot, writes the image, and then registers it, as shown in Figure 12-13.

Figure 12-13

Creating the image using recimg

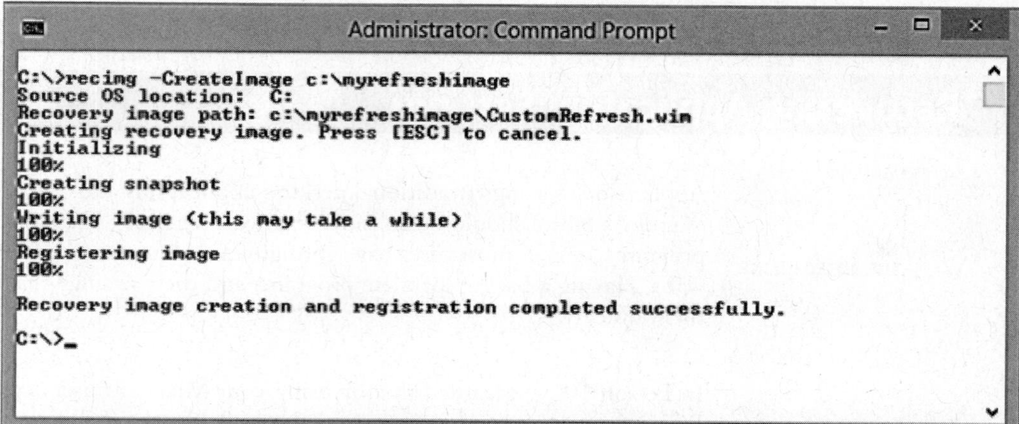

8. Type **exit** to close the command prompt.

SKILL SUMMARY

IN THIS LESSON, YOU LEARNED:

- You can use PC Reset, PC Refresh, and recimg.exe to return your computer to a known state. PC Reset removes everything and reinstalls Windows; PC Refresh refreshes your PC without affecting your files; recimg.exe creates a new image that includes your traditional desktop applications.
- PC Reset removes all your personal data, applications (traditional and Windows apps), and custom settings.
- PC Refresh enables you to keep your personal data, Windows Store apps, and basic settings. It does not preserve your PC settings, any file type associations, display settings, or traditional applications that were installed from a disc or a website; but it places an HTML file on your desktop to help you reinstall them.
- recimg.exe creates an image that is used for future PC Refreshes, so you can keep your traditional applications.
- Windows 7 File Recovery, previously named Windows Backup and Restore, has been superseded in favor of File History, but you can still use it in Windows 8.

- A Windows 8 File Recovery drive can provide enough of a boot environment to get you back into the system so you can begin the troubleshooting process.
- A Windows 8 System Restore provides an option for backing up your settings and registry values via restore points. Windows 8 automatically creates restore points every 7 days, but you can create one manually any time you want.
- File History is an application that is designed to replace the Windows Backup and Restore feature. It works by scanning changes to your personal files and then backing them up. When it is time to restore the files, you can use a simple restore interface to select the version of the file you want to recover.
- User profiles are a collection of settings that enable you to customize how you want Windows 8 to look and function. They are stored in the *%systemdrive%\users\%username%* location on your hard drive.
- The process for recovering from a corrupted local and roaming profile.

Knowledge Assessment

Multiple Choice

Select the correct answer for each of the following questions.

1. Which of the following tools enables you to return your PC back to its original state when you first purchased it or set it up?
   a. PC Reset
   b. recimg.exe
   c. recimage.exe
   d. PC Refresh
2. Which of the following tools keeps your settings and traditional applications by creating an image of your PC after it's configured with the apps and settings you want to use?
   a. PC Refresh
   b. PC Reset
   c. recimg.exe
   d. recimg.msi
3. Which term best describes the former term used for Windows 7 File Recovery?
   a. Windows File Recovery Service
   b. Windows Backup and Restore
   c. Backup
   d. Windows 7 Backup
4. What is the minimum amount of storage space required to re-create a Windows 8 File Recovery drive?
   a. 100 MB
   b. 250 MB
   c. 256 MB
   d. 156 MB

5. How frequently does Windows 8 automatically create restore points?
   a. Every 4 days
   b. Every 5 days
   c. Every 30 days
   d. Every 7 days
6. Which feature in Windows 8 is used to create a restore point?
   a. System Restore
   b. PC Refresh
   c. PC Reset
   d. System Point Restore
7. Which of the following does File History not back up? (Select all that apply.)
   a. System files
   b. Documents
   c. Application files
   d. Registry settings
8. Which of the following terms best describes an application designed to replace the Windows 7 Backup and Restore feature?
   a. SkyDrive
   b. SkyDrive Pro
   c. File History
   d. Windows 8 Backup and Restore
9. Which of the following programs restores files through a familiar File Explorer interface?
   a. SkyDrive
   b. File Explorer History
   c. File History
   d. Windows 8 Backup and Restore
10. Which of the following timeframes best represents the point at which you should create a restore point?
    a. Daily
    b. Weekly
    c. After performing a major system event
    d. Prior to performing a major system event

Best Answer

Choose the letter that corresponds to the best answer. More than one answer choice may achieve the goal. Select the BEST answer.

1. Which of the following tools is considered the best Windows 8 native tool to use to restore your traditional applications?
   a. True Image
   b. Group Policy
   c. recimg.exe
   d. PC Refresh
2. Which of the following approaches is considered most effective to decommission an older computer before donating it to charity?
   a. PC Reset
   b. PC Refresh
   c. Purchase a third-party disk wipe tool
   d. Move all the data off of the hard drive and reinstall Windows manually

3. Which of the following best represents the time when you should create a manual restore point?
   a. After completing the installation of a new application
   b. One day before performing an installation of a new application
   c. Two days before performing an installation of a new application
   d. Let Windows 8 perform an automatic restore point on its regularly scheduled interval
4. Which of the following tools best represents the preferred method to back up your important documents so that you can find and restore a previous version quickly?
   a. SkyDrive
   b. SkyDrive Pro
   c. File History
   d. Windows 7 Backup and Restore
5. Which of the following commands creates an image of your computer that also includes your traditional applications? This image is then used by PC Refresh.
   a. `recimg -CreateImage c:\myrefreshimage`
   b. `recimg -CreateImag c:\myrefreshimage`
   c. `recimg -CreateImage c:\`
   d. `recimage -CreateImage c:\myrefreshimage`

Matching and Identification

1. Match the following terms with the related description or usage.

   _______ a) File History
   _______ b) PC Refresh
   _______ c) PC Reset
   _______ d) recimg.exe
   _______ e) SkyDrive Pro
   _______ f) Windows 7 File Recovery
   _______ g) Windows 8 File Recovery drive
   _______ h) Windows 8 System Restore
   _______ i) user profile
   _______ j) restore point

   1. Windows 8 automatically creates these every 7 days.
   2. This is a collection of settings that enables you to customize how you want Windows 8 to look and function.
   3. This provides enough of a boot environment to get you back into the PC so you can begin troubleshooting. It requires at least 256 MB of space.
   4. This is a private library that provides a repository for storing your work documents.
   5. This is used when you want to remove all your personal data, applications, and custom settings prior to donating or recycling your PC.
   6. This is an application that consults the NTFS change journal instead of scanning, opening, and reading directories on a volume.
   7. This creates an HTML file on your desktop to assist you with reinstalling applications.
   8. This creates an image of your PC that can be used by PC Refresh to return your system to a known state, including your traditional applications.
   9. This is the new term for the feature that was previously named Windows Backup and Restore.
   10. This saves information about your drives, registry settings, programs, and files in the form of restore points.

Build a List

1. Specify the correct order of the steps that must be completed to create an image using recimg.exe.
   ________ Log in with Administrative privileges.
   ________ Press the **Windows logo key + q**, change context to Apps, and type **cmd**.
   ________ Set up the computer with the traditional applications and personal settings you want.
   ________ Right-click the command prompt icon and select **Run as Administrator**.
   ________ Type **md c:\\<*foldername*>**.
   ________ When prompted by the *User Account Control* dialog box, select **Yes**.
   ________ `c:\recimg -CreateImage c:\` <*foldername*>

2. Specify the correct order of the steps that must be completed to enable File History on Windows 8.
   ________ From *Results*, choose **File History**.
   ________ Log in with local Administrative privileges.
   ________ Click **Turn On**.
   ________ Press the **Windows logo key** + **w** and then type **File History**.
   ________ Connect an external drive.

3. Specify the correct order of the steps that must be completed to create a system restore point.
   ________ Click **Apply** and then click **OK**.
   ________ Click **Create** to create a new restore point.
   ________ Click **Create**.
   ________ Drag the slider to set the maximum disk space you want to use, click **Apply**, and then click **OK**.
   ________ Type a description for the restore point.
   ________ Press the **Windows logo key + w** and then type **System Restore**.
   ________ Click **Create a Restore Point From the Results**.
   ________ Click **Configure** and make sure the option *Turn on system protection* is enabled.
   ________ Log in with local Administrative privileges.

Choose an Option

1. Identify the option that writes random patterns on each sector of the drive.

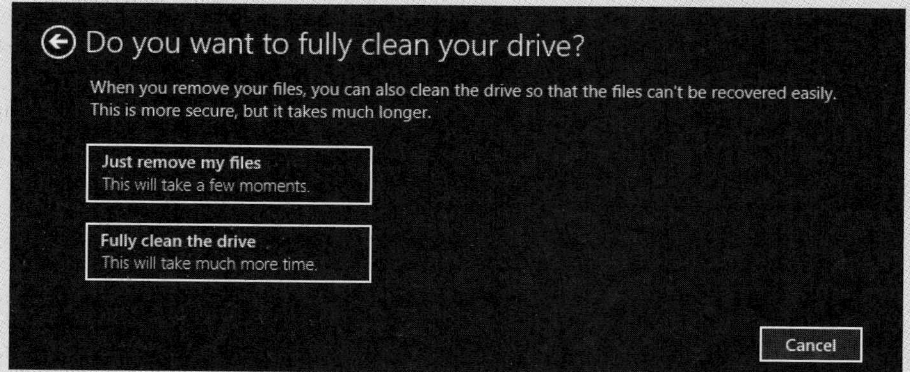

Business Case Scenarios

Scenario 12-1: Recovering your Traditional Desktop Applications After Running PC Refresh

You restored a PC using PC Refresh, but the user no longer has access to traditional applications. He does have access to his Windows Store apps, basic settings, and personalization settings, however. You want to figure out a way to use PC Refresh yet still maintain the settings as well as the traditional applications installed on the PC. Is this possible? If so, explain how you would do it.

Scenario 12-2: Restoring Files

Support staff members have been complaining about the amount of time they are spending restoring selected users' files on their Windows 8 PCs. The users are pretty technically savvy and can perform the tasks themselves, but you don't want to give them Administrative privileges on their PCs. What solution would you recommend?

Managing Endpoint Security

70-688 EXAM OBJECTIVE

Objective 3.4 – Manage endpoint security. This objective may include, but is not limited to: Resolve endpoint security issues; manage updates using Windows Update; manage client security using Windows Defender; manage client security using the Microsoft System Center 2012 Endpoint Protection client; configure application reputation.

LESSON HEADING	EXAM OBJECTIVE
Managing Endpoint Security	
Managing Updates Using Windows Update	Manage updates using Windows Update
Managing Windows Server Update Services (WSUS) 4.0 using Windows Server 2012	Manage updates using Windows Update
Determining a Deployment Strategy	
Reviewing the Update Services Console	
Understanding Server	
Configuring Clients to Use WSUS	
Using Computer Groups with WSUS	
Selecting Server-Side Versus Client-Side Targeting	
Approving and Installing Updates on the Client Computers	
Managing Client Security Using Windows Defender	Manage client security using Windows Defender
Exploring the Home tab	
Exploring the Update tab	
Exploring the History tab	
Exploring the Settings tab	
Understanding the Microsoft Active Protection Service	
Managing Client Security Using the Microsoft SCCM 2012 Endpoint Protection Client	Manage client security using the Microsoft System Center 2012 Endpoint Client
Configuring Application Reputation	Configure application reputation

Resolving Endpoint Security Issues	Resolve endpoint security issues
Resolving Endpoint Security Issues Using Action Center	
Resolving Endpoint Security Issues Using Windows Defender	
Resolving Endpoint Security Issues Using Windows Firewall	
Resolving Endpoint Security Issues with Third-Party Software	

KEY TERMS

Action Center
Application Reputation
autonomous (distribution) mode
client-side targeting
downstream servers
Microsoft Active Protection Service (MAPS)
replica mode
server-side targeting
synchronization
System Center Endpoint Protection (SCEP) client
upstream server
Windows Defender
Windows Server Update Services (WSUS)
Windows Update

Managing Endpoint Security

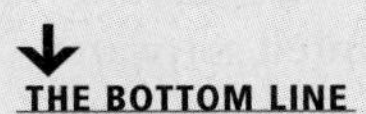

Managing the security of your clients involves a multi-layered approach. Managing the security of your computers involves a multi-layered approach. To ensure your systems are protected, you need to make sure you have the latest service packs and patches for the operating system and the current updates for Microsoft and third-party applications to maintain stability. You can accomplish this using Windows Update on each Windows 8 computer or using ***Windows Server Update Services (WSUS)*** to manage and approve your updates from a central server.

To protect against malware, spyware, and viruses, you need real-time protection that can be provided by Windows Defender or through antimalware policies created and deployed to System Center Endpoint Protection (SCEP) clients.

Application Reputation provides protection from downloading malware through the use of SmartScreen, which is used in Internet Explorer and File Explorer. In this lesson, you learn more about how each of these works.

Managing Updates Using Windows Update

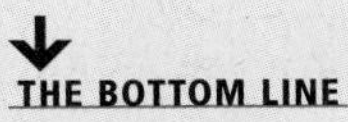

Windows Update provides your Windows 8 users with a way to keep their computers current by checking a designated server. The server provides software that patches security issues, installs updates that make Windows and your applications more stable, fixes issues with existing Windows programs, and provides new features. The server can be hosted by Microsoft or it can be set up and managed in your organization by running the Windows Server Update Services (WSUS).

MORE INFORMATION

At one point, Windows Update was the source for downloading the latest service pack and patches for Windows operating systems. Microsoft Update was used for other updates related to MS Office programs. Over the years, these have basically been merged under the Microsoft Update name.

CERTIFICATION READY
Manage updates using Windows Update
Objective 3.4

On a Windows 8 computer, you can access the Windows Update feature though the Control Panel (*Control Panel > Windows Update*).

From the Windows Update window (see Figure 13-1), you can check for updates, change settings, view the updated history, see installed updates, and restore hidden updates.

Figure 13-1
Viewing Windows updates

Windows updates are organized into the following categories:

- **Important updates:** These updates are designed to maintain computer security and reliability. Examples might include a patch for a security issue that allows an unauthenticated remote attacker to gain control of your system or update to your definition files used to detect viruses, spyware, and other unwanted software.
- **Recommended updates:** These updates are designed to keep your computer running smoothly.
- **Optional updates:** These are optional updates such as installing a codec pack that enables you to view RAW camera files or troubleshooting an incorrect keyboard layout for computers that run a multi-language version of Windows 8.

When you first install Windows 8, you have the option to choose how you want Windows Update to function. It's possible to make changes after Windows 8 is installed unless your Administrator has disabled this option via a Local Group policy or a Domain-based Group policy for your user and/or computer account.

Group Policy settings related to Windows Update can be found in the following locations:

- *Computer Configuration > Policies\Administrative Templates > Windows Components > Windows Update > Configure Automatic Updates*
- *User Configuration > Policies > Administrative Templates > Windows Components > Windows Update > Configure Automatic Updates*

REVIEW YOUR WINDOWS UPDATE SETTINGS

GET READY. To review your Windows Update settings on a Windows 8 computer, perform the following steps:

1. Log in with local Administrative privileges.
2. Press the **Windows logo key + I** and from the menu, choose **Control Panel**.
3. Click **System and Security > Windows Update**.
4. In the *left* pane, click the **Change settings** link.

5. Under *Important updates,* click the **drop-down arrow** to review the options for installing important updates.
6. Click **Cancel** to exit and leave your existing setting for Windows Update configured to *Install updates automatically (recommended)*.

The options for Windows Update include:

- **Install updates automatically:** Updates are automatically downloaded in the background and are automatically installed based on the maintenance window specified. Windows runs automatic maintenance daily at 3:00AM (this is the default, but it can be changed) to perform tasks such as system diagnostics, security scanning, and software updates. Automatic maintenance occurs only if your computer is idle.
- **Download updates but let me choose whether to install them:** Updates are automatically downloaded in the background. You also have the option to receive updates the same way you receive your important updates.
- **Check for updates but let me choose whether to download and install them.** Windows checks for updates but lets you decide whether to download and install them.
- **Never check for updates (not recommended):** Windows does not check, download, or install important updates.

MORE INFORMATION

Microsoft releases security and other patches for the software and operating systems on the second Tuesday of each month. This day, called Patch Tuesday, is used to roll out patches designed to fix recently discovered security holes.

From the Windows Update dialog box, you can also perform the following tasks by selecting the appropriate link from the panel on the left (see Figure 13-2):

- **Check for updates:** Selecting this link forces Windows to contact the Windows Update server at Microsoft. When it is completed, you can see how many updates are available along with tracking information about the most recent check for updates and when updates were installed last.
- **View update history:** This link provides you with a list of updates that are installed on your computer, their names, statuses (canceled and succeeded), their importance (important, recommended, and optional), and their installation dates. To remove an update, you can select the *Installed Updates* link at the top of the *history* page.
- **Restore hidden updates:** These are updates that you have informed Windows to not notify you about or install automatically.
- **Installed updates:** Provides information (name, program, version, publisher, and installation date) for all currently installed updates.

Figure 13-2

Viewing the Windows Update links

■ Managing Windows Server Update Services (WSUS) 4.0 Using Windows Server 2012

THE BOTTOM LINE

WSUS provides a centralized server that can be used to manage the deployment of updates from Microsoft. Instead of having each of your Windows 8 computers connect to Microsoft to check for updates, consider using ***Windows Server Update Services (WSUS)***. WSUS enables you to centrally manage the deployment of updates released through Microsoft, track compliance, and provide basic reporting functions.

CERTIFICATION READY
Manage updates using Windows Update
Objective 3.4

The main components of WSUS are:

- **Windows Server Update Services (WSUS):** This is installed on a Windows server behind your perimeter firewall. This service enables you to manage and distribute updates to WSUS clients. It can also update sources for other WSUS servers.
- **Microsoft Update:** This is the Microsoft website WSUS connects to for updates.
- **Update Services console:** This is the console that can be accessed to manage WSUS.

Setting up WSUS involves the following:

1. Determining a deployment strategy.
2. Installing the WSUS server role.
3. Specifying an update source for the WSUS server.
4. Synchronizing updates to the WSUS server.
5. Setting up client computers.
6. Approving and installing updates on the client computers.

Determining a Deployment Strategy

Determining the appropriate deployment strategy for WSUS ensures that you have the right servers installed in the appropriate locations based on how your organization is geographically dispersed. It also helps you recognize when and where to place WSUS to reduce needless traffic across your WAN links.

You can deploy a single WSUS server to connect to the Microsoft Update Servers and download updates. Figure 13-3 shows an example of a single WSUS deployment in which the clients are connecting to a single server running WSUS. The server connects and downloads updates directly from the Microsoft Update servers. The process of connecting and downloading updates is called ***synchronization***. While a single server option works well in a small office environment, it does not scale very well for companies that have their employees located across branch offices.

In situations where you need to service a large number of clients or where your computers are dispersed geographically, you should consider implementing more than one WSUS server. The additional WSUS servers can be configured to obtain their updates from the first WSUS server or they can get them directly from the Microsoft Update servers.

When multiple servers are used, the server that obtains updates from Microsoft is called the ***upstream server***. The server(s) that obtain their updates from the upstream server are called ***downstream servers***. If multiple WSUS servers are used, you need to make sure the server-to-server and server-to-client communications use the Secure Socket Layer (SSL).

Figure 13-4 shows how you might configure multiple WSUS servers when you have a branch office. In this example, the WSUS server at the branch office functions as the

Figure 13-3
Deploying single WSUS server

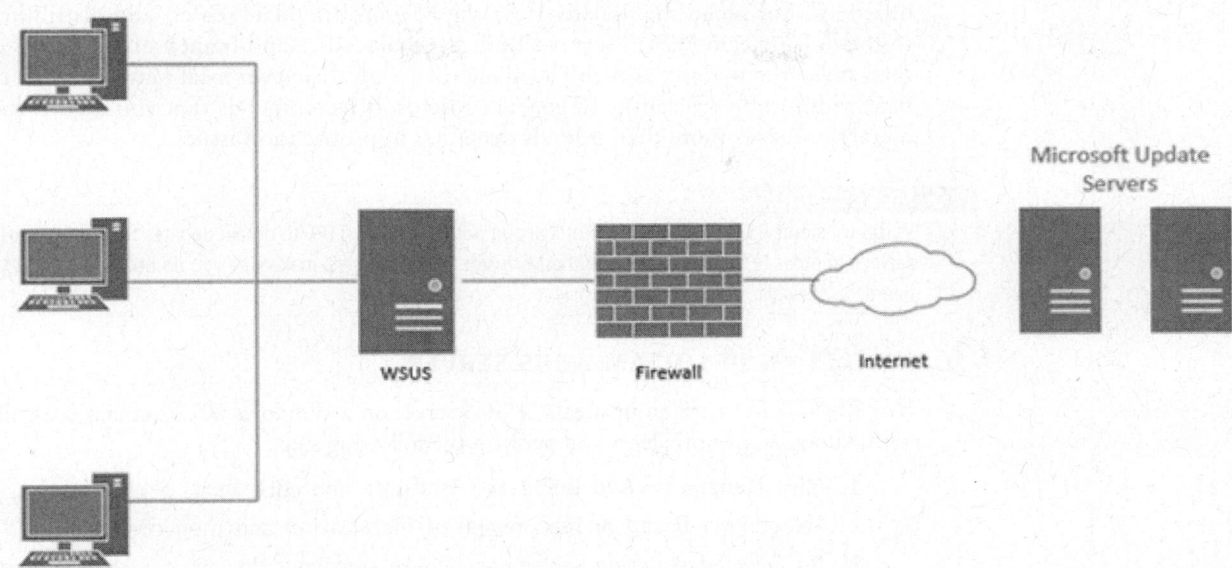

Figure 13-4
Implementing a multiple WSUS Implementation

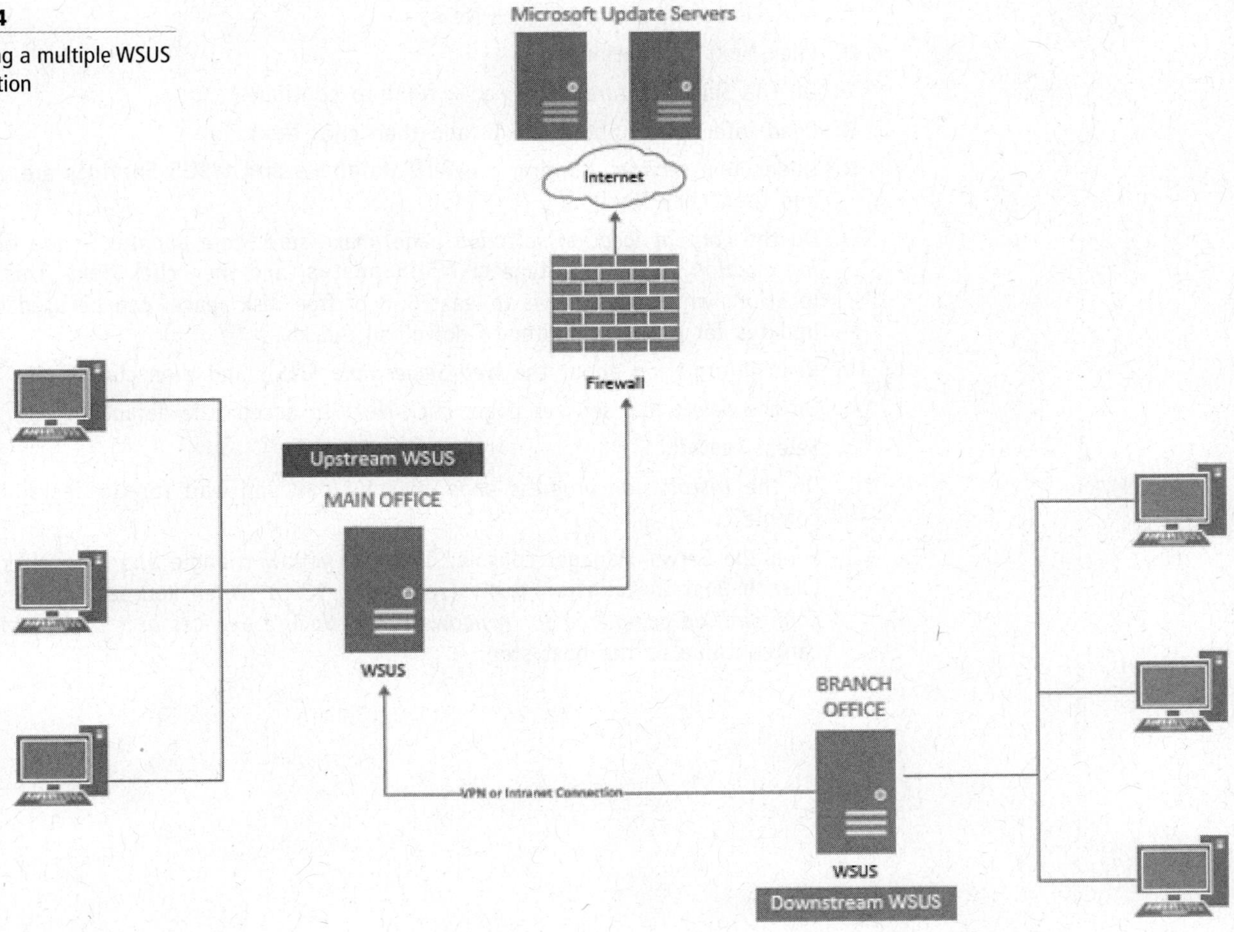

downstream server obtaining its updates from the WSUS server (upstream) at the main office either over a VPN or over an intranet connection. The WSUS server at the main office will download the updates from the Microsoft Update servers and distribute them to the downstream WSUS servers. Both the main office and branch office servers can then make the updates available to their clients on their own local network. This utilizes bandwidth more efficiently. In general, Microsoft recommends that you do not create a hierarchy that is more than 3 levels deep due to propagation issues.

MORE INFORMATION

WSUS uses port 8530 for the HTTP protocol and port 8531 for HTTPS to obtain updates from the Microsoft Update servers. In order to communicate with the Microsoft Update servers, make sure you do not block them at your perimeter firewall.

INSTALL AN UPSTREAM WSUS SERVER

GET READY. To install an upstream WSUS server on a Windows 2012 domain controller, log in with administrative privileges and perform the following steps:

1. Click **Manage > Add Roles and Features** and click **Next.**
2. Select **Role-based** or **feature-based installation** and then click **Next.**
3. On *Select destination server* page, make sure your domain controller is highlighted, and then click **Next.**
4. On the *Select server* roles page, select **Windows Server Update Services.**
5. When you are prompted to install additional features required for WSUS, select **Add Features**, and then click **Next.**
6. Click **Next** to continue.
7. On the *Select features* page, click **Next** to continue.
8. Read information about WSUS, and then click **Next.**
9. Under *Role services,* confirm the **WID Database and WSUS Services** are checked, and then click **Next.**
10. On the *Content location selection* page, make sure *Store updates in the following location* is checked, type **c:\WSUSupdates**, and then click **Next.** This drive location, which must have at least 6GB of free disk space, can be used to store updates for client computer to download quickly.
11. Read information about the *Web Server Role (IIS)*, and then click **Next.**
12. On the *Select role services* page, click **Next** to accept the defaults.
13. Select **Install.**
14. On the *Installation progress* page, select **Close** and wait for the installation to complete.
15. From the Server Manager console, click the yellow triangle and then click **Launch Post-Installation tasks** (see Figure 13-5). When you see the message *Configuration completed for Windows Server Update Services at <servername>*, you can continue to the next step.

Figure 13-5

Launching Post-Installation tasks

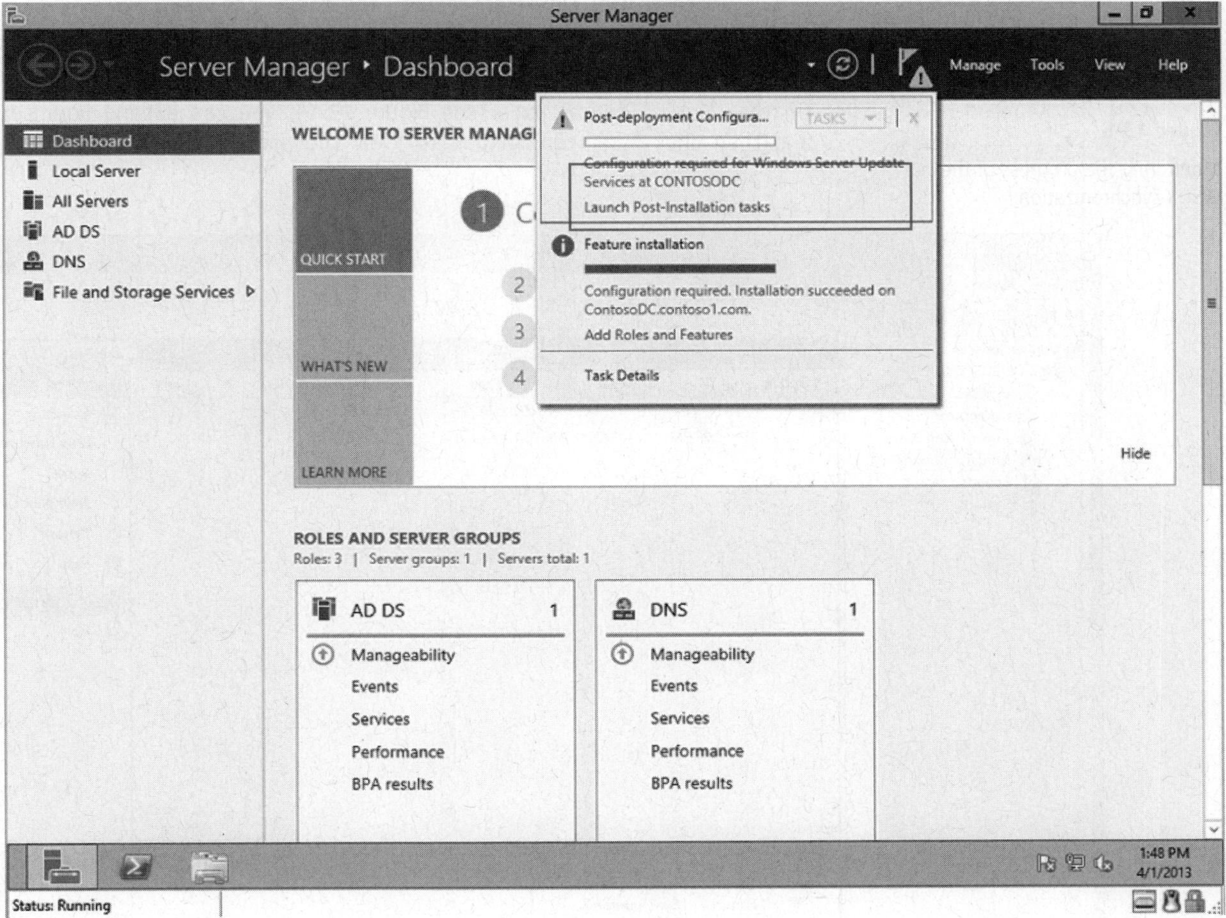

16. Click **Tools > Windows Server Update Services**. When the *Windows Server Update Services* appears, click **Next**. You may need to minimize the Server Manager to see the *Windows Server Update Services Configuration Wizard*.
17. On the *Join the Microsoft Update Improvement Program* page, uncheck the option **Yes, I would like to join the Microsoft Update Improvement Program**, and then click **Next**.
18. On the *Choose Upstream Server,* click **Next** to choose to synchronize this server with Microsoft Update.
19. On the *Specify Proxy Server* page, click **Next**.
20. On the *Connect to Upstream Server* page, click **Start Connecting**.
21. After the server connects, click **Next** to proceed.
22. Select **Download updates only in these languages**, and then choose **English**. Click **Next**.
23. Scroll down and uncheck **Office**. Continue to scroll until you see *Windows*. Uncheck everything except for **Windows 8 Language Packs**, **Windows 8**, and **Windows Defender**. Click **Next** to continue. This reduces the amount of space and time needed to download updates. If this were a real production server, you would download the application and operating system updates to match your needs.

24. On the *Choose Classifications* page, accept the defaults and click **Next**. This ensures you obtain the Critical Updates, Definition Updates, and Security Updates.
25. On the *Set Sync Schedule* page, click **Next** to accept the default setting.
26. Select **Begin initial synchronization**, and then click **Next**.
27. Click **Finish**. Your system synchronizes with the Microsoft Update Servers in the background.
28. On the *Update Services* page (see Figure 13-6), you can expand your server name, and then click **Synchronizations to view the progress**.

Figure 13-6

Monitoring the progress of the WSUS synchronization

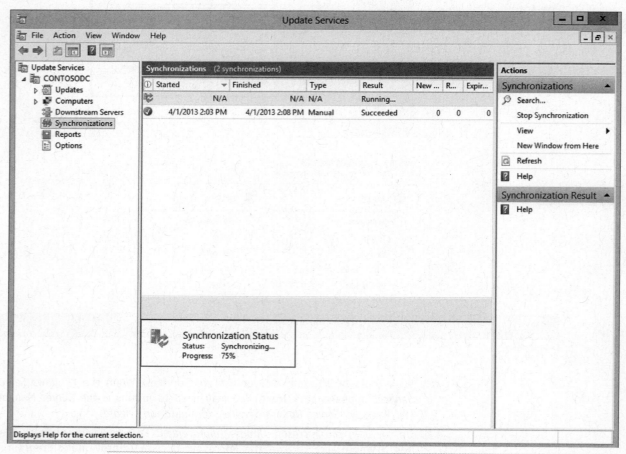

Now that you have your upstream server configured, you can set up a downstream WSUS server on another computer in your domain. In the exercise that follows, you use a nondomain controller (for example, the member server).

INSTALL A DOWNSTREAM WSUS SERVER

GET READY. To install a downstream WSUS server on a Windows member server, log in with administrative privileges and perform the following steps:

1. Click **Manage** > **Add Roles and Features**, and then click **Next**.
2. Select **role-based** or **feature-based installation**, and then click **Next**.
3. On *Select destination server* page, make sure your member server is highlighted, and then click **Next**.

4. On the *Select server roles page,* select **Windows Server Update Services**.
5. When you are prompted to install additional features required for WSUS, select **Add Features**, and then click **Next**.
6. Click **Next** to continue.
7. On the *Select features* page, click **Next** to continue.
8. Read information about WSUS, and then click **Next**.
9. Under *Role services,* confirm the **WID Database** and **WSUS Services** are checked, and then click **Next**.
10. On the *Content location selection* page, make sure *Store updates in the following location* is checked, type **c:\WSUSupdates**, and then click **Next**. This drive location, which must have at least 6GB of free disk space can be used to store updates for client computer to download quickly.
11. Read information about the *Web Server Role (IIS)*, and then click **Next**.
12. On the *Select role services* page, click **Next** to accept the defaults.
13. Select **Install**.
14. On the *Installation progress* page, select **Close** and wait for the installation to complete.
15. From the Server Manager console, click the yellow triangle and then click **Launch Post-Installation tasks**. When you see the message *Configuration completed for Windows Server Update Services at <servername>*, you can continue to the next step.
16. Click **Tools > Windows Server Update Services**. When the Windows Server Update Services appears, click **Next**. You may need to minimize the Server Manager to see the *Windows Server Update Services Configuration Wizard.*
17. On the *Choose Upstream Server,* select **Synchronize from another Windows Server Update Services server**. In the *Server name* field, type the name of the server you set up WSUS on in the previous exercise, and then click **Next**.
19. On the *Specify Proxy Server* page, click **Next**.
20. On the *Connect to Upstream Server* page, click **Start Connecting**.
21. After the server connects, click **Next** to proceed.
22. On the *Choose Languages* page, click **Next** to accept the default setting *Download updates only in these languages* and *English*.
23. On the *Set Sync Schedule* page, click **Next** to accept the default setting.
24. Select **Begin initial synchronization**, and then click **Next**.
25. Click **Finish**. Your system synchronizes with the upstream server in the background.
26. On the *Update Services* page, you can expand your server name, and then click **Synchronizations** to view the progress.

When the downstream WSUS server synchronizes with the upstream WSUS server, it downloads updates in the form of metadata and files. The update metadata can be found in the WSUS database. The update files are stored on either the WSUS server or on the Microsoft Update servers. The location is determined when you set up WSUS. In the earlier examples, we configured the WSUS server to store the updates in the c:\WSUSUpdates folder.

If the server is a downstream server, the products (Office, Developer Tools, Exchange, Skype, System Center, Windows, and so on) and classifications (critical updates, definition updates, drivers, security updates, and so on) included with the synchronization are set up on the upstream server.

The first time the downstream server synchronizes, it downloads all of the updates you specified. After the first synchronization has completed, the server downloads only updates made since the last synchronization.

Now that you have installed an upstream and a downstream WSUS server, you might wonder which components are installed with WSUS. Here is a brief overview of what each does:

- **.NET Framework 4.5:** Provides core support for running ASP.NET 4.5 standalone applications and applications that are integrated with IIS.
- **Remote Server Administration Tools:** This includes snap-ins and command-line tools for remotely managing roles and features.
- **Web Server (IIS):** WSUS is an ASP.NET web service application and requires IIS to deliver access to the services it provides.
- **Windows Internal Database (WID) used by WSUS:** This is a relational data store used only by Windows roles and features.
- **Windows Process Activation Service:** This generalizes the IIS process model and removes the dependency on HTTP.

Reviewing the Update Services Console

After completing the installation, you can access the Update Services console. In Server Manager, choose *Tools > Windows Server Update Services.* The following provides you with an overview of what is included in the console (see Figure 13-7) after expanding the server name folder.

Figure 13-7

Reviewing the folders in the Update Services console

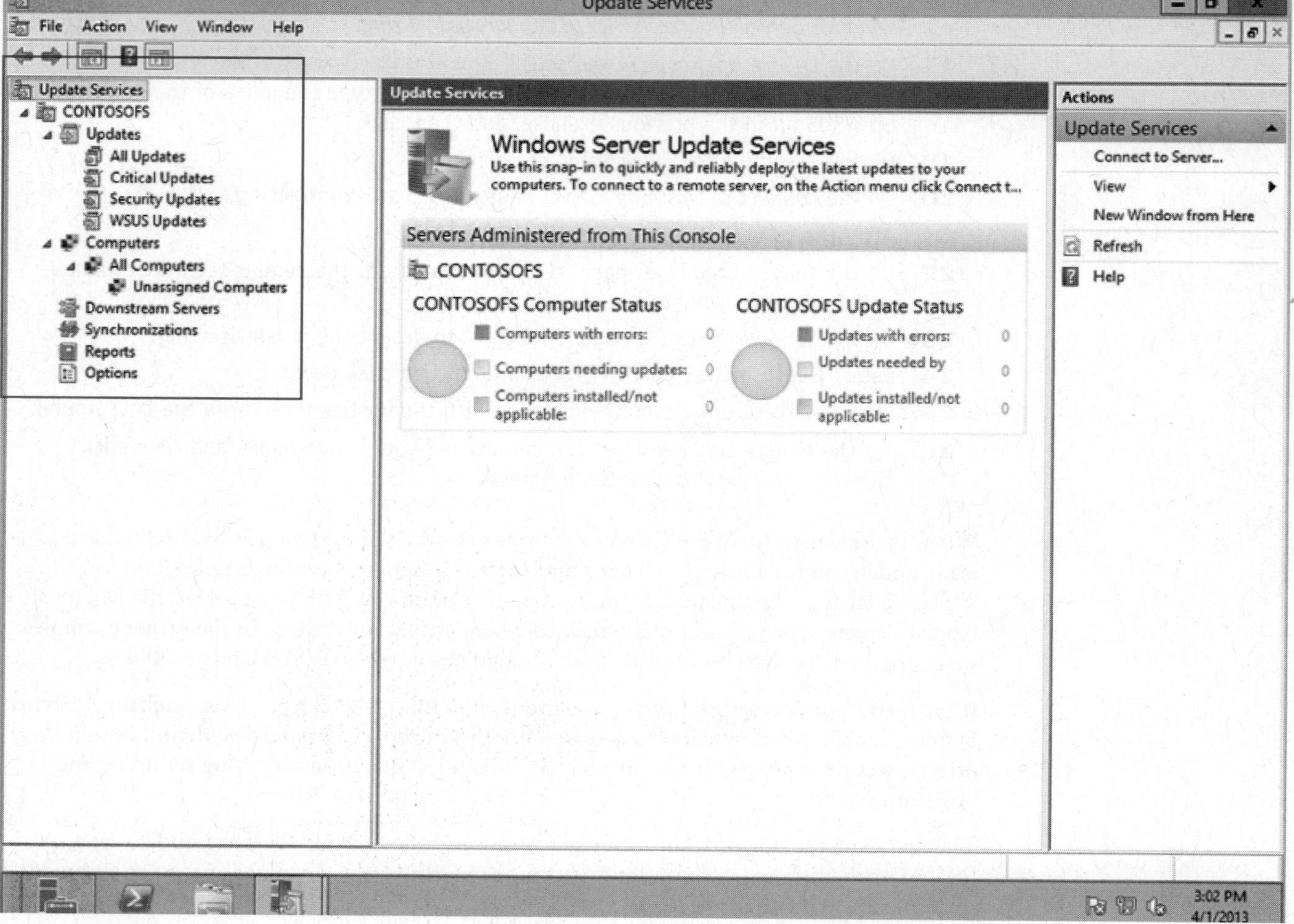

- **Updates:** Updates, used to repair and/or replace software, consist of metadata (properties of the actual updated data) that allows you to determine its uses and the update files that are required to install the update on a computer. These updates are categorized under the following nodes: All Updates, Critical Updates, Security Updates, and WSUS Updates.
- **Computers:** These groups are created by default during the WSUS installation. Groups enable you to target your updates to specific computers and to stagger your rollout of updates. You do not see any computers in the console until you have configured the clients to use WSUS.
  - **All Computers:** Includes all computers.
  - **Unassigned Computers:** If a computer is not assigned to a group, it is added to this node the first time it contacts the WSUS server.
- **Downstream servers:** This lists the downstream servers that obtain their update files, metadata, and approvals from this WSUS server instead of from Microsoft Update or Windows Update.
- **Synchronizations:** During synchronization, the WSUS server downloads updates in the form of metadata and files from an update source. This can be another WSUS server or from the Microsoft servers and Windows Update servers.
- **Reports:** These reports allow you to monitor updates, computers, and synchronization results. You can also roll up data from downstream servers.
- **Options:** This folder provides access to tools you can use to modify settings on the WSUS server. Using the tools provided, you can specify how you want to approve the installation of updates, change your synchronization schedule, clean up old computers, update files from the server, and choose how data is displayed in the Update Services console.

Understanding Server

When you have both upstream and a downstream WSUS servers run on your network, you might want to control how update approvals, settings, computers, and groups are managed. To do this, you must first understand the two modes WSUS can run in: replica and autonomous.

As you learned from setting up the upstream and downstream WSUS servers earlier, you have two options about where you obtained your updates. You can synchronize directly from the Microsoft Update servers or from another WSUS server on your network. The choice you did not have to make at the time was whether or not your downstream WSUS server was going to run in replica or autonomous mode. By default, your downstream WSUS server was automatically set to run in in autonomous (distribution) mode.

In ***replica mode*** a WSUS server mirrors update approvals, settings, computers, and groups from the upstream server. In other words, the downstream server cannot be used to approve updates; they must be performed on the upstream server.

If you are operating the WSUS server in ***autonomous (distribution) mode***, it enables you to configure separate update approval settings while still retrieving updates from the upstream WSUS server.

Now that you understand the difference between the two, there might come a time when you decide that you want to manage the approval of all updates from the upstream server. This is common in situations where you have a downstream WSUS server at a branch office that has no IT support staff. If that happens, you need to understand how to configure your downstream WSUS server to run in replica mode.

CONFIGURE A DOWNSTREAM WSUS SERVER TO RUN IN REPLICA MODE

GET READY. To assign your downstream WSUS server to run in Replica mode, log in to your member server with Administrative privileges, and perform the following steps:

1. The *Server Manager* console opens automatically. If it does not open, on the task bar, click the **Server Manager** icon.
2. Click **Tools** > **Windows Server Update Services**.
3. From the pane on the left, click **Options**, and then choose **Update Source and Proxy Server**.
4. Select **This server is a replica of the upstream server**, and then click **OK**.
5. From the *left* pane, expand **Updates**, and then click the **All Updates** folder.
6. In the *middle* pane, change the status to **Any** and click **Refresh** (see Figure 13-8).

Figure 13-8

Reviewing All Updates

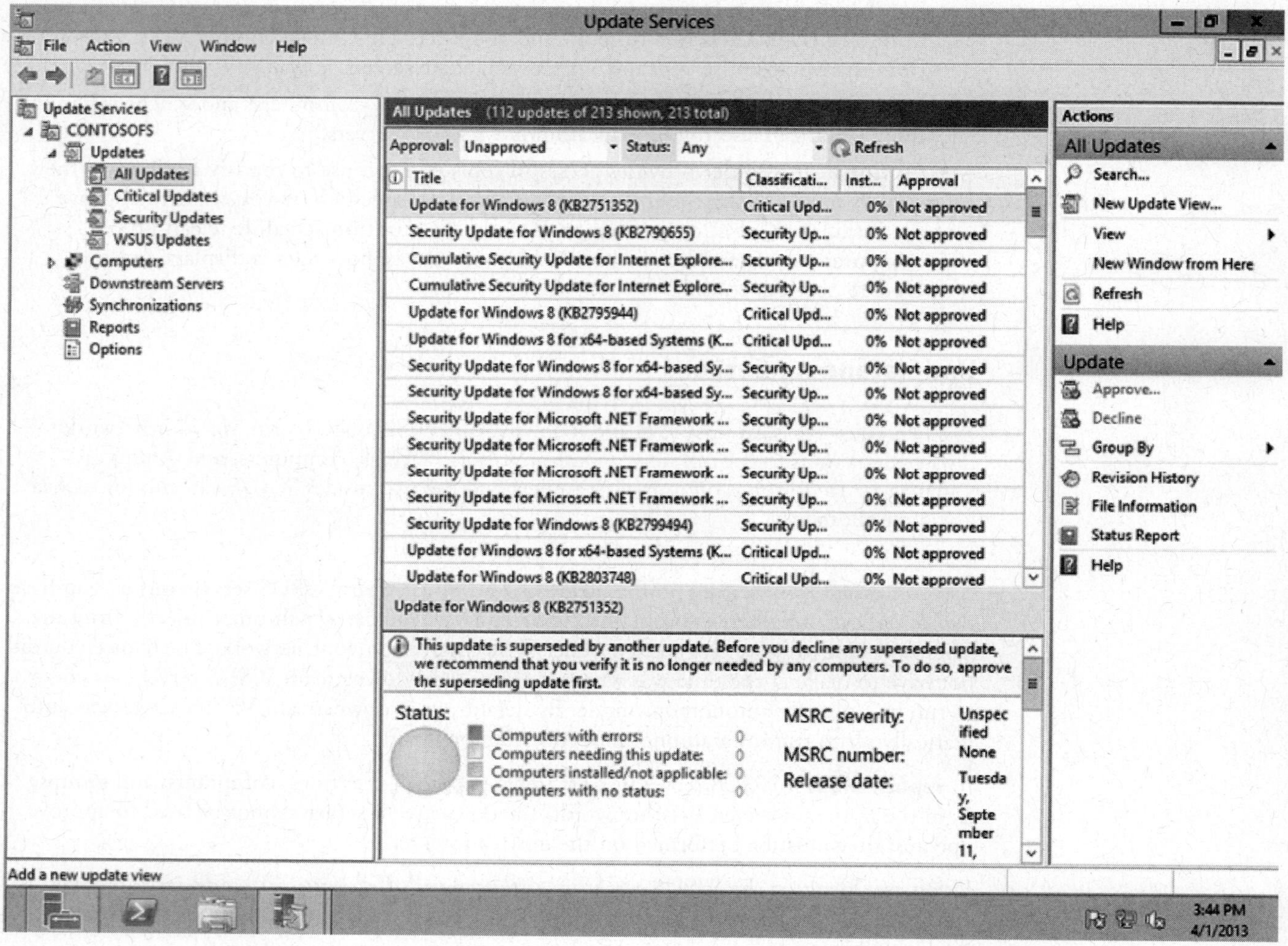

7. Right-click the first update in the list. In the menu that appears, you notice that the option to *Approve* or *Decline* the update is disabled. The downstream server has been configured in replica mode earlier. Updates can be approved only on the upstream server.
8. Close the **Update Services** console.

Configuring Clients to Use WSUS

For clients to obtain their information from your WSUS servers, you need to first configure them. By default, your computers are configured to communicate directly with the Microsoft Update servers. With an Active Directory domain present, you can create a Group Policy Object to configure your clients.

CREATE A GPO TO ENABLE AUTOUPDATE FOR CLIENT COMPUTERS

GET READY. To create a GPO to enable AutoUpdate for client computers in an Active Directory domain, log in with Administrative credentials, and then on your domain controller, perform the following steps:

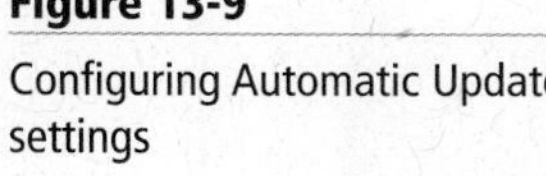

TAKE NOTE*

This can be performed on a Windows 8 client with Administrative tools or at the Domain Controller for the domain using the Group Policy Management console.

1. The *Server Manager* console opens automatically. If it does not open, on the task bar, click the **Server Manager** icon.
2. Click **Tools > Group Policy Management**.
3. Right-click the **Group Policy Objects** folder and select **New**.
4. In the *Name* field, type **WSUS AutoUpdate**, and then click **OK**.
5. Expand the **Group Policy Objects** folder, right-click **WSUS AutoUpdate**, and then select **Edit**.
6. Expand the **Computer Configuration > Policies > Administrative Templates > Windows Components > Windows Update**.
7. In the *details* pane, double-click **Configure Automatic Updates**.
8. Under *Configure Automatic Updates*, click **Enabled** and under *Configure Automatic updating*, review the options.
9. Under *Configure automatic updating*, make sure **3-Auto download and notify for install** is visible. Read the information in the *help* panel to understand how this setting works. Click **OK** when finished (see Figure 13-9).

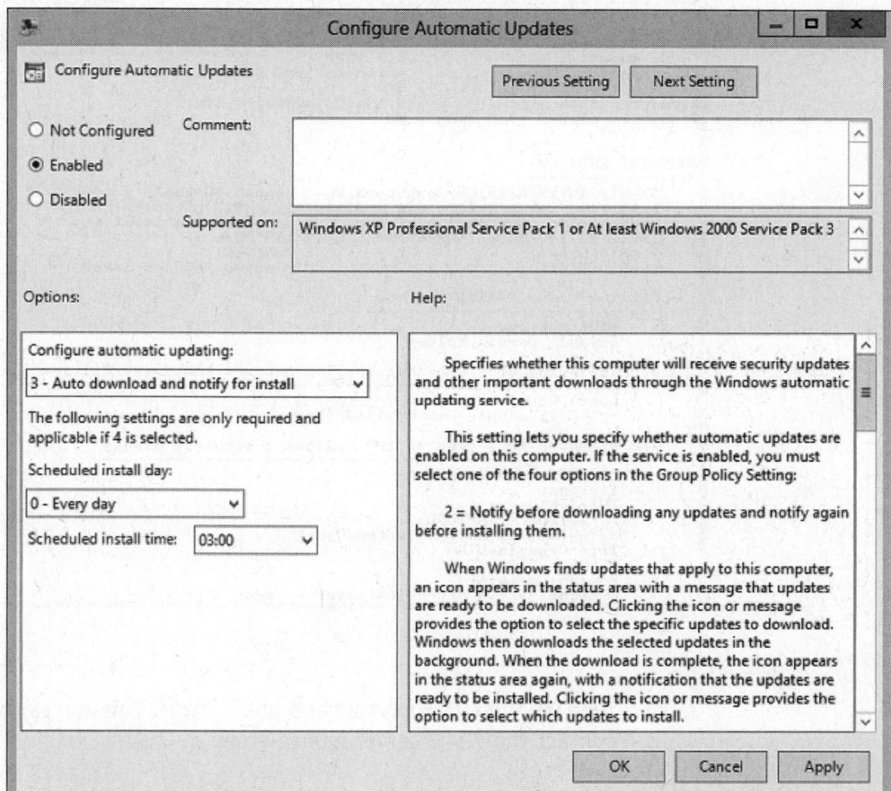

Figure 13-9

Configuring Automatic Update settings

10. Double-click **Specify intranet Microsoft update service location**.
11. Under *Specify intranet Microsoft update service location,* click **Enabled** and then type the URL of the upstream WSUS server you set up earlier. For example, if your domain controller's name is ContosoDC, you type **http://ContosoDC:8530**. 8530 is the default port used by WSUS.
12. For the *intranet statistics server,* type the same information.
13. Click **OK**.
14. Close the **Group Policy Management Editor**.
15. Right-click the domain container (contoso.com) and select **Link an existing GPO**.
16. Choose **WSUS AutoUpdate**, and then click **OK**.
17. Close the **Group Policy Management** console.
18. Restart your Windows 8 computer and then log in with Administrative credentials to the domain.
19. In the Windows 8 *Start* screen, type **cmd**. In *Results,* right-click **Command Prompt**, and then choose **Run as administrator**.
20. From the *Command Prompt window,* type **gpresult /r** and press **Enter**. The *WSUS AutoUpdate GPO* should appear (see Figure 13-10) under the *Computer Settings > Applied Group Policy Objects* section of the report. If it does not, type **gpupdate /force** and they try **gpresult /r** again.

TAKE NOTE*

Perform these steps on a Windows 8 computer that is a member of the Active Directory domain.

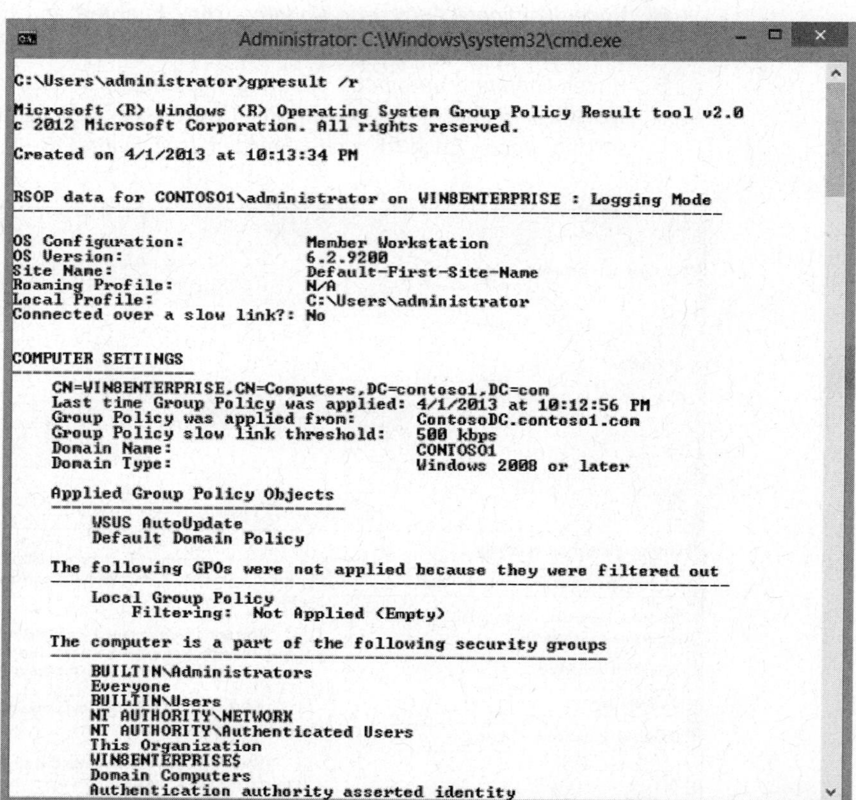

Figure 13-10
Running gpresult /r

21. Type **wuauclt /detectnow** and press **Enter**. This forces the Windows 8 computer to contact the WSUS server immediately.

22. Open the **Update Service** console on the domain controller running WSUS (**Server Manager > Tools > Windows Server Update Services**).
23. Expand the **Computers > All Computers** group. You can see the computer under the *Unassigned Computers* group.

Using Computer Groups with WSUS

After configuring your clients to use WSUS, organize them into computer groups. This enables you to target specific systems for updates. WSUS comes with two built-in groups: All Computers and Unassigned Computers. If you don't have a need to configure and manage your computers separately, you can stay with these groups. If you want to test the impact the updates will have on your computers and any line of business applications before rolling them out to your entire organization, then new groups should be complete.

Here are a few things to note about computer groups:

- If a computer is not assigned to a specific group, it appears in the Unassigned Computers group in the console.
- A computer can be a member of more than one group, and groups can be built in a hierarchical structure.
- If you create a group hierarchy, an update rolled out to a parent group is also distributed to child groups.

CREATE A GROUP IN WSUS

GET READY. To create a group on your domain controller running WSUS, log in with Administrative privileges, and then perform the following steps:

1. Open the **Update Services** console if you closed it earlier (**Server Manager > Tools > Windows Server Update Services**).
2. Expand the **Computers** node, right-click **All Computers**, and then select **Add Computer Group**.
3. In the *Name* field, type **IT Staff**, and then click **Add**.
4. Confirm the group appears under the **All Computers** node. Keep the *Update Services* console open to use in the next exercise.

Selecting Server-Side Versus Client-Side Targeting

Computers can be assigned to groups using either server-side targeting or client-side targeting. ***Server-side targeting*** involves moving clients to computer groups using the Update Services console. ***Client-side targeting*** involves using Group Policy for domain computers or Local Group Policy Editor for nondomain computers. When using client-side targeting, you configure the computers to add themselves automatically to the computer groups by specifying the group in the Computer Configuration \ Policies \ Administrative Tools \ Windows Components \ Windows Update \ Enable client-side targeting policy. Client-side targeting works well when you organize your computers into organizational units based on their configuration or function.

These settings (see Figure 13-11) are configured on the WSUS Server via *Update Services > Options > Computers.*

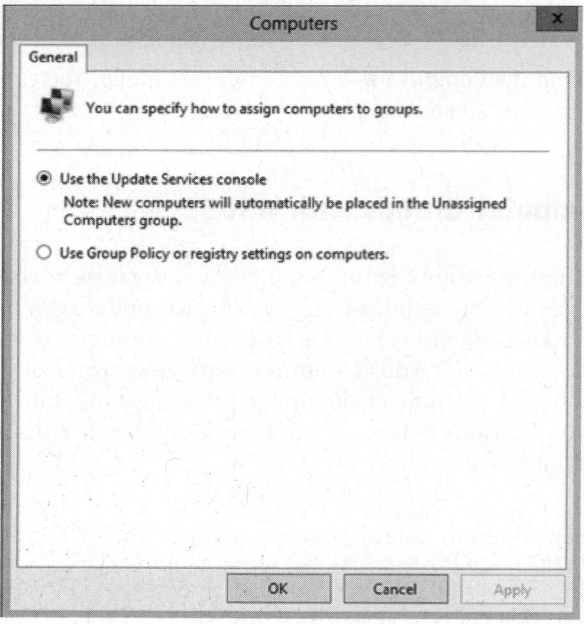

Figure 13-11

Enabling server-side versus client-side targeting on the WSUS server

Selecting the *Use the Update Services* console is using server-side targeting; computers are automatically added to the Unassigned Computers group. The other option, *Use Group Policy or registry settings on computers*, configures the WSUS server to support client-side targeting.

USE SERVER-SIDE TARGETING TO MOVE A COMPUTER TO A GROUP

GET READY. To use server-side targeting, on your domain controller running WSUS, log in with Administrative privileges, and then perform the following steps:

1. From the *Update Services* console, expand **Computers**.
2. In the *Unassigned Computers* group, right-click the **Windows 8 computer** and choose **Change Membership**.
3. Select **IT Staff**, and then click **OK** to add the computer to the group.
4. Click the **IT Staff** group, and in the *middle* pane, confirm the computer appears. Keep the *Update Services* console open to use in the next exercise.

Approving and Installing Updates on the Client Computers

Updates downloaded to the upstream server will not be distributed to WSUS clients automatically. As the WSUS administrator, you have to approve them first. If you look under *Options > Automatic Approval*, you can see the following default WSUS settings:

- **Update Rules:** Under this tab, you can specify rules for automatically approving new updates when they are synchronized. The default rule approves security and critical updates for all computers.
- **Advanced tab:** The following options are configured by default under this tab: Automatically approve updates to the WSUS product, Automatically approve new revisions of updates that are already approved, and Automatically decline updates when a new revision causes them to expire.

As the administrator, you can change which updates are automatically detected, which ones are automatically approved, and which groups of computers are targeted to receive the updates.

APPROVE AND DEPLOY WSUS UPDATES

GET READY. To approve and deploy WSUS updates, on your domain controller running WSUS, log in with Administrative privileges, and then perform the following steps:

1. From the *Update Services* console, expand **Updates**, and then click **All Updates**.
2. Set the *Status* to **Needed** (see Figure 13-12), and then click **Refresh**.

Figure 13-12

Setting the Status to Needed updates

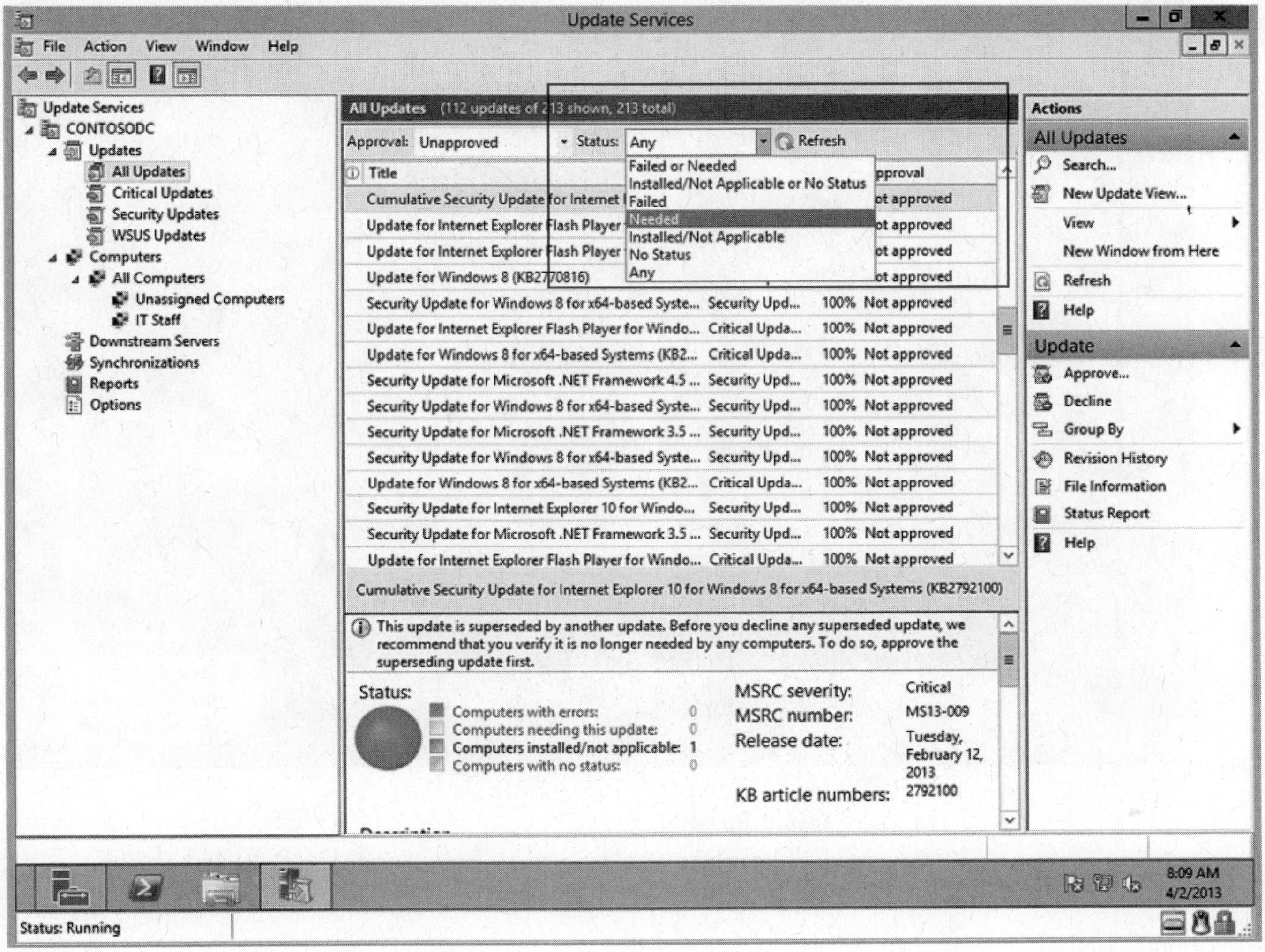

3. Right-click one of the updates, and then choose **Approve**.
4. In the *Approve* Updates box, click **IT Staff** > **Approved for Install**.
5. Click **OK**.
6. When the approval process completes, click **Close**.

   On the Windows 8 Client

7. Log on to a Windows 8 computer that is a member of the domain.
8. In the Windows 8 *Start* screen, type **cmd**. In *Results,* right-click **Command Prompt**, and then choose **Run as administrator**.
9. From the *Command Prompt window*, type **wuauclt /detectnow**, and then press **Enter**. Close the *Command Prompt window*. This causes the client to detect available

updates, automatically queue them for download via Background Intelligent Transfer Service (BITS), and then present a notification to install the updates on the client.

10. Right-click the notification icon and select **Open Windows Update** (see Figure 13-13).

Figure 13-13

Opening Windows Update via the Notification icon

11. Click **Install Updates**.
12. If you are prompted after the updates are completed, click **Restart now** to complete the installation of the update.

Managing Client Security Using Windows Defender

THE BOTTOM LINE

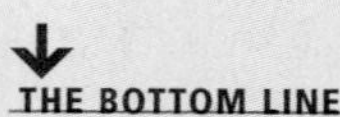

Windows Defender is designed to protect your computer against viruses, spyware, and other types of malware. It protects against these threats by providing real-time protection in which it notifies you if malware attempts to install itself on your computer or when an application tries to change critical settings.

It can also be configured to scan your computer on a regular basis and remove or quarantine malware it finds.

MORE INFORMATION

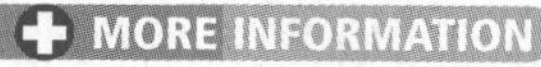

Windows Defender automatically disables itself if you install another antivirus product.

CERTIFICATION READY
Manage client security using Windows Defender
Objective 3.4

At the heart of Windows Defender are its definition files, which are downloaded from Windows Update. The definition files, which contain information about potential threats, are used by Windows Defender to notify you of potential threats to your system.

To access Windows Defender from the Windows 8S menu, type *Windows Defender* and choose it from the *Results*. When Windows Defender opens, you see the screen in Figure 13-14.

Figure 13-14

Viewing the Windows Defender Home tab

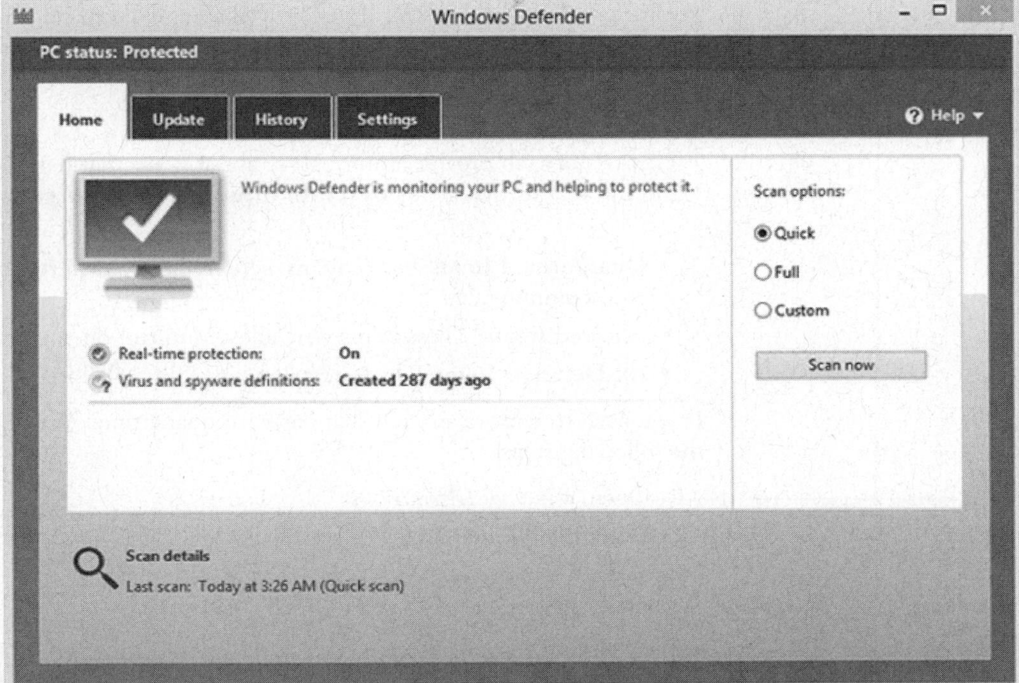

Exploring the Home Tab

- **Status of Real-time protection:** Real-time protection uses signature detection methodology and heuristics to monitor and catch malware behavior. Signature detection uses a vendor's definition files to detect malicious programs. If the program contains code that matches the signature, the program most likely contains the virus. This works well when the threat has already been identified, but what happens in between the time the virus is released and the definition file is made available? That's where heuristics can help. It is used to monitor for suspicious activity by a program. Suspicious activity includes a program trying to copy itself into another program, a program trying to write to the disk directly, or a program trying to manipulate critical system files required by the operating system. These are indicators of possible malware activity that heuristics can detect.
- **Virus and spyware definitions:** When a new virus is discovered, Microsoft creates a new virus signature/definition update. Each definition file contains a piece of the actual virus code that is used to detect a specific virus or malware. During scans, the content on the computer is compared to information in the definition files. Because new viruses are created every day and existing viruses are modified regularly, it's important to keep your definitions updated.
- **Scan options (Quick, Full, and Custom):** A Quick scan checks the areas that malicious software, including viruses, spyware, and unwanted software are most likely to infect. A Full scan checks all the files on your disk including running programs. A Custom scan is designed to check only locations and files you specify.
- **Scan Details:** This area of the Home tab provides information on when the last scan was performed on the computer.

Exploring the Update Tab

Selecting the Update tab provides you with information about your virus and spyware definitions. It is important to keep these current to ensure your computer is protected at all times. The Update tab provides information about when the definition files were created, the last time you updated them, and the current version numbers for the virus and spyware definitions. Windows Defender updates the definition files automatically, but you can manually check for updates by clicking Update on this tab.

Exploring the History Tab

This History tab provides information about items that have been detected in the past and the actions that were taken with them. There are categories of items here:

- **Quarantined Items:** These items were not allowed to run but were not removed from your computer.
- **Allowed Items:** These items were allowed to run on your computer.
- **All Detected Items:** These items provide a list of all items detected on your computer.

If you need to remove an item that has been quarantined (see Figure 13-15), you can perform the following steps:

1. Open *Windows Defender.*
2. Select the *History Tab.*
3. Select *Quarantined Items.*

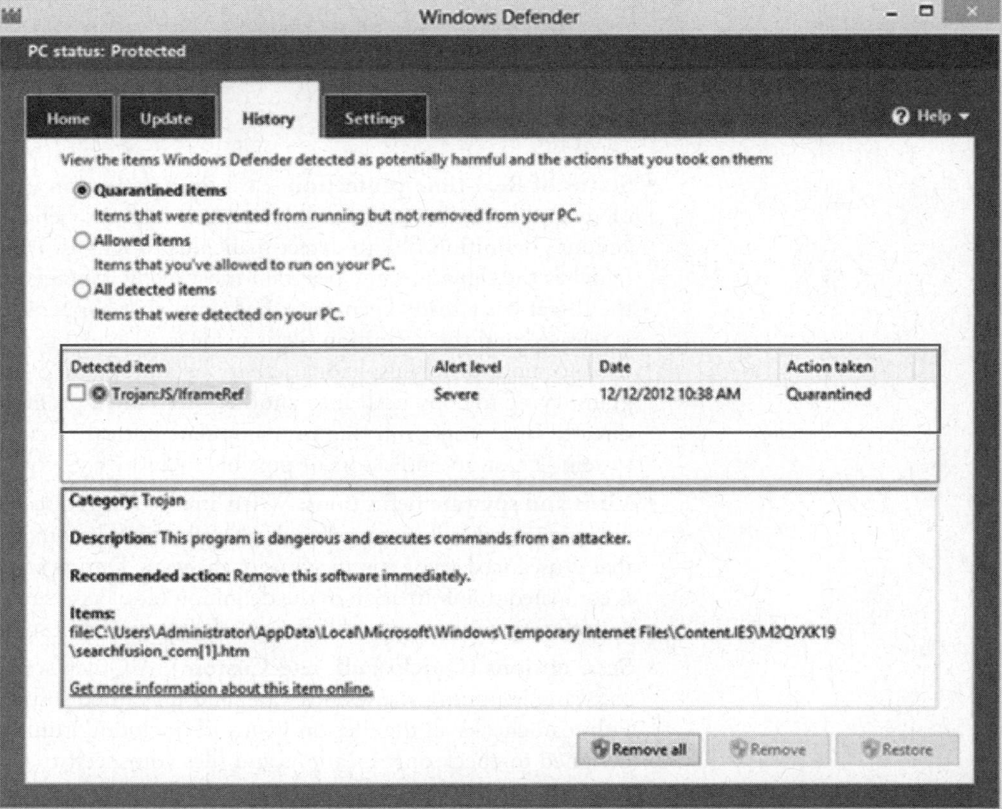

Figure 13-15
Removing a quarantined item

4. Click *View Details.*
5. Select the detected item and read the description (see Figure 13-13).
6. Select *Remove.*

Exploring the Settings Tab

The Settings tab is where you can fine tune how Windows Defender works. In this tab, you can:

- Enable or disable real-time protection.
- Select the files and locations you want to exclude from the scanning process.
- Select the file types you want to exclude from the scan.
- Select the processes you want to exclude.
- Configure Advanced settings that include enabling scans of archive files (cab/zip), scanning removable drives, creating system restore points, allowing users to view full history results, and establishing how long you want to hold quarantine files before they are removed. By default, Windows Defender scans archive files and removes quarantined files after three months.
- Turn on Windows Defender.

Understanding the Microsoft Active Protection Service

On the Settings tab, you can also determine whether you want to participate in the ***Microsoft Active Protection Service (MAPS)***. MAPS is an online community that can help you decide how to respond to certain threat types and it serves as a resource to help stop the spread of new viruses and malware. The information that you send helps Microsoft create new definition files. MAPS also sends you alerts when unclassified software is detected on your computer. There are three options to choose from:

- **I don't want to join MAPS:** Selecting this option means no information is sent to Microsoft.
- **Basic Membership:** This option sends information to Microsoft about where the software came from, the actions you took, and whether the actions you took were successful. This is enabled by default.
- **Advanced Membership:** This option sends Basic membership information such as the location of the software, file names, how the software operates, and how it has impacted your computer.

Windows Defender can also be configured via the Local Group Policy Editor (see Figure 13-16) or Group Policy Management Editor (AD domains). The following policies are located in the *Computer Configuration\Administrative Templates\Windows Components\Windows Defender* node:

- **Check for New Signatures before Scheduled Scans:** When enabled, Windows Defender checks for new signatures before running the scan.
- **Turn off Windows Defender:** This setting turns Windows Defender on or off.
- **Turn off Real-Time Monitoring:** This setting controls whether Windows Defender monitors your system in real-time and alerts you malware for potentially unwanted software attempts to install or run on the computer.
- **Turn off Routinely Taking Action:** This setting determines whether Windows Defender automatically takes action on malware that it identifies.
- **Configure Microsoft Active Protection Service Reporting:** This setting determines the type of membership you use with MAPS. Options include *No Membership, Basic Membership*, or *Advanced Membership.*

Figure 13-16

Viewing the Local Group Policy settings for Windows Defender

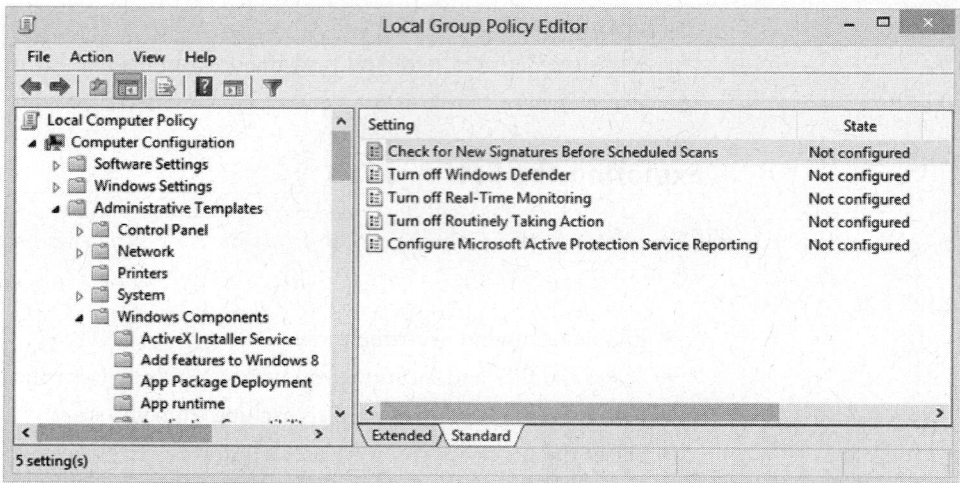

SCHEDULE A WINDOWS DEFENDER SCAN

GET READY. To schedule a Windows Defender scan, log in with Administrative privileges, and perform the following steps:

1. Press the **Windows logo key** + r and in the *Run* dialog box, type **taskschd.msc**.
2. In the left pane, expand the **Task Scheduler Library** > **Microsoft** > **Windows** > **Windows Defender**.
3. Double-click the **Windows Defender Scheduled Scan** (see Figure 13-17).

Figure 13-17

Opening the Windows Defender Scheduled Scan

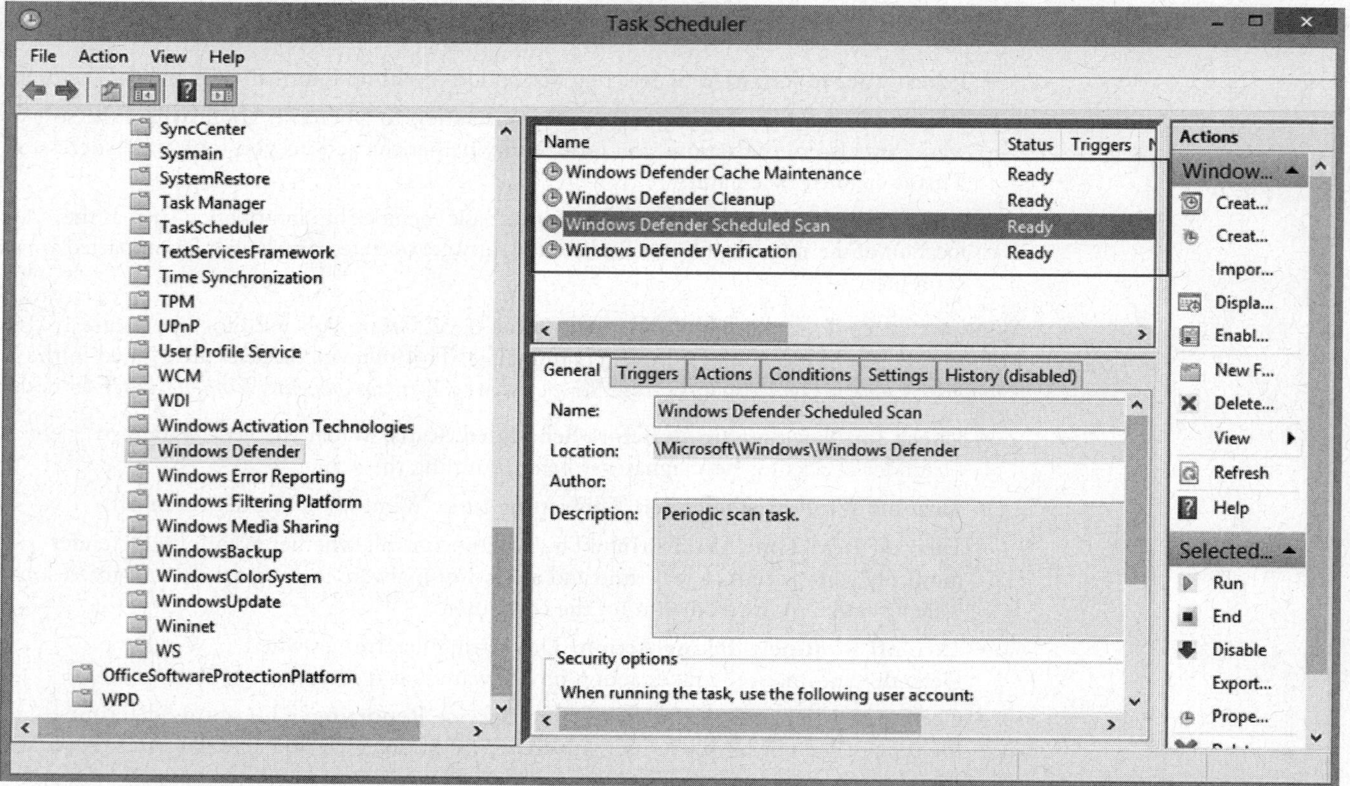

4. Click the **Triggers** tab and then click **New**.
5. In the *Begin the task* field, choose **On a schedule**.
6. Under *Settings*, select **One time** and in the *Start* field, change the time to 5 minutes from your current time.
7. Make sure the e **Enabled** check box is checked, and then click **OK**.
8. To close the *Windows Defender Scheduled Scan Properties* dialog box, click **OK**.
9. (Figure 13-18). Open **Windows Defender** to see the status of the scan on the Home tab. Click **Cancel scan**.

Figure 13-18

Cancelling the scheduled scan

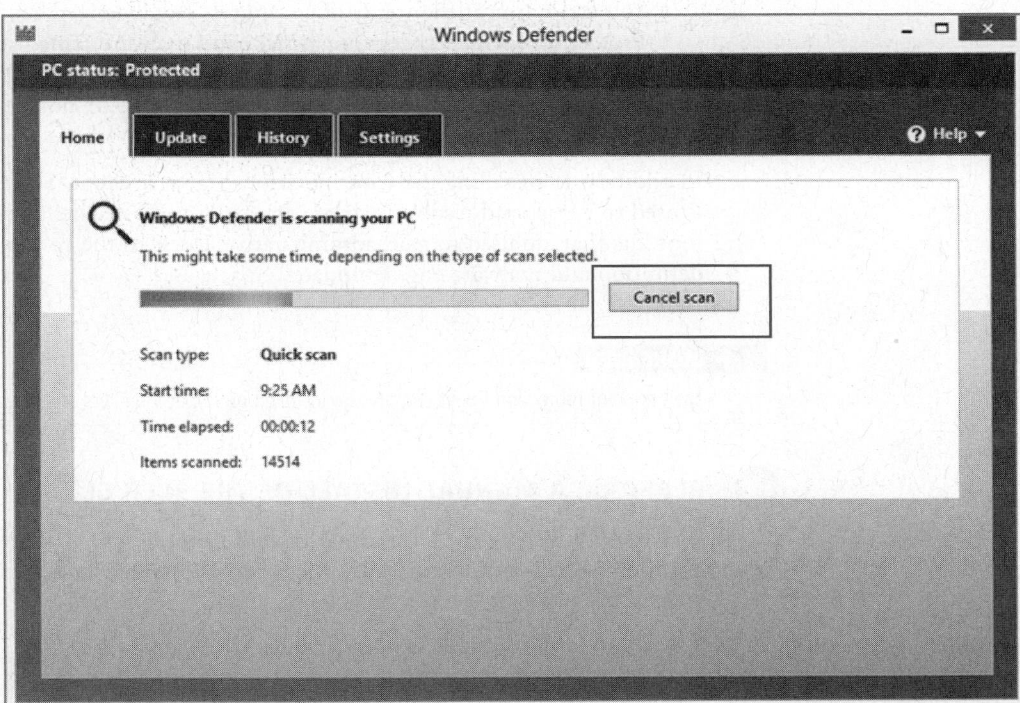

Managing Client Security Using SCCM 2012 Endpoint Protection Client

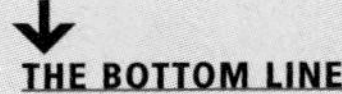
THE BOTTOM LINE

SCEP, integrated with System Center Configuration Manager 2012 (SCCM), provides a central point of management for deploying and managing malware threats.

System Center Endpoint Protection (SCEP) client, a product in the Microsoft System Center 2012 suite, is designed to protect clients and servers from malware threats. Although many of the products were offered as standalone versions in previous releases, SCEP is now integrated with the System Center Configuration Manager. SCCM provides a central console for managing application delivery, device management, and security. By integrating SCEP with the Configuration Manager, you now have the ability to take advantage of its remediation and compliance capabilities, as well as the protection features provided by Endpoint Protection.

CERTIFICATION READY
Manage client security using Microsoft System Center 2012 Endpoint Client
Objective 3.4

Using Endpoint Protection with Configuration Manager, you can manage your antimalware policies and Windows Firewall security for client computers and servers and monitor compliance and security across your entire organization. This provides the following capabilities and benefits:

You can target antimalware policies and Windows Firewall settings to selected computers.

- You can use Configuration Manager Software updates to obtain the latest definition files and keep your client computers current.
- You can send email notifications, use in-console monitoring, and view reports when malware is detected on client computers.
- You can monitor the status of computers (total active clients protected by Endpoint Protection), which clients are at risk, and malware remediation status (failed remediation, full scans required, client settings modified by malware, malware remediated in the last 24 hours, status of deployed antimalware policies, the definition status on computers, and so on).

In addition to installing the Configuration Manager client, SCEP installs its own client that is used to detect and resolve malware and spyware. The client also detects and addresses root kits that are used to gain administrative access to the computer and perform automatic definition and malware engine updates.

MORE INFO
The Endpoint Protection Client can also be installed on Hyper-V servers and guest machines.

PERFORM A MANUAL INSTALL OF THE SCEP CLIENT

GET READY. To perform a manual installation of the SCEP client, log in to your Windows 8 computer with administrative privileges, and perform the following steps:

TAKE NOTE*
This requires an installation of System Center Configuration Manager 2012 to gain access to the shared folder.

1. Connect to the SCCM 2012 Server at \\servername\SMS_sitecode\client.
2. Double-click the **scepinstall** file.
3. When the *System Center 2012 Endpoint Protection Installation Wizard* starts, click **Next**.
4. On the *Licensing* screen, click **I accept**.
5. Select **I do not want to join the program at this time**, and then click **Next**.
6. Enable the option **if no firewall is turned on, turn on the Windows Firewall (recommended)**, and then click **Next**.
7. Click **Install**.
8. Click **Finish**. SCEM installs the latest virus and spyware definitions from Microsoft and performs a quick scan (see Figure 13-19).

Figure 13-19

Performing Quick scan with the System Center Endpoint Client

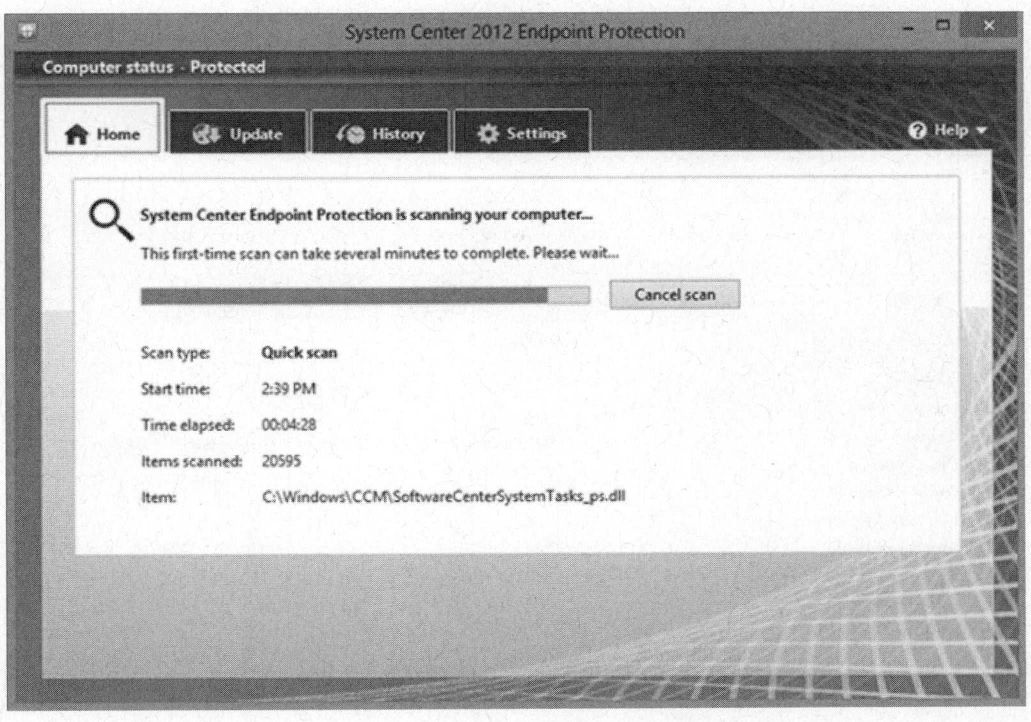

To manage malware, you create antimalware policies that contain settings used for Endpoint Protection Client configurations. You then deploy these policies to your computers and monitor them from the *Configuration Manager\System Center 2012 Endpoint Protection Status* node.

The basic steps to create an antimalware policy are as follows:

1. Expand *Assets and Compliance.*
2. Double-click *Overview.*
3. Expand *Endpoint Protection.*
4. Right-click *Antimalware Policies,* and then click Create Antimalware Policy.

CREATE AN ANTIMALWARE POLICY

GET READY. To create an antimalware policy, log in to your server running SCCM 2012, and perform the following steps:

TAKE NOTE*

This requires an installation of System Center Configuration Manager 2012.

1. Open the **Configuration Manager** console and right-click **Antimalware Policies.** Choose **Create Antimalware Policy** (see Figure 13-20).
2. In the *Name* field, type a name and description for the policy. For example, **SCEPMalwarePolicy.**
3. Click each link in the *left* pane to configure the policy according to your requirements.

Figure 13-20

Creating an antimalware policy

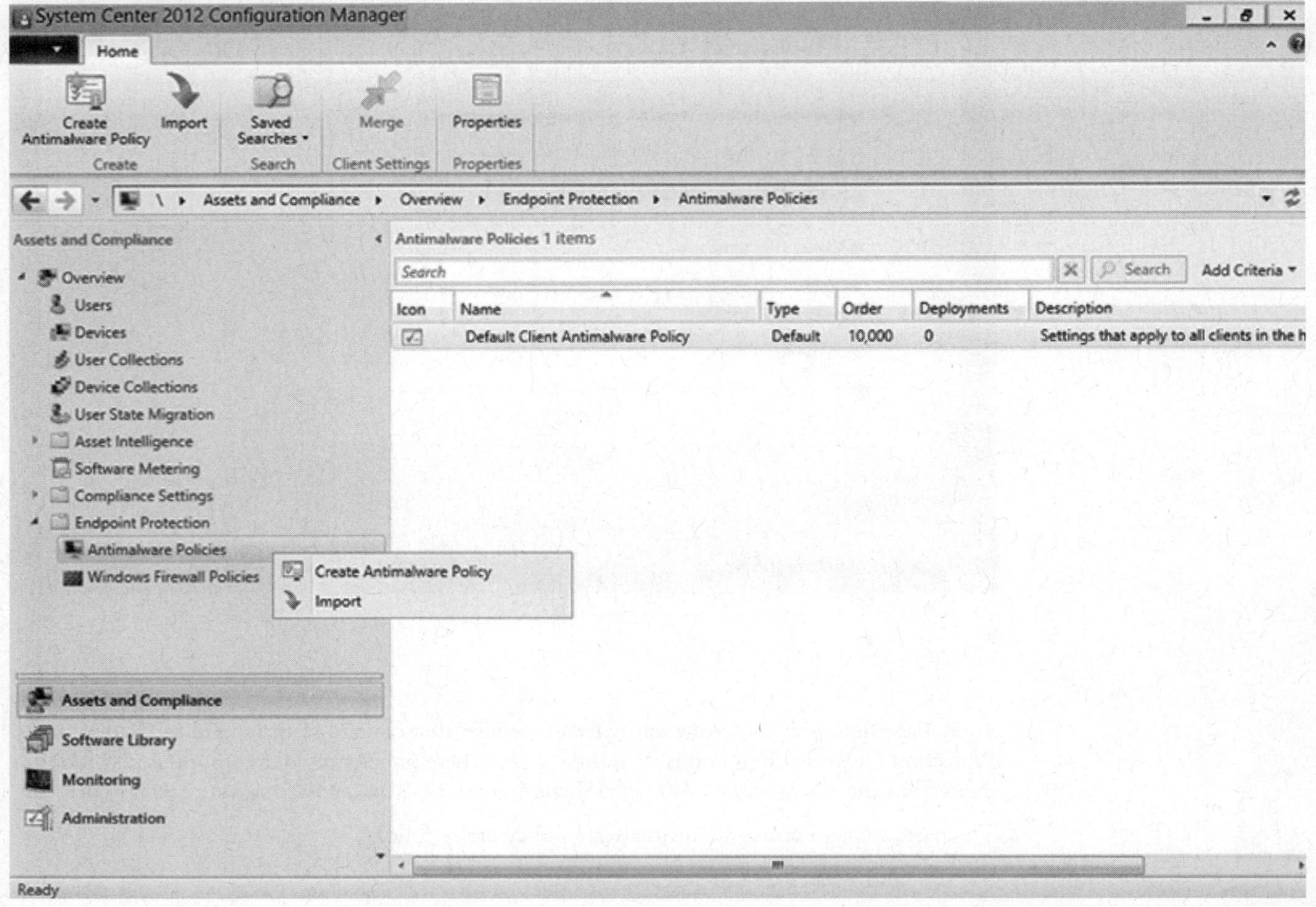

The following provides information about each of the settings for the antimalware policy:

- **Scheduled scans:** Settings here determine the scan type (quick/full) to use and whether or not to enable randomized scans to prevent computers from sending their antimalware scan results to the Configuration Manager database.
- **Scan settings:** Settings here determine whether to scan mapped drives on the client when running a full scan.
- **Default actions:** Settings here determine how to respond when malware is detected on the client. Options include using the action recommended in the definition file, quarantining the malware, and removing it or allowing it.
- **Real-time protection:** Settings here are used to configure real-time protection, determine whether you want to scan system files, download files and attachments, and allow users on client computers to configure real-time protection settings on their client.
- **Exclusion settings:** Settings here determine which files and folders you want to exclude from the Endpoint Protection scans.
- **Advanced:** Settings here enable you to create a system restore point before computers are cleaned. Show notification messages to users when they need to run full scans, download the latest Endpoint Protection software, quarantine settings, and determine whether you allow users to exclude files, folders, and file types, and whether they can view the full history results.

- **Threat Overrides:** Settings here determine remediation actions to take based on the threat ID.
- **Definition Updates:** Settings here determine the source for definition and engine scanning updates, the frequency the client checks for definitions, and whether to force definition updates to clients who have missed a certain number of consecutive updates.
- **Security:** Provides information on which administrative users have permission for the antimalware policy.

To deploy the policy to your client computers, perform the following steps:

1. Right-click the **SCEPMalwarePolicy** you created earlier.
2. Click **Deploy**.
3. Choose the collection (see Figure 13-21) you want to deploy the policy to and then click **OK**.

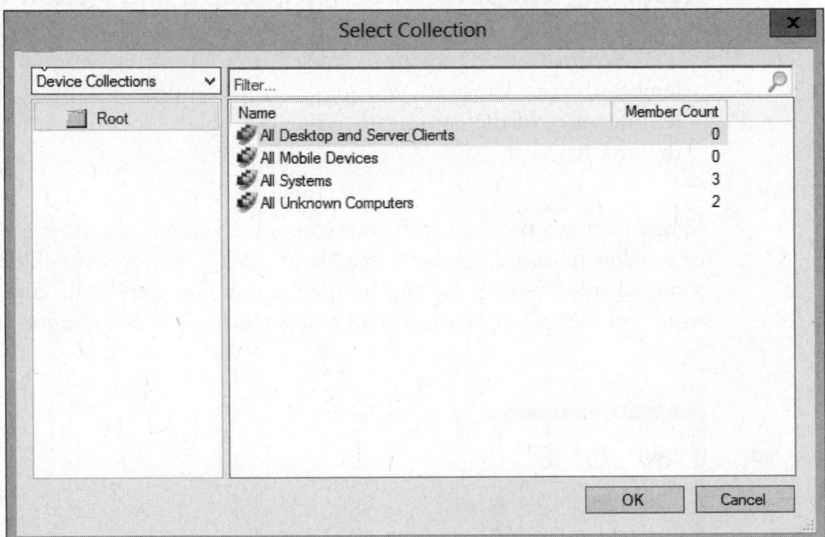

Figure 13-21

Deploying antimalware policy: choosing a collection

Configuring Application Reputation

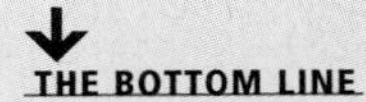

THE BOTTOM LINE

Application Reputation provides an early warning system to address the gap between the release of a new malware and the point in which antimalware products can recognize them.

In Windows 8, ***Application Reputation*** is designed to provide protection from downloading malware and phishing attacks. With new malware and phishing attacks appearing on a daily basis, there is always a gap between their release and the point at which they can be detected and blocked by anti-virus programs.

CERTIFICATION READY
Configure application reputation
Objective 3.4

Application reputation is the early warning system that alerts you before running unrecognized applications or downloading files from the Internet during this in-between period.

In Lesson 2 you learned how SmartScreen was used with Internet Explorer. Windows 8 also uses SmartScreen in File Explorer to double-check any executable files you attempt to run and use. The same principles discussed in Lesson 2 apply with File Explorer. You can adjust SmartScreen settings via the Action Center discussed in the next section.

Resolving Endpoint Security Issues

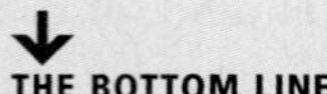

THE BOTTOM LINE

Windows 8 provides several tools to help manage endpoint security issues. These include Action Center, Windows Defender, Windows Firewall, and third-party applications.

CERTIFICATION READY
Resolve endpoint security issues
Objective 3.4

Windows 8 provides the following tools for monitoring and resolving endpoint security issues. The information provided and the process you use to troubleshoot is explained in the sections that follow:

- Action Center
- Windows Defender
- Windows Firewall

Resolving Endpoint Security Issues Using Action Center

The ***Action Center*** provides a central location for viewing notifications regarding problems with your hardware and software. It also provides information related to security and maintenance of the computer. When a problem does occur, you receive a notification in the task bar.

When there is a problem with your computer, you will see either a red x on the Action Center icon or a yellow message. The red x (see Figure 13-22) indicates a problem that needs to be addressed soon, whereas a yellow message indicates a task that you should consider addressing. Right-click the icon, and then select *Open Action Center* to view more information about the problem.

Figure 13-22
Viewing the Action Center red flag notice

Action Center is organized into two areas when it comes to reporting problems. They include the Security category and the Maintenance Category (see Figure 13-23).

Under the Security section, you can view information about the status of Windows Firewall, Windows Update, and Windows Defender. If these security features are not controlled by a Group Policy, you can configure them via the interface. Red indicates a warning message that should be addressed now, whereas Orange indicates something that you should consider addressing to improve the overall performance and stability of your system.

In Figure 13-23, a critical message indicates the Windows Firewall is turned off or set up incorrectly. Selecting *Turn on now* removes this message from the console, assuming the firewall was accidently turned off. In the case of the Windows Update message, there are additional updates available. Because Windows Update is controlled by the system administrator (via Group Policy), the option to change settings has been disabled on this computer.

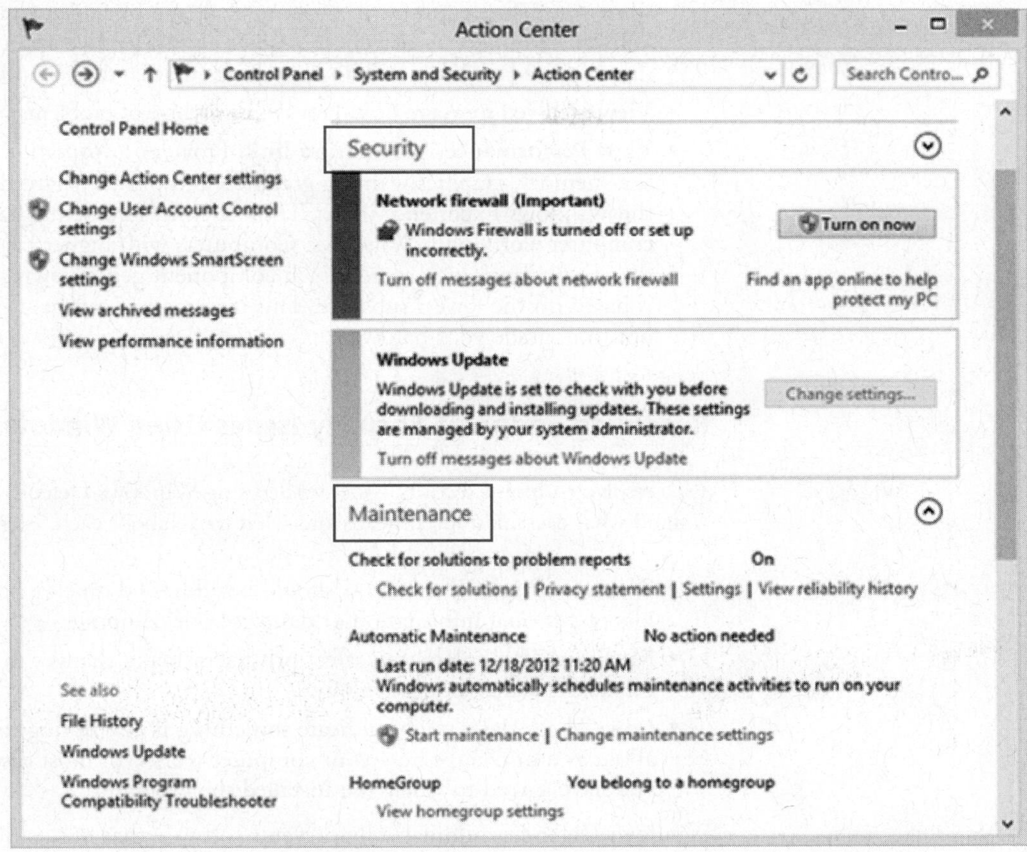

Figure 13-23

Reviewing the Security and Maintenance areas of Action Center

The Maintenance section provides you with the ability to:

- **Check for solutions to problem reports:** When you send problem reports to Microsoft, you receive solutions when they become available. These reports typically contain the name and version of an app that is not working and the date and time the problem occurred. They also include diagnostic information to help determine the cause of the problem.
- **Start automatic maintenance and change settings:** Automatic maintenance is scheduled to run daily at 3:00 AM to perform tasks such as software updates, security scanning, and system diagnostics.
- **View HomeGroup settings:** This allows you to change your network location, leave the HomeGroup, and make changes to advanced sharing settings.
- **Manage File History:** This allows you to change settings, restore personal files, and initiate a copy of files.
- **Drive status:** This provides information about the overall health of your drives.
- **Device software problems:** This provides information about the overall health of your devices.

In the left pane, you can configure additional settings.

- **Change User Account Control (UAC) settings:** This link allows you to make changes to the UAC settings, which are designed to prevent unauthorized changes to your computer. It does this by prompting you for permission before performing a task. The default setting is to notify you when programs try to make changes to your computer.
- **Change Windows SmartScreen settings:** This link allows you to make changes to the Windows SmartScreen feature. SmartScreen is designed to provide warnings before you run unrecognized apps or download files from the Internet. The default setting is to

warn you before running an unrecognized app but not require administrative approval. You can modify settings here to require administrative approval before running an unrecognized app or not doing anything (that is, turn Windows SmartScreen off).

- **View archived message link:** Provides an archive of problems you have reported to Microsoft.
- **View Performance information link:** Provides information on how your processor, memory, graphics, gaming graphics, and primary hard disk perform based on the Windows Experience index. These are measurements that tell you how well your computer works with Windows. Computers with higher base scores perform better than those with lower base scores. Each component gets its own subscore; the total base score is based off the lowest subscore. This information can be used to determine whether or not to upgrade your hardware.

Resolving Endpoint Security Issues Using Windows Defender

To resolve endpoint security issues while using Windows Defender, it's important to understand what each alert level means and what to do about each. Alert levels are as follows:

- **Severe or High:** These alerts should be addressed quickly because they can result in the loss of personal information or damage your computer.
- **Medium:** These alerts can affect privacy or make changes to your computer that can impact its use in a negative way.
- **Low:** These alerts might indicate something is attempting to collection information about you or change how your computer works. In most cases, this is something that you have agreed to when you installed the program.

Windows Defender automatically prevents software that results in Severe or High alerts from running, and it places these things into the Quarantine Items category. For Medium and Low alerts, you need to do a little more research. If you don't trust the publisher of the software, you can either block it from running or uninstall it. In each case, Windows Defender provides information about the detected item, provides you with a description of the program, and provides you with the recommended action to perform. For example, in the case of a Trojan virus, you see it is tagged with a severe alert level. Windows Defender also informs you the program is dangerous and executes commands from an attacker. The recommended action is to remove this software immediately.

Resolving Endpoint Security Issues Using Windows Firewall

Issues with Windows Firewall typically revolve around allowing apps to communicate through the firewall. To resolve problems, open the Windows Firewall (*Control Panel > System and Security > Windows Firewall*) and check its current settings.

As you can see in Figure 13-24, Windows Firewall is designed to block all connections to apps that are not on the list of allowed apps and notifies you when it blocks a new app.

In the left pane, you can select *Allow an app or feature through the Windows Firewall.* In the dialog box that appears, you can add, change, or remove allowed apps and ports by selecting the *Change settings* button. In general, it is more of a risk to add an app to the list of allowed apps then it is to open a port. Ports stay open until you close them, whereas apps use the communication link only when they need it.

The process of adding an app or opening a port is called unblocking. This enables the app to communicate through the firewall.

Figure 13-24

Viewing Windows Firewall settings

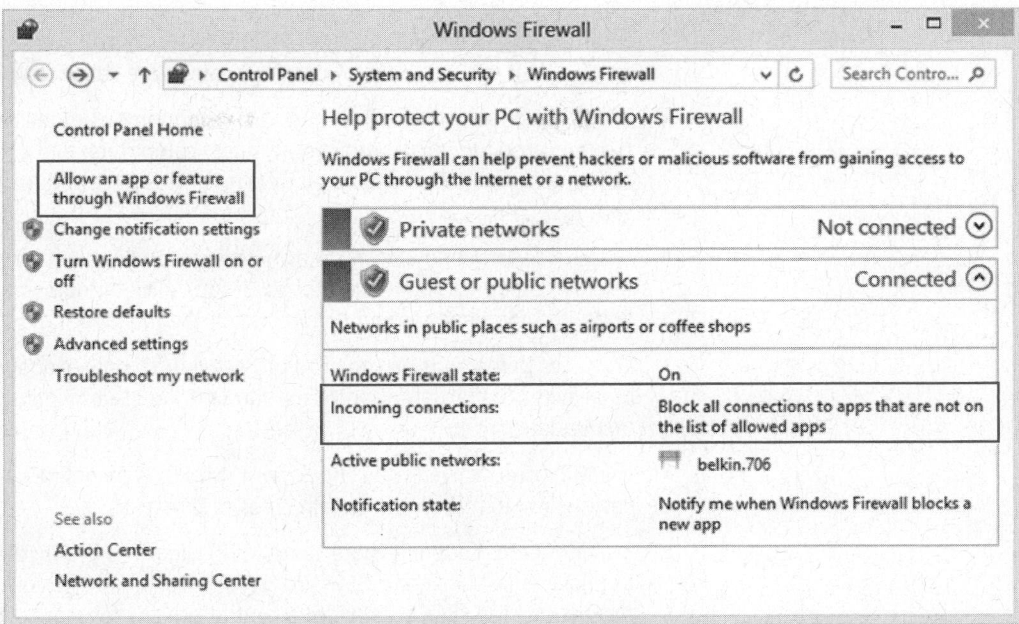

In situations where an Administrator has configured the Windows Firewall with Advanced features, you need to review the Inbound, Outbound, and Connection Security rules to determine whether there are conditions set to allow the traffic that you want to pass. In some situations, you may have a rule that allows your computer to interact with another one only if it is using IPsec to encrypt and authenticate the session. In these situations, you need to review the Connection Security rules to see whether there are further constraints that might help you resolve the problem.

Resolving Endpoint Security Issues with Third-Party Software

If you use third-party software (firewalls, anti-virus, malware, and so on), you need to consult the appropriate product documentation to determine your options. Windows Defender is designed to disable itself when it detects another anti-virus or malware program running. If you use other third-party apps, consider how these interact with each other, ensure you have the latest updates and patches, and ensure you have the latest versions of the software.

SKILL SUMMARY

IN THIS LESSON YOU LEARNED:

- Managing the security of your computers involves a multi-layered approach. This requires the latest service packs and patches that protect against malware, spyware, and viruses.
- Windows Update provides you with a way to keep your computers current by downloading and installing updates from the Windows Update site. Alternatively, you can centralize the administration, approval, and deployment of updates by using Windows Server Update Services (WSUS).

- Servers that obtain updates from Microsoft are called upstream servers and those that receive their updates from an upstream server are called downstream servers.
- WSUS supports both replica mode and autonomous mode configurations. Replica mode mirrors update approvals, settings, computers, and groups from the upstream server, whereas autonomous mode allows you to configure separate update approval settings.
- Server-side targeting involves moving clients to computer groups using the Update Service console; client-side targeting utilizes Group Policy for domain computers and Local Group Policy for nondomain computers to assign them to specific groups.
- Windows Defender is designed to protect your computer against viruses, spyware, and other types of malware in real-time through the use of virus signature updates and definition updates.
- The Microsoft Active Protection Service (MAPS) is an online community that can help you decide how to respond to certain types of threats.
- System Center Endpoint Protection (SCEP) client is a product available via System Center Configuration Manager (SCCM) 2012. It is designed to protect clients and servers against malware threats. SCCM provides a central console for managing application delivery, device management, and security across your organization.
- Application reputation is designed to provide protection from downloading malware and from phishing attacks. It provides a safety mechanism during the gap period between the release of a new virus and the release of virus definition protection files.
- Action Center provides a central location for viewing notifications regarding problems with your hardware and software and information related to the security and maintenance of your PC.

■ Knowledge Assessment

Multiple Choice

Select the correct answer for each of the following questions.

1. Which of the following can protect your PC against malware? Select all that apply.
   - **a.** Windows Defender
   - **b.** SCEP client
   - **c.** File History
   - **d.** SmartScreen
2. Microsoft releases a new code pack that enables you to view RAW camera files. What category of update does this fall under?
   - **a.** Recommended updates
   - **b.** Important updates
   - **c.** Optional updates
   - **d.** Suggested updates

3. Which is the correct location where you can configure how Windows Update functions?
   a. Control Panel > System > Windows Update
   b. Control Panel > System and Security > Windows Update
   c. Control Panel > System > Security > Windows Update
   d. Control Panel > Network and Internet > Windows Update

4. Which of the following is true about a replica mode WSUS server? Select all that apply.
   a. It mirrors update approvals, settings, computers, and groups from the upstream server.
   b. It mirrors update approvals, settings, computers, and groups from the downstream server.
   c. It can be used to approve updates.
   d. It cannot be used to approve updates.

5. Which of the following best describes server-side targeting? Select all that apply.
   a. Uses the Update Services console to move computers into computer groups.
   b. Uses Local Group Policy editor to create a group policy designating the computer group to add the computer to.
   c. Uses Group Policy Management console to create a group policy designating the computer group to add the computer to.
   d. Results in computers initially being added to the Unassigned Computers group.

6. Which command when run on a Windows 8 client detects available updates from the WSUS server, queues them, and then presents a notification to install the updates.
   a. `wuauclt /detect`
   b. `wuauclt /detectnow`
   c. `wuauclt /force`
   d. `wuauclt /renew`

7. Which of the following are scan options available in Windows Defender? Select all that apply.
   a. Quick
   b. Full
   c. Optional
   d. Custom

8. Which tab is the location of the quarantined items Windows Defender finds?
   a. Home tab
   b. History tab
   c. Update tab
   d. Settings tab

9. Which is the name of the SCEP client install file?
   a. scepinstall.exe
   b. scep.exe
   c. SCEPclient.exe
   d. clientEP.exe

10. Which of the following is an early warning system that alerts you before running unrecognized applications or downloading files from the Internet?
   a. Application Reputation
   b. Action Center
   c. SCEP Center
   d. Windows Defender

Best Answer

Choose the letter that corresponds to the best answer. More than one answer choice may achieve the goal. Select the BEST answer.

1. To ensure computers in three branch offices (with no IT support onsite) receive Windows Updates on a regular basis along with those in a main office, which WSUS configuration provides the best solution with the least amount of administrative for the approval and distribution of updates and the least amount of traffic over the WAN link?
   a. Single WSUS server at main office. Branch office PCs configured to use this server.
   b. WSUS server at main office and downstream WSUS servers at each branch office running in autonomous mode. PCs configured to use the local WSUS server.
   c. WSUS server at main office and downstream WSUS servers at each branch office running in replica mode. PCs configured to use the local WSUS server.
   d. WSUS server at main office and downstream WSUS servers at two branch offices running in replica mode and one running in autonomous mode.
2. Which solution is best to protect 100 PCs in a network against malware and to ensure they run the latest definition files while also monitoring them for compliance?
   a. Configure Automatic Updates.
   b. Install Windows Defender.
   c. Install SCEP client.
   d. Install SCEP client, enable Endpoint protection via SCCM 2012, and create and deploy an antimalware policy.
3. Which of the following should you implement to provide the highest level of protection for your clients and servers?
   a. Windows Firewall
   b. Windows Firewall + Windows Defender
   c. Windows Firewall + Windows Defender + SCEP
   d. Windows Firewall + Windows Defender + SCEP + Antimalware policy
4. Which Windows Update option ensures your system receives and uses the most current updates?
   a. Install updates but let me choose whether to install them.
   b. Download updates but let me choose whether to install them.
   c. Check for updates but let me choose whether to download and install them.
   d. Centrally approve and deploy updates using WSUS.
5. Which MAPS option provides you with the best option for responding to and stopping the spread of new viruses and malware?
   a. Basic membership
   b. Advanced membership
   c. Not joining MAPS
   d. Configuring Advanced Membership on one PC and not joining MAPS on the rest of your computers.

Matching and Identification

1. Match the following terms with the related description or usage.
   _______ **a)** Application Reputation
   _______ **b)** Action Center
   _______ **c)** Autonomous mode
   _______ **d)** Client-side targeting
   _______ **e)** Downstream server
   _______ **f)** MAPS

_________ g) Replica mode
_________ h) Server-side targeting
_________ i) Synchronization
_________ j) Upstream server

1. Uses group policies to configure computers to add themselves automatically to computer groups in the Update Services console.
2. Provides a central location for viewing notifications regarding problems with your hardware and software. It also provides information related to the security and maintenance of your computer.
3. WSUS servers that obtain their updates from a WSUS server that has been configured to obtain its updates directly from Microsoft.
4. Involves moving clients to computer groups using the Update Services console.
5. The process of connecting and downloading updates.
6. This WSUS server mode enables you to configure separate update approval settings while still retrieving updates from the upstream WSUS server.
7. An online community that can help you decide how to respond to certain types of threats.
8. A mode in which the WSUS server mirrors update approvals, settings, computers, and groups from the upstream server.
9. A WSUS server that obtains its updates directly from Microsoft.
10. The early warning system that alerts you before running unrecognized applications or downloading files from the Internet during the time between a release of a virus and definitions to protect against it.

Build a List

1. Identify the six basic steps, in order, for setting up a WSUS Server
   _________ Specify an update source for the WSUS server.
   _________ Synchronize updates to the WSU server.
   _________ Determine a deployment strategy.
   _________ Install the WSUS server role.
   _________ Set up client computers.
   _________ Approve and install updates on client computers.

2. Identify the five steps, in order, to create a computer group in WSUS from the Update Services console:
   _________ Expand the Computers node, right-click All Computers, and select Add Computer Group.
   _________ Confirm the group appears under All Computer node.
   _________ Open Update services console.
   _________ Type a name and click Add.
   _________ Log in with Administrative privileges.

3. In order of first to last, identify the six basic steps for removing a quarantined item in Windows Defender.
   _________ Select Quarantined Items.
   _________ Open Windows Defender.
   _________ Select the detected item and read description.
   _________ Click View Details.
   _________ Select the History tab.
   _________ Select Remove.

Choose an Option

1. Which tab should you select to view items quarantined by Windows Defender?

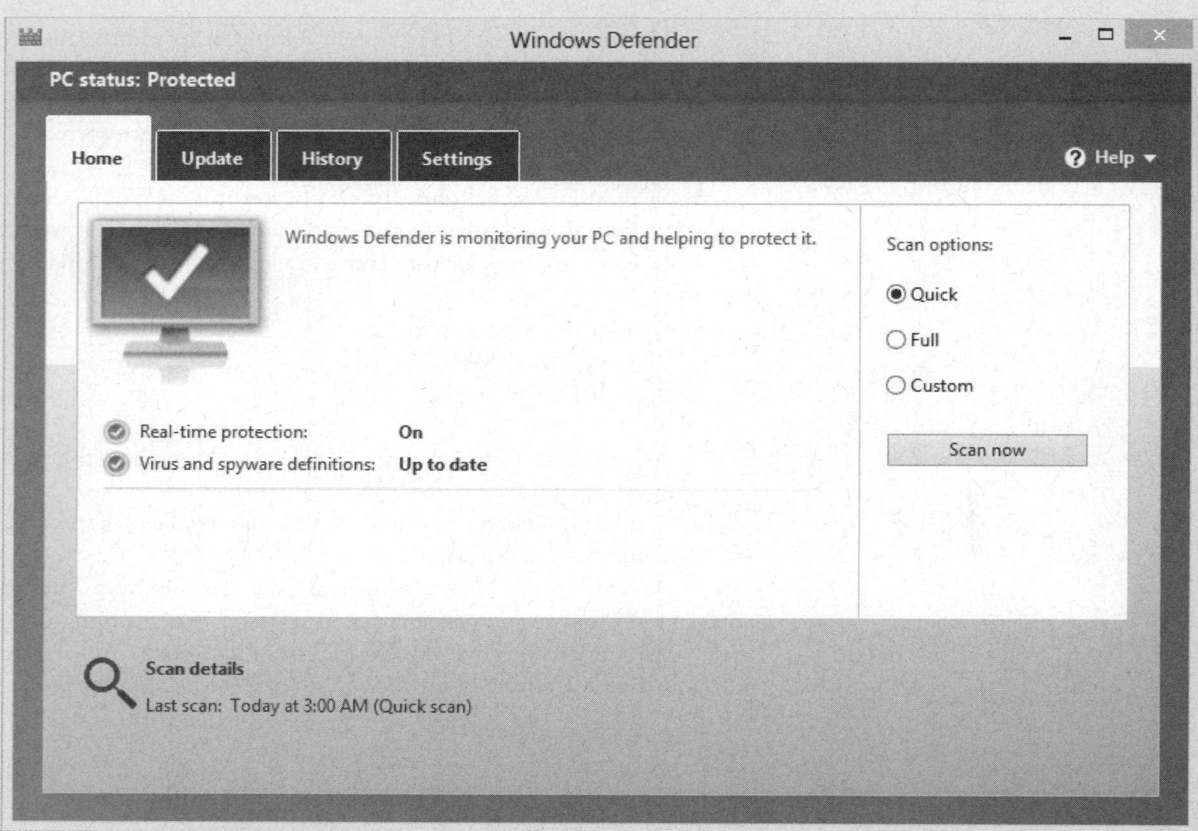

■ Business Case Scenarios

Scenario 13-1: Windows Defender Quarantine

After working on a Windows 8 computer running Windows Defender, it maintains quarantined files from the past several months. Is it possible to configure the computer to remove quarantined files on a weekly basis? If so, explain the steps involved.

Scenario 13-2: WSUS

WSUS server is set up at a branch office that gets its updates from a WSUS server at the main office. The option to approve updates is not available on the branch office server, yet it receives updates from the WSUS server at the main office on a regular basis. What is the problem?

Managing Clients by Using Windows Intune

70-688 EXAM OBJECTIVE

Objective 4.1 – Manage clients by using Windows Intune: This objective may include but is not limited to: Manage updates and update groups; configure the company portal; monitor on-network and off-network machines; manage asset inventory.

LESSON HEADING	EXAM OBJECTIVE
Introducing Windows Intune	
Exploring Windows Intune Configuration Requirements	
Managing Updates and Update Groups	Manage updates and update groups
Configuring the Company Portal	Configure the company portal
Monitoring On-Network and Off-Network Machines	Monitor on-network and off-network machines
Managing Asset Inventory in Windows Intune	Manage asset inventory

KEY TERMS

Automatic Approval rules
criteria membership
direct membership
product categories
recipients
update classifications
Windows Intune Groups
Windows Intune Company Portal
Windows Intune Cloud + On-Premise Configuration
Windows Intune Stand-Alone Cloud Configuration
Windows Intune + System Center Configuration Manager
Windows Intune Tenant Administrator
Windows Intune Service Administrator

■ Introducing Windows Intune

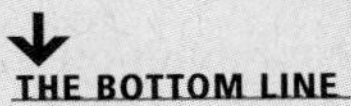

Windows Intune is a cloud-based management solution that allows you to manage your computers when they are not inside your corporate network. Windows Intune helps you manage your computers and mobile devices through a web console. It provides the tools, reports, and licenses to ensure your computers are always current and protected. For mobile devices, it also allows you to manage your remote workforce by working through Exchange ActiveSync or directly through Windows Intune.

Windows Intune can be operated in cloud-only mode or in a new unified configuration option that integrates the cloud-based environment with Microsoft System Center 2012 Configuration Manager Service Pack 1.

Windows Intune utilizes a subscription model in which you are charged on a per-user basis.

Here are some of the things you can do with this cloud-based management solution:

- Manage your mobile devices and computers through a web-based console anywhere at any time through Exchange ActiveSync and System Center 2012 Configuration Manager.
- Manage your Windows Intune subscription, add new users and security groups, set up and manage service settings, and access service status via a Windows Intune Account portal.
- Assess the overall health of devices across your organization using the Windows Intune administrator console.
- Organize users and devices into groups (geographically, by department, and by hardware characteristics).
- Manage updates for computers in your organization.
- Enhance security of your managed devices by providing real-time protection, by keeping virus definitions current, and by automatically running scheduled scans.
- Access the overall health of your managed devices through the use of alerts.
- Deploy policies to secure data on mobile devices to determine which mobile devices can connect, enroll, rename, and un-enroll devices.
- Wipe mobile devices in case they are stolen.
- Deploy software and detect and manage software installed on computers.
- Manage licenses purchased through Microsoft volume Licensing agreements.
- Run reports on software, hardware, and software licenses to help confirm current needs and to plan for the future.
- Provide a cloud-based, self-service portal where users can enroll and manage their devices, search for and install software applications, and request help.

Exploring Windows Intune Configuration Requirements

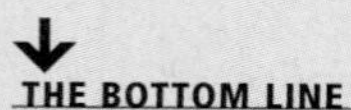

Windows Intune deploys a client agent on each device that you want to manage. The Windows Intune agent communicates back to the Windows Intune administration console, allowing you to inventory software and hardware assets in your organization.

Windows Intune can be deployed with the following configurations:

- ***Windows Intune Stand-Alone Cloud Configuration:*** With this configuration, you have to administer your computers and devices (Windows 8, Windows RT, Windows Phone 8, and Apple iOS) through the Administrator console. Although this configuration allows you to create and manage policies, inventory your devices, and upload and publish software, it does not support the discovery of mobile devices.
- ***Windows Intune Cloud + On-Premise Configuration:*** This configuration integrates Windows Intune with your existing Active Directory and Exchange environment. With this configuration, you can discover mobile devices using Exchange ActiveSync,

synchronize your user accounts with your Active Directory, and manage your mobile devices through Windows Intune.

- ***Windows Intune + System Center Configuration Manager:*** This configuration allows you to manage your computers and mobile devices from the System Center Configuration Manager 2012 console.

Deploying the Windows Intune Client

You can install the Windows Intune client on computers running Windows XP Professional (SP3), Windows Vista (Enterprise, Ultimate, or Business Edition), Windows 7 (Enterprise, Ultimate, or Professional), and Windows 8 (Professional and Enterprise). You can deploy the Windows Intune client on both physical computers and virtual machines.

Before installing the Windows Intune client, you need to consider how you want to handle malware. If you have existing software that protects against these types of threats, Windows Intune Endpoint Protection detects the software and does not install the Endpoint component.

The following options are available for deploying the client:

- **Administrator Deployment:** Using this option, you basically download the client software and manually install it on the target computers. You can automate the process by using Group Policy if you need to install it on a large number of computers.
- **User-Initiated Enrollment for Computers:** Using this option, users can self-enroll their computers through the Windows Intune company portal.
- **Install the client software as part of an image:** Using this option, you can deploy the Windows Intune client as part of a system image deployment. The computer is automatically enrolled when the image is installed.

PERFORM AN ADMINISTRATOR DEPLOYMENT OF THE WINDOWS INTUNE CLIENT

GET READY. You need to agree to and set up a Windows Intune account to complete this exercise. To complete an administrative deployment of the Windows Intune client on a Windows 8 computer, perform the following steps.

1. Log in to the Windows 8 computer on which you want to install the Windows Intune Client software.
2. Open Internet Explorer and type **https://admin.manage.microsoft.com** into the address field, and then press **Enter**.
3. If the message *This application requires Microsoft Silverlight* appears, click **Get Microsoft Silverlight**, and then select **Run**.
4. To accept the licensing agreement, click **Install now**.
5. On the *Enable Microsoft Update* page, click **Next**.
6. In the Windows Intune console's *left* pane, click **Administration**.
7. Click **Client Software Download**.
8. On the *Client Software Download* page, click **Download Client Software** (see Figure 14-1).

Figure 14-1
Downloading Windows Intune client software

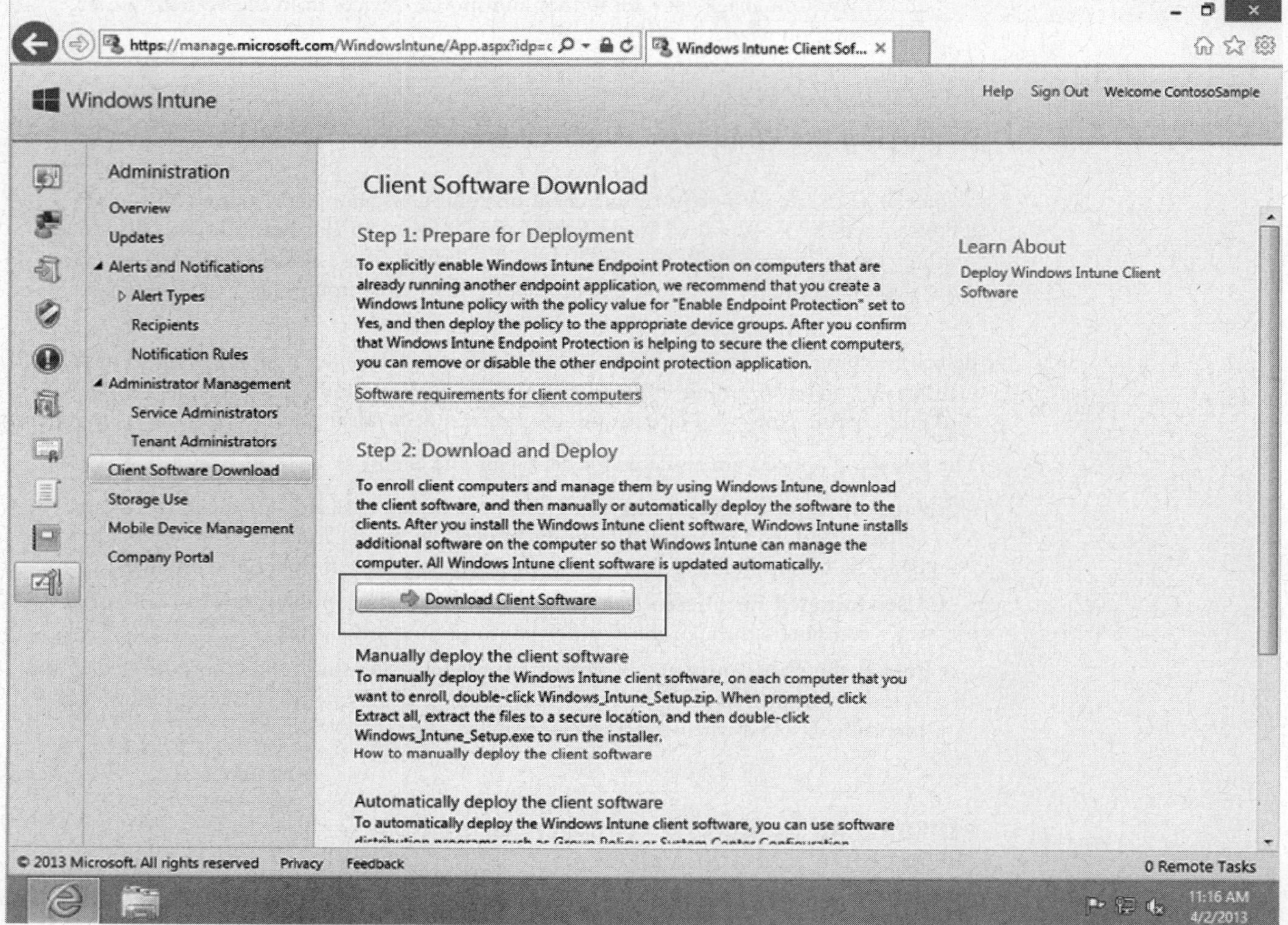

9. From the Windows Internet Explorer box, click **Save as**.
10. In the *Save As* box, click **Desktop** and then click **Save**. This places a file named *Windows_Intune_Setup.zip* on your desktop.
11. Minimize the Windows Intune console and then right-click the **Windows_Intune_Setup.zip** file, and then click **Extract All**.
12. In the *Select a Destination and Extract Files box,* click **Extract**. After the extraction has completed, you should see two files: *Windows_Intune_Setup.exe* and *WindowsIntune.accountcert*. These files must be kept together at all times. The WindowsIntune.accountcert is used by the setup program.
13. Double-click **Windows_Intune_Setup.exe**.
14. When the *Windows Intune Setup Wizard* opens, click **Next**.
15. Click **Finish**. Windows Intune continues to update and install software on the computer. You can use the computer while the process continues in the background.
16. Maximize the Windows Intune console and then click in the left pane. When the pane slides out, click Groups > All Devices.

When the installation is done, you should see the computer name listed (see Figure 14-2). Leave the Windows Intune Administrator console open to use in the next exercise.

Figure 14-2

Viewing the computer as it appears in the Windows Intune administrator console

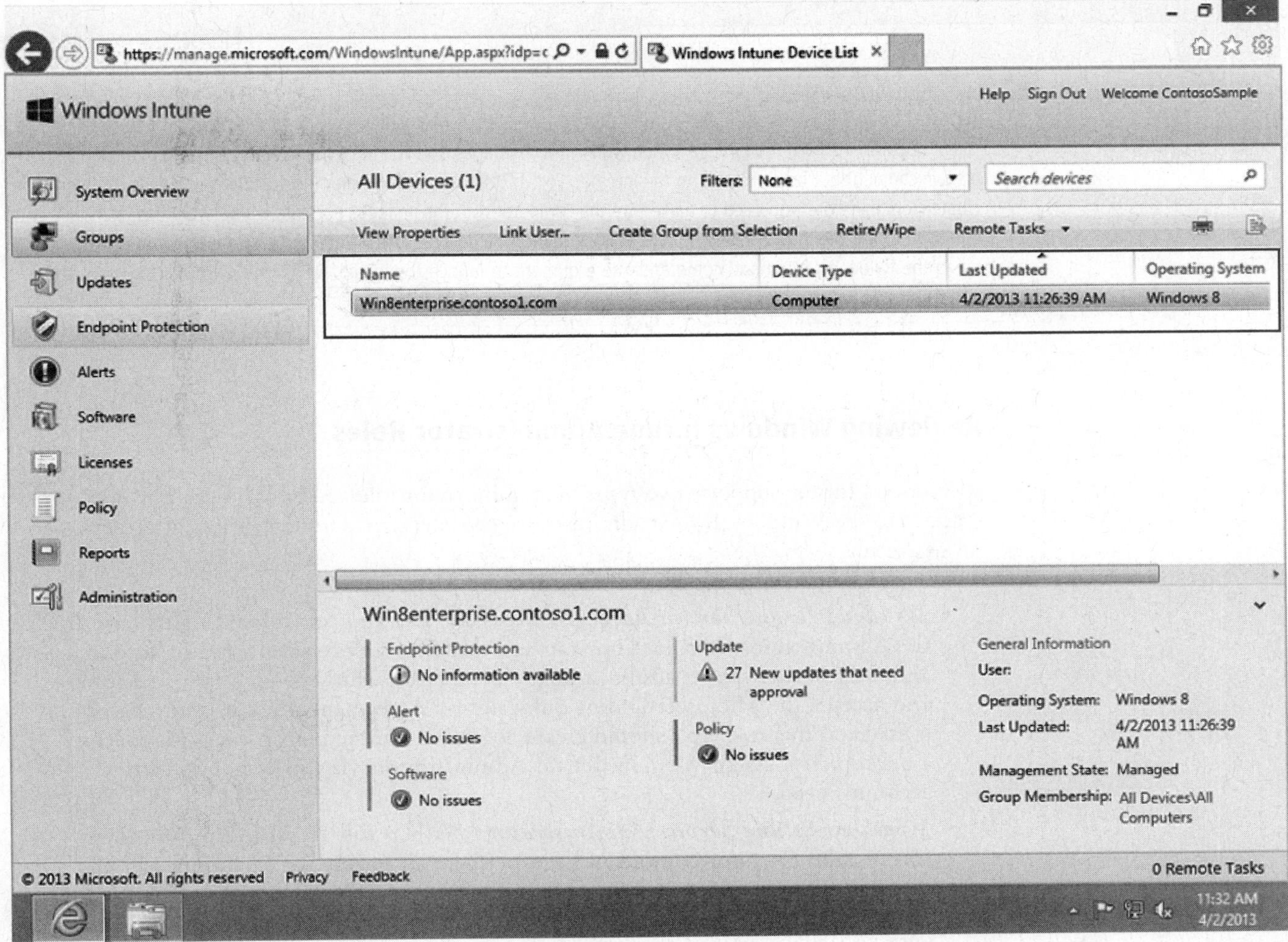

MORE INFORMATION

After the installation has completed, the protection and update agents continue to perform additional setup and configuration steps. This includes downloading the required malware definitions and any other agent updates. The computer should appear in the Windows Intune administrator console in a few minutes, but it can take up to 30 minutes to complete the inventory and status updates process.

In the previous exercise, you performed an Administrative deployment, and the Windows 8 computer was enrolled as part of the installation. If you wanted to allow your users to self-enroll their computers, they would need to be an administrator on the local computer, connect to the Windows Intune portal using an Internet Explorer browser, and use a Microsoft Online ID. To learn more about how self-enroll works, visit Microsoft and search *Windows Intune User-Initiated Enrollment for Computers.* When performing this process, following are the general steps:

1. Click *All My Devices.*

2. Click *Enroll your computer.*
3. Click *Download Software.*
4. Click *Run.*
5. Click *Next to.* To start the Windows Intune Setup Wizard, click *Next.*
6. Click *Finish when.* When the installation is completed, click *Finish.*

MORE INFORMATION

To install the Windows Intune Client as part of an image, search Microsoft's website for *Windows Intune Installing the Client Software as Part of an Image.* When working with images, you will most likely deploy them to multiple computers, which might not be connected to the Internet. For an installation of the client to complete, you need an Internet connection; therefore, you need to make sure the computer with the image is not enrolled before it has been fully deployed to the client. To accomplish this, you can perform a delayed installation of the Windows Intune client by using the following command command-line argument to launch the install: `Windows_Intune_Setup.exe /PrepareEnroll`.

Reviewing Windows Intune Administrator Roles

Windows Intune supports two types of Administrator roles. Although both can gain access to the Windows Intune administrator console, they do differ in the tasks they can execute:

- ***Windows Intune Tenant Administrator*** role: Has full control and rights regarding the Administrator console. They can add or delete service administrator accounts and assign other tenant administrators. The person who sets up Windows Intune and accepts the Microsoft Online Subscription Agreement when it is purchased is assigned this role. You should create at least one more person with this role as a backup. You assign Window Tenant Administrators via the Windows Intune account portal.
- ***Windows Intune Service Administrator*** role: Has full access to the Windows Intune administrator console and can perform all operations including adding or deleting another Services Administrator account. They cannot modify data in the console but instead can only view the data it contains and run reports. Windows Intune Service Administrators are assigned via the Windows Intune Administrator console.

Managing Updates and Update Groups

THE BOTTOM LINE

To make the process of deploying Windows Intune policies, software packages, and software updates more efficient, consider using Windows Intune Groups. ***Windows Intune Groups***, which are used to quickly organize and manage your computers and users, are created and managed in the Groups workspace. These groups apply only to Windows Intune and are completely separate from Active Directory groups, although you can use AD security groups as part of a query to select members when creating a group. After your groups are set up, you can deploy Windows Intune policies, software packages, and software updates to them.

CERTIFICATION READY
Manage updates and update groups
Objective 4.1

You can create groups that include users and you can create groups that include devices. What you cannot do is include users and devices in the same group. Most administrators create groups that are organized in one or more of the following ways:

- Geographical organization: Portland, Seattle, Los Angeles
- Departmental organization: Executives, Human Resources, Marketing
- Physical organization: Desktops, Laptops

In the Groups workspace (see Figure 14-3) you see the default groups created for devices and for users when Windows Intune is initially setup. For example, you will find the Windows 8 computer you installed the Windows Intune Client software on earlier, under the *All Computers* group.

Figure 14-3
Exploring the Groups workspace

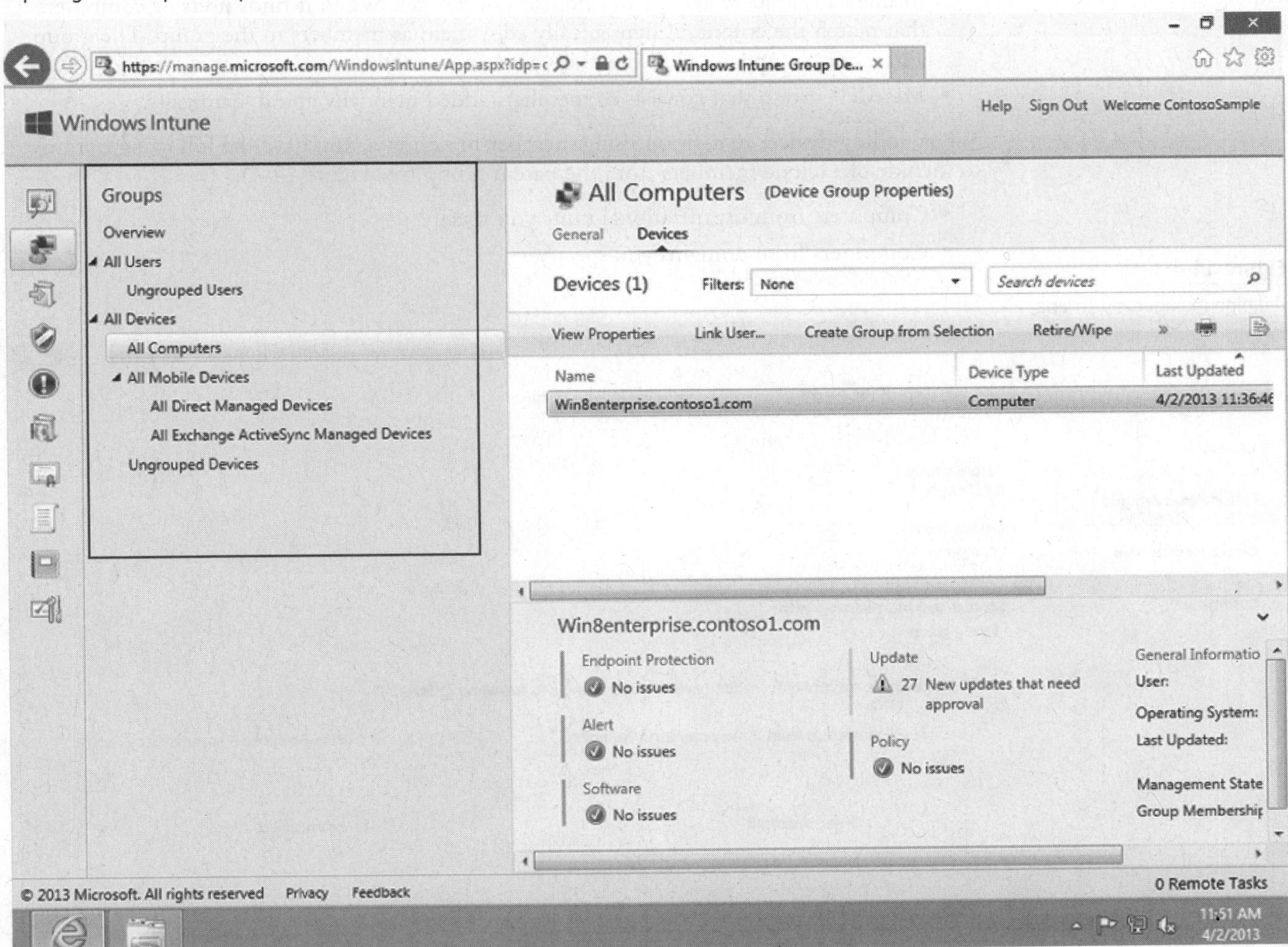

After a closer look, you should see there is a hierarchy for the groups. For example, the All Direct Managed Devices and the All Exchange ActiveSync Managed Devices are child groups under the parent All Mobile Devices. You can deploy software updates, policies, and software applications to multiple groups or to a parent group while excluding one or more child groups. You can also add and exclude specific group members.

> **MORE INFORMATION**
> To protect your production environment, consider creating a test computer group that can be used to roll out and trial new updates. Once in place, you can select the members from within the Windows Intune console. This should be reflective of the different operating systems you want to test on. Even though computers are added to the new group, they still retain their membership in any other groups. This allows you to still assign updates to them without impacting other computers in those groups.

When setting up a group in Windows Intune, you have the option to manually or dynamically add users or devices to a group. You can also take a mixed approach and use both methods when creating a group.

- ***Direct membership:*** The process of manually adding users or devices from within the Windows Intune console. You manually include and exclude specific members from the group.
- ***Criteria membership:*** This involves defining certain types of criteria that Windows Intune runs a query against to find users or devices. When it finds users or computers that match the criteria, it dynamically adds them as members to the group. The group automatically updates with members as changes occur.
- **Mixed:** A group that consists of members added manually and dynamically.

When adding devices to a group using membership criteria, you have the following options to include or exclude members from the parent group (see Figure 14-4):

- Computers from organizational units you specify
- Computers from domains you specify

Figure 14-4

Defining membership criteria

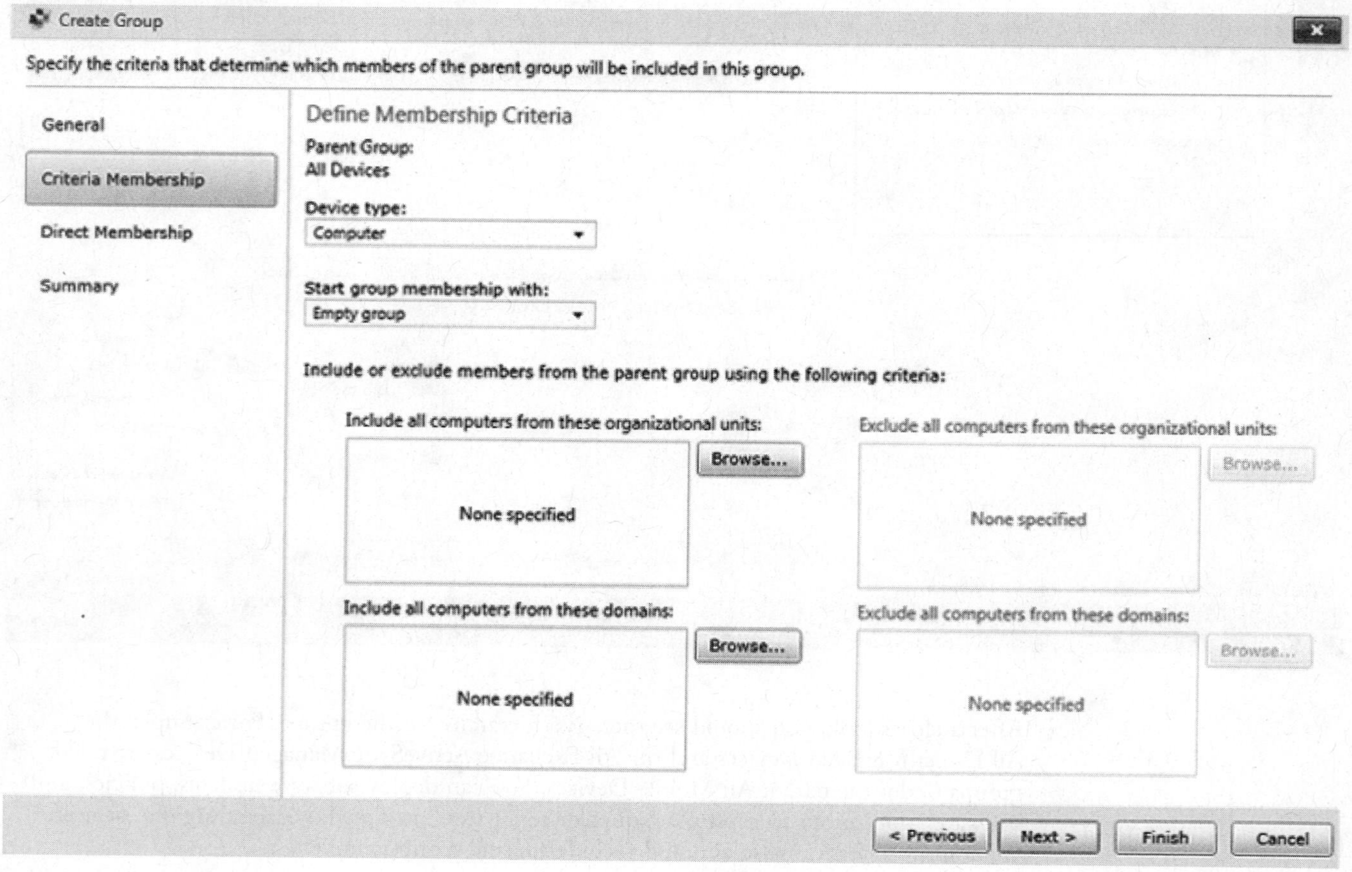

When defining direct membership, you have the option to include or exclude specific members form groups you specify.

Group membership is recursive. This means that if you use a dynamic membership query and set the criteria that a user is a member of an AD DS security group named marketing to be included in the group, you can pick up additional indirect users in the query. For example, if Mary is a member of the Marketing Interns security group and the Marketing Interns security group is a member of the Marketing security group, then she is included in your query and added to the Marketing group.

CREATE A DEVICE GROUP USING DIRECT MEMBERSHIP

GET READY. To create a device group using Direct-based membership, from the Windows Intune Administrator console, perform the following steps:

1. Log in to the **Windows Intune Administrator** console at https://admin.manage.microsoft.com.
2. In the *left* pane, select the **Groups**.
3. Under the *Tasks* menu, click the **Create Group** (see Figure 14-5).

Figure 14-5

Viewing the Create Group link

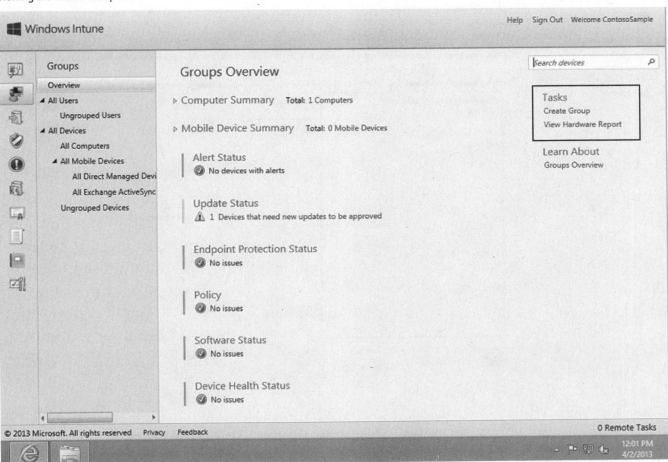

4. In the *Group name* field, type **My Test Group.**
5. In the *Description* field, type **Computers used to test deployments of new updates.**
6. Under *Select a parent group,* click **All Devices.**
7. Click **Next.**
8. On the *Define Membership Criteria* page, click **Next.**
9. On the *Define Direct Membership* screen, click **Browse.** Be careful to select the *Browse* button that is just to the right of the *Include specific members* field. If you select the one on the far right, you will exclude specific members.
10. Choose the Windows 8 computer on which you installed the Windows Intune client software in the earlier exercise, and then click **Add.** Your Windows 8 computer should appear in the *Include specific members* column (see Figure 14-6). Click **OK** to continue.

Figure 14-6

Adding a computer to MyTestGroup

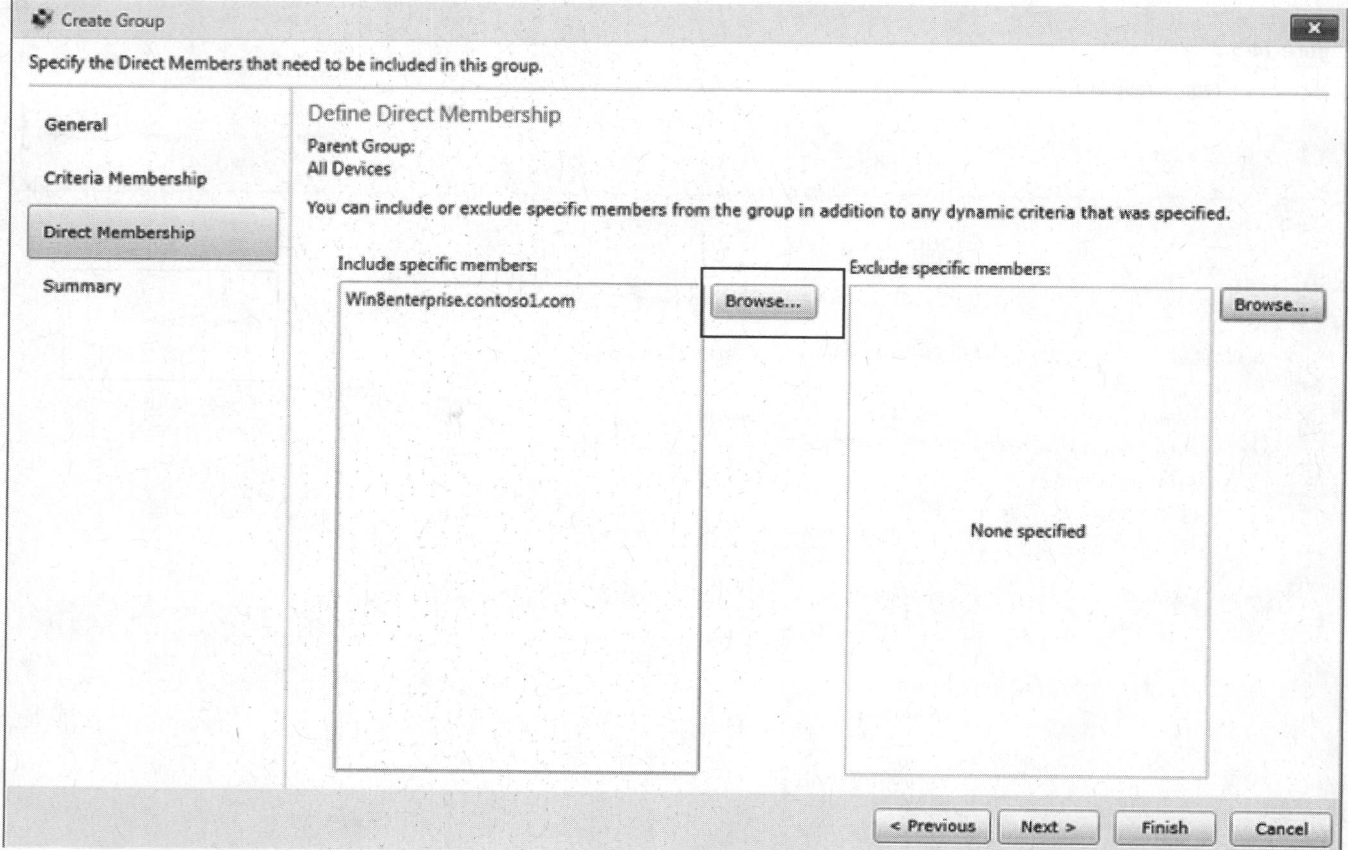

11. On the *Define Direct Membership* page, click **Next.**
12. Review the *General Criteria Membership and Direct Membership summary* page, and then click **Finish.**

13. Under *Groups*, click **My Test Group**, and then click **Devices** (see Figure 14-7). The computer should appear as a member of the group.

Figure 14-7

Viewing members of the My Test Group

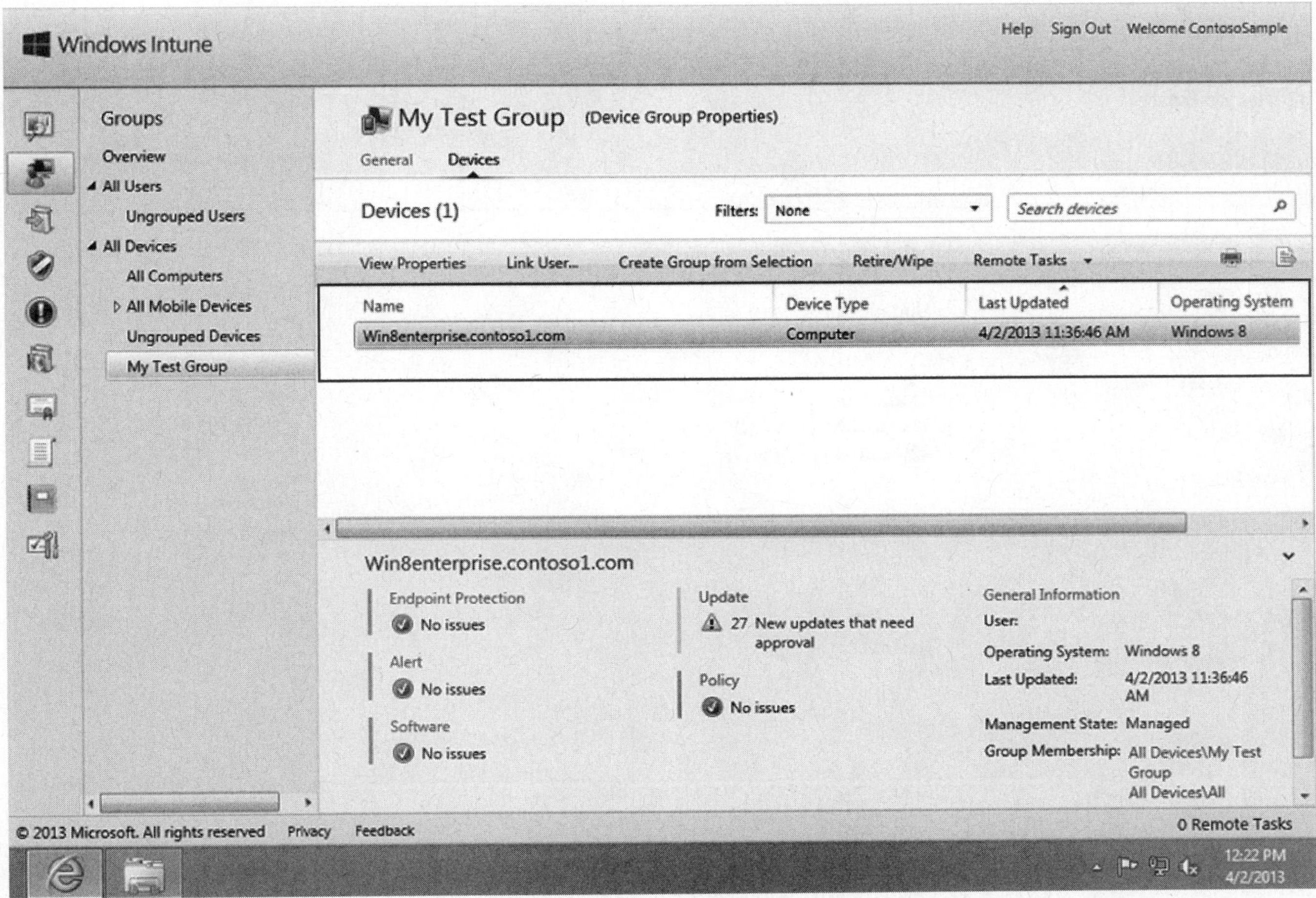

MANAGING UPDATES IN WINDOWS INTUNE

In Windows Intune, updates are managed via the Updates workspace (see Figure 14-8).

CERTIFICATION READY
Manage updates and update groups
Objective 4.1

When you are in the Update workspace, you can view any pending updates, approve or decline updates, configure the automatic approval settings, and set the deadline for update installation in automatic approval rules. From the workspace, you can approve not only Microsoft updates but also non-Microsoft updates.

When working with updates, not all of them are applicable to your situation. To help streamline the process of managing updates, Windows Intune breaks the updates into separate ***product categories*** and ***update classifications***. Product categories are used to organize software by product name, whereas update classifications are arranged around the specific type of update (service pack, critical update, and definition update). Windows Intune checks for updates only on the products and update classifications you select.

Examples of product categories are:

- Antigen
- Biztalk Server

- Exchange
- Office
- SQL Server
- Windows

Figure 14-8

Managing update in the Updates workspace

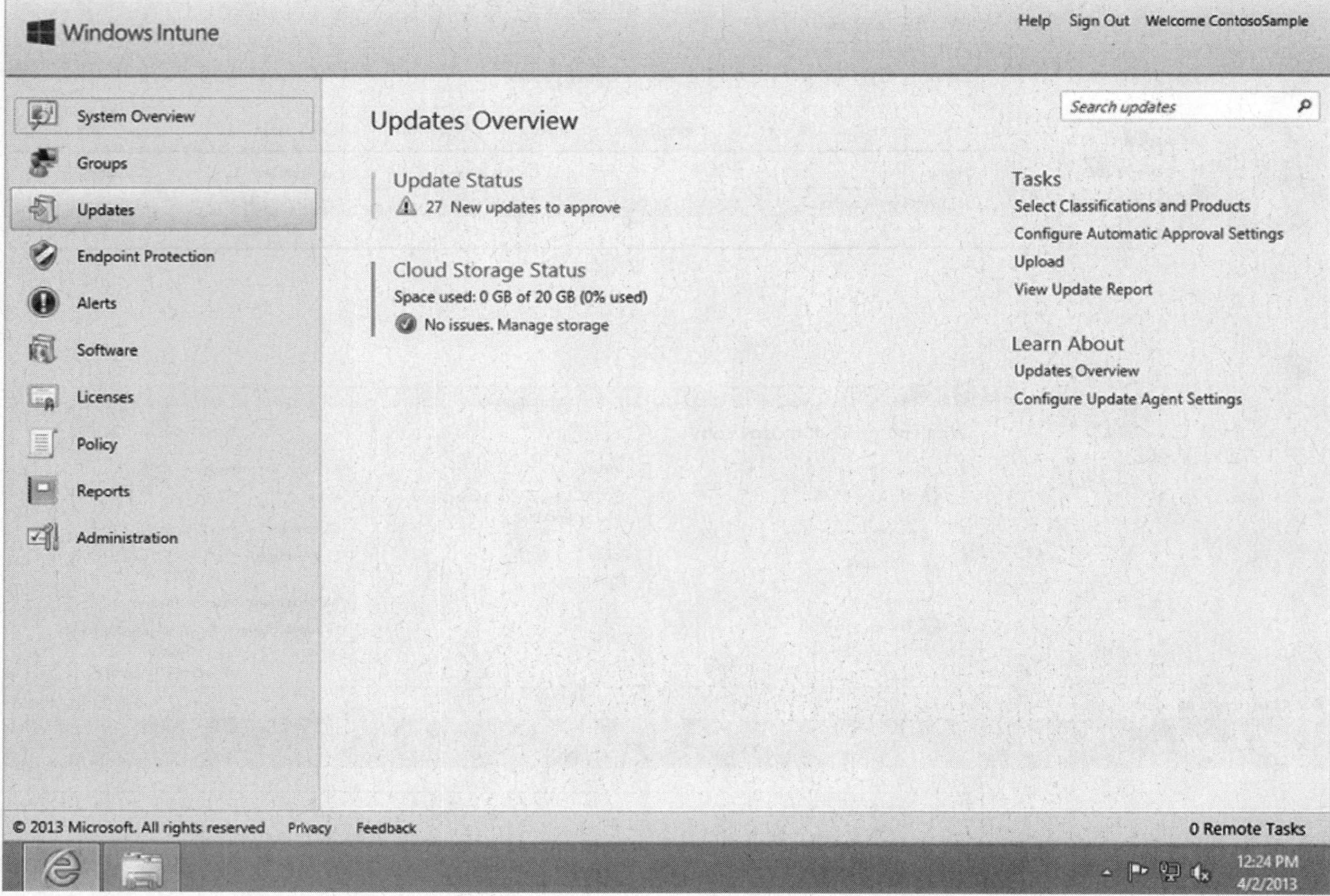

Examples of update classifications are:

- **Critical Updates:** Fixes for a specific problem addressing a critical nonsecurity bug.
- **Security Updates:** Fixes for a product-specific, security-related vulnerability.
- **Definition Updates:** Frequent software updates that contain additions to a product's definition database.
- **Feature Packs:** New product functionality; distributed outside of the product release; usually these are included in the next full release of the product.
- **Service Packs:** A tested cumulative set of all hotfixes, security updates, critical updates, and some customer-requested design and feature changes.
- **Tools:** Utility or features that can help accomplish a task or set of tasks.
- **Update Rollups:** A tested cumulative set of all hotfixes, security updates, critical updates, and updates packaged for easy deployment. These are typically

designed to target a specific area such as security or a component of a specific product.

- **Updates:** Fixes a specific problem that addresses a noncritical, nonsecurity issue.

REVIEW PRODUCT CATEGORIES AND CLASSIFICATIONS

GET READY. To review products and classifications, perform the following steps:

1. Log in to the **Windows Intune Administrator** console at https://admin.manage.microsoft.com.
2. In the *left* pane, click **Administration.**
3. Click **Updates** (see Figure 14-9).

Figure 14-9

Reviewing product categories and update classifications

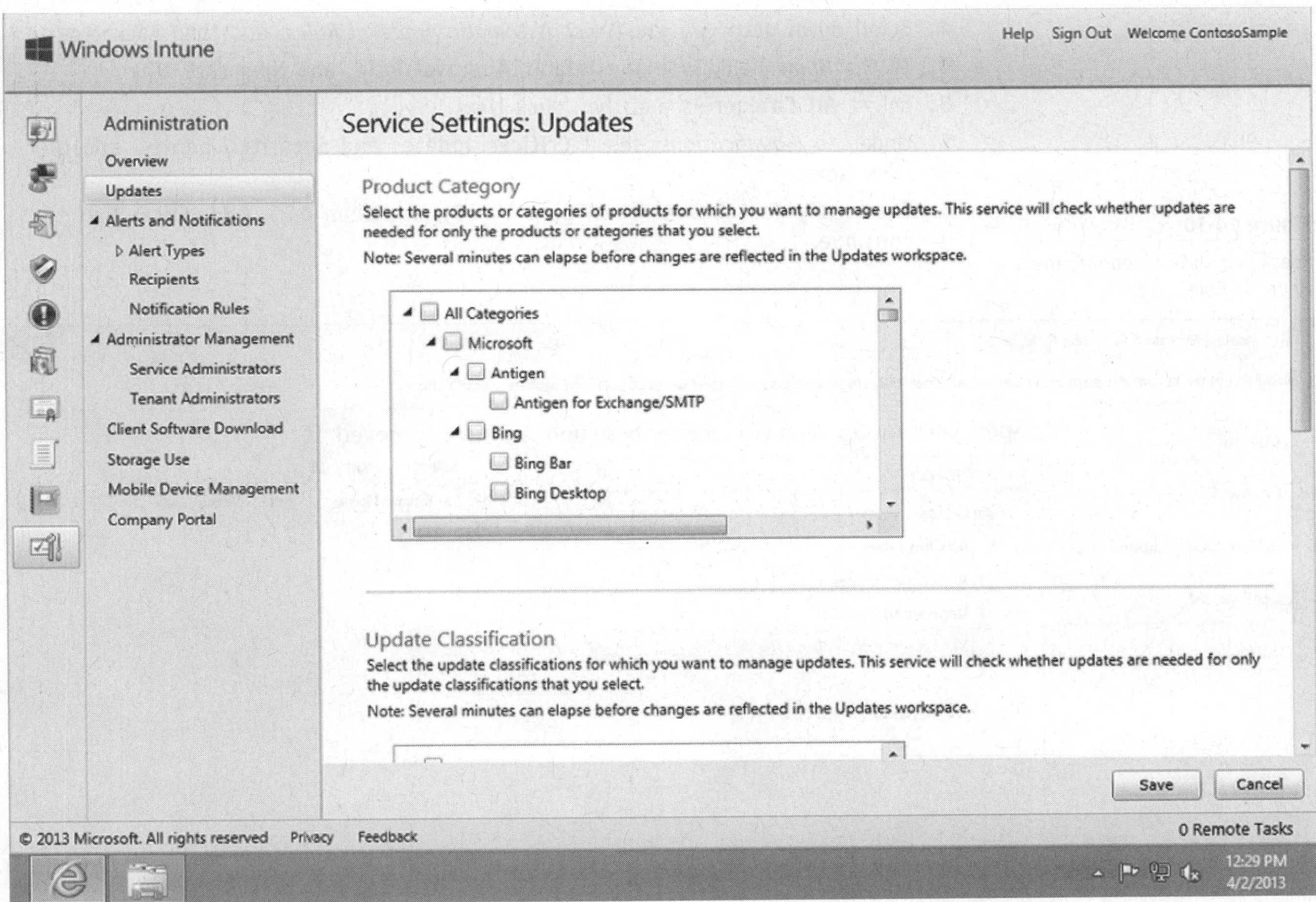

4. Review the product categories that you can filter on, and then review the update classifications you can filter on.
5. Scroll all the way down to the bottom until you see the *Automatic Approval Rules* section.

Understanding the Automatic Update Approval Rule

Creating ***Automatic Approval rules*** can help streamline the management of your computers. When you create a rule, Windows Intune automatically approves installation of all critical and security updates as soon as Microsoft releases them. This ensures your clients are updated as soon as possible.

CREATE AN AUTOMATIC UPDATE APPROVAL RULE

GET READY. To create an Automatic Update approval rule, perform the following steps:

1. If you still have your console open from the previous exercise, skip to Step 4; otherwise, log in to the **Windows Intune Administrator** console at: https://admin.manage.microsoft.com.
2. In the *left* pane, click **Administration.**
3. Click **Updates.**
4. Scroll down until you see *Select Automatic Approval Rules,* and then click **New.**
5. In the *Name* field, type **My Default Approval Rule**, and then click **Next.**
6. Select **All Categories** and then click **Next.**
7. Under *All Classifications,* select **Critical Updates and Security Updates**, and then click **Next.**
8. Choose **My Test Group** (see Figure 14-10), and then click **Add**. Click **Next** to continue.

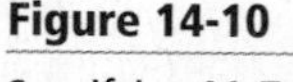

Figure 14-10

Specifying MyTestGroup for the Approval Rule

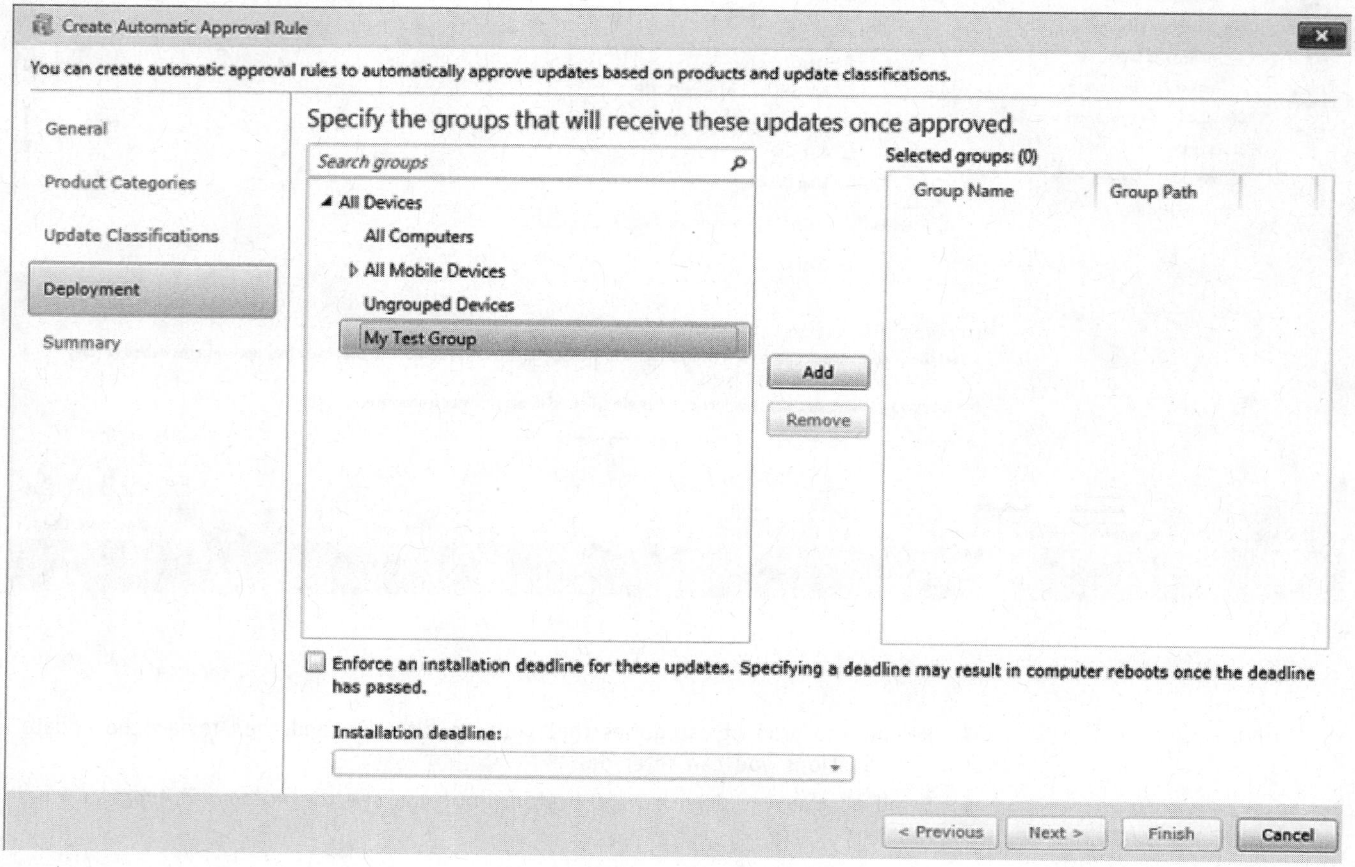

9. Review the information summary and click **Finish**.
10. Confirm your new rule appears under the *Automatic Approval* rules section (see Figure 14-11).

Figure 14-11

Confirming your Automatic Update approval rule

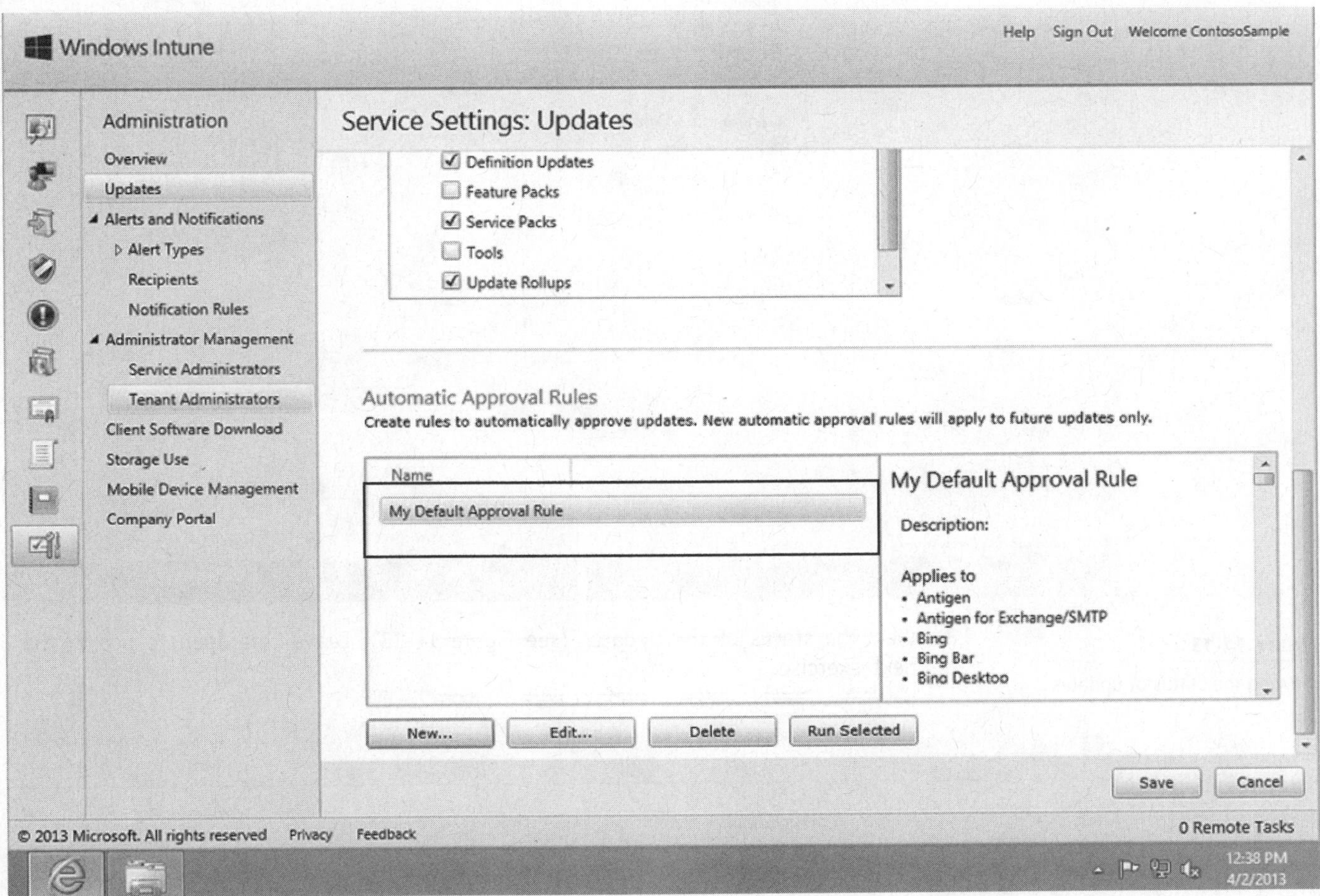

11. Click **Run Selected** and then click **Save**. This forces the rule to evaluate updates on all computers that run Windows Intune agents in the group you specified. After the review, the updates are made available to the computers in the group when they next check in. By default, the Windows Intune agent checks in every 8 hours for updates. When they do, they are instructed by Windows Intune to install the updates. If you click save, the rule applies only to future updates as they are released.

MORE INFORMATION

The frequency an agent checks for updates is configured via the Policy workspace. The recommended setting is 8 hours, but you can set it from 8 to 22 hours.

12. In the *left* pane, click **Updates** (see Figure 14-12).

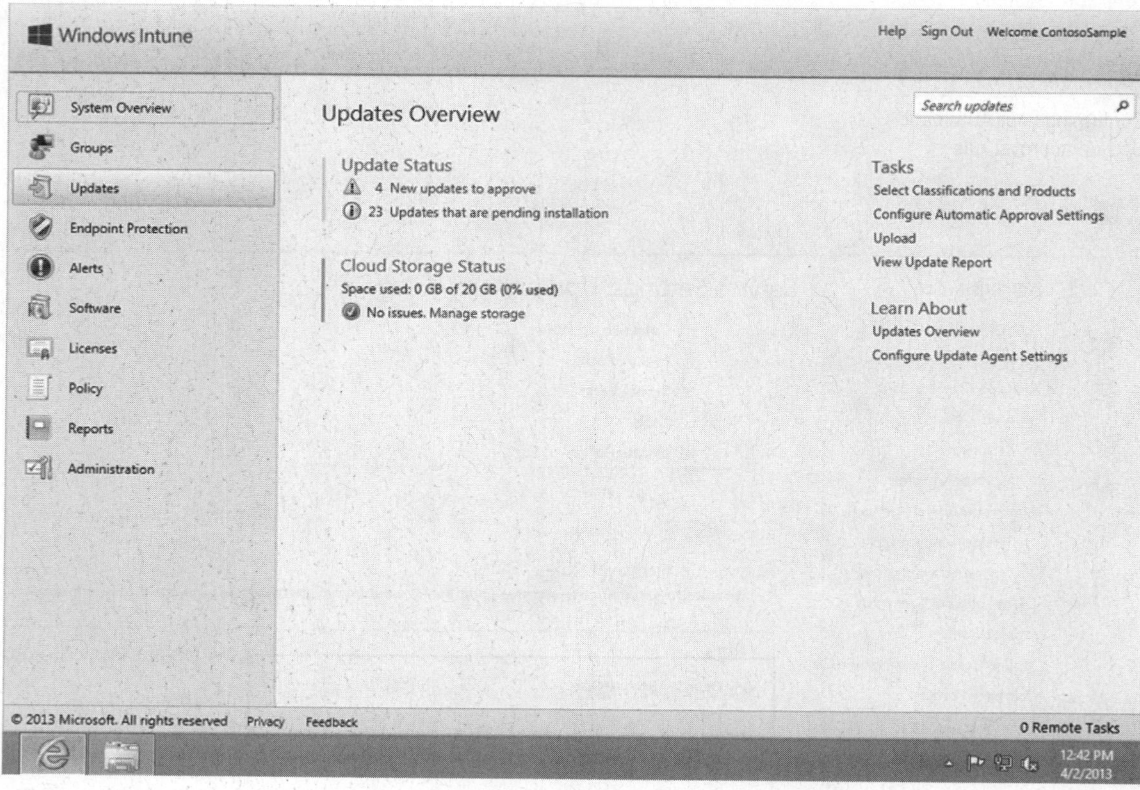

Figure 14-12

Selecting the Updates workspace

13. View the status of the updates (see Figure 14-13). Leave this open to use in the next exercise.

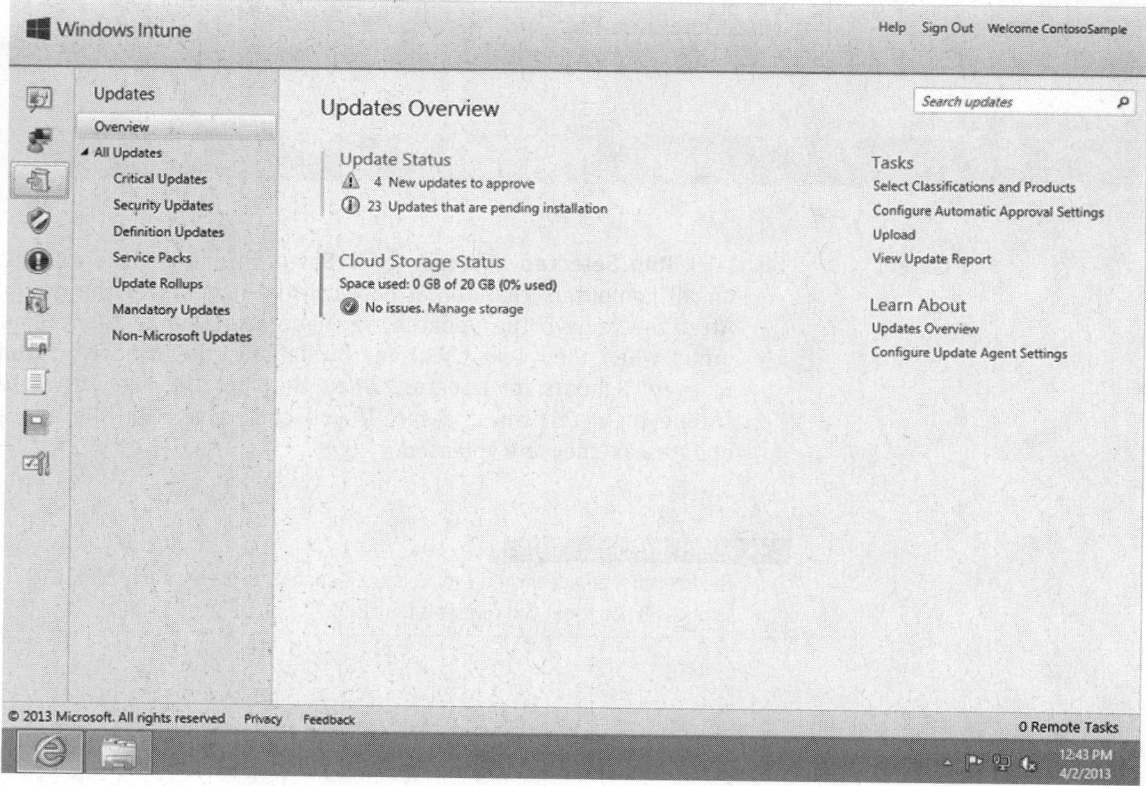

Figure 14-13

Viewing the status of updates

Approving Updates Manually

Some updates you might want to review and manage a little closer before approving and deploying them. In these situations, you perform a manual update from the Update workspace.

In Windows Intune, you can manage updates from Microsoft Update and from third parties. Microsoft updates are included in the Windows Intune console, whereas third-party updates require additional setup. When approving a Microsoft update, you can approve it for an individual group or for multiple groups. To approve an update for multiple groups, you take advantage of the parent and child group hierarchy you read about earlier. For example, you can approve the update for the All Computers group and its child groups receive the updates via inheritance.

MORE INFORMATION

To select multiple groups, you can use the Ctrl or Shift key when selecting the updates to approve.

APPROVE AN UPDATE MANUALLY

GET READY. To approve an update manually, perform the following steps:

1. Log in to the **Windows Intune Administrator** console at: https://admin.manage.microsoft.com.
2. In the *left* pane, click **Updates**.
3. Under *Update Status,* click **New updates to approve** (see Figure 14-14).

Figure 14-14

Viewing the updates to approve

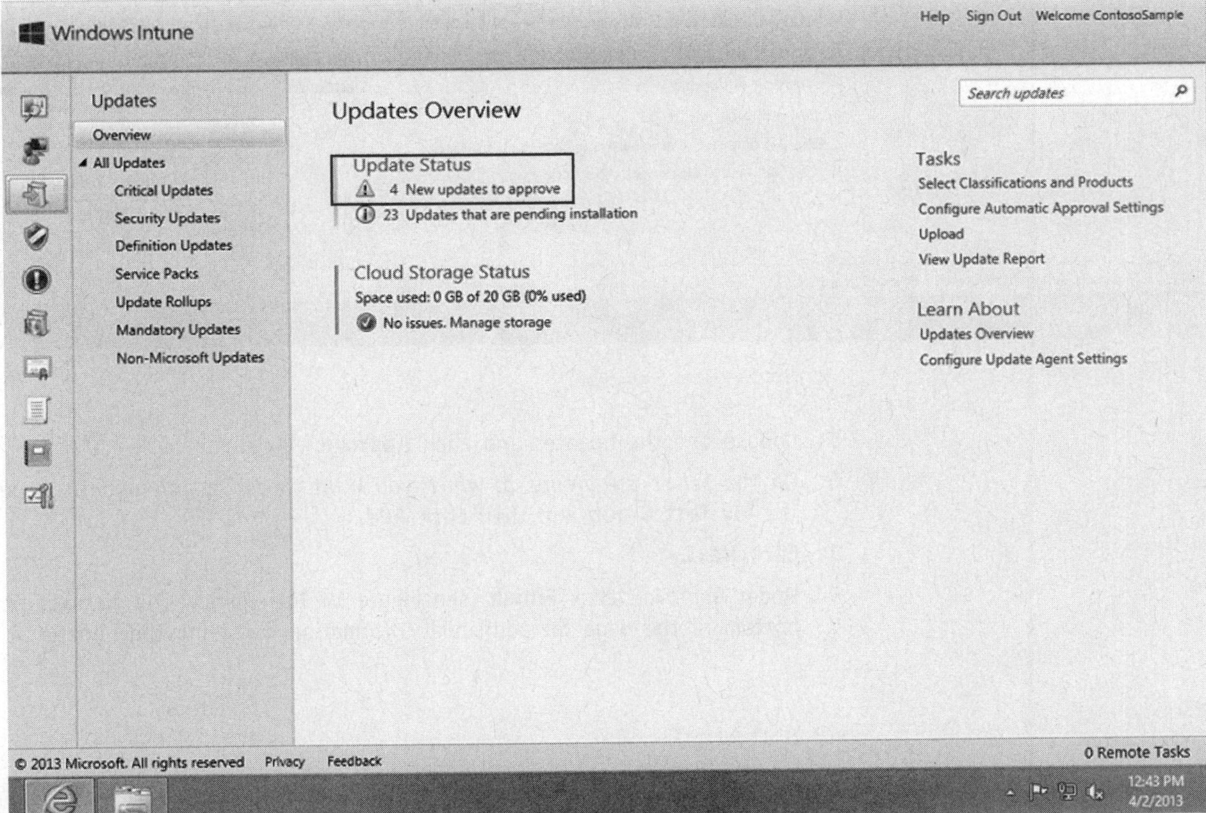

4. Click one of the updates to review additional information about it. In Figure 14-15, you can see the updates available for Windows 8 running the Windows Intune agent. By clicking on the name of the update, you can see how many computers need that specific update. By selecting the *Computers that need this update to be approved* link under *Current status*, you can see the name of the actual computer the update is applied to.

Figure 14-15

Reviewing updates that are available

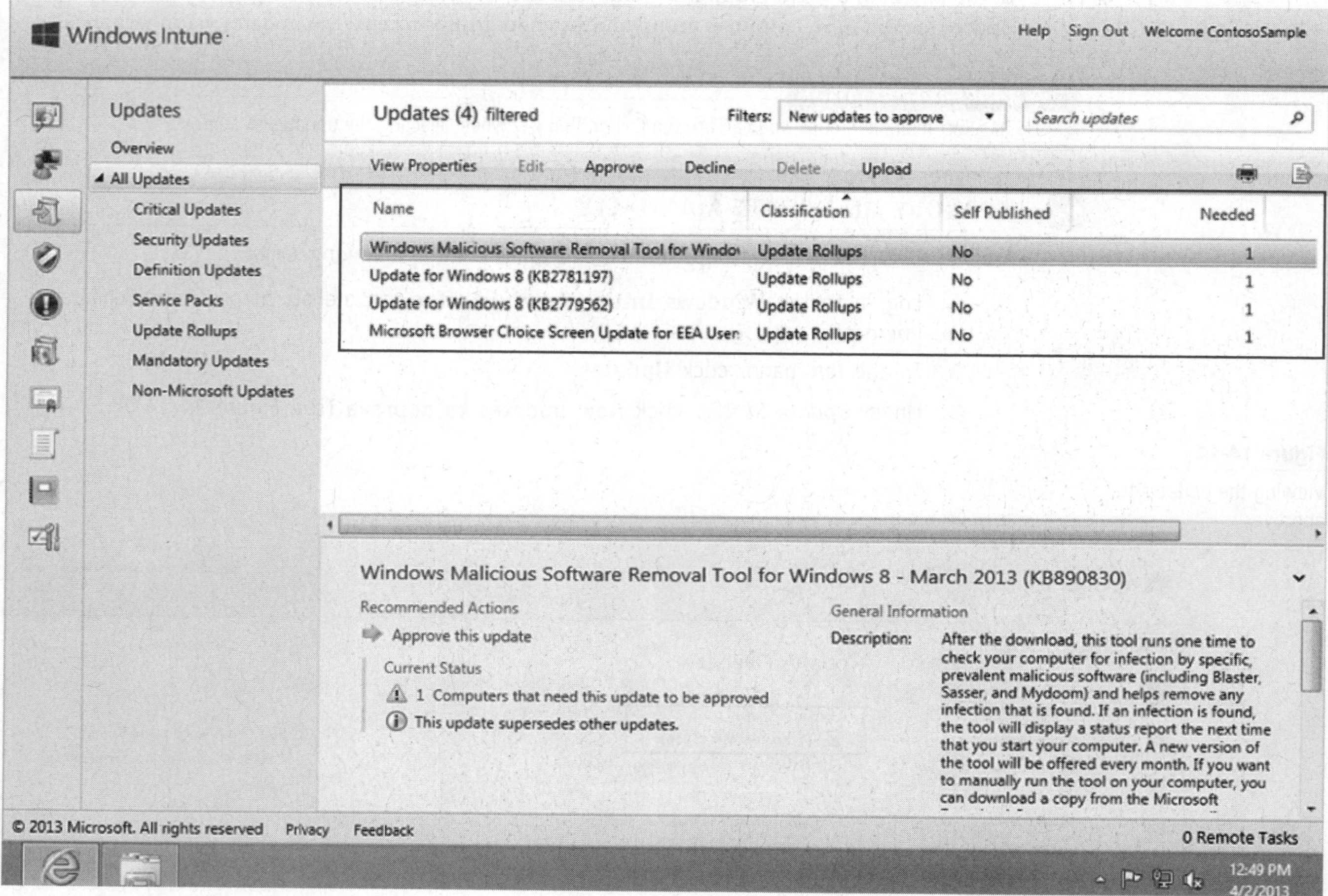

5. Choose one the updates and click **Approve**.
6. On the *Select the groups to which you want to deploy this update,* page choose the **My Test Group** and then click **Add**.
7. Click **Next**.
8. Under *Approval,* click **Finish** (see Figure 14-16). Review the message at the bottom of the page for additional information regarding the updates.

Figure 14-16

Handling additional update requirements

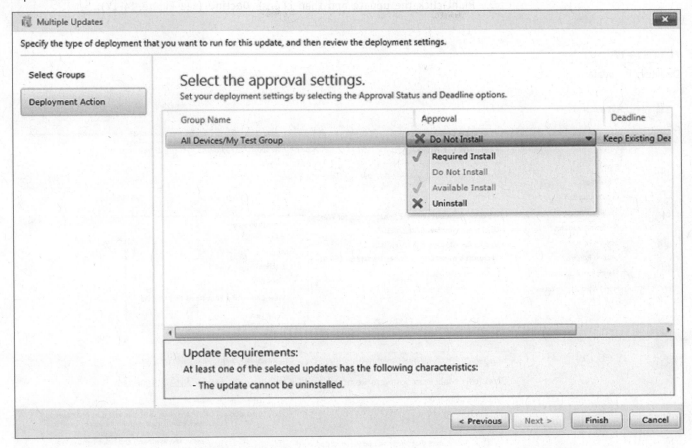

9. Click **Finish**.

Declining Updates

In the previous sections, you learned the process for approving updates either manually or automatically via the Automatic Approval rules. You can also decline an update. When you decline an update, the following happens:

- All approvals for the update are removed.
- The update is hidden in default views in the Update console.
- Any associated reported data is lost.

DECLINE AN UPDATE

GET READY. To decline an update, perform the following steps:

1. Log in to the **Windows Intune Administrator** console at https://admin.manage.microsoft.com.
2. In the *left* pane, click **Updates.**

3. Under *Update Status,* click **New updates to approve.**
4. Choose the update and review its description.
5. Right-click the update and then choose **Decline** (see Figure 14-17).

Figure 14-17
Declining an update

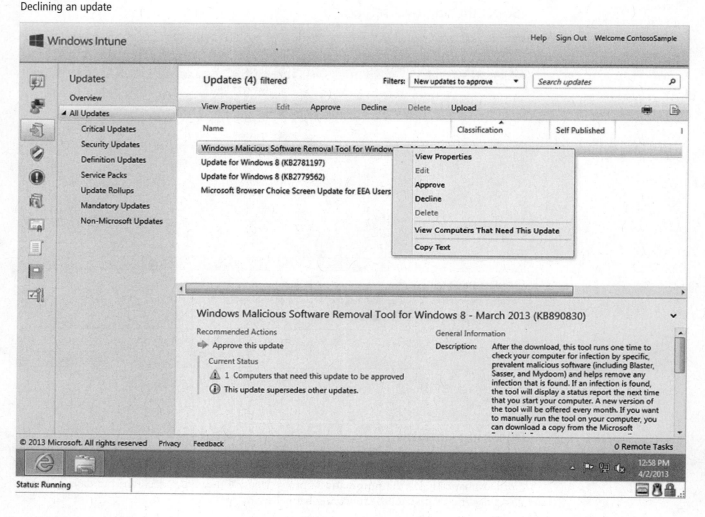

6. After reading the warning prompt, click **Decline.**

Configuring the Company Portal

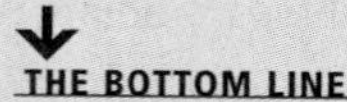

The ***Windows Intune Company Portal*** provides self-service connection point for users to request help and select apps to install. It gives users access to perform self-service tasks, such as adding or removing their computers from Windows Intune, selecting applications to install (made available to them by the Administrator), and contacting the technical support administrator.

Exploring the Company Portal from a User's Perspective

When a user connects to the company portal, he has the option to install a Company Portal app on his computer from the Windows Store. This will create a tile on the user's Start menu (see Figure 14-18).

Figure 14-18

Viewing a company portal tile

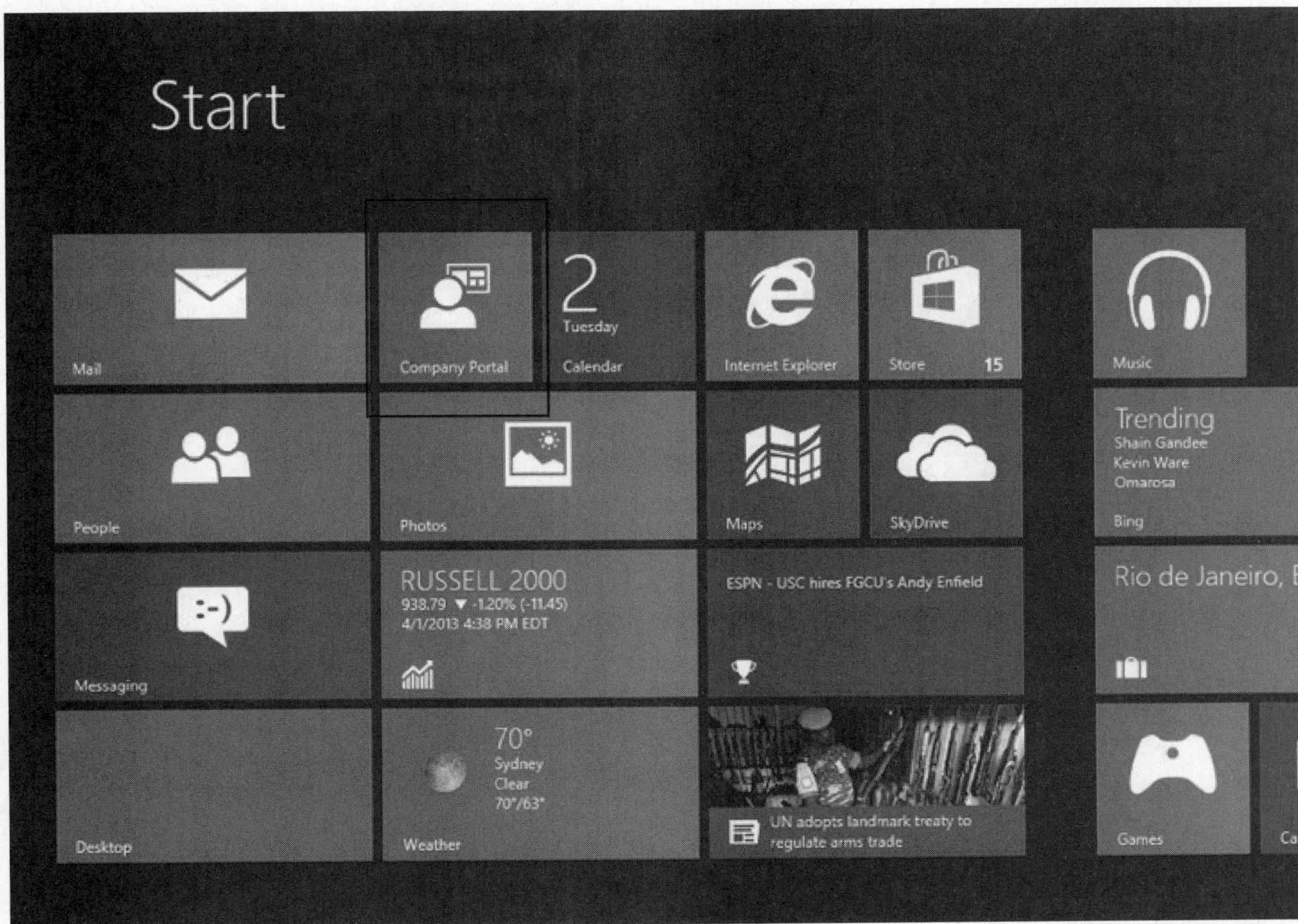

When the user clicks on the tile, he needs to log in using his assigned Windows Intune user name and password. After he is authenticated, the company portal page appears (see Figure 14-19).

CERTIFICATION READY
Configure the company portal
Objective 4.1

If the user clicks the Apps tile, he is prompted to visit the Windows Store to install the Company Portal app. After completing the installation, a new Company Portal tile is placed on the Windows 8 Start menu. The user can then access the portal through this app.

Figure 14-19

Viewing a sample company portal from the user's perspective

Clicking on the *New Apps* icon enables users to view the most recently published apps made available to them via Windows Intune. Selecting an app presents the user with a prompt (see Figure 14-20) to confirm the computer and device they want to install the app on and then perform the installation process.

After it is installed, the app appears as a tile on the company portal page.

+ MORE INFORMATION

Applications can be installed on a remote as well as a local computer. To monitor progress, you can see the application install status on the Apps page of your company portal.

Figure 14-20
Installing App Prompt

Customizing the Company Portal

You can modify the look and feel of the company portal (see Figure 14-21) through the Windows Intune Administrator console.

Figure 14-21
Configuring the company portal

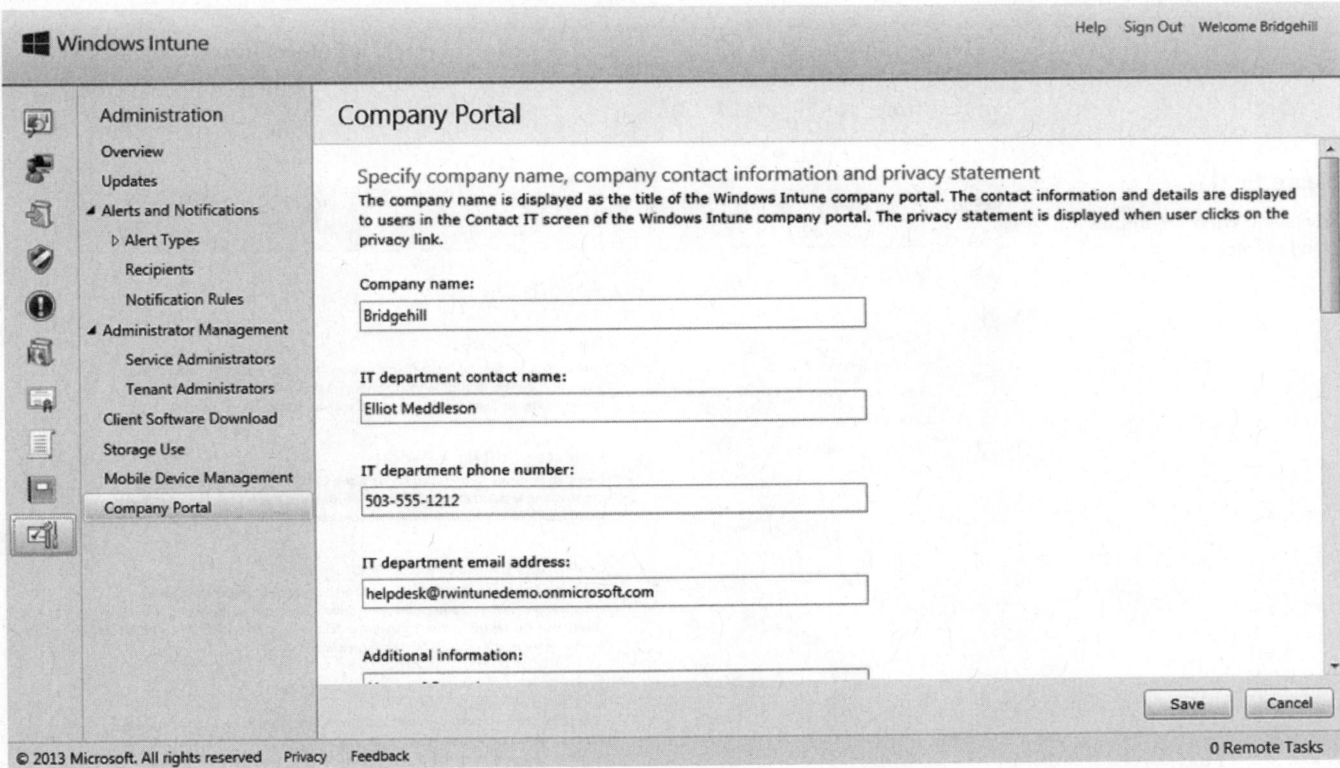

When customizing the portal, information that can be customized includes:

- **Company name:** Appears as the title of your company portal.
- **IT Department contact name:** Appears on the Contact IT tile.
- **IT department phone number:** Appears on the Contact IT tile.

- **IT department email address:** Appears on the Contact IT tile.
- **Additional Information** (such as hours of operation): Appears on the Contact IT tile.
- **Support website URL:** Specifies the website and website name that users can contact for support (name and URL). This can include your IT department phone number, email address, and any additional information you want to provide. Only the name, not the URL, is displayed on the Contact ID page.
- **Theme color:** Customize the theme color and choose a background for the Company Portal app.

■ Monitoring On-Network and Off-Network Machines

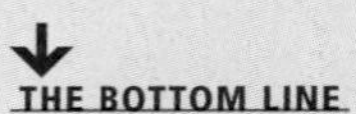

Computers configured with the Windows Intune agent can be tracked both on and off the corporate network. As computers are configured with the Windows Intune agent, they start to report back to Windows Intune. Because Windows Intune is cloud-based, users do not have to be attached to your corporate network to receive updates, patches, or help removing malware.

CERTIFICATION READY
Monitor on-network and off-network machines
Objective 4.1

Using Windows Intune, you can monitor your on-network and off-network machines through standard reports and you do so in real-time.

Reviewing Standard Reports in Windows Intune

Windows Intune offers several types of reports. Although Windows Intune provides a snapshot of your machines through its reporting feature, you should also monitor them in real time (see Figure 14-22).

Figure 14-22

Reviewing Windows Intune standard reports

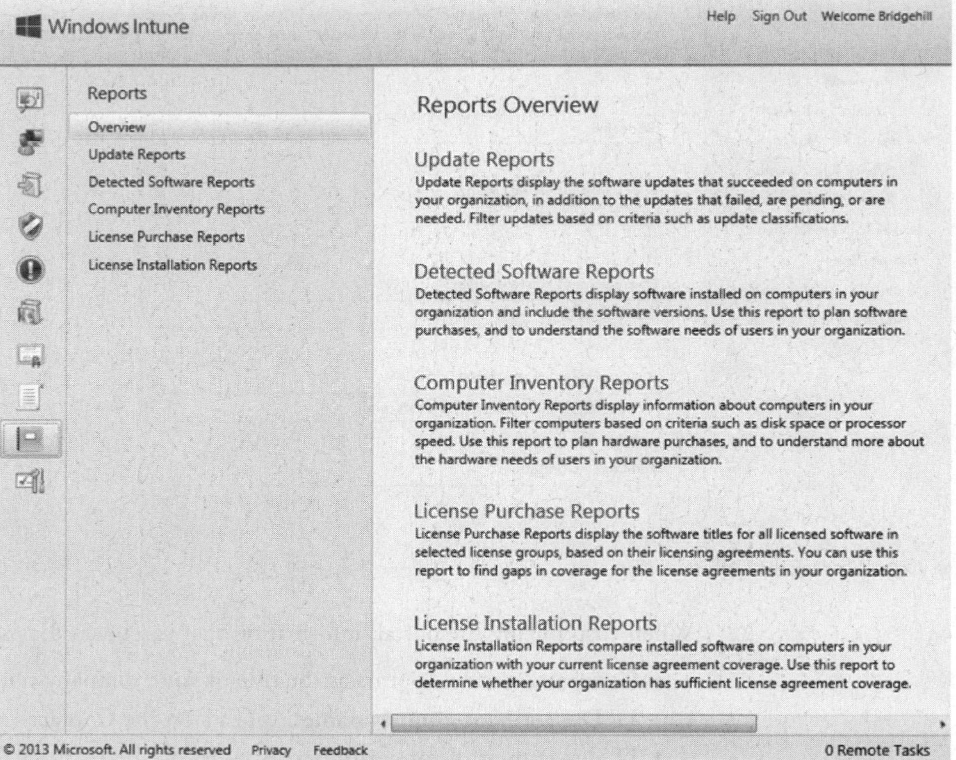

Following are the Windows Intune report types:

- **Update Reports:** Provide information about software updates that succeeded, failed, and are currently pending or those that are needed on computers in your organization.
- **Detected Software Reports:** Provide information about software installed on computers in your organization.
- **Computer Inventory Reports:** Provide information about hardware used in your organization.
- **License Purchase Reports:** Display licensed software titles across your organization.
- **License Installation Reports:** Compare installed software with your current licensing agreement.

You use Windows Intune Alerts and reports to:

- Identify computers that are not running Endpoint Protection Software.
- Identify computers running another malware protection product.
- Investigate and troubleshoot malware activity.
- Identify computers that need updates or computers where updates have failed to install.

The Alerts workspace is designed to help you quickly assess the overall health of the computers in your organization. The Alerts workspace enables you to perform the following functions:

- Configure alert types.
- Select recipients for email notifications.
- Associate recipients with notification rules.

Configuring Alert Types

The Windows Intune Alerts workspace can be used to monitor and manage the overall health of your computers. By using the alerts, you can gain a better understanding of how your computers run and take the necessary steps quickly before a problem impacts your end user's productivity.

There are over 180 alert types available in Windows Intune. Based on your organization's needs, you can enable the alert types you think are important and disable those that are not appropriate for your network environment. You can also configure alert thresholds that are used to determine how often an alert is triggered before it is displayed.

Selecting an alert (see Figure 14-23) provides you with additional information in the bottom pane.

Figure 14-23

Viewing alert types

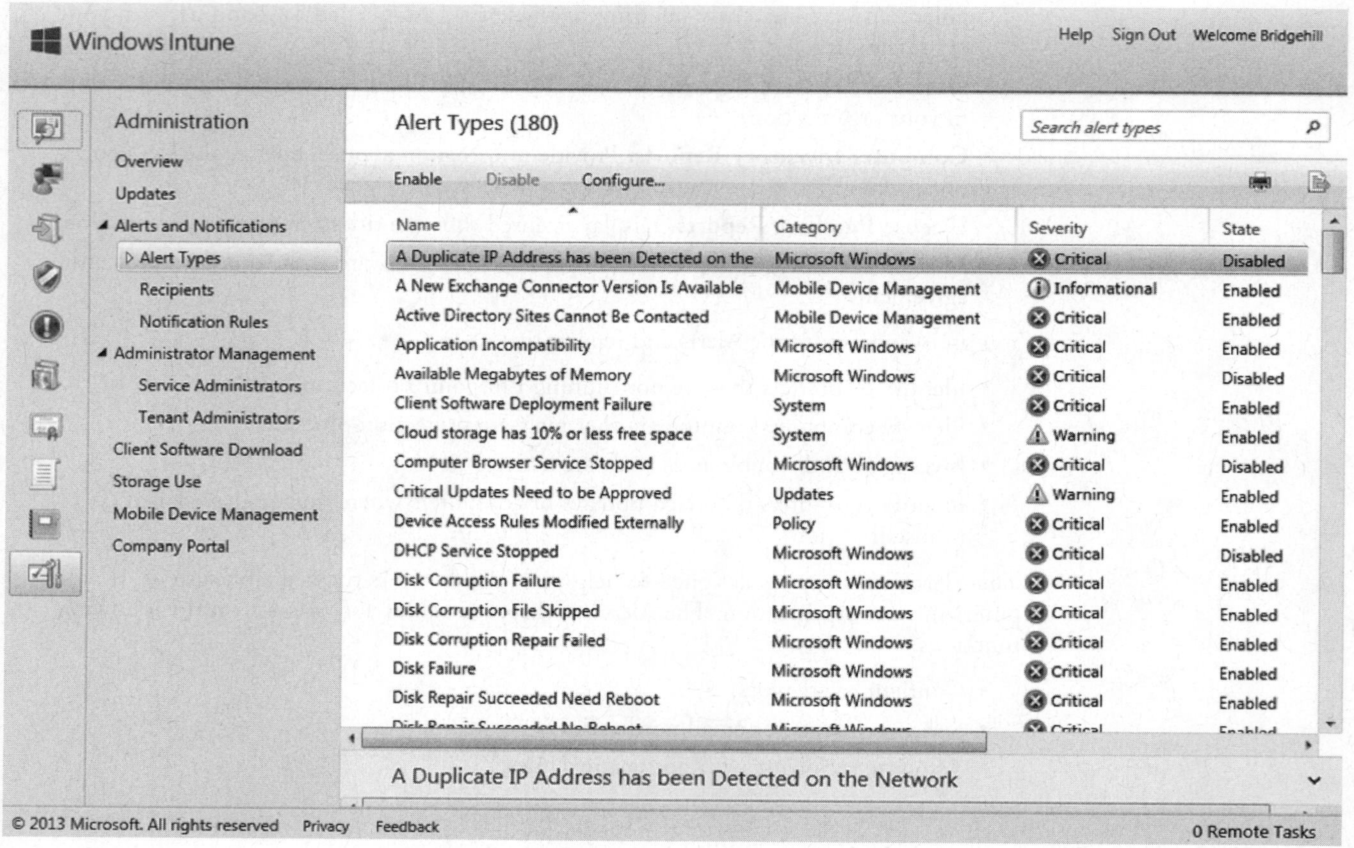

Selecting Recipients

Recipients are individuals who you assign to receive email notifications when alerts occur. Recipients are assigned in the *Administration > Alerts and Notifications > Recipients* location of the Windows Intune Administrator console. To add a new recipient, just select *Add* and type the recipient's email address and specify the language to use for email notification. After you have a list of recipients in place, you need to select Notifications Rules.

Windows Intune has five notification rules that you can target to a recipient. They include:

- All Alerts
- Critical Alerts
- Informational Alerts
- Remote Assistance Requests
- Warning Alerts

To add a recipient to one of these alert types, from the menu, choose *Administration > Alerts and Notifications > Notifications Rules. Under Notification Rules,* click the alert type, and then click *Select Recipients* (see Figure 14-24). Select the box next to each recipient that you want to receive email notifications specified by the rule and click *OK*.

Figure 14-24

Selecting recipients for alert types

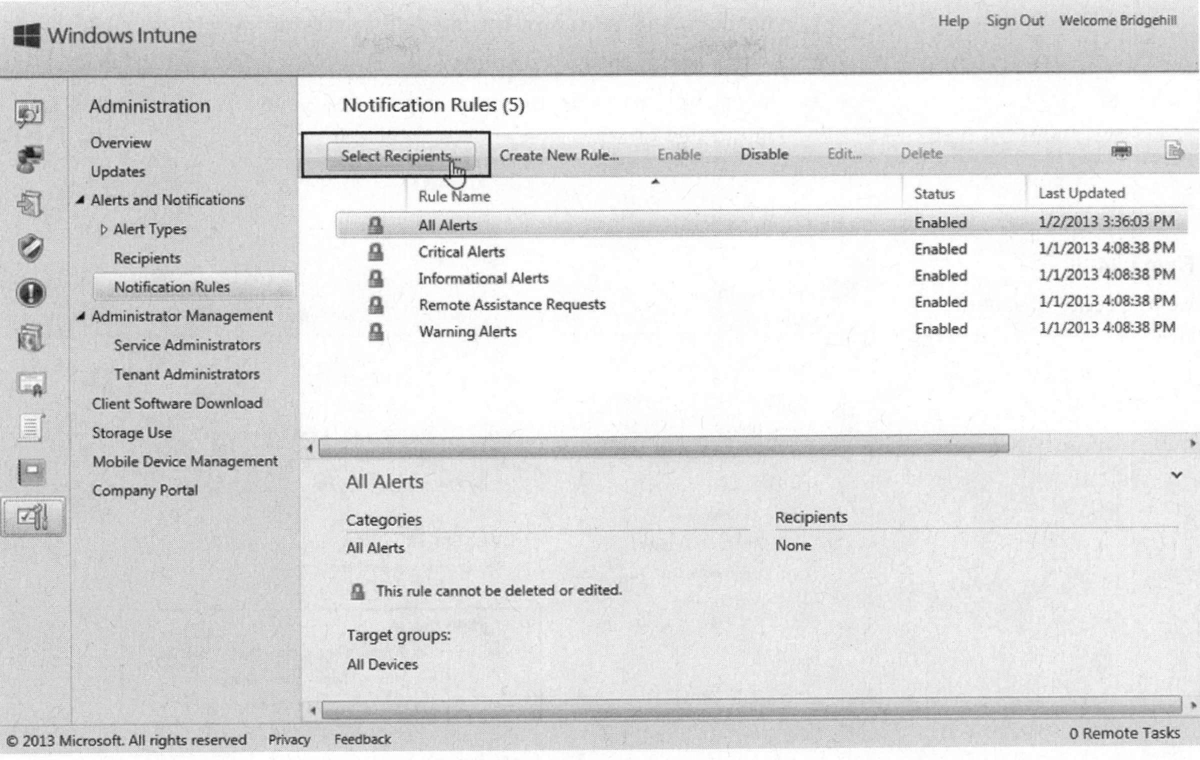

In addition to receiving alerts via email, you can also view alerts directly from within the Windows Intune console via the Alerts workspace (see Figure 14-25).

Figure 14-25

Monitoring alerts

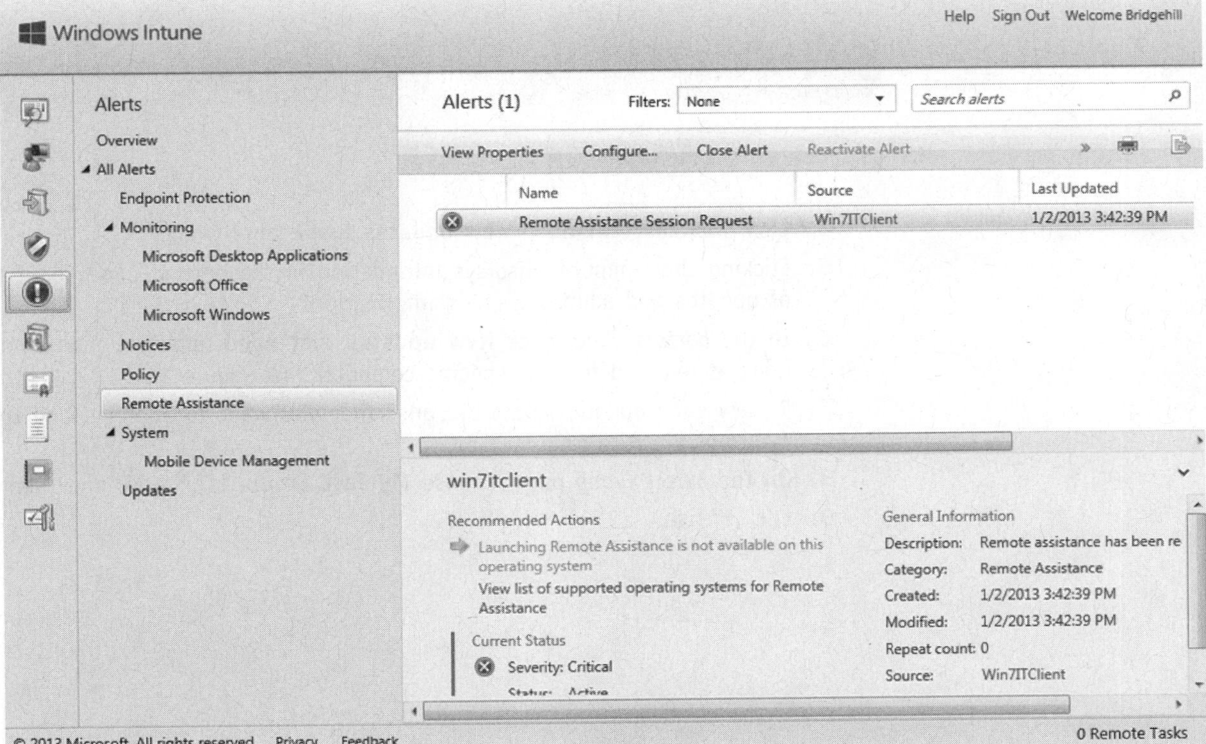

IDENTIFY COMPUTERS THAT NEED UPDATES

GET READY. To identify computers that need updates, perform the following steps:

1. Log in to the **Windows Intune Administrator** console.
2. In the *left* pane, click **Groups**.
3. Under the *Update Status* pane, notice the yellow warning status icon (see Figure 14-26).

Figure 14-26

Viewing devices that need updates

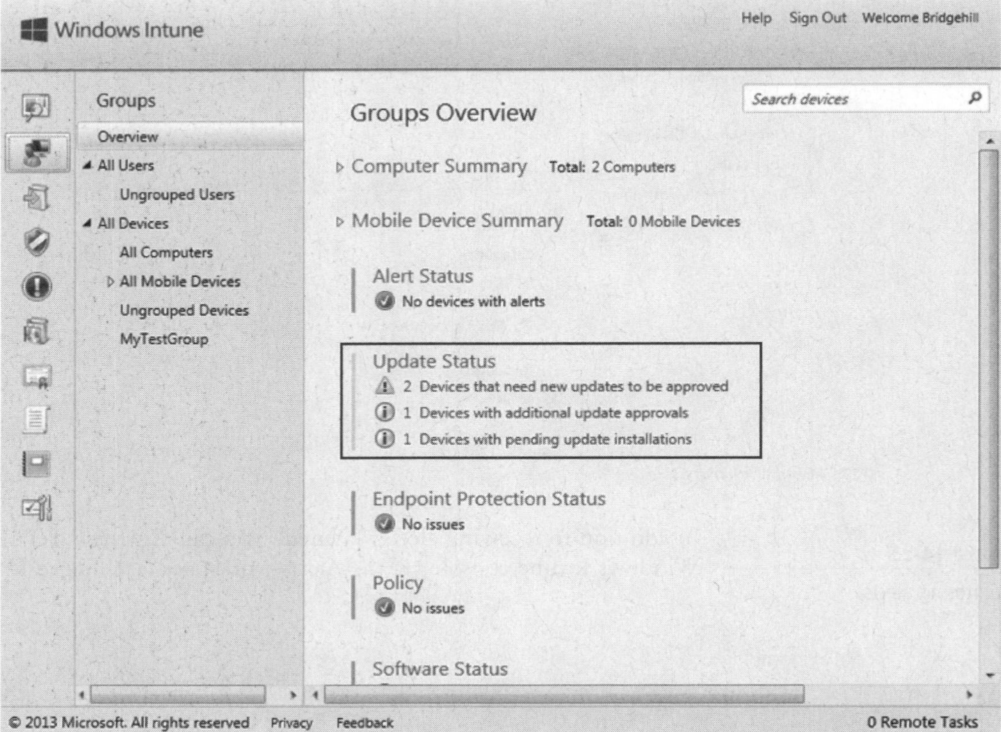

4. Click **Devices that need new updates to be approved.**
5. Clicking the computer displays information in the bottom pane about the number of updates and additional alert information.
6. In the *bottom* pane, click **New updates that need approval** shows you the updates required for this specific computer (see Figure 14-27).
7. Review each update, select the ones that you want to approve, and then click **Approve.**
8. On the *Select Group* page, choose **My Test Group**, click **Add**, and then click **Next.**
9. Click **Finish.**

Figure 14-27

Viewing updates that need to be approved

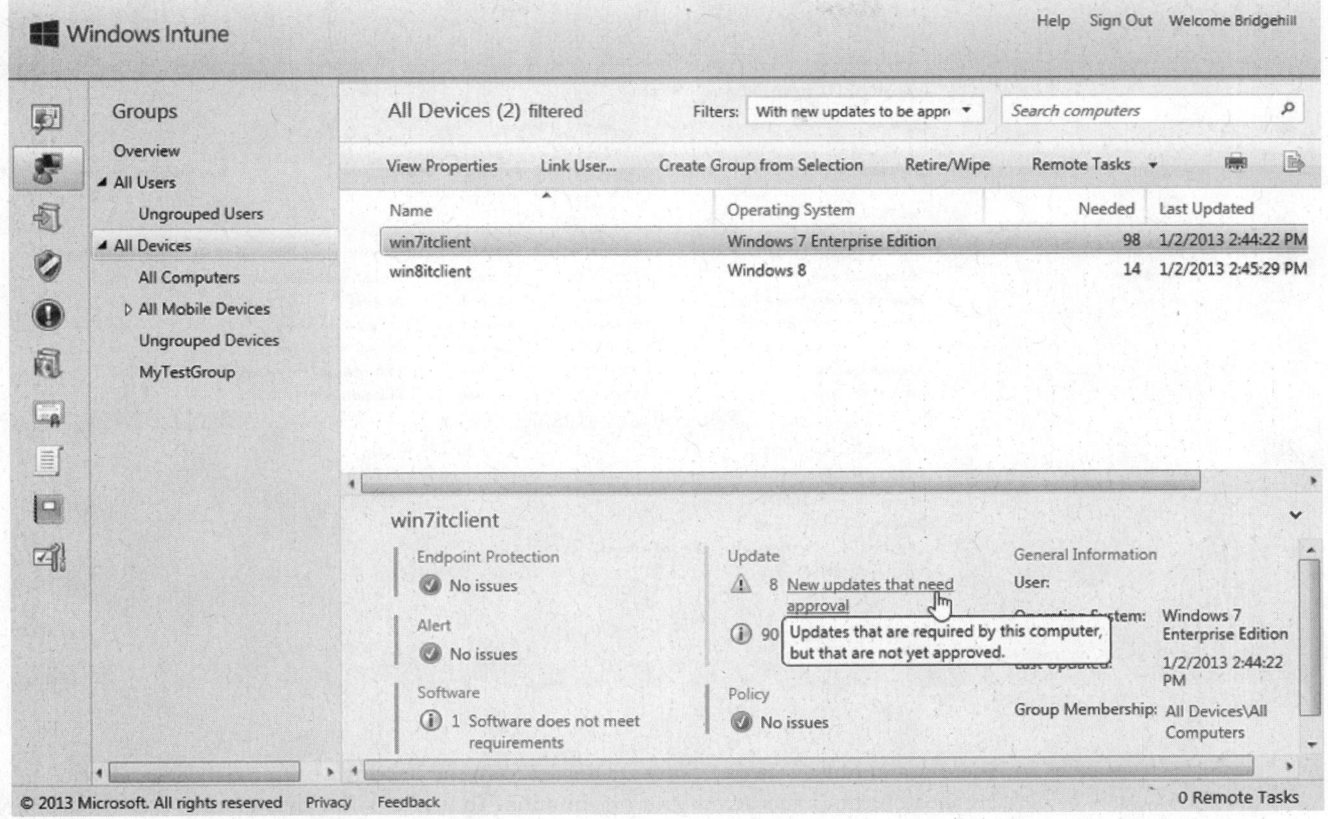

Managing Asset Inventory In Windows Intune

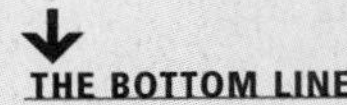

Understanding software and hardware assets can aid in the planning and deployment process of new software and hardware across your organization. Managing your assets means knowing what software and hardware your organization has.

CERTIFICATION READY
Manage asset inventory
Objective 4.1

You can use software inventory to effectively manage the software and licenses used in your organization. This provides information such as the:

- Types of software installed on computers
- Number of copies installed
- Version of software installed
- Publisher
- Category of Software

Reviewing Software Assets

Figure 14-28 shows an example of software information collected from a single Windows 8 virtual machine that runs the Windows Intune agent. This was accessed in the Groups workspace for a Windows 8 computer. From here, you can view the information, print it out, or export it to a CSV or HTML file for further analysis.

Figure 14-28

Collecting software with the Windows Intune agent

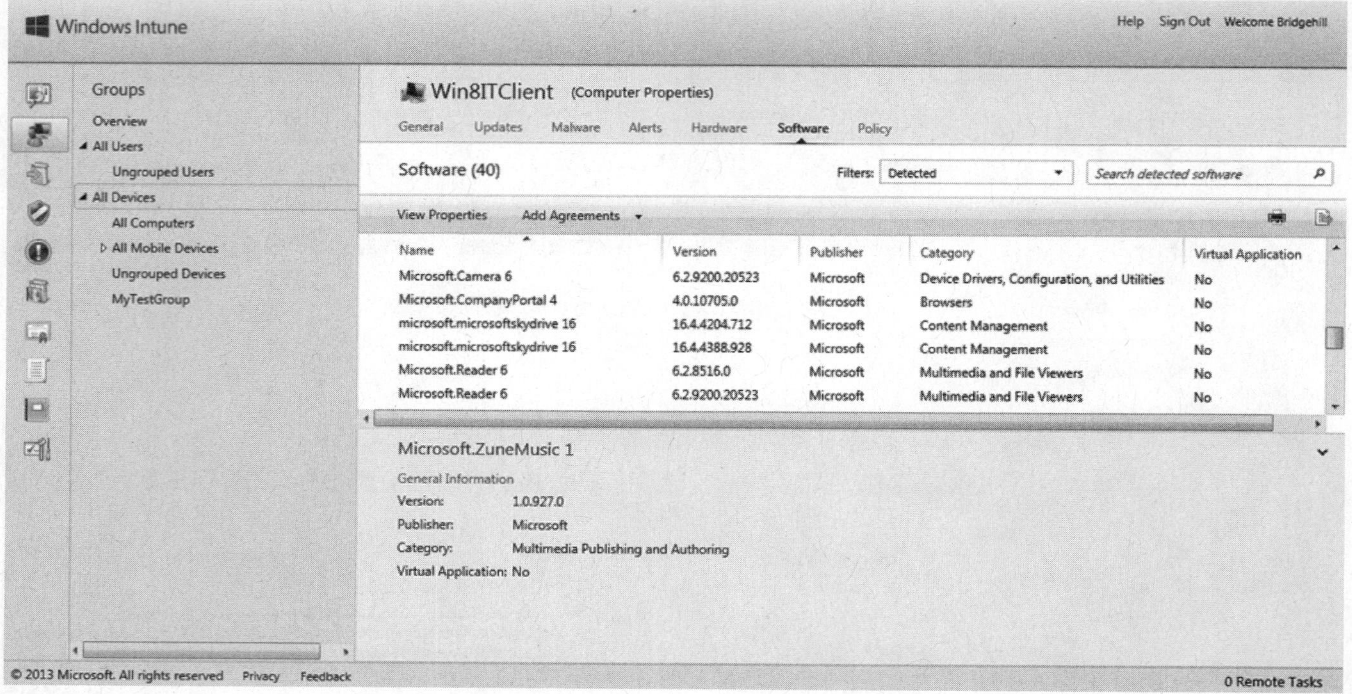

You can also run a Detected Software Report from the Reports workspace to view software installed on computers across your organization. To further refine the report, you can select only software that meets selected criteria (device group, publisher, and/or category). Categories can include browsers, multimedia and file viewers, and operating system and components.

CREATE A DETECTED SOFTWARE REPORT

GET READY. To create a detected software report, perform the following steps:

1. Log in to the **Windows Intune Administrator** console.
2. In the left pane, click **Reports** > **Detected Software Reports**.
3. Under *Select publishers*, click **Edit**.
4. Select **Include only the following**, choose **Microsoft**, and then click **OK**.
5. Under *Select categories*, click **Edit**.
6. Select **Include only the following**, choose **Browser** and **Operating System and Components**, and then click **OK**. See Figure 14-29.

Figure 14-29

Setting the Detected Software Report criteria

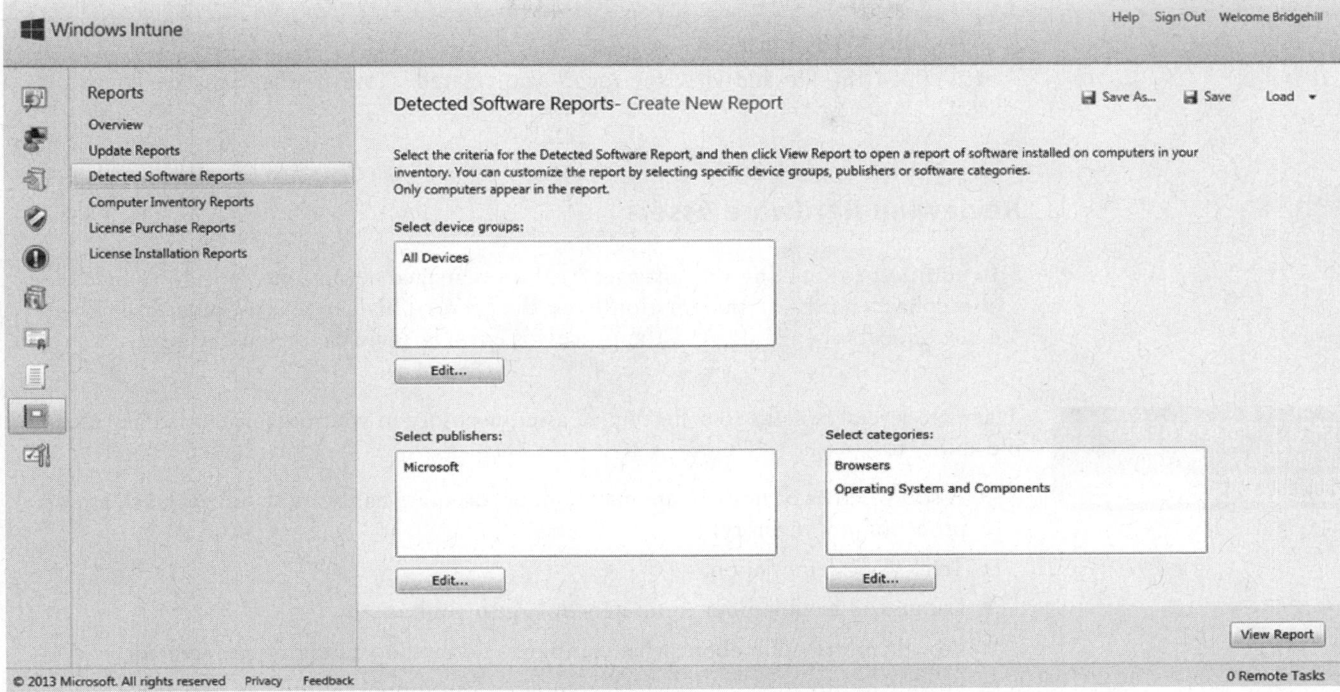

7. Click **View Report.**
8. Move your mouse over the icon in the upper right hand corner and click **Export** (see Figure 14-30).

Figure 14-30

Exporting the report

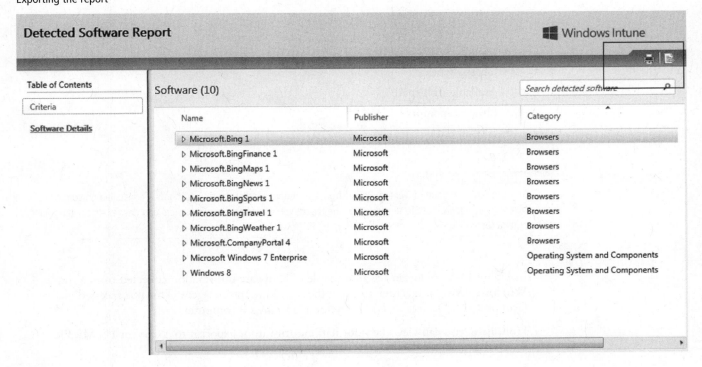

Detected Software Report

Windows Intune

Table of Contents

Criteria

Software Details

Software (10)

Search detected software

Name	Publisher	Category
Microsoft.Bing 1	Microsoft	Browsers
Microsoft.BingFinance 1	Microsoft	Browsers
Microsoft.BingMaps 1	Microsoft	Browsers
Microsoft.BingNews 1	Microsoft	Browsers
Microsoft.BingSports 1	Microsoft	Browsers
Microsoft.BingTravel 1	Microsoft	Browsers
Microsoft.BingWeather 1	Microsoft	Browsers
Microsoft.CompanyPortal 4	Microsoft	Browsers
Microsoft Windows 7 Enterprise	Microsoft	Operating System and Components
Windows 8	Microsoft	Operating System and Components

9. On the *Select the export format for your data* page, click the **down arrow** and choose **.html**. Click **Export**.
10. Choose Desktop as the location to save your file to, and then type **MyWin8Report**.
11. Click **Close**.
12. Open the file and view the report you created. Close it when you are done.

Reviewing Hardware Assets

In addition to tracking the software used on managed computers, Windows Intune also collects hardware information from the agent. This happens automatically or on a customizable schedule, and the process is entirely invisible to the end user.

CERTIFICATION READY
Manage asset inventory
Objective 4.1

There are several benefits to collecting an asset inventory in your organization. They include the ability to:

- Assess whether or not you are maintaining corporate hardware standards (such as processor and memory).
- Track asset depreciation.
- Locate and troubleshoot computers in large organizations.
- Provide information about what computers need an operating system upgrade.
- Provide information about which computers can support a software package.
- Identify computers with common hardware characteristics to aid in deployment of software.

The following information can be collected and reported on both mobile devices and managed computers:

- Operating systems
- Manufacturers
- Models
- Chassis types
- Available disk space
- Physical memory
- CPU speed

MORE INFORMATION
You can run a Computer Inventory Report from the Reports workspace to view hardware installed on computers across your organization. To further refine the report, you can select only computers and devices that meet selected criteria (operating system, model, chassis type, CPU speed, and so on).

In Figure 14-31, you can see an example of hardware information collected from a single Windows 8 virtual machine running the Windows Intune agent. This was accessed via Groups > All Devices > Hardware for a Windows 8 computer.

From here, you can view the information, print it, or export it to a CSV or HTML file for further analysis.

Figure 14-31

Collecting computer hardware information

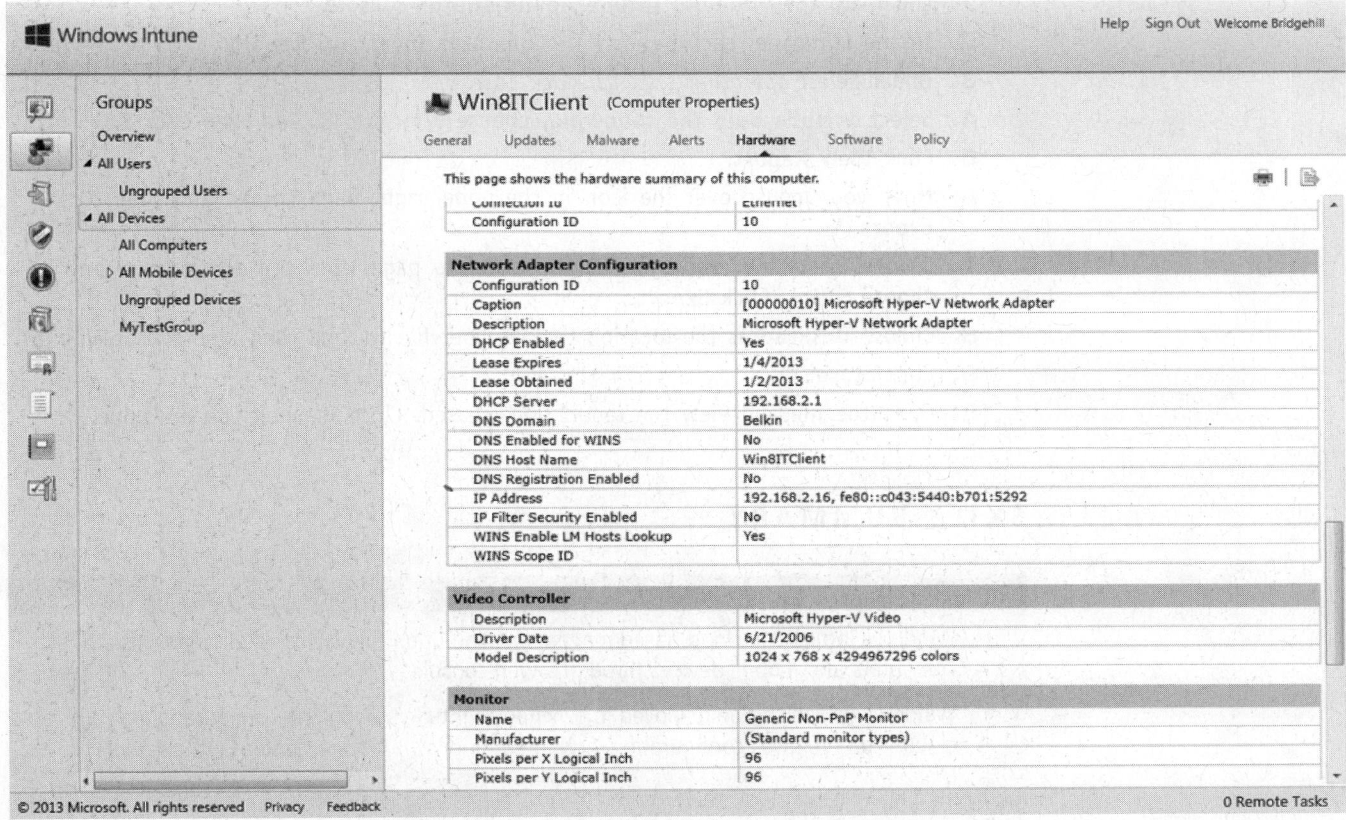

The information provided is broken into the following sections in the report:

- **System:** Name, Manufacturer, Model, Physical memory, Last User to log on
- **System Enclosure:** Chassis type, Serial Number SMBIOS Asset Tag
- **BIOS:** Name, Version, Manufacturer, Release Date
- **Processor:** Name, Architecture, Clock Speed
- **Physical Disk:** Name, Manufacturer Model, Caption, Partitions, Size, interface type
- **Logical Disks:** Name, Drive Type
- **Network Adapter:** Name, Manufacturer, Product Name, MAC Address, Speed, Connection Status
- **Network Adapter Configuration:** DHCP enabled, DHCP Server address, IP address, leaser information, IP address information, IPsec status
- **Video Controller:** Description, Drive Date, model
- **Monitor:** Name, Manufacturer, Pixels per inch, screen height/width
- **Printers:** Name, Share status, local/network, driver name
- **Physical Memory:** Capacity

CREATE A COMPUTER INVENTORY REPORT

GET READY. To create a computer inventory report, perform the following steps:

1. Log in to the **Windows Intune Administrator** console.
2. In the *left* pane, click **Reports** > **Computer Inventory Reports**.
3. Under *Select operating systems,* click **Edit**.
4. Select **Include only the following**, choose **Windows 8**, and then click **OK**.
5. Click **View Report**.
6. Move your mouse over the icon in the upper right hand corner, and then click **Export**.
7. On the *Select the export format for your data* page, click the **down arrow** and choose **.html**. Click **Export**.
8. Choose **Desktop** as the location to save your file to, and then type **MyWin8InvRpt**.
9. Click **Close**.
10. Open the file and view the report you created. Close it when you are done.

SKILL SUMMARY

IN THIS LESSON YOU LEARNED:

- Windows Intune is a cloud-based management solution that helps you manage your computers and mobile devices through a web console.
- Windows Intune can be deployed in a Windows Intune standalone configuration, a cloud+ on premises configuration, and integrated with System Center Configuration Manager.
- You can deploy the Windows Intune agent to both physical and virtual PCs.
- Windows Intune Tenant Administrator and the Windows Intune Service Administrator are the key administrative accounts in Windows Intune.
- Windows Intune uses groups to manage updates. These groups can include users, computers and mobile devices; however, a single group cannot contain both at the same time.
- You can deploy software updates, policies, and software applications to groups and based on the hierarchy, members of child groups can also receive the updates.
- Direct-based membership involves manually entering members of groups, whereas Criteria (dynamic query) members are automatically managed via membership in security groups you specify during setup of the group.
- Windows Intune is based on the concept of workspaces. The Update workspace is used to view, approve, decline, and configure automatic approval rules.
- Automatic approval rules are used to streamline the approval of updates. When you create a rule, Windows Intune automatically approves installation of all Critical and Security updates as soon as they are released by Microsoft.
- Windows Intune provides a portal to allow users to perform self-service tasks, such as adding and removing computers Windows Intune manages, selecting applications to install, and requesting technical support.
- Windows Intune provides real-time information on hardware and software used across the organization and standard reports to help you forecast needs.

Knowledge Assessment

Multiple Choice

Select the correct answer for each of the following questions.

1. On which operating system can you install the Windows Intune? Choose all that apply.
   a. Windows XP Professional (SP3)
   b. Windows Vista Business Edition
   c. Windows 8 Professional (physical computer)
   d. Windows 8 Consumer (virtual client)
2. Which command is used to perform a delayed installation of the Windows Intune client when working with images?
   a. `Windows_Intune_Setup.exe / DelayEnroll`
   b. `Windows_Intune_Setup.exe / DelayedEnroll`
   c. `Windows_Intune_Setup.exe / PrepareEnroll`
   d. `Windows_Intune_Setup.exe / PreparedEnroll`
3. Which administrator role in Windows Intune can create and delete ALL other types of accounts?
   a. Windows Intune Service administrator role
   b. Windows Intune User Management Administrator role
   c. Windows Intune Tenant Administrator
   d. Windows Intune SuperAdmin Role
4. Which of the following are true about Update groups? Chose all that apply.
   a. They can be organized geographically.
   b. They are managed via the Updates workspace.
   c. They can mix both users and devices in the same group.
   d. They are managed as part of a group hierarchy structure.
5. Which type of group is created manually in the Windows Intune administrator console?
   a. dynamic query-based group
   b. direct-based group
   c. security group
   d. dynamic group
6. Which types of updates are designed to fix a specific problem addressing a critical nonsecurity-related bug?
   a. Security update
   b. Definition update
   c. Critical update
   d. Feature pack
7. Which are true statements about using Automatic Update Approval rules? Choose all that apply.
   a. They streamline only critical updates.
   b. They streamline critical and security updates to as soon as they are released by Microsoft.
   c. They cannot be used in Windows Intune on Windows 7 computers.
   d. They are created in the Administrator workspace in the Windows Intune Admin console.
8. Which task cannot be performed when using the Windows Intune Company Portal?
   a. Adding a computer to Windows Intune
   b. Removing a computer from Windows Intune
   c. Contacting Technical Support
   d. Installing Windows applications made available to other users by the Windows Intune Administrator
9. Which Windows Intune report provides information about software updates that have failed?
   a. License Purchase Reports.
   b. Update Reports.

c. Detected Software Reports.
d. Software Update Reports.

10. How many alert types are available in Windows Intune?
    a. 20
    b. 60
    c. 100
    d. Over 180

Best Answer

Choose the letter that corresponds to the best answer. More than one answer choice may achieve the goal. Select the BEST answer.

1. Which method is best for sharing hardware information with an employer who provides information on 20 computers and who wants to see which operating systems are currently installed and which require additional memory upgrades?
   a. Take a screen shot of each computer's hardware settings via the Groups workspace.
   b. Visit each computer and record the information manually.
   c. Export hardware information obtained on each computer from the Groups workspace to a CSV file and send it via email.
   d. Create a Computer Inventory report and set the criteria to only show computers running those operating systems with a selected amount of memory.
2. A Windows Server 2012 Active Directory-based network of 10 technically adept users uses which method to roll out the Windows Intune client that best fits its deployment needs?
   a. User-Initiated Enrollment of computers.
   b. Install the client as part of an image.
   c. Download and install the client on each user's computer.
   d. Download and install the client on each user's computer via Group Policy.
3. Users and devices are distributed across two states. They use both laptops and desktops. Which is the best approach to organize them using the Windows Intune group structure?
   a. Set up one group for Laptops and another for Desktops.
   b. Set up State 1 and State 2 groups, and then set up Laptops and Desktop groups as child groups under each.
   c. Set up State 1 and State 2 groups.
   d. Use the default settings for groups configured by Windows Intune when it is first installed.
4. Which option provides the best approach for rolling out critical updates to user devices when there are only 30 users on a Windows Intune subscription?
   a. Manually check and approve updates for each individual user.
   b. Create an Automatic Update approval rule and test it against a TestGroup before deploying to the rest of the company.
   c. Create an Automatic Update approval rule and deploy it to all computers.
   d. Run an Updates report weekly to identify the computers that need updates, and then manually approve them.
5. Which Windows Intune report provides the most applicable information regarding the software installed on your users' devices of your company's license agreement?
   a. Update Reports
   b. Detected Software Reports
   c. License Purchase Reports
   d. License Installation Reports

Matching and Identification

1. Match the following terms with the related description or usage.
   ________ a) Automatic Update Approval rule
   ________ b) Dynamic Query based membership

_________ c) Product Categories
_________ d) Update Classifications
_________ e) Windows Intune Tenant Administrator
_________ f) Windows Intune Service Administrator
_________ g) Critical update
_________ h) Service Pack
_________ i) Windows Intune Groups
_________ j) Update Reports

1. Provides information about software updates that succeed, fail, are currently pending, or are needed on computers.
2. Windows Intune runs a query based on certain criteria to find users or devices. After they are found, they are dynamically added to the group.
3. Windows Intune uses to automatically approve installation of all Critical and Security updates as soon as they are released from Microsoft.
4. A tested cumulative set of all hot fixes, security updates, critical updates, and some customer-requested design and feature changes.
5. Fixes for a specific problem addressing a critical non-security related bug.
6. Has full access to the Windows Intune administrator console, but cannot modify it.
7. Sets up Windows Intune and accepted the Microsoft Subscription agreement.
8. Examples of these include Critical updates, Security updates, and Definition updates.
9. Used to quickly organize and manage your computers and users and can be created in the Groups workspace.
10. Examples of these include Antigen, Biztalk Server, Exchange, Office, and SQL Server.

2. In order of first to last, identify the seven basic ways to decline an update.
_________ After reading the warning prompt, select Decline.
_________ Select the Updates workspace.
_________ Select the Updates Overview page.
_________ Open the Windows Intune Administrator console.
_________ Select the update and review its description.
_________ In the menu, select Decline.
_________ Under the Updates status (middle pane), select new updates to approve.

3. In order of first to last, identify the ten steps to create a Computer Inventory report that includes the Windows 8 operating system as the criteria, and save it as an html file to your desktop.
_________ Log in to the Windows Administrator console.
_________ Select View Report.
_________ Select the Reports icon.
_________ Select Export by moving your mouse over the icon in the upper right hand corner.
_________ In the Navigation pane, click Computer Inventory Reports.
_________ Select .html as the export format and click Export.
_________ Under Select Operating systems, select Edit.
_________ Type a name for the report and save it to your desktop.
_________ Select Include only the following and select the Windows 8 check box. Click OK.
_________ Click Close.

4. In order of first to last, identify the ten basic steps to create an Automatic Update Approval rule for a specific user group named MyTestGroup.
_________ Log in to the Windows Intune Administrator console.
_________ In the left pain, select Administration.
_________ Select Updates.
_________ Select All Categories, and then click Next. -
_________ Select MyTestGroup, and then click Add. Click Next. -

_________ Select Critical Updates and Security Updates, and then click Next.
_________ Click New to create the rule.
_________ Type a name and description for the rule.
_________ Click Finish.
_________ Confirm your new rule appears under the Automatic Approval rules section.

Choose an Option

1. Which icon do you select to access the Updates workspace to view a pending installation of a service pack?

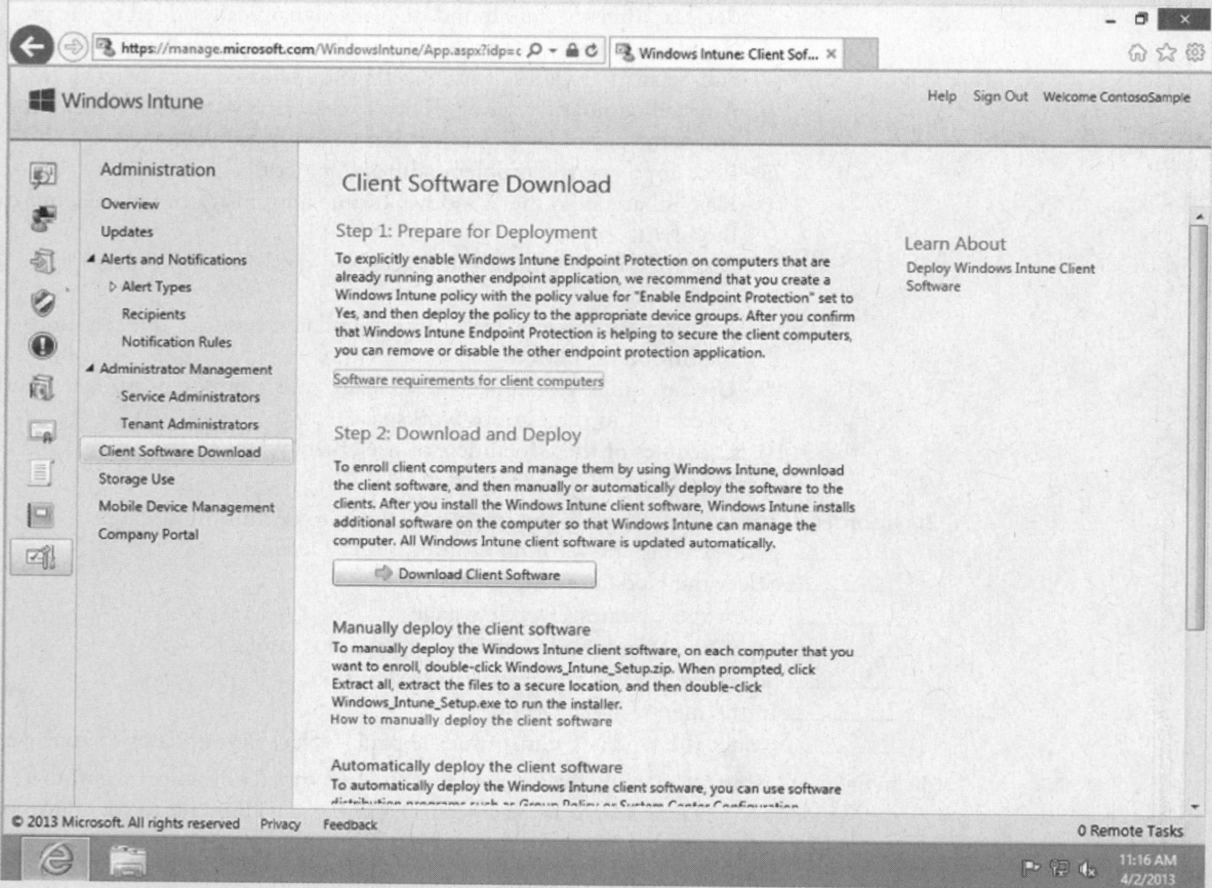

■ Business Case Scenarios

Scenario 14-1: Missing Update

To deploy a specific update after having researched it the day before and after returning to the Updates workspace in the Administrator console, where you can't find it in the default view, what do you determine happened?

Scenario 14-2: Windows Intune Administration

If you cannot modify data after logging into the Windows Intune Administration Console, but you can view the data and run reports, what is the problem?

Managing Public Cloud Services

LESSON 15

70-688 EXAM OBJECTIVE

Objective 4.2 – Manage public cloud services. This objective may include, but is not limited to: Manage Windows Live services including trusted PC, storage, SkyDrive/Live Mesh apps, and groups; implement Office 365 using the Office 365 desktop setup; manage Office 365.

Lesson Heading	Exam Objective
Introducing Public Cloud Services	
Managing Windows Live Services	Manage Windows Live services including trusted PC, storage, SkyDrive/ Live Mesh apps, and groups
Using SkyDrive Groups / SkyDrive Pro	
Using Groups in SkyDrive	
Reviewing Trusted PC Requirements	
Implementing Office Professional Plus Using Office 365	Implement Office 365 using the Office 365 desktop setup
Reviewing Methods for Deploying Office 2013	
Installing Office Professional 2013 on Windows 8	
Managing Office 365	Manage Office 365

KEY TERMS

asset library
cloud
fetching
Global Administrator
group
Office 365
Office 2013
SkyDrive Pro
trusted PC
User Management Administrator

■ Introducing Public Cloud Services

Public cloud services provide a way to access information from anywhere at any time. There are many definitions for the cloud. Microsoft defines a ***cloud*** as a Web-based service that is hosted outside of your organization. This means the information technology infrastructure (hardware, servers, software, and so on) is located somewhere other than your office and is managed by a third party (such as hosted). If you use mobile banking—accessing web-based email or storing your photos online in one of the many services provided—you are interacting with "the cloud."

Using public cloud services such as SkyDrive and Office 365 enable you to take advantage of hosted solutions. This means users have the ability to access their information from anywhere at any time across multiple devices. By using cloud-based services, your users can collaborate via calendars, email, and through document sharing. From an administrative perspective, it means you gain access to services and programs without the additional overhead of maintenance and software upgrades.

In this lesson, we take a look at options for managing your Windows Live services (SkyDrive Groups and trusted PC) and the steps needed to implement and manage Office 365.

■ Managing Windows Live Services

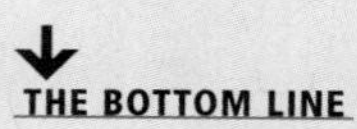

SkyDrive and trusted PCs provide you access to your files and settings when moving between your Windows 8 devices. In Lesson 3, you discovered the benefits of using SkyDrive and the SkyDrive desktop app. From any browser, you can access your SkyDrive account and create files, upload files, and share documents. With the SkyDrive desktop app, you have the ability to gain access to any file on your computer remotely through a process called ***fetching***. As you continue to explore SkyDrive, you can share your content with friends and coworkers. To help you organize and manage your content with others, you create SkyDrive groups.

In addition to managing content stored in SkyDrive, Microsoft provides you with the ability to trust a PC. A ***trusted PC*** is a Microsoft account security feature. Only trusted PCs are allowed to synchronize passwords and can be used to easily reset your password should you forget it.

Using SkyDrive Groups / SkyDrive Pro

After storing your content, you eventually need to share it with other family members or coworkers. SkyDrive groups provide an excellent way for you to communicate and share your files, calendar, and photos with others. A ***group*** consists of users who communicate and share documents with each other.

When you set up a group in SkyDrive, the group is provided a unique URL and email address. Members of the group can access all group information available on the group's site. When you invite someone to become a member of the group, he receives group emails and can view group documents and photos. The group is provided a central place to store and work on documents together and members can make it easy to find documents and folders by pinning them to the group's profile page.

Each group gets its own OneNote notebook. You can copy notes, links, images, and maps and use them to brainstorm ideas in real time.

Groups with up to 40 members can use Messenger to conduct group conversations. Members can also see the email address and online status of other members. Messenger is

CERTIFICATION READY
Manage Windows Live services including trusted PC, storage, SkyDrive / Live Mesh apps, and groups
Objective 4.2

enabled by default for a group, but if it is turned off, you cannot turn it back on for the group.

Members and other people invited to the group can send email messages to each other using the group's email address and if necessary, you can ban selected people from group email messages.

When groups are deleted, all documents, photos, and other information are permanently deleted. The group web address is not available to use again for 60 days.

CREATE A SKYDRIVE GROUP

GET READY. To create a SkyDrive group, log in to your Windows 8 computer with your Microsoft user account, and perform the following steps:

1. In the Windows 8 *Start* menu, click the **Internet Explorer** tile, and then in the browser's *address* field, type **http://www.skydrive.com.**
2. In the menu on the left, click **Groups.**
3. In the *Group name* field, type a name for your group and then type the same or different name in the *Group email* field. This uses *@groups.live.com* as part of the group's email address. For example, projectx2013 uses projectx2013@groups.live.com as the group's email address.
4. Click **Create group.**
   Microsoft will check to make sure the email address is valid. If you used an address that is already in use, you will be asked to enter a different name.
5. From the menu at the top, click **Group actions > Invite people.**
6. In the *Invite people to join this group* field, type the email address of people you want to invite, and then click **Invite.**
   If you are adding multiple email addresses, use a comma between each.
7. Users receive an email with the subject line: *<yourname> wants you to join the group <groupname>*. After clicking the **View group** link provided in the email, they will log in with their Microsoft user account and then access SkyDrive. Figure 15-1 shows what a group member sees when connecting to the website.

Figure 15-1

Viewing the Groups page

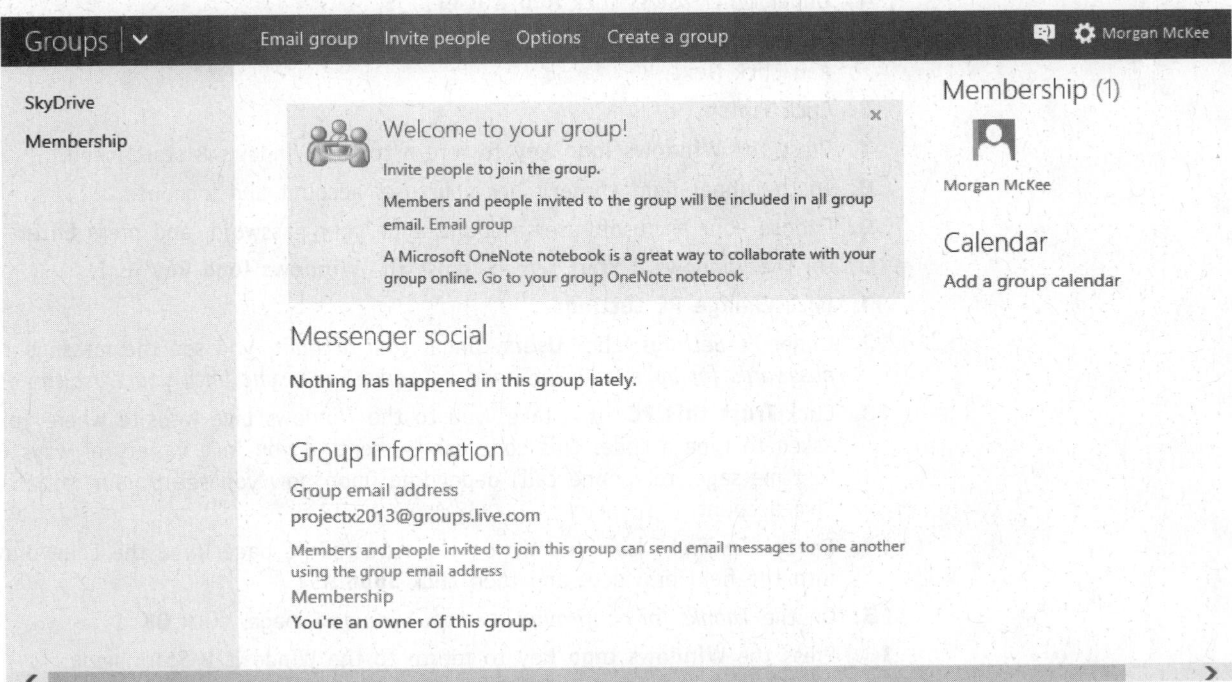

CERTIFICATION READY
Manage Windows Live services including trusted PC, storage, SkyDrive / Live Mesh apps, and groups
Objective 4.2

SkyDrive Pro is a private library that provides a repository for storing your work documents. It is included in the Office 2013 product suite when integrated with Office 365. The data can be stored in the cloud (SharePoint Online) or on your company's SharePoint 2013 server depending upon the configuration you decide to implement. Using SkyDrive Pro, you can:

- Store and manage your private documents.
- Sync your library across your computers and mobile devices, allowing you to access them offline.
- Share your documents with others to allow them to review or edit your documents.

Reviewing Trusted PC Requirements

Lesson 10 discussed how you can synchronize your settings across multiple PCs or devices when using your Microsoft user account. In addition to synchronizing personalized settings (colors, themes, app settings, and browser history), you can also synchronize your passwords. This requires that you set up your computer as a trusted PC.

A trusted PC is a computer or device that you have added to the password reset information for your Microsoft user account. Microsoft can use this information to verify the identity of the person using the computer. If you forget your password or an unauthorized person gains access to the information, you can reset the password from any trusted PC. In general, you should designate only private computers and devices as trusted PCs.

TRUST YOUR PC

GET READY. To trust a new PC, log in to your Windows 8 computer with administrative privileges, and perform the following steps:

1. In the Windows 8 *Start* menu, press the **Windows logo key + I.**
2. Click **Change PC settings.**
3. Under *PC Settings*, click **Users.**
4. Under *Other users,* click **Add a user.**
5. On the *Add a user* screen, type the email address for your Microsoft user account and click **Next.**
6. Click **Finish.**
7. Press the **Windows logo key** to return to the Windows 8 start menu.
8. In the upper right corner, click your user account and log out.
9. Choose your Microsoft user account, type your password, and press **Enter.**
10. On the Windows 8 Start screen, press the **Windows logo key + I.**
11. Click **Change PC settings.**
12. Under *PC Settings*, click **Users.** Under *Your account,* you see the message *Your saved passwords for apps, websites, and networks won't sync until you trust this PC.*
13. Click **Trust this PC.** This takes you to the Windows Live website where you will be asked to type a code. This code can be sent to you in a variety of ways (email, text message, telephone call) depending upon how you setup your initial Windows Live account.
14. On the *Confirm <computername> as a trusted PC* page, type the code provided into the field provided, and then click **Submit.**
15. On the *Thanks for confirming <computername>* page, click **OK.**
16. Press the **Windows logo key** to return to the Windows 8 Start menu.

The next time you log into the computer, you will have the option to synchronize your password and any other settings on the computer that you choose.

Implementing Office 2013 Using Office 365

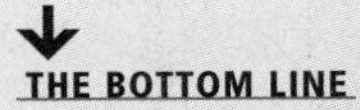

THE BOTTOM LINE

Office 365 is a subscription-based service that offers various services and software that enable you to collaborate and store documents online. When implemented with ***Office 2013***, users can work either online or offline and take advantage of the full features available with the desktop applications in the Office suite.

CERTIFICATION READY
Implement Office 365 using Office 365 desktop setup
Objective 4.2

Office 365 offers several different plans designed for small, midsize, and enterprise-level businesses. The Office 365 Small Business Premium (25 users), Office 365 Midsize Business (300 users), and Office 365 Enterprise E3 (unlimited users) plans include a subscription for Office 2013 for up to five PCs/Macs. Office 2013 includes desktop versions of the following applications:

- Microsoft Access 2013
- Microsoft OneNote 2013
- Microsoft Excel 2013
- Microsoft Word 2013
- Microsoft Outlook 2013
- Microsoft PowerPoint 2013
- Microsoft Publisher 2013
- SkyDrive Pro 2013
- Microsoft InfoPath (not available with the Small Business Premium plan)
- Microsoft Lync 2013

Office 365 manages the licenses for Office 2013 through an online portal by indicating which Office 365 users have the ability to install the program during the setup of the user's account. In the Office 365 portal, you can delete a user to free up a licenses, remove a license from a user if his job changes, or assign a license for a user after the account is set up. You can also review which licenses are assigned to a user and purchase more if necessary.

The next section reviews the different methods available for deploying Office 2013 to your users.

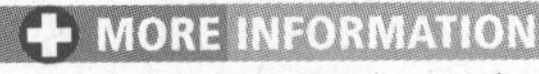

MORE INFORMATION

To learn more about what is included and pricing for Office 365, visit Microsoft and search *Office 365 plans*.

Reviewing Methods for Deploying Office 2013

There are several options available for deploying Office 2013. The option you choose depends on the infrastructure you already have in place and the level of IT support available in your organization.

The options you can choose are:

- **Deploying directly from the Office 365 portal:** This option is designed for organizations that do not have IT resources; it has a self-service approach. When this option is used, you can download and install only the 32-bit version of Office 2013.
- **Deploying from a network share:** This requires basic IT administration skills and works well in situations where you have a slow network connection. When this option is used, you have the option to deploy both 32-bit and 64-bit versions of Office 2013.

- **Deploying using Group Policy or Microsoft System Center Configuration Manager:** These two methods are designed to leverage Active Directory and should be used when deploying to large groups of users.

Following is a brief overview of the steps involved to deploy Office 2013 directly from the Office 365 portal. In the exercise that follows, you look at the following steps in more detail:

1. Administrator signs up for Microsoft Office 365, sets a new domain name, creates user accounts, and assigns licenses to each user.
2. Administrator sends users their temporary passwords by email.
3. Users sign into the Office 365 portal and set up a new password.
4. Users download and configure their desktops with Office 2013 (32-bit version).

Following is a brief overview of the steps involved to deploy from Office 365 from a network share:

1. Administrator signs up for Microsoft Office 365, sets a new domain name, creates user accounts, and assigns licenses to each user.
2. Administrator downloads Office 2013 (32-bit or 64-bit version) from the Office 365 portal to a local computer.
3. Administrator creates a network share (\\servername\Office2013\Source) and then extracts the files into the share using the following command:

   ```
   MicrosoftOffice.exe /extract:"c:\Office2013\Source
   ```
4. Administrator downloads the Office 2013 Administrative template files and the Office Customization Tool (OCT) files. Visit Microsoft's website and search for *Office 2013 Administrative Templates* to find these files. The OCT tool is used to create a setup customization file for the Office package.
5. Administrator double-clicks the AdminTemplates.exe file and completes the install, and then copies the \Admin folder to the \\servername\Office2013\Source folder.
6. Administrator runs the following command to start the Office Customization Tool (OCT):

   ```
   \\servername\Office2013\Source\setup.exe /admin
   ```
7. Administrator customizes Office and saves the changes to the customization (.msp) file, and then places the customization file into the Updates folder located in \\server\Office2013\Source.
8. Administrator notifies users to sign into the Office 365 portal and set up their new passwords.
9. Users then run MicrosoftOffice.exe from the network share.

MORE INFORMATION

During the Office 365 setup process, you create a Microsoft Online Service ID for your account. This email address and password combination is used to sign in to Office 365. Adding new users means you are adding them to the company's Office 365 subscription and creating a new Microsoft Online Services ID for each user. These new users are assigned a temporary password and are asked to change it when they first log in.

ADD A NEW USER TO YOUR OFFICE 365 PORTAL

GET READY. To add a new user in Office 365, log in to your Office 365 portal as the Administrator, and perform the following steps:

1. From the menu on the left, click **users and groups** (see Figure 15-2).
2. In the *middle* pane, click + to create a new Office 365 user.
3. Under *details*, type the user's **First name**, **Last name**, and their **User name** in the fields provided and then click **next**.

Figure 15-2

Adding new users

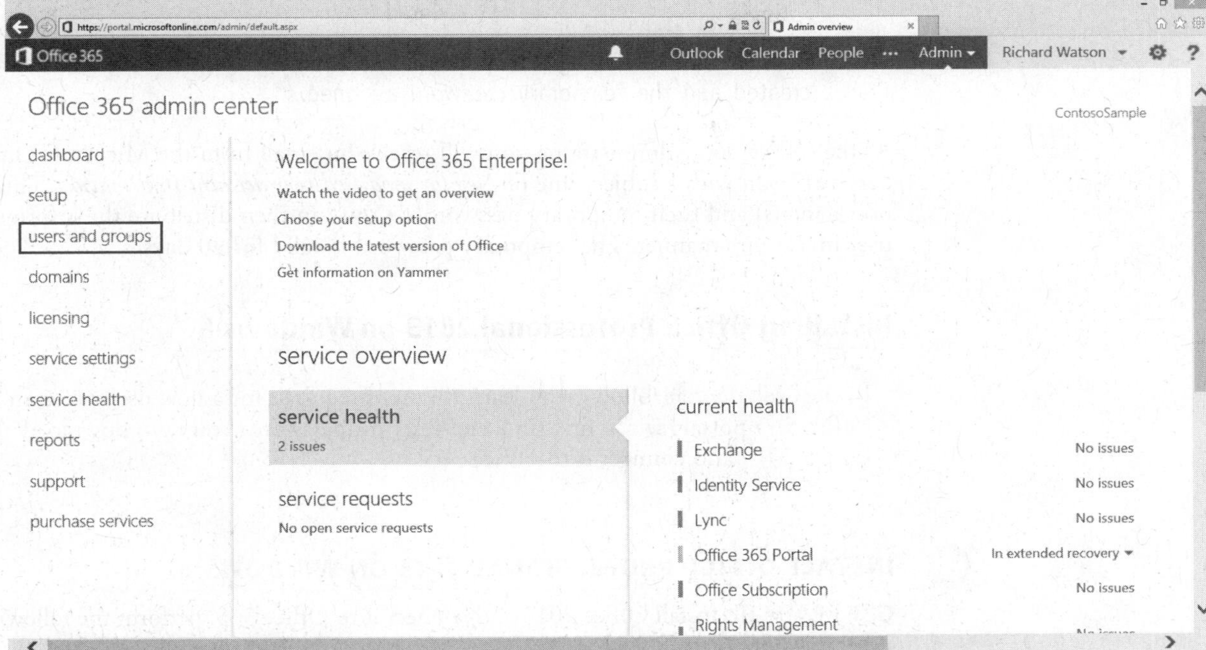

4. Under *Assign role,* select **No** when prompted to assign the user administrative permissions. Under *Set user location,* choose the user's geographic location and then click **next**.
5. Under *Assign licenses,* select the applications (see Figure 15-3), and then click **next**.

Figure 15-3

Assigning licenses

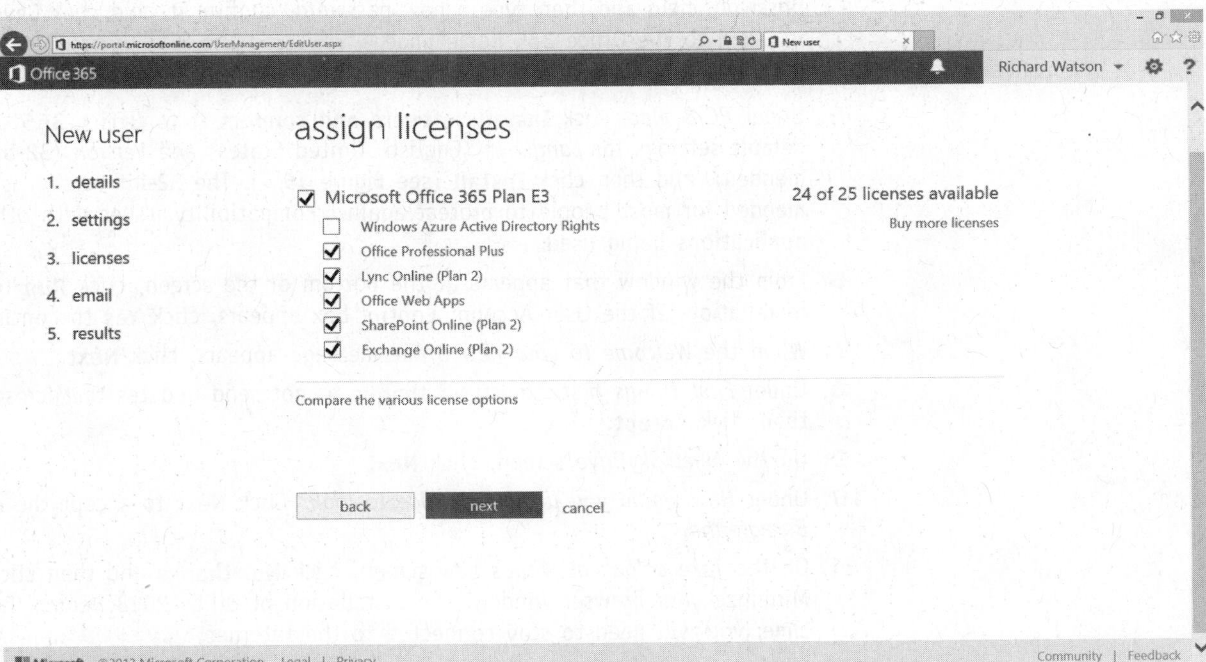

6. Under *send results in email,* select **Send email**, and then click **create**. By default, your email address (the Office 365 Administrator) is entered. To send a copy of the email to the user you are creating the account for, in the field provided, type his email address.
7. Review the *Results* page, and then click **Finish**. You should see the user name you created and the temporary password assigned.

As the Office 365 Administrator, you will receive an email from the Microsoft Online Services Team with a subject line of *New or modified user account information.* This shows the user name(s) and their temporary password(s). You can then distribute the information to the user in a secure manner. The temporary password is valid for 90 days.

Installing Office Professional 2013 on Windows 8

In the exercise that follows, you learn the steps required for a new user to log in to the Office 365 portal for the first time and reset his password. You then download and install Office 2013 and connect it to Office 365.

INSTALL OFFICE PROFESSIONAL 2013 ON WINDOWS 8

GET READY. To install Office 2013 and connect it to Office 365, perform the following steps:
Reset the Temporary Password

1. Log in to the Windows 8 computer where you want to install Office 2013 and open the Internet Explorer browser.
2. In the Internet Explorer *address* field, type **https://portal.microsoftonline.com**.
3. In the *User ID* field, type the user name you assigned to the account (in Step 3 of the previous exercise) and then type the temporary password you received. Click **Sign-in**.
4. *On the Update password* screen, type the user's temporary password in the *Old password* field and then type a new password, confirm it, and click **Save**. The user is taken to the Office 365 home page.

Downloading and Install Office 2013

5. Under *PC & Mac*, click **Install software and connect it to Office 365**. Accept the default settings for *Language* (English, United States) and *Version* (32-bit recommended), and then click **Install** (see Figure 15-4). The 32-bit version is recommended for most people to protect against compatibility issues with other 32-bit applications being used.
6. From the window that appears at the bottom of the screen, click **Run** to start the installation. If the User Account Control box appears, click **Yes** to continue.
7. When the *Welcome to your new Office* message appears, click **Next**.
8. Under *First things first,* select **No thanks** to not send updates to Microsoft, and then click **Accept**.
9. On the *Meet SkyDrive* screen, click **Next**.
10. Under *How would you like your office to look?* Click **Next** to accept the default *No Background*.
11. On the *Take a look at what's new* screen, click **No, thanks** and then click **All done!** Minimize your browser window. The installation of Office 2013 begins. During this time, you will need to stay connected to the Internet.
12. When the message *You're good to go* appears, click **All done!**

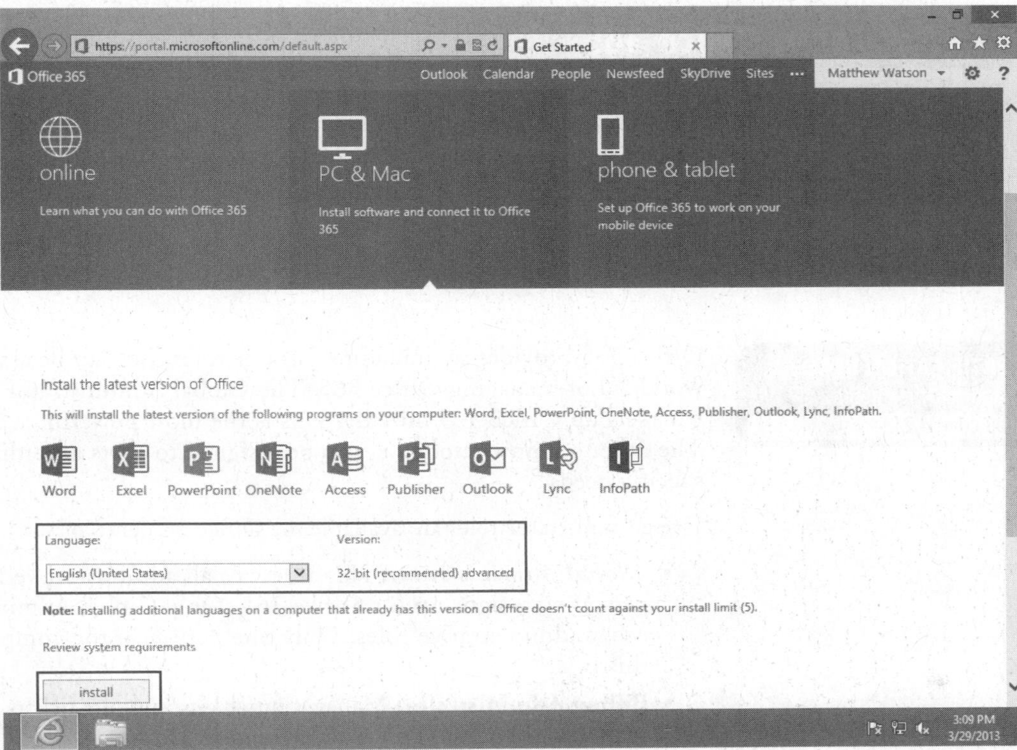

Figure 15-4
Selecting the Install link

13. Press the **Windows logo key** to toggle to the Windows 8 Start menu. A tile is created for each of the Office applications (see Figure 15-5) as part of the installation of Office 2013.

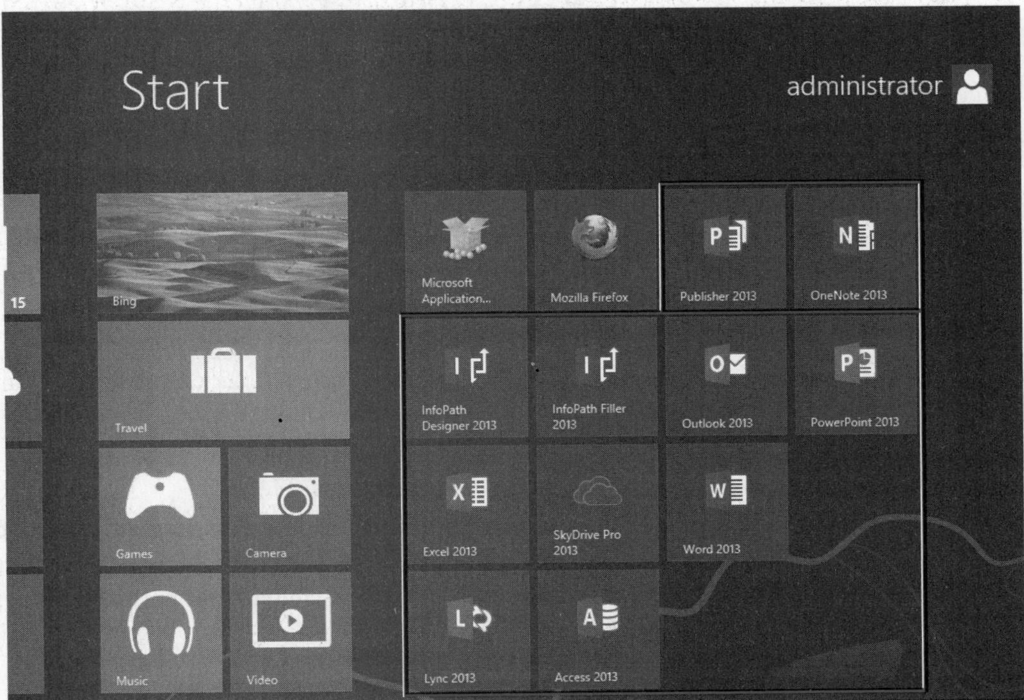

Figure 15-5
Reviewing the Office 2013 tiles

Managing Office 365

THE BOTTOM LINE

Office 365 is managed by a web console that enables you to set up and manage users and their software regardless of where they connect. The person who signs up your company for Office 365 is the ***Global Administrator*** by default. This person can then grant administrator permissions to other users in the organization as needed to distribute the workload.

CERTIFICATION READY
Manage Office 365
Objective 4.2

Office 365 provides several administrator roles that can be assigned to help distribute the workload of managing Office 365. The Global Administrator is assigned to the person who sets up Office 365 initially. This is the most powerful account in the organization. The other administrator roles can be assigned to users according to your organization's specific needs.

Five administrator roles are available for Office 365 enterprises:

- ***Global Administrator:*** Has access to all administrative features. This is the person who signs up for Office 365. Only Global Administrators can assign other administrative roles. Only one person in the company can serve in this role.
- **Billing Administrator:** Manages purchases, support tickets, and subscriptions and monitors the overall health of the services.
- **Password Administrator:** Manages requests for services, resets passwords, and monitors the overall health of the services. Users in this role can reset passwords only for users and other Password Administrators.
- **Service Administrator:** Manages service requests and monitors overall health of services.
- ***User Management Administrator:*** Manages user accounts and user groups, resets passwords, and manages service requests. User Management Administrators can also monitor the overall health of services. They cannot reset passwords for Billing, Global, or Service Administrators and they cannot delete a Global Administrator or create other administrators.

ASSIGN A USER TO A PASSWORD ADMINISTRATOR ROLE IN OFFICE 365

TAKE NOTE*
You must log in with an account that has the Global Administrator's role assigned to perform these steps.

GET READY. To assign a user to a Password Administrator role in Office 365, log in to your Office 365 portal as with the Global Administrator's account, and perform the following steps:

1. From the menu on the left, click **users and groups.**
2. Under the *DISPLAY NAME* column, click the user you want to assign the administrative role to.
3. From the menu on the left, click **settings.**
4. Under *Assign role,* select **Yes.**
5. Click the down arrow and choose **Password administrator** (see Figure 15-6).
6. Under *Alternate email address,* type an email to use in case you forget your password, and then scroll to the bottom of the page and click **Save.**
7. Click **Save.**

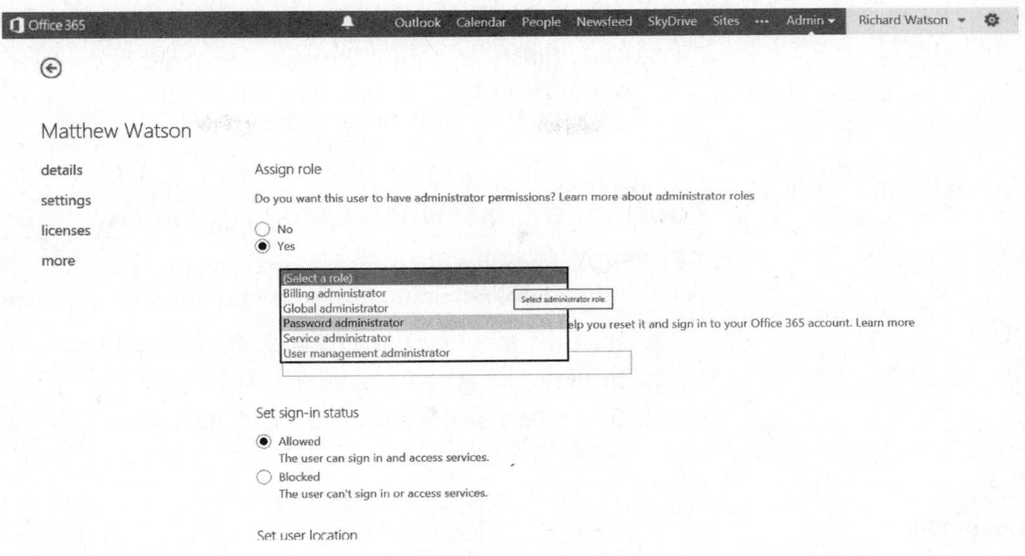

Figure 15-6

Assigning the Password Administrator role

Following are some of the general administrative tasks you will perform in Office 365:

- Reset a user's password.
- Configure a password expiration policy.
- View the overall health of Office 365. Personalize the default SharePoint team site.

RESET A USER'S PASSWORD IN OFFICE 365

GET READY. To reset a user's password in Office 365, log in to your Office 365 portal as the Global Administrator, and perform the following steps:

1. From the menu on the left, click **users and groups.**
2. Under the *DISPLAY NAME* column, select the checkbox next to the user you want to reset the password for.
3. In the menu that appears (see Figure 15-7), under *quick steps,* click **Reset passwords.**

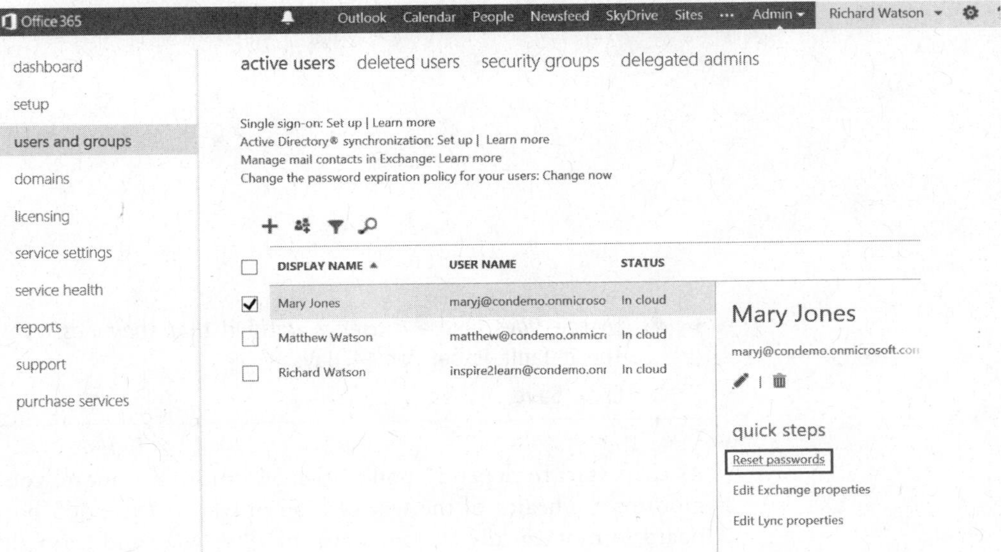

Figure 15-7

Resetting the user's password

4. On the *send results in email* screen, click **reset password**.
5. Click **finish**. The user's temporary password is displayed and mailed to the address you used in the previous step. This information is provided to the user who can now log in to their Office 365 account.

CONFIGURE A PASSWORD EXPIRATION POLICY IN OFFICE 365

GET READY. To configure a password expiration policy in Office 365, log in to your Office 365 portal as the Global Administrator, and perform the following steps:

1. From the menu on the left, click **service settings**.
2. In the menu at the top, click **passwords.**
3. In the *Days before passwords expire* field (see Figure 15-8), type **100.** The default is set to 90 days.

Figure 15-8

Changing the password expiration policy

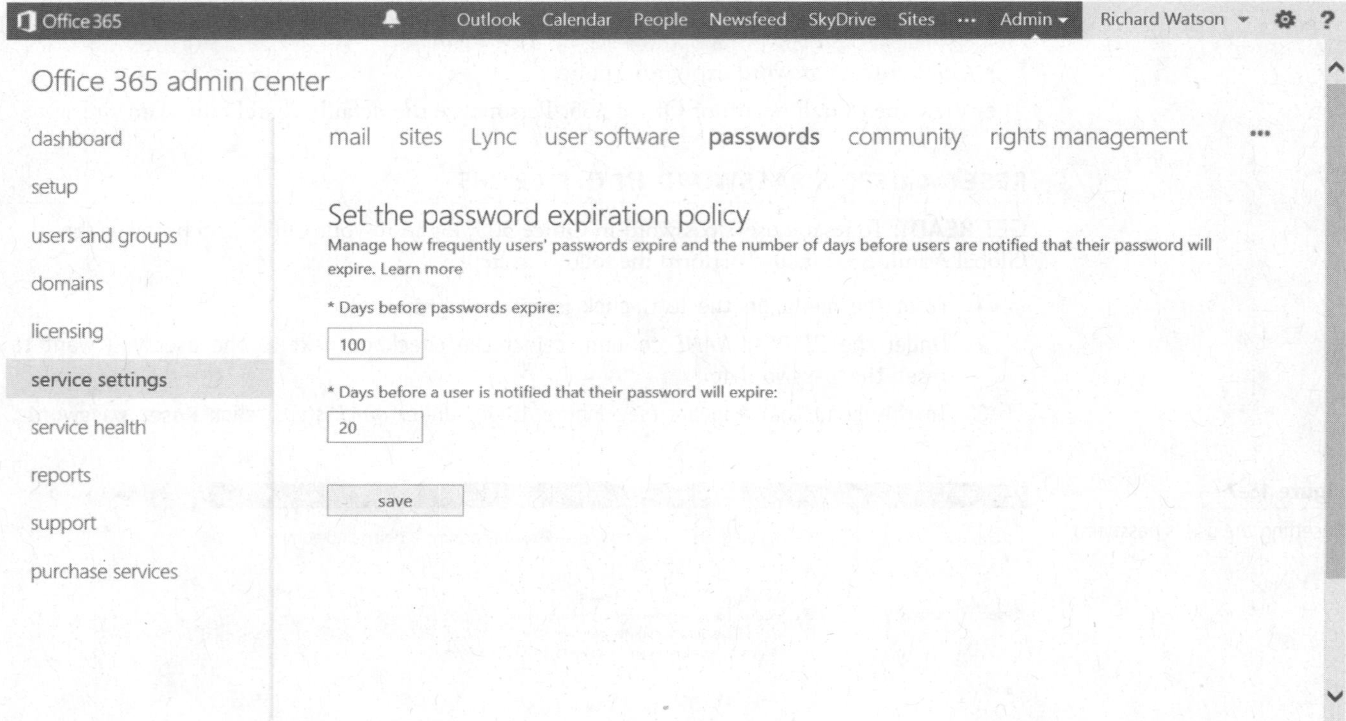

4. In the *Days before a user is notified that their password will expire* field, type **20.** The default is set for 14 days.
5. Click **Save.**

As users start to depend upon Office 365 more and more, you will want to make sure you monitor the health of the services you provide. Office 365 provides an excellent dashboard to monitor the current status of all services and learn about any upcoming planned maintenance.

VIEW THE OVERALL HEALTH OF OFFICE 365

GET READY. To view the overall health of Office 365, log in to your Office 365 portal as the Global Administrator, and perform the following steps:

1. In the menu on the left, click **service health** to view the current status of the services provided by Office 365 (see Figure 15-9).

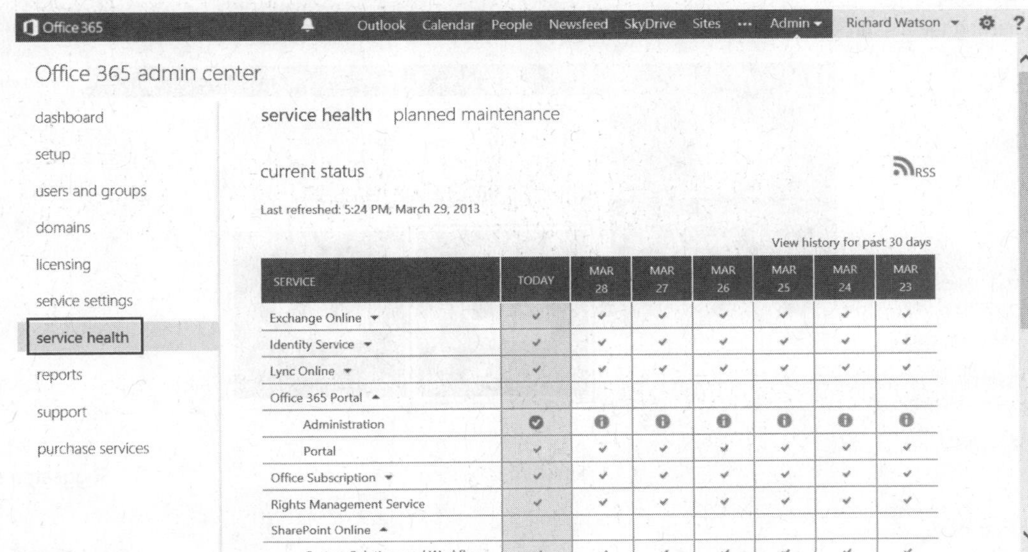

Figure 15-9
Reviewing the status of Office 365 services

2. In the menu at the top, click **planned maintenance** to determine whether there is an upcoming maintenance planned (see Figure 15-10).

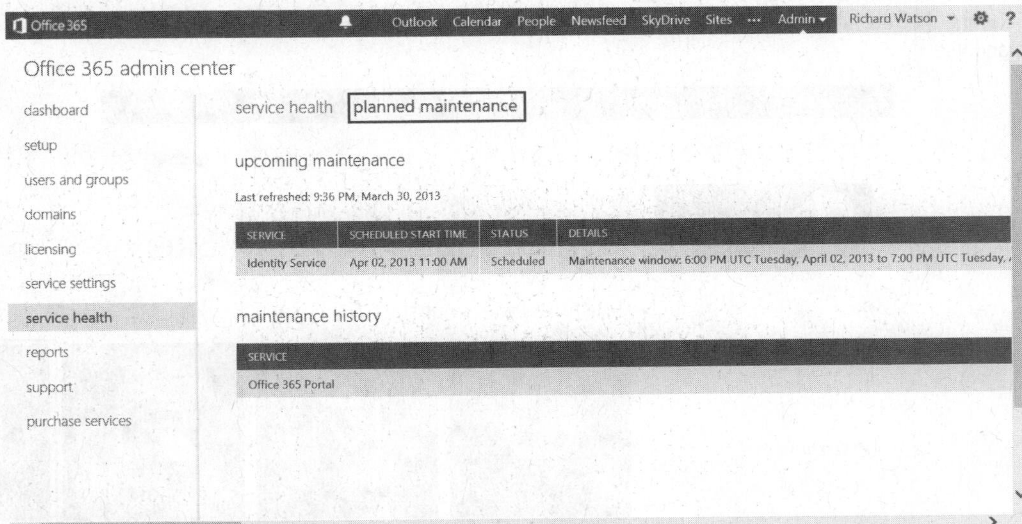

Figure 15-10
Viewing planned maintenance schedules

When Office 365 is set up, a SharePoint team site is configured for you. This is where you can collaborate on projects and share documents. However, the default site can be personalized.

PERSONALIZE THE DEFAULT SHAREPOINT TEAM SITE

GET READY. To personalize the default SharePoint team site in Office 365, log in to your Office 365 portal as the Global Administrator, and perform the following steps:

1. In the menu at the top, click **Sites**.
2. Click the **Team Site** tile (see Figure 15-11).

Figure 15-11

Selecting the default Team Site

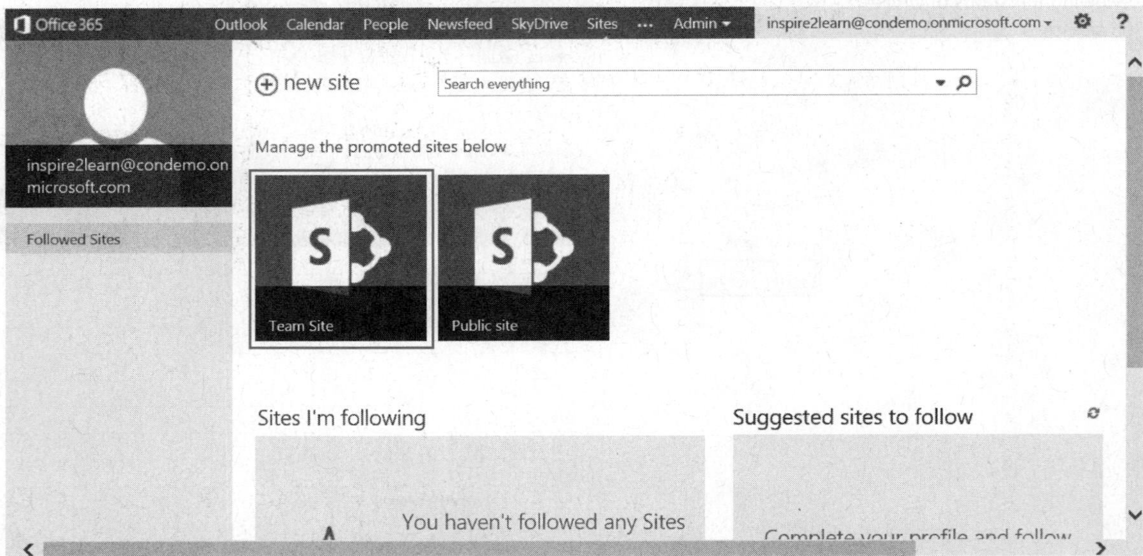

3. Click the **What's your style?** tile (see Figure 15-12).

Figure 15-12

Selecting the Your site. Your brand. tile

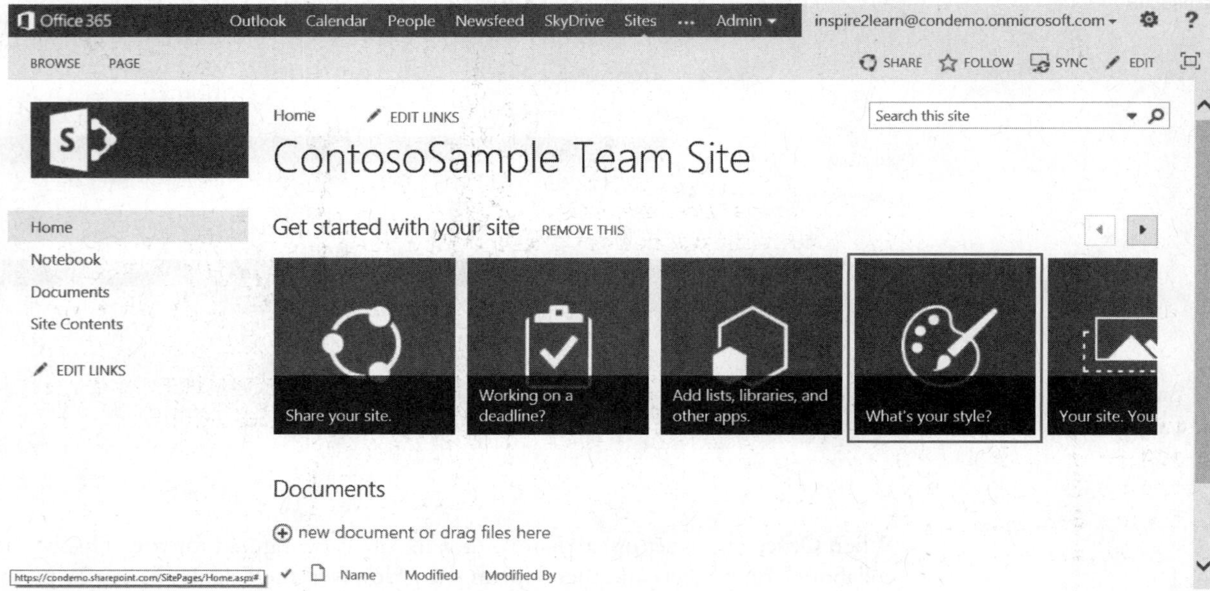

4. Scroll down and click the **Breeze** template.
5. On the *Site Settings > Change the look* screen, click **Try it out.**
6. In the upper right corner, click **Yes, keep it.**
7. Click the **Add lists, libraries, and other apps** tile.
8. Under *Noteworthy*, click the **Document Library** tile.
9. In the *Adding Document Library* box, type **Sales** for the name, and then click **Create**. This creates a sales ***asset library***, which is used to store audio, video, or picture files.
10. In the left pane, under *Recent*, click **Sales** (see Figure 15-13).

Figure 15-13

Selecting the Sales document library

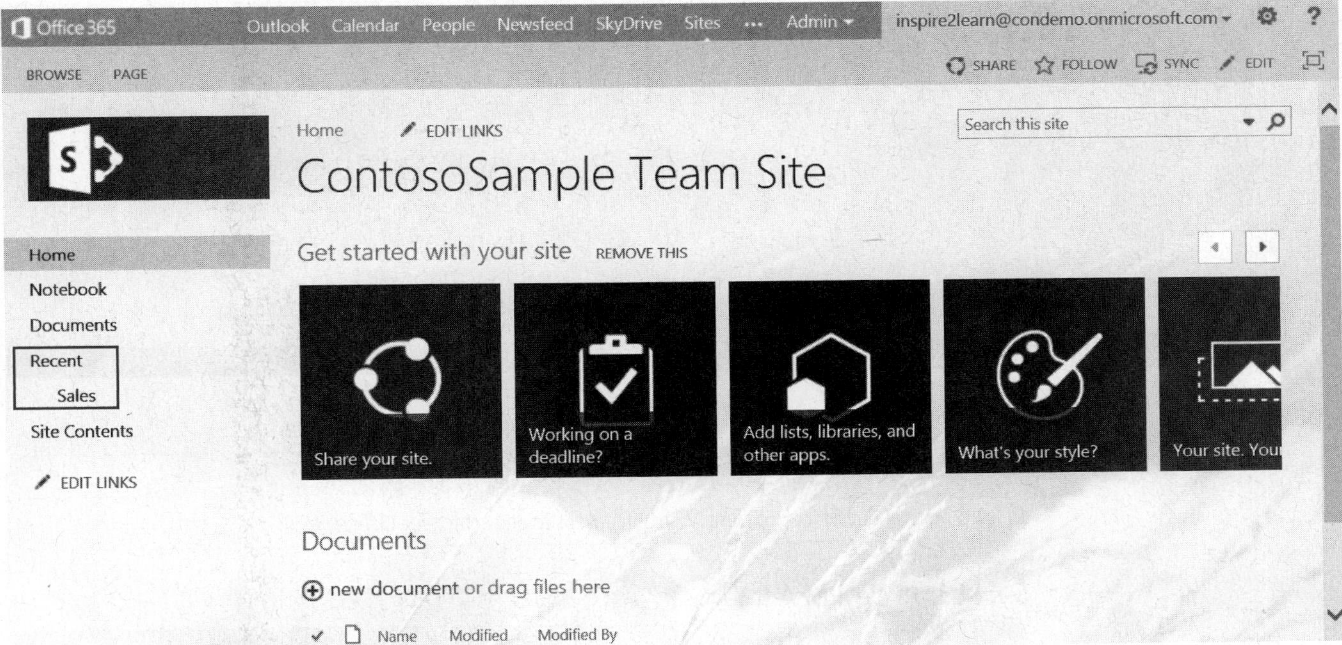

12. Click + **new document.**
13. Under *Create a new file*, click **Word document.**
14. In the *Document Name* field, type **Sales Forecast Q3** and then click **OK.**
15. Type **Sales are good** into the document and in the upper, left corner, click the **Save** icon. Click the **X** to close the document (see Figure 15-14). You can also drag files from your desktop directly into the Sales document library.

Figure 15-14

Saving and closing the Word document

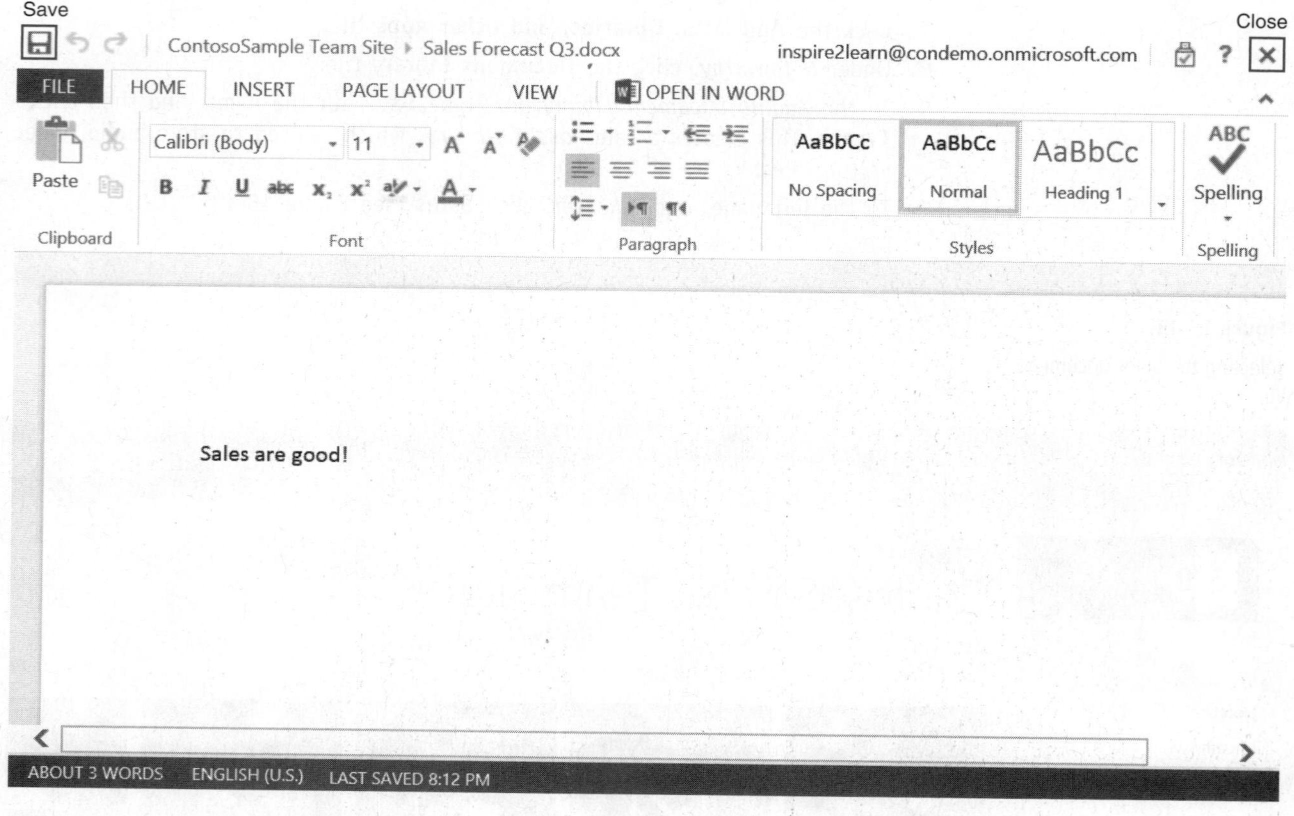

16. In the *left* pane, click **Home** to return to your Team Site.

MORE INFORMATION

To learn more about Office 365, visit Microsoft's website and search for *Office 365*

SKILL SUMMARY

IN THIS LESSON YOU LEARNED:

- A cloud is a web-based service that is hosted outside of an organization.
- Use groups in SkyDrive to communicate and share documents more effectively. When you set up a group, it is provided a unique URL and email address. Members of the group can access all group information on the group's site.
- SkyDrive group members can take advantage of OneNote to copy notes, links, images, and maps to brainstorm ideas.
- SkyDrive group members can use Messenger to conduct group conversations. If you disable the feature, you cannot turn it back on for the group.
- A trusted PC is a computer or device that you have added the password reset information for your Microsoft user account. If you forget your password or an unauthorized person gains access to the information, you can reset the password from any trusted PC.
- Office 365, when combined with Office 2013, allows users to collaborate on documents, work online or offline, and gain access to email, calendars, and documents for their trusted devices.

- You can deploy Office 2013 directly from the Office 365 portal, from a network share, using Group Policy, or with System Center Configuration Manager.
- You can create user accounts, reset user passwords, configure password expiration policies, and view the overall health of your Office 365 installation using tools available from within the Office 365 portal.
- Install Office 2013 directly from the Office 365 portal onto a Windows 8 computer.
- There are five administrator roles in Office 365: Global Administrator, Billing Administrator, Password Administrator, Service Administrator, and User Management Administrator.
- Perform a basic customization of a SharePoint team site in Office 365 by installing a new template to change the appearance, adding a new document library, and then creating a file within the library.

Knowledge Assessment

Multiple Choice

Select the correct answer for each of the following questions.

1. Which of the following cannot be synched with a Windows 8 PC that is not trusted?
   a. Desktop themes
   b. Language preferences
   c. App settings
   d. Passwords
2. Which of the following represents ways you can deploy Office 2013 available from Office 365? Select all that apply.
   a. Directly from the Office 365 portal
   b. From a network share
   c. Using Group Policy
   d. Using System Configuration Manager
3. The person who signs up for the Office 365 subscription is assigned which role by default?
   a. Global Administrator
   b. User Management Administrator
   c. Billing Administrator
   d. Service Administrator
4. The default password expiration policy in Office 365 sets passwords to expire after how many days?
   a. 30 days
   b. 60 days
   c. 120 days
   d. 90 days
5. Which Office 365 administrative role can monitor the overall health of Office 365 services? Select all that apply.
   a. Password Administrator
   b. Global Administrator
   c. User Management Administrator
   d. Billing Administrator

6. By default, when a new Office 365 user account is created, where is the user name and temporary password emailed to?
   a. Global administrator's email address
   b. User's email address
   c. All administrators in Office 365
   d. To both the user and the Global Administrator's email address.
7. Which of the following happens after a user is added to a group in SkyDrive? Choose all that apply.
   a. Users can access files that have been shared for other groups.
   b. Users can access your SkyDrive files.
   c. Users can communicate with other members of the group.
   d. Users receive email asking them to join the group.
8. Which administrator role should you assign to an Office 365 user who needs to manage support tickets for Office 365 only?
   a. Service Administrator
   b. User Management Administrator
   c. Billing Administrator
   d. Global Administrator
9. Which of the following happens when you add a new user to Office 365? Choose all that apply.
   a. The user is added to your company's Office 365 subscription.
   b. They are assigned the Global Administrator role.
   c. The user receives a temporary password.
   d. The user is assigned to the Users group in AD Users and Computers.
10. Which version(s) of Office 2013 does Microsoft recommend you install when working with Office 365 to protect against compatibility issues?
   a. 16-bit version
   b. 32-bit version
   c. 64-bit version
   d. Both the 32-bit and 64-bit versions

Best Answer

Choose the letter that corresponds to the best answer. More than one answer choice may achieve the goal. Select the BEST answer.

1. Which option works best when deploying Office 365 in an organization that does not have dedicated IT staff?
   a. Deploy directly from the Office 365 portal
   b. Deploy from a network share
   c. Deploy using Group Policy
   d. Deploy using SCCM
2. Which of the following allows SkyDrive group members to perform group conversations?
   a. Lync
   b. Messenger
   c. SkyDrive Chat
   d. SkyDrive Internet Messaging client
3. If you leave the Office 365 password expiration policy at its default setting, how often do users have to change their passwords?
   a. Every 90 days.
   b. Set Every 30 days.
   c. Set Every 60 days.
   d. Every 45 days.

4. Which of the following are correct regarding SkyDrive Groups? Select all that apply.
   a. Deleting a group prevents you from using the same web address for 60 days.
   b. Members of the same group can send email messages to each other using the group's email address.
   c. Deleting a group also deletes the group's documents, photos, and other information.
   d. Deleting a group prevents you from using the same web address for 90 days.
5. After setting up a user's account in Office 365, how does he have access to the temporary password before it expires?
   a. 30 days
   b. 90 days
   c. 120 days
   d. 100 days

Matching and Identification

1. Match the following terms with the related description or usage.
   _____ **a)** Asset Library
   _____ **b)** Global Administrator
   _____ **c)** User Management Administrator
   _____ **d)** Group Policy
   _____ **e)** Office 2013
   _____ **f)** Office Customization Tool
   _____ **g)** Messenger
   _____ **h)** SkyDrive
   _____ **i)** Trusted PC
   _____ **j)** Billing Administrator
   1. This role is assigned to the person who signs up for Office 365.
   2. Allows you to customize Office 2013 before deploying it to users.
   3. Can be used to deploy Office 2013 in an Active Directory-based network.
   4. This manages Office 365 subscriptions and purchases.
   5. Available in SkyDrive groups to conduct group chats.
   6. Allows you to sync passwords among your Windows 8 devices.
   7. Can be installed directly from the Office 365 portal.
   8. Used to store audio, video, or picture files in a SharePoint team site.
   9. Allows users to sync files and create groups to share documents.
   10. Manages user accounts and groups. Cannot reset passwords for Billing, Global, or Service Administrators, and he cannot delete a Global Administrator.

Build a List

1. In order of first to last, configure a trusted PC.
   ________ Type the code you receive into the field provided on the Windows Live website to confirm it is trusted.
   ________ Log in with your Microsoft user account.
   ________ Under *PC settings,* click Users.
   ________ Press the Windows logo key + I and click Change PC Settings.
   ________ Click the Trust this PC link
2. In order of first to last, deploy Office 2013 directly from the Office 365 portal:
   ________ Administrator sends users temporary passwords.
   ________ Users download and configure their desktops with Office 2013 (32-bit version).
   ________ Administrator signs up for Office 365, sets new domain name, creates user accounts, and assigns licenses to each user.
   ________ Users sign in to Office 365 portal with temporary password and creates a new password.

3. In order of first to last, add a new user to your Office 365 portal.
   _______ In the menu on the left, click **users and groups.**
   _______ Under *details,* type the user's **First name, Last name,** and their **User name** in the fields provided and then click **next**.
   _______ In the middle pane, click + to create a new Office 365 user.
   _______ Under *Assign licenses,* select the applications, and then click **next.**
   _______ Under *Assign* role, select **No** when prompted to assign the user administrative permissions. Under *Set user location,* choose the user's geographic location and then click **next.**
   _______ Under *send results in email,* select **Send email**, and then click **create.**
   _______ Review the Results page and then click **Finish**.

Choose an Option

1. Which option should you click to configure password expiration policies for your Office 365 users?

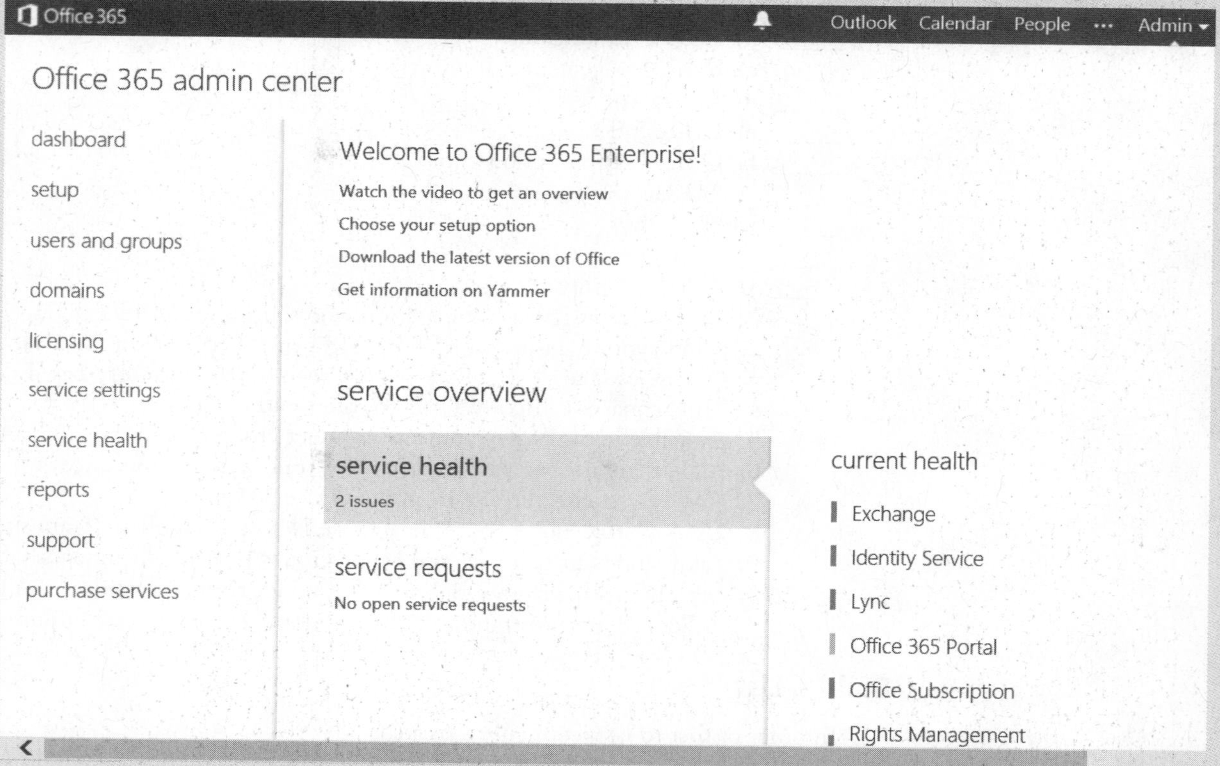

Business Case Scenarios

Scenario 15-1: Sync Problems

Multiple computers run Windows 8, and they are synched across the same Microsoft user account. On one of the devices, you notice that the option to synch passwords is disabled. Why?

Scenario 15-2: Installing Office 2013 from the Office 365 Portal

A company does not have an IT department but would like to install and use Office 2013 with Office 365. Active Directory is not set up and the company does not need to customize the installation for users. Which approach should you recommend?

Managing and Maintaining Clients by Using MDOP

LESSON 16

70-688 EXAM OBJECTIVE

Objective 4.3 – Monitor and maintain clients by using MDOP. This objective may include but is not limited to: Remediate startup issues using the Diagnostics and Recovery Toolkit (DaRT); monitor clients using System Center Desktop Error Monitoring; manage the App-V client; manage BitLocker and BitLocker To Go using Microsoft BitLocker Administration and Monitoring (MBAM).

LESSON HEADING	EXAM OBJECTIVE
Remediating Startup Issues Using Dart 8	Remediate startup issues using the Diagnostics and Recovery Toolkit (DaRT)
Understanding the DaRT 8.0 Recovery Image Tool	
Reviewing the Tools included with DaRT	
Monitoring Clients Using Desktop Error Monitoring	Monitor clients using System Center Desktop Error Monitoring
Exploring Desktop Error Monitoring	
Initiating Desktop Error Monitoring	
Managing the App-V Client	Manage the App-V client
Exploring the App-V 5 Components	
Exploring the App-V 5 Console	
Troubleshooting Issues with the Publishing Server	
Managing BitLocker and BitLocker To Go Using MBAM	Manage BitLocker and BitLocker To Go using Microsoft BitLocker Administration and Monitoring (MBAM)
Understanding MBAM 1.0 Components	
Reviewing Deployment Options for MBAM	
Reviewing MBAM Next Steps	
Reviewing MBAM 2 Features	

KEY TERMS

App-V 5 Client
App-V 5 Sequencer
App-V 5 Server
App-V Shared Content Store
Connection Groups
Microsoft BitLocker Administration and Monitoring (MBAM)
Microsoft Desktop Optimization Pack (MDOP)
Microsoft Diagnostics and Recovery Took Kit (DaRT)
Microsoft System Center Desktop Error Monitoring (DEM)
Publishing Server

Remediating Startup Issues Using DaRT 8

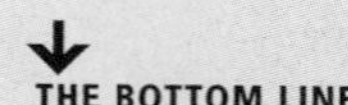

The Microsoft Diagnostics and Recovery Took Kit (DaRT) 8 provides the tools needed to diagnose and recover Windows systems when they do not boot.

CERTIFICATION READY
Remediate startup issues using DaRT
Objective 4.3

The ***Microsoft Diagnostics and Recovery Toolset (DaRT)*** 8 is part of the ***Microsoft Desktop Optimization Pack (MDOP)***. DaRT provides you with a set of tools that diagnose and recover your Windows systems when they are offline.

Following are some of the things you can do with DaRT 8:

- Review the computer's event logs.
- Determine the cause of a computer crash.
- Recover boot volumes and restore the master boot record.
- Restore files that are accidentally deleted.
- Reset or change a local administrator's password.
- Uninstall hot fixes and service packs.
- Detect and remove malware and root kits.

Before starting this activity, install the Windows Assessment and Deployment Kit (Windows ADK) if it is not already installed on your Windows 8 computer. Visit Microsoft's website and search for *ADK for Windows 8.*

INSTALL THE MICROSOFT DIAGNOSTICS AND RECOVERY TOOL KIT (DART) 8

GET READY. To install the Microsoft Diagnostic and Recovery Toolset (DaRT) 8, log in to your Windows 8 computer with administrative privileges, and perform the following steps:

1. Insert the **Microsoft Desktop Optimization Pack 2012 DVD**; if the DVD does not automatically open, right-click the DVD drive and choose **Auto-Play**. In the menu, click **Run launcher.hta**.
2. In the *MDOP* menu, click **Microsoft Diagnostics and Recovery Toolset** (see Figure 16-1).

Figure 16-1

Selecting the DaRT 8 from the MDOP menu

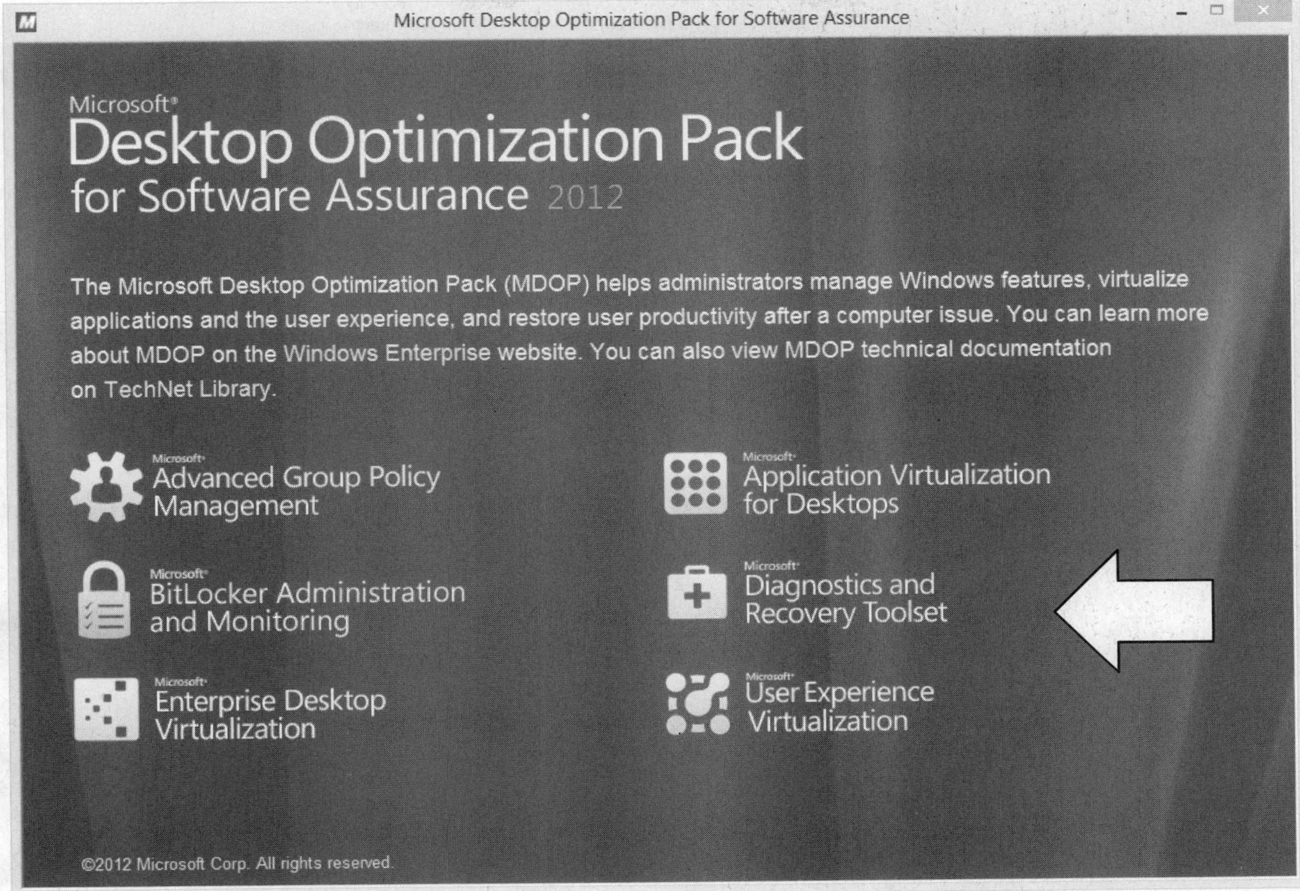

3. Under the *DaRT 8 for Windows 8 and Windows Server 2012* menu, click **DaRT 8: 64-bit** (see Figure 16-2).
4. When the Microsoft *DaRT 8.0 Setup Wizard* screen appears, click **Next**.
5. On the *End-User License Agreement* screen, click **I Agree**.
6. Select **Use Microsoft Update when I check for updates (recommended)**, and then click **Next**. This ensures you have the latest updates for the DaRT 8 toolset.
7. On the *Select Installation Folder* screen, click **Next**.

   The default installation folder is *c:\Program Files\Microsoft DaRT 8*.

MORE INFORMATION

You can click Disk Space to determine available space on other drives along with the amount of space required for DaRT 8 prior to selecting the folder.

8. On the *Setup Options* screen, click **Next**.
9. Click **Install**.
10. Click **Finish**.
11. Close the **Microsoft Diagnostics and Recovery Toolset** box.

Figure 16-2

Selecting the 64-bit version of DaRT 8 for installation

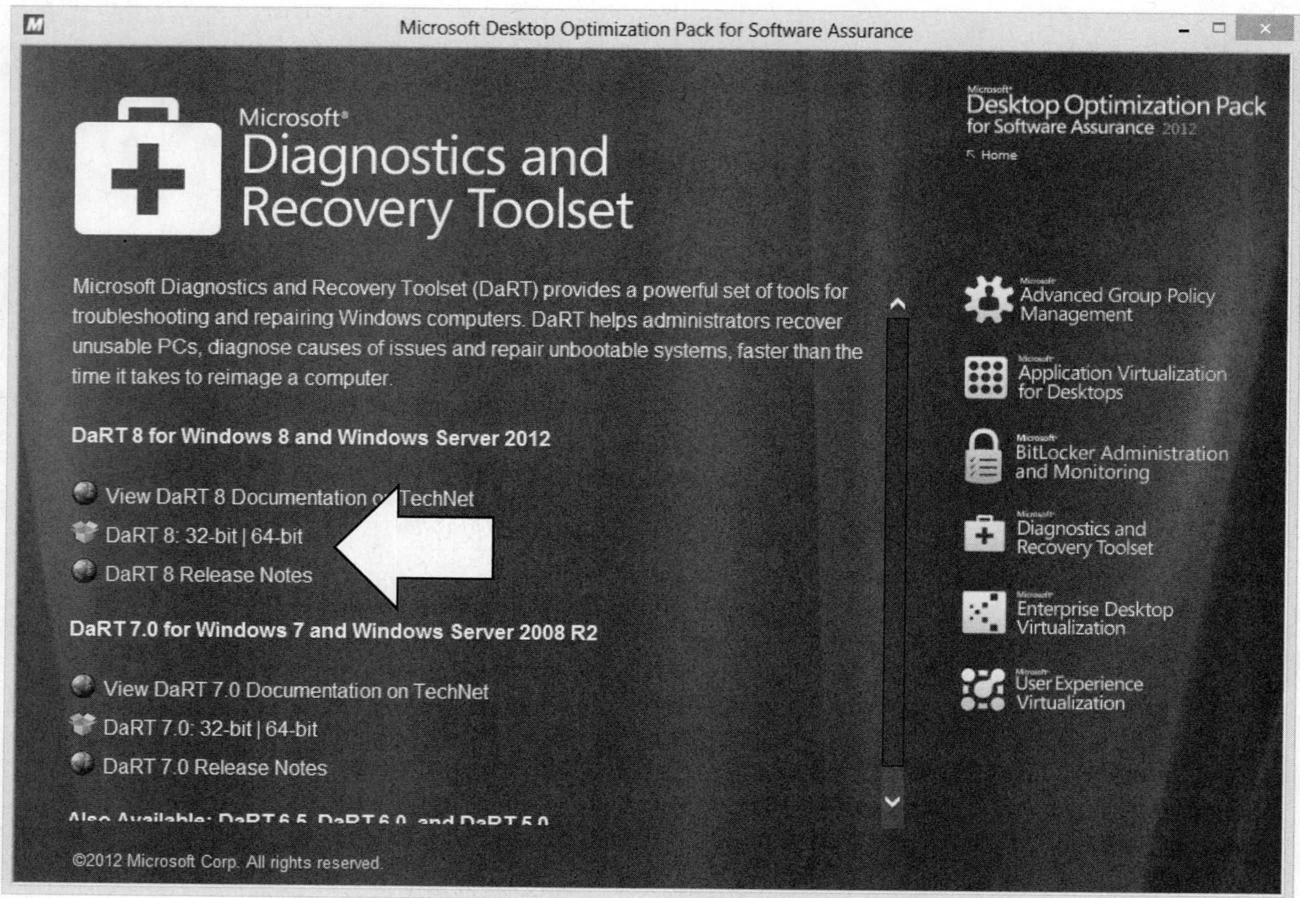

MORE INFORMATION

You should install the Windows 8 debugging tools after you complete the installation of the DaRT kit. The Crash Analysis tool uses these tools to debug drivers, applications, and services. They can be found on Microsoft's website by searching for *Download and Install Debugging Tools for Windows.*

TAKE NOTE*

Using the wizard, you can create International Organization for Standardization (IOS) files and Windows Image Format (WIM) images. You can also use Windows PowerShell to create a script that captures the options you select while running the wizard. To rebuild recovery images, use the same settings in the future.

Understanding the DaRT 8.0 Recovery Image Tool

The DaRT 8.0 Recovery Image tool creates a bootable image that contains the DaRT. When creating the recovery image, you need to decide which tools to include on the image. If you are an administrator, you will probably want to include all of the tools on the media that you will use to troubleshoot your user's computers. When troubleshooting computers remotely, you might want to disable tools such as Disk Wipe and Registry Editor.

Using the DaRT Recovery Image tool, you can create a 32-bit and 64-bit DaRT recovery image from the same computer; however, you cannot create one image that works for both architectures on the same media. To run DaRT on a Windows 8 x64 PC, you need at least 2.5 GB of memory on a Windows 8 x32 PC 1.5GB of memory, and on Windows Server, you need a minimum of 1GB.

MORE INFORMATION

If you want to bypass the wizard and create a recovery image by using Windows PowerShell, you can learn more by visiting Microsoft's website and searching for *How to Use a Windows PowerShell Script to Create the Recovery Image*.

Following is an overview of the steps for creating a DaRT Recovery Image:

1. Start the DaRT Recovery Image Wizard (DaRTImage.exe).
2. Choose the type of DaRT Recovery image you want to create.
3. Provide the path to the matching Windows 8 media files.
4. Select the tools you want to include with the image.
5. On the Crash Analyzer Tab/Advanced options page, include the Windows 8 Debugging Tools.
6. Download the latest malware definitions for Windows Defender.
7. Set the default path and name for the recovery image.
8. Select *Create to generate the image files (ISO, WIM).*
9. Burn the image to bootable media (CD, DVD, and USB Flash Drive).

CREATE A DART RECOVERY IMAGE

GET READY. To create a DaRT 8 recovery image and burn it to a DVD, log in to your Windows 8 computer with administrative privileges, perform the following steps:

1. In the Windows 8 *Start* menu, click the **DaRT Recovery Image** tile.
2. Read the information about the wizard, and then click **Next**.
3. On the *Windows 8 Media* screen, select **Create 64-bit DaRT image** and specify the root path to your Windows 8 installation media (see Figure 16-3). Click **Next** to continue.

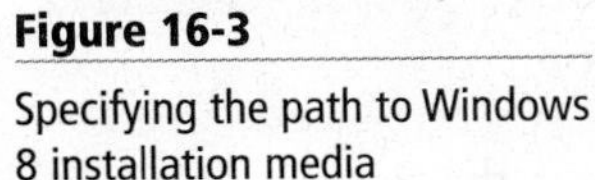

Figure 16-3

Specifying the path to Windows 8 installation media

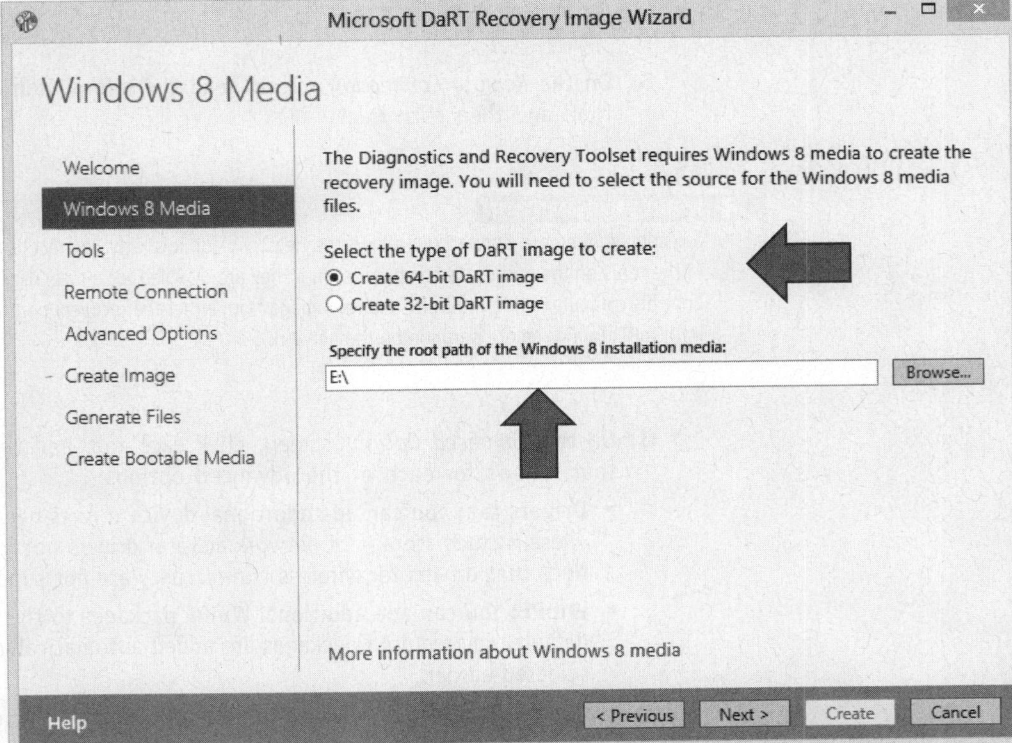

4. On the *Tools* screen click **Next** to install all of the tools available (see Figure 16-4).

Figure 16-4

Selecting all DaRT 8 tools

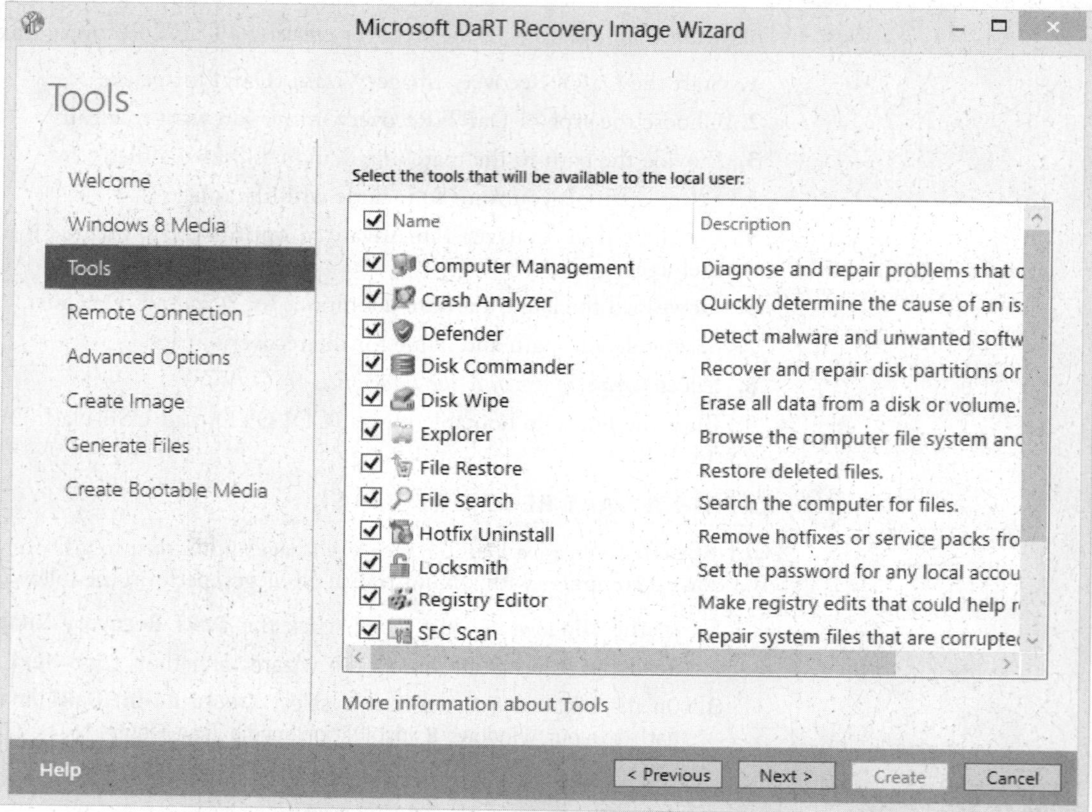

5. On the *Remote Connection* screen, read the information about the *Remove Connection* tool, and then click **Next.**

MORE INFORMATION

Selecting *All Remote Connections* allows the Helpdesk administrator connect to the DaRT tools remotely and use all of the tools on the end user's computer even if they are disabled for a local user. The end user would need to first boot his computer using the DaRT recovery image from either the recovery partition on the local computer or boot into DaRT from a remote partition on the network.

6. On the *Advanced Options* screen, click each tab, and then read the explanation that follows for each of the advanced options:
   - **Drivers tab:** You can add additional device drivers needed to repair the computer. These include storage or network adapter drivers not included with Windows 8. Note that drivers for wireless connectivity are not supported in DaRT.
   - **WinPE:** You can add additional WinPE packages to the image if you choose. By default, any required packages are added automatically based on the tools you selected earlier.
   - **Crash Analyzer:** If you download and install the Windows 8 debugging tools on your computer, the Wizard includes them. You can also click the *Download*

the Debugging Tools link or use the *Debugging Tools from the computer that is being debugged*.

- **Defender:** Options on this tab allow you to download and install the latest definitions, or, you can choose to download them later. If you select *Download the latest definitions (Recommended)*, the definitions are added to the DaRT recovery image. If you select to download later, they are not included in the image.

7. Under the *Crash Analyzer* tab, be sure the option **Use the Debugging Tools from the computer that is being debugged.** selected, and on the *Defender* tab, be sure **Download the latest definitions** is selected. Then, click **Next**.
8. On the *Create Image* screen, review the defaults for the *Output folder* and *Image name*. Make sure *Create WIM (Windows Imaging Format), Create ISO, and Create a Windows PowerShell script* options are selected (see Figure 16-5). Click **Create** to generate the DaRT image.

Figure 16-5

Creating the DaRT 8 image

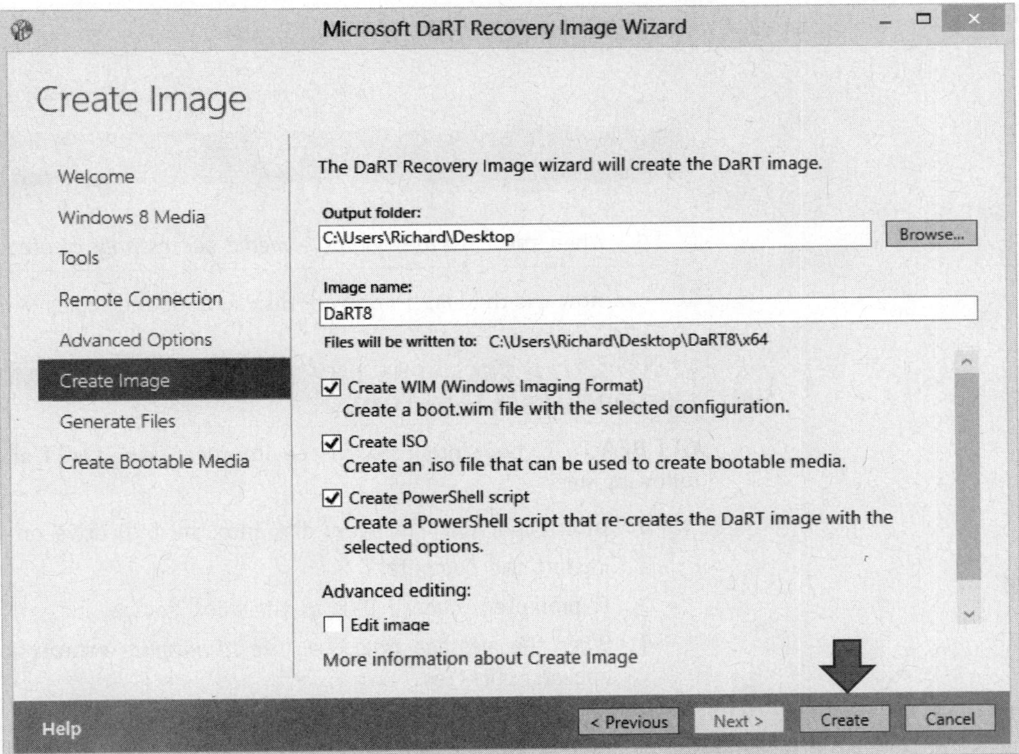

9. When the message *The DaRT image was successfully created* appears, click **Next**.
10. On the *Create Bootable Media* screen, click **Open Folder** to view the files created. You should see the Windows Image file (boot.wim), the Disc Image file (DaRT8.iso), and the Windows PowerShell script (DaRT8.ps1).
11. Close the folder and return to the DaRT Recovery Image Wizard.
12. Insert a blank recordable DVD.
13. Click **Create Bootable Media** (see Figure 16-6).

Figure 16-6
Creating bootable media

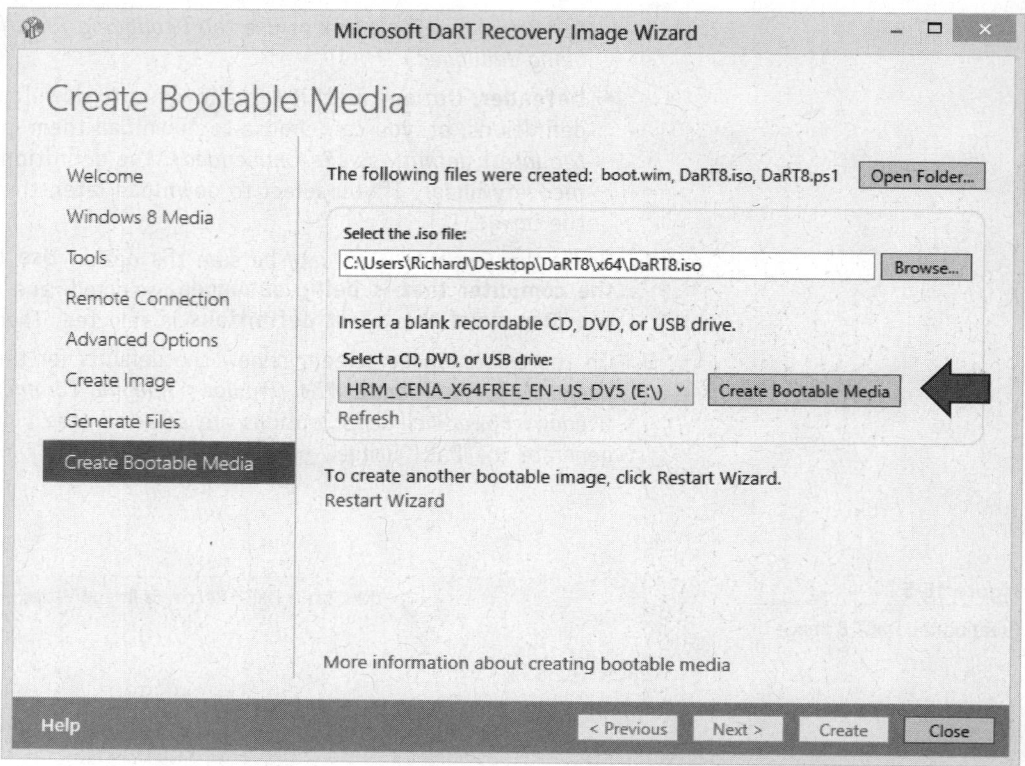

14. When the message *Bootable media successfully created* appears, click **Close.**

You can now use the DaRT recovery disk to boot and repair Windows 8.

BOOT INTO A RECOVERY ENVIRONMENT USING DART AND EXPLORE AVAILABLE TOOLS

GET READY. To boot into a recovery environment using DaRT and run a virus scan, perform the following steps.

1. Insert your DaRT recovery disk into the DVD drive on your Windows 8 computer.
2. Restart the computer.
3. If prompted, choose DVD as the **boot device.**
4. When the message *Would you like to initialize network connectivity in the background?* appears, click **Yes.**
5. On the *Choose your keyboard layout* screen, click **US.**
6. On the *Choose an option* screen, click **Troubleshoot** (see Figure 16-7).
7. On the *Troubleshoot* screen, click the **Microsoft Diagnostics and Recovery Toolset.**
8. On the *Recovery Tool* screen, click **Windows 8.**
9. In the *Diagnostics and Recovery Toolset* window, click **Defender** (see Figure 16-8).
10. After the virus scan has completed, close the **Windows Defender** program.
11. Click **Explorer** and then confirm you can browse through the directories on the computer's hard drive. Close the **Explorer** box when you are done.
12. Click **Computer Management.** In the *Computer Management* console, you can expand the Event Viewer to search your Windows logs for errors. From *Services and Drivers,* you can view and disable services that might cause problems or use Disk Management to view the health of your partitions and volumes. Close the **Computer Management** console.

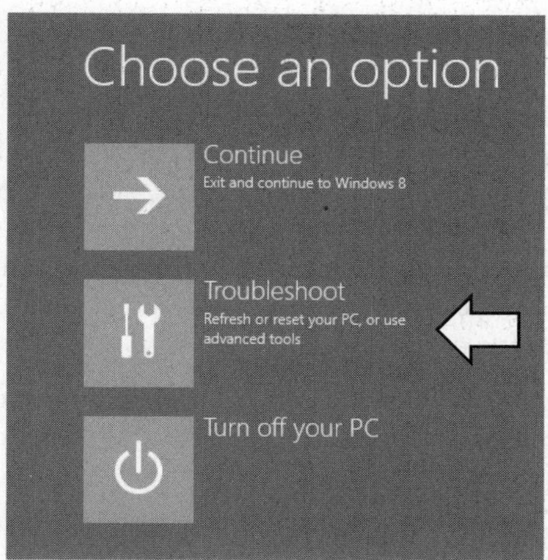

Figure 16-7
Choosing the Troubleshoot option

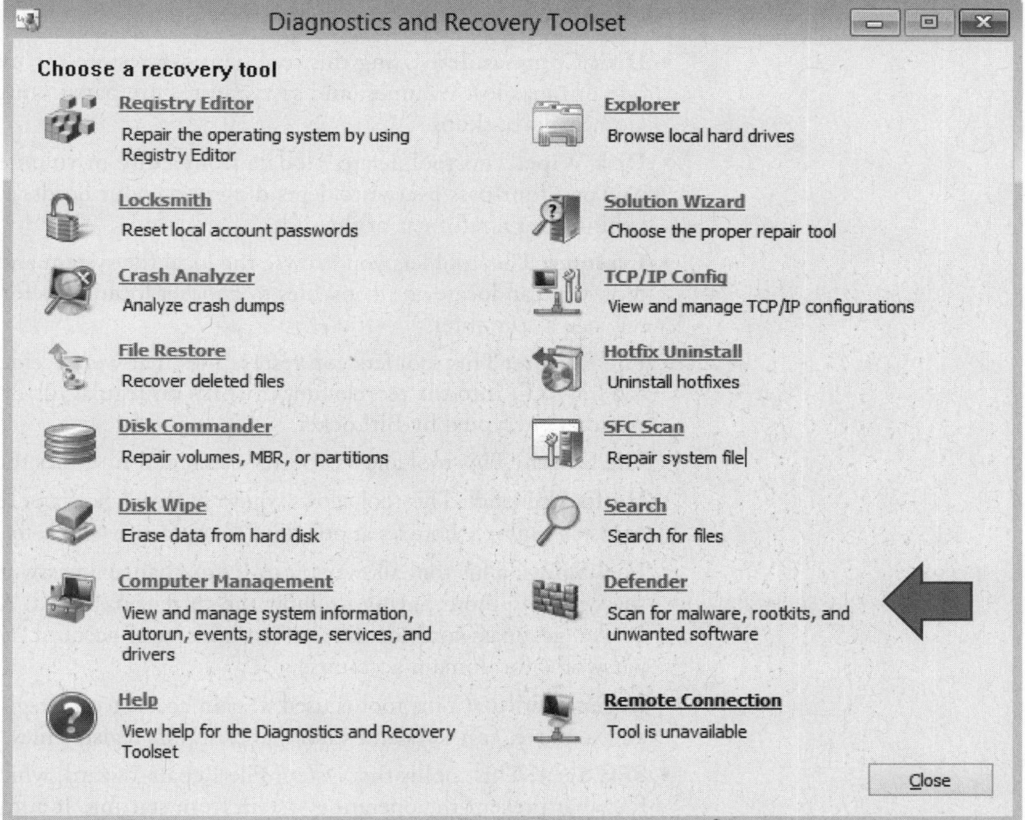

Figure 16-8
Selecting available tools

TAKE NOTE*

You can use the DaRT Recovery Image tool to create both 32/64-bit DaRT recovery images from the same computer, but you cannot create one image that works for both architectures on the same media.

13. From the *Diagnostics and Recovery Toolset* window, click **Close**.
14. Remove the DaRT recovery disk from the computer's DVD drive.
15. On the *Choose an option* screen, click **Continue** to exit and continue to Windows 8.

If you use a Windows 8 (64-bit) DaRT recovery disk to boot into a computer running a Windows 8 (32-bit) operating system, you can run some of the tools, but others will not be available.

Reviewing the Tools Included with DaRT

As an administrator, it is important to familiarize yourself with the tools available in DaRT. Understanding what each tool is used for can make troubleshooting more efficient and less stressful when you are faced with a recovery situation on a production computer.

When you boot into a computer with the DaRT recovery disk, you will have access to a variety of troubleshooting tools. In the earlier exercise, you had the opportunity to explore just a few of those available. The following provides a closer look at all of the tools on the recovery disk:

- **Computer Management:** This is a collection of administrative tools that can be used to troubleshoot the computer. For example, you can use it to view event logs and manage services and drivers.
- **Crash Analyzer:** This tool can be used to determine the cause of a computer failure. It does this by analyzing the memory dump file for the driver that caused the operating system to fail. You can then use the Computer Management tool to disable the driver.
- **Defender:** You can use this tool to detect and remove malware. It works especially well when it comes to detecting rootkits.
- **Disk Commander:** Using this tool, you can restore the master boot record, recover one or more lost volumes, and save and restore partition tables to and from Disk Command backups.
- **Disk Wipe:** This tool deletes all data from a disk or volume. You can use either a single-pass or a four-pass overwrite depending upon your needs. This wipes data that is left behind after a reformat of the disk.
- **Explorer:** This tool lets you browse the local file system and network shares. Using this tool, you can locate and copy files to another location before attempting to repair or reimage a computer.
- **File Restore:** This tool lets you restore files that were accidentally deleted or were too big to fit into the recycle bin. It works on regular disk volumes, lost volumes and volumes encrypted by BitLocker.
- **File Search:** This tool allows you to search and find files that need to be recovered.
- **Hotfix Uninstall:** This tool allows you to remove a hotfix or service pack. Although you can uninstall multiple hotfixes at one time, best practice will be to uninstall the one at a time.
- **LockSmith:** This tool allows you to set or change a password for any local account on the system without having to know the current password. Although it can be used to set or change a password for the local administrator account, it does not allow you to set passwords for domain accounts.
- **Register Editor:** This tool is used to gain access to the registry. Using this tool, you can add, remove, edit keys and values, and import registry files.
- **SFC Scan:** This tool is the System File Repair Wizard, which is used to repair system files that prevent the operating system from starting. It automatically repairs missing or corrupt files but can be configured to prompt you before performing a repair.
- **Solution Wizard:** This wizard presents a series of questions to determine the best tool to use for a given situation.
- **TCP/IP Config:** A system booted with a DaRT disk automatically obtains its TCP/IP information from a DHCP sever. If a DHCP server cannot be bound, you can use TCP/IP Config to manually configure the TCP/IP settings by first selecting a network adapter and then configuring the IP address and DNS Server for the selected adapter.

MORE INFORMATION

To learn more about how to use each of these recovering tools, visit Microsoft's website and search for *DaRT 8 Overview.*

Monitoring Clients Using Desktop Error Monitoring

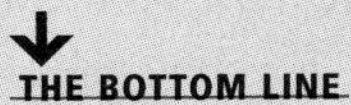
THE BOTTOM LINE

Application and computer failure can dramatically impact a user's productivity. Unfortunately, in many cases, the failure is not reported because the user simply reboots their computer or just restarts their application. If administrators are not aware of the problem, any information that might have been collected is lost.

System Center Desktop Error Monitoring (DEM), a core component of the Microsoft Desktop Optimization Pack (MDOP), is designed to capture all application and operating system failures that are typically under reported by end users. DEM leverages the Windows Error Reporting function that is available on all Windows-based computers by redirecting the information to a central server on your network (see Figure 16-9).

Figure 16-9

Reporting errors to a centralized Windows DEM server

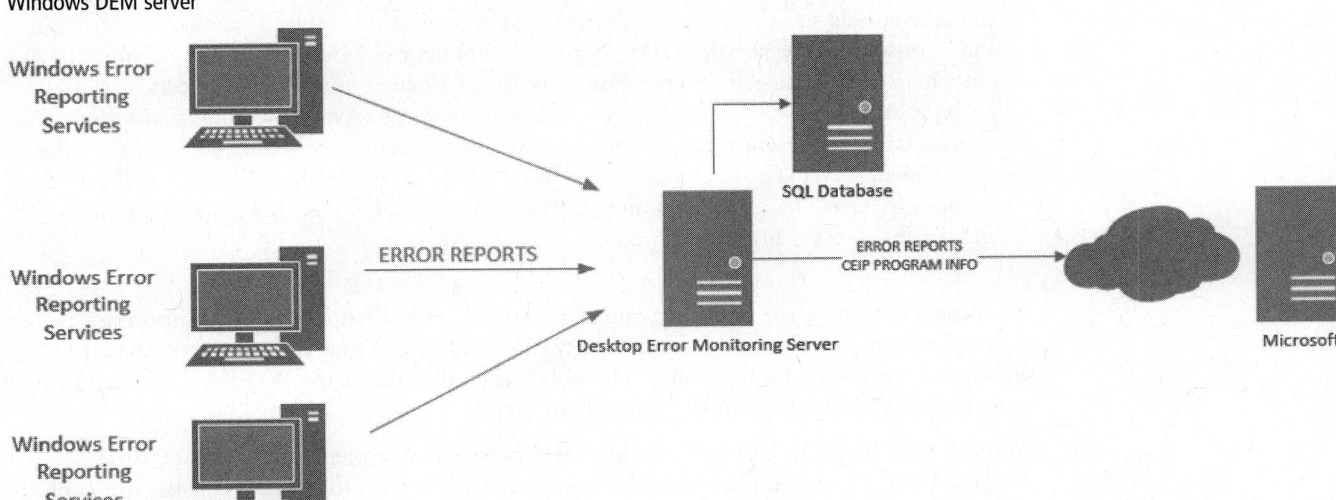

CERTIFICATION READY
Monitor clients using System Center Desktop Error Monitoring
Objective 4.3

In the past when an application "hung," Windows Error Reporting displayed a message asking the user if he wanted to send a report to Microsoft. Unfortunately, the majority of users promptly closed the dialog box and rebooted their computers. They did not always mention something to their help desk technicians or network administrators, resulting in the information being lost without any way to track it.

Regardless of whether the information is reported, the user loses time either waiting for the computer to reboot or, needing to recreate some of the data that might have been corrupted during the crash. The end result is that the root problem behind the failure was not fixed and the data that could have helped target and resolve the problem has been lost.

Exploring Desktop Error Monitoring

With DEM, Windows error reporting information can now be redirected to a Microsoft SQL server database without an agent being installed on the client computers. This is accomplished with Group Policy.

Using the reporting capabilities native to SQL, you can query the data and create reports to diagnose problems. The DEM server can automatically download a link to the latest troubleshooting and knowledge information to help you diagnose and solve system and application crashes. You can also configure DEM to report information directly to Microsoft and download the latest information on how to troubleshoot and resolve the errors you submit.

Here are some things you can do with DEM:

- Determine which applications in your organization produce the most problems.
- Proactively manage critical errors in real-time. This allows you to resolve problems and address them before rolling out new systems.
- More effectively target updates and patch deployments with information you collect.
- Decrease the time needed to collect and review crash detail information and obtain links to resources to troubleshoot and resolve problems found.

Initiating Desktop Error Monitoring

To use DEM, you need to redirect error reporting on the client computer to a centralized server. This enables you to monitor and streamline your reports. DEM uses the Operations Manager to help monitor services, devices, and operations for multiple computers from a single console. The Operations Manager is a component of Microsoft System Center 2012. The Operations Manager's infrastructure consists of a management server, operational database, and a data warehouse database. The management server is the focal point for administering your computers. When you open the Operations console, you connect to the management server. The operational database is a SQL server database that stores all the monitoring data. The data warehouse database is also a SQL server that stores monitoring and alerting data for historical purposes.

To initiate desktop error reporting, run the System Center Desktop Error Monitoring Wizard, which creates a set of Group Policy Objects (GPOs) that you can then integrate into a company-wide Group Policy. The policy is used to direct the Windows error reporting information from each client to a centralized server.

You can then use SQL Server Reporting Services to generate predefined and/or custom reports. For example, you can view the top errors collected on the network or the top applications with errors. To further streamline the reporting process, you can configure and schedule selected reports to be sent via a distribution list to key individuals in your organization.

MORE INFORMATION

For a detailed look at the policy and its specific settings, visit Microsoft's website and search for: *Desktop Error Monitoring tour.*

Managing the App-V Client

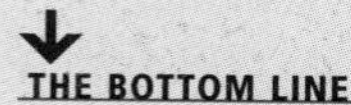

The App-V Client is used to download, update, and run virtual applications on your computer. To manage the client and virtual applications use the App-V Client Management console.

CERTIFICATION READY
Manage the App-V client
Objective 4.3

Through the App-V Client Management console you can update and download virtual applications, view the packages for the current user, and see the applications that make up a virtual package. The App-V Client software can be found on the Microsoft Desktop Optimization Pack (MDOP).

Exploring the App-V 5 Components

Before looking at the process for managing the App-V 5 Client, it is important to first understand the components you typically see in an App-V 5 environment.

App-V components include the following:

- ***App-V 5 Sequencer:*** The App-V Sequencer is software that converts applications into virtual packages. These packages can be added to the package library in the App-V Management console. The App-V Sequencer should be installed on a computer running a virtual machine. This process involves installing the sequencer pre-requisites, installing the App-V Sequencer tool and then taking a snapshot. By taking a snapshot of the machine, you can sequence an application and then return to a clean starting point before sequencing your next application.
- ***App-V 5 Client:*** The App-V Client is used to run the virtualized application on the computer. Through the client, the user is able to interact with icons and double-click file types to start a virtualized app package. The client is also used to obtain the virtual apps from the App-V Management server. There are two types of clients: Client for Remote Desktop Services (used on the RD Session Host Server systems) and the App-V Client, which runs on all other computers.

  You can deploy the Client manually on each computer or you can use an electronic software distribution system, Group Policy, or script the installation.
- ***App-V 5 Shared Content Store:*** The App-V Client typically obtains the virtual application content from the App-V Management Server and then caches it before it starts the app. If the client is configured to use a Shared Content Store, the package contents are not saved to the computer but instead are streamed.
- ***App-V 5 Server:*** The App-V server is comprised of five roles: Management Server, Management Database, Publishing Server, Reporting Server, and the Reporting Database. The Management Server provides the overall management functionality, and the ***Publishing Server*** is used to host and stream virtual apps.

TAKE NOTE*

The following steps require an App-V Server with the Management Server, Management Database, Publishing Server, Reporting Server, and the Reporting Database present on the network. The App-V server installation files can be found on the MDOP disk. The App-V server, which cannot run on a domain controller, also requires a SQL Server 2012 database to store information. The App-V server should have virtual apps available to users who connect from the App-V 5 client.

INSTALL THE APP-V 5.0 CLIENT

GET READY. To install the App-V 5.0 Client, perform the following steps:

1. Insert the **Microsoft Desktop Optimization Pack 2012 DVD**; if the DVD does not automatically open, right-click the **DVD** drive and choose **Auto-Play**. In the menu, click **Run launcher.hta**.
2. In the *MDOP* menu, click **Microsoft Application Virtualization for Desktops**.
3. Under the *App-V 5.0 category,* click **App-V 5.0 Client**.
4. Click **Install** (see Figure 16-10).
5. On the *Software License Terms* screen, select **I accept the license terms**, and then click **Next**.
6. When prompted to use *Microsoft Update*, select **I don't want to use Microsoft Update**, and then click **Next**.
7. On the *Customer Experience Improvement Program* screen, select **I don't want to join the program at this time**, and then click **Install**.
8. When you see the message *Setup completed successfully,* click **Close**. Close the *MDOP* box.

Figure 16-10

Installing the App-V 5.0 Client

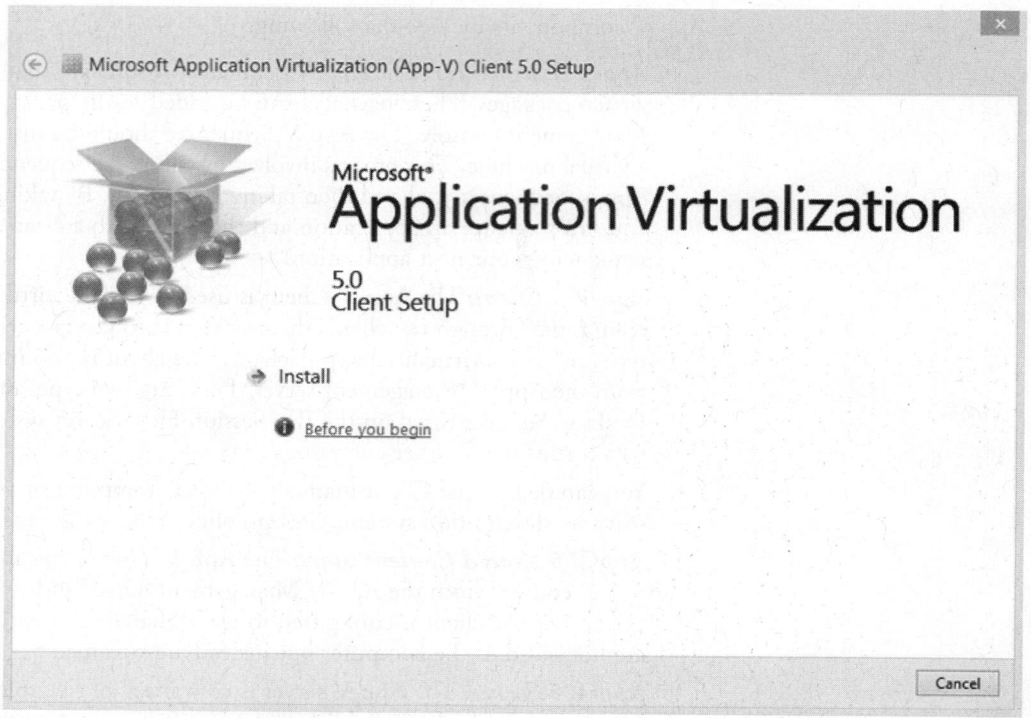

9. Press the **Windows log key** to toggle to the Windows 8 *Start* menu. In the *Start* menu, type **Windows PowerShell**. From the *Results*, choose **Windows PowerShell**.
10. In the *Windows PowerShell* window, type the following command and then press **Enter**:
    ```
    import-module AppvClient
    ```
11. In the *Windows PowerShell* window, type the following command and then press **Enter**:
    ```
    Add-AppvPublishingServer -Name <appvserver name> -URL
    http://<appv-servername:port#>
    ```
    For example, if your App-V server is named *contosoFS* and the Publishing Server is configured to use port number *64531* when it is initially set up, type:
    ```
    Add-AppvPublishingServer -name contosoFS -url http://
    contosoFS:64531
    ```
12. Close the *Windows PowerShell* window.
13. Press the **Windows logo key** to toggle to the Windows 8 *Start* menu, and then click the **Microsoft Application Virtualization client** tile.
14. When the program opens, you see the **virtual application management** console (see Figure 16-11).
15. Click the **Download** tile to download virtual applications that have been made available to you from the App-V Publishing Server.
16. From the menu, click **VIRTUAL APPS** and confirm app(s) were downloaded.
17. Close the *virtual application management* console and press the **Windows logo key** to toggle to your Windows 8 *Start* menu. The virtual application appears as a tile on your Windows 8 Start menu.

MORE INFORMATION

You can use the Windows PowerShell `Get-AppVClientPackage` cmdlet to return a list of all the App-V packages currently on the system. To remove the package, you can type `Remove-AppVClientPackage <name>`.

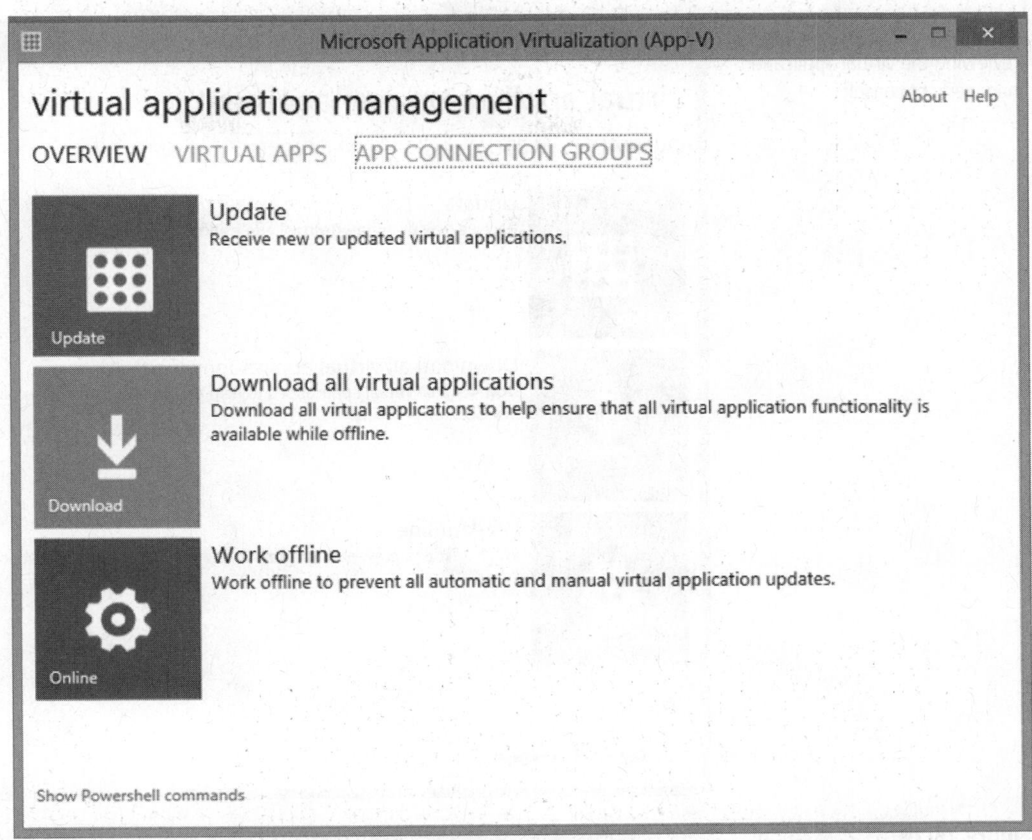

Figure 16-11
Opening the virtual application management console

Exploring the App-V 5 Management Console

To ensure you have the latest virtual applications and updates from your App-V server, you need to have a good understanding of what is available within the virtual application management console.

The virtual application management console (see Figure 16-12) has three menu items across the top.

The Overview tab contains the following three elements:

- **Update:** You select the Update tile to receive a new virtualized app package or to refresh a virtualized app. When you perform a refresh, you see the current version of the virtualized package.
- **Download all virtual applications:** You select this tile to download all of the packages that have been provisioned for the user.
- **Work offline:** You can use this tile when you don't want to allow automatic or manual virtual application updates.

The VIRTUAL APPS tab is used to view all of the packages that have been published to the user. You can also select the package to see the applications that it contains. For example, in the Firefox v17 package (see Figure 16-13), you can see it contains a single application (Mozilla Firefox). You can also start and stop package downloads and repair user state information. This deletes any user data associated with the package.

The APP CONNECTION GROUPS tab displays the connection groups that are available to the user. ***Connection Groups*** are used to group one or more App-V packages. These packages

Figure 16-12

Reviewing the virtual application management console

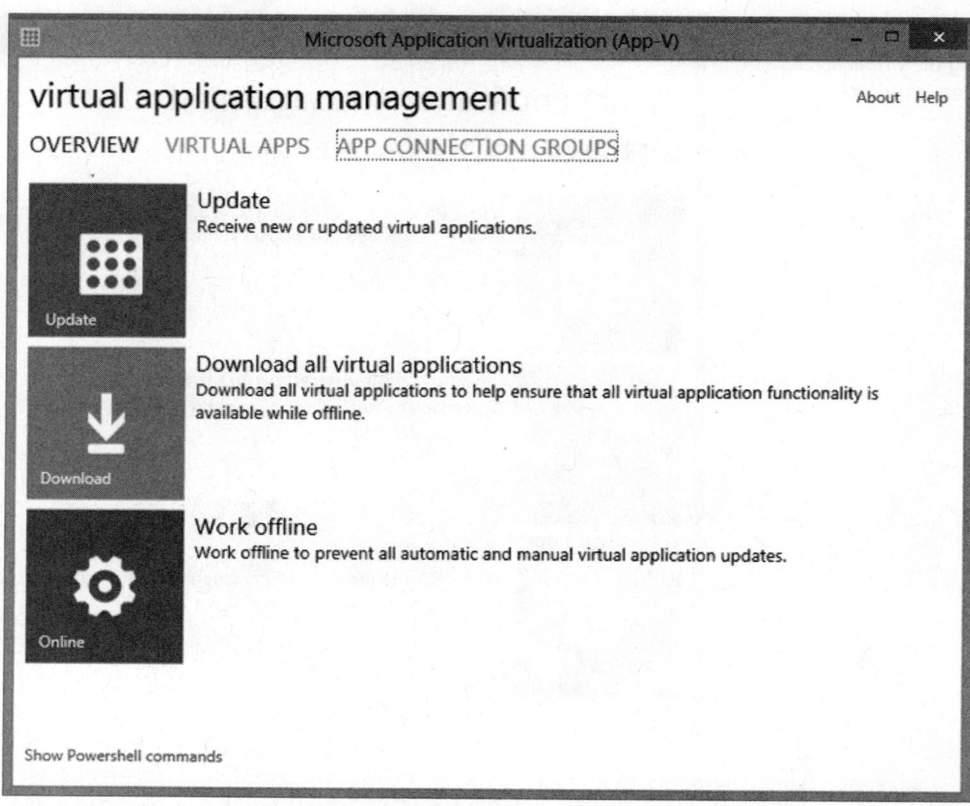

Figure 16-13

Viewing the Firefox application included in a virtual package

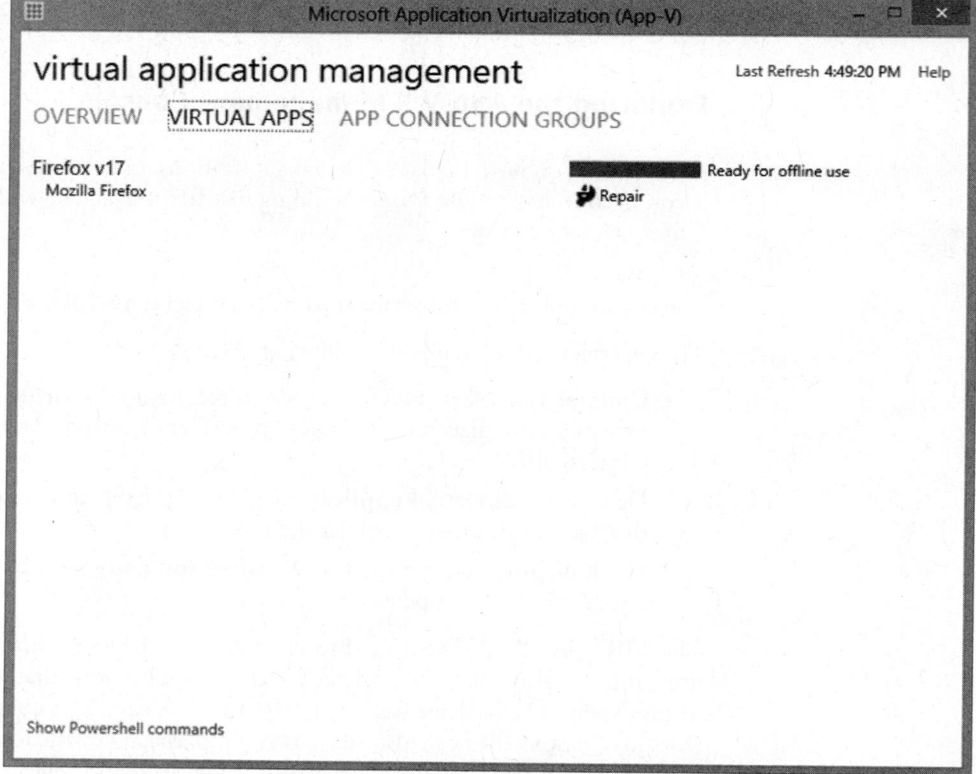

can then interact with one another while still maintaining isolation from the rest of the system. By selecting one of the groups, you will see all of the packages assigned to it. You can also start and stop a package download and repair the user state information from this tab.

MORE INFORMATION

For more information on installing the App-V 5 client using a script or using the Windows Installer (.msi), visit Microsoft's TechNet website.

Troubleshooting Issues with the Publishing Server

In situations where the virtual applications are not available after performing a refresh, you can check several things to troubleshoot the problem. App-V creates new event logs, Windows PowerShell can be used to confirm port numbers, and you can check in Internet Information Services Manager to determine whether key services are running.

A good place to start troubleshooting is to review the App-V Client Event logs to obtain additional information based on any errors identified. These are added as part of the installation of the App-V Client software (see Figure 16-14).

Figure 16-14

Reviewing additional logs added after App-V 5 Client installation

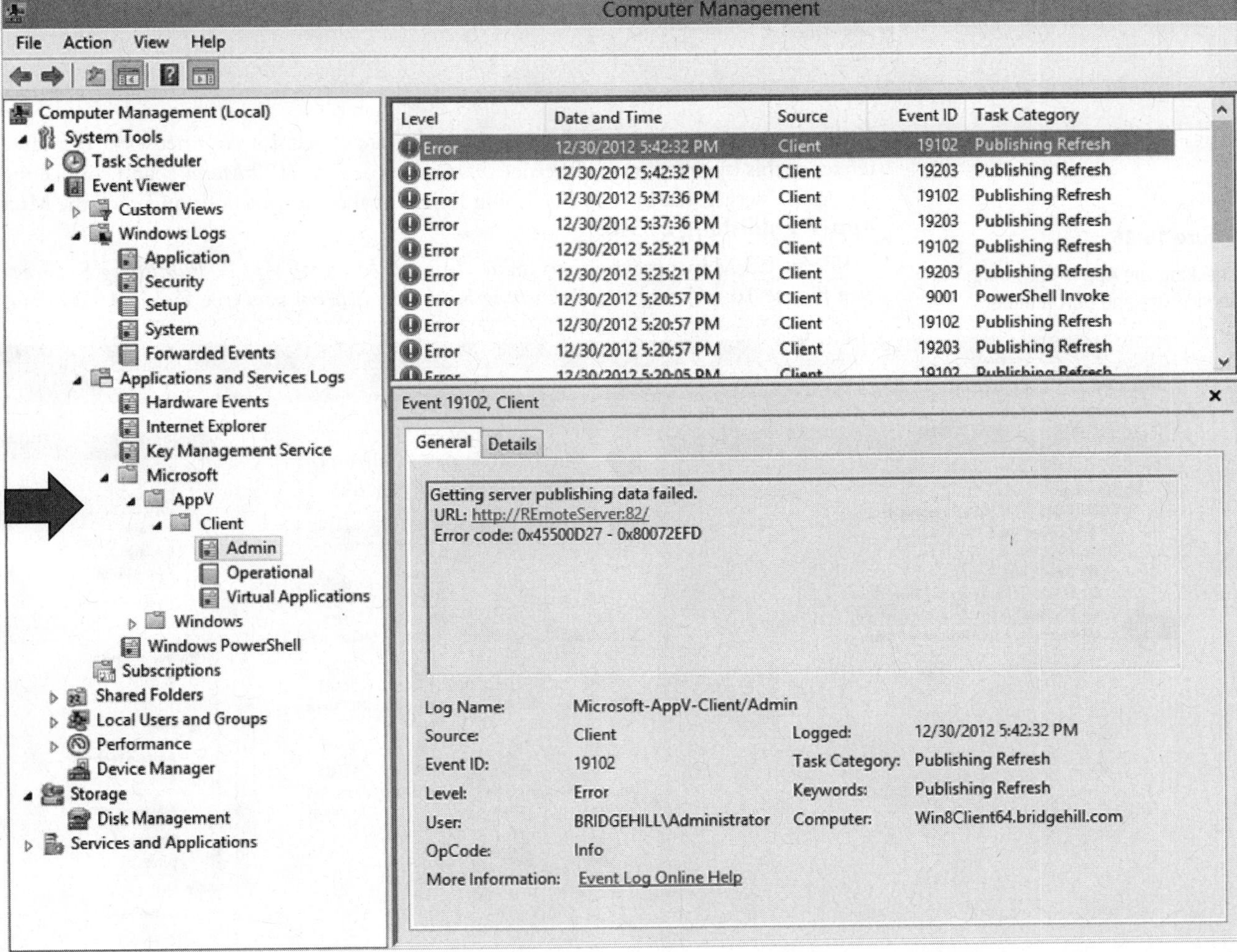

For example, in Figure 16-14, you can see a client having problems accessing the App-V publishing server. To continue to troubleshoot this, you can use Windows PowerShell to see what port the App-V Publishing server is configured to use from your App-V Client's perspective.

Use Windows PowerShell to confirm current settings on the client (Publishing server URL and port number):

1. Open an elevated Windows PowerShell command prompt.

2. Type `Get-AppvPublishingServer` and press **Enter**. Figure 16-15 shows that the Publishing Server is called contosofs and is listening on port 64531.

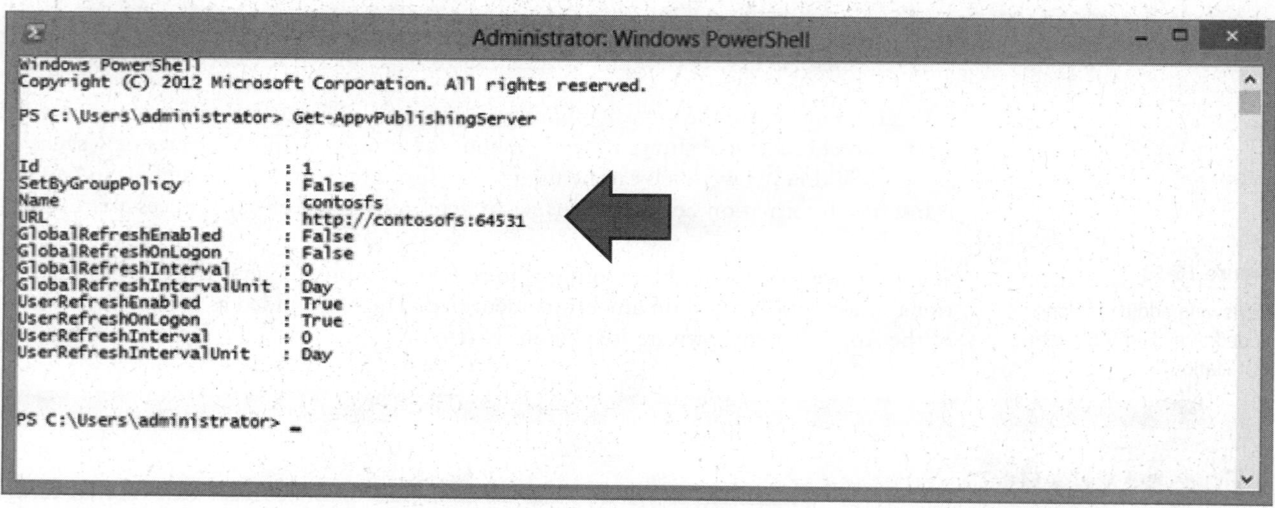

Figure 16-15

Running the Get-AppvPublishingServer cmdlet

3. Verify that the server name and the port number are correct for your network. You can cross-reference this by opening the Internet *Information Services (IIS) Manager* and connecting to the App-V server that has the Publishing Role. Expand the *Sites* node and click the **Microsoft App-V Publishing Service**.
4. While in IIS Manager, check to make sure the *Microsoft App-V Publishing Service* site (see Figure 16-16) and the *Publishing Server application pool* (see Figure 16-17) are

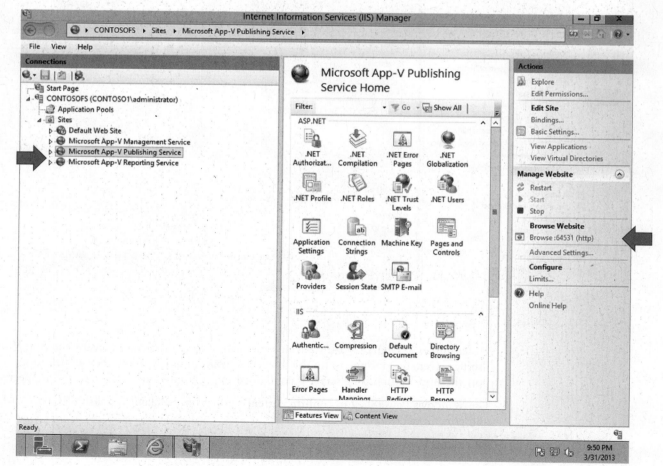

Figure 16-16

Checking the App-V Publishing Service site and port number

running. An application pool provides you with a way to isolate websites that are hosted on the same server. Each application pool is given its own set of server resources.

Figure 16-17

Checking the App-VPublishing pool

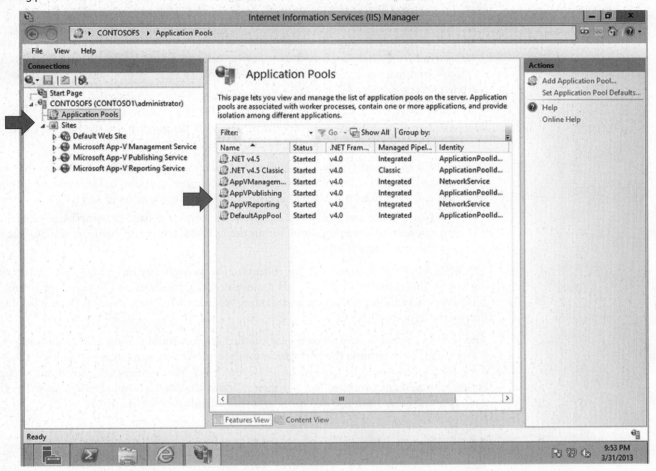

You should also review the incoming rules on the Windows Firewall if it enabled on the computer that runs the Publishing Server role.

If a rule is not in place, you must create a new rule that allows traffic directed to the TCP port the Publishing Server is listening on. For example, this is TCP port 64531 for contosofs.

Managing BitLocker and BitLocker to Go Using MBAM

MBAM provides a single interface to manage BitLocker and BitLocker To Go policies, reports compliance across your organization, and centralizes recovery keys.

CERTIFICATION READY
Manage BitLocker and BitLocker To Go using MBAM
Objective 4.3

The ***Microsoft BitLocker Administration and Monitoring (MBAM)*** tool provides you with a single interface to manage BitLocker encryption policies, simplifies deployment and key recovering, centralizes provisioning, and assesses compliance and encryption status across computers in your organization. You can find the tool as part of the Microsoft Desktop Optimization Pack (MDOP) 2012 kit.

Understanding MBAM 1.0 Components

To deploy MBAM in your organization, it is important to understand the MBAM architecture and how each component communicates with the other. There are three key components for MBAM: They include the Administration and Monitoring Server, the MBAM Client and the Policy template. The MBAM Administration and Monitoring Server installed on Windows Server 2012 holds the Administration and Management web services. The website is used to review compliance status, audit BitLocker client activity, and manage hardware capabilities. It can also be used to access the BitLocker recovery keys.

The MBAM Administration and Monitoring Server is designed to use the Recovery and Hardware Database and the Compliance and Audit Database.

- The Recovery and Hardware Database maintains recovery key data for clients that are managed by BitLocker Administration and Monitoring. It also holds hardware information collected from the MBAM agent running on the client computers.
- The Compliance and Audit Database holds information used in compliance reporting; you can access the reports from within the MBAM Admin tool or from the SQL Server Reporting Services (SSRS).

The MBAM Client is responsible for collecting the recovery key information for the operating system drive, fixed data drives, and removable USB drives, using Group Policy to enforce BitLocker encryption parameters, and sending recovery, hardware, and compliance information to the appropriate entities.

The Policy template is used to configure the BitLocker Administration and Monitoring client policies used to determine the encryption policy options you want to apply for BitLocker drive encryption. It can be used with the Group Policy Management and Advanced Group Policy Management consoles. You can then monitor the client compliance against the policies and report status at both the enterprise and the individual computer levels.

Reviewing Deployment Options for MBAM

You can deploy MBAM on a single server or you can use a more distributed topology that consists of three, four, or five computers each holding one or more MBAM roles. The type of topology used has an impact on the number of MBAM Clients you can support. Setting up MBAM on a single server is recommended for testing purposes only.

In a three-node deployment (supports up to 55,000 MBAM clients), the Administration and Monitoring Server is installed on one server (see Figure 16-18). The Recovery and

Figure 16-18

Reviewing the three-node MBAM deployment

Hardware Database, the Compliance and Audit Database, and the Compliance and Audit Reports are maintained on a second server. The MBAM Group Policy template is installed on a third computer (server/client) that can modify the settings. MBAM settings are managed via the MBAM Policy template, which is integrated into a Group Policy Object on a Domain Controller. The Group Policy object is then distributed via a domain controller to your MBAM Clients.

In a four-node deployment (supports up to 110,000 MBAM Clients), the Administration and Monitoring Server feature is installed on two servers that are part of a Network Load Balancing cluster (see Figure 16-19). The Recovery and Hardware Database, the Compliance and Audit Database, and the Compliance and Audit Reports are maintained on the third server.

Figure 16-19

Reviewing the four-node MBAM deployment

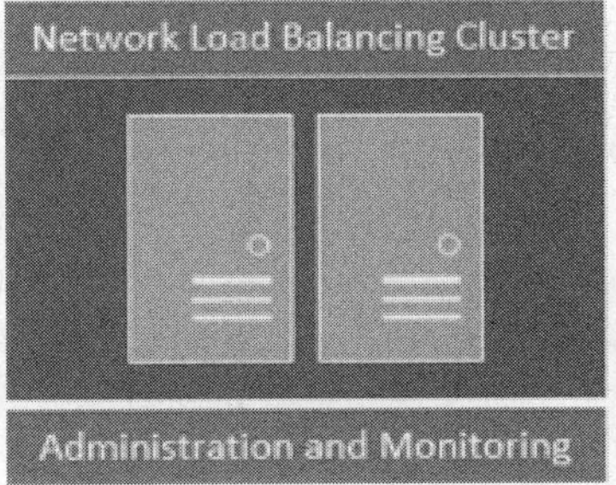

The MBAM Group Policy template is installed on the fourth computer (server/client). It can modify the MBAM settings via the MBAM Policy template, which is integrated into a Group Policy Object on a domain controller. The Group Policy object is then distributed via a domain controller to your MBAM clients.

In a five-node deployment (supports 135,000 MBAM clients), you still install the Administration and Monitoring Server feature using two servers that are members of a Network Load Balancing cluster (see Figure 16-20). You split out the Recovery and Hardware database to its own server. Then you host the Compliance and Audit Database along with the Compliance and Audit Reports feature on another server. Finally, the MBAM Group Policy template is installed on a computer (server/client) that can modify them. MBAM settings are managed via the MBAM Policy template, which is integrated into a Group Policy Object on a domain controller. The Group Policy object is then distributed via a domain controller to your MBAM Clients.

Figure 16-20

Reviewing the five-node MBAM deployment

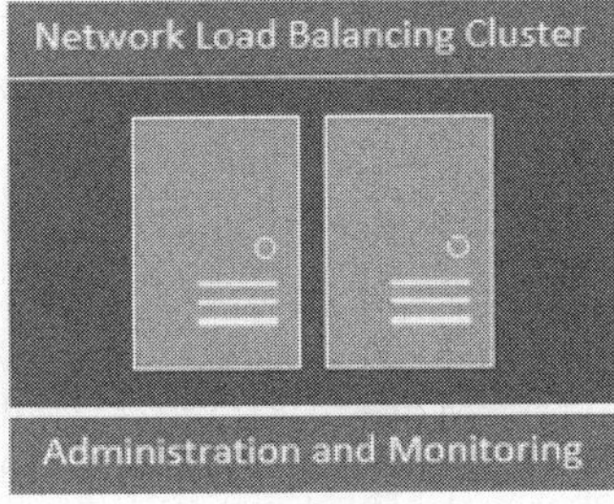

INSTALL MBAM ON WINDOWS SERVER 2012

GET READY. To install MBAM on Windows Server 2012, login with Administrative privileges, perform the following steps:

1. Insert the **Microsoft Desktop Optimization Pack (MDOP) 2012 DVD**; if the DVD does not automatically open, right-click the **DVD** drive and choose **Auto-Play**. In the menu, click **Run launcher.hta**.
2. In the *MDOP* menu, click **Microsoft BitLocker Administration and Monitoring** (see Figure 16-21).

Figure 16-21

Installing the BitLocker Administration and Monitoring tool

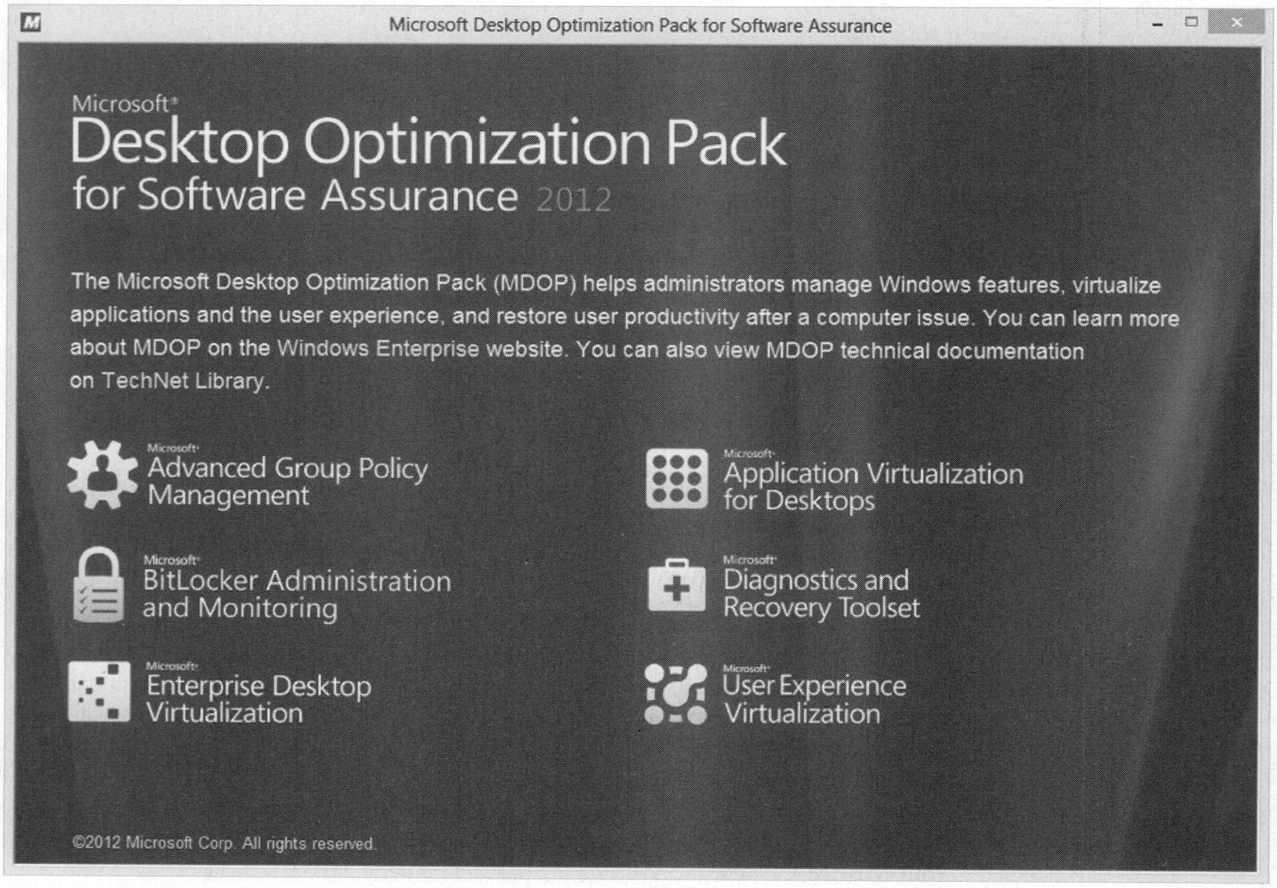

TAKE NOTE*

You must have Windows Server 2012 installed in an Active Directory domain and complete the prerequisites prior to installing MBAM 1.0. You can find them at Microsoft's website by searching for *MBAM 1.0 Deployment Prerequisites.* If the prerequisites are not installed, you cannot continue the installation of MBAM until they are addressed.

3. Under the *MBAM category,* click **MBAM Server: 64-bit.**
4. When the *BitLocker Administration and Monitoring* screen appears click **Start.**
5. On the *End User License Agreement* screen, select **I accept**, and then click **Next.**

6. Under *Select features to install*, click **Next**. This installs the Recovery and Hardware Database, Compliance and Audit Database, Compliance and Audit Reports, Administration and Monitoring Server, and the Policy Template features.
7. If you see the message *Installation cannot continue* (see Figure 16-22) you need to address the prerequisites to continue the installation. Minimize the screen, install the prerequisites, and then click **Check Prerequisites Again**. If no other messages appear, click **Next** to continue.

Figure 16-22

Warning you about prerequisites you must complete

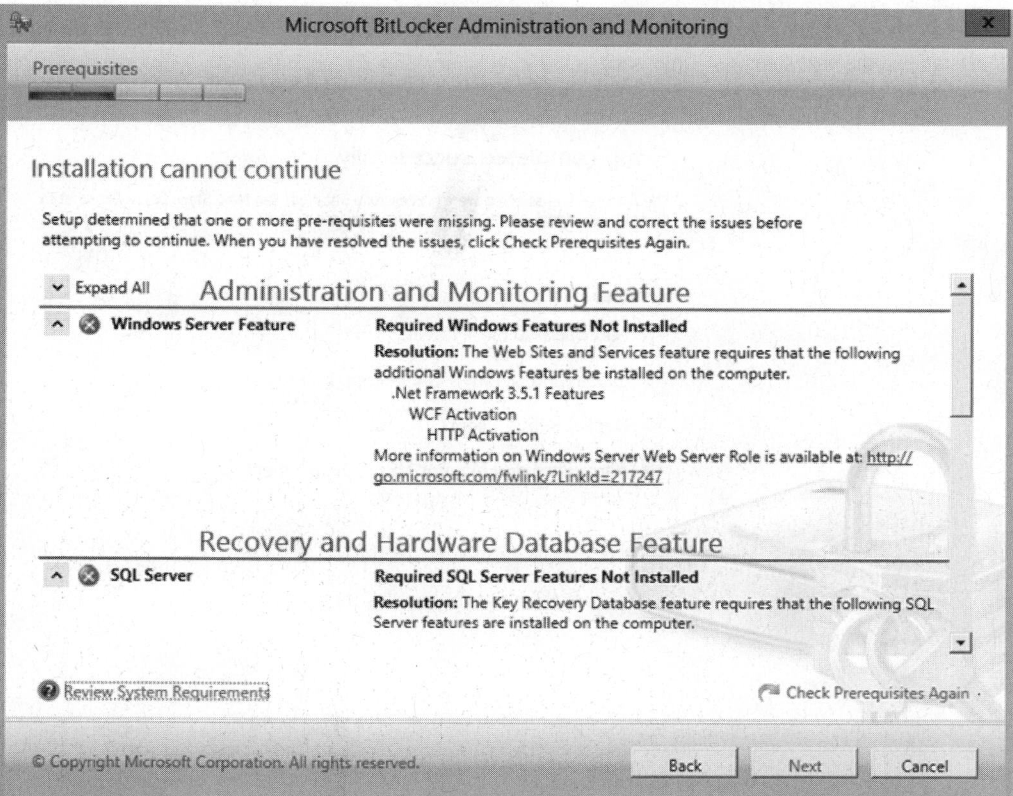

8. On the *Configure network communication security* screen, select **Do not encrypt network communication**, and then click **Next**.
9. On the *Configure the Recovery and Hardware database*, type the SQL Server instance (for example, ContosoFS), and then click **Next**.
10. On the Configure *Compliance and Audit database*, type the SQL Server instance (for example, ContosoFS), and then click **Next**.
11. On the *Configure the Compliance and Audit Reports* screen, type the name of the SQL server (for example, ContosoFS), and then click **Next**.
12. On the *Configure the Administration and Monitoring Server*, under *Port Binding* type **80**, and then click **Next**. If there is a website configured on your system that is already using port 80, you can change this to 81.
13. On the *Microsoft Update Opt-In* page, select **Use Microsoft Update when I check for updates (Recommended)**, and then click **Next**.
14. Review the *Installation Summary* and click **Install**. The initial installation of your MBAM server is complete.

Reviewing MBAM Next Steps

After completing the initial installation of MBAM, you need to perform a series of post tasks.

After the installation of MBAM is completed, you need to perform several post-installation tasks. These differ from company to company. The information that follows provides you with the details about what is involved to customize the system to your specific requirements (see Figure 16-23).

Figure 16-23

Understanding the next steps in the MBAM configuration

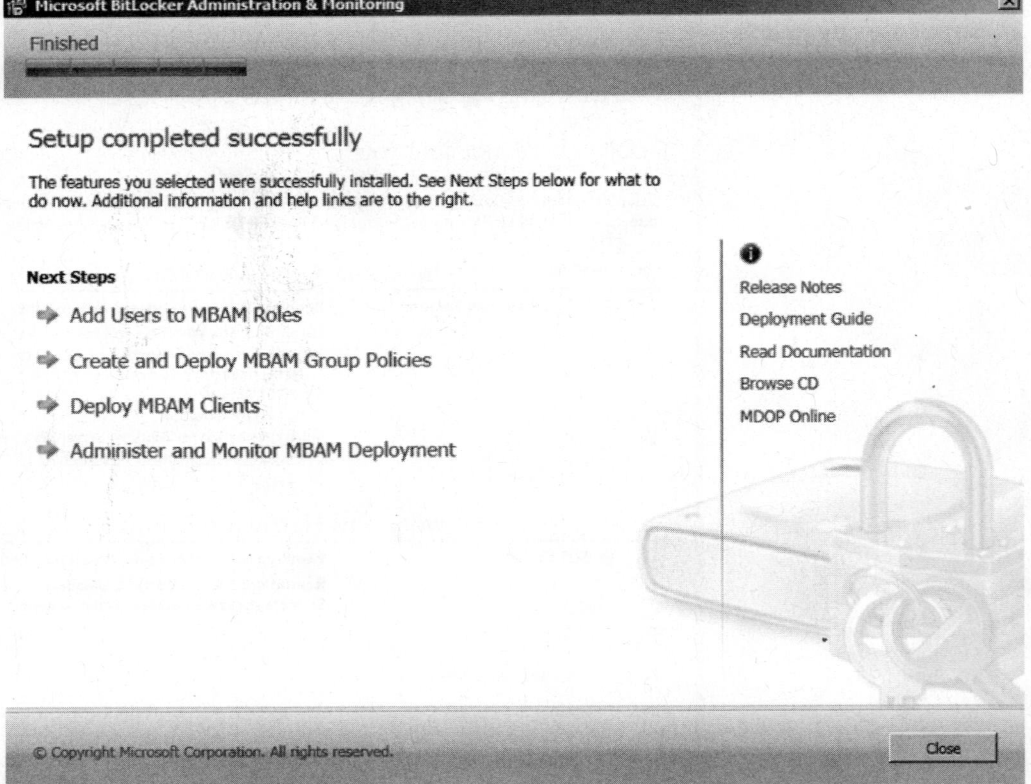

Here are some of the post-installation tasks and the options you need to use:

- **Add Users to MBAM Roles:** Administrative users need to be granted access to the MBAM server features by assigning them to the groups below after setup is complete. You should assign them first to Active Directory security groups and then make those groups members of the appropriate MBAM local administrative group(s) that follow:
  a. **MBAM System Administrators Group:** Members of this group have full access to all BitLocker Administration and Monitoring features on the MBAM administration website.
  b. **MBAM Hardware Users Group:** Members of this group have access to the hardware capability features in the MBAM administration website.
  c. **MBAM Helpdesk Users Group:** Members of this group have access to Helpdesk features, including the ability to manage the Trusted Platform Module (TPM) and Drive Recovery options in the MBAM administration website. They must fill in all fields when they use either option.
  d. **MBAM Advanced Helpdesk Users Group:** Members of this group have access to the Helpdesk features, including the ability to manage the TPM and Drive Recovery

options. They are not required to fill in all the fields when they use either of the options.

e. **MBAM Report Users Group:** Members of this group have access to the Compliance and Audit Reports in the MBAM administration website.

- **Create and Deploy MBAM Group Policies:** MBAM integrates with the policy under the Computer Configuration \ Policies \ Administrative Templates \ Windows Components \ MDOP MBAM (BitLocker Management) node (see Figure 16-24).

  This template can be installed on any computer that can run the Group Policy Management console or Advanced Group Policy Management. If this is installed on a different computer, you will need to start the MBAM Installation Wizard, deselect all MBAM features except for the Policy template, and then continue the installation.

Figure 16-24

Reviewing the BitLocker MBAM Group Policy settings

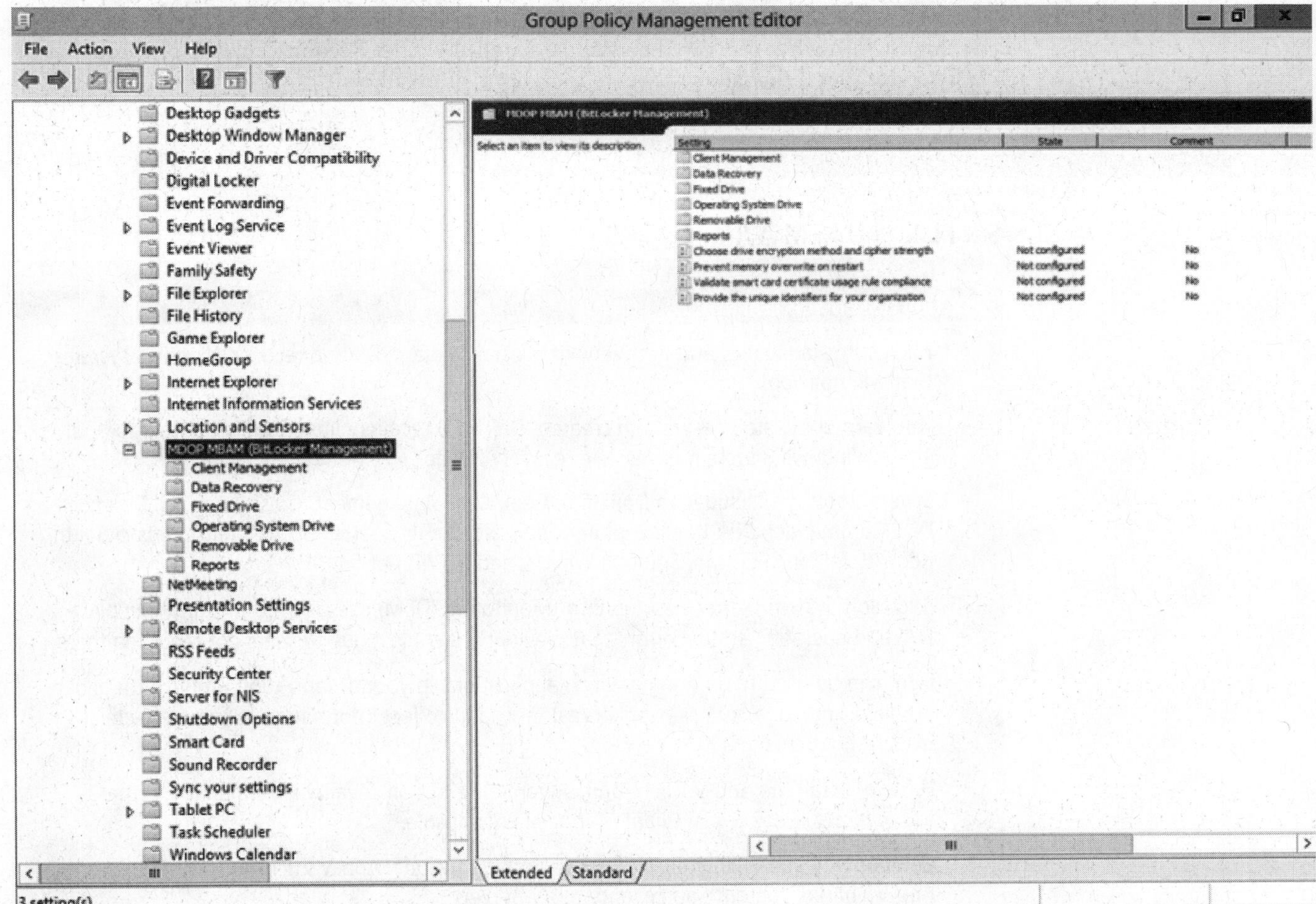

- **Deploy MBAM Clients:** After you configure the Group Policy, you can deploy the MBAM Client installer files. This can be accomplished through System Center 2012 Configuration Manager or by using Active Directory services. There are two files available (MBAMClient-64bit.msi and MBAMClient-32bit.msi). To learn more about deploying the MBAM client as part of a Windows Deployment, visit Microsoft's website and search for: *Deploying MBAM clients using Active Directory.*
- **Administer and Monitor MBAM Deployment:** This option allows you to view the *Recover access to an encrypted drive* form (used by users to regain access to their computer or encrypted drive). You can also view the *Manage TPM* form. This form

is designed to help users whose TPM has locked them out and no longer accepts their PIN. You typically use the *Recover access to an encrypted drive* form to gain access to the computer and then the *Manage TPM* form to allow the user to manage his TPM. The Hardware option allows you to manage a master hardware inventory and designate whether or not hardware models are capable or incapable in regards to performing BitLocker encryption.

Reviewing MBAM 2 Features

MBAM 2.0 is currently in beta at the time of this writing, but it is expected to provide better compliance features and improvements in security. It also offers both standalone integration and integration with System Center Configuration Manager (SCCM). Using SCCM, you can see BitLocker reports and hardware management integrated within SCCM while recovery keys can be handled via the Recovery console or through a self-service portal that allows users to look up their own keys.

SKILL SUMMARY

IN THIS LESSON YOU LEARNED:

- Microsoft Diagnostics and Recovery kit is used to diagnose and recover Windows systems that will not boot.
- You learned the steps needed to create a DaRT 8.0 recovery image tool and how to boot into a Windows 8 system to test the recovery image.
- Several tools are included in DaRT 8.0: Computer Management, Crash Analyzer, Defender, Disk Commander, Disk Wipe, Explorer, File Restore, File Search, Hotfix Uninstall, LockSmith, Registry Editor, SFC Scan, Solution Wizard, and TCP/IP Config.
- Microsoft System Center Desktop Error Monitoring (DEM) can be used to capture application and operating system errors that previously were lost due to users not reporting them.
- DEM can be used to determine which applications in your organization produce the most problems, manage critical errors in real time, and collect information to more effectively troubleshoot crashes.
- How to install the App-V Client and explored the options available to manage virtual applications in the App-V Client Management console.
- Components of a typical App-V implementation include: App-V Client, App-V sequencer, App-V Shared Content Source, and App-V Servers.
- Use the steps for troubleshooting problems with the Publisher server when your App-V Client does not have access to virtual apps that should be available to it.
- Microsoft BitLocker Administration and Monitoring (MBAM) provide a centralized single interface for managing encryption policies across your organization.
- The three components of MBAM include the Administration and Monitoring Server, the MBAM client, and the Policy template.
- You can set up different topologies to deploy MBAM to a single server for testing only and three-node, four-node, and five-node configurations.

Knowledge Assessment

Multiple Choice

Select the correct answer for each of the following questions.

1. Which of the following is prerequisite before installing the DaRT Kit on Windows 8?
   a. SCCM
   b. Service Pack 2
   c. Windows Assessment and Deployment Kit (Windows ADK)
   d. RSAT
2. Which DaRT tool can be used to change the password for any local account on the system without having to know the password for the account?
   a. File Restore
   b. LockSmith
   c. DaRT Password Recovery
   d. User Account Reset
3. Which software converts applications into virtual packages?
   a. App-V Client
   b. App-V Shared Content Store
   c. App-V Sequencer
   d. App-V Server
4. Which MBAM database holds recovery key information collected from MBAM agents?
   a. Compliance and Audit Database
   b. Recovery and Hardware Database
   c. Policy Template Database
   d. Client Recovery Database
5. Which Windows PowerShell command can you run from an elevated mode to confirm the URL for the publishing server name and its port number?
   a. Get-AppvPublishingServer
   b. Get-AppvPubServer
   c. Set-AppvPublishingServer
   d. Set-AppvPubServer
6. Which of the following are components in an MBAM 1.0 environment? Choose all that apply.
   a. Administration and Monitoring Server
   b. Policy template
   c. MBAM Client
   d. MBAM Redirector Client
7. How many clients can a four–node MBAM deployment support?
   a. 50,000
   b. 110,000
   c. 130,000
   d. 200,000
8. In which deployment type should you install the Administration and Monitoring server on two servers as part of a Network Load Balancing cluster, and then place the Recovery and Hardware Database, the Compliance and Audit Database, and the Compliance and Audit Reports on a third server?
   a. Five-node
   b. Two-node
   c. Three-node
   d. Four-node

9. Members of which group have full access to all BitLocker Administration and Monitoring features in the MBAM Administration website?
   a. MBAM Helpdesk users group
   b. MBAM Advanced Helpdesk users group
   c. MBAM Report users group
   d. MBAM System Administrators group

10. Which of the following topologies is recommended for MBAM testing purposes only?
    a. Single server
    b. Five-node
    c. Three-node
    d. Four-node

Best Answer

Choose the letter that corresponds to the best answer. More than one answer choice may achieve the goal. Select the BEST answer.

1. You want to deploy MBAM in a topology that supports growth. You currently have 100,000 clients. What topology should you deploy if you expect growth of 20,000 clients per year?
   a. Three-node
   b. Four-node
   c. Five-node
   d. Single-node

2. Which option provides the best solution for monitoring and capturing errors from crashes on your users' PCs?
   a. Ask users to report problems to you when they occur.
   b. Set up a website and ask users to visit it and submit problems when they occur.
   c. Review event logs on PCs after a crash has occurred.
   d. Set up DEM to use Windows Error Reporting to centralize reporting and management of crash information.

3. Which is the quickest way to identify the Publishing Server and its associated port number from an App-V Client?
   a. Review the computer's registry.
   b. Review the packages installed by launching the App-V Client and navigating to the appropriate tab.
   c. Contact the administrator in charge of App-V and ask.
   d. Run the `Get-AppVClientPackage` cmdlet on your machine.

4. Which tool provides you with the best information about why a computer has crashed when using DaRT?
   a. Computer Management
   b. Crash Analyzer
   c. SFC Scan
   d. Registry Editor

5. Which is the best way to deploy MBAM clients to 100 Windows 8 computers if your administrators are inexperienced with SCCM?
   a. Perform a manual installation.
   b. Use System Center 2012 Configuration Manager.
   c. Use Group Policy.
   d. Set up a share and asking users to connect and install.

Matching and Identification

1. Match the following terms with the related description or usage.

_______ **a)** App-V Client
_______ **b)** DaRT
_______ **c)** App-V Sequencer
_______ **d)** LockSmith
_______ **e)** MBAM
_______ **f)** Crash Analyzer
_______ **g)** App-V Shared Content Store
_______ **h)** Publishing Server
_______ **i)** DEM
_______ **j)** MBAM client

1. Allows you to set or change a password for any local account on the system.
2. Provides a single interface for managing BitLocker encryption policies.
3. Used by the App-V Client to stream content instead of downloading it.
4. Designed to capture application and operating system failures by leveraging the Windows Error Reporting function.
5. Used to host and stream virtual apps.
6. Responsible for collecting the recovery key information for the operating system drive, fixed data drives, and removable USB drives.
7. Used to analyze the memory dump file for the driver that caused an operating system to crash.
8. Can be managed via the App-V Client management console.
9. Provides you with a set of tools that can be used to diagnose and recover your Windows systems when they are offline.
10. Software that converts applications into virtual packages.

Build a List

1. In order of first to last, identify the steps to create a DaRT Recovery Image.

_______ Select Create to generate the image files (ISO and WIM).
_______ On the Crash Analyzer tab Advanced options page, include the Windows 8 Debugging tools.
_______ Choose the type of DaRT Recovery image you want to create.
_______ Select the tools you want to include in the image.
_______ Burn the image to bootable media.
_______ Provide the path to the matching Windows 8 media files.
_______ Download the latest malware definitions for Windows Defender.
_______ Set the default path and name for the recovery image.
_______ Start the DaRT Recovery Image Wizard.

2. In order of first to last, identify the steps to boot into a recovery environment using DaRT:

_______ Select the tool you want to use from the DaRT tool kit.
_______ Select the target operating system Windows 8.
_______ Select Microsoft Diagnostics and Recovery Toolset.
_______ Select Troubleshoot.
_______ Choose your keyboard layout.
_______ Select Yes if you are asked to initialize network connectivity in the background.
_______ Select the boot device if prompted.
_______ Restart the computer.
_______ Ensure your computer is configured to boot from a DVD drive or USB bootable device.

3. In order of first to last, identify the steps to install the App-V 5.0 Client.
   _______ Under the App-V 5.0 category, click App-V 5.0 Client.
   _______ When you see the message Setup completed successfully click Close. Close the MDOP box.
   _______ Press the Windows logo key to toggle to the Windows 8 start menu. In the Start menu, type Windows PowerShell. Choose Windows PowerShell from the Results.
   _______ Insert the Microsoft Desktop Optimization Pack (MDOP) 2012 DVD.
   _______ Click Install.
   _______ When prompted to use Microsoft Update, select I don't want to use Microsoft Update, and then click Next.
   _______ On the MDOP menu, click Microsoft Application Virtualization for Desktops.
   _______ On the Software License Terms screen, select I accept the license terms, and then click Next.
   _______ On the Customer Experience Improvement Program screen, select I don't want to join the program at this time and then click Install.
   _______ In the Windows PowerShell window, type the following commands and then close the Windows PowerShell window:
   ```
   import-module AppVClient, Add-AppvPublishingServer -Name
   <appvserver name> -URL http://a<appv-servername:port#>
   ```
   _______ Press the Windows logo key to toggle to the Windows 8 Start menu. The Microsoft Application Virtualization client tile indicates the install has completed.

Choose an Option

1. Where do you click in the virtual application management console to see the packages published to the user and the applications included in a specific package?

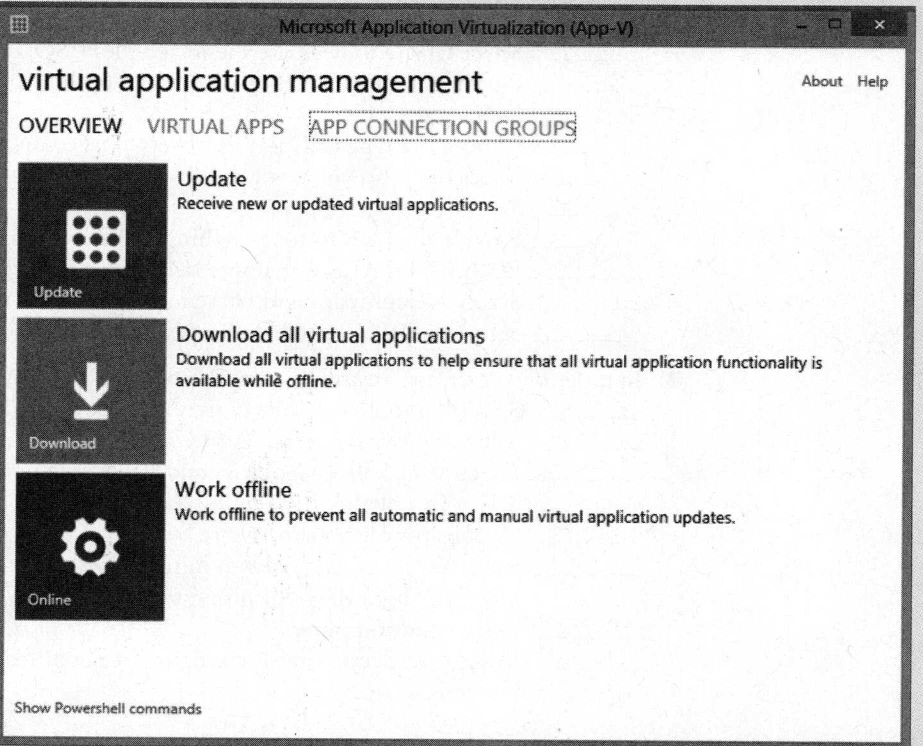

Figure 16-12
App-V 5.0 virtual application management console

Business Case Scenarios

Scenario 16-1: Lost Password

An administrator who just joined the company a week ago was terminated. Unfortunately, the computer he was working on needs to be accessed but the employee refused to provide it when he left. How should you address this issue without having to reinstall the operating system?

Scenario 16-2: Virtual Apps Not Publishing to App-V Client

You have set up an App-V Client, but the apps published for the user are not showing up in the virtual application management console. How do you troubleshoot this problem?

Appendix A
Exam 70-688 Managing and Maintaining Windows 8

EXAM OBJECTIVE	OBJECTIVE NUMBER	LESSON NUMBER
Design an Installation and Application Strategy		
Design an operating system installation strategy	1.1	1
Design an application strategy for desktop applications	1.2	2
Design an application strategy for cloud applications	1.3	3
Design a solution for user settings NOTE: The 1.4 objective item "USMT 5.0/WET" is covered in Lesson 1, in the sections "Exploring the User State Migration Tool (USMT) 5.0" and "Using Windows Easy Transfer."	1.4	4
Maintain Resource Access		
Design for network connectivity	2.1	5
Design for remote access	2.2	6
Design for authentication and authorization	2.3	7
Manage data storage	2.4	8
Manage data security	2.5	9
Maintain Windows Clients and Devices		
Manage hardware and printers	3.1	10
Manage mobile devices	3.2	11
Design a recovery solution	3.3	12
Manage endpoint security	3.4	13
Manage Windows 8 Using Cloud Services and Microsoft Desktop Optimization Pack		
Manage clients by using Windows Intune	4.1	14
Manage public cloud services	4.2	15
Monitor and maintain clients by using MDOP	4.3	16

Index

A

B

C

D

E

F

N

O

P

T

U

V

W